Economics
A Student's Guide

John Beardshaw

Senior Lecturer in Economics, Southgate Technical College

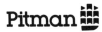
Pitman

PITMAN PUBLISHING
128 Long Acre, London, WC2E 9AN

A Division of Longman Group UK Limited

First published in Great Britain 1984
Second edition 1989
Reprinted 1989, 1990, 1991

British Library Cataloguing in Publication Data
Beardshaw, John
  Economics: a student's guide. – 2nd ed.
  1. Economics
  I. Title
  330

ISBN 0 273 03013 2

Printed and bound in Singapore

Back cover photograph by Peter Ewell.

Line illustrations Lyn Williams

Contents

iii

Contents

Contents

Preface to the second edition

I believe that it has been more difficult to prepare the second edition than write the first one. There have been the usual tasks of updating, amending and correcting but the real problem has been that so much has changed. This has been a result of the *political* change in perspectives brought about in the Thatcher/Reagan years. Those familiar with the first edition will probably find this increased recognition of the value judgement element in modern economics the biggest difference in the second.

The chief objective of the book is, as before, to bridge the gap between the excellent but complex texts which extend well beyond 'A' Level and the understandable but inadequate texts which rely on description rather than analysis. 'A' Level economics today is such a vast subject that it makes this book also suitable for all those who are considering a career with an economics element. As such it is directly relevant to first year degree students, those taking professional examinations, such as those of the accountancy bodies and the Institute of Bankers, and to BTEC courses at Higher and National level.

What is new

The second edition will instantly appear different from the first since it is laid out in double columns and is in colour. However, much more fundamental changes are to be found.

There are two main lots·of changes which have been incorporated into the second edition. First are the changes in the teaching of economics which have come about in recent years and second are the developments in economics itself. Undoubtedly the trend in teaching has been a much greater emphasis on the real-world documentary approach and this trend is bound to continue and develop. To this end a series of data-response sections have been added to the book which both illuminate and develop the material in the chapters. The wealth of real-world data in the first edition has been revised and extended. A workbook to accompany the second edition is published concurrently with it.

However, the main task of a textbook such as this remains the development of the basic concepts of economics. Reliance on case-study material is not without its dangers. Some topics are just too important to be left to the student to glean from case study examples. The danger of missing the point or misunderstanding and hence impeding student progress often means an explicit exposition must be provided.

The second trend we must consider is the developments in the subject matter of economics. The 1980s saw free-market economics resurgent. The application of monetarist ideas in economic policy was followed by neoclassical (or new classical) policies. In particular there has been the swing away from the policies of Keynesian demand-management towards supply-side policies. It is a major aim of the second edition to integrate fully these developments into the text. The various concepts of aggregate demand and supply are fully explained and not just produced like rabbits out of a hat.

The book is particularly strong in its treatment both of macroeconomics and of monetary economics. Whereas most treatments seem to separate theory and practice, an attempt has been made to develop an understanding of the economy using real data to illustrate the basic ideas.

The reader will find a full treatment of the issues in modern economics such as the arguments between neo-Keynesians and neo-classicists. There is also a section on Marxist economics. This, once again, emphasises the approach the book uses to economics issues, seeing them as a debate rather than received truth.

Another feature of the book is its attention to the international aspects of the economics. Thus, while of necessity the UK economy is the main source of examples there are copious references to, and statistics drawn from, other economies. The book has also been strengthened by the addition of a chapter on development economics.

I have tried to eliminate any lingering elements of sexism which remained. The subject abounds in gender-specific terms such 'manpower', 'businessman' and so on. My endeavours were *encouraged* by my editors Liz Hartley and Tania Hackett!

New chapters

There are three new chapters in the second edition and the chapter on monetary and income analysis has been completely rewritten. Readers will find new chapters on the concept of aggregate equilibrium in the economy, development economics and radical economics and Marxism.

The workbook

Published at the same time as the second edition is a workbook. This is jointly written with Andy Ross. In this the student will find more data-response problems together with essays and multiple-choice tests. There is also a section on study skills and exam technique. The combination of the two books provides the student with a comprehensive preparation for economics exams.

Data-response sections

At the end of each chapter there is a data-response section. It is obviously important for students to develop their competence with these because this type of problem is used in most economics exams and other forms of assessment. It has been the intention in creating these sections to utilise the material employed as fully as possible. There are, therefore, often many more questions than could possibly be answered in the time allowed in an exam. The reader should not be discouraged if these sections require more than 45 minutes effort!

Each data-response section is linked to the material in the preceding chapter. But it is in the nature of such problems that they 'spill-out' into other areas. In some cases, therefore, the student may have to roam far-and-wide through the book to answer a particular question. As with the chapters the data-response sections are graduated and you are likely to find the later questions in each section more demanding.

It is hoped that students at all levels will find these sections rewarding at all stages of their studies. For example, the data response section at the end of chapter one can be attempted by those who have only worked their way through the first chapter. However, it is hoped that students at the end of their course of studies will find this section equally demanding. It is an old quip in economics that the questions remain the same but we constantly change the answers!

How to use this book

The first thing to say is that no one book can pass an economics examination for a student. Whilst this book attempts to lay out the framework and provide all the theory which is necessary, a *select bibliography* of other works is included at the end of the book. However, even if the student were to read and digest all of these works, it must still be said that he or she can, and will, only do well if a consistent attempt to keep up to date is maintained. The student, whether in the UK or overseas, is in fact surrounded by an embarrassment of riches. In the UK alone there are four good daily papers and a number of excellent periodicals. In addition to this radio and television usually provide a stream of well-informed reporting.

The student is also directed to the section of the bibliography on official publications and statistics. These provide much of the raw material of the subject: too long has the subject been taught divorced from the real world! Additionally, the student should not neglect the wealth of free literature which is available, such as the reviews published by the major banks and the *Economic Progress Reports* of the Treasury.

As far as this book is concerned, a *graduated approach* to learning has been adopted. The first part of the book deals with the fundamentals of the subject and with its basic vocabulary; as such it could form the basis of an introductory course. The remaining two parts then develop the main areas of the subject. This graduated approach has also been adopted within the chapters. The basic concepts are fully explained and illustrated but the level of difficulty tends to increase towards the end of each chapter. Thus the student should not feel discouraged if often the later pages of a chapter are energetic; it is possible to proceed to the next chapter so long as the fundamentals have been absorbed.

The author is well aware that few students ever read a textbook from cover to cover. Therefore, although the book has a well-planned structure, many of the chapters may be taken in their own right as a discrete treatment of their subjects.

Another problem which seems endemic to economics is that it often appears difficult for the student to appreciate parts of the subject without understanding the whole. In an attempt to cope with this difficulty the author has made copious use of *cross-referencing* in the book so that ideas may be traced backwards and forwards through the text. The author makes no apologies for frequent recapitulation of ideas and concepts throughout the book. It is hoped that the *summaries* at the end of each chapter may act both as a revision aid and a method of reinforcing essential ideas.

In conclusion

To those about to set out on the study of economics may I say that you are likely to find it the most rewarding and frustrating of subjects. However there has never been a greater need for us to understand and to overcome the economic problems which face and divide us. For those of you embarking on this journey may I say 'good luck and bon voyage'.

August 1988   JSB

Acknowledgements

I must first thank Andy Ross of Ealing College of Higher Education, where he works on the economics degree course. Andy is largely responsible for the Section on welfare economics as well as much of the chapters on monetary and income analysis, policy and equilibrium and the chapter on radical economics. He has also saved me from many of my worst errors elsewhere in the book. Any mistakes are, of course, all my own work.

Thanks to Malcolm Bowler for the computer program at the end of Chapter 31 and for mathematical advice at various points.

In several places I have drawn on the work done by David Palfreman and myself for our book *The Organisation in its Environment* published by Pitman. I have also drawn on work done by Chris Faux and myself for our BTEC Workbook and our book of documentary case studies, *Organisations in the UK*. My thanks to David and Chris for the help and co-operation.

I must also thank the newspapers and others who have given their permissions to use the extracts and articles in the data response sections. Thank yous also to the Central Statistical Office, the Bank of England, the World Bank and the Statistical Unit of the London and Scottish Clearing Banks for permission to use their statistics.

In addition, I must express my gratitude to my good friend Lester Bennett of Lester Bennett Associates for his advice on the presentation of this new edition.

Thanks also to all at Pitman, especially my editor Liz Hartley for help, advice, criticism, *patience* and lunches.

DEDICATED TO LILLIAN

1

Introduction
I Economics and the economy: an overview

1

Introduction: What is economics about?

The subject matter of economics

Defining economics

Economics is as old as the human race: it is probably the first art which man acquired. When some cavemen went out to hunt while others remained to defend the fire, or when skins were traded for flint axes, we had economics. But economics as an academic discipline is relatively new: the first major book on economics, Adam Smith's *The Wealth of Nations*, was published in 1776. Since that time the subject has developed rapidly and there are now many branches of the subject, such as microeconomics, international economics and econometrics as well as many competing schools of thought.

There is an economic aspect to almost any topic we care to mention – education, religion, employment, housing, transport, defence, etc. Economics is a comprehensive theory of how the society works. But, as such, it is difficult to define. The great classical economist Alfred Marshall defined economics as 'the study of man in the everyday business of life'.

This is rather too vague a definition. Any definition should take account of the guiding idea in economics which is *scarcity*. Virtually everything is scarce; not just diamonds or oil but also bread and water. How can we say this?

The answer is that one only has to look around the world to realise that there are not enough resources to give people all they want. It is not only the very poor who feel deprived; even the relatively well-off seem to want more. Thus when we use the word scarcity we mean that:

All resources are scarce in the sense that there are not enough to fill everyone's wants to the point of satiety.

We therefore have limited resources, both in rich countries and poor countries. The economist's job is to evaluate the choices that exist for the use of these resources. Thus we have another characteristic of economics; it is concerned with *choice*.

Another aspect of the problem is people themselves; they do not just want more food or clothing, they want particular types of food, specific items of clothing and so on.

We have now assembled the three vital ingredients in our definition, *people, scarcity* and *choice*. Thus we could define economics as:

The human science which studies the relationship between scarce resources and the various uses which compete for these resources.

The central economic problems

There are many economic problems which we encounter every day – poverty, inflation, **3** unemployment, etc. However if we use the term *the* Economic Problem we are referring to the overall problem of the scarcity of resources. Each society is faced with this, be they people still living a Stone Age life in New Guinea, people in the USSR, the USA, Poland or Argentina. Each society has to choose how to make the best use of scarce resources. The great American economist Paul Samuelson said that every economic society has to answer three fundamental questions, 'What?', 'How?' and 'For whom?'

What? What goods are to be produced with the scarce resources – clothes, food, cars, submarines, television sets, etc.?

How? Given that we have basic resources of labour, land, etc., how should we combine them to produce the goods and services which we want?

For whom? Once we have produced goods and services we then have to decide how to distribute them amongst the people in the economy.

Economic goods

All the things which people want are lumped together by economists and termed economic goods.

Economic goods are those which are scarce in relation to the demand for them.

As such this definition encompasses almost all the resources in the world: to not be an economic good a resource would have to be not scarce. About the only thing which fits happily into this category is air.

Wealth and welfare

One alternative definition of economics is that it is the study of wealth. By wealth the economist means all the real physical assets which make up our standard of living – clothes, houses, food, roads, schools, hospitals, cars, oil tankers, etc. One of the primary concerns of economics is to increase the wealth of a society, i.e. to increase the stock of economic goods. However, in addition to wealth we must also consider welfare.

The concept of welfare is concerned with the whole state of well-being. Thus it is not only concerned with more economic goods but also with public health, hours of work, with law and order, and so on. It is not difficult to see that it would be possible to increase the level of wealth in a society while decreasing its level of welfare. For example, if everyone were to work 50 per cent longer per day the country's wealth would be increased, but it is doubtful if its welfare would, because people would be over-tired, their health would break down, and so on.

Modern economics has tried to take account not only of the output of economic goods but also of economic 'bads' such as pollution. The *wealth/welfare connotation* is thus a complex aspect of the subject.

The problem of money

Money is an essential component of the modern economy, but it is not, as many people think, the *whole* subject matter of economics. Indeed we can have an economic society without money. Also, if we consider economics to be the study of wealth, it is at once obvious that we could print twice as much money without altering the real wealth of the economy. The subject matter of economics is therefore much broader than the study of money.

Relationships with other disciplines

There is an old saying: 'If two or three economists are gathered together in one place, there you will find four or five opinions.'

The reasons for disagreements in economics are: *firstly*, that in many areas, for example inflation, there is genuine disagreement over the theory; *secondly*, that economists are also human beings and have their own prejudices and preferences; and, *thirdly*, that economics is influenced by many other disciplines. Fairly obviously, economics is influenced by politics and also by sociology; less obviously, it is influenced by physics, chemistry and the other natural sciences. The last point can be easily demonstrated by mentioning how the developments in nuclear physics have influenced economic life today. It is small wonder, therefore, that it is difficult to arrive at a *purely* economic decision.

It has traditionally been the view that when economists pronounce on problems, they should minimise value judgments, i.e. personal opinions. While this is true, we should guard against throwing the baby out with the bathwater. If it is suggested that an economist might spend months or years studying a problem such as taxation or inflation and that at the end of this time his viewpoint is worth no more than that of someone who has not given a moment's thought to these problems, then this is clearly nonsense. It is on a par with suggesting that we take a popular vote to decide whether we should have gas-cooled nuclear reactors or advanced water-cooled reactors. The reason we study the subject is so that we shall be better informed.

Methodology in economics

Positive and normative statements

Consider the following statements.

a) The rate of inflation is greater this year than last year.

b) The UK's rate of economic growth is greater than West Germany's.

c) Liverpool deserve to win the League this year.

d) The reintroduction of the death penalty would reduce the number of murders by deterring people from the crime.

e) Old age pensions ought to be increased.

f) The UK has a deficit on her balance of payments.

Which of the above statements are 'true'? How do we establish their validity? The answer is that certain of the questions can be proved or disproved by reference to the facts. Such a statement is termed a *positive* statement.

A positive statement is one which can be tested by reference to the facts.

Many statements, however, cannot be so tested because they involve value judgments. Such statements are usually concerned with the 'ought' problems; for example, in our list above we said that old age pensions 'ought' to be raised. Such statements are termed *normative*.

A normative statement is one which cannot be tested purely by reference to the facts.

A normative statement may or may not be untrue; however it cannot be demonstrated to be correct or incorrect by reference to the facts.

If you refer back to the list you may now be able to see which are positive statements. Obviously *a*), *b*) and *f*) are definitely positive statements, but what of the rest? We find that with normative statements they often have positive aspects to them. Take the most obvious example in the list, statement *c*). Is it a positive or a normative statement? The answer is that it depends upon the time of year you make the statement. In May all the games would have been played and the team with the most points would 'deserve' to win the League.

We will find with the two remaining statements that, although seemingly normative, they have positive aspects. 'Ought' we to raise old age pensions? Ultimately this is a normative problem, but there are many positive problems we might investigate, such as what is the rate of inflation, what has happened to pensioners' real incomes, and so on. If we consider the most emotive of the statements, the one about the death penalty, we will also find that there are positive questions we could answer such as, 'Has the murder rate decreased in those states in the USA where the death penalty has been reintroduced?' When such positive evidence is introduced we see that we begin to have a better understanding and so, too, reduce the normative element.

For many years after the Second World War economics was dominated by the positive approach to the subject. Indeed one of the most **5** famous textbooks, Lipsey's *An Introduction to Positive Economics* draws its title from this. There is now a growing opposition to positivism and to hypothetico-deductive methodology. Increasingly there is a recognition that economics is a value laden subject. In some ways we may therefore have returned to the subject of *political economy* in which economics had its origins. However in saying that there may be value judgements in economics we must be careful not to state that problems are simply 'a matter of opinion' when there are many elements which we can answer scientifically.

Scientific method

We say we attempt to test our economic ideas scientifically, but how is this done? Scientific method begins with the formulation of a theory about behaviour. For example, we may put

forward the idea that the demand for a good is determined by its price. On the basis of this we may reason that as the price is increased, demand goes down, while if the price is decreased the demand will go up. This then gives us a *hypothesis* which can be tested on observed behaviour. This testing of ideas on the evidence is known as *empiricism*. Having made our observations we may then:

a) confirm our theory;
b) reject it;
c) amend it in the light of the evidence.

This process is shown in diagrammatic form in Fig. 1.1.

Ceteris paribus

This is the Latin expression which means *all other things remaining constant*. This is an essential component of scientific method. In physics, for example, if we wished to test the effects of temperature upon a body we would not simultaneously change the pressure, altitude, etc. It is the same in economics; if, for example, we wish to examine the effect of price on demand we do not simultaneously change incomes, tastes, etc. Therefore, when formulating economic principles, we are usually careful to state that such and such will happen, *ceteris paribus*.

This principle presents particular problems in the social sciences because, whereas in the natural sciences we can undertake laboratory experiments, this is not possible where human society is concerned – we cannot command all social factors except one to stand still. This does not mean, however, that we have to abandon scientific method; rather, we should work harder to refine it in relation to the subject.

Human behaviour

It can be argued that since economics is concerned with human behaviour, it is impossible to reach any firm conclusions. This may be so if we consider the behaviour of *one* person, since human beings are unpredictable and may react in opposite ways to the same stimulus. How-

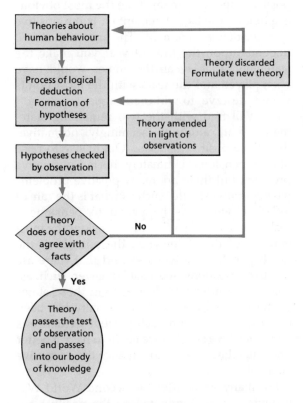

6   Fig. 1.1 *The scientific testing of theories*

ever, while individuals are unpredictable, people in large numbers are not. If, for example, we increase people's income it is possible that any particular individual may or may not spend more. However if we examine what happens to a million people as their income increases it is possible to conclude that, overall, their expenditure will increase. Thus, examining a large number of people's behaviour allows us to take advantage of the *law of large numbers*. This law predicts that the random behaviour of one person in a large group will be offset by the random behaviour of another, so that we are able to make definite predictions about the behaviour of the group as a whole.

Different answers to the same questions

We stated earlier in this chapter that each society has to answer three fundamental economic questions. 'What?', 'How?' and 'For whom?' While there are a million variations on answers to these questions, when we look around the world we find that there are only a limited number of ways in which societies have set about answering them. We will now examine these briefly.

Tradition and command

For most of human history the 'What?', 'How?' and 'For whom?' has been solved by the twin forces of tradition and command. To illustrate this let us consider feudal society. *What* crop should be planted and *how* should it be grown? The answer is that the same crops were always planted and always grown in the same manner. The decisions that could not be taken by tradition were taken by command. The king or the lord of the manor simply ordered people what to do. The *for whom* question was answered in a similar manner, with the nobility taking most of the wealth, leaving a bare minimum for the rest.

It is easy to scoff at feudal society, but it should be remembered that this form of organisation

lasted for hundreds of years, while our own system has lasted for a relatively short period of time and is now under great strain.

We do not usually include tradition and command in our classification of economic societies today, but it should not be thought that such societies have disappeared. Obviously in many less developed countries, and even in some wealthy countries such as Saudi Arabia, tradition and command are still important. Indeed, tradition and command are also still important in our own society. For example, patterns of consumption are largely a matter of tradition, and command is by no means absent.

Free enterprise: the price system

The feudal society we have described was largely a non-monetary society; people did not work for wages but merely to produce their food. They did not pay rent for their land; instead they worked for so many days in the lord's fields. Money was only used for the relatively small percentage of things which the local economy could not produce. However, over a period of several hundred years this changed and there was a monetisation of the economy: people grew food not to eat but to sell; labourers worked for wages; rent was paid for land; taxes were paid to the king. Thus was developed the price system.

The price system is the situation where the economic decisions in the economy are reached through the workings of the market.

Thus, everything – houses, labour, food, land, etc. – came to have its market price, and it was through the workings of market prices that the 'What?', 'How?' and 'For whom?' decisions were taken. There were no central committees organising shoe production or regulating wages, but this resulted not in chaos but order. People, by being willing to spend money, signalled to producers what it was they wished to be produced. The 'How?' question was answered because one producer had to compete with others to supply the market: if that producer could not produce as cheaply as possible then custom would be lost to competitors. The 'For whom?' question was answered by the fact that anyone who had the money and was willing to spend it could receive the goods produced.

The study of the price system forms much of the subject matter of economics and, hence, of this book. It should be said, however, that the free market, or free enterprise system, as envisaged by the classical economists such as Adam Smith and Alfred Marshall, has been much modified by the growth of large monopolistic businesses and unions. It would probably be more accurate today to describe the market system as capitalism rather than free enterprise.

Collectivism

In the twentieth century there has grown up a new economic order, known as *collectivism*.

Collectivism is the system whereby economic decisions are taken collectively by planning committees and implemented through direction of resources either centrally or at local level.

Under this system planning committees are appointed and they provide the answers to our three central questions. Thus committees take the decision on whether, for example, more cars or more tractors should be produced. They solve the 'How?' problem by directing labour and other resources into certain areas of production and, at the end of the day, they decide the 'For whom?' problem not by pricing but by allotting goods and services on the grounds of social and political priorities.

In the world today we associate collectivism mainly with communist states such as the USSR and China. However collectivism need not

mean the state socialism of those countries. Possibly the most socialist and collectivist form of organisation is to be found in some of the kibbutzim in Israel, but no one suggests calling Israel a communist state.

The mixed economy

By a mixed economy we mean one in which some economic decisions are taken by the market mechanism and some collectively. To this mixture we might also add a dash of 'tradition and command'.

All economies are mixed to some extent: there are some free markets in the USSR; there are collectivist decisions in the USA. We might thus arrange the economies of the world in a spectrum stretching from those which are predominantly collectivist to those which are mainly free market or capitalist. This is shown in Fig. 1.2. Thus, on the left we see Albania and the USSR and at the right we see the USA and Japan.

When we use the term mixed economy it is usually applied to economies where there is a significant component of both collectivism and free enterprise.

Despite the fact that all economies are mixed, we usually reserve the term for economies where there is a reasonable balance between the various methods of running the economy. It is a term, therefore, which is well illustrated by the UK, Sweden and other Western European economies.

There are some economists, notable amongst them John Kenneth Galbraith, who would reject these classifications and argue in favour of new classifications. Galbraith, for example, sees great similarities between the way decisions are taken

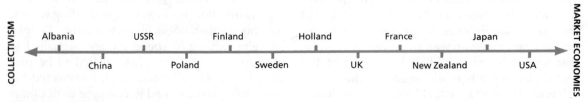

Fig. 1.2 *All economies are mixed but some are more mixed than others*

in state planning committees and the way in which the modern large business corporation takes decisions.

Conclusion: why study economics?

In this final section of the chapter is a plea to avoid the OBE, the One Big Explanation for the economy. We have all met people who will tell us 'the whole trouble with the economy is trade unions', 'the whole trouble with the economy is management', 'there is only one thing which causes inflation', and so on. If you just glance through the pages of this book you will see that economics is a vast and often complex subject and many of the problems are, as yet, imperfectly understood. This should only encourage our wish to study and so to understand.

We study economics in the belief that through understanding we will be able to increase the wealth and welfare of society, and with the conviction that knowledge is better than opinion, analysis better than supposition. What we understand about economics is terribly im-portant; it influences us all. We can put this need no better than it was put in 1936 by John Maynard Keynes in the closing words of the most influential economics book of the century, *The General Theory of Employment, Interest and Money*.

The ideas of economists and political philosophers, both when they are right and when they are wrong, are more powerful than is commonly understood. Indeed the world is ruled by little else. Practical men, who believe themselves to be quite exempt from any intellectual influences, are usually the slaves of some defunct economist. Madmen in authority, who hear voices in the air are distilling their frenzy from some academic scribbler of a few years back. I am sure that the power of vested interests is vastly exaggerated compared with the gradual encroachment of ideas. Not indeed, immediately but after a certain interval; for in the field of economic and political philosophy there are not many who are influenced by new theories after they are twenty-five or thirty years of age, so that ideas which civil servants and politicians and even agitators apply to current events are not likely to be the newest. But, soon or late, it is ideas, not vested interests which are dangerous for good or evil.

Summary

1 Economics is the human science which studies the relationship between scarce resources and the various uses which compete for these resources.
2 All economic societies have to answer three fundamental questions: 'What shall be produced?', 'How shall it be produced?' and 'For whom?'
3 Wealth is the stock of physical assets while welfare is the general state of well-being.
4 It is difficult to arrive at 'pure' economic decisions since the economic problems are closely bound up with political, sociological and other problems.
5 Great emphasis is placed in economics on separating positive from normative problems.
6 There are four main categories of economic society; those run by:
   a) tradition and command;
   b) the market mechanism;
   c) collectivism; and
   d) a mixture of the other methods, i.e. the mixed economy.
7 The study of economics is of fundamental importance to the well-being of society.

9

Questions

1   Comment upon the economic aspects of sport, leisure, religion, transport, television and education.
2   List five economic goods whose production also involves economic 'bads'.
3   Why may economists agree on theory but disagree on policy?
4   Make positive and normative statements about:
   a) the distribution of income;
   b) inflation;
   c) industrial relations;
   d) health care.
5   Discuss the emotive content in the following terms: free enterprise; communism; trade unions; hard work; monopolies; gambling and money lending.
6   List five goods or services you have used today and say by which of the economic systems – free enterprise, collectivism, etc. – they were produced.
7   What criteria would you use for assessing the effectiveness of an economic society? Are they all positive or are some normative?
8   Why have you chosen to study economics?

Data response   Defining economics

Read the following statements carefully. They are all concerned with the subject matter of economics and economic society and about the study of economics.

The great object of the political economy of every country, is to increase the riches and power of that country.
Adam Smith *The Wealth of Nations*

The history of all hitherto existing society is the history of class struggles. Freeman and slave, patrician and plebian, lord and serf, guild master and journeyman, in a word, oppressor and oppressed, stood in constant opposition to each other, carried on an uninterrupted, now hidden, now open fight, a fight that each time ended, either in a revolutionary reconstitution of society at large, or in the common ruin of the contending classes.
Karl Marx and Friedrich Engels *The Communist Manifesto*

The science of Political Economy as we have it in England may be defined as the science of the business, such as business is in large productive and trading communities.
Walter Bagehot *Economic Studies*

Economics is a study of mankind in the ordinary business of life.
Alfred Marshall *Principles of Economics*

Economic life is an organisation of producers to satisfy the wants of consumers.
John Hicks *The Social Framework*

Economics is a science which studies human behaviour as a relationship between ends and scarce means which have alternative uses.
Lionel Robbins *An Essay on the Nature and Significance of Economic Science*

The economist's value judgements doubtless influence the subjects he works on and perhaps also at times the conclusions he reaches . . . Yet this does not alter the fundamental point that, in principle there are no value judgements in economics.
Milton Friedman *Value Judgements in Economics*

Less than a century ago a treatise on economics began with a sentence such as, 'Economics is a study of mankind in the ordinary business of life'. Today it will often begin, 'This unavoidably lengthy treatise is devoted to an examination of an economy in which the second derivatives of the utility function possess a finite number of discontinuities. To keep the problem manageable, I assume that each individual consumes only two goods, and dies after one Robertsonian week. Only elementary mathematical tools such as topology will be employed, incessantly.'
George J. Stigler *The Intellectual and the Market Place*

'Do you have anything on economics?' asked a colleague in his local bookshop. 'Over there', replied the assistant, 'beyond fiction.'
Anonymous. Quoted in *Financial Times* 9.11.81.

Having studied these statements, say which of the statements you consider is the best description of economic society and the study of economics. Explain the reasons for your choice as fully as possible. You should also explain your reasons for rejecting the other statements.

(All the above statements, including the last one, have something important to say about economics. If you are only just starting to study the subject you may find understanding them and explaining what they mean difficult. However if you have read the first chapter you should be able make some sense of them. This would be a very good exercise to return to at the end of your studies.)

2
Mathematical techniques in economics

Statistical figures referring to economic events are historical data. They tell us what happened in a non-repeatable historical case
Ludwig Edler von Mises

He uses statistics like a drunken man uses lamp-posts – for support rather than illumination.
Andrew Lang

Economics makes extensive use of statistics and mathematics. There is now a branch of economics called *econometrics* which is the application of mathematics to economic theories. Students are often daunted by mathematical techniques and therefore in this chapter we will attempt to explain the basic techniques which are used in a study of the subject at this level.

The use and abuse of statistics

Numbers often appear to have a magical authority about them. Politicians and economists produce statistics to 'prove' their case. However we must treat figures with caution for three reasons. Firstly there may be inaccuracies in the compilation of data and, secondly, figures can be 'presented' in such a way as to distort them. This does not mean that we abandon statistics; rather that we need to study them more carefully in order to appreciate what they really do mean. Thirdly, the compilation of statistics usually reflects a particular way of looking at a problem and thus they seldom speak for themselves.

We will first consider the visual presentation of data.

Visual deception

The choice of scale in graphs can be deceptive. Figure 2.1 is taken from Chapter 10. Both graphs show the same information but because of the different scales used, a very different impression is gained from *a*) than is from *b*).

Figure 2.2 shows a graph as it might appear in a newspaper. This gives an extremely misleading impression but is typical of the way statistics are presented in the media. The vertical axis, as you see, does not start at zero but at 500 and the gap in the horizontal axis with the graph plunging through it gives the impression that the figures have broken some sort of barrier when, in fact, none exists.

Numerical deception

Consider the following two statements.

In the last four years the size of the national debt has grown by no less than £25 billion.

In the last four years the size of the national debt has shrunk from 6 per cent of the national income to 3 per cent of the national income.

Which of the statements is correct? The answer is that they both may be. What we see is that the way in which the change in the national debt is represented has been chosen to support two different viewpoints.

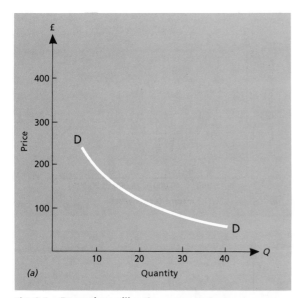

(a)

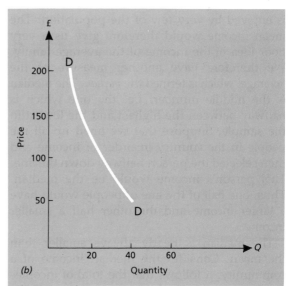

(b)

Fig. 2.1 *Deceptive calibrations on graphs*

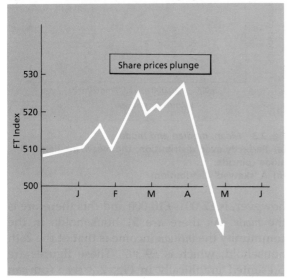

Share prices plunge

Fig. 2.2 *Visual deception*
The graph of share prices gives a misleading impression of the magnitude of changes in the index of share prices in the first six months of the year.

Averages and distribution

Most people are familiar with the view of an average, or to use the correct name, an *arithmetic mean*. Table 2.1 shows figures for the GDP of various countries. You can see that the average figure (GDP divided by population) gives a very different impression of the economies involved than the aggregate figure for GDP. However, the average figure can also be misleading. Does the fact that GDP/head in the United Arab Emirates is nearly three times as high as that of the UK mean that the typical citizen there enjoys a living standard three times as high as the average Briton? No! This is not the case because we also need to know about the distribution of income in the two countries.

Table 2.1 Population and income (1984)

Country	Population (millions)	GDP ($m)	GDP/head ($)
India	749·2	162 280	217
Nigeria	96·5	73 450	761
Greece	9·9	29 550	2 984
UK	56·4	425 370	7 542
Germany	61·2	613 160	10 019
Japan	120·0	1 255 006	10 458
Sweden	8·3	91 880	11 070
USA	237·0	3 634 600	15 336
United Arab Emirates	1·3	28 840	22 185

Source: World Development Report, *IBRD*

Means and medians

Means can be very misleading. For example, in many countries the bulk of the national income **13** is enjoyed by very few of the population. The mean income would therefore give us a very poor idea of the income of the average family. We therefore have another measure of the 'average' which is termed the *median*. The median is the middle number, i.e. the one which is halfway between the highest and the lowest in the sample. Suppose that we lined up all the people in the country in order of income and then selected the person halfway down the line. This person's income would be the median. Thus, one half of the line of people would have a larger income and the other half a smaller income.

The median is nearly always smaller than the mean. Consider the median income of a community. It follows that the total of incomes for the poorer half of the community must be smaller than that of the richer half.

Table 2.2 Distribution of household incomes

Number of households	Annual income (£)
1	less than 3 000
3	3 001– 4 000
5	4 001– 5 000
7	5 001– 7 000
13	7 001–10 000
12	10 001–15 000
7	15 001–25 000
2	25 001–50 000
1	more than 50 000
Total 51	650 000

The mode

Another measure of the 'average' exists and this is termed the *mode*. The mode is the most commonly occurring figure in the sample. We can further explain these concepts by taking a numerical example. Table 2.2 shows the distribution of annual incomes in a community of 51 households. The total income for the community is £650 000 so that this gives an arithmetic *mean* of £12 745 per household. The most commonly occurring level of income,

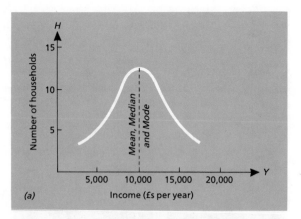

(a)

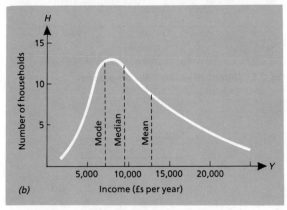

(b)

Fig. 2.3 *Mean, median and mode*
(a) Perfectly even distribution; the mean, median and mode coincide.
(b) A 'skewed' distribution.

however, is £7 001–£10 000 and this therefore is the *mode*. As there are 51 households in the community the *median* income is that of the 26th household, which is £9 307. These figures are presented graphically in Fig. 2.3 (*b*). You can see that the mode is the highest point of the distribution curve, whilst the median and mean are displaced to the right. This is referred to as 'skewedness'. By comparison, Fig. 2.3 (*a*) shows how the curve would look if there were a totally even distribution.

The existence of these various measures of the average should warn us to treat statistics with care. The mode or the median may give a much better idea of the typical unit in a sample than does the arithmetic mean.

Indices

What is an index number?

Index numbers or indices are another commonly used statistical technique in economics. An index is a method of expressing the change of a number of variables through the movement of one number. The technique consists of selecting a base, which is given the value of 100, and then expressing all subsequent changes as a movement of this number. This is most easily explained by taking the change in just one variable. Say, for example, that we consider the output of cars in the economy (see Table 2.3). If year 1 is adopted as the base, then this is given the value of 100. In year 2 production is 15 per cent higher and therefore the index becomes 115, and so on. The table records a fall in production in year 4 below the level of year 1, and so the index number is less than 100. As you can see in Table 2.3, it is rather easier to judge the magnitude of the changes by looking at the index number than by looking at the output figures.

Table 2.3 **Index of car production**

Year	Output of cars	Index number
1	1 502 304	100
2	1 727 609	115
3	1 906 003	127
4	1 400 005	93
5	1 679 294	112
6	1 699 024	113

Weighting

Index numbers are usually used to measure the movement of many things simultaneously. In our example so far we have used the output of just one commodity, cars, and there is therefore no problem involved. However if we wished to compile an index of all industrial production the output of many different commodities would have to be measured.

However when we come to consider a number of factors simultaneously we have to assign to them some measure of their relative importance. This is referred to as *weighting*. Table 2.4 gives a simplified example of how this may be done. Here we are concerned with five industries. In year 1 each industry's output has an index of 100, but in year 2 industry A's output has risen to 115, while that of industry B has fallen to 90, and so on. If we then add up the five index numbers in column (3) and average them out by dividing by five, we see that the index number for year 2 is 106. However this could be misleading since industry B might be more important than industry C.

How, therefore, do we decide whether the 15 per cent rise in industry A is more significant than the 10 per cent fall in industry B? As a measure of their relative importance we have taken the number of people they employ, and this is shown in column (4). To weight the index we now multiply the index number by the weight. This gives a value of 230 for industry A and 630 for industry B, and so on. When this has been done we total the figures in column (5) and divide by the sum of the weights. Thus we arrive at an overall index number of 99 for year 2.

Thus the unweighted index made it appear that industrial output overall had risen, while the weighted index shows that it has fallen. This is because the rises in output were in the industries which employed few people, while the industries which employed more experienced falls in output.

Table 2.4 **Weighting an index**

Industry	Index of output, year 1	Index of output, year 2	Weight (No. of people employed)	Year 2 index multiplied by weight ((3) × (4))
(1)	(2)	(3)	(4)	(5)
A	100	115	2	230
B	100	90	7	630
C	100	95	9	855
D	100	120	2	240
E	100	110	3	330
Total	500	530	23	2 285
Index	100	106	–	99

Price indices

The most frequently used index is that which measures prices, the retail price index (RPI). In this we have to combine the movements in prices of thousands of different commodities. This is described in detail in Chapter 33. The weighting technique, however, is exactly as described above.

Econometrics

If we use mathematical and statistical techniques to analyse economic problems then this is termed *econometrics*. In this section we will consider some of the more commonly used techniques. You should be familiar with these if you are to gain a firm grasp of the subject.

Symbols

We make use of symbols in economics. In so doing we are adopting a kind of shorthand. The symbols are common to most economics books so that once they are learnt they should help us to speed up our writing on the subject. Typical examples of such symbols are:

Y = income
Q = output or quantity
S = savings

Unfortunately arrays of symbols in texts can look forbidding but the student should remember that they are not in themselves mathematical, just abbreviations.

Functions

We will often find that the magnitude of one factor is affected by another. For example, the demand for a good is affected by its price. In mathematical terms we could say that demand is a *function* of price. This can be written as:

$Q = f(P)$

where Q is the quantity demanded and P the price.

Often the value of the factor we are considering will be affected by several variables. These we can add to the function. Thus, for example,

$Q = f(P, Y, P_1 \ldots P_{n-1}).$

This tells us that demand is a function of the price of the commodity (P), consumers' income (Y) and the price of other commodities ($P_1 \ldots P_{n-1}$).

Writing things in this fashion is, again, just a form of shorthand because *no values* have been ascribed to P, Y, etc. Once we put in values, we obtain one of two kinds of function.

a) Linear functions. This is where, if we plotted the figures as a graph, we would obtain a straight line. For example, consider the function:

$C = 0.8Y$

where C is total consumer spending and Y is income. This expression tells us that consumption is always 0.8 (80 per cent) of income. This would produce a straight line graph.

b)Non-linear functions. Any function which does not give a straight line when plotted as a graph is a non-linear function. Students up to GCE A level will not be required to handle non-linear functions in examinations. However the student who wishes to venture into computer modelling will have to become adept at handling them.

Graphs

The economist makes extensive use of graphs. These are both an illustration and a means of analysis. Once again the practised economist will tell you that they are also a form of shorthand and a method by which, often complex, relationships can be reduced to a few lines on a page.

Graphs are a method of showing the relationship of one variable to another. On the horizontal (or x) axis of the graph we place the independent variable, and on the vertical (or y) axis we place the dependent variable.

Consider the following figures:

Year	Sales of product Z (thousands/year)
1980	5
1981	10
1982	12
1983	7
1984	14

Which is the independent variable? Obviously it is time (the year) since that depends upon no other factor, whereas the quantity of sales *depends* upon the year we are considering. Thus if we plot these figures on a graph we obtain Fig. 2.4.

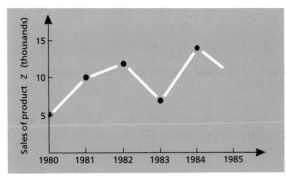

Fig. 2.4 *The dependent variable*
The independent variable (time) is plotted on the *x* axis and the dependent variable (sales of Z) on the *y* axis.

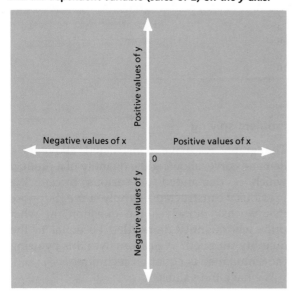

Fig. 2.5 *Plotting positive and negative values of* x *and* y

The figures in the table can be referred to as *discrete* data because they give a *separate* piece of information for each year. The information given by the graph is *continuous data* because we can obtain information for any point between 1980 and 1984.

The graph in Fig. 2.4 shows only positive values of *x* and *y*. However it is possible to have graphs with negative values, in which case the axes (or coordinates) would be as shown in Fig. 2.5. We will come across such graphs. Figure 17.2 (Chapter 17) shows negative values for *y* when we plot the marginal revenue of a business, and Fig. 5.8 (Chapter 5) shows negative values for *x*.

Equations and graphs

If we have the equation for two related variables, such as the quantity of a good supplied and its price, then we can plot a graph to show them. Suppose we have the equation:

$$P = 2Q$$

Then in order to plot the graph we have to ask ourselves what if the value of Q were 1, what if it were 2, and so on. Knowing that Q is always half the value of P, we would obtain the figures in Table 2.5.

Table 2.5 Values of *P* and *Q* (1)

Values of Q (x)	Values of P (y)
1	2
2	4
3	6
4	8
5	10

What values must we assign to P and Q? That need not concern us at the moment. We can simply have them as one unit of P or two units of P and so on. We can decide later whether we are talking about pennies or kilograms or tonnes.

If we plot the figures in Table 2.5, we obtain the graph in Fig. 2.6. The graph slopes upwards from left to right. This is said to be a direct, or **17**

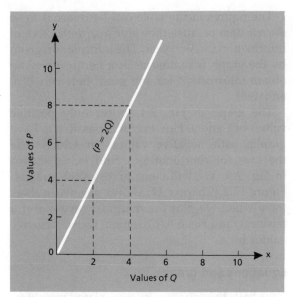

Fig. 2.6 *The slope of a line given by the equation:* *P = 2Q*

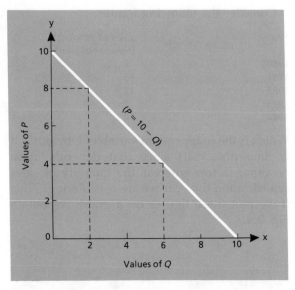

Fig. 2.7 *The slope of a line given by the equation:* *P = 10−Q*

positive, slope since as the value of P increases so does the value of Q.

The graph we have drawn is an example of a supply curve. In plotting it we have departed from mathematical convention because Q has been placed on the x axis. However, it is, strictly speaking, the dependent variable because the quantity supplied *depends* upon the price and so should go on the y axis. The reason for plotting it as we have is that when economists such as Alfred Marshall first began to plot supply and demand curves, they plotted them in this way. If they were plotted as they should be they would appear very unfamiliar to economists. We will therefore adhere to this convention for demand and supply curves. However, elsewhere we keep to the correct mathematical convention.

Suppose that we have a function which is:

$$P = 10 - Q$$

Now what happens if we ask ourselves the question what is the value of P if Q is 1? We obtain the result that P must be 9. If we continue for other values of Q then we obtain the figures in Table 2.6. If these figures are plotted as a graph, as in Fig. 2.7, we see that this produces a

downward sloping line. This is referred to as an inverse or negative slope since as the value of Q *increases*, the value of P *decreases*.

Table 2.6 Values of *P* and *Q* (2)

Values of Q (x)	Values of P (y)
2	8
4	6
6	4
8	2
10	0

Problem solving

The graph we have constructed above is a demand curve, showing the quantity of a product which is demanded at various prices. We previously constructed a supply curve. Suppose that we ask ourselves the question, at what price will quantity demanded be equal to the quantity supplied? We can answer this by using the simultaneous equation technique.

We have the values

$$P = 2Q \text{ (supply)} \tag{1}$$

18

and

$$P = 10 - Q \text{ (demand)} \qquad (2)$$

The price (P) for demand and supply will be the same when:

$$2Q = 10 - Q \qquad (3)$$

If we move all the Qs to one side of the equation and the numbers to the other, we obtain:

$$3Q = 10 \qquad (4)$$

Thus

$$Q = 3\tfrac{1}{3} \qquad (5)$$

To obtain the value for P we now need only insert the value of Q into expression (1) and we obtain:

$$P = 2 \times 3\tfrac{1}{3}$$
$$P = 6\tfrac{2}{3}$$

We can check that this result is correct by doing a similar exercise with expression (2).

$$P = 10 - 3\tfrac{1}{3}$$
$$P = 6\tfrac{2}{3}$$

Thus the quantity is the same for both supply and demand when price = $6\tfrac{2}{3}$. You can check that this is so by superimposing Fig. 2.6 on Fig 2.7. You will see that this is the point where the two curves intersect. The student who is unsure about this analysis should now attempt the relevant questions at the end of the chapter. It is important to master this, because questions are set on it.

The approach we have adopted here might be criticised as being too specific to one set of problems (demand and supply). Many books prefer to conduct this analysis in purely abstract terms of x and y. We have adopted the price and quantity approach because this is the most usual area for problems. However the student should remember that the mathematics can be applied to any linear functions.

Correlation

Correlation exists when there is a connection between two variables. We establish the existence of a correlation by collecting information.

Figure 2.8 shows two *scatter diagrams*. Both diagrams show information about the same group of 20 male adults. Figure 2.8 (*a*) depicts the

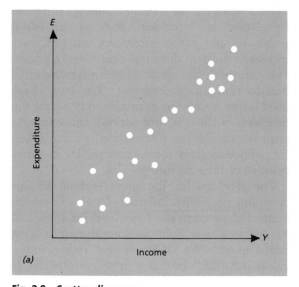

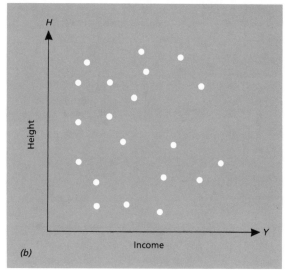

Fig. 2.8 *Scatter diagrams*
(*a*) This shows a possible correlation between the income of the 20 persons in the sample and their expenditure.
(*b*) There is no correlation between income and height.

relationship between income and expenditure while Fig. 2.8 (*b*) shows the relationship between income and height. It is clear that there is a possible correlation between income and expenditure, but none between income and height.

Regression

To measure the relationship between two variables when correlation appears to exist, we need to indulge in a *regression analysis*. How this is done is illustrated in Fig. 2.9. Here we have drawn two regression lines. This has been done visually to obtain a *line of best fit*. Visually they both may appear sound, but if we wish to find the best regression line then we must obtain the so-called line of *least squares*. This is done by drawing a line from each of the dots to the regression lines A and B. We then measure the length of each line and *square* it. Then the total of these squares is found for the two regression lines. The regression line with the smaller total is the better fit. In this case it is line A.

The slope of the regression line now tells us the *regression coefficient* of the two variables.

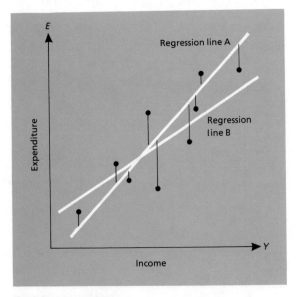

Fig. 2.9 *Least squares*
The line of best fit is the one which has the smallest total of the squares of the distances of the dots from it.

In our example we have shown the regression of expenditure on income. This could be, for example:

$$E = 0.6Y$$

telling us that expenditure (*E*) is 0.6 of income (*Y*).

Correlation and causation

The fact that there appears to be a correlation between two variables does not prove that one *causes* the other. Two major problems exist.

a) Wrong-way causation. It is a proven fact that in the cities of northern Germany there is a correlation in the number of babies born and the number of storks' nests. Should this then be taken as proof that storks do indeed bring babies? The causation is, of course, the wrong way round. Cities that have more children have more houses and, therefore, more chimneys for storks to build their nests in.

*b) Spurious causation.*It is a statistical fact that during the 1970s there was a positive correlation between the rise in the cost of living in London and the number of foreign tourists visiting the city. Does this therefore prove that rising prices caused more people to visit London? Here the correlation is 'spurious' because increased prices do not cause increased tourism, and increased tourism does not cause rising prices. They are both the result of more fundamental broader-ranging phenomena. We have here used rather humorous examples to illustrate the problem, but it is a very serious and common error in the subject. Correlation is often taken by politicians (and some economists) as proof positive of their argument.

Consider one of the most serious of our economic problems, inflation. One can demonstrate a close correlation between inflation and the rise in wages. Politicians are therefore often heard to say 'We all know that rising wages cause inflation.' Is this a true correlation? Is it a wrong-way causation or is it a spurious correlation? At the same time we can show a strong positive correlation between increases in the money stock and rising prices. Some politicians (often the same ones) therefore state with equal confidence, 'Increases in the money supply cause inflation.' A moment's reflection will tell you that if it is increased wages which are *the* cause of inflation it cannot at the same time be increases in the money stock.

It would be presumptuous of us to suggest a glib answer to the above problem, being, as it is, one of the most thorny in modern economics, but we hope by the end of the book to have done so. Suffice it to say that *correlation is not causation*. In addition to correlation, we need an explanation of *why* one factor relates to another.

Summary

1 Numerical and statistical information can be used both to inform and deceive.
2 There are several types of 'average'. These are the mean, the median and the mode.
3 Index numbers are a method of expressing the change in a number of variables through the movement of one number. They are frequently used to measure such things as the price level.
4 Symbols are used in economics as a convenient means of abbreviation.
5 Functions can be used to express the relationship of one variable to another.
6 Equations can be used to draw graphs.
7 Correlation in a graph does not imply causation.

Questions

1 Define the following: mean; median; mode; index numbers; correlation.
2 Suppose that you wanted to describe the 'average' intelligence of the population. What measure(s) would you use and why? If instead you wanted to describe the average ownership of wealth in the economy, how would your choice of measure differ and why?
3 Construct a graph which is calculated to deceive someone, for example showing changes in the exchange rate in the last 12 months.
4 Re-read the section on page 12 on numerical deception and then explain how the same information could lead to the two seemingly contradictory statements.
5 Describe how an index might be compiled to measure prices.
6 Construct a graph and on it draw the line which would illustrate the following functions: $y = 3x$ and $y = 10 - x$. State the value of x and y where the two lines intersect.
7 Construct a graph to illustrate the following function:

$$y = 4 + \frac{5}{x}$$

8 In the following situations, determine the points at which x and y are equal, i.e. where the graphs would intersect.

a) $y = 1 + 3x$
$y = 25 - x$

b) $y = 20 + 5x$
$y = 100 - x$
c) $y = 10 + x$
$y = 2x - 40$

Data response Maps and models

Study carefully the maps shown in Fig. 2.10. These both show areas of London around the King's Cross area; one is an extract from the Streetfinder map and the other is based on the Underground map.

1 a) What means of presenting information is used in the two illustrations?

b) How would the producer of the illustrations go about presenting the information?

c) In what ways can these presentations be seen as 'model building'?

2 Explain as fully as possible what the use of models is in economics.

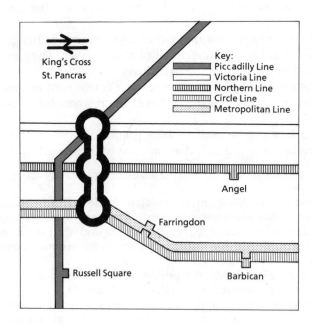

Fig. 2.10 (a)

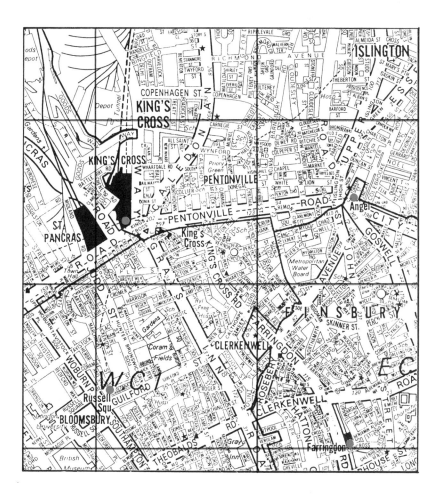

Fig. 2.10 (*b*)

3

The economic problem: resources and their exploitation

The economic problem, as one may call it for short, the problem of want and poverty and the economic struggle between classes and nations is nothing but a transitory and unnecessary muddle.
J.M. Keynes, *Essays in Persuasion*

The economic problem

The problem restated

We saw in Chapter 1 that the fundamental economic problem is the *scarcity* of all resources. Therefore all economic decisions involve *choice* in terms of *what* to produce, *how* to produce it and *who* will receive the output thus produced. We must now turn to another aspect of the economic problem – the insatiability of human wants.

It is literally impossible to satisfy human wants because as one economic want is satisfied another appears to be created. We may liken this to a see-saw with, on the one hand, the *finite* resources of the world while on the other hand are *infinite* wants (see Fig. 3.1). It may be possible to satisfy human *needs*, so that we could say, for example, a person needs three shirts, two pairs of shoes, good health care, etc., but this is not the same thing as human *wants*. If we give people enough to eat then they appear to *want* better or different foods; if we give them

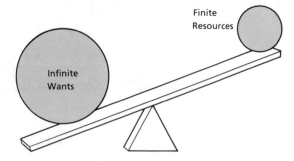

Fig. 3.1 *The economic problem: finite resources and infinite wants*

enough to wear then they want more fashionable clothes, and so on. Thus, in this sense, the economic problem is *insoluble*. Possibly the only people for whom the economic problem could be solved are those that have rejected the material world, such as monks or hermits.

Conspicuous consumption

The subject of insatiability of human wants has been the subject of much thought in economics.

24

The great American economist Thorstein Veblen (1857–1929), in his book *The Theory of the Leisure Class,* first described what is termed *conspicuous consumption.* This refers to the tendency of those above the subsistence level, i.e. the 'leisure class', to be mainly concerned with impressing others through standards of living, taste and dress. To the extent to which this is true, people may therefore reject strict economic rationality in living their lives. It should not be thought that this is exclusively a feature of modern society; the Roman empire was much given to conspicuous consumption, as are many primitive tribes today.

In more recent times Professor Galbraith has pointed out that in most advanced industrial economies most people have gone beyond the level of physical necessity. Consumers may be observed to flit from one purchase to another in response to pressures of fashion and advertising. In opposition to this it may be pointed out that many people say that there are many things they still *need* as well as *want.* This is undeniably so amongst the poor of the world. On the other hand without such theories as Veblen's it would be impossible to explain much consumer behaviour in the modern world.

The factors of production

The sum total of the economic resources which we have in order to provide for our economic wants are termed the *factors of production.* Traditionally economists have classified these under four headings. They are:

a) labour
b) land $\Big\}$ primary factors;
c) capital
d) enterprise $\Big\}$ secondary factors.

The first two are termed primary factors since they are not the result of the economic process; they are, so to speak, what we have to start with. The secondary factors, however, are a consequence of an economic system.

Labour

Labour may be defined as the exercise of human mental and physical effort in the production of goods and services.

Included in this definition is all the labour which people undertake for reward, either in the form of wages and salaries or income from self-employment. We would not, therefore, include housework or the efforts of do-it-yourself enthusiasts, even though these may be hard work. The exclusion of these items creates no real problems in an advanced economy, but in an underdeveloped country, where there is considerable subsistence agriculture, special allowance may have to be made for this (see page 91).

In more technical terms the *working population* constitutes the supply of labour. This is discussed in Chapter 4 on demography (see pages 47 to 48).

Land

Land may be defined as all the free gifts of nature.

As such, land constitutes the *space* in which to organise economic activity and the *resources* provided by nature. Thus, included within the definition are all mineral resources, climate, soil fertility, etc. The sea, since it is a resource both for fishing and mineral exploitation, would also fall within the definition of land. The economist, therefore, uses the word 'land' in a special way.

In practice it may be very difficult to separate land from other factors of production such as capital but, theoretically, it has two unique features which distinguish it.

Firstly, it is *fixed in supply.* Since, as we saw above, the sea is included in the definition, we are thus talking about the whole of the planet, and it is obvious that we can never acquire more land in this sense.

Secondly, land has no cost of production. The *individual* who is trying to *rent* a piece of land may have to pay a great deal of money, but it never cost *society* as a whole anything to produce land. This last point may seem rather abstract **25** but forms an important component of some political ideologies such as Marxism.

Capital

We define capital as the stock of wealth existing at any one time.

As such, capital consists of all the real *physical* assets of society. An alternative formulation would be:

Capital is all those goods which are used in the production of further wealth.

Capital can be divided into *fixed capital*, which is such things as buildings, roads, machinery, etc., and *working*, or *circulating*, *capital* which consists of stocks of raw materials and semi-manufactured goods. The distinction is that fixed capital continues through many rounds of production while working capital is used up in one round; for example, a machine for canning beans would be fixed capital, while *stocks* of beans to go into the cans would be circulating capital.

As stated previously, capital is a secondary factor of production, which means that it is a result of the economic system. Capital has been created by individuals *forgoing current consumption*, i.e. people have refrained from consuming all their wealth immediately and have *saved* resources which can then be used in the production of further wealth. Suppose we consider a very simple economy in which the individual's wealth consists entirely of potatoes. If the individual is able to refrain from consuming all the potatoes, then these may be planted and, thus, produce more wealth in the future. From this example it can be seen that a capital good is defined, not from what it is, but from what it does, i.e. in our example the potato is a capital good if it is used in the production of more potatoes.

Enterprise

Some economists have cast doubt on whether enterprise is a separate factor of production. However we still have to explain the vital role fulfilled by the *entrepreneur*. Enterprise fulfils two vital functions.

a) **It hires and combines the other factors of production.**
b) **It takes a risk by producing goods in anticipation of demand.**

It may be fairly easy to identify the role of the entrepreneur in a small business. However in a large business the *entrepreneurial function* will be split up between many managers and departments, as well as being shared with the shareholders of the company. Despite the difficulties involved in identifying the entrepreneur, the role of enterprise is clearly vital to the economic process since it is the *decision-making factor*. It therefore provides an important tool in our understanding of how businesses work.

Factor incomes

The various incomes which the factors receive can also be termed *factor rewards* or *factor returns*. Labour receives *wages and salaries*, land earns *rent*, capital earns *interest* and enterprise earns *profit*. In practice it is difficult to separate them precisely; for example, the 'rent' of a building is actually the rent for the land plus the interest on the capital, which is the building itself.

Division of labour

Specialisation

The expression 'division of labour' refers to the dividing up of economic tasks into specialisations. Thus few workers these days produce the whole commodity but only undertake particular parts of the production process. This factor lies at the very heart of the modern exchange economy.

The enormous advantages of division of labour were early recognised by Adam Smith and he illustrated them by the use of, what is now possibly, the most famous example in economics –

pin making. In *The Wealth of Nations* he described pin making thus.

One man draws out the wire, another straights it, a third cuts it, a fourth points it, a fifth grinds it; to make the head requires two or three distinct operations, to put it on is another peculiar business, to whiten the pin is another, it is even a trade by itself to put them into paper.

The resulting increase in output is phenomenal.

It is important to grasp the significance of this idea of specialisation. It is not necessary that any new technique be invented; the specialisation itself will result in increases in production. The ultimate extension of the principle is that of the specialisation of nations, which is the basis of the theory of international trade.

Advantages of division of labour

a) Increase in skill and dexterity. Practice makes perfect, as the saying goes; the constant repetition of tasks means that they can be done more expertly. This is well illustrated by the skill demonstrated in a job such as typing.

b) Time saving. If a person has to do many different tasks then a considerable period of time is taken *between* operations. Time can also be saved in the training of people. If, for example, a person has to be trained as an engineer this takes many years, but a person can quickly be trained to fulfil one operation in the engineering process.

c) Individual aptitudes. Division of labour allows people to do what they are best at. Some people are physically very strong, while others have good mental aptitudes. With division of labour there is a greater chance that people will be able to concentrate on those things at which they are best.

d) Use of machinery. As tasks become subdivided it becomes worthwhile using machinery, which is a further saving of effort. For example, consider wine production: if production is only a few hundred bottles then specialist bottling equipment is hardly justified; but if we are thinking of specialising in bottling tens of

thousands of bottles, then it become worthwhile using a specialist machine to do this.

Disadvantages of division of labour

Economic life without division of labour is inconceivable. Thus when we speak of its disadvantages it should be realised that these are not arguments against specialisation but rather problems associated with it.

a) Interdependency. Specialisation inevitably means that one is dependent upon other people. In the UK today we are dependent for our food upon people thousands of miles away and beyond our control.

b) Dislocation. Because of interdependency the possibilities for dislocation are very great. For example, a strike by a key group of workers such as the miners can bring the whole country to a halt.

c) Unemployment. Specialisation means that for many people their training and experience is narrow. This can mean that if that skill is no longer required it is very difficult for the person to find alternative work.

d) Alienation. This refers to the estrangement many workers feel from their work. If, for example, a person's job is simply to tighten wheel nuts on a car production line, it is understandable that he or she should feel bored or even hostile towards the work. This will therefore have had repercussions on labour relations and productivity. Some manufacturers such as Volvo have undertaken job enrichment schemes, putting division of labour into reverse, as it were, in order that people may have more varied tasks.

The alienation of the workforce is a major part of Marxist sociology. The capitalist would reply that although jobs may be dull, working hours are made shorter and leisure is enriched by greater wealth. However alienation is not a problem that should be ignored, either at work or in society in general, and a nation with as poor a record of industrial relations as the UK had until recently could do well to study the problem more carefully.

Economies of scale

Economies of scale exist when the expansion of a firm or industry allows the product to be produced at a lower unit cost. As such, economies of scale are a development of the division of labour. Economies of scale are only possible if there is sufficient demand for the product. For example, we would hardly expect to find scale economies in the production of artificial limbs, because there simply are not enough of them demanded. As Adam Smith put it, 'the extent of division of labour is limited by the size of the market'.

Internal and external economies of scale

Internal economies of scale are those obtained within one organisation, while external economies are those which are gained when a number of organisations group together in an area. Industries such as chemicals and cars provide good examples of internal economies, where the industry is dominated by a few large organisations. Historically, the most famous example of external economies of scale was the cotton industry in Lancashire, where many hundreds of businesses concentrated in a small area made up the industry. A more up-to-date example might be the grouping of firms offering specialist financial services in the City of London.

Types of internal economy

a) *Indivisibilities*. These may occur when a large firm is able to take advantage of an industrial process which cannot be reproduced on a small scale. For example, many of the modern colour printing processes are not available on a small scale.

b) *Increased dimensions*. In some cases it is simply a case of bigger is better. For example, an engine which is twice as powerful does not cost twice as much to build or use twice as much material. This is partly due to area/volume relationships. For example, if we square the dimensions of a ship we will cube its volume, i.e. its ability to carry cargo, while we will only square its resistance to motion. Hence large ships are much more efficient than small ships, which at least partly accounts for the trend towards bulk cargo carriers.

c) *Economies of linked processes*. Technical economies are also sometimes gained by linking processes together, e.g. in the iron and steel industry, where iron and steel production is carried out in the same plant, thus saving both transport and fuel costs.

d) *Commercial*. A large-scale organisation may be able to make fuller use of sales and distribution facilities than a small-scale one. For example, a company with a large transport fleet will probably be able to ensure that they transport mainly full loads, whereas a small business may have to hire transport or despatch part-loads. A large firm may also be able to use its commercial power to obtain preferential rates for raw materials and transport. This is usually known as 'bulk buying'.

e) *Organisational*. As a firm becomes larger, the day-to-day organisation can be delegated to office staff, leaving managers free to concentrate on the important tasks. When a firm is large enough to have a management staff they will be able to specialise in different functions such as accounting, law and market research.

f) *Financial*. Large organisations often find it cheaper and easier to borrow money than small ones.

g) *Risk bearing*. All firms run risks, but risks taken in large numbers become more predictable. In addition to this, if an organisation is so large as to be a monopoly, this considerably reduces its commercial risks.

h) *Overhead processes*. For some products very large overhead costs or processes must be undertaken to develop a product, for example an airliner. Clearly these costs can only be justified if large numbers of units are subsequently produced.

i) *Diversification*. Most economies of scale are concerned with specialisation and concentration. However as a firm becomes very large it may be able to safeguard its position by diversifying its products, processes, markets and the location of production.

For any product we consider, the various processes which are needed to produce it may not have the same optimal scale of production. For example, a large blast furnace may produce 75 tonnes of pig iron but a steel furnace may only be able to handle 30 tonnes; we would thus need more than one steel furnace for every blast furnace. In fact the smallest optimal size for the whole process is the lowest common multiple of the individual processes involved. In our steel-making example this would give us a plant consisting of two blast furnaces and five steel furnaces.

$$2 \times 75 \text{ tonnes} = 150 \text{ tonnes}$$
$$5 \times 30 \text{ tonnes} = 150 \text{ tonnes}$$

Thus the smallest optimal size is 150 tonnes.

Types of external economy

a) Economies of concentration. When a number of firms in the same industry band together in an area they can derive a great deal of mutual advantage from each other. Advantages might include a pool of skilled workers, a better *infrastructure* (such as transport, specialised warehousing, banking, etc.) and the stimulation of improvements. The lack of such external economies is a serious handicap to less developed countries.

b) Economies of information. Under this heading we could consider the setting up of specialist research facilities and the publication of specialist journals.

c) Economies of disintegration. This refers to the splitting-off or subcontracting of specialist processes. A simple example is to be seen in the high street of most towns where there are specialist photocopying firms.

It should be stressed that what are external economies at one time may be internal at another. To use the last example, small firms may not be able to justify the cost of a sophisticated photo-copier, but as they expand there may be enough work to allow them to purchase their own machine.

Efficiency and economies of scale

Where an economy of scale leads to a fall in unit costs because less *resources* are used to produce a unit of a commodity, then this is economically beneficial to society. If, for example, a large furnace uses less fuel per tonne of steel produced than a small one, then society benefits through a more efficient use of scarce fuel resources. It is possible, however, for a firm to achieve economies through such things as bulk-buying, where its buying power is used to bargain for a lower price. This benefits the firm because its costs will be lower, but it does not benefit society since there is no saving of resources involved.

Diseconomies of scale

Diseconomies of scale occur when the size of a business becomes so large that, rather than decreasing, the unit cost of production becomes greater. This comes about because all possible economies of scale have been exhausted. Thus, achieving the best size of business is not simply a question of getting bigger but of attaining the optimal size of business or plant.

The typical size of plant will vary greatly from industry to industry. In capital-intensive industries such as chemicals the typical unit may be very large, but in an industry like agriculture the optimum size of farm is quickly reached and, beyond this, diseconomies set in.

Economies of scale and returns to scale

Confusion frequently arises between economies of scale and returns to scale. *Economies of scale* reduce the unit *cost* of production as the scale of production increases, while *returns to scale* are concerned with *physical* input and output relationships. If, for example, the input of factors of production were to increase by 100 per cent but output were to increase by 150 per cent, we would be said to be experiencing *increasing*   29 *returns to scale*. Conversely, if inputs were to be increased by 100 per cent but output were to increase by less than this, then we would be experiencing *decreasing returns to scale*.

Increasing returns to scale should result in decreasing costs. However it does not follow that every economy of scale which reduces costs is a result of a return to scale. To take the most obvious example, bulk-buying may be a cost economy to the business but it does not involve returns to scale since no change in the input/output relationship is involved.

The new technology

Improvements in technology are obviously of fundamental importance to the economy. We have learnt that improved technology brings improved productivity and is therefore beneficial. However the impact of the *new technology* of microprocessors is likely to be so massive that it is worthwhile considering this as a constraint upon the economy.

The silicon chip has unleashed such power to process information and control activity and functions of all kinds that it is virtually impossible to foretell where it will lead. Facsimile copiers can now transmit letters without the need for the postman; microprocessor-controlled lathes can undertake the most precise and complex of engineering tasks; robots can assemble electrical components; and still the possibilities have hardly been tapped. It could be argued that our technological knowledge has run ahead of our economic and financial understanding.

Many people view the technology with alarm, seeing it purely as a method of making workers redundant . What will the future hold, though? Will microprocessors free us from the drudgery of work and create a new Utopia, or will they create vast wealth for those who are able to exploit them, and unemployment for millions of others?

Economic history tells us that vast leaps in technology have been made before, as in the industrial revolution. For example, within 10 years of its invention each spinning jenny was able to replace 100 workers. In the wake of the industrial revolution there was poverty and misery for millions, but in the long run the expansion of the economy was able to provide employment for all (labour is after all our most valuable resource) and a higher standard of living. Thus we may see our present problems as those of adjustment, although we must also bear in mind that a return to full employment depends upon a renewed expansion of the economy.

Increasing costs and diminishing returns

We have been examining factors which help people to exploit the resources of the world. However the basic law of economics is that of scarcity. We must now consider the factors which place constraints upon our exploitation of resources.

The law of diminishing returns

Why can we not grow all the world's food in one garden? A silly question perhaps, but it ilustrates a very important principle..We can get a greater output from a garden of fixed size by working longer hours or adding more seeds, etc., but the *extra* output we obtain will rapidly diminish. Indeed, if we just go on dumping more and more seeds in the garden, total output may even go down. The principle involved here is known as the *law of diminishing returns*. This law is one of the most important and fundamental principles involved in economics. We may state it thus:

If one factor of production is fixed in supply and successive units of a variable factor are added to it, then the extra output derived from the employment of each successive unit of the variable factor must, after a time, decline.

We can illustrate this by the use of a simple numerical example. Suppose that the fixed factor of production is a farm (land). If no labour is employed then there will be no output. Now let us see what happens if people are employed. Suppose that one person is employed in the first year, two in the second, and so on. Table 3.1 shows the resulting output from the various combinations of the factors. The first person results in 2000 tonnes of produce. When two people are employed output rises to 5000 tonnes, so that the second person has resulted in 3000 extra tonnes being produced. However after this, diminishing returns set in and the employment of a third person only results in 2000 tonnes more being produced, while a fourth person adds just 1000 tonnes to production. Were a fifth person to be employed there would be no extra output at all.

The law of diminishing returns comes about because each successive unit of the variable factor has less of the fixed factor to work with.

The law of diminishing returns may be offset by improvements in technology, but it cannot be repealed.

Table 3.1 The law of diminishing returns

Number of people employed	Total output (tonnes)	Extra output added by each additional unit of labour
0	0	
		2000
1	2000	
		3000
2	5000	
		2000
3	7000	
		1000
4	8000	
		0
5	8000	

The short-run and the long-run

At any particular time any business must have at least one of the factors of production in fixed supply. For example, the buildings which a firm uses cannot be expanded overnight, so that if the firm wants to obtain more output it must use more of the variable factors such as labour.

The period of time in which at least one factor is fixed in supply is defined as the short-run.

Given time, all the factors may be varied, i.e. new buildings can be constructed, more land acquired, etc.

The period of time in which all factors may be varied and in which firms may enter or leave the industry is defined as the long-run.

The length of time involved will vary from business to business. Obviously it will take much longer for an oil refinery to vary its fixed factors by constructing a new refinery than it would, for example, for a farmer to rent more land.

The law of diminishing returns is thus a *short-run phenomenon* becuse, by definition, it is concerned with a situation in which at least one factor is fixed in supply. However, there is what we might term a *very* long-run validity to the law, since we cannot indefinitely expand *all* the factors of production since all factors are limited in supply.

The law of increasing costs

The law of diminishing returns concerns what happens to output if one factor remains fixed; *the law of increasing costs* examines what happens to production, and therefore to costs, as all factors of production are increased.

Let us imagine we are faced with the choice which Hermann Goering gave the German people in 1936; we can produce either guns or butter. Table 3.2 shows a list of alternative possibilities.

Table 3.2 Increasing costs: a production possibility schedule

Possibility	Guns (thousands)	Butter (millions of kg)
A	15	0
B	14	5
C	10	10
D	5	14
E	0	15

If we start at possibility C, where we are producing 10 000 guns and 10 million kg of butter, and then try to produce more guns, this involves switching resources from farming to industry. To reach possibility B we have had to give up 5 million kg of butter to gain 4000 guns. If we want still more guns, to reach possibility A we have to give up 5 million kg of butter to gain only 1000 guns. Thus the cost of guns in terms of butter has risen sharply.

It would also work the other way. If we started from possibility C and tried to increase our output of butter, the cost in terms of guns not produced would become greater and greater. Figure 3.2 shows this graphically. As we move to either end of the *production possibility* boundary (or frontier) we can see that it is necessary to give up a greater distance on one axis to gain a smaller distance on the other axis. Why should this be? It is because as we concentrate more and more resources on the output of a particular commodity, the resources we use become less and less suitable. For example, if we tried to produce more and more butter we must, inevitably, be forced to graze cows on land which is more and more unsuitable.

Increasing costs have been looked at here from the point of view of society as a whole, but any trading organisation could easily become aware of it. If, for example, Fords tried to double the capacity of their plant at Dagenham they would immediately suffer from increasing costs as they would have to pay higher wages, to attract labour in from greater distances, and higher rents, to attract land away from other uses. Increasing costs can therefore come about as a result of two factors:

a) the use of less and less suitable resources;
b) the increased competition for resources.

It must be pointed out, however, that for any individual firm these effects are more likely to be the effects of shorter term 'local' adjustments rather than a long-term general increase in the demand for resources. For example, once sufficient people have moved it might be possible to reduce wages to former levels.

Opportunity cost

Limited resources have alternative uses; for example, the bricks and labour we use to build a house could have been used to build a factory or a hospital. Thus the cost of any product may be looked at in terms of other opportunities forgone. In the example of guns and butter used above, any movement along the production possibility line tells us the *opportunity cost* of guns in terms of butter or vice versa.

It is possible for opportunity costs to be zero. For example, from the point of view of the economy any job is worth doing rather than having labour unemployed. This may not be so to the individual if the wage offered is lower than unemployment benefit.

The production possibility boundary

If we plot the figures in Table 3.2 as a graph we obtain Fig. 3.2. This is termed a production

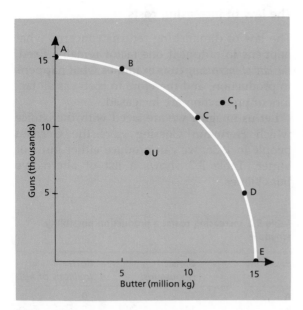

Fig. 3.2 *Production possibility boundary*
Society can attain any combination of guns and butter on line AE or any combination within it such as U, but is unable to attain a position beyond line AE such as C₁.

possibility boundary (or frontier) because it shows the limit of what it is possible to produce with present resources. Society may attain any point on the line, such as point C, or, through the unemployment or inefficient use of resources, any point within the frontier, such as U.

However point C_1 is unattainable at present. Point C_1 may become attainable as the production possibility shifts rightwards as a result of economic growth and improvements in technology.

You will note that the line is bowed outwards (concave to the origin). This is because of the law of increasing costs. A few moments experimenting with a ruler on the graph will show you that the rate of exchange of guns for butter, or vice versa, worsens continually as we move up or down the line. This is the typical shape for a production possibility boundary.

Three possibilities for a line

To check that you have understood this idea let us consider the three possibilities for the shape of the production possibility line. These are illustrated in Fig. 3.3. In Fig. 3.3 (a) as we move down the vertical axis each 20 units of X given up gains smaller and smaller amounts of Y. Moving from position A to position B we give up 20 units of Y but gain 50 units of X. However, as we move from position B to position C 20 units of Y given up now only gains us 22 units of X. The ratio of exchange continues to deteriorate until the last 20 units of Y given up only gains three units of X. Review your understanding of this principle by considering it in reverse, i.e. as we move from point F to point E it only costs three units of X given up to gain 20 units of Y but moving from position B to position A involves giving up 50 units of X to gain 20 units of Y. Thus the ratio of exchange of X for Y (or Y for X) deteriorates whichever way we move along a line which is *concave* to the origin of the graph. Such a line illustrates *increasing costs* (or diminishing returns).

In Fig. 3.3 (b) we show a *constant cost case*, i.e. that product X can be exchanged for product Y at a constant rate. You will find various applications of such a line in this book. (*See* Figs 37.1 and 37.3.)

If we look at a line which is bowed inwards (convex to the origin) this shows *increasing returns* (or decreasing costs), i.e. the ratio of exchange of X for Y (or Y for X) gets better as we move towards the ends of the line. In Fig. 3.3 (c) moving from position A to position B involves giving up 20 units of Y to gain six units of X but the next 20 units of Y given up gains eight units of X and so on until the last 20 units of Y given up gains us 52 units of X. This could come about if, for example, specialising in X allowed us to gain more and more economies of scale. Again check your understanding of the principle by moving the other way along the line and seeing that the ratio of exchange of Y for X also improves, i.e. the

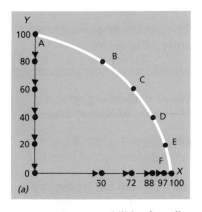 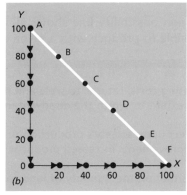 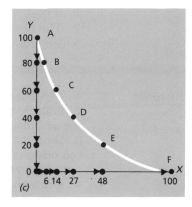

Fig. 3.3 *Three possibilities for a line*

first 20 units of Y cost us 52 units of X given up but the next 20 only 21 and so on. As we have stated above, a production possibility line is most likely to be concave, but we shall encounter various applications of these properties of lines throughout the book.

Conclusion

Choice and the economist

The student can be forgiven for finding the principles in this chapter contradictory; increasing costs for example seems to contradict economies of scale. It is necessary to realise that the economic world not only places *constraints* upon us but also *enables* us to deal with problems. Each situation therefore demands a *choice* of the best circumstances for that particular case. It is the task of the economist to assist in this choice by evaluating the possibilities.

Summary

1   The economic problem is that of infinite human wants but only limited resources with which to fulfil them.

2   Economic resources are traditionally divided into the four factors of production: labour, land, capital and enterprise.

3   Division of labour is the subdivision of the economic process into specialist tasks. The resultant increase in output is the basis of economic prosperity.

4   Economies of scale exist when the production of a product in large numbers allows its unit cost to be decreased. There are both external and internal economies of scale.

5   The law of diminishing returns states that if one factor is fixed in supply, but more and more units of a variable factor are employed, the resultant extra output will decrease.

6   The law of increasing costs is encountered when one type of production is expanded at the cost of others. It comes about because less suitable resources have to be used and because increased competition for resources drives up their cost.

7   The production possibility line shows all the combinations of products which it is possible to produce with a given quantity of resources.

Questions

1   Define increasing costs, returns to scale and the law of diminishing returns.

2   Evaluate the extent to which the disadvantages of division of labour outweigh the advantages.

3   Show the effect upon society's production possibility line in Fig. 3.2 if technological improvements increased productivity in the production of guns but not of butter.

4   If in a given situation the quantity of land could be increased but labour could not, would the law of diminishing returns still operate? Explain your answer.

5   Assess the extent to which each of the following products is affected by

available economies of scale: petroleum; milk; bespoke tailoring; cars; frozen peas; coal; luxury yachts.

6   Evaluate the role which prices play in helping to answer the economic problem.

7   Consider the opportunity cost of:

  a) a student's attendance at college;
  b) the development of Trident nuclear missiles;
  c) raising old age pensions;
  d) the construction of the M25 motorway around London.

Data response   The JSB Audiomax Speaker Company ▬▬▬▬▬▬▬▬▬▬▬

Table 3.3 presents information for the JSB Audiomax Speaker Company showing how the cost of producing loudspeakers varies with the output produced per week.

Table 3.3 Costs of the JSB Audiomax Speaker Company

Units of output produced per week	Total costs of production (£)
1009	85 025
1998	110 014
3004	130 010
4014	160 002
4997	209 889
6011	280 015
7003	370 000
7990	479 917

1   From this information construct a graph to show how the cost of producing a loudspeaker (*unit* or *average cost*) varies with the quantity of loudspeakers produced each week.

2   State the range of output over which the company experiences:
  a) increasing returns to scale
  b) decreasing returns to scale.

3   What is the most productively efficient level of output for JSB?

4   Distinguish between economies of scale and returns to scale.

5   What economies of scale are likely to be available to JSB?

4

Demography

Population is the human basis of the whole of economics. In this chapter we shall consider both the world and UK aspects of population. This statistical study of the characteristics of human populations is termed *demography*.

World population

The population explosion

Since the eighteenth century the world has undergone a population explosion. The impact of the population explosion on all aspects of human life – economic, legal, social and political – is so immense as to almost defy analysis. The population question is the all-important backdrop against which all human activities are played. For the firm it provides one of its essential resources, labour, as well as the markets for its goods and services. Government organisations must also base their plans on their estimates of changes in the future population. Although it would appear that population growth has stabilised in many Western countries, the continuing growth of world population poses some of the most imponderable questions for the future.

What is meant by the population explosion is demonstrated graphically by Fig. 4.1. It can be seen from this graph that estimated world

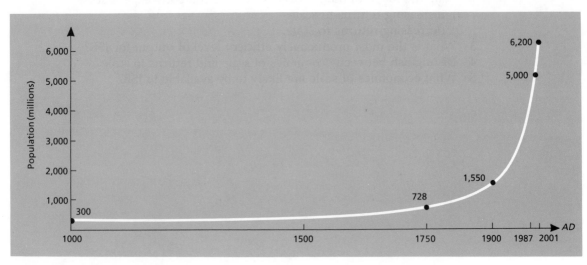

population was 300 million in AD 1000 and that this slowly rose to around 728 million in AD 1750. Population then began to rise much more quickly, reaching 5000 million by 1987. Estimates for the year 2000 envisage an increase to 6200 million. This means that population will have risen over 20-fold in the last 1000 years, having been almost static for the previous 20 000 years of human history. Moreover the majority of this growth will have taken place in 100 years. Although figures for the rate of population increase show some signs of slowing, they nonetheless indicate very great potential for growth. As total world population hit 5000 million in 1987 the rate of increase meant that population was still growing at the rate of 1 million every five days, or 1 billion every 12 years.

T.R. Malthus (1766–1834)

Accurate population figures for the UK start with the first census of 1801. Three years earlier Malthus published the first major work on population. This was entitled *An Essay on the Principle of Population as it Affects the Future Improvement of Society*. Malthus had noted the quickening growth of the UK population and was also aware of the principle of diminishing returns as expounded by Adam Smith and other political economists. Malthus wrote that:

Population when unchecked, increases in a geometrical ratio [1, 2, 4, 8, 16, etc.] Subsistence increases only in an arithmetical ratio [1, 2, 3, 4, etc.] A slight acquaintance with numbers will show the immensity of the first power in comparison with the second.

Since the amount of land on the planet is fixed, this would mean that there would be less and less food to feed each person. This would continue until population growth was halted by 'positive checks' of 'war, pestilence and famine'. This would give more food per person so that population would increase again, thus causing positive checks to set in again, and so on. Thus the gloomy forecast of Malthus was that world population would forever fluctuate around the point when most of it is on the point of starving to death. This is termed a *subsistence equilibrium*.

For a number of reasons these pessimistic forecasts did not come true in the UK. Through technological improvements, industry and agriculture became more productive, the New World and Australia provided room for expansion, and, towards the end of the nineteenth century, parents in the UK began to limit the size of their families. Moreover, there is a debate in economic history as to whether population growth stimulated economic growth or vice versa.

You must note that the law of diminishing returns cannot be repealed, only offset. When one looks at much of the Third World today, one might be forgiven for thinking that Malthus was only too right.

The rich and the poor

There is a growing disparity between the rich areas of the world and the poor, both in proportional and aggregate terms, i.e. the poor are poorer than they have ever been before. Population provides one of the major clues as to why this is so. It would appear that in some countries of the world, e.g. Zaire, however fast the gross national product (GNP) grows, population grows faster, and, therefore, the country is poorer in terms of GNP per head. The countries for which this is true are illustrated in Table 4.1. As a region the worst affected is Sub-Saharan Africa where the entire area has experienced negative growth over the past 20 years. Looking at the countries in Table 4.1 you may well be aware that many have had their problems compounded by wars. It is also the case that many of these countries are now also burdened with large amounts of international debt.

Asia (excluding the USSR), South America and Africa together occupy about 55 per cent of the land surface of the Earth and have about 70 per cent of its population, whereas Europe, North America and Australasia occupy 45 per cent of the Earth and have only 30 per cent of the population. By the end of the century it is likely that the first of these two areas will have 80 per cent of the population and the second only 20 per cent. Obviously the poorer areas **37**

Table 4.1 Countries experiencing negative growth in GNP per capita

Country	GNP per capita (average annual growth %) 1965–1984
Zaire	−1·6
Niger	−1·3
Central African Republic	−0·1
Madagascar	−1·6
Ghana	−1·9
Senegal	−0·5
Zambia	−1·3
El Salvador	−0·6
Nicaragua	−1·5
Peru	−0·1
Jamaica	−0·4
Chile	−0·1
Libya	−1·1

Source: IBRD

will need enormous advances in agricultural and industrial techniques to cope with this rise, but most of the expertise and the capital is possessed by the richer countries. It is because of this that many people consider that a great fall in the birth rate in the poor nations is the only way out of this cycle of poverty for them. It is possible, however, that continued population growth in poor countries will only increase the bargaining power of the richer nations in world markets, thereby making the problems even worse.

The order of nations in the international tables in this chapter may appear curious. They are listed from the poor to the rich according to the World Bank's tables of GNP/head.

Factors influencing the size of population

Population is affected by three main influences: the birth rate; the death rate; and by migration, i.e. the net figure derived from immigration and emigration. This is illustrated in Fig. 4.2.

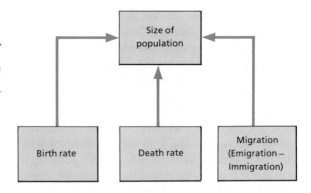

Fig. 4.2 *Factors influencing population*

Birth rate

Table 4.2 gives figures for the birth rate for various countries. Birth rates are usually expressed as a rate per thousand of the population. For example, in 1984 the birth rate in the UK was 13.0, i.e. in 1984 for every thousand people in the country 13 births took place, whereas in India the rate was 33 per thousand. This is sometimes called a *crude birth rate* since it simply records the number of live births, no allowance being made for infant mortality or other circumstances.

Table 4.2 Birth rates, selected countries

Country	Crude birth rate per thousand of population 1965	1984
India	45	33
Kenya	51	53
Mexico	45	33
Ireland	22	19
UK	18	13
USA	19	16
France	18	14
West Germany	18	10

Source: IBRD

Death rate

Death rates are normally expressed as the number of people in the country that died in a year per thousand of the population. This is sometimes called the *crude death rate* because it takes no account of the age of the person at death; they could be three months old or 90 years. Table 4.3 shows death rates for various countries.

Table 4.3 Death rates, selected countries

Country	Crude death rate per thousand of population	
	1965	*1984*
India	21	12
Kenya	21	13
Ghana	20	14
Mexico	11	7
Ireland	12	9
UK	12	12
USA	9	9

Source: IBRD

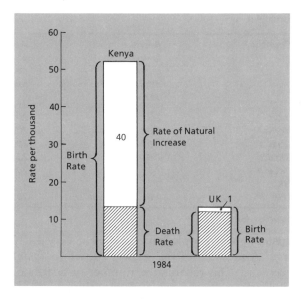

Fig. 4.3 *Rates of natural increase in population*
The rate for Kenya is 40 per thousand (4.0%) whereas the rate for the UK is only 1 per thousand (0.1%)

Net reproduction rate

The *net reproduction rate* (NRR) measures the number of daughters a newborn girl will bear during her lifetime after making assumptions about fertility and expectation of life. The NRR therefore measures the extent to which a given collection of newborn girls will reproduce themselves. A NRR of 1 indicates that fertility in a society is at replacement rate.

A way of presenting the change in society can be arrived at by comparing the birth rate with the death rate; this gives a simple measure of the *rate of natural increase* or *decrease*. This can be illustrated by superimposing one bar diagram on another. Figure 4.3 does this for both the UK and Kenya. As you can see there was virtually no growth of population in the UK in 1984, with a rate of natural increase of only 1 per thousand or 0·1 per cent per year, but in Kenya the rate was 40 per thousand.

However, the concept of a *stationary population* is slightly more complex. It is one in which not only are the birth rates and death rates equal but they must have remained so for some time and the age structure constant.

Another measure of the potential for population growth is that of *population momentum*. This measures the tendency for a population to go on growing even after the NRR has reached 1. This can be so because past high growth rates may have produced a population with a high proportion of women in the childbearing years. For example, if we assume that in 1988 the population of India was 770 million and that NRR was also 1 in that year then the level of *stationary population* would be 1349 million and this would not be until the year 2150! In this case this yields a *population momentum* of approximately 1.8.

Table 4.4 gathers together some of these measures. From this you can see that our assumptions about India proved to be very optimistic. The projected year in which the NRR will reach 1 is not until 2010 and the projected *stationary population* 1700 million.

Infant mortality

It is often misleading to speak of the average expectation of life, since for much of human

Table 4.4

Country	Average annual growth of population % 1973–84	Assumed year of reaching net reproduction rate of 1	Population momentum 1985	Total period fertility rate 1984
India	2·3	2010	1·7	4·6
Kenya	4·0	2030	2·1	7·9
Ghana	2·6	2030	1·9	6·4
Mexico	2·9	2010	1·9	4·4
Ireland	1·3	2005	1·4	2·7
UK	0·1	2010	1·1	1·8
USA	1·0	2010	1·3	1·8

Source: IBRD

history most people have died at a very early age. A measure of this exists, known as *infant mortality*. This records the number of deaths of children under the age of 12 months expressed as number per thousand of children in this age group. Historically this was very significant in the UK. In the early eighteenth century over half of the children born died before the age of one and four out of five died before the age of five. In 1951 the rate of infant mortality in the UK was 31·1 and by 1984 this had fallen to 10·0. The lowest rate in the world is enjoyed by Japan, at only 6 per thousand.

Table 4.5 gives infant mortality rates for various countries in 1984. The worst rate in 1984 was that in Mali at 176. This means that one in five children died before the age of one, a 30-fold greater mortality than in Japan.

Table 4.5 Infant mortality rates, selected countries

Country	Infant mortality rate (aged 0–1) 1984
Mali	176
India	90
Ghana	95
Mexico	51
Ireland	10
UK	10
USA	11
Japan	6

Source: IBRD

Fertility rate

Even when a population is increasing, this may be misleading since the growth of population may be due to increasing longevity so that, although there are more people, they may be concentrated in the older age groups so that the future increase of society is threatened. To overcome this we can consider the *total period fertility rate* (TPFR). This measures the average number of children born per woman of child-bearing years (defined as aged 15 to 50) that would result if women survived to the end of their reproductive period. It is necessary for the rate to be 2·0 or above if society is to continue to have the ability to reproduce itself. Table 4.6 shows the fertility rate for various countries. You can see that the advanced industrial economies are losing the ability to reproduce themselves while the potential for population growth in less developed countries is enormous.

Table 4.6 Fertility rates, selected countries

Country	Total period fertility rate 1984
Kenya	7·9
India	4·6
Ghana	6·4
Mexico	4·4
Ireland	2·7
UK	1·8
USA	1·8
West Germany	1·4

Marriage and size of family

As the vast majority of births are to married women, the number of marriages taking place obviously has an effect upon the number of births. However, in the UK, the percentage of people marrying has remained fairly constant, around 88 per cent.

The age at which people marry may also have an effect. In recent years the tendency has been for people to marry younger. Thus there are more potential child-bearing years and, in addition to this, women tend to be biologically more fertile in their teens and twenties (these trends were significantly modified in the 1970s – see below).

However, the most significant factor in UK population over the last century has been the trend to smaller families. The reasons for this will be examined later, but we may note here the change from the five-to-six child family in 1870 to the present two-to-three child family. Today there is also a social pattern to the size of family.

Social class 1 (professional, e.g. doctors, lawyers, clerics, etc.) are most prone to have three-to-five children, but social class 5 (semi-skilled and unskilled employees) are more likely to have families of six and upwards. Overall, there is an inverse relation between social class and size of family. This is not only true for the UK but also for many other Western countries.

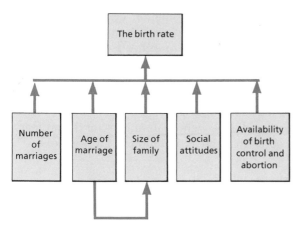

Fig. 4.4 *Influences on the birth rate*

Ireland, however, continues to have a large average size of family.

The factors influencing the birth rate are summarised in Fig. 4.4.

Migration

If immigration is compared with emigration, a figure of net outflow or inflow of migrants is arrived at. Demographically, migration has not been a significant factor in the UK. On the other hand North America is an area where immigration has been very important, whereas emigration *from* Ireland has actually been responsible for a decline in its population. Only on two occasions has the UK been a net gainer by migration, first during the 1930s and then during the 1950s and early 1960s.

The net inflow in the 1930s is explained by two factors: firstly, by people who had emigrated to the colonies returning because of the depression; secondly, in the 1930s there was a large flow of refugees coming from Nazi Europe. Successive waves of immigrants from the new Commonwealth countries account for the inflow in the 1950s and early 1960s. Although the net figure is not significant, the fact that many were from very different ethnic backgrounds has posed particular social and political problems. Economically the immigrants have filled a vital role in providing labour for the economy.

One factor to be borne in mind is that immigrants are predominantly of working age and therefore swell the ranks of the productive part of society. Balanced against this is the fact that the emigrants which the UK has lost have often been highly trained and dynamic; this has sometimes been called the 'brain drain'.

The growth of the UK population

The first census of the UK was conducted in 1801 and one was held every ten years thereafter, with the exception of 1941. These ten-year censuses are now usually followed by a more detailed census of 10 per cent of the population **41**

Table 4.7 Population growth in the UK

	Population of England, Wales and Scotland (thousands)	Percentage increase per decade
1801	10 501	
		13·9
1871	26 072	
		11·5
1911	40 891	
		4·3
1941 (estimate)	46 605	
		5·8
1971	53 720	
		0·8
1981	54 129	
		2·1
2001 (estimate)	57 193	

five years later. Before 1801 calculations and estimates are few and unreliable and come from such things as the Domesday Book (1086) the poll tax of Richard II (1379) and the calculations of Gregory King (1690).

The UK population grew rapidly up to the 1870s, at which time the rate of increase began to slow down. The 1914–18 war marked a great watershed, after which the growth of population came almost to a halt. Since 1945 the rate of population growth has fluctuated, but is hovering just above zero at present (see Table 4.7).

The period of rapid growth

The explanation of the rapid growth of population up to the 1870s is to be found in the decline of the death rate (see Table 4.8). This is because the birth rate remained almost constant up to the 1870s and the UK was a net loser by migration throughout this period. In 1750 the rate of natural increase was little over 0·2 per cent. The death rate then began to drop dramatically, so that by 1851 the rate of natural increase was around 1·3 per cent, i.e. it had increased more than six-fold.

Table 4.8 Crude death rates, UK

Year	Crude death rate
1750	33·0
1851	22·7
1911	13·8
1947	12·6
1970	12·3
1980	12·2
1985	11·9

One of the main reasons advanced to explain this decline in the death rate is the improvement in medical knowledge and provision, together with the elimination of many epidemic diseases such as plague, smallpox, typhus, typhoid and cholera in the nineteenth century. In addition to this there were improvements in diet, housing, clothing and water supply. It has even been argued that the reimposition of the gin tax in 1751 had a significant effect. However these do not provide an adequate explanation. With the possible exception of the gin tax, none of these factors was effective early enough to account for the change in the death rate. The origins of population growth therefore remain a controversial issue. It is worth bearing in mind that most people died before the age of five, and it was a decline in this infant mortality, for whatever reasons, that affected death rate at least as significantly as increasing longevity. The growth of population certainly coincided with the quickening of economic activity in the industrial revolution, either as cause or effect. This was also the time when the urbanisation of the UK population began. People flocked from the countryside to the towns, and from the south to the north of England. However in the towns the conditions were so insanitary for the ordinary people that the expectation of life was low.

The decline in the size of the family

After the 1870s the expectation of life continued to increase and therefore reasons for the decrease in the rate of population growth are to be found in the birth rate. It was from this time onwards that people began to limit the size of their families. It has been argued that up to this time people had seen children as a source of income, and when child labour was forbidden they were discouraged from bearing children. While this argument is of dubious value, it is certainly true that the new Education Acts of 1870 and 1876 increased the cost of bringing up children. Perhaps it was the decline in infant mortality that caused people to take a different economic attitude towards children, but certainly from this time parents began to want higher standards for their children and realised that limiting the size of their family would make this possible. The new age of Victorian prosperity presented many goods which competed for the income of households, and one way to have more income left to buy them was to have fewer children.

Doubtless, many people had smaller families simply because this became the social norm. The emancipation of women and the availability of birth control also played a part, as did the tendency for people to marry at a later age. It took time, however, for the knowledge and availability of contraception to filter down the social structure.

The 1914–18 war was a great watershed in demographic trends, as in all other aspects of society. After 1918 population growth became much slower. In addition to the influences discussed above, the great economic depression in the 1930s also dissuaded people from having children. Although there has been some increase

in the size of the family since the 1939–45 war, it would appear that the smaller family is here to stay (see Table 4.9).

Population since 1945

Looked at in the long term, the changes in population since 1945 may appear small and to be a continuation of previous trends. However small aggregate changes may bring with them profound changes in the structure of population, with important consequences for the economy. The 1939–45 war brought large numbers of women into industry and they have stayed there, thereby affecting both production and consumption. Similarly, the 'baby-boom' of the late 1940s brought changes in education and public services.

The rise in the birth rate immediately after the war may be partly due to families being reunited. However there were more significant longer-term reasons. One such reason was people getting married younger. This may be accounted for by increased prosperity and the improved opportunities for married women to work. With increased prosperity it was possible to afford both more consumer goods *and* children. A larger family became a smaller proportionate burden, especially when the benefits of the welfare state, for example family allowances (1946) and national health insurance (1948), are taken into account. Once again one should not discount the importance of social fashion in parents' choice of the size of their family.

As predicted, the high birth rates of the late 1940s were followed by lower rates in the 1950s. However in the 1960s the birth rate began to rise more rapidly than predicted. This was followed by a fall in the birth rate in the late 1970s to the all-time low of 11·6. This may have been partly due to the fact that child-bearing became a longer and more expensive task. The school leaving age was raised to 16 in 1972, in addition to which the proportion of students continuing into further and higher education increased sharply. Despite the conditions of economic stagnation people still continued to expect a

Table 4.9 Crude birth rates, UK

Year	Crude birth rate	Year	Crude birth rate
1871	35·5	1965	17·6
1911	24·5	1970	16·1
1933	14·4	1975	12·3
1947	20·5	1977	11·6
1950	15·9	1979	13·0
1955	15·0	1981	13·0
1961	17·4	1983	12·8
1963	19·2	1985	13·3

rising standard of living. This may have been a further motive for limiting the size of the family or for having no children at all. In addition to this, the decline in the birth rate was influenced by a decreasing proportion of people marrying (17·2 per thousand in 1972, 13·9 per thousand in 1985) and by an increase in the average age at which people married (25 for men and 22 for women). It is difficult to assess the role of birth control and abortion in this, but certainly the increased availability and efficacy of birth control must have had a depressing effect on the birth rate. In 1984 in Great Britain there were 146 000 legal abortions. This compares with a total 730 000 live births. Abortion is particularly prevalent where the *mother* is under 20 years of age. In 1984 34 per cent of all conceptions to this age group ended in abortion.

Death rates have declined since 1945 as a result of long-term environmental improvements. In 1985 the death rate was 11·9. Migration has varied as an influence on population. Immediately after the war there was a wave of emigration from the UK, with many people going to Canada, Australia and New Zealand. The flow of immigrants from the Commonwealth made the UK a gainer by migration. However, the net figure, having considered both immigration and emigration, is much smaller than is commonly supposed. In the period 1951–61 the net gain was a mere 6000 while the period 1961–71 saw a net loss of 23 000. It is estimated

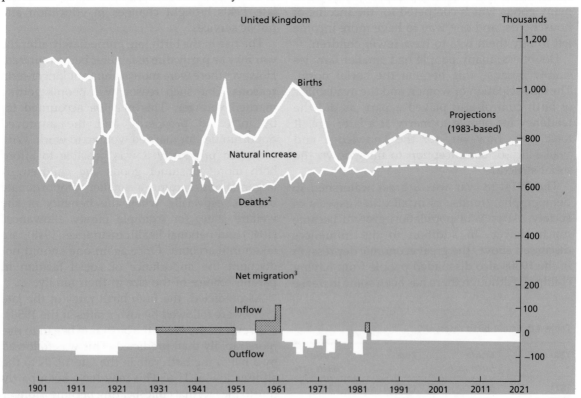

Fig. 4.5 *Population changes and projections*[1]
[1] Deaths and births up to 1984 relate to calendar years. Projections and migration figures relate to 12-month period ending on 30 June in each year shown.
[2] The dots on this line cover the periods 1914–1918 and 1939–1945 which include deaths of non-civilian and merchant seamen who died outside the country.
[3] Figures before 1961 show net civilian migration and other changes; figures from 1961 show net civilian migration only. *Sources: Office of Population Censuses and Surveys; Government Actuary's Department*

that in the period 1983–91 there will be a net loss of 27 000. Fig. 4.5 shows the past and future rates of natural increase and decrease and the net figure for migration for the UK.

The structure of the UK population

When we come to analyse population structure we can split it up by age, sex, occupation and geographical distribution.

The age and sex distribution of the population

This refers to the number of people of each sex in each age group. The most important divisions are 0–15, 16–64 and 65 and over. The relative size of the 16–64 group is important because it is from here that the majority of the working population is drawn (see Table 4.10).

Table 4.10 Age distribution of the population of the UK

	Under 16 population (millions)	(%)	16–64 population (millions)	(%)	Over 65 population (millions)	(%)
1931	10·1*	22·0	32·5*	70·7	3·4	7·3
1951	13·2	26·3	31·5	62·7	5·5	11·0
1961	14·6	27·7	31·9	60·5	6·2	11·8
1971	15·7	28·3	32·5	58·6	7·3	13·1
1981	14·5	25·7	33·4	59·2	8·5	15·1
1985	13·6	24·1	34·4	60·7	8·6	15·2

*estimated
Source: Annual Abstract of Statistics

Both age and sex distribution in society can be presented as a pyramid. In a population where there was an even age and sex distribution a smooth pyramid would be the result. The population is divided between men and women and then between age groups at five-year

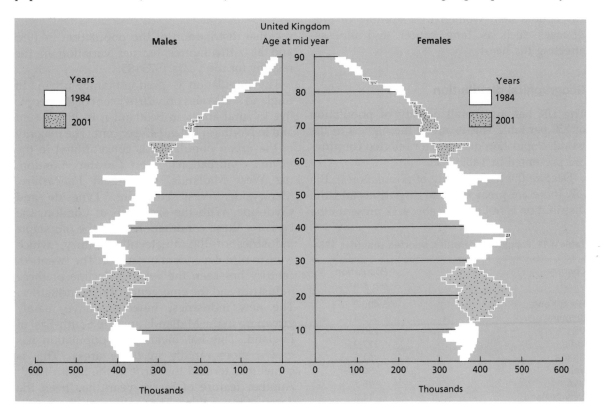

Fig. 4.6 *Population by sex and age, 1984 and 2001 1983-based projections*
Source: *Office of Population Censuses and Surveys; Government Actuary's Department*

intervals. Increasing mortality in the older age groups narrows the pyramid until at the age of 90 there is virtually no-one left. Decline in the birth rate would pinch in the bottom of the pyramid. This is well illustrated by Fig. 4.6.

The number of male births to female births does not usually vary much, with about 105 boys born for every 100 girls. Subsequently, mortality is greater for males in every age group, so that by the age of 85 there are 330 women for every 100 men. There are at present 1½ million more women in the country than men. The expectation of life varies. At present a man can expect to live 71·4 years, a woman 77·2. Life expectation has risen continuously since 1901, when men could expect 48·1 years and women 51·18. The discrepancy in the expectation of life of men and women is explained by a number of factors; men work in more hazardous occupations, more men are killed in wars, and men are more susceptible than women to a number of fatal diseases such as lung cancer and illnesses affecting the heart.

Geographical distribution

The UK has an overall density of population of 230 per km². This is one of the highest in the world. Population densities for selected countries are presented in Table 4.11.

Despite the high density of population in the UK there are great regional disparities and the distribution is not static. Table 4.12 presents the

Table 4.11 Population densities, selected countries 1984

Country	Population per km²
Hong Kong	5 400·0
Belgium	319·4
UK	230·0
India	227·9
Ghana	51·5
Ireland	50·0
USA	25·3
New Zealand	11·9
Australia	2·0

Source: IBRD

Table 4.12 Geographical distribution of population, UK 1985

Region	Total population (thousands) 1985	Regional variation (net in thousands) 1975–85
North	3 086	−67
Yorkshire and Humberside	4 903	−25
East Midlands	3 897	+135
East Anglia	1 965	+172
South-East	17 192	+177
(Greater London)	(6 768)	−411
South-West	4 501	+244
West Midlands	5 183	−2
North-West	6 386	−195
Wales	2 812	+17
Scotland	5 137	−69
Northern Ireland	1 558	+19
Total	56 619	—

Source: Regional Trends, *Employment Gazette*, HMSO

regional distribution of the population in 1985 and also the figures for net variation in the regions for the years 1975–85.

The population is predominantly urban. In England and Wales only 20 per cent of the people live in rural areas, in Scotland it is 28 per cent and in Northern Ireland 45 per cent. The majority of the urban population is concentrated in the major conurbations, i.e. Greater London, the West Midlands, South-East Lancashire, Merseyside, West Yorkshire, Tyneside and Clydeside. With the exception of London, the basis for these conurbations was the old staple industries of the nineteenth century, which were in turn dependent upon coal. The twentieth century has seen the relative decline of these industries and the emergence of new industries. The new industries, however, have mainly grown up in the Midlands and the South-East of England. This has meant that population has grown more rapidly in these areas. This is sometimes termed the 'drift to the South-East'. Another feature of recent years has been the decay of inner cities. Thus, although the South-East has gained population, London has lost people as they have moved out to the home counties such as Hertfordshire, Buckinghamshire and Berkshire. In these home counties population has grown more than 30 per cent in the last 15 years. These people remain, however, to a great extent economically dependent on London.

A separate trend has been the depopulation of rural areas such as northern Scotland. Here population has actually declined. As it is the young people who move away, the age structure of these areas is left most distorted. However, North Sea oil had attracted people to North-East Scotland but this trend has now ceased with the decline in the fortunes of the oil industry.

The occupational distribution of population

This describes the distribution of the working population between different occupations. The working population comprises all those people between the ages of 16 and 65 (60 for women) who are working or available for work, and thus includes the registered unemployed. Also included in the figure are those over 65 who are still working. However, housewives not otherwise employed, those living off private means and those unable to work, e.g. the chronically sick, the insane and those in prison, are excluded from the working population.

The working population in the UK in 1985 was 48·7 per cent of the total population and 40.4 per cent of the working population were women. The percentage of women working is the highest figure for any developed country. The reason for this is that many married women entered the working population during the 1939–45 war and this practice has continued and increased since then.

The industries in which people are employed (see Table 4.13) may be classified as:

a) primary – extraction of raw materials, agriculture, fishing etc;

b) secondary – all manufacturing processes;

c) tertiary – the provision of services, e.g. finance, education, the civil service and the armed forces.

Table 4.13 Occupational distribution of the UK population 1985

Industry	Number of people (*thousands*)	(%)
Agriculture, forestry and fishing	329	1·2
Mining, quarrying etc.	496	1·8
Electricity, gas and water supply	311	1·1
Manufacturing	5 431	19·7
Construction	947	3·4
Distributive trades	3 351	12·1
Hotels and catering	1 045	3·8
Transport and communication	1 286	4·7
Banking, finance, insurance etc	1 946	7·1
Public administration	3 058	11·1
Education	1 542	5·6
Other services	1 724	6·2
HM Forces	325	1·2
Self employed*	2 623	9·5
Unemployed	3 179	11·5
Working population	27 593	100·0

* With or without employees. Self employed are involved in a wide variety of industries.

Source: *Annual Abstract of Statistics*

As a rule an under-developed country would have a large percentage of its total population working and concentrated mainly in primary industries. An advanced economy would have a smaller percentage working population with a larger tertiary sector. In the UK the tertiary sector represents about 59 per cent of the working population. The proportion of the population which is available for work is affected by demographic factors such as the age structure of the population and by other factors such as society's attitude to women working, the school leaving age and the retirement age. If we say that this makes everyone between the ages 16 and 65 for men and 16 and 60 for women *potentially* available for work then, in the UK, this was 33·9 million people in 1986. However, the percentage of people which constitute the working population, as officially defined, was 27·6 million. The percentage of the total population which constitutes the working population rose from 46·1 per cent in 1966 to 48·7 per cent in 1986. This was because of the changing age structure of the population and also because of an increasing proportion of women working. It is for these reasons that it was possible to see both the number of people working increasing at the same time as the number of people unemployed. (*See* Table 4.14.)

Over the last 100 years there has been a sharp decrease in the percentage of people employed in agriculture, forestry and fishing. The UK now has one of the smallest percentages employed in these occupations of any country. Domestic services also used to be very important, but they have now almost entirely disappeared. There have been large increases in those employed in commerce, the professional services, public administration, manufacturing and the armed forces. This has been caused by the industrialisation of society and rising real incomes which have given people money to spend on a wider range of goods and services. The growing complexity of society has increased the numbers of those engaged in administration. This is also associated with the rise in the influence of the state in economic and social life. Today the government disposes of over two-fifths of the national income; hence there is a growing army of civil servants and other state employees.

In recent years there have been dramatic changes in the occupational distribution of population. The percentage of those employed in manufacturing has dropped dramatically from 37.1 per cent in 1960 to only 21·5 per cent in 1987. This is associated with the *de-industrialisation* of the economy and also the depression in manufacturing industries brought about by imports. There has also been some increase in the number involved in primary industries because of North Sea oil. Overall there is a marked trend to a reliance on tertiary industries, the growth areas being financial and professional services. Tourism is also now a major industry.

Demographic constraints

Consequences of the changing structure of population

For the last two centuries UK population has been increasing in size, and ageing. Most discussion has centred on the consequences of this, but now the future of the UK population seems less certain. It is therefore necessary to consider the consequences of the various alternatives.

If the population is *increasing in size* then, other things being equal, there is less land and other resources available per head. In the short term this could lead to a tendency to import more goods, thus worsening the balance of payments. On the other hand there would be an increasing domestic market for goods which could lead to increasing economies of scale. In the nineteenth century the UK's population growth was accompanied by great technological improvements. Thus increasing population was attended by increasing prosperity.

A *declining* population would, other things being equal, lead to more resources being available per head. It is possible, however, that, lacking the stimulus of population growth, there would be less incentive to improve technology. This could have an adverse effect on the long-term prospects of the economy.

If the population was *becoming younger* then there would be a smaller dependent population of old people, and a changing pattern of consumption away from geriatric hospitals and the like to a greater demand for schools, pop records, etc. In addition, a younger population would be more flexible and dynamic and more able to take advantage of technological change. There would also be a greater mobility of labour, both occupational and geographical.

Throughout this century *up to the 1970s the population of the UK has been ageing*. There has also been a rising percentage of young people. Consequently the working population has had to provide for a growing *dependent population*.

This has meant both more schools and more old age pensions. The ageing of the population has also made it less mobile and less able to take advantage of technological change. In addition there has been growing competition for resources such as houses and land.

The growth of the tertiary sector has also meant that there is a smaller and smaller percentage of the working population involved in the manufacture of goods. The building of more schools and more senior citizens' homes both make demands on the nation's capital. Although education might be regarded as increasing society's productivity in the long-run, services for the old do not do so. When these factors are considered together, they may partly account for the UK's depressing economic growth figures since the 1950s.

The *changing geographical distribution* of the population also has economic and social consequences. In an area of declining population it is usually the young and active who move away, leaving a distorted population structure behind them with an even more intractable unemployment problem.

A major problem is now also posed by people moving out of the inner-city areas. The decay of the inner-cities is now a major social and economic headache. Inner-cities tend to have much higher costs than rural and suburban areas. For example, the cost of homes, roads, social services and so on are all considerably greater in cities. The departure of people, especially the better-off, decreases the tax (or rate) revenue in these areas while costs escalate and this makes local government ever more difficult. Table 4.12 illustrates the dramatic decline in the population of London.

The future structure of population

Predictions about the future population are produced by making *population projections* which are forecasts of the future trend of population. Such projections have to take into account many *variables* such as the death rate, birth rate and the extent of migration. In order to make pre-

dictions we must make *assumptions* about these variables. The predictions may thus prove faulty, either because we have selected the wrong variables or because our assumptions prove incorrect. Despite these problems it is essential to make predictions about the future population because we need to plan for such things as schools and hospitals.

Although current estimates are being revised downwards, world population continues to increase and there will still be many hundreds of millions more mouths to feed in the next half-century. However, due to a combination of circumstances, demography will actually be working in favour of the UK over the next 25 years. The dependency ratio (the ratio of dependent population to working population) reached a peak in 1974 and is now declining.

Since the mid-1960s the number of births has been declining and the fertility rate has dropped to 1.8. The number of children under 15 has fallen since 1973. It remains to be seen whether the slight upturn in the birth rate after 1978 will affect this. The fertility rate remained at this low level until the baby-boom of the early 1960s reached child-bearing age. In addition to this, the number of people reaching retiring age will soon begin to decline. This is because there was a sharp fall in the birth rate after the 1914–18 war and, although there was a rise in the rate immediately afterwards, the inter-war period as a whole was one of low birth rates. There are also the deaths of many young people in the 1939–45 war to consider. Therefore, there will be fewer people in retirement in the 1990s. Unless there are great breakthroughs in medicine, the death rate will decline very little. There is also a trend to a unisex death rate as women become more prone to fatal accidents, heart attacks and lung cancer. This could also check the rise in the dependent population. As a result of these factors, dependence will decrease and the average age of the population is likely to fall from the present 33·7 years to 31·5 in 1995. The potential labour force will continue to grow so long as the number passing into it at 16 exceeds those leaving it at retiring age (*see* Fig. 4.6).

49

However the dependency ratio could be misleading if a larger number of people go on to higher education or there is a rise in the number of the very old (since they make the greatest demand on welfare services). Recent work at the Office of Population, Censuses and Surveys suggests this will not be so; educational activity, it suggests, has passed its peak and, although it rose in the late 1980s, it did not reach the levels of the mid-1970s. Similarly it is envisaged that hospital activity for the very old will decline continuously until the end of the century. This picture is complicated by the increasing cost of medical services as improved knowledge makes new techniques available. However, it is possible to conclude that in *numerical* terms the UK's dependency burden will decline until the end of the century. Beyond this it is difficult to make any forecasts.

The optimum population

The concept of the optimum population

The optimum population may be defined as that size and structure of population which is most conducive to the betterment of the wealth and welfare of a society.

If a population is too small in relation to resources, under-population exists; if it is too large, a country is suffering from over-population. However it is very difficult to quantify these ideas. The most obvious measure to consider is the GNP per capita of a country. We saw that for some countries in the world GNP per capita has indeed been declining (*see* Table 4.1). There are no simple rules about the relationship of people and the availability of resources. Singapore has turned the seeming disadvantage of over-population into an advantage by industrialisation. Conversely, New Zealand has turned the apparent disadvantage of under-population to its advantage through agriculture. The idea of optimum population must, therefore, also depend upon the level of technology, the amount of capital per head and the ability of a population to adapt to change.

We cannot, therefore, state the optimum population as anything as simple as so many people per square kilometre. Optimum levels of population are therefore not comparable from one country to another. What is right for an industrial country is not right for an agricultural one. Neither is the optimum level static. Two centuries ago the UK would have been disastrously over-populated with 56 million people, but technological change and capitalisation has proceeded at a rate sufficient to ensure that national income has gone up faster than population.

Diminishing returns

We can relate the concept of optimum population to the law of diminishing returns (*see* page 30). If we assume that all other things remain constant, then it would follow that, as the population of a country grows and grows, there must come a point at which diminishing returns set in. This is illustrated in Fig. 4.7. Thus we have defined optimum population as that size of population where average output per person is greatest.

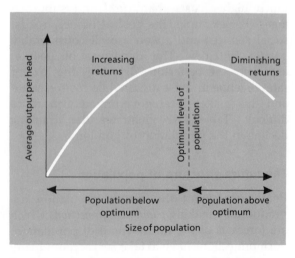

Fig. 4.7 *The growth of population and diminishing returns*

However other things may not remain constant. If we allow for improving technology or the discovery of new resources, then the optimum level of population will rise. The peak of the curve in Fig. 4.7 will move to the right.

On the other hand we must recognise that if improvements in technology only offset diminishing returns, there is a constant need to improve technology if we are to prevent the onset of falling productivity. When we consider diminishing returns on a *global scale* in the light of the continuing explosion of population, it is easy to appreciate the concern many authorities feel that Malthus's predictions may yet come true.

Environmental concerns

The measures we have attempted to use for optimum population are fraught with difficulties. The idea of average output per head is very hard to quantify. In addition to this we should be aware that GNP per head is not concomitant with the standard of living, so that it does not follow that if GNP per head increases the average standard of living is improving.

On a broader scale there is increasing concern about the effect of increasing population upon the global environment. Finite resources such as oil, copper, tin, etc., are rapidly becoming depleted and there is no way in which they can be replaced. Renewable resources such as fish-stocks and timber are being despoiled at a frightening rate. In addition to these very serious concerns, even if we are able to keep economic production increasing, we are also accelerating the problems of pollution of the environment. Thus, although our level of wealth increases, the level of welfare may decline.

A supporter of an environmental interest group such as Greenpeace might, therefore, give a very different definition of optimum population than that given by most economists. The commission headed by the Norwegian Prime Minister Mrs Gro Harland Bruntland in 1987 produced a report which stressed the fragile balance which exists between the human race and the environment.

Is the UK over-populated?

It is a common fallacy to believe that, since the UK is very *crowded*, it must therefore be over-populated. This is not necessarily so. Indeed, despite the rise in population over the last two centuries, the average standard of living has continued to improve. It would seem unlikely therefore that the UK is, as yet, over-populated. On the other hand some commentators would see the recent stagnation in the economy as evidence that the UK must be at, or near, to its optimum level of population.

However, it might also be worth bearing in mind that there is practically zero population growth in the UK and other Western European countries. Many people fear that this may have an adverse effect on the economy, i.e. it might lose the spur to economic growth and the dynamism that population growth provides. On the other hand it might provide the breathing space in which the UK may solve the long-term structural problems of its economy.

Summary

1 The population explosion is the most significant factor in the human history of the last 200 years.
2 The overall size of the population is influenced by the birth rate, the death rate and the level of migration.
3 The birth rate is influenced by the age of marriage, the number of marriages and the availability of contraception and abortion.
4 UK population grew rapidly up to 1870. After this the rate of increase

51

slowed until 1945. The growth of population accelerated after 1945 but at present is almost static.

5 The age and sex distribution of population can be shown in a population pyramid. The UK population is concentrated in the major conurbations. The occupational distribution of the UK population is characterised by the decline of manufacturing industries and the rise of tertiary industries.

6 For most of this century the dependent population has been increasing, but this will not be so during the last years of the century.

7 The optimum level of population may be defined as that size and structure of population which is most conducive to the betterment of its wealth and welfare.

Questions

1 Describe the factors which have influenced the average size of family in the UK since 1945.

2 Discuss the view that the size of population is not as significant as its age, sex and geographical distribution.

3 Explain the problems involved in making forecasts of future population.

4 Consider the figures in Table 4.11 and then comment upon the relationship between the density of population and the level of prosperity.

5 Describe the problems involved in defining the optimum level of population.

6 Having studied the figures in Table 4.12, describe as fully as possible the reasons for the discrepancies between the regions.

7 To what extent do you think that the ideas of Malthus are relevant to current world problems?

Data response   Population and prosperity

Study the figures contained in Table 4.14.

Table 4.14 Income, area and population

Country	Population (millions) 1985	Area (thousands of square kilometres)	GNP per capita Dollars 1985	Average annual growth (%) 1965–85	Average annual growth of population (%) 1980–85
India	765·1	3 288	270	1·7	2·2
Ghana	12·7	239	380	−2·2	3·3
Brazil	135·6	8 512	1 640	4·3	2·3
Mexico	78·8	1 973	2 080	2·7	2·6
Singapore	2·6	1	7 420	7·6	1·2
Saudi Arabia	11·5	2 150	8 850	5·3	4·2
United Arab Emirates	1·4	84	19 270	..	6·2
Ireland	3·6	70	4 850	2·2	0·9
UK	56·5	245	8 460	1·6	0·1
USA	239·3	9 363	16 690	1·7	1·0
France	55·2	547	9 540	2·8	0·6
West Germany	61·0	249	10 940	2·7	−0·2
Japan	120·8	372	11 300	4·7	0·7
USSR	277·4	22 402	4 550	4·0	0·9

1   Identify the following. The country which:
   a) has the greatest density of population.
   b) has the least density of population.
   c) experienced the greatest percentage growth in population.
   d) experienced the smallest percentage growth in population.
   e) experienced the greatest percentage growth in GNP/capita.
   f) experienced the smallest growth in GNP/capita.
2   On the basis of these figures comment on the relationship between density of population and the level of prosperity.
3   Using these figures as illustration comment on the concept of the optimum population.
4   What other information would be useful in order to arrive at answers to questions 2 & 3 and why?

5

The basis of the market economy

Fundamentally, there are only two ways of co-ordinating the economic activities of millions. One is central direction involving the use of coercion – the technique of the army and the modern totalitarian state. The other is voluntary cooperation of individuals – the technique of the market place.

Milton Friedman

What is a cynic? A man who knows the price of everything, and the value of nothing.

Oscar Wilde

The price system

Micro- and macroeconomics

Due largely to the work of the great economist John Maynard Keynes, it has been customary to divide economic theory into *microeconomics* and *macroeconomics*. As its name implies microeconomics is concerned with small parts of the economy and the inter-relationships between these parts, while macroeconomics is concerned with the behaviour of broad aggregates affecting the whole economy. A microeconomic topic therefore might be explaining movements in the prices of shoes or whether there has been under investment in manufacturing vis á vis the service sector. Macroeconomic topics come under the four headings of inflation, unemployment, the balance of payments and growth.

Obviously macroeconomic explanations are not necessarily separate from microeconomic explanations, e.g. the growth of the economy is most likely to have been affected by the allocation of investment funds across the various sectors of the economy; unemployment will be affected by the decline and rise of individual industries. But the fundamental reason for a distinction being made is the notion that broad aggregates might behave differently from the way that is predicted by theories based on observing the behaviour of individual markets. For example, a cut in wages in one industry may make it profitable for employers in that industry to employ more workers, but Keynes suggested that a cut in wages across the economy as a whole might reduce the *aggregate* demand for goods and services hence forcing all employers to cut back on production and hence workers.

Since the late 1960s, there has been a reaction to the macro/micro distinction; monetarists in particular have attempted to explain all economic phenomena in terms of theories based upon explanations of how individual markets function, i.e. microeconomic theory. You should in any case be aware that the 'big small' distinction often made between macro and micro economics is misleading. For example in a famous definition of microeconomic theory by Laidler we read; *'General Equilibrium theory tries to describe how a market economy as a whole would operate'*.

54

General equilibrium is considered to be a microeconomic topic in that it studies the allocation of resources as determined by relative prices. It ignores the problems associated with the disequilibrium of aggregate supply and demand which gives rise to macroeconomic considerations. As monetarists do not feel there is any particular problem with such aggregate disequilibrium it follows that they do place much stress on the macro/micro distinction. To them much of macroeconomics is simply 'bad' microeconomics.

In this chapter we will concern ourselves with the essentials of the price mechanism which forms the nub of microeconomic theory. At the end of the chapter we will further consider General Equilibrium theory.

Assumptions about human behaviour

In examining the functioning of the price system we are not dealing with abstract forces but with people. It is therefore necessary to set out the assumptions we make about human behaviour.

Firstly we assume that people are *maximisers*: they try to gain as much wealth or pleasure as possible. Those things for which people strive, be they goods, services or leisure, are said to give utility. Perhaps in a true socialist state people would strive for the greatest good of all, but this is not generally true of our society. In saying this we are implying that people are primarily *economic* creatures. If political, religious or aesthetic motives overcame people's acquisitive instincts then most of our theories on markets and production would begin to break down. By and large, however, the picture of acquisitive society seems to hold true. In addition to this we also assume that people are *rational*, i.e. they will stop to consider which course of action will give them the greatest utility for the least cost. This somewhat unlovely portrait of humankind is not a suggestion of how people should be but an observation of how they are!

We also assume that people are *competitive*. This is different from acquisitiveness, for it implies that people want to do better than other people. We can also see from this that people are *individualistic*. In a competitive society such as ours not only are people forced to compete but also the good working of the system depends upon them doing so.

In addition to assuming that people generally compete to gain as much utility as they can, we also assume that they do not like work. Work is said to have *disutility* and therefore people have to be paid to encourage them to undertake it. There are people who do like work, but in general if people are offered the same money for shorter hours of work they would accept it.

The price system

When we speak of the price system we mean situations where the vital economic decisions are taken through the medium of prices. A market price is the result of the interaction between the consumers' demand for a good and the supply of that product by producers. However in order to produce goods the producers must have used factors of production. Ultimately all factors in the economy are owned by consumers, so that the producers must buy the use of these factors from consumers. There are therefore, in addition to markets for products, markets for the factors of production. This is illustrated in Fig. 5.1. This shows the critical importance of prices as the *connecting*, or *communicating*, mechanism between consumers and producers.

Consumer sovereignty

In the price system it is sometimes said that the 'consumer is king', meaning that a consumer decides what is to be produced by being willing to spend money on those particular goods. It is probably more accurate to say that there is a joint sovereignty between the consumer and the producer, because the producer's behaviour and objectives will also have a great influence on the market.

The price system is also said, by some people, to be democratic in that every day consumers 'vote' for what they want to be produced by spending their money. Although to some extent

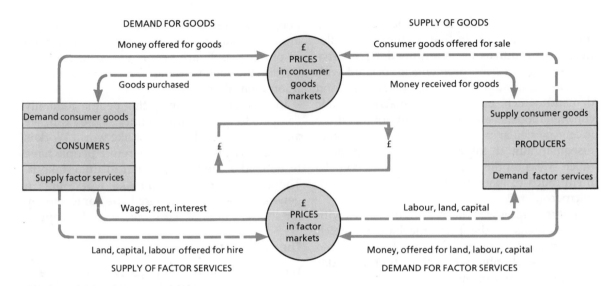

Fig. 5.1 *The price system*
The prices of consumer goods and services are determined by the interaction of consumer demand and supply from producers. Similarly, the price of factors of production is determined by the interaction of producers' demand for factor services and the supply of factors of production from consumers.

this is true, it is considerably modified by the fact that money 'votes' in the economy are unevenly distributed. Thus those with a high income have more 'voting' power than those who are poor.

Market prices

Much of economics is concerned with the behaviour of market prices. Many criticisms can be made of prices as a method of allocating goods and services, but before we can assess the strengths and weaknesses of the price system we must understand its functioning. We will therefore examine the demand and supply of goods and then the formation of market prices.

Demand

Market demand

The demand for a commodity is the *quantity* of the good which is purchased over a specific period of *time* at a certain *price*. Thus there are three elements to demand: price, quantity and time. This is the *effective demand* for a good, i.e. the desire to buy the good, backed by the ability to do so – it is no use considering a person's demand for a product if they do not have the money to realise it.

We may distinguish between *ex ante* demand and *ex post* demand. *Ex ante* demand is the quantity consumers will wish to demand at a particular price, while *ex post* demand is the amount they actually succeed in buying. The difference between the two may be brought about, for example, by a deficiency of supply in the market (see below, excess demand, page 62).

Ceteris paribus, it is usually the case that as the price of the commodity is lowered, so a greater quantity will be demanded. A formal analysis of the reasons for this is contained in Chapter 9. However at this point we may consider the relevance of the *law of diminishing marginal utility*.

Utility defined

We have used the word utility several times. This is another word which economists use in a special sense. It simply means the satisfaction which people derive from consuming goods or services. However a good does not have to be 'useful' in the conventional sense; for example, cigarettes possess utility to the smoker even though they are harmful.

Marginal utility

The law of diminishing marginal utility states:

Other things being constant, as more and more units of a commodity are consumed the additional satisfaction, or utility, derived from the consumption of each successive unit will decrease.

For example, if one has nothing to drink all day, the utility of a glass of water would be very high indeed and in consequence one would be willing to pay a high price for it. However as one proceeded to drink a second, third and fourth glass of water the extra utility derived from each would become less. In this case one might have been willing to pay a great deal for the first glass of water but, as one continues to consume, the price one would be willing to pay would decrease because one would be deriving a smaller utility from each successive glass. This helps to clear up the puzzle of why we are willing to pay so little for bread, which is a necessity, and so much for diamonds, which have little practical value. The answer is that we have so much bread that the extra utility derived from another loaf is small, whereas we have so few diamonds that each one has a high marginal utility. Thus this principle helps to explain why more of a good is demanded at a lower price. The extra sales come from existing buyers, who buy more, and new buyers, who could not afford, or who did not think the good was worth buying at, the higher price.

We must be careful to state our definition of the law with the *ceteris paribus* conditions that 'all other things remain constant'. It is worthwhile considering the factors which may offset the law of diminishing marginal utility.

a) Time. The law only operates over a certain period of time. This is related to the nature of the commodity. For example, if we are considering food, then if a person has not had a meal for several hours they will place a high value on food. They will then not require another meal immediately, but after several hours they will be equally willing to buy another meal. If, on the other hand, we consider a product such as a car, if a person has just bought a new car it will be a long time before they are willing to buy another one.

b) Income. The utility someone derives from consuming a product may be altered if their income is changed. To continue the example of cars used above, a substantial increase in a person's income may make them willing to buy another car shortly after the purchase of a new one. Different levels of income also influence the utility a person derives from the consumption of a commodity. For example, the acquisition of a new pair of shoes may give little extra satisfaction to a millionaire, but may give a great deal of utility to a poor person.

c) Addiction. The law also depends upon the fact that consumption of a commodity does *not* alter the nature of successive units. For example, smokers may find that the more they smoke the more they want to smoke. The product need not necessarily be narcotic; for example the avid philatelist may find a growing compulsion in stamp collecting.

There is, however, a long-term validity to the law. The smoker can only smoke so many cigarettes in a day, and even the millionaire's demand for the new cars and swimming pools must eventually be satisfied.

The demand curve

The data in Table 5.1 is a hypothetical *demand schedule* for commodity X. It illustrates the *first law of demand*.

All other things remaining constant, more of a good will be demanded at a lower price.

Such information is usually expressed as a graph called a demand curve. As you can see in Fig. 5.2, the graph marked DD slopes downwards **57**

Table 5.1 Demand schedule for commodity X

	Price of commodity X (£/kg)	Quantity of X demanded (kg/week)
A	5	110
B	4	120
C	3	150
D	2	200
E	1	250

from left to right; this is almost invariably the case. The relationship between price and the quantity demanded is an *inverse* relationship since as price *goes down* the quantity demanded *goes up*. If the price is lowered from £3 per kg to £2 per kg, then the quantity demanded grows from 150 kg to 200 kg per week. This can be shown as a movement down the existing demand curve from C to D. This is termed an *extension* of demand. Conversely, if the price of X were raised then this could be shown as a movement up the curve which is termed a *contraction* of demand. An extension or contraction of demand is brought about by a change in the price of the commodity under consideration *and by nothing else.*

An increase in demand

Suppose that the product X was wheat, and there was a failure of the potato crop. People would then wish to buy more wheat, even though the price of wheat had not fallen. This is shown as a shift of the demand curve to the right. In Fig. 5.3 this is the move from DD to D_1D_1: as a result of this, at the price of £3, 150 kg are demanded instead of 100, as we have moved from point C to C_1. A movement of the demand curve in this manner is termed an *increase* in demand. If the curve were to move leftwards, for example from D_1D_1 to DD, this would be termed a *decrease*. An increase or decrease in demand is brought about by a factor other than a change in the price in the commodity under consideration.

It is important not to confuse an *increase* in demand with an *extension* of demand. An extension of demand (sometimes referred to as an increase in the quantity demanded) is brought

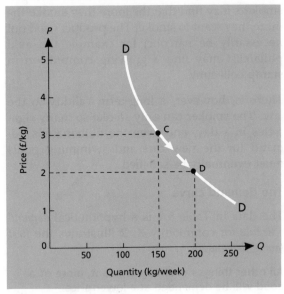

Fig. 5.2 *A demand curve*
A fall in the price of X from £3 to £2 per kg increases the quantity demanded from 150 to 200 kg/week.

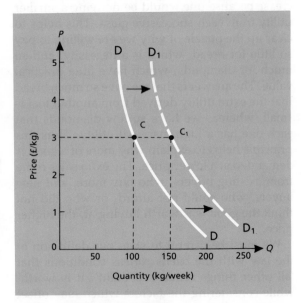

Fig. 5.3 *An increase in demand*
The shift of the curve from DD to D_1D_1 shows that more is demanded at every price, e.g. demand at £3/kg increases from 100 to 150 kg/week.

about by a fall in the price of the product, whereas an increase in demand is brought about by a change in any other factor affecting demand *except* the price of the product.

Total revenue

The total revenue is the total sales receipts in a market at a particular price. In Table 5.1 you can see that if the price were £3 per kg then the quantity demanded would be 150 kg per week. Consequently the total revenue would be £450. Thus we can say that:

Total revenue (*TR*) = Price (*P*) × Quantity (*Q*)

If the price were lowered to £2 then the total revenue ($P \times Q$) would be £400. You can see in Fig. 5.2 that the total revenue can be represented as a rectangle drawn under the demand curve (represented by the dotted lines).

Supply

Market supply

We will now turn to the other side of the market, which is supply. By supply we mean the quantity of a commodity that suppliers will wish to supply at a particular price. This is illustrated by Table 5.2. As you can see, the higher the price is, the greater the quantity the supplier will wish to supply. If the price decreases there will come a price (£1) at which suppliers are not willing to supply because they cannot make a profit at this point.

Table 5.2 Supply schedule for commodity X

	Price of commodity X (£/kg)	Quantity of X suppliers will wish to supply (kg/week)
A	5	240
B	4	200
C	3	150
D	2	90
E	1	0

The first principle of supply is that, all other things remaining constant, a greater quantity will be supplied at a higher price because at a higher price increased costs can be incurred.

We explain this by saying that a greater quantity is supplied at a higher price because, as the price increases, organisations which could not produce profitably at the lower price would find it possible to do so at a higher price. One way of looking at this is that as price goes up, less and less efficient firms are brought into the industry. A good example of this is provided by North Sea oil. The UK's oil costs four or five times as much to extract as Saudi Arabian oil. The low prices of the 1950s and early 1960s would certainly not have allowed the UK to extract the oil profitably, but as the price rocketed in the 1970s it became possible for her to produce oil.

When asked why more is supplied at a higher price, students frequently reply 'because increased profits can be made'. This you can now see is not so. The organisations which could make a profit at the lower prices do indeed make more profit, but the extra supply comes from the marginal firms which are now brought into the industry.

The supply curve

As with demand, we can plot the supply information as a graph. This is illustrated in Fig. 5.4. As you can see the supply curve slopes upwards from left to right. This is a *direct* relationship, i.e. as price *goes up* the quantity supplied will *go up*. If the price increases from £2 per kg to £3 per kg, then the quantity suppliers are willing to supply goes up from 90 kg to 150 kg. As with the demand curve, this movement along the supply curve from D to C is called an *extension* of supply. A movement down the curve would be called a *contraction* of supply. As with demand, an extension or contraction is brought about by a change of the price of the commodity under consideration and nothing else.

The reasons for the shape of the supply curve are examined in more detail in Part Two of this book. We may note here, however, that we **59**

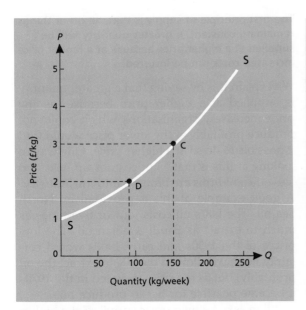

Fig. 5.4 *A supply curve*
An increase in the price of X from £2 to £3 per kg causes the quantity supplied to increase from 90 to 150 kg/week.

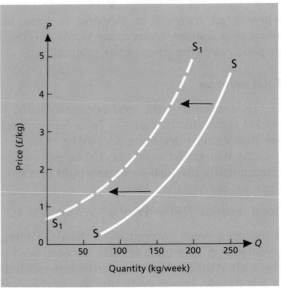

Fig. 5.5 *A decrease in supply*
The shift of the supply curve leftwards from SS to S_1S_1 shows that less is supplied at every price.

have already dealt in Chapter 3 with two principles – the law of diminishing returns and the principle of increasing costs – which would suggest that costs increase with supply.

The determinants of supply

The theory of supply forms the basis of Sections II and III of this book. However it is convenient here to simply list the factors which can influence the supply of a commodity.

a) Price. The most important determinant of supply is price. As we have just seen, a change in price will cause a movement up or down the supply curve. The remaining determinants of supply can be termed the *conditions of supply*. A change in the conditions of supply causes an increase or decrease in supply, shifting the supply curve leftwards or rightwards. For example, suppose that the product we are considering is tomatoes, then very bad weather would have the effect of decreasing the supply. In Fig. 5.5 you can see that this has the effect of

shifting the supply curve leftwards. Conversely, unexpectedly good growing weather would shift the curve rightwards.

b) Price of factors of production. Since output is produced by combining the factors of production, their price is an important determinant of supply. An increase in the price of a factor will increase the *costs* of a firm and this shifts the supply curve leftwards. This could be illustrated by the rise in costs brought about by increased oil prices in the 1970s.

c) The price of other commodities. If, for example, there is a rise in the price of barley but not of wheat, this will tend to decrease the supply (shift the curve leftwards) of wheat because farmers will switch from wheat to barley production. Economic theory envisages resources switching easily and rapidly from one type of production to another in response to price changes. In practice, though, this may be a slow and often painful process.

d) Technology. Changes in the level of technology also affect supply. An improvement in technology allows us to produce more goods with less factors of production. This would therefore have the effect of shifting the supply curve to the right. This has been well illustrated in recent years by the effect of microchip technology upon the supply of things such as pocket calculators, watches and personal computers.

e) Tastes of producers. In theory suppliers are perfectly rational beings only interested in obtaining the highest return for their efforts. However producers may have preferences and be willing to tolerate lower returns if, for example, they find the business stimulating or worthwhile or socially prestigious. Conversely producers may avoid unpleasant lines of work.

f) Exogenous factors. Supply can be affected by conditions outside market forces. Perhaps the most obvious example of this would be the weather.

Regressive supply curves

Supply curves usually slope upwards from left to right. Sometimes, however, they change direction, as in Fig. 5.6, and are said to become *regressive*; this might be the case with the supply of labour where there may be a high *leisure preference*. In coal-mining for example, where the job is extremely unpleasant, it has often been noticed that as wage rates have been increased miners have worked shorter hours. This is because instead of taking the increased wage rate in money the miners are taking it in increased leisure.

A similar effect may be observed in some undeveloped peasant economies where producers have a static view of the income that they require. In these circumstances a rise in the price of the crop they produce causes them to grow less because they can now obtain the same income from a smaller crop.

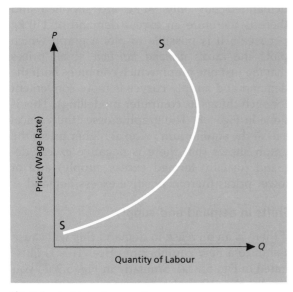

Fig. 5.6 *A regressive supply curve*
As the wage rate continues to rise people eventually work shorter hours, preferring to take the improvement in wages as increased leisure rather than increased income.

Equilibrium prices

The formation of an equilibrium price

We shall now combine our analysis of demand and supply to show how a competitive market price is determined. Table 5.3 combines the demand and supply schedules. The motives of consumers and producers are different in that the consumer wishes to buy cheaply while the supplier wishes to obtain the highest price possible. Let us examine how these differences are reconciled.

Table 5.3 The determination of the equilibrium price

	Price of commodity X (£/kg)	Quantity demanded of X (kg/week)	Quantity supplied of X (kg/week)	Pressure on price
A	5	110	240	Downward
B	4	120	200	Downward
C	3	150	150	Neutral
D	2	200	90	Upward
E	1	250	0	Upward

If, for example, we examine line A in Table 5.3, here the price is £5 per kg and 240 kg will be supplied per week. However at this price **61** consumers are only willing to buy 110 kg. Thus unsold stocks of goods begin to pile up. Suppliers will therefore be forced to reduce their prices to try and get rid of the surplus. There is a downward pressure on prices. Conversely, if we examine line D, where the price is £2 per kg, suppliers are only willing to supply 90 kg per week but consumers are trying to buy 200 kg per week. There are therefore many disappointed customers, and producers realise that they can raise their prices. There is thus an upward pressure on price. If we continue the process we can see that there is only one price where there is neither upward nor downward pressure on price. This is termed the equilibrium price.

The equilibrium price is the price at which the wishes of buyers and sellers coincide.

If we superimpose the supply curve on the demand curve we can see, in Fig. 5.7, that the equilibrium price occurs where the two curves cross. The surplus supply and the shortage of supply at any other price can be shown as the gap between the two curves. The arrows in Fig.

5.7 show the equilibrium forces which are at work pushing the price towards the equilibrium.

Equilibrium prices ration out the scarce supply of goods and services. There are no great queues of people demanding the best cuts of meat at butchers; a price of £10 per kg for fillet steak ensures that only the rich or those who derive great utility from beefsteak buy the meat. Neither are there vast unsold stocks of meat at the butchers, the equilibrium price having balanced the demand and supply. It might be argued that the price mechanism is socially unjust but if we do away with price as a rationing mechanism we only have to put something else, perhaps equally unacceptable, in its place.

Excess demand and supply

If the price is above the equilibrium then more will be supplied than is demanded, this surplus of supply over demand being termed *excess supply*. Conversely, if the price is below the equilibrium then this will result in a situation of *excess demand*. For example, in Table 5.3, if the price is £2 per kg, then 200 kg per week are demanded but only 90 kg are supplied and there is therefore an excess demand of 110 kg per week. It is possible to plot a graph which plots the *excess demand function* at all prices (having just one graph which combines both the demand and supply curves is more convenient for such things as computer modelling). This is done in Fig. 5.8. The graph crosses the vertical axis at the equilibrium price; at higher prices the graph shows that there is negative excess demand (usually termed excess supply) and at lower prices there is positive excess demand.

Shifts in demand and supply

If there is an increase in demand this will cause a shift to a new equilibrium price. This is illustrated in Fig. 5.9 (*a*). Similarly in Fig. 5.9 (*b*) you can see the effect of a decrease in supply upon the equilibrium price.

The problems associated with changes in equilibrium price are discussed at more length in Chapter 11.

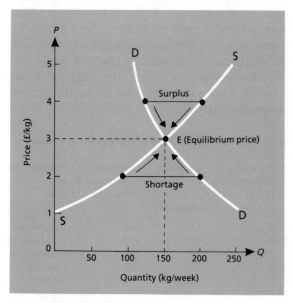

Fig. 5.7 *The equilibrium price*
At the price of £3/kg the quantity which is offered for sale is equal to the quantity people are willing to buy
at that price.

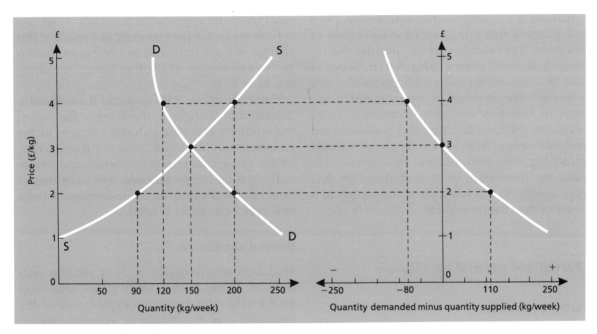

Fig. 5.8 *The excess demand curve*
If the quantity supplied is subtracted from the quantity demanded it gives the excess demand function, e.g. at a price of
£4/kg 120 kg are demanded but 200 kg are supplied, giving a negative excess demand (excess supply) of 80 kg.

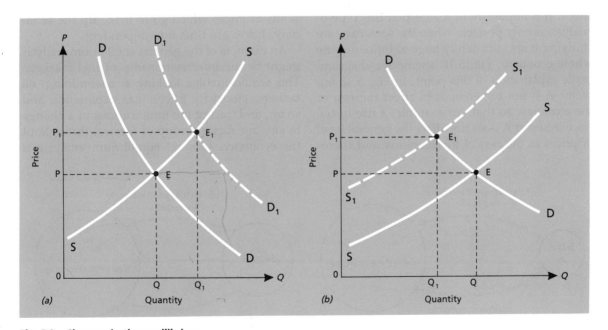

Fig. 5.9 *Changes in the equilibrium*
A shift of either the demand or the supply curve creates a new equilibrium price.
(*a*) An increase in demand gives a higher price and a greater quantity
(*b*) A decrease in supply gives a higher price and lower quantity.

If there is a change in the equilibrium price and quantity this brings about a *reallocation* of resources. For example, let us consider the increase in demand shown in Fig. 5.9 (*a*). Suppose that this shows an increased preference for tomatoes. The increase in demand raises the price of tomatoes and this encourages more people to produce them so that resources are switched away from other forms of market gardening and into tomato production. No planning committee or central direction has been necessary; this has come about simply as a result of the change in price.

Partial and general equilibrium

Partial equilibrium

The analysis we have been using so far in this chapter is termed *partial equilibrium analysis*. It is termed partial because it only deals with one small part of the economy, e.g. the price of shoes. It is important to realise that this type of analysis is only possible when the sector we are studying is *not* sufficiently large to influence the whole economy. Fig. 5.10 attempts a diagrammatic explanation of this point. In Fig. 5.10 (*a*), sector A is not big enough to affect the rest of the economy, so that, for example, a rise in the price in sector A does not affect the general level of prices in the rest of the economy and there-

fore there is no appreciable 'feedback' to section A from the rest of the economy as a result of this change. We are thus able to keep to our *ceteris paribus* assumption of all other things remaining constant.

However, in Fig. 5.10 (*b*), sector B is sufficiently large that changes in it influence the rest of the economy and that induced changes in the economy then 'feed back' to sector B and so on. Under these circumstances partial equilibrium analysis is no longer possible. We have moved from microeconomics to macroeconomics and a new type of analysis is needed.

General equilibrium

Macroeconomic analysis is dealt with in later sections of the book. However we may note here that a microeconomic explanation of the functioning of the whole of economy exists. This is termed the *general equilibrium*. This is illustrated in Fig. 5.11. Here we imagine that rather than just looking at the determination of one price we have the thousands upon thousands of prices which go to make up the economy. Prices are thus interdependent.

An example of the general equilibrium analysis might be the interrelationship of fuel markets. This would involve looking at coal-mining, oil tankers, electricity prices, gas exploration and so on, and tracing the ramifications of a change in any one factor (group of factors) throughout the economy. General equilibrium analysis is

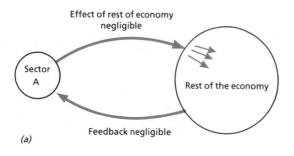

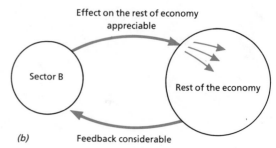

Fig. 5.10 *Partial equilibrium analysis*
Partial equilibrium analysis is possible in (*a*), where we may assume *ceteris paribus*, but feedback effects make it impossible in (*b*).

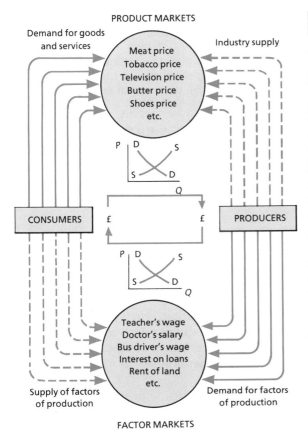

PRODUCT MARKETS

Demand for goods and services

Industry supply

Meat price
Tobacco price
Television price
Butter price
Shoes price
etc.

CONSUMERS £ £ PRODUCERS

Teacher's wage
Doctor's salary
Bus driver's wage
Interest on loans
Rent of land
etc.

Supply of factors of production

Demand for factors of production

FACTOR MARKETS

Fig. 5.11 *The general equilibrium*

much more complicated than partial equilibrium analysis because the possibility of feedback between sectors now exists.

This effect was illustrated by the rise in oil prices in 1978. The OPEC countries attempted to double prices. The price of a barrel of oil might be considered a microeconomic phenomenon; however, oil was such an important product to most countries that the price rise was sufficient to push their economies into depression. Thus a microeconomic phenomenon became a macroeconomic one.

The credit for the discovery of general equilibrium analysis is usually given to the great French economist Léon Walras (1834–1910). However the development of it had to wait for the use of matrix algebra, which was the work of Wassily Leontief (1906–   ).

The price system assessed

The price system provides an answer to the fundamental problem of any economic society. Through prices the economy decides *what* to produce, i.e. anything people are willing to spend money on that can be produced profitably. We have also seen that *how* things are produced is also dependent on prices, since it involves producers buying the services of the factors of production in factor markets. The income generated in these factor markets also determines *who* will have the money to buy the goods which are produced.

We will now consider briefly some of the major problems associated with the operation of an economy through the price system. A fuller treatment of this must wait until we have considered all the aspects of the market.

The distribution of income

A serious problem associated with the market system is that income is very unevenly divided amongst the population. In theory people's income is determined by demand and supply in the factor markets but, apart from the serious inefficiencies involved in these markets, a person's income is influenced by inheritance.

Such are the inequalities in income that nearly all governments are forced to intervene in markets to alleviate the worst excesses. For example, the provision of old age pensions in the UK is necessary to avoid mass poverty amongst the old.

Dangerous products

A minor interference with the market system that is forced on nearly all governments is the regulation of dangerous products. Thus, for example, governments may forbid the sale of firearms or dangerous drugs.

Competition

The picture of the economy we have been developing in this chapter depends upon there **65** being *competition* between suppliers. This, said Adam Smith, along with the *'invisible hand'* of self-interest, leads to an optimum allocation of resources. But the invisible hand will not work if there is not free competition. When we turn to examine the economy we find that there are many monopolies and restrictions upon trade.

A monopoly [said Smith] granted either to an individual or a trading company has the same effect as a secret in trade or manufactures. The monopolists, by keeping the market constantly understocked, by never supplying the effectual demand, sell their commodities much above the natural price, and raise their emoluments, whether they consist in wages or profit, greatly above their natural rate.

Despite these reservations we continue to study the market because it provides a model by which we can judge the economic inefficiency of the real world.

Summary

1 The price system is a method of operating the economy through the medium of market prices.
2 The first law of demand tells us that, *ceteris paribus*, more of a product is demanded at a lower price.
3 The law of diminishing marginal utility states that, *ceteris paribus*, as more and more of a commodity is consumed the extra utility derived declines.
4 A change in price, *ceteris paribus*, causes an *extension* or *contraction* of demand, while a change in any other determinant causes an *increase* or *decrease* of demand.
5 The first principle of supply is that, *ceteris paribus*, a greater quantity is supplied at a higher price because at a higher price increased costs can be incurred.
6 An increase or decrease in supply is caused by a change in one of the conditions of supply.
7 The determinants of supply are price – the price of factors of production and the price of other commodities – the state of technology, the tastes of producers, and other exogenous factors.
8 The equilibrium price is the price at which the wishes of buyers and sellers coincide.
9 At any price other than the equilibrium there is either upward or downward pressure on price caused by either excess demand or excess supply.
10 Partial equilibrium analysis is only possible when there are no 'feedback' effects between the sector being considered and the rest of the economy.
11 Our view of the price system as a method of achieving the optimum allocation of resources is modified by problems associated with the distribution of income and by the lack of competition in the economy.

Questions

1 Describe the factors which determine the supply of wheat.
2 Make a list of as many cases as you can of where the government intervenes with the automatic working of the price system, e.g. food and drugs legislation.

3   Describe precisely how excess supply in a market causes the price to fall.
4   What would happen to the market demand for steak as the result of each of the following?
   a) an increase in the average income per head.
   b) an increase in the size of population.
   c) increased advertising for lamb and pork.
   d) an increase in the price of lamb.
   e) a decrease in the price of pork.
5   What would happen to the equilibrium price and quantity of butter if:
   a) the price of margarine increased?
   b) the cost of producing butter increased?
6   Discuss the problems associated with using the price mechanism as a way to deal with:
   a) the allocation of university places;
   b) traffic problems in cities.
7   Explain the difference between partial equilibrium and general equilibrium analysis.
8   'When some people are very wealthy while others are poor, the whole notion of consumer sovereignty in a market economy is misleading and prejudicial.' Discuss.
9   St Thomas Aquinas in the thirteenth century wrote: 'To sell a thing for more than it's worth or to buy it for less than it's worth, is in itself unjust and unlawful.' Discuss the problems which might be associated with the application of this view to a modern economy.
10 Suppose that a demand curve is given by the equation $y = 1000 - x$ and the supply curve by the equation $y = 100 + 2x$.
   a) what will be the equilibrium price?
   b) What is the excess demand or supply if the price is: (i) 900; (ii) 400?
   c) Devise an equation for the excess demand function based on the demand and supply schedules in this example.
(Remember y = price and x = quantity).

Data response   Equilibrium prices ━━━━━━━━━━━━━━━━━━━━━━━━━━━━━━━━━━━

The following figures give the demand and supply schedules for product Z.

Price of Z (£/kg)	Quantity demanded of Z (kg/week)	Quantity supplied of Z (kg/week)
9	100	800
7	300	600
5	500	400
3	700	200
1	900	0

From these figures:
   a) draw the demand and supply curves.
   b) determine and state the equilibrium price.
   c) what is the excess demand or supply if the price is: (i) £7 per kg; (ii) £2 per kg?
   d) suppose that demand were now to increase by 50 per cent at every price.   **67**

Draw the new demand curve and determine the new equilibrium price.

e) from the original figures, construct the excess demand function.

f) from the original demand curve calculate the total revenue to be gained from the sale of product Z at £1, £2, £3, etc. Then plot this information on a graph, putting total revenue on a vertical axis and quantity on the horizontal axis. State the quantity at which total revenue is maximised.

6

The mixed economy

The imperatives of technology and organisation, not the images of ideology, are what determine the shape of economic society.

J. K. Galbraith

As we saw in the first chapter, all economies of the world can be said to be 'mixed' to a greater or lesser degree. However we usually reserve the term for those economies where there is both a large proportion of a market economy, together with a significant proportion of state control. It is thus a term which can be applied to most of the countries of Western Europe.

The most famous mixed economy in the world is that of the UK because it was in the UK that the form first evolved. If therefore we wish to understand how mixed economies came into being and what are their central features, a study of the UK economy is a good starting place.

The origins of the mixed economy

The decline of the free market

The economy of the UK in the nineteenth century was one in which people and organisations were in a state of unfettered competition. It was believed that the economy would operate best if the government did not intervene in it. Such beliefs were based on the writings of Adam Smith (1723–90), who argued that *competition* was the best regulator of the economy. The belief that internal and external trade should be left to regulate itself became known by the French expression *laissez-faire*.

Adam Smith saw the economy as made up of millions of individuals and small businesses guided by an *invisible hand*.

Every individual endeavours to employ his capital so that its produce may be of greatest value. He generally neither intends to promote the public interest, nor knows how he is promoting it. He intends only his own security, only his own gain. And he is led in this by an invisible hand to promote an end which was no part of his intention. By pursuing his own interest he frequently promotes that of society more effectively than when he really intends to promote it.

To Smith, therefore, the economy was a *self-regulating structure*. For this to happen properly he believed that government should interfere in the economy as little as possible, for interference disturbed the mechanism of the market.

It is often thought that free competiton is the 'natural' state of the economy. This is not so: it is almost entirely a nineteenth-century phenom-enon. Before this time monarchs felt free to regulate the economy as they saw fit. On the other hand in the twentieth century the economy is dominated by the government and by giant business organisations. Only in a few sectors of the economy could free competition be said to exist today.

In his book *The Wealth of Nations* Smith argued that the many taxes and regulations which surrounded the commerce of the country hin-dered its growth. Business organisations should be free to pursue profit, restricted only by the competition of other business organisations.

From about 1815 onwards government began to pursue this policy. The UK, already a wealthy country, grew wealthier still. The success of industries such as textiles and iron appeared to prove the wisdom of Adam Smith. Belief in the 'free market' system became the dominant economic ideology.

However as the nineteenth century progressed it became apparent that the free market system had two major defects.

a) Although efficient at producing some products such as food and clothing, the free market system failed to produce effectively things such as sanitation or education.

b) Competition could easily disappear and give way to monopoly.

It was to combat these two problems that the state began to intervene in the economy. In the case of *a*) the government did not take a conscious decision to depart from laissez-faire philosophy; rather action was forced upon it by the severity of the problems. This is well illustrated by the 1848 Public Health Act. In this case cholera epidemics forced the government to promote better drainage and sanitation. In the case of *b*) there was a more conscious effort to regulate monopolies. This may be illustrated by the measures, which began as early as 1840, to regulate the activities of railway companies.

Thus the nineteenth century presents a picture of governments believing in a free market economy but being forced to regulate its most serious excesses.

The effects of the 1914–18 war

The 1914–18 war thrust upon the government the control of the economy. Until this time wars had been fought on a free enterprise basis, if we can use the expression, with volunteer armies and little disruption of the domestic economy. Gradually the government had to assume control of more and more of the economy. The railways were taken over, agriculture was completely controlled, the iron and steel industry was directed and conscription was introduced.

However after 1918 the government immediately tried to return to a market economy. In 1921 a depression started in the UK and in 1929 it turned into a worldwide slump which the market economy seemed powerless to cure.

The Keynesian revolution

Between 1921 and 1939 the average level of unemployment was 14 per cent; it never fell below 10 per cent and in the worst years was over 20 per cent. Conventional economic theory concentrated on the demand for resources. This held that if there was unemployment it was because wages were too high. Thus the way to cure unemployment was to cut wages and prices, thereby making people more willing to buy goods and employers more willing to employ people. *Say's law* further maintained that if the market mechanism was allowed to work it would ensure the full employment of all resources and that this was the 'natural' equilibrium for the economy.

The writings of John Maynard Keynes (1883–1946) are the most important contribution to economic thinking in the twentieth century. Despite the fact that during the 1930s the economy was patently not self-regulating, Keynes realised that the ideas of classical economics were still doughty opponents. In 1934 he wrote:

The strength of the self-adjusting school depends on its having behind it almost the whole body of economic thinking and doctrine of the past 100 years. This is a formidable power. It is the product of acute minds and has persuaded and convinced the great majority of the intelligent and disinterested persons who have studied it. It has vast prestige and a more far reaching influence than is obvious. For it lies behind the education and habitual modes of thought not only of economists, but of banks and businessmen and civil servants and politicians of all parties.

Keynes was English and worked for many years at Cambridge University. His views on the economy, however, were so radical that they were not accepted by governments in the 1930s. In his most famous book *The General Theory of Employment, Interest and Money* (1936) Keynes analysed the workings of the economy and put forward his solution to unemployment.

Keynes maintained that it was not the demand for individual resources which was important but the *level* of total (aggregate) demand in the economy. He said that a fall in the level of demand would lead to over-production; this would lead to the accumulation of stocks (inventories) and, as this happened, people would be thrown out of work. The unemployed would lose their purchasing power and therefore the level of demand would sink still further, and so on. Cutting wages, therefore, would not cure unemployment: it would make it worse.

Since it would appear that the economy was no longer self-regulating, there was a clear case for government intervention. Keynes' solution was that, if there was a shortfall in demand in the economy, the government should make it up by public spending. In order to do this the government would have to spend beyond its means (a budget deficit). In the 1930s this solution was not acceptable. As Galbraith has written: 'To spend money to create jobs seemed profligate; to urge a budget deficit as a good thing seemed insane.' It took the 1939–45 war to bring Keynes's ideas into the operation of government policy.

Socialism

Keynes was a 'conservative revolutionary': his concern was to show not how the capitalist system could be abolished but how it could be modified. Thus the post-Keynesian capitalist society has been even more successful than its predecessor. The fact that Keynes argued for government intervention in the economy does *not* make him a socialist. Socialists are those who believe that the means of production should be publicly owned. Socialism is therefore a different strand in the development of the mixed economy. Although much socialist thinking is based on the works of Marx, in the UK socialism has tended to be constitutional rather than revolutionary. Socialist thinking in the UK probably owes more to *Sidney and Beatrice Webb*

and other great *Fabian* socialists than to Marx and Lenin.

The effect of the 1939–45 war

From the outset of the 1939–45 war the government took over the direction of the economy: industries were taken over, labour was directed, food was rationed. The UK could be said to have had a *centrally-planned economy*. The realisation spread that the government could intervene successfully in the economy. Keynes's ideas at last came to be accepted. Both the major political parties during the war committed themselves to the maintenance of a high and stable level of employment once peace was achieved. This was to be achieved by Keynesian techniques of the management of the level of aggregate demand. The fact that it was a Labour government which was elected in 1945 meant that an element of socialism was also introduced into the economy.

The welfare state

You do not have to be a socialist to believe that everyone is entitled to education, health services and social security. The origins of the welfare state might be traced back to *Lloyd George* and beyond, but its immediate progenitor was the *Beveridge Report* of 1942. This recommended a national health scheme for 'every citizen without exception, without remuneration limit and without an economic barrier'. Beveridge also stated that the basis for comprehensive social security must be the certainty of a continuing high level of employment. A White Paper, *Employment Policy*, which embodied this idea, was published in 1944 and accepted by both the major political parties. Subsequently, full employment was to become a first priority for all governments. The wheel had come full circle from the workhouses of 1834 which were designed to be so unpleasant that they would force people to find work. The age of laissez-faire had passed away.

The components of the mixed economy

What emerged from this period of Labour **71**

government was an economy which was a compound of socialist ideas, Keynesian management and capitalism. It was truly a mixed economy. Hence we might summarise the main components of the mixed economy thus.

a) A free enterprise sector, where economic decisions are taken through the workings of the market.

b) Government regulation of the economy through its budgets, etc.

c) Public ownership of some industries.

d) Welfare services, either provided by the state or supplied through state administered schemes.

In this list *a*) constitutes the *private sector* of the economy whilst *b*) to *d*) are the *public sector*.

The monetarist counter-revolution

During the 1970s many western economies were faced with the dual pressures of rising inflation and rising unemployment. Keynesian demand management policies seemed powerless to deal with these problems. Some economists came to believe that Keynes's ideas were flawed and that control of the money supply and a return to free market economics was the only way to restore the economy. The popular name, at the time, for these economists was *monetarists* but the counter-revolution was much wider than monetarism. It might be better to refer to those advocating a return to market values as the *new classicists*.

The result of the application of these ideas was a rigorous drive back towards a *price orientated economy*. This trend was known to most people as *privatisation* and had a profound effect upon the economy. Thus the late 1970s might be seen as the high-water mark for government intervention. However, whatever its political complexion, it is impossible for a government not to play a massive role in a modern economy.

The remaining sections of this chapter consider the various ways in which the government intervenes in the UK economy.

Management of the economy

The objectives of economic policy

Whatever political party is in power, four main objectives of policy are pursued.

a) Control of inflation.

b) Reduction of unemployment.

c) Promotion of economic growth.

d) Attainment of a favourable balance of payments.

These objectives are not in dispute; they are concerned with the 'good housekeeping' of the economy. Different governments may, however, place different degrees of importance on individual objectives. Thus, for example, a Labour government might place a higher priority on reducing unemployment than a Conservative one. In addition to these generally agreed objectives, more 'political' economic policies might be pursued, such as the redistribution of income. There are three areas of action in which the government can pursue its economic policies: fiscal policy, monetary policy and direct intervention.

Fiscal policy

The term fiscal policy is used to describe the regulation of the economy through government taxes and spending. The most important aspect of this is the overall relationship between taxes and spending. If the government spends more money in a year than it collects in taxes, the situation is referred to as a *budget deficit*. A deficit has an expansionary, or inflationary, effect upon the economy. Conversely, a situation where the government collects more in taxes than it spends is referred to as a *budget surplus*. A surplus has a restraining, or deflationary, effect upon the economy.

If the government spends more money than it collects in taxes, so that it is in deficit, the budget is financed by *borrowing*. The amount of money which the government may be forced to borrow in a year is referred to as the *public-sector borrow-ing requirement* (PSBR). In the 1970s the PSBR became very large and governments since then have tried to restrain its growth.

Monetary policy

This is the regulation of the economy through the control of the *quantity of money* available and through the *price of money*, i.e. the rate of interest borrowers will have to pay. Expanding the quantity of money and lowering the rate of interest should stimulate spending in the econ-omy and is thus expansionary, or inflationary. Conversely, restricting the quantity of money and raising the rate of interest should have a restraining, or deflationary, effect upon the economy.

It might be thought that, because the govern-ment controls the printing of banknotes, it is easy for it to control the quantity of money. This, however, is not so because most spending in the economy is not done with banknotes but with bank deposits. The amount of this 'cheque money' is determined by the banking system and can only be affected indirectly by the gover-ment. The government does, however, have a great effect upon the rate of interest because all other interest rates in the economy tend to move in line with the rates of interest set by the Bank of England. In addition to this the govern-ment has a similarly large effect upon interest rates since it is the biggest borrower in the economy.

Direct intervention

This expression is used to describe the many different ways in which the government, through legislation, spending or sanctions, tries to im-pose its economic policy directly upon the economy. Both fiscal and monetary policy are attempts to *create conditions* in the economy which will cause industry and people to react in a way which is in line with the government's wishes. Direct intervention, on the other hand, seeks to *impose the government's will* directly upon the economy, leaving people no choice. A

good example of this would be the imposition of a statutory prices and incomes policy.

Provision of goods and services

Many of the things which individuals use are provided either by *central* or *local government*; for example, most people's health care and edu-cation is provided by the state. These services are not, of course, free, since we pay for them indirectly through taxes and insurance schemes. The state also provides goods and services to the public on a commercial or semi-commercial basis, i.e. they are *sold* to the public. These products, such as postal services and rail travel, are usually provided by public corporations.

Many essential services are supplied by the governments. These may be controlled directly by *central government*, e.g. defence and motor-way construction. Alternatively the service may be decided upon by central government but administered by local government, e.g. edu-cation. Services such as street lighting and refuse collection may be entirely controlled by local authorities. On the other hand, services may be provided by bodies set up by the government but which are not regarded as either central or local government bodies. An example of these are health authorities. Such bodies are termed QUANGOs (quasi-autonomous non-govern-mental organisations).

Public goods and services

Public goods are those where consumption of the product by one person does not diminish the consumption by others. The classic example of this is that of a lighthouse, where the fact that the light guides one ship does not detract from its ability to guide others. More significantly in the modern economy, such things as defence and street lighting might be considered public goods.

Merit goods and services

These are products which are allocated to the **73**

members of the public according to their merit (or need). Thus, for example, health services are not given to everyone, only those who need (or merit) them because of ill-health. Similarly, education is not given to everyone equally. Educational opportunities are only made available to those between the age of 5 and 16 and to those whose achievements in examinations qualify them for higher education. There are several problems involved in defining merit goods. These are discussed in Chapter 26.

Nationalised industries

Many of the major industries in the UK have been nationalised. Legally they may be termed public corporations. These and their subsequent privatisation, form the subject of a separate chapter in the book (see Chapter 19).

The mixed enterprise

A mixed enterprise is one which retains a private sector form (e.g. Plc) but is wholly or partly owned by the government. The most famous example of this was BP (British Petroleum) in which the government owned 51 per cent of the shares. These were sold off in a number of slices until the government's shareholding was eliminated.

During the 1970s there was a rapid growth in the number of mixed enterprises and the National Enterprise Board (NEB) was set up by the Labour government in 1974. This public corporation owned and controlled the shares acquired by the government in limited companies. Mixed enterprises are normally counted as part of the private sector of the economy, not the public.

The NEB grew very rapidly during the late 1970s, acquiring shares in dozens of companies which were often in financial difficulties. The Conservative government of 1979, however, decided to decrease the role of the NEB and sell the shares it owned. This was partly because they wished to raise money to reduce government borrowing and partly because they believed that the state should play a smaller part in the

economy. By 1988 the one major shareholding left to the government was in the Rover Group (formerly British Leyland). In March 1988 British Aerospace made an offer to buy out the government's shares.

The prospect for the mixed economy

We can look at the prospect for the mixed economy in political, economic or technological terms. Considering the economic point of view first, the central problem is the failure of Keynesian management of the economy. Keynes's analysis centred on the *macroeconomy* and was based on the short-term management of demand.

This worked reasonably well until the 1960s, but since that time there has been a conspicuous failure to solve the twin problems of inflation and unemployment. In recent years governments here tried *microeconomic programmes*, trying to encourage potential growth wherever it can be found in the economy.

Economic policy, however, must function within the political framework. In practice this gives the consumers very little economic choice. However detailed the platform is on which a government is elected, it will only roughly approximate to the wishes of even its own supporters. Politics also places another constraint upon the mixed economy. At least once every five years the government must seek re-election. It is possible to argue that any major economic policy should last for much longer than this and therefore the real welfare of the country is being subjected to the government of the day's desire to ensure re-election. Thus politicians are led to ask themselves what most people want, while the economist would maintain that the correct question should be 'What do people want most?'

The election of the Thatcher government in 1979 was to have a radical effect upon the development of the mixed economy. The government was strongly opposed to all forms of collectivism and economic interventionism. This led to a return to market-centred economics and to the round of privatisations. Margaret Thatcher's achievement in being re-elected for a third term allowed this push of policy to continue into areas previously considered sacrosanct such as the health service. The shape of the economy in 1989 was profoundly different from that of 1979.

A third factor shaping the economy which may be independent of political and economic ideology is technology.

It is obvious that technology, and in particular the revolution in microprocessing, is having a very profound effect upon our lives. There are many people, however, who believe that the revolution in technology has also brought about a revolution in the economic order and created a new decision-making process. Foremost amongst the advocates of this point of view is Professor J. K. Galbraith.

Galbraith maintains that power has passed from company directors, shareholders, trade unionists, voters and even the government to the *technostructure*. It is argued that in all advanced states power rests with those who have the high level of skill and information which is necessary to operate in a large corporation or government department. James Burnham in his book *The Managerial Revolution* (1941) argued that the new ruling class would not be capitalists or communists, but those who had expert technological skills. The argument is developed in Galbraith's books *The New Industrial State* and *The Age of Uncertainty*. While this is probably an extreme point of view, it cannot be doubted that the new technology, particularly that of the silicon chip, is transforming our lives.

Despite the changes wrought by the Conservative governments of the 1980s the UK economy was still a mixed economy with the public sector accounting for over 40 per cent of GDP. The mixed economy stands poised between the two ideologies of capitalism and collectivism, pulled this way and that by differing political opinions. In addition to this it has to cope with the rising power of the technocrat both in multinational corporations and in government departments.

Summary

1   Despite a belief in laissez-faire, governments of the nineteenth century were forced to intervene in the economy.
2   Classical economics proved unable to explain or cure the mass unemployment of the 1920s and 1930s.
3   Keynes's insights into the workings of the economy revolutionised the subject.
4   The Labour government of 1945 was largely responsible for the shape of the economy for the subsequent 30 years.
5   The mixed economy is a compound of laissez-faire, government management, public ownership and welfare state.
6   The government controls the economy through fiscal policy, monetary policy and direct intervention.
7   A profound change of direction came about in the 1980s through privatisation and measures to make the economy more market orientated.
8   In the late-twentieth century the mixed economy faces new problems, in particular those of the new technostructure. The role of the state is once more a subject of great political controversy.

Questions

1   Trace the development of the mixed economy.
2   Which of the following are:
   a) public goods;
   b) merit goods;
   c) neither?
Lighthouses; public broadcasting; roads; education; dental care; electricity; council houses; defence; old age pensions; toothpaste; rail travel; and public libraries. Which of these did you have difficulty categorising and why?
3   Do you agree with Galbraith's assertion that we are now governed by technocrats? Give reasons for your answer.
4   What effect has the 'privatisation' of nationalised industries had upon the mixed economy?
5   Economic activities can take place in:
   a) the public sector;
   b) the private sector; or
   c) both sectors of the economy.
Coal-mining, for example, is almost entirely a public sector activity whilst shoe manufacture is entirely in the private sector, and armaments manufacture takes place in both sectors. Give three more examples for a), b) and c) respectively which illustrate these categories.

Data response   The size of the public sector

1   For each of the years shown in Table 6.1 state which country had:
   a) the largest public sector
   b) the largest percentage of GDP devoted to transfer payments
2   Which three countries had the largest budget deficits in 1985.
3   Which countries had a larger public sector than the UK in 1985.
4   Explain what is meant by the indexing of transfer payments? Which countries in the sample would find this most burdensome and why?
5   What reasons are there for the growth of public sector expenditure from 1965–85? Why are there such differences in the size of public sectors?
6   Explain what is meant by the term the 'crowding out' of investment?

Table 6.1 The growth of the public sector. (All figures are % GDP)

Country	Total government outlay			Public consumption			Transfer payments			General government financial balance Surplus (+)/Deficit (−)			Gross domestic investment			Average annual growth in GDP/capita
	1965	1975	1985	1965	1975	1985	1965	1975	1985	1965	1975	1985	1965	1975	1985	1965–85
Sweden	38·3	48·9	64·5	18·0	23·0	27·0	20·3	25·9	37·5	3·0	2·7	−0·3	27·0	24·0	19·0	1·8
Netherlands	40·7	52·8	60·2	15·0	16·0	16·0	25·5	36·8	44·2	1·0	−3·0	−5·6	27·0	24·0	20·0	2·0
Italy	34·3	43·2	58·4	15·0	16·0	19·0	19·3	27·2	39·4	−6·0	−12·4	−11·2	20·0	19·0	19·0	2·6
Belgium	33·5	44·5	54·4	13·0	15·0	17·0	20·5	29·5	37·4	−2·0	−4·7	−9·2	23·0	19·0	15·0	2·8
France	38·5	43·5	52·4	13·0	14·0	16·0	25·5	29·5	36·4	−2·0	−2·2	−2·9	25·0	22·0	19·0	2·8
UK	35·3	47·3	47·7	17·0	21·0	21·0	18·3	26·3	26·7	−2·0	−4·7	−2·6	20·0	18·0	17·0	1·6
Germany	36·7	48·9	47·2	15·0	18·0	20·0	21·7	30·9	27·2	−1·7	−5·7	−1·2	28·0	25·0	20·0	2·7
USA	28·5	34·6	36·7	17·0	17·0	18·0	11·5	17·6	18·7	2·1	−4·1	−3·5	20·0	19·0	19·0	1·7
Japan	19·1	27·3	32·7	8·0	9·0	10·0	11·1	18·3	22·7	3·1	−2·7	−0·9	32·0	31·0	28·0	4·7
Switzerland	20·1	28·7	30·9	10·0	11·0	13·0	10·1	17·7	17·9	N/A	N/A	N/A	30·0	28·0	24·0	1·4

Source: OECD and IBRD statistics

7   From the figures does there appear to be any connection between the size of the public sector and the growth of GDP?

8   What do you expect to happen to the size of the public sector in the countries mentioned in the Table over the next five years? Explain your reasoning.

9   Why do different economies place greater or lesser emphasis on public sector activity?

10   What factors do you consider to be most important in affecting the development of the mixed economy?

11   What other information would be useful in assessing the performance of the mixed economy?

7
National income

We have seen already that micro- and macro-economics are different approaches to the study of the economy. Macroeconomics is concerned with *aggregate* economic phenomena and processes. National income gives us a measure of those aggregates. In this chapter we will outline the main components of national income and consider some of the difficulties involved in measuring it. Subsequently (Section V) we will examine the factors which determine the size of national income.

The circular flow of national income

The national product

National product is a term we use to describe the total of all the wealth produced, distributed and consumed in an economy over a specific period of time.

There are several different measures of national product, the most commonly used being gross domestic product (GDP), gross national product (GNP) and net national product (NNP). In the UK the data relating to national income is collected together in *National Accounts* prepared by the Central Statistical Office. This annual publication is more commonly called the 'Blue Book'. Most countries outside the Communist Bloc use similar measurements. Quarterly summaries for the leading 24 industrialised nations can be found in the *OECD Economic Outlook*.

The national product (or national income) is a *flow with respect to time*, i.e. it is so many billions of pounds *per year*. It is not a count of the static wealth of the community. Its size is of vital importance to the well-being of society because such things as employment and the standard of living are determined by it.

The circular flow

To understand the various measures of national product it is necessary to understand the nature of the macroeconomy. Figure 7.1 illustrates a

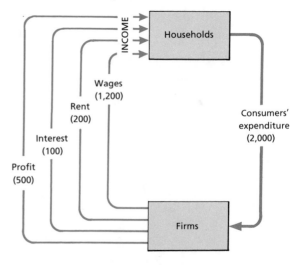

Fig. 7.1 *The circular flow of income*
National income is the same total as consumers' expenditure.

simple view of the economy in which there is no foreign trade and no government intervention. Here we see two of the main components of the macroeconomy, households and firms. These components are identified not by who they are but by what they do, i.e. firms produce while households consume. Everyone in the economy must belong to a 'household' since everyone must consume. The households also own the factors of production. In order to produce, firms must buy factor services from households. In return for the factor services, firms pay households wages, rent, interest and profit. The size of these payments will give us the cost of producing and therefore the value of the national product.

This payment for factor services is known as *income* and can be abbreviated to the letter Y. We shall see later that this corresponds to the GDP measure of national product.

Since we have included profits in the factor payments it can be seen that we could also arrive at the value of the national product by measuring the amount of money spent on it. Thus if we totalled all consumers' expenditure (C) on the right-hand side of Fig. 7.1 it should be equal to all the factor incomes on the left-hand side. We therefore have two methods of measuring the national product, either by measuring *national income* or *national expenditure*.

If we return to Fig. 7.1 again it should be obvious why this view of the economy is often referred to as the circular flow of income. Firms receive money from households which they then pay out as wages, etc. This income is spent creating more income for firms and so on. *Everyone's income is someone else's expenditure.*

Two methods of measurement

A simple example will show the similarity of the two-fold method of measuring national product to double entry bookkeeping. Table 7.1 shows a simplified balance sheet for a farm. The profit reverts to the farmer as householder, i.e. it is the farmer's income. It is then spent in the same way as other factor incomes.

Table 7.1 Balance sheet of a farm

Sales (consumers' expenditure)		Costs (factor earnings)	
Sales of wheat	£1000	Wages	£600
		Rent	100
		Interest	50
		Profit	250
Total	£1000	Total	£1000

If the economy just consisted of 2 million such farms then we could arrive at the national product by aggregating all their balance sheets. This has been done in Table 7.2

Table 7.2 National product

Sales (consumers' expenditure)		Costs (factor incomes)	
Sales of wheat (2m × £1000)	£2000m	Wages (2m × £600)	£1200m
		Rent (2m × £100)	200m
		Interest (2m × £50)	100m
		Profit (2m × £250)	500m
National expenditure	£2000m	National income	£2000m

Thus we can see that the two sides of the balance sheet give two different ways of arriving at the same measure for national product, and we can conclude that:

National income = National expenditure

When we come to look at the actual statistics for the national product we shall see that both these measures are used. A third measure of national product exists and this is arrived at by totalling the *value added* by each industry in the country.

A third measure

Many products must go through several stages of production before they reach their *final* form. **79**

Consider a product such as bread; first we must produce wheat; this must then be ground into flour; the flour must be baked into bread; and finally the product must be sold to the customer. The total value of bread to the national product will be its *final* selling price. The expenditure method of calculating national product involves totalling all expenditure on *final* products. Bread is obviously a final product because it is consumed and disappears from the economy. However, many *intermediate* products are bought and sold and if we examine their value we can determine the *value added* to the economy by each industry and we also arrive at another measure of national product, which is termed *national output*.

When calculating the national product by the *output* method it is important to avoid *double counting*. Let us pursue our bread example a little farther. The farmer produces wheat by employing the factors of production – land, labour, etc. The wheat is then sold for £1000. The miller then *adds value* to it by milling it and sells it for £1300. What is the value to the economy of the miller's contribution? It is £1300 minus the £1000 he paid for the wheat.

Therefore if we wish to calculate the value added to the economy by an industry we arrive at it by taking the value of its output and subtracting the cost of the raw materials or intermediate products it had to buy in order to produce its output. Thus the value added by an industry is the factor services it has applied to

the product. The payment for these services – wages, rent, interest and profit – returns to the households as income.

Table 7.3 illustrates a value-added method of calculating the national product.

The stages of production

Figure 7.2 uses the same example of bread-making to show that all three methods of calculating the national income can be reconciled. The value of the national product can be shown as the expenditure by households of £2500 on bread. The same figure can be arrived at by totalling the value added by each of the four stages of production. The national product can also be measured as the flows of income to households in return for the factor services. The national product is a measure of the wealth (in our example bread) produced in the economy over a certain period. We can now see that there are three methods of arriving at a measure of the same thing. Thus we can write:

National income = National expenditure = National output

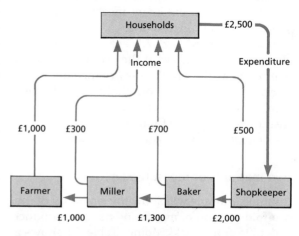

Table 7.3 The value-added method

Type of industry	Value of output	Cost of intermediate goods	Value added (*factor services*)
Farming	£1000	0	£1000
Milling	1300	£1000	300
Baking	2000	1300	700
Retailing	2500(a)	2000	500
	£6800	£5300	£2500(b)

(a) National product by final expenditure method.
(b) National product by value-added method.

Fig. 7.2 The stages of production
National income (£1000 + £300 + £700 + £500)
= national expenditure (£2500) = national output
[£1000 + (£1300 − £1000) +
(£2000 − £1300) + (£2500 − £2000)].

The components of national income

So far we have been considering a very simple economy which produces only consumer goods and has no government intervention and no foreign trade. However all these things must be included in the actual calculation of national income or product. We will consider each of these in turn.

Capital goods

In order to produce consumer goods we need capital goods in the form of buildings, machines and stocks. Therefore an economy must produce not only consumer goods (C) but also investment, or capital, goods (I). We count both consumer goods and investment goods as part of the gross national product (GNP). Although we may not actually 'consume' factories or machines, if our stock of them increases then the economy has become wealthier because we have a greater ability to produce wealth. We therefore need to count investment goods as part of the national product. From this we can see that national product is going to be equal to the output of consumer goods plus investment goods (C+I).

Final goods

When we are calculating the national product we therefore need to include all *final goods*. For example, bread is a final good because it is not made into anything else, but is consumed. In the same way bakers' ovens are final goods because they are not made into anything else and they are also 'consumed' by being used to produce bread. Stocks of raw materials, or intermediate goods, may also enter into the evaluation of the national product. If at the end of the year our stocks of raw materials, etc., are greater than at the beginning of the year then we have obviously become wealthier. Therefore we include in the calculation of the national product the value of the *physical* increase in our stocks. (Stocks are also often referred to as *inventories*.)

Gross and net output

The output in capital goods in any particular period is referred to as *capital formation*. Capital goods may be either *fixed capital*, such as buildings and machinery, or *circulating capital* in the form of stocks of raw materials and intermediate goods. In national income accounts these two items are considered separately. The output of buildings and machinery is shown as *gross domestic fixed capital formation*. The change in circulating capital is recorded as the *value of physical increase in stocks and work in progress* (this may be either a positive or negative value depending upon whether inventories have increased or decreased during the year).

If we consider capital goods such as roads, buildings and machinery, it is obvious that as we use them they wear out. Therefore every year we must produce a certain amount of capital goods simply to replace those which are wearing out. The output of all capital goods during the year might therefore be referred to as *gross capital formation*. However, when we have made allowances for the wearing out of capital we arrive at a figure known as *net capital formation*. The allowance made for the wearing out or *depreciation* of capital is known as *capital consumption*.

There are therefore two measures of the national product. If we simply count up the output of all final products – both consumer goods and investment goods – we will arrive at a measure which is known as gross national product (GNP), but if we make an allowance for capital consumption then we arrive at a measure known as net national product (NNP).

The government and the national product

We have so far considered expenditure by households on consumer goods, as well as the expenditure on capital goods. However the largest single consumer of all types of goods is the government. Therefore, when we are calculating national expenditure, as well as consumer spending (C) and private investment spending (I) we add all government expenditure

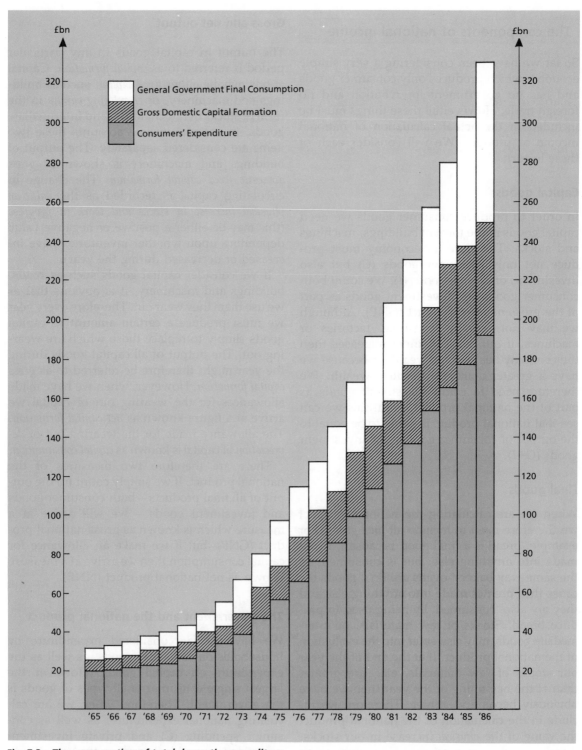

£bn

£bn

General Government Final Consumption

Gross Domestic Capital Formation

Consumers' Expenditure

'65 '66 '67 '68 '69 '70 '71 '72 '73 '74 '75 '76 '77 '78 '79 '80 '81 '82 '83 '84 '85 '86

82   Fig. 7.3   *The consumption of total domestic expenditure*

on goods and services (*G*), so that the total demand for goods and services will now be *C* + *I* + *G*.

Included within government expenditure are such things as the cost of new schools and the salaries of school teachers and the people in the services, and the cost of tanks and guns. In short it is the wages of all government employees plus goods (medicines, paper, roads, etc.) which the government buys from the private sector.

This does not, however, include *all* government spending. We do not include items such as expenditure on old age pensions or sickness benefits. These are termed *transfer payments*. The reason for this is that these are not payments for *current* productive services and therefore have nothing to do with the creation of the national product in the current year. Similarly we do not include payment of interest on the national debt.

Figure 7.3 shows the proportions of total domestic expenditure which the various components of national expenditure represent. You will note that the proportion represented by government expenditure has gradually increased over the years.

Foreign trade and the national product

So far the economy we have considered has been a *closed economy*. The UK, however, is an *open economy*, i.e. one which trades with the rest of the world. Of all countries in the world the UK is one of the most dependent on foreign trade. In 1988 exports (*X*) of goods and services were equivalent to 30 per cent of the gross domestic product and imports (*M*) to 33 per cent.

The sale of UK goods and services abroad creates income for people in this country and we therefore include that in our calculation of the national product. On the other hand much of what is spent in the UK is expenditure on imported goods and services which creates income for people overseas. This is therefore subtracted from the national product. When we have done this we can arrive at a full statement for all the components of the national product, which is:

$$Y = C + I + G + (X - M)$$

It will be obvious from this that the overall size of the national product can be either increased or decreased by the net effect of foreign trade. However, although foreign trade is enormously important, the import and export of goods and services are usually roughly equivalent, so that the net effect of foreign trade has only a small effect on the overall size of the national product. It has been the tendency of the UK and most other industrialised economies for a greater and greater proportion of the national product to be exported and imported.

It is a common fallacy that it is only the export of goods which earns money for the country; the sale of services such as banking, insurance and tourism are also a major source of overseas income for the UK.

National income accounts

We have already seen that the value of the national product can be arrived at in three different ways. In this section we shall consider how these three different methods are actually presented in the national income accounts.

National expenditure method

Table 7.4 shows the expenditure calculation. It is the method which most clearly shows the components of national income as we have explained them.

a) Consumers' expenditure. This includes all consumers' expenditure on goods and services, except for the purchase of new houses which is included in *gross fixed capital formation*, although this item does include an imputed rent for owner-occupied dwellings.

b) General government final consumption. This includes all current expenditure by central and **83** local government on goods and services, including the wages and salaries of government employees. Excluded from this figure are all expenditure by government trading bodies, e.g. harbours, water supply, etc.; expenditure on grants, subsidies, interest and transfer payments; expenditure on fixed assets; and expenditure on loans and loan repayments.

c) *Gross fixed capital formation.* This is expenditure on fixed assets (buildings, machinery, vehicles, etc.) either for replacing or adding to the stock of existing fixed assets. This is the major part of the *investment* which takes place in the economy.

d) *The value of physical increases in stocks and*

Table 7.4 Gross national product of the UK by category of expenditure, 1986

Item	£m
Consumers' expenditure (C)	234 167
General government final consumption (G)	79 423
Gross domestic fixed capital formation (I)	64 227
Value of physical increase in stocks and work in progress (I)	551
Total domestic expenditure (TDE)	378 368
Exports of goods and services (X)	97 835
Total final expenditure (TFE)	476 203
less Imports of goods and services (M)	−101 308
Gross domestic product (GDP) at market prices	374 895
Factor cost adjustments:	
less Taxes on expenditure	−62 273
Subsidies	6 467
Gross domestic product (GDP) at factor cost	319 089
Net property income from abroad	4 686
Gross national product (GNP) at factor cost	323 775
less Capital consumption	−46 004
National income, i.e. net national product (NNP)	277 771

Source: CSO, United Kingdom National Accounts, *HMSO*

work in progress. As explained previously (see page 81) we include in the calculation of the national product the change in the *quantity* of stocks, or inventories, during the course of the year. This may be either a positive or a negative figure. As you can see in Table 7.4, in 1986 it was plus £551 million.

e) *Total domestic expenditure (TDE).* If all these items are totalled they give a measure known as total domestic expenditure.

f) *Exports and imports.* If we add expenditure on exports to the TDE we then arrive at a measure known as *total final expenditure* (TFE). It is so called because it represents the total of all spending on *final* goods. However, much of the final expenditure is on imported goods and we therefore subtract spending on imports. Having done this we arrive at a measure known as *gross domestic product at market prices.*

g) *Gross domestic product (GDP).* The gross domestic product at market prices is the value of the national product (net of foreign trade) in terms of money actually spent. This, however, is misleading since the price of many articles includes taxes on expenditure or subsidies. Therefore in order to obtain the value of the national product in terms of the resources used to produce it we must make *factor cost adjustments.* In order to do this we must subtract the taxes on expenditure levied by the government and add on the amount of subsidies. When this has been done we arrive at a figure known as *gross domestic product at factor cost.* This is the most commonly used measure of national product and you will see that it appears in all three modes of measurement.

h) *Gross national product (GNP).* The GDP represents the extent to which resources (or factors) are used in the economy. National product, however, can be affected by rent, profit, interest and dividends paid to, or received from, overseas. This is shown in Table 7.4 as *net property income from abroad.* This figure may be either positive or negative. When this has been taken into account we arrive at the *gross national product at factor cost.*

i) *Net national product (NNP).* As previously

explained the capital stock of a country wears out. Part of the gross fixed capital formation is, therefore, to replace worn out capital and is referred to as *capital consumption*. When this has been subtracted we arrive at a figure known as the net national product.

Thus, summarising the above, we can say that:

$$Y = C + I + G + (X - M)$$

National income method

Table 7.5 illustrates the second method by which national product is measured. Here you can see that income from all different sources is totalled to give *total domestic income*.

The *imputed charge for the consumption of non-trading capital* is, principally, the imputed rent for owner-occupied houses. To arrive at the

Table 7.5 Gross national product of the UK by category of income, 1986

Item	£m
Income from employment	209 445
Income from self-employment	34 340
Gross trading profits of companies	50 785
Gross trading profits of public corporations	8 126
Gross trading profits of general government enterprises	161
Rent	22 497
Imputed charge for consumption of non-trading capital	3 026
Total domestic income	328 380
less Stock appreciation	−2 331
Gross domestic product (GDP) (income based)	326 049
Residual error	−6 960
Gross domestic product (GDP) (expenditure based*)	319 089
Net property income from abroad	4 686
Gross national product (GNP) (at factor cost)	323 775
less Capital consumption	−46 004
National income, i.e. net national product (NNP)	277 771

Source: United Kingdom National Accounts *HMSO*
*See Table 7.4

GDP an amount for *stock appreciation* must be deducted. Goods held in stock throughout the year may appreciate in value; to include this increase would exaggerate their value (in terms of factor cost). This may be contrasted with the value of *physical increase in stocks* in Table 7.4, where there was an allowance for a change in the physical *quantity* of stocks.

When the GDP has been calculated by the income method it may be compared with the GDP obtained by the expenditure method. The difference is shown as the *residual error*, which is a measure of the statistical inaccuracy between the two methods. At £6960 million it may seem like a large amount but this is only 2 per cent of the GDP.

By making the same adjustments as in Table 7.4 we can then arrive at the figures for GNP and NNP. (*See* Fig. 7.4 overleaf.)

Personal income

Not all the income in the economy is received by individuals; some is earned by companies and not distributed and some is received by government. A measure of *personal income* is arrived at by totalling income *before tax* from all sources, including transfer payments such as national insurance benefits. In 1986 total personal income was £326 710 million, compared with a GDP of $319 089 million. However, much of this personal income is subject to tax. If income taxes and national insurance contributions are taken away we arrive at a measure known as *personal disposable income* (PDI).

Personal disposable income is a significant measure. It will be watched by retailers as an indicator of likely spending. It is also important to individuals since it will determine how much money they have left in their pockets to spend. Disposable income is divided between consumer spending and saving. In 1986 PDI was £257 512 million, of which £23 345 million was saved. Thus 9·1 per cent of PDI was saved. This is termed the *savings ratio*. The savings ratio increased significantly in the late 1970s but then decreased again in the 1980s.

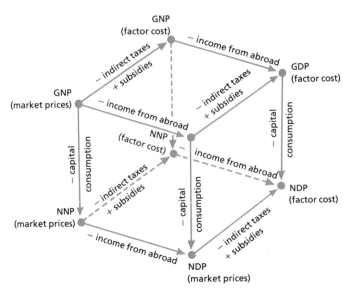

Fig. 7.4 *Measures of National Product*
Starting from GNP at market prices in the top left of the diagram it can be seen how other measures are derived.
GNP = Gross National Product; GDP = Gross Domestic Product; NDP = Net Domestic Product; NNP = Net National Product

You will note that the amount of PDI actually spent (£234 167 million) corresponds to the item *consumers' expenditure* in Table 7.4.

National output method

The final method by which national product is calculated is to total the contributions made by the various sectors (industries) of the economy. This is illustrated in Table 7.6, where, as you can see, the largest contribution comes from manufacturing. This contribution of manufacturing has, however, declined relatively in recent years as service industries have grown in importance. Petroleum and natural gas is a recent arrival to the table. As can be seen from the table, North Sea oil and gas is now of major importance to the economy.

When calculating the GDP in this manner it is necessary to avoid *double counting*. To do this only the value added by each business should be included (see pages 79–80); for example, the value of the steel in motor vehicles should not be included if it has already been counted in the steel industry. In Table 7.6 the figures for the

Table 7.6 Gross domestic product of the UK by industry, 1986

Item	£m
Agriculture, forestry and fishing	5 941
Energy and water supply	23 808
(of which oil and gas extraction)	(8 996)
Manufacturing	80 281
Construction	20 976
Distribution, hotels and catering: repairs	46 587
Transport	14 832
Communication	8 922
Banking finance, insurance business services and leasing	51 513
Ownership of dwellings	18 873
Public administration, national defence and social security	23 578
Education and health services	29 510
Other services	20 963
Total	345 784
less Stock appreciation	−2 331
less Adjustment for financial services	−17 404
Gross domestic product (GDP)	326 049
Residual error	−6 960
Gross domestic product (GDP) (expenditure based)	319 089

Source: United Kingdom National Accounts *HMSO*.

various sectors are shown before allowance has been made for their net interest payment to the financial sector. This is allowed for as the composite figure, *adjustment for financial services*. After this and the residual error have been allowed for we arrive at the GDP at factor cost. By then making adjustments for net property income from abroad and for capital consumption we can arrive at the GNP and the NNP.

A digression: income and wealth

The various measures of the national product give us a tally of the nation's income for a year. However this does not measure the nation's wealth. The nation has a great stock of capital goods. We still benefit from the works of our forebears – the railway system built in the Victorian age, the stock of buildings created over centuries, the roads, the power stations and so on. This stock of national capital is the sum total of everything that has been preserved from all that has been produced throughout our economic history.

Table 7.7 gives an estimate of the capital stock of the nation in 1986. We do not include in this calculation such things as the art treasures of the nation because they cannot be accurately valued. Also excluded is one of our most valuable assets – the skill of the workforce, which we might describe as our 'human capital'. Obviously this is impossible to value, although it is vital to our economy.

If we were assessing someone's wealth, one of the first things we would look at would be how much money they had and also whether they owned stocks and shares. However these are excluded from the calculation of national wealth. Why? The answer is because we have already counted them in the form of real wealth such as buildings and machines. Money and other *financial assets* are only *claims upon* wealth. For example, the reality of British Petroleum is its physical plant, etc., not the shares by which it is owned. If by some chance all the shares were to be destroyed, BP would still be there.

Table 7.7 The UK's net capital stock at replacement cost 1986

Item	£bn
Personal sector	319·1
Industrial and commercial companies	314·2
Financial companies and institutions	52·3
Public corporations	129·1
Central government	69·4
Local authorities	177·7
Total	1062·2

Source: CSO, United Kingdom National Accounts, *HMSO*

Conversely the physical destruction of a nation's capital, for example by war, would leave it impoverished even though the shares remained intact. Similarly varying the amount of money in the economy does not make it any richer or poorer.

When we examine Table 7.7 we see that the national wealth is several times as great as the national product. Does this mean that the national income figures are unimportant? We might answer this by looking at an individual. Individuals' real capital in the form of houses, cars, furniture, clothes, etc., are part of the living standard they enjoy. However if we were to remove their income they would rapidly lose the ability to enjoy them. So it is with the nation. We could not live for long on capital and it is therefore the national income which is all-important. The national income will also determine whether we are able to add to our wealth or not. If there is a large amount of net capital formation (see page 81) then the nation is becoming wealthier and can look forward to a higher standard of living.

Problems and international comparisons

In this final section of the chapter we consider some of the difficulties that arise when we attempt to take any measure of the national product as a guide to the standard of living. We will also look at problems associated with comparing the national product of one country with that of another.

Inflation and the GDP deflator

A major problem we face when comparing one year's national product with another is that of inflation. If, for example, the national product were to grow by 10 per cent, but at the same time there was inflation of 10 per cent, then in *real* terms the national product would not have grown at all.

It is useful to have a measure of *real national product* in *constant cost* terms, which can be calculated by *deflating* the figures by the amount of inflation that has taken place. We usually measure inflation by means of index numbers. The best known index is the retail price index (RPI). This is, however, not an appropriate measure for the purpose of deflating the national product because it only measures consumers' expenditure and, as we have seen, the national product also includes expenditure on investment and expenditure by the government. Therefore a more complex index is needed and this is termed the *GDP deflator*. The present series is based on 1980.

Let us consider an example. The GDP in current prices was £94·3 billion in 1975, £196·0 billion in 1980 and £319·1 billon in 1986. The GDP deflator for these years was 51·9, 100·0 and 144·3 respectively. To express the GDP in constant price terms we divide by the deflator and multiply by 100. Thus we obtain:

$$1975 \quad \frac{£94·3}{51·9} \times \frac{100}{1} = £181·7bn$$

$$1980 \quad \frac{£196·0}{100·0} \times \frac{100}{1} = £196·0bn$$

$$1986 \quad \frac{£319·1}{144·3} \times \frac{100}{1} = £221·1bn$$

Thus the 'real value' of the GDP in 1986 was £221·1 billion in terms of 1980 prices, rather than

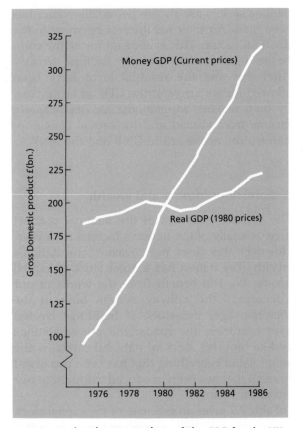

Fig. 7.5 *Real and money values of the GDP for the UK*

its current value of £319·1 billion. Put another way, the real value of the GDP increased by 13 per cent between 1980 and 1986 while its monetary value increased by 63 per cent.

Figure 7.5 compares the real and monetary values of the GDP since 1975. As you can see if we go back beyond the year of 1980 then the 'real value' of the GDP is greater than the money value because prices were lower then.

Rapid rates of inflation in the 1970s and early 1980s greatly increased the discrepancies between 'real' and money values of the GDP and complicated comparisons with other countries. Figure 7.5 dramatically illustrates the difference between the two measures. The graph of money GDP shows an almost runaway growth in national product. However, when we turn to the graph of real GDP we see that it is much

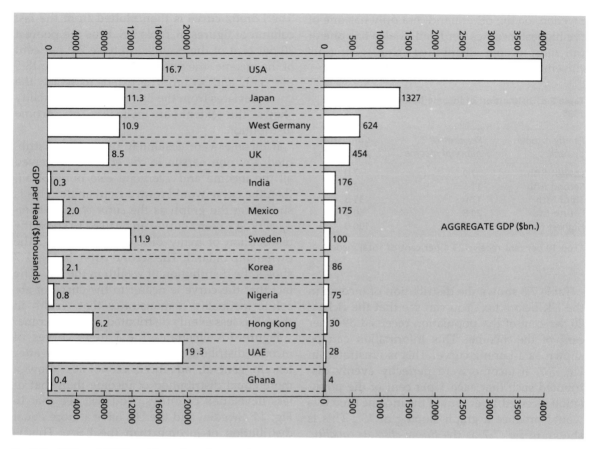

Fig. 7.6 *GDP and GDP/head for selected countries, 1985*

flatter and that around the early 1980s was actually declining.

National income per head

Figure 7.6 shows the national income of various countries in 1985. You can see that the USA had by far the highest national income.

The picture is modified, however, when we consider the number of people in a country. India, for example, had a GDP of $176 billion while Sweden's GDP was $100 billion. However India's GDP had to be shared amongst 765 million people, giving an average income per head of only $270 per year, while in Sweden, with only 8·4 million people, the income per head of $11 890 was amongst the highest in the world. The oil-rich United Arab Emirates (UAE) present

an even sharper contrast, with 1·4 million inhabitants enjoying an average income of $19 270 per year, one of the highest in the world. (*See* comments on exchange rates, page 92).

The distribution of income

Although national income per head gives us a good basis for comparison between countries, this too may be a misleading guide to the standard of living because income may be very unevenly distributed within the country. India, as we saw, had a per capita income of only $270 per year, but income is also badly distributed, with a few rich people and millions of desperately poor. In many poor countries the uneven distribution of income is further compounded by excessive government expenditure on arms. **89**

Sweden, on the other hand, not only has one of the highest incomes per head, it also has one of the most evenly distributed, thus giving its citizens a very high standard of living.

Table 7.8 Distribution of income before tax in the UK, 1985

Family income by rank	Per cent of national income	Cumulative percentage
Lowest fifth	7·0	7·0
Second fifth	11·5	18·5
Third fifth	17·0	35·5
Fourth fifth	24·8	60·3
Highest fifth*	39·7	100·0

*Top 10 per cent receive 23·4 per cent of total income.

Table 7.8 shows the distribution of income in the UK before tax. You can see that the richest 20 per cent of the population received 39·7 per cent of the income. This information can be shown as a Lorenz curve. This is illustrated in Fig. 7.7. If income were perfectly evenly distributed such that each 1 per cent of the population received 1 per cent of the income then this would produce a graph sloping at 45°. This is shown in Fig. 7.7 as the *line of absolute equality*.

The Lorenz curve is then plotted from the last column of figures in Table 7.8, thus the poorest 20 per cent of the population have 7·0 per cent of the income, the poorest 40 per cent have 18·5 per cent, and so on. The extent to which the curve deviates from the line of absolute equality shows the extent of inequality of income distribution.

If income were absolutely unequally distributed, i.e. one person in the economy received all the income and everyone else none at all, then the curve would form a right angle. This is shown on the graph as the *curve of absolute inequality*. A Lorenz curve can be used to show the distribution of many different things, e.g. the ownership of land. The second curve in Fig. 7.7 shows the distribution of wealth in the UK. The fact that the curve is nearer to the curve of absolute inequality demonstrates that wealth in the UK is less evenly distributed than is income.

Figure 7.8 illustrates the Lorenz curves of income distribution for various countries after tax. In general, advanced economies show a more equal distribution of income than that of less developed countries. You will see that in Fig. 7.8 Sweden and the UK have a more equal distribution of income than the USA. This is

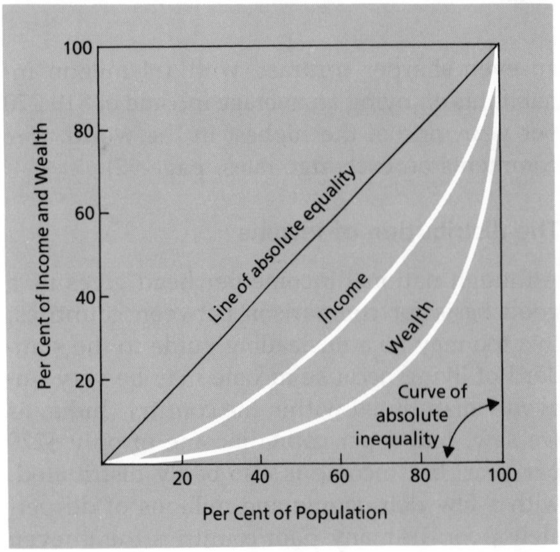

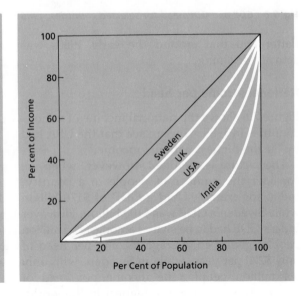

Fig. 7.7 *Distribution of income and wealth in the UK, 1985*

Fig. 7.8 *Income distribution in various countries*

because the distribution in these countries has been modified by a progressive system of taxation. This refutes the contention of Pareto, an Italian-Swiss economist, that there is an inevitable tendency for income to be distributed in the same way, irrespective of the stage of development, the political system and taxation.

Government expenditure

As we have seen, government expenditure is a major component of the GDP. Table 7.9 gives government expenditure for selected nations. It may seem strange that there are such large percentage differences between countries with similar living standards. Sweden and Switzerland are often regarded as having the highest living standards within the OECD area. The differences in government expenditure can partly be explained by their different approaches to problems. In Sweden and the Netherlands, for example, there is heavy government expenditure on transfer payments such as old age pensions and sickness benefits, whereas in the USA and Switzerland they are mainly paid for on an individual basis.

Table 7.9 Government expenditure in various countries as a percentage of GDP, 1985

Country	%
Sweden	64·5
Netherlands	60·2
France	52·4
UK	47·7
West Germany	47·2
USA	36·7
Japan	32·7
Switzerland	30·9

The type of government expenditure affects living standards. Expenditure on defence, for example, brings no immediate improvement to living standards whereas expenditure on hospitals does. Many of the poorest countries of the world have their living standards depressed because the majority of the governments' budget goes on arms expenditure and upon debt interest.

Non-monetary transactions

National income accounts measure only those transactions where money changes hands. This may omit activities which are economically beneficial. Housewives, for example, contribute much to our economy, but their effort is not measured. Conversely, if housewives suddenly decided to send all their washing to the laundry the value of national income would increase, although there would be no 'real' difference in the services the economy was enjoying.

This problem assumes more significant dimensions if there is a substantial amount of subsistence agriculture in the economy, i.e. people producing and consuming their own food. In an advanced economy the effect of people growing their own vegetables is insignificant. However many less developed economies find it necessary to add a significant proportion to their national income calculations to allow for this. In Kenya, for example, 25 per cent is added to the national income to allow for subsistence agriculture in the economy. This is termed the *non-monetary sector*.

Tax evasion

Many transactions may go unrecorded because people are seeking to evade taxes – people may 'moonlight' by doing a second job which they do not declare. In the UK this is known as the 'black economy' and is an increasing problem. Some estimates place a value on these transactions equal to 10 per cent of the GDP. However the significance of the problem is much greater in many of the less developed countries where governments may find great difficulty in monitoring the transactions which are taking place in the economy.

Leisure

Leisure is also a complicating factor when we are trying to assess or compare living standards. If, for example, the GDP were to remain constant but the average working week were to decline then we could say that the quality of life had improved, even though this would not show up in the GDP figures. These variations in the working week tend to exaggerate further the disparities between countries. For example the GDP/head of the USA is approximately 50 per cent higher than that of the UK, but the working week is shorter in the USA. Thus the disparity in standards is greater than it appears.

We might also consider the proportion of the population which works. In the UK 48.7 per cent of the population are in the working population. This is the highest figure in the EEC and much higher than in the USA. However in a less developed country the proportion of the population working would be even higher.

Difficulties in international comparisons

In addition to the problems caused by the distribution of income, non-monetary transactions and differing effects of government expenditure, particular problems are caused by exchange rates.

In this chapter we have made comparisons in US dollars. Up until 1971 the value of the dollar was fixed and was therefore a useful common unit of account. All national income figures could be converted at the existing rate of exchange. However at the moment most countries' exchange rates 'float', i.e. their values change from day to day. The figures which were used to construct Fig. 7.8 were based on the exchange rates of that year (1985). However, this was at a time when the dollar was somewhat overvalued. After that date the dollar plunged dramatically and currencies such as the yen and the deutschemark appreciated. Table 7.9 uses the 1985 data but applies the exchange rates of early 1988.

Compare the figures in Table 7.9 with those in Fig. 7.6. As you can see this has a dramatic effect upon the figures. Japan now has the highest GDP per head.

When we are considering a large number of nations, each of whose exchange rates is varying, the possibilities for inaccuracy are multiplied. Comparisons with Eastern Bloc countries are made even more difficult because the exchange

Table 7.9 GDP and GDP per head in selected countries. 1985 figures with 1988 exchange rates

Country	GDP $bn	GDP/capita $
Japan	2 410.0	20 513
West Germany	1 034.0	18 103
UK	575.0	10 726

rates stated by the government often overstate the value of the currency by 100 per cent or more.

National income and welfare

The problems considered above should persuade us to treat measures of national income cautiously. We should also guard against equating increases in *wealth* with increases in *welfare*. We have already noted that factors such as the distribution of income may modify our view of the standard of living in a country. However to gain a fuller appreciation of the standard of life in a nation we should consider such things as the expectation of life, the crime rate, the standard of health care, etc. We must also remember that producing more economic 'goods' such as cars will also give rise to more economic 'bads' such as pollution.

In recent years attempts have been made to arrive at an alternative measure of the national product which takes into account both the unseen 'pluses', such as leisure, and the 'minuses', such as pollution. The most notable contribution has come from Nordhaus and Tobin in their work *Is Growth Obsolete?* Here a new measure is put forward, termed a *measure of economic welfare* (MEW). This measure demonstrates that welfare has advanced much less rapidly than gross domestic product. These matters are further considered in Chapter 27.

In 1984 the *Economist* published a survey it had conducted in which it had attempted to rank 23 countries in order of their desirability as places to live and work. ('Nirvana By Numbers', 6 January, 1984.)

The survey included many quantifiable

GDP per capita 1981, US$ Overall rank from _Economist_ survey

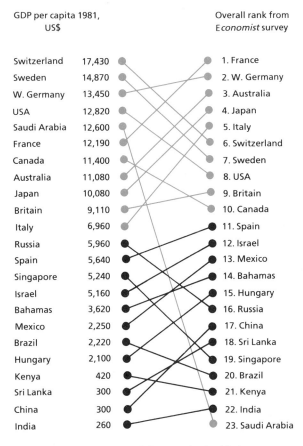

	GDP per capita 1981, US$		Overall rank from _Economist_ survey
Switzerland	17,430		1. France
Sweden	14,870		2. W. Germany
W. Germany	13,450		3. Australia
USA	12,820		4. Japan
Saudi Arabia	12,600		5. Italy
France	12,190		6. Switzerland
Canada	11,400		7. Sweden
Australia	11,080		8. USA
Japan	10,080		9. Britain
Britain	9,110		10. Canada
Italy	6,960		11. Spain
Russia	5,960		12. Israel
Spain	5,640		13. Mexico
Singapore	5,240		14. Bahamas
Israel	5,160		15. Hungary
Bahamas	3,620		16. Russia
Mexico	2,250		17. China
Brazil	2,220		18. Sri Lanka
Hungary	2,100		19. Singapore
Kenya	420		20. Brazil
Sri Lanka	300		21. Kenya
China	300		22. India
India	260		23. Saudi Arabia

Fig. 7.9 _Two measures of the standard of living_

measures such as infant mortality, climate, number of doctors per thousand people and so on. However, it also asked people to rank their preferences, e.g. would they put good health care above political stability, low taxes above adequate defence and so on. This was done 'blind' so that respondents did not know which countries they were considering. The results of the survey are shown in Fig. 7.9. The right hand column shows the _Economist_ ranking and the left hand column the ranking in order of GDP per capita.

The interesting point to emerge from this survey is that, with one notable exception, the ranking produced by the survey did not differ widely from the GDP per capita ranking. As you can see from Fig. 7.9 the top ten in the _Economist_ ranking could all be found in the first eleven in the GDP per capita ranking. The odd one out is Saudi Arabia which, while having a high income per head, was deemed to be a less attractive place to live than all the other countries in the survey.

We might conclude from this that, with all its shortcomings, GDP per capita is at least a reasonable place to start an assessment of a country's living standard.

Summary

1 National income is a measure of the wealth produced, distributed and consumed over a given period of time.

2 Income, expenditure and output are different methods of measuring the same entity.

3 Capital goods form part of the national product. An allowance must be made for depreciation and this is termed capital consumption.

4 Government expenditure and the net figure from foreign trade also form part of the national product.

5 The components of national product may be summarised as:

$$Y = C + I + G + (X - M)$$

6 National expenditure at factor cost is the total of all expenditure on final goods plus any change in the volume of stocks less taxes on expenditure plus subsidies.

7   National income is the total of all incomes excluding transfer payments and stock appreciation.

8   When calculating the national output care must be taken that there is no double counting, i.e. only the *value added* by each industry should be included.

9   Changes in 'real' value of national product can be arrived at by using the GDP deflator.

10   Problems are caused in the interpretation of national income accounts by:
   a) size of population;
   b) distribution of income;
   c) government expenditure;
   d) non-monetary transactions;
   e) tax evasion;
   f) leisure.

Questions

1   $Y = C + I + G + (X - M)$. Give the precise names of all the terms in this identity.

2   Distinguish between gross and net investment. Why is the level of net investment so important? Why is money not considered capital?

3   Distinguish between wealth and income.

4   More people are turning to 'do-it-yourself' for household improvements. Does the GDP (which includes the cost of DIY components) therefore over- or under-estimate the 'true' value of the national product.

5   In 1978 Subtopia had a GDP of $7750 million which had risen to $21 000 million by 1988. Over the same period of GDP deflator rose from 100 to 250. Meanwhile population had also increased from 54·2 million to 58·7 million. What was the change in the real GDP/capita in Subtopia over this period?

6   Imagine that a simple economy produces nothing but wheat. Total output is 1000 tonnes at a price of £50 per tonne. What is the value of the GDP for the economy? Suppose that output rises to 11 000 tonnes but the price falls to £42 per tonne. Devise a 'deflator index' which will demonstrate the real change in GDP.

7   Suppose that West Germany has a GDP of DM1000 billion and a population of 61 million, whereas the UK has a GDP of £244 billion and a population of 56 million. The exchange rate is £1 = DM3. Compare their relative prosperity. What other information would be useful in order to assess the standard of living in the two countries?

8   Explain how it is possible for the standard of living to improve in a society if there is no increase in the real GDP.

9   List and evaluate the factors which you consider most important in determining the level of welfare in a society.

10   Consider the graph of real national income in Fig. 7.5. How do you account for the drop in real GDP around 1980–81?

Data response   National income accounts

Table 7.10 presents all the figures necessary for the calculation of the Gross National Product by the expenditure method. It also contains some figures only relevant to other methods of calculation.

1   Prepare a statement of national product by the expenditure method. This should show:

a) GDP at market prices
b) GDP at factor cost.
c) GNP at factor cost
d) Net national product.

Table 7.10 Figures for the calculation of GNP

National income accounts	£ million
Imputed charge for the consumption of non-trading capital	230
Value of physical increase in stocks and work in progress	+461
Gross trading profits of companies	4 750
Exports of goods and services	6 614
Adjustment for financial services	249
Net property income from abroad	+450
Consumers' expenditure	23 120
Subsidies	571
Exports of goods and services	6 614
Capital consumption	3 000
Stock appreciation	+507
Imports of goods and services	6 972
General government final consumption	6 011
Gross domestic fixed capital formation	6 630
Total domestic expenditure	36 222
Taxes on expenditure	4 922

2 Discuss the difficulties involved in compiling national income accounts.
3 What information other than national income data would be useful in attempting to assess the standard of living in a country?

2

The microeconomic system
II Markets and prices

8

The price system

*We must look at the price system as a
mechanism for communicating information if
we want to understand its real function.*
Friedrich August von Hayek

The first part of this book was a general survey of some of the important areas of the subject. We now commence our detailed study of economics. In the next three sections we will be concerned with the study of microeconomics. This is primarily an analysis of *how markets work*. The remaining four sections of the book, in Part Three, then deal with macroeconomic topics.

The circular flow compared with the price system

It is tempting to try to reconcile the micro- and macroeconomic views of the subject. Figure 8.1 recapitulates the view of the price system as put forward in Chapter 5 and the circular flow of income from Chapter 7. With some slight amendments to the nomenclature, the two can apparently be made compatible. Indeed this is done in some textbooks. This, however, is misleading since the two views tell us different things about the economy. In the price system diagram you can see that the 'arrows' of demand and supply collide to form market prices and factor prices. This view of the economy is helpful in explaining how the price of a product is determined, as well as how the *relative* prices of products are determined and how they change; for example, it tells us how the price of carrots might change as a result of a change in the price

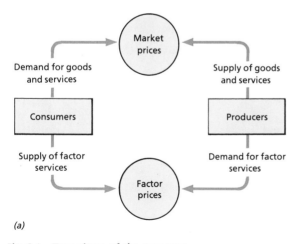

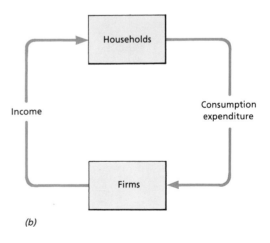

(a)

(b)

Fig. 8.1 *Two views of the economy*
(a) **The microeconomic view: the price system.**
(b) **The macroeconomic view: the circular flow of income. The apparent similarity is deceiving.**

of cauliflowers. However it has little to tell us about how the general level of all prices is determined. For this we must turn to the macro view.

In the circular flow diagram we see a dynamic, i.e. moving, view of the economy. Here expenditure gives rise to income and income gives rise to expenditure which are passed round in an endless flow. There is no clash of opposing forces as in the price system view.

Which view is correct? The answer is that neither presents a totally satisfactory picture of all aspects of the economy. The price system view is good for explaining some aspects and the circular flow view for others.

The circular flow view of the economy is the work of Keynes and his followers from the 1930s. It is sometimes termed *modern*, or the *new*, economics. The price system view is that developed by the classical economists from Adam Smith onwards. There is an unfortunate tendency for economists (and politicians) to take up entrenched positions and insist that one view of the economy is superior to all others. This is mistaken because, at present, no one theory can fully explain all that occurs in the economy. Students should look at all theories and use those parts of them which can be *proved* to be reasonable. This has, in fact, been the basis of mainstream economics since the 1939–45 war. The blending of the old ideas of the classicists and the ideas of modern economics has been termed the *neo-classical synthesis*.

Market prices and factor prices

As we now continue to study the workings of the price system it should be remembered that it explains not only the price of consumer goods and services, such as food or cars, but also the price of factors of production. Thus, as we shall see, wages and rent can be treated as a price in the same way as can the price of a bar of chocolate. In Fig. 8.2 you can see that the price of a product (chocolate) can be treated in just the same way as the price of a factor (wages). Therefore as we study the price system we are looking at an explanation, not just of how the price of certain things is formed but how the price of everything in the economy is determined.

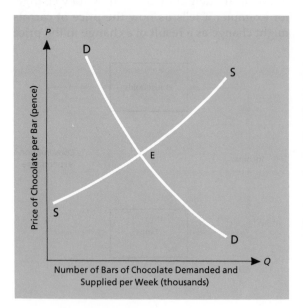

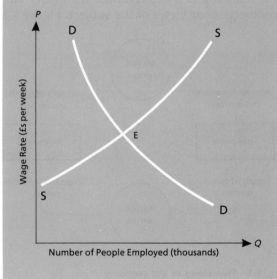

Fig. 8.2 *The price of a product can be treated in the same way as the price of a factor*

Why study the market?

We study the market because it provides answers to the three fundamental questions of economic society – 'What?', 'How?' and 'For whom?' With all the shortcomings it is still the most complete explanation of how economic society functions. It offers an explanation of not only consumers' behaviour but also that of businesses as well.

When it comes to assessing the market system we shall see that there are two different sets of problems. Firstly, there are those which are concerned with influences within the system itself. Thus, for example, we can demonstrate how imperfections in markets, such as the existence of monopoly, lead to an inefficient use of resources and a loss of 'welfare'. In this respect the price system is most important in giving us a reference standard by which we can judge economic efficiency. Secondly there are the normative questions which lie outside the system. Two of these have already been considered. There is the distribution of wealth and income, both of which, as we have seen, are very unevenly distributed; the theory of the price system has nothing to say about this. There is also the problem that the price system does not seem terribly good at providing such items as defence and education. Once again we are here concerned with society making *normative* judgements about what *ought* to be provided. These problems form the subject of Section IV of the book where we consider modern welfare economics.

Summary

1   The price system and the circular flow present alternative views of the economy, neither of which is completely satisfactory.
2   The price system explains the price of all things in the economy.
3   The price system gives not only an explanation of the economy but also a measure of its efficiency.
4   The main areas of shortcoming in the price system form the subject matter of modern welfare economics.

Questions

1   Examine Fig. 8.1 and then state which problems the circular flow diagram leaves unanswered and which problems the price system diagram does not answer.
2   List five items which you think the price system provides well and five which it provides badly. Give reasons for your choices.
3   Give four examples of how the government interferes in the price system.

Data response   How well does the price system work?

All the following short extracts were taken from national newspapers on 26 July 1988.

The first is concerned with the hold-ups at Gatwick Airport and the demand for more night time flights:

Extract 1
So 'the good of the many must override the interests of the few' must it? . . . Holidays abroad are not a necessity but a good night's sleep is and there has to be a limit to the amount of torment holiday makers are allowed to cause.

Extract from a letter to the *Guardian*   **101**

Extract 2

The Royal College of Nursing heavily criticised the government for failing to fund the nurses' pay award as they had promised. 'The community needs more health care and desperately needs to attract and retain staff. Everyone is agreed that there is nothing more critical than people's health' said RCN spokesman . . .

Home affairs page of the *Daily Telegraph*

Extract 3

Government funding of the revolutionary Hotol space project, an invention that could give Britain a lead in world space technology, is being halted.

The decision drew widespread condemnation of Britain's policy on space and claims that the Government was placing short-term cash savings ahead of long-term industrial development.

Front page article in *The Times*

Extract 4

A survey by the Halifax Building Society shows that the rise in house prices continues unabated. Increases of over 20 per cent are the norm throughout the south-east.

Reported in the *Daily Express*

Extract 5

The Minister for Trade and Industry, Lord Young, was urged to intervene in the Rank-Hovis-McDougall take-over bid. John Smith the Labour spokesman demanded that it be referred to the Monopolies and Mergers Commission.

From the City page of the *Independent*

Extract 6

Mrs Thatcher may yet come to regret her remark that 'there is no such thing as society, there are only individuals'.

Comment on the parliamentary pages of *New Statesman*

Extract 7

The government yesterday prepared the ground for private firms to take over the running of some services in remand centres within the next three years.

Home News page of the *Guardian*

Extract 8

0% finance when you buy a new Citroen 2CV

Advert in the *Daily Mail*

With reference to *all* the items comment on the use of market forces and prices as a method of dealing with the Economic Problem. In your answer make clear which goods and services you believe the market system provides well and which not so well. Also explain in what ways governments may deal with the shortcomings of the market system.

The fact that all these extracts were taken in one day should also tell you that newspapers are filled with items relative to our study of the subject. Learn to read them regularly.

9

Demand and utility

All men know the utility of useful things; but they do not know the utility of futility.
Chuang-tzu, 369–286 BC

Revealed preferences is just a funny way of saying that individuals do whatever individuals do, and whatever they do, economists call it utility maximisation.

Lester Thurow

Market demand and individual demand

In this chapter we will complete our look at the theory of demand. The first part of the chapter deals with the fundamentals of market demand; it is extremely important for the student to understand these. In the remainder of the chapter we look at the theory of individual demand. There is no incompatibility between the two, since if we are able to explain individual demand we can explain market demand. The market demand curve can be seen as a horizontal summation of individual demand curves. This is illustrated in Fig. 9.1

The reader may find the sections on utility rather taxing but it is worth persevering, not only because of the topic itself but also for the techniques which are developed which will be used in later sections.

Determinants of demand

The first law of demand . . . again

We have so far examined market demand and stated that it is the total *quantity* of a product which is demanded at a particular *price* over a given period of *time*. The first law of demand

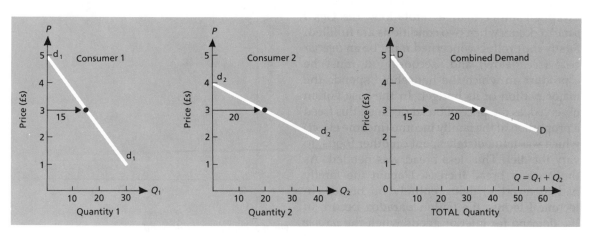

Fig. 9.1 *The market demand curve is a horizontal summation of individual demand curves*
At any price, e.g. £3, we add the quantities demanded by each consumer to produce the market demand.

tells us that, *ceteris paribus*, a greater quantity will be demanded if the price is lowered. This is the most important determinant of demand; the determinants of demand other than price are referred to as the *conditions of demand*.

There are a number of exceptions to the first law of demand, i.e. situations when a fall in the price of a good actually *causes* people to buy less of it, or a rise in price *causes* them to buy more.

a) *Exception 1 – goods demanded for their price*. With some expensive items, e.g. a Rolls Royce or Chanel perfume, the consumer may buy the commodity because it is expensive, i.e. the price is part of the attraction of the article and a rise in price may render it more attractive. In everyday language, the effect is often referred to as 'snob value'.

b) *Exception 2 – expectation of a further change in price*. You may also observe a perverse demand relationship where purchasers believe that a change in price is the herald of further price changes. On a stock exchange, for example, a rise in the price of a share often tempts people to buy it and vice versa.

c) *Exception 3 – Giffen goods*. Sir Robert Giffen, a nineteenth-century statistician and economist, noticed that a fall in the price of bread caused the labouring classes to buy less bread and vice versa. Giffen saw this as a refutation of the first law of demand. It is now recognised as an exception rather than a refutation. *The Giffen paradox* occurs when two conditions are fulfilled. Firstly the product concerned must be an *inferior good* (see below) and, secondly, it must be a product on which the household spends the major portion of its budget. In the case Giffen observed, as the price of bread declined this freed a proportion of the family income (income effect) which was immediately spent on other foods, to vary the diet. Thus less bread was needed. As the price of bread increased again the family had to revert to living entirely on bread. (In technical terms, the Giffen paradox occurs in the demand for inferior goods when the *income effect* outweighs the *price effect*. This is explained in more detail below.)

Income

Since *effective* demand is the desire to buy a good backed by the ability to do so, it is obvious that there must be a relationship between the demand for a firm's product and the consumer's purchasing power. Purchasing power is usually closely linked to income. The nature of the relationship between income and demand will depend upon the type of product considered and the level of consumers' income. Under normal circumstances a rise in income is hardly likely to send most consumers out to buy more bread, whereas it might cause them to buy a new car.

Ceteris paribus if the demand for a commodity increases as income increases it is said to be a normal good.

In Fig. 9.2 line (*a*) represents the *income demand curve* for normal goods. As you can see demand rises continuously with income. However, the graph tends to flatten out at higher levels of income because people will not want more and more cars and more and more swimming pools etc. For some normal goods the income demand

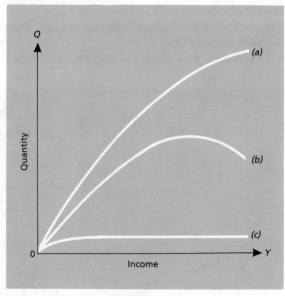

Fig. 9.2 *Income and demand*
(a) Normal goods. (b) Inferior goods. (c) Inexpensive foodstuff, e.g. salt.

curve will flatten very quickly as people reach their desired level of consumption of, say, fresh vegetables.

With a small number of products, usually inexpensive foodstuffs such as salt, the demand tends to remain constant at all but the very lowest levels of income. The income demand curve for such products is shown by line (*c*) in Fig. 9.2.

The final possibility, Fig. 9.2 (*b*), is that demand will decline as income increases. Such products are termed *inferior goods* and may be defined as follows:

Ceteris paribus **if, as income rises, the demand for a product goes down it is said to be an inferior good.**

The effect may be observed with products such as bread and potatoes. At low levels of income people will tend to consume large amounts of these products but, as their incomes rise, they will buy other foods – more meat, fish, etc. – and thus require less bread and potatoes.

You should note that the demand for inferior goods behaves like the demand for normal goods at lower levels of income. All inferior goods start

out as normal goods and only become inferior as income continues to rise. For example, cotton sheets might be considered inferior if, as you become very wealthy, you substitute silk sheets. In other words the goods are not intrinsically inferior; it is the commodity's relationship with income which is inferior. However it is commodities such as bread and potatoes which are usually termed inferior since here the relationship of *market* demand with the community's income is inferior, whereas the demand for a product such as cotton sheets is not. (*See* also page 130.)

The price of other goods

The demand for all goods is interrelated in the sense that they all compete for consumers' limited income. This relationship is obviously too generalised to be measured, but there are two particular interrelationships of demand which may be quantified, they are where goods are *substitutes* one for another or are *complementary*. Examples of substitute commodities would be tea and coffee, or butter and margarine.

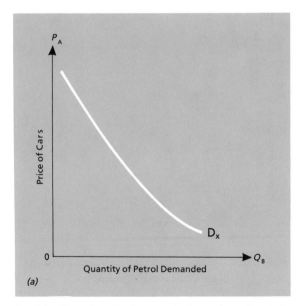

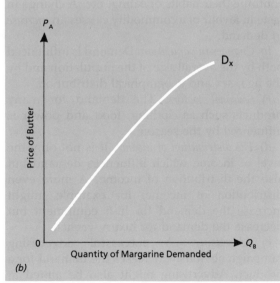

Fig. 9.3 *The price of other goods determines demand*
(*a*) **Complements. A fall in the price of cars increases the demand for petrol.**
(*b*) **Substitutes. A rise in the price of butter causes an increase in the demand for margarine.**

The case of complementary or *joint demand* is illustrated by commodities such as cars and petrol, or strawberries and cream. In all these cases there is a relationship between the price of one commodity and the demand for the other. This is illustrated in Fig. 9.3. In Fig. 9.3 (*a*) you can see that as the price of cars is lowered so the demand for petrol increases, whereas in Fig. 9.3 (*b*) as the price of butter increases so the demand for margarine increases.

In the case of the determinants of demand we have discussed above – price, income and the price of other goods – the relationships are quantifiable and we have been able to illustrate them with graphs. In the next chapter we will place precise mathematical values upon these relationships. However there are many factors which influence demand which are not so readily quantifiable. Some of these are considered below.

Other factors influencing demand

a) *Tastes, habits and customs*. These are extremely important as most people tend to continue their habits of eating, etc. A change in taste in favour of a commodity causes an *increase* in demand.

b) *Changes in population*. Demand is influenced both by the overall size of the population and by the age, sex and geographical distribution.

c) *Seasonal factors*. The demand for many products such as clothing, food and power is influenced by the season.

d) *The distribution of income*. It is not only the level of income which influences demand but also the distribution of income. A more even distribution of income, for example, might increase the demand for hi-fi equipment but decrease the demand for luxury yachts.

e) *Advertising*. A successful advertising campaign obviously increases the demand for a product. Advertising might also be aimed at making the demand for a product less elastic (see Chapter 10).

f) *Government influences*. The government frequently influences demand, an example of this being the government's legislation making it compulsory to wear seat belts. This increases the demand for them. Conversely, the government might prohibit or restrict the purchase of some goods, e.g. firearms.

Students are often tempted to say that supply is a determinant of demand; this is *not* so. Supply influences demand only via the *price* of a commodity. Similarly, indirect taxes such as VAT are not a demand but a supply influence since they affect the cost of production (see Chapter 11).

An increase in demand

A change in the price of a commodity can be shown to result in a movement up or down the demand curve. However if we change one of the conditions of demand this will cause an increase or decrease in demand which can be shown as a movement to the right, or left, of the whole demand curve. Figure 9.4 shows an increase in demand for commodity X. The circumstances which might have caused such an increase are:

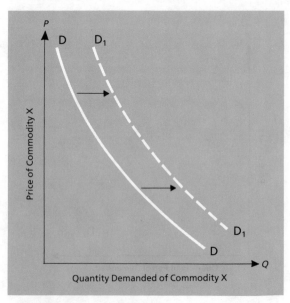

Fig. 9.4 *An increase in demand*
This is brought about by a change in the conditions of demand, *not* by a fall in the price of commodity X.

a) a rise in consumers' income if X is a normal good;

b) a fall in consumers' income if X is an inferior good;

c) a fall in the price of a complement;

d) a rise in the price of a substitute;

e) other circumstances such as a successful advertising campaign.

Demand and marginal utility

Two approaches

We will now turn to analyse more closely the theory of why individuals or households spend their money as they do. Two major explanations of *consumer behaviour* are current; neither presents a totally complete picture. This is hardly surprising since we are trying to explain individual behaviour. The first approach is the *marginal utility*, or *cardinalist*, *approach*. Secondly we shall look at *indifference curve analysis*, which is also termed the *ordinalist approach*. In the last part of the chapter we shall consider more recent developments in theory such as *revealed preference*.

Marginal utility

We have already encountered the law of diminishing marginal utility (see page 57) which tells us that as more of a commodity is consumed, the *extra* utility derived from the consumption of each successive unit becomes smaller. This is only true if all other factors such as income remain unchanged. In the nineteenth century many economists, among them Alfred Marshall, believed that it was possible for utility to be measured in cardinal numbers. Hence these economists are termed cardinalists. For example, we might say that a person derives 10 utils of utility from consuming the first unit of a commodity, 8 utils from the second, and so on.

In fact it is impractical to measure utility in this manner since it is a matter of subjective judgement how much utility a person is deriving.

However, we can still learn something by following this approach a little further.

Equi-marginal utility

Table 9.1 gives some hypothetical figures showing the total and marginal utility derived by a consumer from consumption of product X. Consuming 1 unit of X gives 15 utils of satisfaction, consuming 2 units gives 25 utils, and so on. The figures for marginal utility decline as each successive unit is consumed. If the consumer goes on consuming more and more units, eventually we see that the sixth unit yields no extra satisfaction at all, and, should a seventh unit be consumed, total utility actually decreases so that marginal utility becomes negative. Negative utility is referred to as *disutility*.

Table 9.1 Diminishing marginal utility

Units of X consumed	Total utility (utils)	Marginal utility (utils)
0	0	
1	15	15
2	25	10
3	33	8
4	38	5
5	40	2
6	40	0
7	39	−1

If we assume that consumers are *utility maximisers*, i.e. they wish to obtain as much utility as they can then, subject to no other constraints, the consumer in Table 9.1 would consume 5 units of X where total utility is greatest. However we must now consider two complicating factors.

a) The consumer's income is limited.

b) The consumer must distribute expenditure between many different commodities.

Assume that the consumer has a choice between two products, X and Y. If X and Y both cost £1.00 each, and the consumer has £1.00 to spend, then, obviously, the commodity which yields the greatest utility will be bought. If we **107** were to apply this principle to each successive unit of the consumer's spending, then we could conclude that utility will be maximised when income has been allocated in such a way that the utility derived from one extra pound's worth of X is equal to the utility derived from the consumption of one extra pound's worth of Y. If this condition is not fulfilled then the consumer could obviously increase the total utility derived by switching expenditure from X to Y or vice versa. For example, a consumer would not spend a pound more on vegetables if it was considered that the same pound spent on meat would give more satisfaction, or in the reverse situation would not spend a pound extra on meat if they considered that the same pound spent on vegetables would yield greater satisfaction.

The extra satisfaction derived from the consumption of one more unit of X is its marginal utility which we can write as MU_X and that of Y as MU_Y, etc. We must also consider the relative price of X and Y which we can write as P_X and P_Y. We can then see that the utility maximising condition is fulfilled when:

$$\frac{MU_X}{P_X} = \frac{MU_Y}{P_Y}$$

Any number of commodities may then be added to the equation. Table 9.2 gives hypothetical marginal utility figures for a consumer who wishes to distribute expenditure of £44.00 between three commodities, X, Y and Z.

Table 9.2 Equi-marginal utility

kg consumed	Marginal utility derived from each kg of		
	X (£8/kg)	Y (£4/kg)	Z (£2/kg)
1	72	60	64
2	48	44	56
3	40	32	40
4	36	24	28
5	32	20	16
6	20	8	12
7	12	4	8

In order to maximise utility, the consumer must distribute available income so that:

$$\frac{MU_X}{P_X} = \frac{MU_Y}{P_Y} = \frac{MU_Z}{P_Z}$$

By studying the table you can see that this yields a selection where the consumer buys 2 kg of X, 4 kg of Y and 6 kg of Z. Hence:

$$\frac{48}{8} = \frac{24}{4} = \frac{12}{2}$$

If the consumer wishes to spend all the £44.00 it is impossible to distribute it any other way which would yield greater total utility. You can check this by totalling the marginal utilities for various other combinations.

This theorem, which we may term the *concept of equi-marginal utilities*, should be carefully studied by the student, for it frequently forms the basis of data response or multiple choice questions.

The demand curve

The marginal utility approach gives us a rationalisation of the demand curve. Suppose that, starting from a condition of equilibrium, the price of X falls relative to Y. We now have a condition where the utility from the last penny spent on X will be greater than the utility from the last penny spent on Y. Mathematically this can be written as:

$$\frac{MU_X}{P_X} > \frac{MU_Y}{P_Y}$$

In order to restore the equilibrium the consumer will buy more of X (and less of Y), thus reducing the marginal utility of X. The consumer will continue substituting X for Y until equilibrium is achieved. Thus we have attained the normal demand relationship that, other things being equal, as the price of X falls, more of it is bought. We have therefore a normal downward-sloping demand curve. The demand curve we have derived is the *individual's* demand curve for a product. The *market* demand curve can be then obtained by aggregating all the individual demand curves.

The explanation we have obtained here is of the *price* (or *substitution*) effect.

Indifference curve analysis

The ordinalist approach

The marginal utility approach is subject to the major criticism that we have never found a satisfactory way of quantifying utility. In the 1930s a group of economists, including Sir John Hicks and Sir Roy Allen, came to believe that cardinal measurement of utility was not necessary. They argued that demand behaviour could be explained with ordinal numbers (that is first, second, third and so on). This is because, it is argued, individuals are able to rank their preferences, saying that they would prefer this bundle of goods to that bundle of goods and so on. Finite measurement of utility therefore becomes unnecessary and it is sufficient simply to place in order consumers' preferences. To explain this we must investigate indifference curves.

Indifference curves

In order to explain indifference curves we will again make the simplifying assumption that the consumer only buys two goods, X and Y. Table 9.3 gives a number of combinations of X and Y which the consumer considers to give equal satisfaction; for example, combination C of 8X and 20Y is thought to yield the same satisfaction as D where 12X and 10Y are consumed. The consumer is thus said to be *indifferent* as to which combination they have – hence the name given to this type of analysis.

Figure 9.5 gives a graphical representation of the figures in Table 9.3. Before proceeding any

Table 9.3 An indifference schedule

Combination	Units of X	Units of Y
A	0	50
B	4	32
C	8	20
D	12	10
E	16	4
F	20	0

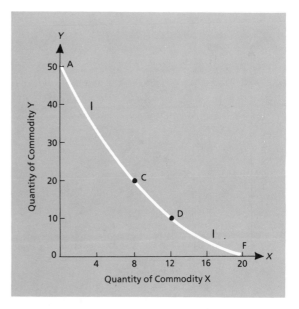

Fig. 9.5   *An indifference curve*
At each point on the indifference curve the consumer believes that the same amount of utility is received.

further with the analysis we must pause to consider several important features of indifference curves.

a) Indifference curves slope downwards from left to right. Since we assume that consumers are rational then we must conclude that if consumers give up some of X they will want more of Y. This will therefore imply a negative, or inverse, slope for the indifference curve. This is illustrated in Fig. 9.5. If the curve were to slope upwards from left to right, this would imply that as a consumer gave up some of X he or she could only keep their level of utility constant by also giving up some of Y! This is clearly nonsense because it is illogical to assume that consumption of less of both goods can leave total utility undiminished.

b) Indifference curves are convex to the origin. You will notice in Fig. 9.5 that the indifference curve bends inwards towards the origin. This is because as consumers give up more of X they want relatively more and more of Y to compensate them.

c) The marginal rate of substitution. As noted **109**

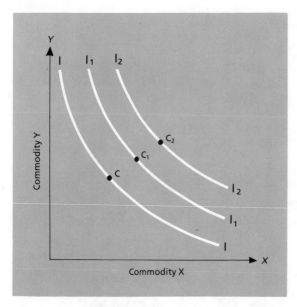

Fig. 9.6 *An indifference map*
Each move to the right yields greater total utility. Thus
C_1 gives more utility than C and so on. It is possible to
construct an infinite number of curves.

above the consumer requires more of X in return
for Y (or vice versa) as they move along the
indifference curve. In other words the rate of
exchange of X for Y changes along the whole
length of the curve.

**The rate at which a consumer is willing to exchange
one unit of one product for units of another is
termed the marginal rate of substitution. It is given
by the slope of the indifference curve.**

d) An indifference map. If we construct another
indifference curve to the right of the original
one (see Fig. 9.6) this must show a situation
where the consumer derives greater total utility,
since at each point on the curve the consumer is
receiving both more of X and Y. We can say that:

**Any movement of the indifference curve to the
right is a movement to greater total utility.**

Thus in Fig. 9.6 point C_1 must yield more utility
than point C, and so on. We are here at the
heart of the ordinalist approach; we do not need
to know how much utility the consumer obtains
on indifference curve I to know that more

is obtained on curve I_1 and more still on I_2. A
series of indifference curves such as those in
Fig. 9.6 is known as an indifference map.

e) An infinite number of curves. Given a consumer's scale of preferences, it is possible to
construct any number of indifference curves on
the indifference map. In each case a rightward
shift gives more utility.

f) Indifference curves never cross. It would be a
logical absurdity for indifference curves to cross
since this would imply that a consumer was
equally happy with, for example, two combinations of X and Y, both of which have the same
quantity of X but different quantities of Y.

The budget line

The indifference curve shows us consumer
preferences but it does not show us the situation
in the market place. Here the consumer is constrained by *income* and by the *prices* of X and Y.
They can both be shown by a *budget line*. Suppose

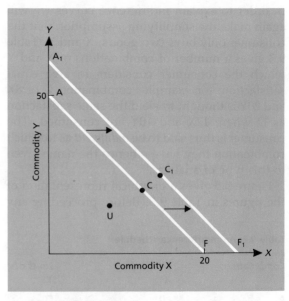

Fig. 9.7 *The budget line*
A budget of £100 and prices for Y of £2/unit and for X
of £5/unit gives a budget line AF, showing the ratio of
prices of 1:2·5. The consumer can attain any positioin on
the line, e.g. C, or within it, e.g. U. Line A_1F_1 shows an
increase in the budget.

that product X costs £5.00 per unit and product Y £2.00 per unit and that the consumer's income is £100.

A budget line shows all the combinations of two products which can be purchased with a given level of income. The slope of the line shows the relative prices of the two goods.

In Fig. 9.7 you can see that the budget line AF stretches from 50 units of Y to 20 units of X. Thus X exchanges for Y at a rate of 2·5:1·0 which is their relative prices. The consumer is able to attain any point on the line, such as point C, or any point within the line, such as point U, where less than all of the budget is spent. However given the constraint of an income of £100 it is not possible to obtain any combination of X and Y to the right of the budget line.

The line A_1F_1 shows the effect of an increase in income on the budget line. The whole line moves rightwards showing that both more of X and more of Y may be consumed. Thus point C_1 which lies on the line A_1F_1 is unobtainable if the budget is limited to £100.

The consumer equilibrium

To demonstrate the consumer's equilibrium, i.e. the point at which the consumer maximises utility with a given budget, we need to combine the indifference map and the budget line. In Fig. 9.8 you can see that the consumer's equilibrium is at point C. This is because, with the budget line AF, it is the indifference curve the farthest to the right that can be reached. At this point the indifference curve I_3 is just tangential to the budget line.

Can we be sure that the indifference curve will be tangential to the budget line? Yes, because we have already shown that there can be an infinite number of indifference curves on an indifference map and therefore one of them must just touch the budget line without cutting, i.e. be at a tangent to it.

Geometry tells us that when a tangent touches a straight line their slopes, at that point, are equal. Now in our model the budget line

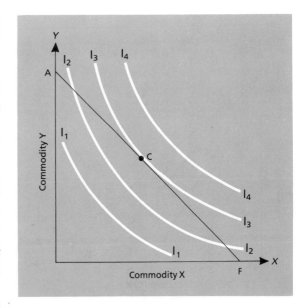

Fig. 9.8 *The consumer equilibrium*
The consumer obtains maximum utility from a budget of AF by choosing the combination of X and Y represented by C, where the marginal rate of substitution is equal to the relative prices of X and Y.

represents relative prices and the slope of the indifference curve the marginal rate of substitution. Thus we can conclude that:

The consumer's utility maximisation equilibrium occurs when relative prices are equal to the marginal rate of substitution.

Applications of indifference curve analysis

Having derived the consumer's equilibrium we can now use this to explain more fully the demand effects which we examined in the earlier part of this chapter.

The price–consumption line

Suppose that the consumer's budget is fixed and there are only two goods to choose from. Figure 9.9 shows us what happens as the price of X falls relative to Y. The original situation is

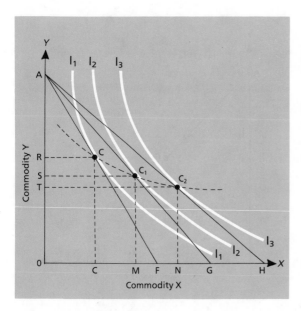

Fig. 9.9 *The price effect*
As the price of X falls, the budget line shifts from AF to AG to AH and the consumer shifts from C to C_1 to C_2, substituting X for Y. CC_1C_2 is the price–consumption line.

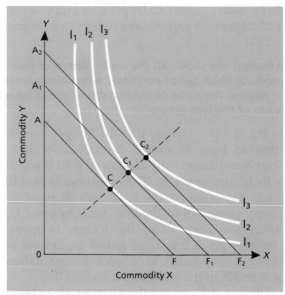

Fig. 9.10 *The income effect*
A rise in the consumer's income shifts the budget line outwards and equilibrium shifts from C to C_1 to C_2 as more of both X and Y are consumed. Line CC_1C_2 is the income–consumption line.

shown by budget line AF where the consumer's equilibrium is at point C. As the price of X falls so the budget line pivots to AG and the consumer's equilibrium now changes to C_1. A further fall in the price of X relative to Y moves the budget line to AH and the consumer's equilibrium to C_2. Thus as the price of X has fallen relative to Y, so consumption of Y has fallen from OR to OS and then to OT, whilst consumption of X has grown from OC to OM and then to ON. These changes can be broken down into *substitution* and *income* effects.

The dotted line which joins points C, C_1 and C_2 shows how consumption alters in relation to price changes and is known as a *price–consumption line*.

Effect of a rise in income

We saw in Fig 9.7 above that the effect of an increase in income is to shift the budget line outwards. This being the case, it can be seen in Fig 9.10 that as the budget line shifts outwards

so the consumer moves to indifference curves further and further to the right. Thus as the budget line has shifted from AF to A_1F_1, and the equilibrium has changed from C to C_1, a further increase to A_2F_2 shifts the equilibrium to C_2. Thus the effect of an increase in income is to increase the demand for both Y and X, provided that they are both normal goods. This accords with what we said earlier in the chapter; you can see that Fig. 9.10 provides evidence for the income demand curve illustrated in Fig. 9.2(*a*).

Distinguishing between substitution and income effects

As the price of a product falls people may buy more of it for two reasons.

a) It is cheaper (substitution effect).
b) The fall in price in effect leaves them more income to spend (income effect).

By using indifference curve analysis it is possible to distinguish between the magnitude of these

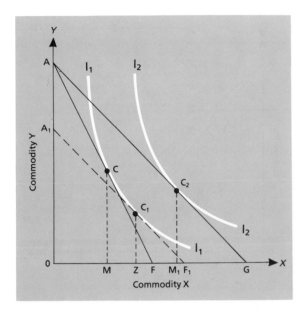

Fig. 9.11 *Separating income and substitution effects* Increase in demand, MZ, is due to substitution effect and ZM$_1$ to income effect. This is determined by projecting a hypothetical budget line A$_1$F$_1$ which is parallel to the new budget line AG and tangential to the original indifference line I$_1$.

effects. In Fig. 9.11 AF represents the original budget line and C the original equilibrium. The shift of the budget line to AG shows the effect of a fall in the price of X. As you can see this moves the consumer to a new equilibrium C$_2$ on indifference curve I$_2$; this means that the consumption of X increases from OM to OM$_1$. But how much of this increase is due to the fall in price and how much to the income effect of the fall in price making the consumer better off? In order to distinguish the two we project a new budget line A$_1$F$_1$ which is parallel to AG and tangential to the original indifference curve I$_1$. Remember, the fall in price increases the real income of consumers by leaving more money to spend. The line we have drawn, A$_1$F$_1$, shows the new relative prices of X and Y but at the original indifference curve. This will tell us how much of X the consumer would have bought at that price if real income had *not* been increased. It can be seen that at equilibrium C$_1$ OZ units of X would have been consumed. Thus the increase

MZ is due to the substitution effect, while the rest of the increase in consumption at C$_2$, i.e. ZM$_1$, is due to the income effect alone.

Derivation of the demand curve

We can now use indifference curves to show how an individual's demand curve is derived. The upper portion of Fig. 9.12 shows the effect of a price change similar to that in Fig 9.9. In this case we can see that the price–consumption line shows how demand for X grows as its price falls relative to Y. The lower portion of Fig. 9.12 plots the price of X against the demand for it. If we

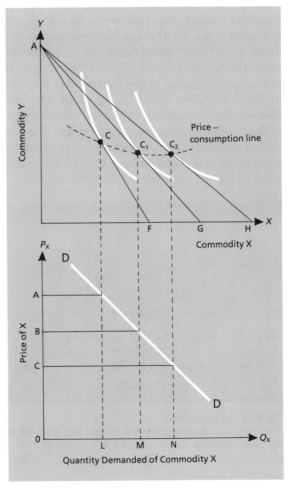

Fig. 9.12 *The derivation of the individual demand curve*

113

correlate quantities of X demanded along the price consumption line with the various prices on the demand curve we can see that we derive a normal downward-sloping demand curve. Thus as price has fallen from OA to OB to OC, so demand has expanded from OL to OM to ON.

As we concluded with marginal utility analysis, so we may also conclude here; if we can derive an individual's demand curve we can also derive a market demand curve by aggregating all the individual demand curves.

Inferior goods

We have demonstrated that a rise in a consumer's income will lead to an increase in demand. However market observations tell us that this is not always so. In the case of inferior goods demand actually goes down as a result of an increase in income. The inferior goods phenomenon is due to the *income effect* and *not* to the *substitution effect*. In Fig. 9.13 you can observe that, as a result of the particular shape of the indifference curves, as the budget line has shifted outwards from AF to A_1F_1 the consumer's equilibrium has changed from C to C_1 involving a fall in the demand for X from OM to OM_1.

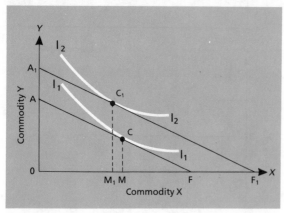

Fig. 9.13 *Inferior goods*
The increase in income shifts the budget line from AF to A_1F_1 but decreases the demand for X from OM to OM_1.

Giffen goods

It will be recalled that Giffen goods are those

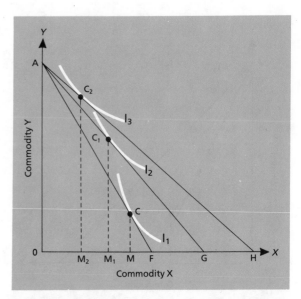

Fig. 9.14 *Giffen goods*
The fall in the price of X is shown by the line pivoting outwards from AF to AG to AH, but instead of demand for X expanding it contracts from OM to OM_1 to OM_2.

where a fall in the price of the good *causes* a fall in the demand. Figure 9.14 shows the fall in price of X by pivoting out the budget line from AF to AG and then to AH. As it can be seen, due to the peculiar shape of the indifference curves where Giffen goods are concerned, the demand for X does not expand but falls from OM to OM_1 and then to OM_2. This has come about because as Giffen goods are inferior there is a negative income effect as their price falls, and because they are such an important part of the household budget the negative income effect has been sufficient to swamp the substitution effect.

Other demand theories

Revealed preference theory

Professor Samuelson developed a theory which was designed to do away with the subjective element which is implicit in the utility theories

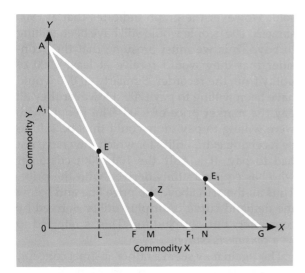

Fig. 9.15 *Revealed preference*
A fall in the price of commodity X pivots the budget line from AF to AG. The consumer moves from E to E₁. Of the increase, LN, in demand, LM may be attributed to the price effect and MN to the income effect.

of both the marginal utility and the indifference curve approach. The only assumption necessary is that the consumer behaves rationally. It is an analysis of consumer behaviour based only on the choices actually made by consumers in various price–income situations. Thus it is based on consumers' *revealed preferences*.

In Fig. 9.15 AF represents the original budget line, with point E the consumer's revealed preference. A fall in the price of X pivots the budget line to AG. The consumer's revealed preference is now for the combination of X and Y represented by E₁. We can analyse this change by projecting a new budget line, parallel to AG and running through the original equilibrium E, i.e. we have projected a set of circumstances where the individual is not able to consume more than was originally consumed but is on a budget line reflecting the new price. The consumer would then have to choose some combination along the line A₁F₁. It would be illogical to choose a combination to the left of E, i.e. along the part of the line A₁E, since this combination was available before the price fell. Logically, therefore, the consumer would choose some

point to the right, for example Z. We are therefore able to attribute the increase in the demand for X of LM to the *price effect* alone, while the remaining increase in demand of MN to the new revealed preference of E₁ must be due to the *income effect*. This analysis can then be extended to derive a demand curve for product X. We are thus able to analyse the effects of changes in price and incomes without reference to measures of utility or indifference curves.

Space precludes a fuller treatment of this theory; the interested reader should consult one of the more advanced texts on the subject.

Modern objections

An element of subjectivity still remains in the revealed preference approach. Also all the theories place a great emphasis upon rationality and the search for utility maximisation. This is often hard to accord with observed behaviour. A possible reason for the difficulty is that consumers are much swayed by differences within a product. For example, the minor differences in brands of washing powder which may seem trivial to the logical economist may be important to the consumer, who is often willing to pay substantially for them. Those who work in advertising are well aware that it is often the *emotional* content of a product which is more important than the *rational*. This does not necessarily contradict our analysis since the emotional satisfaction given by the consumption of a product is part of its utility. It is for this reason that in recent years there has been more emphasis upon examining the *characteristics of goods* as part of their utility.

Market demand and consumers' surplus

Finally we will return to market prices and utility. In Fig. 9.16 £500 represents the market price of video cassette recorders, of which 100 000 are **115**

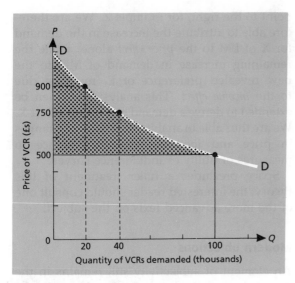

Fig. 9.16 *Consumers' surplus*
The shaded area represents utility which consumers receive but do not pay for.

sold. However the graph indicates that at £900 some 20 000 people would still have been willing to buy. Thus we must presume that they consider that they would receive at least £900 of utility from the recorder. Similarly 40 000 would have been willing to pay £700. However they all pay the market price of £500. The people who were willing to pay more could thus be said to be receiving extra utility for which they have not had to pay. It is only the 100 000th customer who has equated utility derived with the price. Thus all the area above the price line and below the demand curve is surplus utility derived by consumers but not paid for. This is referred to as a *consumers' surplus*.

This again may seem a rather abstract concept, but as we shall see it has important implications for the marketing of goods (see page 219). We shall also see this analysis occurring again in the theory of production.

We have now concluded our look at the theory of demand. Next we turn to the measurement of demand and supply and the analysis of market changes.

Summary

1 The market demand curve is a horizontal summation of individuals' demand curves.

2 Price is the prime determinant of demand and is the basis of the first law of demand.

3 There are three exceptions to the first law of demand:
  a) goods demanded for their price;
  b) where there is an expectation of a further change in price; and
  c) Giffen goods.

4 The conditions of demand are the income of consumers, the price of other goods and other non-quantifiable factors such as advertising and consumers' tastes.

5 The marginal utility (or cardinalist) approach to demand maintains that the consumer maximises utility when the marginal utility of product A divided by its price is equated with the marginal utility of product B divided by its price, and so on.

6 The indifference curve (or ordinalist) approach maintains that the consumer maximises utility when a person's marginal rate of substitution is equated with the relative price of products.

7 Indifference curve analysis can be used to explain price and income effects and to demonstrate the derivation of the demand curve.

8 Revealed preference theory is an attempt to explain consumers' behaviour without having to measure utility.

9 The consumers' surplus is the extra utility enjoyed by consumers which they do not pay for.

Questions

1 Examine the factors which determine the demand for:
a) summer holidays;
b) public transport.

2 Explain Giffen's paradox and state under what condition you would expect to find it in today's world.

3 List the following commodities in order of their responsiveness to increase in income: colour televisions; petrol; wine; cigarettes; potatoes; beef; holiday travel; salt.

4 Assume that a family has a weekly budget of £240 and a choice of only two goods which cost respectively £12 and £8.
a) Construct the family's budget line.
b) Show the effect of the price of the good which costs £12 increasing to £20.
c) In the original situation show the effect of the family's budget increasing to £360.

5 If one wished to avoid the subjective element involved in the marginal utility approach and indifference curve analysis, how could one justify the first law of demand, including the explanation of both the price effect and the income effect?

6 Study Fig. 9.12 which shows the derivation of a normal demand curve and then show how the perverse demand curve for Giffen goods can be derived from Fig. 9.14.

Data response Maximising utility

Study the total utility figures given in Table 9.4 and then answer the following questions.

Table 9.4 Total utility schedules

kg consumed	Cheese (£2/kg)	Fish (£4/kg)	Meat (£5/kg)
		Total utility derived	
1	7	8	16
2	13	16	29
3	17	21	41
4	20·5	25	51
5	22	28·5	59
6	25	31·25	65
7	26	33·5	68

a) Assume that a poor family has a budget of £10, all of which it intends to spend, but only cheese is available. How many kg of cheese will be bought and why? Calculate the consumer's surplus under these conditions.

117

b) A richer family has a budget of £34 and a choice of all three commodities. Explain how they will allocate their expenditure between the three commodities, assuming that they wish to spend all of their budget. (Hint: remember the consumer equilibrium condition under the cardinalist approach.)

c) Do you notice anything unusual about the utility schedule for cheese? Explain your answer.

10

Elasticities of demand and supply

In every thyng I woot,
there lith mesure.

Chaucer, *Troilus* Book 2

Introduction

In previous chapters we have considered how demand and supply determine prices. The first law of demand, for example, tells us that if we lower the price of a commodity, other things being equal, a greater quantity will be demanded. In this chapter we seek to measure and quantify those changes.

Everyone is familiar with the idea that if there is a glut of a commodity its price usually falls. As long ago as the seventeenth century Gregory King, the English writer on population, noted that when there was a good harvest not only did prices fall but farmers appeared to earn less. In other words bad harvests seemed to be better for farmers (*see* page 155). King, without knowing it, was commenting on an application of the principle of elasticity of demand.

Elasticity of demand

Elasticity of demand defined

There are several different types of elasticity. The most important is elasticity of demand, which can also be termed the price elasticity of demand and is sometimes abbreviated to PED. We may define it thus:

Elasticity of demand measures the degree of responsiveness of the quantity demanded of a commodity to changes in its price.

It is worthwhile remembering this definition since it can be readily adapted to give the definition of any other type of elasticity.

Thus elasticity is a *measure* of responsiveness and its measurement depends upon comparing the percentage change in the price with the resultant percentage change in the quantity demanded. It will at once be obvious that in response to a fall in price the resultant change in quantity demanded may be a great deal or very little.

Consider Fig. 10.1. In both cases the price has been cut by the same amount, from £10 to £5, but this has had very different effects upon the quantity demanded. In (*a*) the quantity demanded has expanded a great deal, from 100 units to 300 units, but in (*b*) the demand has only grown from 100 units to 125. Thus the same percentage cut in the price has resulted in different percentage changes in the quantity demanded. Diagram (*a*) is said to illustrate an *elastic* demand because it is *responsive* to price changes, whereas diagram (*b*) illustrates an *inelastic* demand because it is relatively *unresponsive* to price changes. Which category of elasticity the demand for a product falls into depends upon the product we are considering. A 50 per

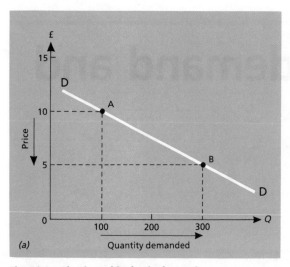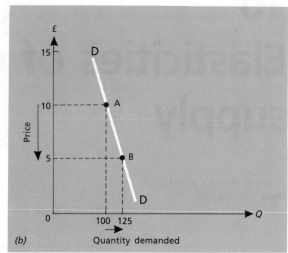

Fig. 10.1 *Elastic and inelastic demand*
(*a*) **Responsive (elastic) demand.** (*b*) **Unresponsive (inelastic) demand.**

cent drop in the price of salt, for example, would hardly send everyone dashing out to the shops, but a 50 per cent drop in the price of cars might well have people queuing at the showrooms. Remember:

It is the demand which is elastic or inelastic, not the product.

Categories of elasticity of demand

There are three categories of elasticity of demand; elastic, inelastic and unitary. Which category any particular demand falls into depends upon the relative percentage changes in price and quantity demanded and the resultant effect upon the total revenue. They may be defined thus.

a) **Demand is elastic when a percentage cut in price brings about a greater percentage expansion in demand so as to increase total revenue.**
b) **Demand is inelastic when a percentage cut in price brings about a smaller percentage expansion in demand so as to decrease total revenue.**
c) **Demand is unitary when a percentage cut in price brings about an exactly equal expansion of demand so as to leave total revenue unchanged.**

Elasticity of demand and total revenue

120 The above definitions of categories of elasticity

may be made clearer by studying Fig. 10.2. Total revenue, it will be recalled from Chapter 5, is always obtained by multiplying the price of the commodity by the quantity demanded. In diagram (*a*) of Fig. 10.2 it can be seen that as price is lowered from £5 to £3 the total revenue is increased from £500 to £900. The shaded rectangle A shows the revenue that has been given up by lowering the price, but you can see that this is greatly outweighed by the shaded rectangle B which is the extra revenue gained from increased sales. This, therefore, is an *elastic* demand because, as the price is lowered, total revenue *increases*. The opposite is the case in diagram (*b*) when, as price is lowered from £100 to £50, total revenue declines from £400 to £250. The demand is therefore *inelastic*.

In diagram (*c*) the cut in price is exactly matched by the increase in quantity and therefore, although the price has fallen from £6 to £2 the total revenue remains *constant* at £48. Area A is exactly equal to area B. We therefore have *unitary* elasticity of demand. If you check the other points on the demand curve in diagram (*c*) you will discover that whatever is done to price, the total revenue remains the same. A graph such as this is called a hyperbola. The curve has the property that any rectangle drawn under it has a constant area (the area represents total

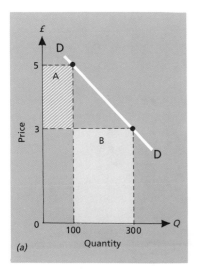
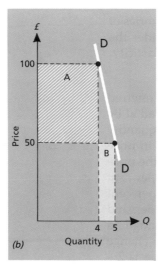
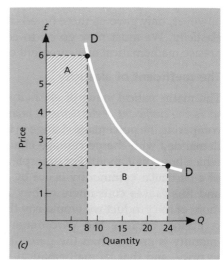

Fig. 10.2 *Elasticities of demand and total revenues*
(*a*) **Elastic demand. Total revenue increases as price falls.**
(*b*) **Inelastic demand. Total revenue decreases as price falls.**
(*c*) **Unitary demand. Total revenue remains constant whatever happens to price.**

revenue); it is therefore referred to as a 'rectangular' hyperbola. Such a curve is asymptotic to the axes, i.e. it gets nearer and nearer to each axis without ever touching. If it were to touch the axis total revenue would fall to zero and it would cease to have the quality of a unitary demand curve.

We have, so far, considered elasticity of demand always with respect to a fall in price. What happens if we raise prices? The answer is that the same rules apply, but in reverse. For example, if it is the case that if price is lowered and total revenue increases and demand is elastic, then it must also be the case that if price is increased and total revenue decreases demand is also elastic. We may summarise the situation thus.

a) **Price decreases –**
    total revenue increases ⎫ **Demand is**
  Price increases –   **elastic.**
    total revenue decreases ⎭

b) **Price decreases –**
    total revenue decreases ⎫ **Demand is**
  Price increases –   **inelastic.**
    total revenue increases ⎭

c) **Price increases –**
    total revenue constant ⎫ **Demand is**
  Price decreases –   **unitary.**
    total revenue constant ⎭

The relationship between price changes and total revenue is, of course, one which is vital to the business organisation. It would obviously be of great benefit to firms to know whether raising their prices or cutting their prices would increase their revenue.

The measurement of elasticity

If you look back over Figs. 10.1 and 10.2 you will see that the elastic demand curves tended to be rather flat whereas the inelastic curves were steep. The appearance of the curves, however, can be most deceptive. In Fig. 2.1 (see page 13) you will see that both demand curves show the same information; one is steep and the other is rather flat simply because the scales have changed.

We have seen already that elasticity may be more accurately categorised by considering the effect of price changes upon total revenue. This, **121** however, only gave us three broad categories of elasticity. We must now go on to consider the precise mathematical measurement of elasticity.

The coefficient of elasticity

The mathematical value of elasticity is referred to as the *coefficient of elasticity*. It is arrived at by comparing the percentage change in the quantity demanded with the percentage change in price which brought it about. For example, if the price of a particular commodity is cut by 10 per cent and this causes consumers to buy 20 per cent more of the product we would say that demand is elastic, because the percentage change in quantity is greater than the percentage change in price, and that its mathematical value is 2 – this was arrived at by dividing the percentage change in quantity by the percentage change in price.

We can write this as:

The coefficient of elasticity of demand (E_D) =
$$\frac{\text{Percentage change in quantity demand}}{\text{Percentage change in price}}$$

In order to calculate the coefficient we must consider some change in demand, i.e. we examine a small movement along the demand curve. In Fig. 10.3 a small part of a demand curve has been extracted so that we may examine it in detail.

In moving from point A to point B on the demand curve the price has fallen from £400 to £350. To calculate this as a percentage we take the original price (*P*) £400 and divide it into the change in price ($\triangle P$) £50 which we are considering and then multiply the result by 100.

$$\text{Percentage change in price} = \frac{\triangle P}{P} \times \frac{100}{1}$$

$$= \frac{50}{400} \times \frac{100}{1}$$

The same thing must then be done for quantity. We can then arrange the formula for the coefficient as follows:

The coefficient of elasticity (E_D) =
$$\frac{\triangle Q/Q \times 100/1}{\triangle P/P \times 100/1}$$

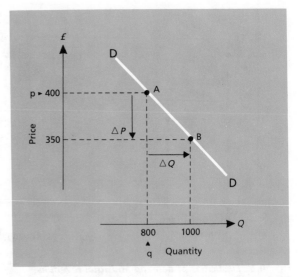

Fig. 10.3   The coefficient of elasticity of demand.
As price falls from £400 to £350 the quantity demanded expands from 800 to 1000.
Thus the original P = £400 and $\triangle P$ = £50, while Q = 800 and $\triangle Q$ = 200.

$$E_D = \frac{200/800}{50/400}$$
$$= 2$$

Since 100/1 is common to both numerator and denominator we may cancel it out, giving us the formula:

$$E_D = \frac{\triangle Q/Q}{\triangle P/P}$$

(We have adopted the abbreviation E_D for the coefficient of elasticity of demand. Some economists use the Greek letter η (eta) as the abbreviation.)

Let us now complete the calculation from Fig. 10.3.

$$E_D = \frac{\triangle Q/Q}{\triangle P/P} = \frac{200/800}{50/400} = \frac{200}{800} \times \frac{400}{50}$$
$$= 2$$

Thus in this example we have a value of 2 for the coefficient. It is simply stated as a number and is independent of the units used to measure price and quantity.

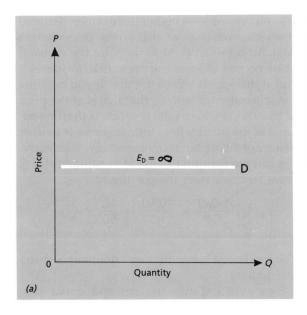

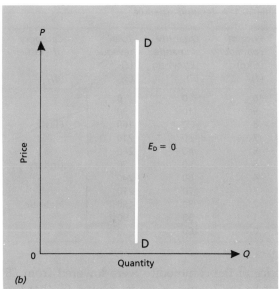

Fig. 10.4 *(a) Infinitely (perfectly) elastic demand. (b) Totally (perfectly) inelastic demand.*

The values of the coefficient

When looking at Fig. 10.3 it might be thought that the value of elasticity is the value of the slope of the demand curve. This is not so. What is being measured is not the slope of the curve but the relative movements along the axes. This is yet another warning not to be deceived by the appearance of the curve.

There are two cases, however, when the slope of the curve does tell us the value of the coefficient. These are shown in Fig. 10.4. In diagram (*a*) the demand curve is horizontal, showing that consumers are willing to buy any amount at this price, but a price of even one penny higher would lead to an infinite reduction in sales. This is termed an infinite (or perfectly) elastic demand and the value of the coefficient is infinity. In diagram (*b*) it would appear that consumers will buy exactly the same amount of the product whatever the price. There is therefore no responsiveness of demand to price changes. This is termed a totally (or perfectly) inelastic demand and the value of the coefficient is zero.

What about the in-between case of unitary demand? If you look back to Fig. 10.2 (*c*) you will see that a curve of constant unitary elasticity is a rectangular hyperbola. In this case the value of the coefficient is one. This is because any percentage cut in price is matched by an exactly corresponding percentage change in the quantity demanded. Therefore the value of the coefficient is always unity (one).

Having considered these three extreme cases we can state the boundaries of the values of the different categories of elasticity.

a) **If the value of the coefficient is greater than one but less than infinity then demand is elastic.**

b) **If the value of the coefficient is exactly equal to one then demand is unitary.**

c) **If the value of the coefficient is less than one but greater than zero then demand is inelastic.**

We can confirm this by considering an example.

An example of elasticity

We can examine all three categories of elasticity by studying the demand schedule in Table 10.1.

The easiest guide to the category of elasticity is the total revenue ($P \times Q$). If, for example, the **123**

Table 10.1 A demand schedule

Price of commodity (£/kg) (1)	Quantity demanded (kg/week) (2)	Total revenue (£) (3)	Category of elasticity (4)
A	10	0	0	
B	9	10	90	
C	8	20	160	Elastic
D	7	30	210	
E	6	40	240	
F	5	50	250	Unitary
G	4	60	240	
H	3	70	210	
I	2	80	160	Inelastic
J	1	90	90	
K	0	100	0	

price of the commodity were lowered from £8 per kg to £7 you can see in column (3) that the revenue would increase from £160 to £210. The price has been lowered and total revenue has increased; demand is therefore *elastic*. Further down the schedule this is not so. If, for example, the price is lowered from £4 to £3 the total revenue *decreases* and demand is, therefore, *inelastic*.

We can confirm these findings by calculating the coefficient.

a) If we lower the price from £8 to £7 the demand changes from 20 kg to 30 kg. We can arrange our calculation thus:

$$E_D = \frac{\triangle Q/Q}{\triangle P/P} = \frac{10/20}{1/8} = \frac{10}{20} \times \frac{8}{1}$$
$$= 4$$

The coefficient is 4, which is greater than one and less than infinity. Demand is therefore elastic.

b) If we lower the price from £4 to £3 the demand changes from 60 kg to 70 kg. We can arrange our calculation thus:

$$E_D = \frac{\triangle Q/Q}{\triangle P/P} = \frac{10/60}{1/4} = \frac{10}{60} \times \frac{4}{1}$$
$$= 2/3$$

The coefficient is 2/3, which is less than one and greater than zero. Demand is therefore inelastic.

In our example, at higher price ranges demand is elastic, while over the lower price ranges demand is inelastic. At some point the demand must be just changing from elastic to inelastic and at this spot it will be unitary. If you examine the schedule you will see that this is at the price of £5 – this is where total revenue is maximised, i.e. it is the point where total revenue is neither rising nor falling but is, momentarily, stationary. We can confirm that demand is unitary at this point by calculating the coefficient.

$$E_D = \frac{\triangle Q/Q}{\triangle P/P} = \frac{10/50}{1/5} = \frac{10}{50} \times \frac{5}{1}$$
$$= 1$$

The coefficient is exactly 1 and demand is therefore unitary.

Figure 10.5 shows the demand curve constructed from the same figures. You will see that it is a straight line although, as we have just shown, it has all three categories of elasticity. How can it be that a demand curve of constant slope can have various elasticities? This is because the elasticity does not depend upon the

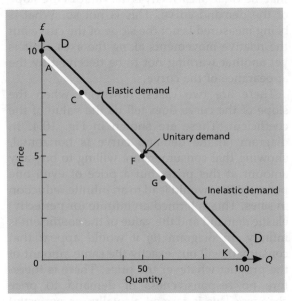

Fig. 10.5 *One demand curve can have all three elasticities*
The value of elasticity decreases from infinity at point A through unity at point F to zero at point K.

slope but upon the proportional changes in price and quantity. Thus if we lower the price from £10 to £9 we are reducing it by 10 per cent, but if we lower it from £2 to £1, although the cut in price is still £1, it is now 50 per cent of the price. Consider, however, the effects that these same price changes would have upon the quantity demanded. Lowering the price from £10 to £9 increases demand from zero to 10 kg. Mathematically this is an infinite increase. Reducing the price from £2 to £1, though, means that demand expands from 80 to 90 kg. This is an increase of only 12·5 per cent. Therefore as we move down the demand curve from A to K, the proportional changes in price become greater but the proportional changes in quantity demanded become smaller.

Elasticity of demand will decrease along the whole length of any downward sloping straight-line demand curve, being infinite where it touches the vertical axis and zero where it touches the horizontal axis.

A note on the value of elasticity

An increase (+) in price will cause a fall (−) in quantity and, conversely, a decrease (−) in price will cause a rise (+) in quantity. If we divide the change of quantity by the change in price the value of the answer must always be negative. This will mean that the greater the negative value of elasticity becomes the greater will be the elasticity. For no better reason than that this appears perverse, the coefficient is therefore always quoted as positive. This can be done by simply omitting the sign. However, intermediate economic texts make the coefficient positive by putting a minus sign in front of the equation, thus:

$$E_D = - \frac{\triangle Q/Q}{\triangle P/P}$$

We will refer to this later in the chapter, but for the time being we will ignore the sign.

Factors determining elasticity

Although we know how to measure elasticity we have not yet discussed the reasons why some demands are elastic and others not so. Why is it, for example, that the demand for wheat is very inelastic while the demand for cakes, which are made from wheat, is much more elastic? The most important determinants of elasticity are discussed below.

Ease of substitution

This is by far the most important determinant of elasticity. If we consider food, for example, we will find that food as a whole has a very inelastic demand but when we consider any particular food, e.g. cream cakes, we will find that the elasticity of demand is much greater. This is because, while we can find no substitute for food, we can always substitute one type of food for another. In general we can conclude that:

The greater the number of substitutes available for a product, the greater will be its elasticity of demand.

It may be thought that elasticity may be determined by whether or not a product is a necessity. To some extent this is true. The 'bare necessities' do tend to have low elasticities of demand. However this can be a misleading idea because what is a luxury to one person may be a necessity to another. Tobacco, for example, can hardly be considered a 'necessity' and yet to many people it is because there is no substitute available.

The idea of necessity determining elasticity is also further undermined when we discover that demand for many luxury goods, for example diamonds, is relatively inelastic. It is not therefore the 'expensiveness' which determines elasticity. Fresh strawberries, for example, which can hardly be the prerogative of millionaires, have a relatively elastic demand. Once again it is the fact that, if there is a close substitute available, the product therefore is not a 'necessity'. **125**

The number of uses

The greater the number of uses to which a commodity can be put, the greater its elasticity of demand

This is because if a product has many uses then there are many different markets on which price changes can exert their effect. There is, therefore, a greater possibility that in some of the markets substitutes may be readily available. Electricity, for example, has many uses – heating, lighting, cooking, etc. A rise in the price of electricity might cause people not only to make economies in all these areas but also to substitute other fuels in some cases.

The proportion of income spent on the product

If the price of a box of matches were to rise by 50 per cent, for example from 2p to 3p, it would discourage very few buyers because such an amount is a minute proportion of their income. However if the price of a car were to rise from £4000 to £6000 it would have an enormous effect upon sales, even though it would be the same percentage increase.

We can state this principle as:

The greater the proportion of income which the price of the product represents the greater its elasticity of demand will tend to be.

If we apply this principle to individual consumers it will be clear that those with high incomes may be less sensitive to changes in the price of products than those with low incomes. Similarly, if we consider the growth in national income over the years it is apparent that products which seemed expensive luxuries some years ago, e.g. colour televisions, are now regarded by many as 'necessities'. This is partly because the product now represents a much smaller proportion of their income.

Time

The period of time we are considering also plays a role in shaping the demand curve. Suppose, for example, that the price of meat rises disproportionately to other foods. Eating habits established over years will be slow to change, but, if the price remains high, people will begin to seek substitutes. We have observed this effect in recent years, as evidenced by the introduction of soya protein and the switch to cheap meats such as hamburgers. This principle we may state as:

Following a change in price, elasticity of demand will tend to be greater in the long-run than the short-run.

Whether or not this is a noticeable effect will depend upon whether or not consumers discover adequate substitutes.

It is also possible to observe the opposite effect. Suppose, for example, that train fares rise sharply and that the public respond by switching to buses, buying bicycles or walking. There is thus a big response to the price change. However after a while the public discover that the buses are too slow, bicycles are unpleasant to ride when it rains and walking is too arduous. Therefore, after a time, they switch back to trains. In this case we have observed the effect of the public finding the substitutes unsuitable and therefore elasticity was *less* in the long-run.

The price of other products

In the previous chapter it was explained how the price of other commodities affects the demand we are considering. A rise in the price of a product will cause the demand for its substitutes to rise and the demand for its complements to fall. The effect of this upon elasticity may be gauged from Fig. 10.6.

In both diagrams in Fig. 10.6 there has been an increase in demand which has moved the demand curve rightwards. In diagram (*a*) it can be seen that the movement of the whole curve to the right has *reduced* its elasticity. In diagram (*b*), however, where demand has increased by a constant percentage (100 per cent) at every price, elasticity has remained constant.

An increase (or decrease) of demand by a constant percentage leaves elasticity unchanged, but a

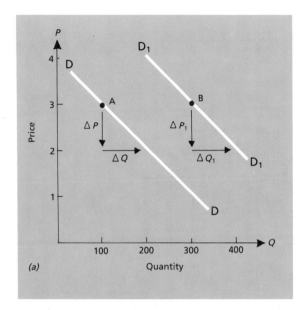

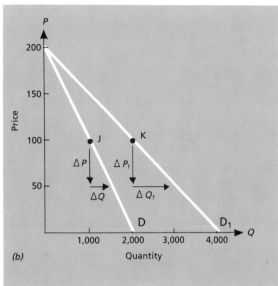

Fig. 10.6 *Elasticity and increases in demand*
If the whole demand curve moves outwards (*a*) then elasticity decreases, but if the demand curve swivels outwards
(*b*) then elasticity remains the same.

(*a*) E_D at A $= \dfrac{100}{100} \times \dfrac{3}{1} = 3$

E_D at B $= \dfrac{100}{300} \times \dfrac{3}{1} = 1$

(*b*) E_D at J $= \dfrac{500}{1000} \times \dfrac{100}{50} = 1$

E_D at K $= \dfrac{1000}{5000} \times \dfrac{100}{50} = 1$

rightwards shift of the curve by a fixed amount reduces elasticity.

Durability

If the price of potatoes rises it is not possible to eat the same potatoes twice. However if the price of furniture rises, we can make our existing tables and chairs last a little longer. Thus we can say:

The greater the durability of a product, the greater its elasticity of demand will tend to be.

Addiction

Where a product is habit forming, for example cigarettes, this will tend to *reduce* its elasticity of demand.

Economic and human constraints

After studying the above determinants you can see that elasticity of demand is determined by many factors. If the list is studied closely, however, it will be seen that nearly all these factors depend upon the possibility of substitution.

The possibility of substitution is restricted by both demand and supply constraints. Firstly there is human nature, with its tastes and aspirations. What may be an acceptable substitute to one person may not be acceptable to another. Secondly there are the physical and economic supply constraints of the natural world. For example, in the 1970s the world had to cope with huge rises in the price of oil and, although there were substitutes, it proved very difficult to adjust to them adequately.

Arc elasticity and point elasticity

Arc and point elasticity defined

The method of calculating elasticity which we have developed measures what is known as *arc* **127**

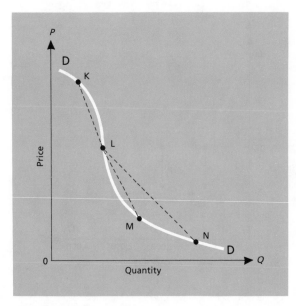

Fig. 10.7 *Arc elasticity*
Arc elasticity measured from point L gives the values of straight lines drawn to other points on the curve, but not the value at L itself.

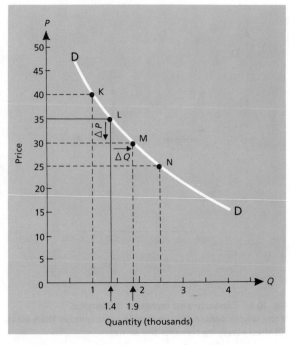

Fig. 10.8 *Application of the arc elasticity formula*
Applying the arc elasticity formula:

$$E_D = \frac{\triangle Q/Q}{\triangle P/P}$$

to calculate E_D at point L will give different values if different arcs are considered. Arc LM gives:

$$E_D = \frac{500/1400}{5/35} = 2 \cdot 5$$

arc LN gives:

$$E_D = \frac{1100/1400}{10/35} = 2 \cdot 75$$

and arc LK gives:

$$E_D = \frac{400/1400}{5/35} = 2$$

elasticity, i.e. it measures the *average* value of a segment (or arc) of a demand curve. This is illustrated in Fig. 10.7.

If we attempt to calculate the value of E_D at L by dropping the price to M we will, instead, get the value of a straight line drawn between these two points. It is obvious from Fig. 10.7 that the value of E_D calculated in this manner will vary with the direction and magnitude of the change considered – the greater the magnitude of the change, the greater will be the inaccuracy of the answer. This is illustrated in Fig. 10.8. If we wish to determine the value of E_D at £35 and we drop the price to £30 we get the value $E_D = 2\cdot50$. If the price is dropped to £25 then $E_D = 2\cdot75$. And if we calculate E_D at £35 by raising the price to £40 then $E_D = 2.00$.

The inaccuracy of the answer is minimised by considering as small a change as possible. If we are able to consider the slope of the curve at one spot we will obtain a value known as *point elasticity*.

a segment of the curve, while point elasticity is the value at any one point on the curve.

The graphical measurement of elasticity

There is a simple graphical way to calculate the coefficient for a straight-line demand curve. If we consider any point on the demand curve, then the value of E_D at the point is equal to the length of the demand curve below that point, divided by the length of the demand curve above it. You can confirm this in Fig. 10.5. At

128 Arc elasticity is the average value of elasticity over

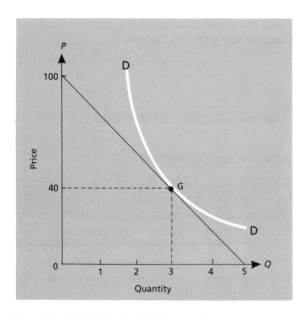

Fig. 10.9 *Elasticity calculated from a tangent*
The value of the coefficient can be determined from a tangent drawn to the demand curve, e.g. at point G the value is the length of the tangent below this point divided by the length of the tangent above it. Thus:

$$E_D = \frac{2}{3}$$

point C the value would be $E_D = 8/2 = 4$, whereas at F the value would be $E_D = 5/5 = 1$ and at G it would be $E_D = 4/6 = 2/3$. These values we already know to be correct.

This same method can be used for a curved line. To calculate the value it is necessary to draw a tangent to the curve at the point we wish to measure. This is illustrated in Fig. 10.9. To calculate E_D at point G of the demand curve, a tangent is drawn touching both of the axes. The value can then be calculated on the length of the tangent below this point divided by the length of the tangent above – in this case $E_D = 2/3$.

This gives us the value for *point* elasticity rather than arc elasticity. However the usefulness of this method is limited by the practical difficulties of drawing an accurate tangent.

The point elasticity formula

This section may be omitted without impairing your understanding of elasticity.

In order to calculate E_D for point elasticity we need to use some simple calculus. We already have:

$$E_D = -\frac{\triangle Q/Q}{\triangle P/P}$$

This can also be written as:

$$E_D = -\frac{P}{Q} \cdot \frac{\triangle Q}{\triangle P}$$

To calculate point elasticity we need to calculate this as:

$$E_D = -\frac{P}{Q} \cdot \frac{dQ}{dP}$$

(Note: the negative sign in the formula of E_D has been re-introduced here.)

The ratio dQ/dP is the derivative of quantity with respect to price, while P and Q are the original price and quantity for which we wish to discover E_D as with arc elasticity.

If we apply this formula to the example used in Fig. 10.8 for the price of £35 and a quantity of 1400 (1·4) (point L) we obtain the following:

$$E_D = -\frac{35}{1.4} \cdot \frac{dQ}{dP}$$

At this point of the curve the value of dQ/dP is -0.09. In order to calculate dQ/dP we must have the equation of the demand curve. In this case it is $Q = 0.002P^2 - 0.23P + 7 \lim 10 \leqslant P \leqslant 50$. When differentiated with respect to P this gives a value of:

$$dQ/dP = 0.004P - 0.23$$

Thus we may undertake the calculation:

$$(0.004 \times 35) - 0.23 \text{ when } P = 35$$

This gives a value of $dQ/dP = -0.09$.

Therefore:

$$E_D = -\frac{35}{1.4} \times -0.09 = 2.25$$

Thus we have a true value for E_D of 2·25 at point L of the curve. If you refer back to Fig. 10.8 you will see that all the values for arc elasticity at this **129** point were approximately correct, but none was absolutely correct.

Straight-line demand curves

If we are considering straight-line demand curves, then none of the problems discussed in the previous sections occur. The formula for arc elasticity will give an absolutely accurate answer. What is more, the answer will not be affected by the magnitude or the direction of any change we consider.

Refer to Table 10.1 (*see* page 124) and calculate the E_D at $P = £8$, but this time increase the price. Having done this, repeat the calculation but drop the price from £8 to £5. The answer remains $E_D = 4$. This is because when the demand curve is straight its slope must be constant. Thus in the equation:

$$E_D = \frac{P}{Q} \cdot \frac{\triangle Q}{\triangle P}$$

the value of $\triangle Q/\triangle P$ must remain constant, irrespective of the change considered.

We have spent a good deal of time examining price elasticity of demand. This is because it is an important, and at times complex, topic. However, having examined it in detail, we will find that we can deal with the other types of elasticity easily and quickly as they all involve similar techniques.

It is important to understand the difference between arc and point elasticity. However you will not be required to *calculate* point elasticity unless you go to higher-level theoretical economics.

If you are asked to calculate the coefficient of elasticity apply the arc formula.

The main points are summarised in Table 10.2.

Income elasticity of demand

Income elasticity defined

In the previous chapter we saw how the demand for a product has several determinants. The most important of these is price, and so far in this chapter we have been concerned with how demand alters in response to price changes. Another determinant of demand is income (Y). The response of demand to changes in income may also be measured.

Income elasticity of demand measures the degree of responsiveness of the quantity demanded of a product to changes in income.

Income elasticity also has a coefficient and this we may state as:

$$E_Y = \frac{\text{Percentage change in quantity demanded}}{\text{Percentage change in income}}$$

This we may write as:

$$E_Y = \frac{\triangle Q/Q}{\triangle Y/Y}$$

where Y = income.

Categories of income elasticity

As was explained in the previous chapter, demand might increase or decrease in response

Table 10.2 Elasticities of demand

Category	Value	Characteristics
Perfectly inelastic	$E_D = 0$	Quantity demanded remains constant as price changes
Inelastic	$0 < E_D < 1$	Proportionate change in quantity is less than proportionate change in price
Unitary	$E_D = 1$	Proportionate change in quantity is the same as proportionate change in price
Elastic	$1 < E_D < \infty$	Proportionate change in quantity is greater than proportionate change in price
Perfectly elastic	$E_D = \infty$	Any amount will be bought at a certain price but none at any higher price

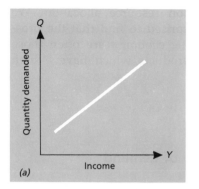
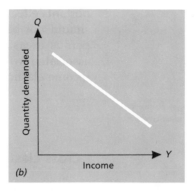
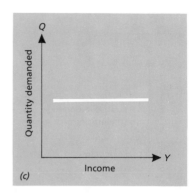

Fig. 10.10 *Income elasticities: three possibilities*
(*a*) Positive income elasticity as demand increases with income, e.g. colour television sets.
(*b*) Negative income elasticity as demand falls with income, e.g. potatoes.
(*c*) Zero income elasticity; demand remains constant as income rises, e.g. salt.

to a rise in income, depending upon whether the product we are considering is a normal good or an inferior good. The demand for normal goods increases with income and so these are both positive movements; consequently the value of the coefficient of income elasticity will be positive. With inferior goods, as income rises demand falls and the value of the coefficient is therefore negative. A third possibility exists, which is that demand will remain constant as income rises (*see* also page 104). In this case there is said to be zero income elasticity. These possibilities are illustrated in Fig. 10.10. (You will note in Fig. 10.10 that quantity demanded is on the *vertical* axis and income on the *horizontal* axis. This is because we have returned to the correct mathematical procedure of placing the *dependent variable* on the vertical axis (*see* pages 17–18).

You will recall that price elasticity of demand is always negative but that we usually omit the sign. Income elasticity can be either positive or negative and it is therefore very important to include the sign (+ or −) when stating the value of the coefficient. Positive income elasticity can still fall into the three categories of elastic, inelastic and unitary. The possibilities are summarised in Table 10.3.

When we examined elasticity of demand we discovered that one demand curve might have all three categories of elasticity. This is also so with income elasticity of demand. Consider a product like potatoes. If an economy is very poor then as income rises people will be pleased to eat more potatoes and therefore potatoes will be a normal good. As income continues to rise people buy other types of food to supplement their diet, the demand for potatoes remains

Table 10.3 Income elasticities

Category	Value	Characteristics
Negative income elasticity	$E_Y < 0$	Demand decreases as income rises
Zero income elasticity	$E_Y = 0$	Demand does not change as income rises or falls
Income inelastic	$0 < E_Y < 1$	Demand rises by a smaller proportion than income
Unit income elasticity	$E_Y = 1$	Demand rises by exactly the same proportion as income
Income elastic	$1 < E_Y < \infty$	Demand rises by a greater proportion than income

131

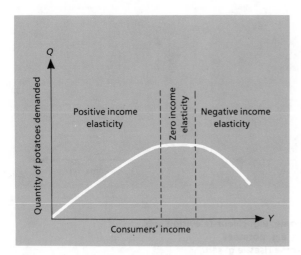

Fig. 10.11 *The demand for potatoes may have all three types of income elasticity*

constant and there is therefore zero income elasticity. As the economy becomes richer people consume such quantities of meat and other vegetables that they need less potatoes. There will now be negative income elasticity of demand for potatoes. This is illustrated in Fig. 10.11

The importance of income elasticity

Economic growth increases the income of a country and this is generally considered to be a good thing. However for those engaged in the production of goods with negative income elasticies, this will mean a declining demand for their product. Even when we consider products with positive income elasticities, there is a great variability of response. For example, with commodities such as food and clothing, although demand may rise with income, it might not rise fast enough to offset improvements in productivity, so that the result may still be unemployment for some in the industry. The booming industries tend to be those making products which have highly income-elastic demands such as televisions, holidays and cars. A downturn in national income, however, may well mean a rapid decline in the demand for these types of goods.

Income elasticity therefore has a most im-

portant effect upon resource allocation. We should not be surprised to find that the prosperous areas of the economy are often those associated with products which have a high income elasticity.

Cross elasticity of demand

The demand for many products is affected by the price of other products. Where this relationship can be measured we may express it as the cross elasticity of demand.

Cross elasticity of demand measures the degree of responsiveness of the quantity demanded of one good (B) to changes in the price of another good (A).

Cross elasticity also has a coefficient and this we may state as:

$E_X =$
Percentage change in quantity demanded of B
_____
Percentage change in price of A

This we may write as:

$$E_X = \frac{\triangle Q_B / Q_B}{\triangle P_A / P_A}$$

In the case of complementary goods, such as cars and petrol, a fall in the price of one will bring about an increase in the demand for the other. Thus we are considering a cut in price $(-)$ bringing about a rise in demand $(+)$. This therefore means that for complements, the E_X is negative. Conversely substitute goods such as butter and margarine might be expected to have a positive E_X because a rise in price of one $(+)$ will bring about a rise in the demand for the other $(+)$ (*see* page 105).

The value of E_X may vary from minus infinity to plus infinity. Goods which are close complements or substitutes will tend to exhibit a high cross elasticity of demand. Conversely when there is little or no relationship between goods then the E_X will be near to zero.

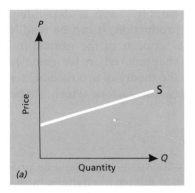 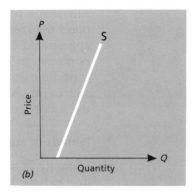 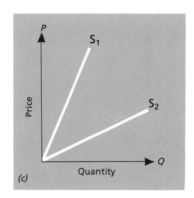

Fig. 10.12 *Elasticity of supply*
(*a*) Elastic. (*b*) Inelastic. (*c*) Unitary.

Elasticity of supply

Elasticity of supply defined

Much of what we have said about elasticity of demand will hold true for elasticity of supply. Indeed the definition is very similar.

Elasticity of supply measures the degree of responsiveness of quantity supplied to changes in price.

The coefficient of the elasticity of supply we may state as:

$E_S =$

$$\frac{\text{Percentage change in the quantity supplied}}{\text{Percentage change in price}}$$

This may be written as:

$$E_S = \frac{\triangle Q/Q}{\triangle P/P}$$

This appears to be identical with the formula for elasticity of demand. However you will recall (*see* page 125) that elasticity of demand is always negative. Elasticity of supply, however, is positive since the supply curve slopes *upwards* from left to right. There is a possibility that we may encounter a backward-bending supply curve (*see* page 61), in which case the backward-sloping position of the supply curve would have negative elasticity.

Supply curves

When we examined demand curves we discovered that it was dangerous to infer elasticity from the slope of the curve. With supply, however, things are much easier. Any straight-line supply curve that meets with the vertical axis will be elastic and its value will lie between one and infinity. A straight-line supply curve that meets the horizontal axis will be inelastic and its value will lie between zero and one. Any straight-line supply curve through the origin will have unitary elasticity.

Thus in Fig. 10.12 both S_1 and S_2 have unitary elasticity. (This is because at any point on the supply curve P, Q and $\triangle P$, $\triangle Q$ form similar triangles with the supply curve.) This you may confirm by experimenting with curves of different slopes. Supply curves of more complex shapes pose similar problems to demand curves. The category of elasticity of supply at any point on a supply curve may be judged by drawing a tangent to the point of the curve we wish to know about. If the tangent hits the vertical axis then supply is elastic at that point. If it hits the horizontal axis, as in Fig. 10.13, then it is inelastic.

The importance of elasticity of supply

Business organisations, the government and public corporations all take a keen interest in **133**

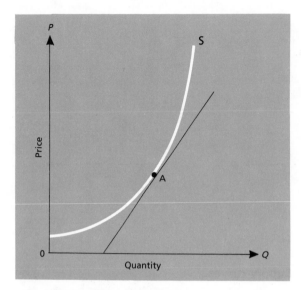

Fig. 10.13 *Elasticity of supply*
The elasticity of supply at point A can be judged from a tangent drawn to the curve at that point.

elasticity of demand and are interested in its precise measurement. This is not hard to understand for they will be interested in how price changes affect their revenues. However no conclusions about total revenue can be arrived at from the supply curve. The precise measurement of E_S is, therefore, of less interest.

Although we have dealt with elasticity of supply only briefly here, it should not be thought that it is unimportant. Indeed, since the long-

run shape of the supply curve is dependent upon the costs of production, it can be readily appreciated that its slope is of the utmost importance. In later chapters, when we come to consider costs and the theory of production, we will be investigating the factors which shape the supply curve.

Periods of supply

Elasticity of supply increases with time as producers have longer to adjust to changes in demand. Alfred Marshall maintained that there were three periods of supply – the *momentary*, *short-run* and *long-run* periods. Perhaps the most famous definition in economics is J. M. Keynes' reply when he was asked to define the long-run; he said 'In the long-run we're all dead.' The more conventional definitions are:

a) **Momentary. In the momentary period supply is fixed and E_S is zero.**
b) **Short-run. In the short-run supply can be varied with the limit of the present fixed costs (buildings, machines, etc.).**
c) **Long-run. In the long-run all costs may be varied and firms may enter or leave the industry.**

Suppose we consider an increase in the demand for candles as a result of a strike in the electricity supply industry. In the *momentary* period we only have whatever stocks of candles already exist in shops. In the *short-run* the existing candle

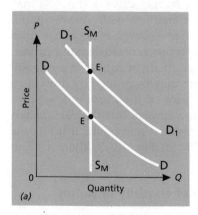

(a)

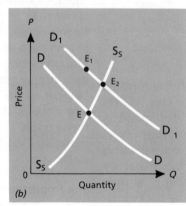

(b)

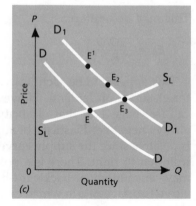

(c)

Fig. 10.14 *Periods of supply*
(a) Momentary period. (b) Short-run period. (c) Long-run period.

factories can work longer hours, take on more labour, etc. If the increase in demand for candles were to be permanent, then in the *long-run* more candle factories could be built.

The effect of periods of supply on costs is discussed in Chapter 15.

Periods of supply and the equilibrium price

If we accept the Marshallian periods of supply then we should be able to observe them in their effect on equilibrium price. Figure 10.14 follows Marshall's analysis. Suppose that the diagram represents the market for fresh fish. In each diagram the effect of the same increase in demand is considered. This increase might have been brought about by, for example, an outbreak of foot and mouth disease causing people to switch to fish.

In each diagram E represents the original equilibrium. In diagram (*a*) the supply of fish is fixed at whatever the present landings are. The only response therefore is for price to rise (E_1) but there is no variation in supply. In diagram (*b*) the fishing industry responds by working longer hours, using more nets, taking on more labour, etc. The price falls from the momentary high of E_1 to E_2 as there is some expansion of supply. Diagram (*c*) shows what happens if there is a long-term increase in demand. Now in response to the increase in demand the industry is able to build more boats (vary the fixed costs) and new businesses enter the industry. The result is that the price falls to E_3 and considerably more is supplied. It was Marshall's contention that E_3 would be higher than E, i.e. that the supply curve is upward sloping. Marshall assumed that the industry had already benefitted from economies of scale and that any expansion of the industry, in relations to others, would cause it to suffer from *increasing costs* (*see* page 31). Since S_L is more elastic than S_M or S_S we may conclude that:

Elasticity of supply tends to increase with time.

It should not be thought that the equilibrium price leaps from E_1 to E_2. More usually it is a gradual process as elasticity of supply increases with time. In the next chapter we will be considering changes in demand and supply. It is worthwhile remembering that when changes occur the effect may occur in three phases, as we have seen here.

Determinants of elasticity of supply

As with demand, there are a number of factors which affect elasticity of supply.

a) *Time*. This is the most significant factor and we have seen how elasticity increases with time.

b) *Factor mobility*. The ease with which factors of production can be moved from one use to another will affect elasticity of supply. The higher the factor mobility, the greater will be the elasticity.

c) *Natural constraints*. The natural world places restrictions upon supply. If, for example, we wish to produce more vintage wine it will take years of maturing before it becomes vintage.

d) *Risk-taking*. The more willing entrepreneurs are to take risks the greater will be the elasticity of supply. This will be partly influenced by the system of incentives in the economy. If, for example, marginal rates of tax are very high this may reduce the elasticity of supply.

Conclusion

This chapter has concentrated on the theoretical aspects of the elasticities of demand and supply. You will find, however, that it is a concept which has widespread uses. It can be applied to exports and imports to assess the effects of depreciation in the currency. The Chancellor of the Exchequer will be concerned with it in determining the level of indirect taxes, and of course firms are vitally concerned with it in their price and output policy. You will find references to it throughout the book and especially in the next two chapters; therefore make sure you have understood this chapter thoroughly.

135

Summary

1   Elasticity of demand measures the responsiveness of quantity demanded to changes in price. Demand may be elastic, inelastic or unitary depending upon whether a cut in price raises, lowers or leaves total revenue unchanged.
2   Any coefficient of elasticity is arrived at by dividing the percentage change in the quantity demanded (or supplied) by the percentage change in the determinant which brought it about (price, income, price of other goods).
3   Elasticity of demand is primarily determined by the ease of substitution.
4   Elasticity measured along a segment of a curve is referred to as *arc elasticity* while elasticity measured at one spot on a curve is *point elasticity*.
5   Income elasticity measures the responsiveness of demand to changes in income and may be positive, negative or zero, depending upon whether quantity demanded goes up, goes down or remains constant as income increases.
6   Cross elasticity measures the responsiveness of the quantity demanded of one good to changes in the price of another. It may be either positive or negative depending upon whether the two products considered are subsitutes or complements.
7   Elasticity of supply may be either elastic, inelastic or unitary depending upon whether, following a price rise, the quantity supplied rises by a greater, smaller or equal percentage.
8   Elasticity of supply increases with time. This can be analysed in Marshall's three supply periods – momentary, short-run and long-run.

Questions

1   Explain the factors which determine elasticity of supply.
2   Compare and contrast the responsiveness of demand of primary products and manufactured products with respect to changes in price and changes in income.
3   Explain how OPEC has exploited its knowledge of the elasticity of demand for oil. Evaluate the success of their policy.
4   Explain how the value of price elasticity of demand will affect the success of the following actions.
   a) Cinema owners increase the price of admission in order to increase their receipts.
   b) London Transport reduces underground train fares to attract more customers and increase their receipts.
5   Consider the following information;

	1980	1981	1982	1983	1984	1985	1986
Disposable income at constant prices	100·0	98·6	98·4	100·6	103·4	106·1	110·6
Cigarette sales (millions)	121·5	120·3	119·1	118·4	115·4	113·6	110·7

Are cigarettes inferior goods? Justify your answer.

If you were to be asked to account for the observed variation in cigarette sales, what additional information would help you?

6   If we have linear demand and supply curves such that:

$$DD = Y = 100 - x$$
and
$$SS = Y = 10 + 2x$$

what will be the E_D and E_S at the equilibrium price? (Remember Y = price and x = quantity.)

7   If you understood the section on point elasticity, then use the information in Fig. 10.8 and page 129 to confirm the principle that E_D can be calculated from a tangent drawn to a point on the demand curve. The E_D can be arrived at by dividing the length of the tangent below point B by the length of the tangent above it. Confirm that, if the tangent runs from $P = 5·056$ to $Q = 4·55$ then, at point B $E_D = 2·25$.

Data response   BEEBOP Trainers ━━

Information in Table 10.4 represents the demand and supply for BEEBOP trainers.

Table 10.4

Price per pair	Quantity of trainers pairs/week	
£	Supplied	Demanded
50.00	20 000	1 250
42.50	16 250	3 125
35.00	12 500	5 000
27.50	8 750	6 875
17.50	3 750	9 375
12.50	1 250	10 625
10.00	0	11 250

From this information:

1   Determine the equilibrium price and quantity of BEEBOP trainers.

2   Calculate the coefficients of the elasticity of demand (E_D) and supply (E_S) at the equilibrium price.

3   What would be the new equilibrium price if demand were to increase by 50 per cent at every price?

4   What is the coefficient of the elasticity of demand (E_D) at the old equilibrium price but on the new demand curve? Explain the observed relationship between this value and the value you calculated for Question 2.

5   Why would it be useful to the owners of BEEBOP to know the elasticity of demand for their product? In what other circumstances is knowledge of the value of elasticity of demand likely to prove useful?

6   What does elasticity of demand tell us about the relative power of consumers, sellers and producers in given market situations?

7   Distinguish between point elasticity of demand and arc elasticity of demand.

137

11

Markets in movement

> We might as reasonably dispute whether it is the upper or the under blade of a pair of scissors that cuts a piece of paper, as whether value is governed by utility or cost of production.
>
> Alfred Marshall

> You can make a parrot the most learned economist in the world; just teach it the words supply and demand.
>
> Anon

In previous chapters we have examined the factors which shape demand and supply curves and the formation of equilibrium prices. We will now go on to analyse how changes in demand and supply affect market prices. We will start by recalling some important points.

Some important ideas reviewed

Here we will give a brief summary of some of the fundamentals established in previous chapters. It is necessary that you fully understand these ideas before proceeding with the rest of this chapter.

Equilibrium price

This occurs where the demand curve cuts the supply curve and is the point at which the wishes of buyers and sellers coincide. Equilibrium prices also have an important allocative and distributive function in a free enterprise economy, helping us to answer the 'What?', 'How?' and 'For whom?' questions. An equilibrium price, however, is not permanent; it lasts only so long as the forces which produced it persist. A change in the conditions of demand or supply will bring about a new equilibrium price.

Ceteris paribus

It is only possible to reach any conclusions so long as we keep the rule of only considering one change at a time. Most statements in microeconomics should be prefaced with the phrase 'all other things remaining constant' or *ceteris paribus*.

Changes in demand and supply

It is important to distinguish between changes in the *quantity demanded or supplied* and changes in *demand and supply*. For example, lowering the price of a good will bring about a rise in the *quantity demanded*; it will not create a new demand. In Fig. 11.1 (*a*) this is seen as a movement along the existing demand curve from A to B. This is termed an *extension of demand*. However if, for example, there is a rise in income such that more is demanded at each price than before, this *shifts* the demand curve to the right as a new demand is created. This termed an *increase in demand*. These principles hold true for supply as well.

A movement along an existing supply curve is termed an extension or contraction of supply and a shift to a new supply curve is termed an increase or decrease in supply. Thus in Fig. 11.1 diagrams (*a*) and (*c*) represent changes in the *quantity* demanded or supplied while (*b*) and (*d*) represent *changes in demand and supply*.

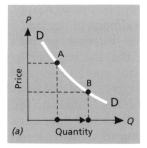 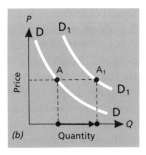 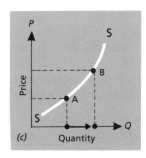 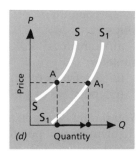

Fig. 11.1 *Changes in quantity demanded or supplied versus changes in demand or supply*
In (*a*) and (*c*) a change in the price of the commodity causes a change in the quantity demanded or supplied. In (*b*) and (*d*) a change in the willingness or ability to demand or supply brings about a new demand or supply such that a different quantity may be demanded or supplied at the same price.

Elasticity

The extent to which the quantity demanded or supplied changes in response to changes in price may vary enormously depending upon the elasticity of demand or supply.

Changes in market price

Four possibilities for change

If we consider all the possible changes in demand and supply it will be apparent that only *four* basic movements in the equilibrium are possible. These are illustrated in Fig. 11.2.

Other things being equal, an increase in demand will bring about an extension of supply so that more is supplied at a higher price (Fig. 11.2 (*a*)). A decrease in demand leads to a contraction of supply with less bought at a lower price (Fig. 11.2 (*b*)). Conversely an increase in supply causes an extension of demand so that more is demanded at a lower price (Fig. 11.2 (*c*)) and a decrease in supply causes a contraction of demand so that less is bought at a higher price (Fig. 11.2 (*d*)).

If you refer back to the determinants of demand and supply you will see what factors might have brought about these changes. Can you match the following four examples with the correct diagrams in Fig. 11.2? Which diagram shows the effect on the market for:

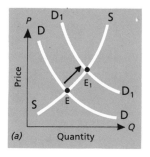 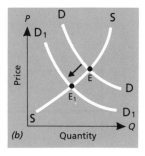 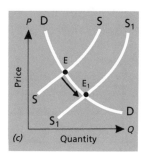 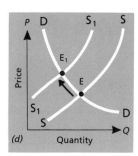

Fig. 11.2 *Changes in the equilibrium*
(*a*) Increase in demand results in more being bought at a higher price.
(*b*) Decrease in demand results in a smaller quantity being bought at a lower price.
(*c*) Increase in supply results in more being supplied at a lower price.
(*d*) Decrease in supply results in less being supplied at a higher price.

139

(*i*) computers of improvements in silicon chips;

(*ii*) tomatoes of an exceptionally poor summer;

(*iii*) beefsteak of a rise in consumers' incomes;

(*iv*) potatoes of a rise in consumers' incomes?

You should have got: (*i*) (*c*); (*ii*) (*d*); (*iii*) (*a*); (*iv*) (*b*). (Remember that potatoes are usually considered an inferior good.)

A common fallacy

A mistaken argument is often advanced which goes something like this. 'If supply increases (Fig. 11.2 (*c*)) the price will fall, but if the price falls then more will be demanded. This rise in demand will then push up the price, increased price will cause less to be demanded and so on. Therefore it is impossible to say what the effect of the original increase in supply will be.'

This argument confuses changes in supply and demand with movements along supply and demand curves. The original increase in supply does not cause demand to change. For example, technological advance means that many more

pocket calculators can be supplied very cheaply. This does not alter the conditions of demand – it does not, for example, increase people's incomes. Instead it means that the suppliers of pocket calculators have many more to sell and this they do by *lowering the price*. This causes a greater *quantity to be demanded*. If there is no further change a new equilibrium will have been reached, with more calculators bought at a lower price.

Complex changes

We were only able to reach any firm conclusions in the analysis above because we stuck to the rule of *ceteris paribus*, i.e. of only considering one change at a time. It is, of course, possible that more than one factor may vary. Suppose, for example, that there is a large rise in the demand for apples because of a successful advertising campaign to promote them. This is followed by an unexpected bumper crop of apples. What will be the final effect upon the equilibrium price? (*See* Fig. 11.3.)

If you study Fig. 11.3 you will see that both

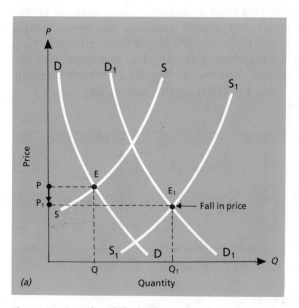

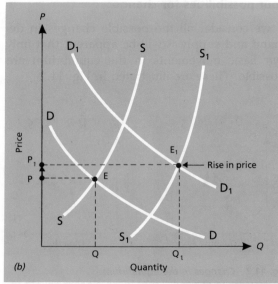

Fig. 11.3 *Complex shifts in demand and supply*
In both cases there is an increase in demand and supply, but in (*a*) this results in a lower equilibrium price and in (*b*) a higher equilibrium price. This is because of the different magnitudes of shifts in demand and supply.

diagrams could illustrate the example we have just mentioned. However although the quantity demanded and supplied increases in both cases, in Fig. 11.3 (*a*) the price falls while in Fig. 11.3 (*b*) it rises.

When multiple shifts in demand and supply curves are considered it is impossible to reach any firm conclusion about the effect on the equilibrium price unless the precise magnitude of the changes is known.

This conclusion has important consequences for anyone undertaking an examination in economics. Suppose you are asked to consider the effect of a number of changes in the demand and supply of a particular product. It is obvious from Fig. 11.3 that no firm conclusion can be reached unless both changes move in the same direction; for example, an increase in supply coupled with a decrease in demand will definitely lower the equilibrium price. What is the solution? The answer is to *explain one change at a time*. In the example used above, for instance, first explain the effect of an increase in demand and draw a diagram to illustrate it. Then explain the effect of the increase in supply and draw *another* diagram to illustrate this. Always keep to the rule of explaining one thing at a time unless you have precise details of the demand and supply.

Multiple choice examinations

If your examination contains a multiple choice element it is quite likely that you may find yourself faced with a diagram similar to Fig. 11.4. In this case we can answer questions about multiple changes in demand and supply because we know the precise magnitude of them (they are shown in the diagram). Suppose the question were:

In Fig. 11.4 O shows the original equilibrium price of margarine. However, many people are discouraged from eating butter because of articles in the press suggesting it is dangerous. This is followed by a large rise in the cost of the oils from which margarine is made. What will be the new equilibrium price? A? B? C? D? E?

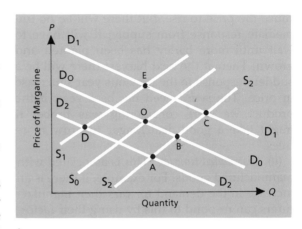

Fig. 11.4

The best way to answer the question is to locate position O and then ignore the other DD and SS curves. Then follow the question one step at a time. The articles in the press will decrease the demand for butter and thus increase the demand for margarine; we are thus at the intersection of S_0S_0 with D_1D_1. The increase in the cost of oils will decrease the supply of margarine. Thus we will move to point E, which is the correct answer.

If there are more questions on the same diagram always remember to return to the original equilibrium O. Then follow the same procedure as outlined above.

The effect of time on prices

Time lags

Supply often takes some time to respond to changes in demand. This *time lag* will vary depending upon the product we are considering. We may distinguish between two types of response.

a) One-period time lag. This is associated with agricultural products, where the supply in one period is dependent upon what the price was in the previous period. Say, for example, that there is an increase in demand for barley. This will **141** cause the price to rise, but there will be no immediate response from supply; it will have to wait until more barley has been planted and grown. Then at the next harvest there will be a sudden response to the previous year's increase in price. The *period* need not be a year; if the product we were considering was timber it might take a good deal longer to grow more trees.

(*b*) *Distributed time lag*. This is associated with manufactured goods. For example, if there is an increase in the demand for cars then manufacturers can respond to this by using their factories more intensively. However if this does not satisfy the demand then supplying more will have to wait upon the building of new factories. The response is thus more complex and *distributed* over time.

Time lags and prices

It is easiest to consider one-period time lags. A possible effect is shown in Fig. 11.5. Suppose that the diagram illustrates the demand and supply of barley. The move from DD to D_1D_1 shows the effect of an increase in the demand for barley. However at the time of harvest the

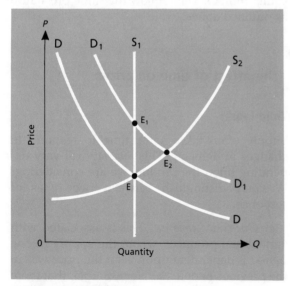

supply of barley is absolutely fixed and can be represented by the vertical supply curve S_1. The only response of the market, therefore, is for the price to rise to E_1, but there is no change in supply. Seeing the increase in demand, however, farmers plant more barley and so next year there is more supplied and we arrive at E_2. The extra supply in year 2 has thus been called forth by the high price in year 1.

This is a development of the idea of elasticity of supply explained on pages 133–35. The further implications of this are discussed at the end of this chapter.

Government interference with equilibrium prices

The problem

We have seen that prices fulfil an allocating function in distributing scarce goods between different uses or consumers. Income, however, is unevenly distributed so that although goods may be readily available people may not be able to buy them. If these goods are the essentials of life it is very hard for a democratic government not to interfere. Suppose, for example, rents are extremely high so that people cannot afford housing. The government could build more houses; this however is very expensive. It is very tempting for the government, therefore, to think that it can get round the problem by freezing the rent of houses below the equilibrium price. It is the object of this section to show that such interferences, almost invariably, have undesirable side effects.

Any price artificially imposed by law may be termed a *fiat* price. Where the authorities stipulate a *maximum* price for a commodity this may be termed a *ceiling price* and where a *minimum* price is stipulated this is termed a *price floor*.

The objectives

Governments do not just freeze prices at a low level; they sometimes maintain them at artificially high levels. It is possible for a government to be fixing some prices too high and some too low at the same time. This is because they have different objectives of policy.

a) *Cheapness*. It may be the objective of the government to keep the price of a product at a level at which it can be afforded by most people.

b) *The maintenance of incomes*. The government may want to keep the incomes of producers at a higher level than that which would be produced by market prices. This is often true of farm incomes.

c) *Price stability*. If there is a wide variation in the price of produce from year to year, e.g. agricultural products, the government may wish to iron out these variations in the interests of both producers and consumers.

Ceiling prices

Governments in many countries have often interfered in the economy to fix the price of a commodity below the equilibrium. Good examples of this are to be found in wartime. In the UK during the 1939–45 war almost everything was in very short supply. If the price of a basic commodity such as meat had been left to find its own level it would have been very high and beyond the means of many of the community. In Fig. 11.6 this is shown as price OT. A ceiling price is shown as OR. At this price consumers will wish to buy ON but suppliers who were willing to supply OM when the price was OT are now only willing to supply OL. There is therefore an excess demand of LN. Thus price is failing to fulfil its *rationing* function and some other method will have to be used. This might lead to long queues outside butchers' shops or to butchers only serving their regular customers. This often happens in Eastern Bloc countries today, where prices are kept down but there is a deficiency of supply. In some cases this is dealt with by only allowing meat to be sold on one day of the week, thus decreasing demand.

a) *Wartime controls*. During the 1939–45 war

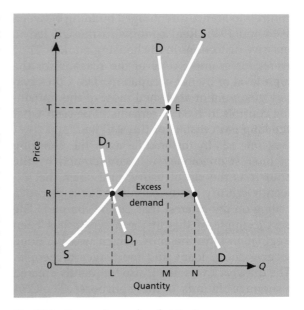

Fig. 11.6 *Excess demand and rationing*
The price set below the equilibrium brings about excess demand of LN. D₁ shows an artificial equilibrium created by the imposition of rationing.

the UK adopted a system of rationing. This meant that in addition to the price, customers also had to have a coupon issued by the government which entitled them to so many ounces of meat per week. Therefore, in effect, a new money-plus-coupon price had been created. Demand could be effectively decreased to equate with supply by regulating the issue of coupons. In Fig. 11.6 this is shown by the new demand curve D_1 and thus an equilibrium, of sorts, was arrived at. This system still had drawbacks; for example, a coupon entitled a person to a number of ounces of meat per week but it did not specify the quality of the meat.

b) *Rent control*. Such interference has not been limited to wartime. In the UK there has been rent control since the 1914–18 war. Rather than providing cheap accommodation for all, this had made it very difficult for many people to rent accommodatioon. Landlords have sold houses rather than let them at low rents and sitting tenants have clung to their accommodation. Thus rent control has had the opposite effect from that which was intended. Similar **143** controls in France discouraged building between 1914 and 1948. Rent controls in the UK led to massive distortions in the housing market. They were, for example, one of the reasons for the high level of owner-occupation. The Conservative government abolished most of the remaining controls in 1988. It remains to be seen what the long-term results of this will be.

c) Interest. In the middle ages the charging of interest on money was condemned by the church as the sin of usury, and since the sixteenth century many countries have placed a ceiling on the interest that can be charged. The best example of this in recent years has been Regulation Q in the USA, which was intended to give cheap loans and mortgages to people. The drawback was that it also frequently created a shortage of funds for these purposes. The USA began to phase out restrictions on interest charges in 1981.

Price floors

If the government establishers a floor below which prices may not fall, and this price is above the equilibrium, then excess supply will be created. This is illustrated in Fig. 11.7. Here the price has been fixed at OT and this has caused demand to contract from OM to OL. However at the higher price suppliers wish to sell more and supply expands to ON. The excess supply is shown as line AB.

We will consider three examples of this.

a) Agricultural prices. In the USA and in Europe governments frequently set guaranteed high prices for agricultural products in order to protect the incomes of farmers. The Common Agricultural Policy (CAP) of the EEC does this and Europeans are familiar with the excess supply it creates in the form of 'butter mountains' and 'wine lakes' (this is discussed in more detail in the next chapter).

b) Minimum wages. Where wages are very low a government may try to improve the lot of workers by insisting on a minimum wage. This may, however, have the effect of encouraging employers to employ fewer people and instead

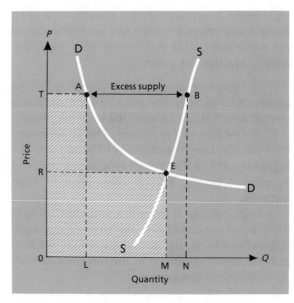

Fig. 11.7 *Excess supply and a price floor*

substitute other factors of production. Thus the workers that remain in employment are better off but others may have lost their jobs. This is illustrated in Fig. 11.7. Here the diagram shows that not only are fewer people employed but also the possibility that the total amount of money paid in wages has declined. If OT is the minimum wage then the total amount paid in wages is OTAL, whereas at the lower wage rate of OR the amount paid is OREM.

In the USA, Milton Friedman has argued that minimum wage regulations have significantly reduced the employment of young blacks and have depressed the total paid in wages, as in Fig. 11.7. In the UK on the other hand, the Wages Councils Act 1969 was passed to set minimum wage levels in a variety of industries, such as agriculture and catering, where wages were low. At one time Wages Councils were laying down the minimum wage levels for 3 million workers. The Conservative government, however, followed Milton Friedman's argument and set about dismantling many of the Wages Councils during the 1980s believing that this would enlarge employment.

c) Exchange rates. Where the external value

(exchange rate) of a currency is fixed by a government it is possible for its price to be set too high (or too low). Suppose that the rurit, the currency of Ruritania, has a real value of 10 rurits = £1; thus 1 rurit = 10p. However the Ruritanian government insists on an exchange rate of 2 rurits = £1. This now values the rurit at 1 rurit = 50p. At this exchange rate Ruritanians will find UK exports and holidays in the UK extremely attractive. However they will not find anyone willing to sell them pounds at this rate unless they are sufficiently desperate for Ruritanian goods to pay five times their true value. Thus commerce between the two countries will be all but impossible.

Many Eastern European countries insist on exchange rates as unrealistic as the one described above. Thus their citizens find it difficult to obtain pounds or dollars to buy imports or to travel abroad. Foreign currency earnings come from tourists who are willing to pay unrealistic exchange rates to visit these countries. Exports and imports usually have to be arranged by special trade agreements between Eastern and Western governments.

Black markets

Whenever a government intervenes to fix a price too high or too low, it means that there is another price at which both buyers and sellers *are* willing to trade. Such *fiat* prices thus tend to bring so-called 'black markets' into being, as people begin to make illegal arrangements to circumvent the government price.

During rationing in the 1939–45 war there were active black markets in the USA, the UK and occupied Europe. Rent control has led to potential tenants making payments to landlords for 'furniture and fittings' or as 'key money' in order to obtain a tenancy. In the USA ceilings on interest payments frequently led banks to offer other inducements to attract accounts. Potential depositors were often offered gifts to open an account, the gifts varying from electric toasters to, on one occasion, a Rolls Royce. The reader may be more familiar with the black mar-

ket in tickets for Wimbledon or the Cup Final.

When we turn to prices set too high we find comparable attempts at circumvention. Anyone who has visited an Eastern European country will be aware of the efforts of residents to buy foreign currency at black market rates. Wages set too high can also cause difficulties; for example, people are often employed illegally thus not only receiving a low wage but also defrauding the government of income tax. Employers also get round legislation by employing outworkers. The rates of pay for such work are often incredibly low. The artificially high prices of the Common Agricultural Policy (CAP) often mean that the EEC itself has to make arrangements to dispose of the excess supply. An example of this is the sale of cut-price butter to the USSR.

Not all these are black markets in the accepted sense, but they do illustrate the difficulties caused by interfering with equilibrium prices.

Price stabilisation

Agricultural products are often subject to *unplanned variations in supply*, i.e. because of the influence of such things as the weather and diseases the actual output in any particular year may be greater or smaller than that which farmers planned. If we consider a product with a relatively inelastic demand, such as wheat, then comparatively small variations in supply may cause large variations in the price. This is illustrated in Fig. 11.8. S_0 represents the planned supply, with farmers happy to produce 20 million tonnes of wheat at £260 per tonne. A bad harvest might decrease the supply to S_2 while a good one might increase it to S_1. High prices in bad years might suit farmers but might cause distress or even famine to consumers. Although consumers might be delighted with low prices in good years, these might result in bankruptcy for many farmers.

It would seem desirable, therefore, to attempt to stabilise prices and incomes. This could be done by a producers' cooperative or by a government agency. Suppose that we have the situation **145**

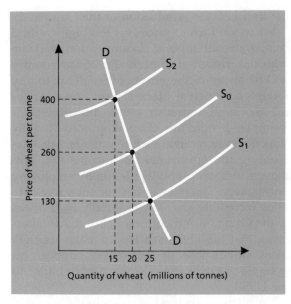

Fig. 11.8 *Price and income stabilisation*

represented by S_1 in Fig. 11.8, with supply totalling 25 million tonnes. If an agency were to buy up 5 million tonnes and store it, this would drive up the price to £260 per tonne. Suppose that in the subsequent year the crop were very poor so that now only 15 million tonnes is produced. By releasing 5 million tonnes from store the agency can keep the price down to £260 per tonne, thus bringing stability and order to the situation.

This policy is not easy to implement because it is difficult to determine the correct price for a product and to be certain in any year how much to buy up or to release. Nevertheless many such schemes have been tried. (This subject is developed in the next chapter.)

Taxes and subsidies

Types of tax

Taxes fall into two main groups, *direct* and *indirect*. Direct taxes are those which are levied directly on people's incomes, the most important being income tax. Indirect taxes are those

which are levied on expenditure. We are here only concerned with *expenditure or outlay taxes* and their effect upon demand and supply. (Taxes are more fully discussed in Chapter 40).

The two most important indirect taxes in the UK are value added tax (VAT) and excise duty. VAT is an *ad valorem* (by value) tax, i.e. it is levied as a percentage of the selling price of the commodity. Excise duty is a specific (or unit) tax which is levied per unit of the commodity, irrespective of its price; for example, the same excise duty is levied per litre of wine irrespective of whether it is ordinary table wine or the finest vintage.

VAT is levied on most goods, with only a few essentials being exempt from it. Excise duty is levied mainly on alcohol, tobacco and petrol (hydrocarbon oils). VAT is levied after excise duty and consequently the purchaser may end up paying a tax on a tax. Thus products such as petrol have both a specific and an ad valorem tax on them.

The effect of a tax

If we wish to demonstrate the effect of a tax upon the demand and supply situation, this is done by moving the *supply* curve vertically *upwards* by the amount of the tax. The tax may be regarded as a cost of production. The producer has to pay rent and wages and now must also pay the tax to the government. The effect of indirect taxes is shown in Fig. 11.9.

In diagram (*a*) £1 specific tax has raised the supply curve from S to S_1. You can see that the new supply curve is £1 above the old curve at every point. In diagram (*b*) the effect of a 50 per cent ad valorem tax is shown and you can see that the new supply curve diverges from the old one as the tax increases with price.

The incidence of a tax

If we use the phrase 'the incidence of taxation' this means who the tax falls upon. The formal (or legal) incidence of a tax is upon the person who is legally responsible for paying it. In the case of alcohol, for example, this is the producer

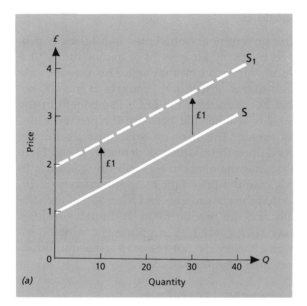 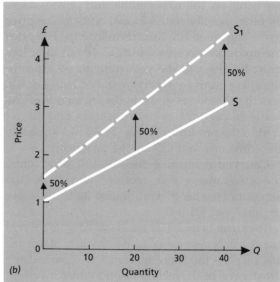

Fig. 11.9 *Taxes and the supply curve*
(a) This shows the effect of a £1 specific tax, while (b) shows the effect of a 50 per cent ad valorem tax.

or importer. It is possible, however, that some or all of the tax may be passed on to the consumer, in which case the incidence is said to be *shifted* so that the *actual incidence* (or *burden*) of the tax is wholly or partly upon the consumer.

It is often thought by the consumer that if the government places a tax upon a commodity the price of that commodity will immediately rise by the amount of the tax. *This is usually not so.* Consider what might happen if a tax of £1 per bottle were placed on wine. If the price were to be put up by £1 consumers would immediately begin to look for substitutes such as beer, spirits or soft drinks. The wine merchants, being worried about their sales, might well reduce their prices. In other words they have absorbed part of the tax. Thus the incidence has been distributed between the producers and consumers of wine.

This situation is analysed in Fig. 11.10. Here you can see that the original price of a bottle of wine was £2.50 and that 25 000 bottles were sold. The imposition of a £1 tax might be expected to raise the price to £3.50. This you can

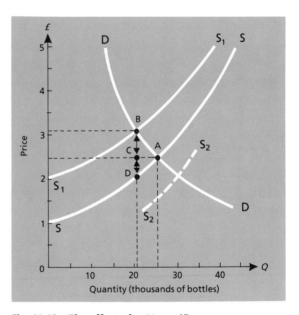

Fig. 11.10 *The effect of a £1 specific tax*
The original equilibrium is at A, with price £2.50 per bottle and 25 000 bottles sold. After the imposition of a £1 tax the new equilibrium price is £3.10 and the quantity sold is 21 000 bottles. S_2 shows the effect of a £1 per unit subsidy.

147

see is not so; the new equilibrium price is £3.10 and the quantity sold is 21 000 bottles. The price to the consumer has thus risen by 60p. The price the producer receives is now £3.10 but £1 of this must be given to the government, so the producer is effectively receiving only £2.10, i.e. 40p less than previously. Thus the incidence of the tax is 60 per cent to the consumer and 40 per cent to the producer. In Fig. 11.10 BC is paid by the consumer and CD by the producer.

Can you determine the amount of revenue the government will receive? It will be the amount of the tax (£1) multiplied by the number of units sold (21 000).

The extent to which the tax is passed on to the consumer will be determined by the elasticity of demand and supply – the more inelastic the demand the greater will be the incidence upon the consumer. Consider what would happen in Fig. 11.10 if the demand curve were vertical. The price would rise to £3.50 and all the tax would be passed on to the consumer. The more elastic is the demand the less the producer will be able to pass on the tax.

Subsidies

The government sometimes subsidises a product by giving an amount of money to the producers for each unit they sell. This was the case with many agricultural products in the UK before her entry into the EEC. The benefit of the subsidy will be split between the producer and consumer. The division will, once again, depend upon the elasticity of demand. In Fig. 11.10 S_2 shows the effect of a £1 per unit subsidy. In this case the price falls to approximately £2.10, so that the consumer is receiving 40p of the subsidy and the producer 60p. Although subsidies may be regarded as supporting an inefficient industry they do not result in a disequilibrium (see also Chapter 12).

Government tax revenues

If the government is trying to raise more revenue it will increase taxes on those products which have *inelastic* demands. If it were to increase the tax on those products with *elastic* demands the money it collected would actually

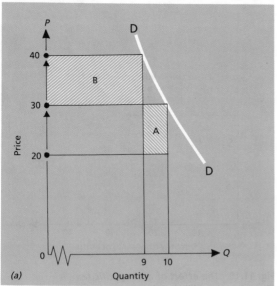

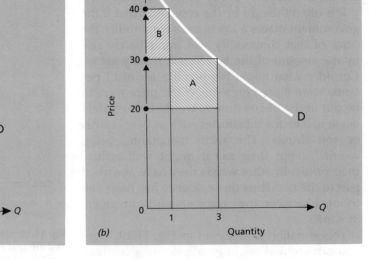

Fig. 11.11 *Revenue from an indirect tax*
(a) Inelastic demand.
(b) Elastic demand.
B is the revenue gained by raising the tax and A the revenue lost. Only if B is greater than A will increasing the tax be worthwhile.

decline. Figure 11.11 illustrates this in a simplified form by omitting the supply curves. In diagram (a) you can see that if the tax is increased from £10 a unit to £20 a unit, tax revenue increases from £100 to £180, but in (b) the same increase in the tax causes revenue to fall from £30 to £20. It would follow, therefore, that if a government wanted to increase its tax revenue from those products with elastic demands it would do best to *lower the tax*. This point was well illustrated when the nineteenth-century UK prime minister Robert Peel reduced the import duties on many commodities and thereby considerably increased the revenues of the exchequer.

Problems with demand and supply analysis

In these last two sections of the chapter we will examine some of the shortcomings of demand and supply analysis and suggest some ways in which these might be remedied. It is necessary for the reader to be aware of these problems, but a thorough study of them belongs in a more advanced course of economics.

Comparative statics

The demand and supply analysis which we have developed so far has been concerned with the formation of an equilibrium price. Any change in the market condition has then moved us to a new equilibrium. For example, the analysis predicts that an increase in supply will lead to a new equilibrium at a lower price with a greater quantity supplied (*see* page 139). We arrive at this conclusion by comparing one static equilibrium with another. This method of analysis is therefore termed *comparative statics*.

It has already been pointed out in this chapter that a time element may enter into the formation of prices (*see* page 142). This being the case, we need a theory which will explain the movement of prices with respect to time. Such a study is termed *dynamic analysis*. We may indeed find

when we use dynamic analysis that a market may never be in a state of equilibrium. This does not mean, however, that we shall abandon comparative static analysis. Comparative statics is a useful way to explain changes in market and is the basis of our understanding of the forces involved, i.e. its predictions are often correct.

Ceteris paribus . . . again

It has been emphasised throughout this section of the book that we can only reach any firm conclusions if we hold all other things constant and just consider the influence of one factor at a time. A moment's reflection will tell us, however, that in the real world all other things are not constant; in reality the demand for a particular product will be the result of the influence of price, incomes, tastes, the price of other goods and dozens of other factors all acting upon prices *simultaneously*. If we were to be limited to our comparative static analysis we should perhaps end up with a situation like Fig. 11.4, with both demand and supply curves shifting upwards and downwards simultaneously. Thus if we wish to enter the real world of economic measurement and forecasting we must have a method of analysis which allows us to combine all these factors together but nevertheless allows us to identify the separate influence of each factor.

Multiple correlation

A demand curve expresses the correlation between the quantity demanded and the price of the product (correlation was explained in Chapter 2). We may say that demand is a function of, i.e. depends upon, price and this we can write as:

$$D = f(P)$$

It is necessary, however, to consider not just one correlation but many. Thus demand will become a function of all the variables which influence it:

$$D = f(P, Y, T, \text{etc.})$$

where P is the price of the commodity, Y is consumers' income, T is consumers' tastes, and we would have to continue for all the other factors which might influence demand. The same could then be done for supply. It at once becomes apparent that this is a complex task.

The astute reader, however, will have noticed that we have already quantified some of these variables. For example, we know the nature of the relationship between demand and income and can measure this as the coefficient of income elasticity. The problem, however, is further complicated by the influence of such things as taste and quality upon price. The quality of a product is extremely difficult to quantify but it is undoubtedly important and some allowance for the effect of changes in quality upon demand must therefore be made.

Exogenous and endogenous variables

The factors which influence price can be divided between *exogenous* and *endogenous*. Endogenous variables are those which are explained *within* the theory; for example, the explanation of how changes of price affect demand is within the theory of demand. Exogenous factors are those which are outside the theory. For example, the weather certainly affects the demand for ice cream and as such we must take account of it; however it is an exogenous variable because, although it affects the demand for ice cream, it is itself unaffected by it.

An exogenous variable which frequently upsets calculations and forecasts is war. Most of the forecasts of the early 1970s proved very inaccurate because they could not foresee the Arab–Israeli conflict of 1973. Inflation may also be regarded as an exogenous variable. If, for example, we are trying to predict the price of a product next year, the estimate of the rate of inflation will be an important factor. In most cases, however, the price of a particular commodity has very little effect on the general level of prices. (This would not be so if we were constructing a macroeconomic model of an economy

for government policy purposes. In this case the rate of inflation could well be said to be largely determined by government policy and would thus be endogenous.)

It might be thought from what has been said that the price of a commodity is affected by everything else in the world. There may be, for example, a remote connection between the price of ball-point pens and the demand for ice cream. However it is so slight that we can ignore it. By selecting the factors which have a *significant* effect upon the market we are considering we will be able to build a model of how that market works.

Towards a dynamic theory of market prices

The cobweb theorem

We may develop a simple dynamic theory of market price by considering the cobweb theorem. Let us return to the example on page 142 where we considered the effect of time lags. We would normally say that supply is a function of price, which we could write as:

$$S_t = f(P_t)$$

where t is the time period we are considering. However it has been pointed out that for some products, especially agricultural ones, it is the price in the previous period which determines the supply. For example, farmers will look at this year's price in determining how much barley to plant for next year. Thus we can write:

$$S_t = f(P_{t-1})$$

i.e. the supply in the period we are considering (S_t) is a function of the price in the previous period (P_{t-1}).

Let us consider the effect this might have upon the market situation. Examine Fig. 11.12,

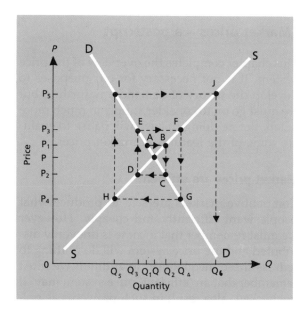

Fig. 11.12 *An unstable or diverging cobweb*
The supply in one time period, e.g. Q_3 is determined by the price in the previous period, i.e. P_2. Thus:

$$S_t = f(P_{t-1})$$

For example:

$$Q_3 = f(P_2)$$

where P and Q represent the equilibrium situation for the market for barley.

Suppose in year 1 that for some reason the crop is less than intended, so that supply is Q_1 (A). This will mean that the price is P_1. You can see that at this price farmers would wish to supply Q_2 (B) and are therefore encouraged to plant this much for year 2. You can see, however, that an output of Q_2 can only be sold for a price of P_2 and so the price falls to this level (C). The low price discourages farmers from planting barley and so they only produce Q_3 in the following year and there is thus a deficiency of supply which drives the price up to P_3. The high price of P_3 encourages farmers to over-produce, and so on. You can see from the graph how the cobweb theorem gets its name.

Thus when we introduce a time lag into the situation we may introduce instability into the system, or even permanent disequilibrium. Figure 11.12 illustrates a *diverging* or *unstable* cobweb. This is brought about because the slope of the supply curve is *less than* (flatter than) the slope of the demand curve. Other possibilities are illustrated in Fig. 11.13. In diagram (*a*) you can

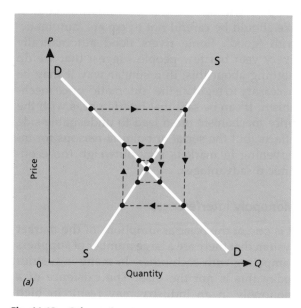

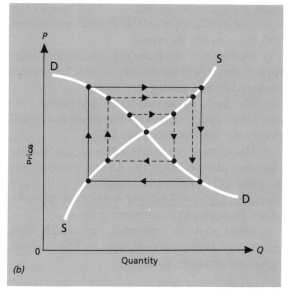

Fig. 11.13 *Other cobwebs*
(*a*) A stable or converging cobweb. (*b*) A cobweb with non-linear oscillations.

see a *converging* or *stable cobweb*. In this situation any disequilibrium will reduce and, other things bring equal, an equilibrium price will eventually be reached. This is brought about when the slope of the supply curve is *greater than* (steeper than) the slope of the demand curve. Diagram (*b*) illustrates what may happen with more complex curves. Here we see what are termed *nonlinear oscillations*. The oscillations finally stabilise when the absolute slopes of the DD and SS curves are equal. If the price and quantity continue to fluctuate around the box indicated by the solid rectangle in Fig. 11.13 (*b*), then we would be experiencing *persistent oscillations*.

These predictions may appear fanciful but were in fact developed from Professor Ezekiel's observations of the 'corn–hogs cycle' in the USA. In this, a low price of corn caused farmers to switch to hogs (pigs) so that corn became dear and hogs cheap. This caused farmers to revert to corn and so on. The inherent instability of some agricultural markets is one of the reasons why governments intervene to aid farmers.

Factors modifying the cobweb

There are a number of factors which modify the extent of oscillations in the market associated with the cobweb theorem.

a) Producers learn from experience and thus do not vary their behaviour to the full extent predicted by the theory.

b) We have examined only *one-period time lags*. *Distributed time lags* on the other hand will modify the cobweb (*see* page 142).

c) The cobweb depends upon actual supply equalling planned supply. As we pointed out on page 145, unplanned variations in supply can occur. These will further modify the cobweb, either diminishing or increasing its effect.

d) Prices may be inflexible, in which case prices may change too slowly to bring about significant changes in supply.

Having considered all these points, we may still conclude that some markets are inherently unstable.

Market prices – a postscript

This chapter completes the overview of the price system. It is not necessary for our purposes to develop the theory of demand any further, but we must go on to consider supply in much more detail. Before doing this we will pause to evaluate some of the features of market prices.

Market prices are efficient

Competitive markets are said to produce what people want efficiently and cheaply. However we must remember that income is unevenly distributed and the price system will do nothing to redress these inequalities. In addition we must remember that an 'efficient' price system may, if unchecked, also result in such problems as pollution. (The welfare implications of market prices are discussed in Chapter 25.).

The system is automatic

Much is often made of the fact that supply decisions seem to happen automatically and that adjustments to changing demand conditions happen without central coordinating bodies. We should be careful not to equate 'automatic' with 'good'. Some rivers flood automatically every year but few people suggest that we do nothing about this; in a similar way it may be necessary to regulate the 'automatic' price mechanism. It can be said that interferences with the price mechanism often lead to undesirable side effects, but the social or political reasons for intervening in markets may outweigh the economic disadvantages.

Monopoly interferences

It is one of the basic assumptions of the market system that there are a large number of suppliers competing with each other. In many industries today this is not the case. The existence of a monopoly in an industry may result in high prices and an inefficient use of resources. The next chapters of the book go on to consider the structure of markets and the effects of monopolistic interferences.

Ignorance

Much of demand and supply analysis assumes that consumers have a perfect knowledge of the market. In practice this is not so and ignorance constitutes a major criticism of the effectiveness of the market mechanism.

Summary

1 Increases or decreases in demand or supply will move the DD and SS curves rightwards or leftwards respectively. If we keep to the rule of *ceteris paribus* there are then only four basic changes which can occur in the equilibrium.
2 Time may affect the ability of supply to respond to changes in demand.
3 Any government interference with equilibrium prices is likely to have undesirable side-effects which often lead to the opposite result from that desired by the government. The side-effects of intervention include the creation of black markets.
4 The incidence of an indirect tax will be determined by the elasticity of demand and supply for the product.
5 The shortcomings of demand and supply analysis place limitations upon its usefulness.
6 The cobweb theorem predicts constant disequilibrium for some markets.

Questions

1 The following information concerns the demand and supply of oranges.

Price (£/box)	Quantity demanded (boxes/week)	Quantity supplied (boxes/week)
8	500	1700
7	800	1200
6	1100	700
5	1400	200
4	1700	0

a) Determine the equilibrium price and quantity.
b) As part of the CAP support system orange growers are guaranteed a price of £7 per box. What are the likely consequences of this?
c) Suppose that in the original situation demand were to increase by 50 per cent at every price. What would be the equilibrium price now?
2 'A decrease in demand leads to a decrease in price.' 'A decrease in price leads to a rise in the quantity demanded.' Reconcile these statements.
3 In July 1987 the price of commodity X was £700 and 60 units were demanded. In July 1988 the price of commodity X was £800 and 80 units were demanded. Show that these observations are consistent with demand and supply analysis.
4 The following information is known about the elasticities of demand of three products X, Y and Z. For X $E_D = 2$, for Y $E_D = 1$ and for Z $E_D = 0.75$. Each bears a

sales tax of 15 per cent. Last year the tax revenues were as follows: product X = £200m; product Y = £100m; and product Z = £300m. This year the government wishes to raise its total revenue from the sales tax on these products to £700m. What advice would you give to the government?

5   Why is the price of some products inherently unstable?

6   Product K has linear demand and supply curves such that $DD = Y = 10 - x$ and $SS = Y = 1 + 2x$. Further suppose that $S_t = f(P_{t-1})$. If the quantity produced in period 2 were to be $Q_s = 1$ what would be the price and quantity supplied of product K in period 3?

Data response   Reforming the CAP

The following is an extract from a newspaper article from early 1988.

Brussels Talks Fail Again

Ministers again returned from Brussels without reaching agreement on farm surpluses. The labyrinthine complexities of the system continue to confuse the casual observer.

The European Commission raised the idea of what is called 'land set-aside'. It was one of four options proposed for reducing the grain mountain, and with it the mountain of cash which has to be paid out to store it. The present reserve of 15 million tonnes is expected to rise to 80 million tonnes by 1991 unless action is taken.

The other options are price reductions to farmers, quota systems and a 'co-responsibility levy' under which farmers are taxed for over-producing.

*Britain's Agriculture Minister, Michael Jopling, has taken the lead in trying to persuade his EEC colleagues to consider 'set-aside'. Under this scheme farmers would, in essence be paid **not** to grow crops on, say, 10 per cent of the acreage.*

The NFU favours a compulsory scheme. The Union argues that under a voluntary scheme farmers will fallow their least productive marginal land with the lowest yields.

Professor Colin Spedding director of the Centre for Agricultural Strategy at Reading University says:
'People already feel that farmers are being paid too much for their produce. If we now pay them to produce nothing, the idea will go down like a lead balloon.'

1   What might happen to grain surpluses over the next few years according to the article?

2   With the aid of a diagram explain how the CAP (Common Agricultural Policy) of the EEC results in surpluses such as that of grain mentioned in the article.

3   With the aid of diagrams explain how the various options mentioned in the article might be expected to reduce the surpluses.

4   Describe a scheme for the support of agriculture which would not create the disequilibriums associated with the present policy.

5   Under the existing EEC support scheme is marginal land being used effectively? In this context explain why a set-aside of 20 per cent of land will not lead to a 20 per cent drop in output.

12
Agricultural prices: a case study

*Here's a farmer that hang'd himself on th'
expectation of plenty.*

Shakespeare, *Macbeth*, II, ii

Introduction

In this chapter we look at the application of demand and supply theory to agriculture. Agriculture has been called the UK's most successful industry; output and productivity have boomed since the 1939–45 war. This has been achieved by extremely interventionist policies on the part of the government; the average Briton supports farmers through artificially high prices and through taxes.

It is, perhaps, a curious paradox that agriculture is the economist's most used example of the marketplace. We use it to illustrate shifts in demand and supply and all the workings of the free market system. But no market is so interfered with as agriculture. Governments, not only in the UK, but in most other nations constantly interfere to regulate and manipulate production and farm incomes. In many nations the quantity of next year's crop is more likely to be affected by government policy than it is by market forces.

Background to agricultural policy

Farming's privileged status can be traced back to the Agriculture Act 1947. The experience of two world wars had taught the UK the danger of being over-reliant on imported foodstuffs.

Agriculture was therefore supported by government grants for improvements, tax relief, fixed prices for milk and 'deficiency' payments on many products to bring prices up to a guaranteed level and enable farmers to compete with imports. The detail of the schemes need not concern us, but we can say that the main effect was a heavy subsidisation of farm prices. The effect of this is shown in Fig. 12.1. Here you can

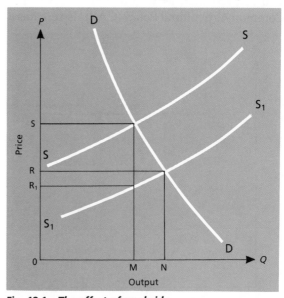

Fig. 12.1 *The effect of a subsidy*
The subsidy reduces the equilibrium price from OS to OR. Of the subsidy, SR is passed on to the consumer and RR₁ is gained by the farmer.

see that, although 'inefficient' farmers are being propped up, no disequilibrium is created because the lower price brought about by the subsidy encourages consumers to buy more. Thus before the subsidy OS was the price and OM the quantity demanded. After the subsidy the price is OR and the quantity demanded is ON. This form of support, as well as helping farm incomes, also benefits the consumer because some of the subsidy comes back to the taxpayer by way of lower prices. This particularly benefits low income groups, to whom the price of food is very important (*see also* page 143).

The UK joins the EEC

Since the UK joined the EEC the system just described has largely disappeared and has been replaced by guaranteed high prices and a variable import levy to keep cheap non-EEC food out of Europe. This is 'cheaper' to the EEC because they only have to buy the surplus supply, while a great deal of disguised 'tax' is thrown on to the consumer by way of artificially high prices. This situation is illustrated in Fig. 12.2. You can see that, as well as being costly, the Common Agricultural Policy (CAP) also creates a

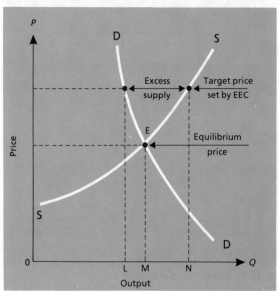

Fig. 12.2 *Excess supply created by guaranteed high prices*

disequilibrium of excess supply, this excess supply being familiar to us as the butter mountain, the wine lake, etc.

It is impossible to sell off the surplus within the EEC because this would depress the price and ruin the policy. It is difficult to sell it on world markets because its price is too high and so it is often 'dumped' on non-competitive markets, such as the USSR, where it has little or no effect on world prices. In doing this the EEC's behaviour might be analysed in a manner similar to that of a discriminating monopolist (*see* page 219).

Assessment of farming policy

The UK and Europe compared

Farming in the UK is different from that in most of Western Europe. There are a number of reasons for this.

a) *Climate*. The UK's cool damp climate favours barley and pasture but rules out crops such as olives, tobacco, vines and maize – all products which soak up much of the CAP budget.

b) *Land*. The UK has much of the poor-quality hill grazing in the EEC and in consequence rears almost 50 per cent of the EEC's sheep.

c) *Land ownership*. The UK has a large average size of farm, three times as large as the average French farm and four times as large as the average West German farm. There are two main reasons for this. Firstly, there is the custom of *primogeniture* in the UK, i.e. a system whereby the first-born inherits the whole of the property, in contrast to the system of *gavelkind* where property is automatically divided up between the surviving relatives. This tends to make UK farms larger and larger and European ones smaller and smaller. Secondly, many UK small farmers were driven from the land by cheap food imported from the Empire.

d) *Workforce*. In the UK only 1·6 per cent of the workforce are employed in agriculture. This is not only the smallest percentage in the EEC; it is the smallest in the world. This compares with 6 per cent in West Germany, 14 per cent in Italy and 30 per cent in Greece.

In view of all these differences there is little wonder that the CAP often seems ill attuned to the UK's needs.

Productivity

Since the 1939–45 war there have been spectacular increases in the productivity of the UK's agriculture, in terms of *output per hectare* and *output per worker*. There are a number of reasons for this.

a) *Breeding*. Better varieties of crops and improved livestock have resulted in large increases in productivity. Since 1947 the average yield of wheat has risen from 2·4 tonnes to 6·3 (1985) tonnes per hectare.

b) *Mechanisation*. In 1947 700 000 people were employed in agriculture in the UK, compared with 309 000 in 1985. This is largely the result of mechanisation, attributable not so much to more machines as to more powerful machines.

c) *Fertilisers and sprays*. The use of fertilisers and pest control agents is thought to account for about 30 per cent of the increased productivity.

d) *Improvements*. The most significant improvement has been improved drainage, but in addition to this there are better buildings, etc.

e) *Innovations*. The introduction of new crops, e.g. rape seed, and of new methods, e.g. zero grazing (keeping livestock indoors all year) have also increased productivity.

Other measures of productivity

There are, however, other measures of productivity and judged by these UK farming has not done so well.

a) *Fuel*. Fertilisers and mechanisation all require power. When fuel was cheap in the 1950s and 1960s this was not an important consideration, but in the high-cost 1970s and 1980s fuel costs became all important. On a technological level, productivity has fallen, with a unit of energy producing a smaller amount of crop than it did 20 years ago.

b) *Input–output*. In 1980 a study by the University of Reading measured productivity as the yield produced for each pound sterling spent. On this measure the UK did very badly compared with Belgium, the Netherlands and Denmark. Belgian farmers, for example, produced £121 of produce for each £100 spent, while UK farmers produced only £87 worth. The reason for this is the *over-capitalisation* of farming. As more and more capital is applied, farming experiences the law of diminishing returns. There is now some evidence to suggest that because of this low cost/low yield farming may be more profitable.

c) *Environmental considerations*. The environment lobby argues that the destructive effects of new farming methods upon the countryside should be included in the input–output analysis. Here there is clearly a divergence between private and public costs and benefits. The welfare economist would argue that the negative externalities of farming are one of the contributory causes of over-production (*see* Chapter 26).

The cost of farming policy

Figure 12.3 summarises the cost of farming support in the EEC. You will find in this diagram three estimates of the cost of the CAP. The estimates differ so widely because different years were used; in addition to this the support given by the EEC is supplemented by support from national governments which may be disguised. The main area of estimation, however, is caused by the fact that the gap between world prices and EEC prices varies widely. In all the estimates you can see that it is *not* chiefly through taxes that the farmer is supported but through the higher prices which consumers are forced to pay for the products. If this point is not clear study Fig. 12.4. In Fig. 12.4 E is the original equilibrium with a market price of OG. The CAP guaranteed-prices policy raises the price to OH. **157**

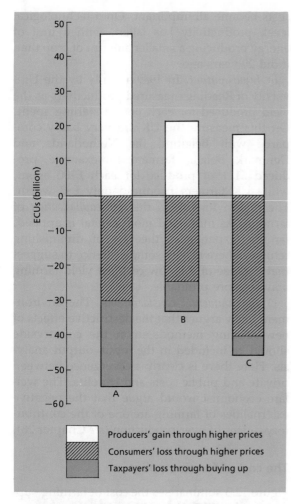

Producers' gain through higher prices

Consumers' loss through higher prices

Taxpayers' loss through buying up

Fig. 12.3 *The estimates of the cost of agricultural intervention*
Sources:
A: Australian Bureau of Agricultural Economics
B: Buckwell, Harvey, Thomson and Parton
C: Tyers and Anderson
1988 1ECU = £1.48
(See also page 161)

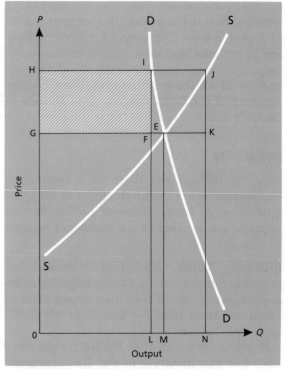

Fig. 12.4 *The cost of guaranteed prices*
Guaranteed minimum prices increase the price from OG to OH. This therefore requires extra expenditure of GHJK. Of this the government pays FIJK to buy up the excess supply, but consumers are forced to spend GHIF extra (the shaded area).

This contracts demand to OL but expands supply to ON. CAP intervention agencies are then forced to buy up the excess supply of IJ. The EEC is thus committed to additional expenditure of FIJK (theoretically it could recover the rest of expenditure LFKN by selling it on the world market). On the other hand consumers are now involved in extra expenditure of GHIF which, as you can see, is greater than FIJK.

In addition to these costs we must also consider the allocative inefficiency involved in producing food surpluses which the market does not want. In the wider sphere we could also consider the damage the policy does to Third World countries who are deprived of markets for their products by the policy.

An alternative policy

Instability in agricultural markets

As we have already seen, prices in markets for agricultural products are inherently unstable because of unplanned variations in supply. This is deemed to be undesirable both to producers and consumers (*see* page 145). Governments therefore usually intervene in agricultural markets, with the object of stabilising both farm incomes and consumer prices. However complete price stabilisation would lead farmers' incomes to vary directly with output, making them high in bumper years and low in times of bad harvest. This is the complete opposite of the normal state of affairs where, because of the inelasticity of demand for agricultural products, farmers' incomes usually vary inversely with output (see the quote which starts this chapter).

A sensible scheme will therefore probably aim not at total stability but rather at limiting fluctuations in prices and incomes.

A suggested scheme

The scheme put forward here is based on Fig. 12.5. Here planned production is 60 000 tonnes per year at a price of £40 per tonne. Actual output, however, varies between 40 000 tonnes and 80 000 tonnes. Given that the demand curve DD is very inelastic this would cause the price to vary from £120 to £16 per tonne. If we assume that the desired income level is that produced where the price is £40 and output 60 000 tonnes, i.e. £2·4m, how do we decide government policy? If we say that it is desired that income (total revenue) is constant whatever the level of output, does this sound familiar? Yes it does; it is the idea of unitary elasticity. We can then form the basis of a policy by constructing a hypothetical demand curve through the intersection of the DD and SS curves. In Fig. 12.5 this is the dotted line labelled $E_D = 1$. This will tell us what has to happen at any price if income is to remain constant at £2·4m.

a) Suppose that the actual output is 80 000 tonnes. In order for farm income to be stable at £2·4m it is necessary for the market price to be £30 instead of £16. However at a price of £30 the public are only willing to buy 67 000 tonnes. It is therefore necessary for the government intervention agency to buy 13 000 tonnes (80 000 −

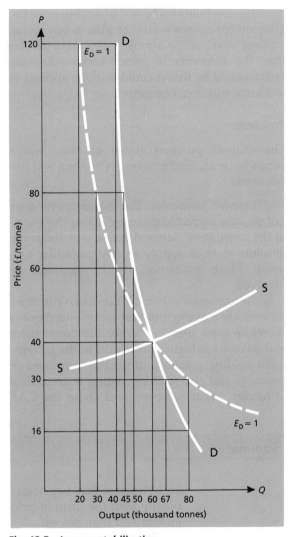

Fig. 12.5 *Income stabilisation*

67 000). This is then added to the government's buffer stocks.

b) Now suppose that actual output is 40 000 tonnes. This would result in a price of £120 per tonne. However if farm incomes are to remain at £2·4m then it is necessary for the price to be £60. A price of £60 is consistent with a demand of 50 000 tonnes and it is therefore necessary for the government to release 10 000 tonnes from its buffer stocks.

If this policy was successfully applied it would reduce price fluctuations and stabilise farm **159** incomes. It would also be self-financing since the government agency would be able to buy cheap and sell dear, unless storage costs were greater than the difference in price. Another limiting factor would be that it could only be applied to products which can be stored.

Problems

The analysis pursued above in many ways seems to be an ideal answer. Why then is it not followed?

a) Imperfect knowledge. The government does not possess perfect knowledge about the shape of the consumers' demand curve, nor about the absolute state of supply at any particular moment. Much estimation would therefore be involved.

b) Political pressure. In most European countries farmers are a strong political lobby and there is therefore great pressure to set the target price and income too high. This results in the government holding greater and greater surpluses of products and the scheme costing a great deal of money. What has been said about the CAP above will bear testimony to the strength of this argument.

c) Administration costs. The cost of running a scheme in terms of both bureaucracy and storage may offset the advantages. This will be very pronounced if the target set is too generous to farmers.

Conclusion

In this chapter we have briefly considered a problem which can be approached through demand and supply analysis. It would be presumptuous of us to maintain that we have provided any definite answers. However what we have shown is that there are many positive areas within the larger normative question of whether or not we should support agriculture and farmers. We have shown that this is an area in which the economist has much to offer. Unfortunately it is obvious that economic logic is often impotent in the face of political power.

Summary

1   UK agriculture has been supported since the 1939–45 war. This support mainly took the form of price subsidies, in contrast with the CAP system of guaranteed high prices.

2   The pattern of agriculture and land ownership in the UK is very different from that in the rest of the EEC, which is one reason why the UK does not fit well into the EEC.

3   Productivity has increased greatly in terms of output per hectare and output per worker. However other measures of productivity show that the UK's productivity has declined.

4   The cost of maintaining UK farmers is greater than that of all the nationalised industries put together.

5   Agricultural markets are inherently unstable so that governments usually intervene to stabilise prices and farm incomes.

6   A suitable policy may be worked out based upon a hypothetical demand curve having unitary elasticity.

7   Agricultural policy is complicated by imperfect knowledge, by political pressure and administrative costs.

Questions
1 Describe the present pattern of agricultural support policies.
2 Discuss the efficiency of quotas as a method of reducing farm surpluses.
3 What are the pros and cons of guaranteed prices for farm products?
4 In Fig. 12.5 what should the government's policy be to maintain farm incomes if the output were to fall to 30 000 tonnes?
5 India has established price ceilings to hold down prices. Why has this aggravated the Indian food problem?
6 The UK is now a net exporter of wheat. In what ways may this be regarded as an allocative inefficiency?
7 Has productivity increased or decreased in UK agriculture since 1939–45? Explain your answer.
8 How does the variable import levy affect the economy?
9 Do you consider it good for a country to be self-sufficient in food and if so why? Would you put any limit upon self-sufficiency as an end of policy?

Data response   Agricultural policy and welfare ━━━━━━━━━━━━━━━━━━━━

Study the information in Table 12.1.

Table 12.1 The costs of the EEC agricultural intervention

	Consumer losses	Taxpayer losses	Producer gains	Deadweight losses
	(1)	(2)	(3)	= (4)
(A) Australian Bureau of Agricultural Economics (1983) (Ten members)				
ECU billions (1982 prices)	30·6	24·9	47·5	
% of GDP	1·2	1·0	1·9	
ECU per person	112·0	90·0	173·0	
(B) Buckwell, Harvey, Thomson and Parton (1980) (Nine members)				
ECU billions	24·8	8·3	22·0	
(C) Tyers and Anderson (1985) (Ten members)				
$ billions (1980 prices)	49·0	2·2	27·2	

Buckwell, Harvey, Thomson and Parton assess only the costs of the CAP proper, the Australian Bureau of Agricultural Economics and Tyers and Anderson also include certain of the member states' national agricultural policies.

Source: Alan Winters The Economic Consequences of Agricultural Support: A Survey. *OECD Economic Studies, Autumn 1987.*

1 Explain what is meant by 'deadweight loss'. Calculate the deadweight loss for all of the estimates in Table 12.1.
2 Construct a demand and supply diagram to illustrate the concept of deadweight loss.
3 In what ways is the CAP damaging to less developed countries?

(You might also like to try Data Response, Chapter 11.)

13

The business organisation: its size, location and form

A living is made, Mr Kemper, by selling something that everybody needs at least once a year. Yes Sir! And a million is made by providing something that everybody needs every day. You artists produce something that nobody needs at any time.

Thornton Wilder, *The Matchmaker*

Types of business organisation

There are many organisations which trade with the public, i.e. supply goods and services in return for money. It is our intention here to deal with *business* organisations. Business organisations are those who exist with the intention of *maximising their profits*. Thus we are at present excluding such organisations as public corporations like the electricity boards or the Post Office because, although they are trading organisations, they are in the *public sector* and do not exist primarily to maximise their profits (*see* Chapter 19).

There are many different types and forms of business, but so long as they exist to maximise their profits the economist lumps them altogether and calls them *firms*.

Plants, firms and industries

The *plant* is the unit of production in industry while the *firm* is the unit of ownership and control. We can perhaps make this distinction clear by taking an example. Ford UK is a firm but it controls 24 different plants in the UK, such as at Dagenham and Bridgend.

An industry is all the firms concerned with a particular line of production. The government's standard industrial classification (SIC) list 49 industries and 111 subgroups of industries. Industries are difficult to define rigorously as one firm may operate in more than one industry.

The classification of firms

There are many ways in which we might classify firms; for example, we could do it by size. However the most important distinction as far as the economist is concerned is the type of competition under which a firm operates, and this forms a major portion of this part of the book. Before turning to this aspect, though, we must first look at the *legal forms of business*. As a prelude to this we will look at the development of the modern business organisation.

The development of the business organisation

As society evolved from feudalism to laissez-faire and then to capitalism, so the forms of business organisations evolved. The earliest forms were the sole trader and the partnership. The joint stock company did not become common until the nineteenth century, although its origins can be found much earlier in the *commercial revoltuion* of the sixteenth and seventeenth centuries. During this period the capitalist system of production became well established, i.e. a system where there was a separation of functions between the capital-providing employer on the one hand and the wage-earning worker on the other.

The joint stock form of organisation developed not from industry but from foreign trade. In order to raise the necessary capital and spread the risk of early trading ventures a company form of organisation was adopted. These were called *chartered companies* because they needed a Royal Charter to establish them. Many businesses without a charter styled themselves companies, but this did not constitute a legal form of organisation. At first they were *regulated companies*, e.g. the Muscovy Company (1553), which were established for one venture. However the joint stock company which had a continuous existence and was run by a board of directors and controlled by its shareholders became much more popular. The most important of these early companies was the East India Company. This was founded in 1600 and became a joint stock company in 1660.

Limited liability (*see* page 165) was first introduced in 1662 but it was only granted to three companies. Dealings in shares took place from the beginning but the first stock exchange was not established until 1778. By this time there was a flourishing capital and insurance market centred on a number of coffee houses in the city of London. The most famous of these was Lloyds. A great speculative boom known as the South Sea Bubble ruined many people and caused the passing of the Bubble Act 1720. This made it illegal to form a company without a charter and effectively hindered the development of companies for many years.

The building of canals (1761 onwards) required vast amounts of capital and so the joint stock form of organisation had to be adopted. By this time companies were formed not by

Royal Charter but by Act of Parliament. The building of railways involved hundreds of joint stock companies and by 1848 their quoted share capital was over £200 million. A few public utilities such as water supply had adopted the joint stock form of organisation but it was not until the mid-nineteenth century that industry generally began to adopt this form. The development of joint stock banking in the UK dates from 1826.

It was obviously inconvenient for Parliament to have to establish so many companies and so legislation was passed to enable companies to be set up more easily by *registration*. The most important acts were the Companies Act 1844, the Limited Liability Act 1855 and the Joint Stock Companies Act 1856. The Companies Act 1862 consolidated the previous legislation and was the basis of company organisation until well into the twentieth century.

Throughout the nineteenth century the family business remained the dominant form of organisation in industry. If such businesses sought company status it was usually for the protection afforded by limited liability and not for the purpose of raising capital. It is interesting to note that at this time, when industry and commerce were finding it necessary to adopt the joint stock form of organisation, the government was also finding it impossible *not* to interfere in the economy; just as the sophistication of industry and commerce needed regulation through company legislation, so the increasingly complex urban world demanded government intervention to ensure adequate drainage, street lighting, education, etc.

Much of the organisation of institutions which evolved at this time, such as hospitals and schools, was modelled on factories. These forms have survived the *scientific revolution* of the twentieth century. We are now on the threshold of great changes in our economy which will be brought about by the *microprocessor revolution*. Perhaps if we are tempted to cling to the forms of organisation of the past we should recall that they originated in the need to exploit large steam engines as a source of power.

163

Legal forms of firms

The sole trader

A sole trader is a business organisation where one person is in business on their own, providing the capital, taking the profit and standing the losses themself. Typical areas of commercial activity for the sole trader are retailing and building, i.e. activities which are not usually capital intensive. Sole traders are often wrongly termed 'one-man businesses'. Sole traders are indeed *owned* by one person but the business may *employ* many people.

Limits are placed on the growth of a sole trader's activities by two main constraints. Firstly, finance: economic growth largely depends on the availability of capital to invest in the business, and the sole traders are limited to what can be provided from their own resources or raised from banks etc. Secondly, organisation: one person has only limited ability to exercise effective control over and take responsibility for an organisation. As a business grows, a larger and more complicated business organisation will generally replace the sole trader.

The sole trader is in a potentially vulnerable financial position. The profits may all accrue to one person but so do the losses, and many sole traders are made bankrupt each year. Limited capital resources often make the sole trader particularly vulnerable, not only to sustained competition from large business units but also to bad capital investments, e.g. a grocer opening a delicatessen in an area which turns out to prefer more mundane food.

It can be argued, however, that a sole trader is able to weather a short reduction in consumer spending far better than a larger business unit. The sole trader can adapt quickly to the level of demand and, if necessary, can make personal economies until business improves.

The sole trader remains the most common business unit in the UK and they are the backbone of the business structure on which the country depends. Nevertheless, in terms of capital and manpower resources employed, sole traders are of limited importance. In recent years the number of sole traders has decreased. The main reasons for this are:

a) lack of capital to invest in new premises, equipment and materials;

b) lack of expertise in every aspect of the business resulting in inefficiency, e.g. the sole traders may be good at selling but bad at administration;

c) lack of advice and guidance about the operations of the business – consultancy is usually too expensive to be considered;

d) competition from chain stores and other larger business units which are able to benefit from various economies of scale;

e) changes in shopping patterns caused by, for example, an increase in the number of married women working and an increase in car ownership;

f) increased overheads resulting from bureaucratic functions imposed by law, e.g. VAT collection, which sole traders are often disinclined and ill-equipped to perform (this is less quantifiable as a reason but still important).

Yet sole traders survive. As a business organisation they offer attractive advantages when compared with others. The initial capital investment may only need to be very small and the legal formalities involved are minimal. In sharp contrast to joint stock companies, they offer financial secrecy and the 'personal touch' (a subjective but often important factor). Sole traders are also able to alter their activities to adapt to the market without legal formality or major organisational problems (see reasons for continuance of the small business at the end of this chapter).

Partnerships

The Partnership Act 1890 defines a partnership as 'the relation which subsists between persons carrying on a business in common with a view of profit'. Many partnerships are very formal organisations, such as a large firm of solicitors or accountants, but two people running a stall in a local Sunday market would almost certainly be in partnership with one another and subject to the same legal rules as a firm of city solicitors with an annual turnover of several hundred thousand pounds.

Partnerships became common with the emergence of economic society, for they are better suited to cope with the demands of modern commercial activity than sole traders, who must provide capital, labour and skill themselves. Two or more persons in partnership can combine their resources and, in theory, form an economically more efficient business unit, producing a better return on the capital invested.

The maximum number of members possible in most partnership is fixed by law at 20. The professional partnerships that are allowed to exceed this number – solicitors, accountants and members of a recognised stock exchange – are often organisations of some size, with considerable capital resources and offering economies of scale and the benefits of specialisation. It would be unusual, however, to find a trading partnership consisting of more than five or six partners, for corporate status as a company with limited liability is usually more attractive.

Quite apart from the rules of professional bodies, which usually prohibit their members from forming a company, a partnership is a business organisation generally more suited to professional people in business together than to manufacturers or traders. In the former, the risk of financial failure is less and consequently unlimited liability is less of a disadvantage. For all but the small trading ventures, or where there are particular reasons for trading as a partnership, registration as a company with limited liability is usually preferred.

The joint stock company

A joint stock company may be described as an organisation consisting of persons who contribute money to a *common stock*, which is employed in some trade or business, and who share the profit or loss arising. This common stock is the capital of the company and the persons who contribute it are its members. The proportion of capital to which each member is entitled is their *share*.

The need for more capital explains both the development of partnerships and, later, the development of joint stock companies. As soon as it became possible to do so, many partnerships chose to become registered joint stock companies with limited liability. Today, in terms of capital and manpower resources employed, the joint stock company is the dominant form of business organisation.

The principle of *limited liability* is extremely important to a company. Limited liability means that an investor's liability to debt is limited to the extent of their shareholding. Thus, for example, if you own 100 £1 shares in a company, in the event of its becoming insolvent, then the most you can lose is the £100 originally invested. This encourages investment because it limits the risk an investor takes to the amount they have actually invested. Without limited liability it is likely that none but the safest business venture would ever attract large-scale investment. In particular, the institutional investors, such as life assurance companies and pension funds, would not hazard their vast funds in any speculative venture and would only invest in the gilt-edged market (government securities).

Public and private companies

The Companies Act 1980 (amended by the Companies Act 1985) completely altered the classification of public and private companies as it had existed since 1908. Previously a private company was defined and a public company was any limited company which did not fall within this definition. The 1980 Act was passed as part of the harmonisation of law programmes within the EEC. By defining a public company for the first time it brings the UK into line with other member states.

To the outsider the most obvious distinction **165**

between public and private limited companies is that a public limited company has the letters PLC after its name as, for example, Marks and Spencer PLC while private limited companies have the abbreviation Ltd after their name. A public limited company may own subsidiaries which are private limited companies. When one company owns and controls others it is often referred to as a *holding company*.

Legally speaking a public company is a company limited by shares (or guarantee) which has been registred as a public company under the Companies Act 1985. It has two or more members and can invite the general public to subscribe for its shares or debentures. It must have a minimum authorised and allotted share capital of (at present) £50 000.

A *private company* is any company which does not satisfy the requirements for a public company. In common with a public company it has two or more members.

Thus the essential *distinction* between a public and a private company is that the former may offer its shares or debentures to the public while the latter cannot. Restrictions on share transfers and the size of membership no longer constitute an essential part of private company status, but there is nothing to prevent private companies retaining such restrictions. It is a criminal offence to invite the general public to subscribe for shares or debentures in a private company.

The private company at present is in some respects a transitional step between the partnership and the public company; typically it is a family business. In common with a public limited company, it possesses the advantage of limited liability, but in common with a partnership it has the disadvantage of only being able to call upon the capital resources of its members (supplemented by possible loans from its bank). Since public companies can offer their shares to the public – the shares of many (but certainly not all) public companies are quoted on the stock exchange – they are able to raise considerable sums of money to finance large-scale operations.

A private company is not under a statutory obligation to hold an annual meeting, although both public and private limited companies must submit annual accounts to the Registrar of Companies. A private company used to be limited to a membership of 50, was unable to invite the public to subscribe for its shares and had by its articles to restrict the right to transfer its shares, e.g. only to existing shareholders. These restrictions on membership and transfer of shares no longer exist. This means that private companies have the prospect of growth and development previously only open to public companies. Non-public share offers, e.g. through business contacts or bankers, are now possible.

Nevertheless, in terms of capital, public companies dwarf private companies, and they have been responsible for the immense growth in investment this century. The typical public company can carry on such diverse activities as manufacture cars, give overdrafts or sell insurance – in other words, there is no such thing as a 'typical' public company.

The location of industry

There are many factors which affect the attractiveness of a location for a firm. These are examned below in two groups: those occurring spontaneously in the economy; and those engineered by the government. We might imagine that organisations weigh all the possible advantages and disadvantages carefully and site their business so as to minimise their costs. It is doubtful whether this is ever totally the case; historical accident might well play a big part in location. For example, William Morris started car manufacture in Oxford because that is where his cycle shop was. Equally, businesspeople tend to be gregarious and will often site their organisation where there are lots of others. However no-one will begin a business or site a new factory without considering some of the following factors.

Spontaneous factors

a) Raw materials. Extractive industries must locate where the raw materials are, and this may in turn attract other industries, e.g. the iron and steel industry was attracted to coalfields and engineering industries were then often attracted to the same location. Thus around Glasgow there were the Lanark coalfield, an iron and steel industry and shipbuilding. Today, when many raw materials are imported, industries frequently locate at ports.

b) *Power*. The woollen industry moved to the West Riding of Yorkshire to utilise the water power from Pennine streams. In the nineteenth century most industries were dependent upon coal as a source of power. Since coal was expensive to transport, they tended to locate on coalfields. Today, most industries use electricity, which is readily available anywhere in the country. This means that the availability of power is not an important locational influence today. An exception to this is the aluminium industry, which uses vast quantities of electric power. The industry is therefore centred on countries where there is lots of cheap hydroelectric power such as Canada and Norway.

c) *Transport*. Historically transport was a vital locational influence. Water transport was the only cheap and reliable means of transporting heavy loads. Most industries, therefore, tended to locate near rivers or the coast. Canals and, later, railways allowed industry to spread to other locations. Today access to good transport facilities is still a locational influence. This is illustrated by the town of Warrington in Cheshire, which has experienced a renaissance in its industrial fortunes partly as a result of standing at the intersection of three main motorways. The most significant development in transport in recent years has been containerisation.

Max Weber, a famous economic historian and sociologist, developed a theory of the location of industry. Weber maintained that industrialists would try to minimise their transport costs. This means that if a commodity *lost weight* during manufacture the industry would tend to locate near the raw materials, whereas if it *gained weight* during manufacture it would tend to locate near the market. Steel is an example of a commodity which loses weight during manufacture. To manufacture steel near the market would mean transporting several tonnes of raw materials but only selling one tonne of finished product. Brewing is an industry in which the product gains weight during manufacture. It is therefore more economical to transport the hops, barley and sugar to the market, where water is added and the brewing takes place. Traditionally brewing was a widely dispersed industry, although in recent years it has become more centralised. Weber's theory is modified by the value of the commodity. Whisky, for example, is so expensive that transport costs are only a small percentage of the price and are therefore not a locational influence.

d) *Markets*. Service industries such as catering, entertainment and professional services have nearly always had to locate near their markets. In the twentieth century many more industries have located with respect to markets, so that today it is one of the most important locational forces. Goods which are fragile and expensive to transport, such as furniture and electrical goods, are better produced near where they are to be sold. The ring of consumer goods industries around London is adequate testimony to the power of the market.

e) *Labour*. It might be thought that the availability of cheap labour would be an important locational influence. It does not appear to be so. The existence of a pool of highly skilled labour may be a locational influence but, increasingly, manual skills can be replaced by automated machinery. An exception to this may be 'footloose' industries. These are industries which are not dependent upon other specific locational influences and are therefore attracted to cheap labour. An example of this is electronic component assembly, but organisations in this field have tended to locate in the suburbs to utilise cheap female labour rather than moving to areas of heavy unemployment which often have a history of industrial unrest.

f) *Industrial inertia*. This is the tendency of an industry to continue to locate itself in an area when the factors which originally located the industry there have ceased to operate. An **167** example of this would be the steel industry in Sheffield, although this may be partly explained by external economies of scale and the existence of skilled labour.

g) Special local circumstances. Such things as climate or topography may affect the location of an industry. The oil terminal at Milford Haven is located there because of the deep-water anchorage available. A further example is provided by the market gardening industry in the Isles of Scilly, located there to take advantage of the early spring.

h) 'Sunrise' industries. This is the term given to industries such as computer software which are associated with the 'new technology'. They could be regarded as 'footloose' industries since they are relatively free from apparent locational constraints. However many of them have become concentrated in the so-called 'software valley' which is the area either side of the M4, stretching from Slough towards Bristol. Reasons that have been suggested for this, apart from the natural gregariousness of business people, are the good communications and, more importantly, the fact that, freed from other obvious constraints, businesspeople have opted to live and work in the pleasant environment of Berkshire and Oxfordshire.

Government influences and the location of industry

The *old staple industries*, such as iron and steel, shipbuilding and coal-mining, have been in decline for most of this century. They tended to be heavily concentrated in the coal-mining area. The operation of free market economics seemed powerless to alleviate the consequent economic distress of these areas. This meant that from the 1930s, the government brought in more and more measures to try to attract industry to these areas. We used to explain things in terms of the decline of the old staple industries and the rise of the new industries such as motor vehicles, electronics and chemicals. However, since the 1970s many of these 'new' industries have been in decline so that previously prosperous areas

such as the West Midlands are now areas of industrial dereliction. Successive governments have tried to combat the decline of both the old and the 'new' industries.

There are today so many legislative controls and financial inducements that the government must be considered one of the most important locational influences upon industry. It is possible to identify four main ways in which the government tries to influence the location of industry.

a) Financial incentives. Financial incentives to encourage organisations to move to depressed areas have existed since the Special Areas Act of 1934. The Distribution of Industry Acts of 1945 and 1950 established Development Areas to replace the Special Areas and made Treasury assistance available for firms establishing there.

The Industry Act of 1972 designated three types of area which would be given assistance. These areas were termed *Special Development Areas* (SDAs), *Development Areas* (DAs) and *Intermediate Areas* (IAs), to which may be added Northern Ireland. The Conservative governments of the 1980s progressively reduced both the money available for regional assistance and also the areas to which it was applied. Figure 13.1 shows the Assisted Areas as they were defined in 1984. In Development Areas grants of 15 per cent of the capital expenditure of projects were available. (Alternatively £3000 for each new job created – whichever was higher.) In 1988 the Department of Trade and Industry (DTI) announced that henceforth all assistance would be discretionary. Figure 13.2 traces the decline in regional assistance. The reasons for this were the government's disinclination to intervene in the economy stemming from its belief that market forces are the best way to ensure a healthy economy, and its desire to cut public expenditure.

In early 1988 the DTI started to call itself the Department for Enterprise when it launched its *Enterprise Initiative*. This was aimed at encouraging self-help and private enterprise in the regions.

The EEC makes some funds available from the European Regional Development Fund

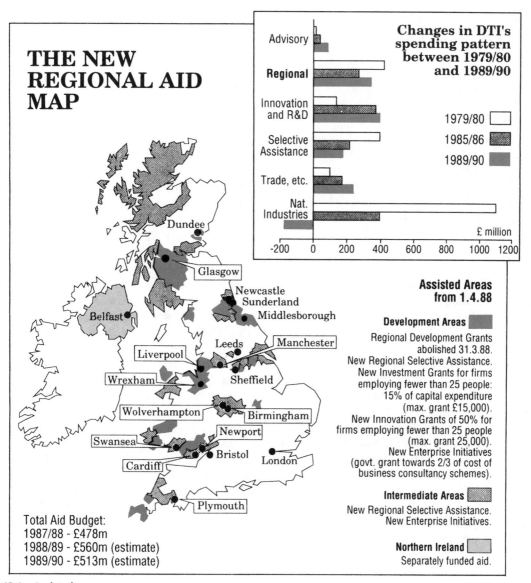

THE NEW REGIONAL AID MAP

Changes in DTI's spending pattern between 1979/80 and 1989/90

Advisory
Regional
Innovation and R&D
Selective Assistance
Trade, etc.
Nat. Industries

1979/80
1985/86
1989/90

£ million

-200 0 200 400 600 800 1000 1200

Dundee
Glasgow
Newcastle
Sunderland
Middlesborough
Belfast
Leeds
Manchester
Liverpool
Wrexham
Sheffield
Wolverhampton
Birmingham
Newport
Swansea
Bristol
London
Cardiff
Plymouth

Assisted Areas from 1.4.88

Development Areas

Regional Development Grants abolished 31.3.88.
New Regional Selective Assistance.
New Investment Grants for firms employing fewer than 25 people:
15% of capital expenditure
(max. grant £15,000).
New Innovation Grants of 50% for firms employing fewer than 25 people
(max. grant £25,000).
New Enterprise Initiatives
(govt. grant towards 2/3 of cost of business consultancy schemes).

Intermediate Areas

New Regional Selective Assistance.
New Enterprise Initiatives.

Northern Ireland

Separately funded aid.

Total Aid Budget:
1987/88 - £478m
1988/89 - £560m (estimate)
1989/90 - £513m (estimate)

Fig. 13.1 *Assisted areas*
Reproduced by kind permission of the DTI

(ERDF); however, the DTI deducts the amount of any ERDF grant from any assistance it may be giving. Whether interventionism works or whether free market forces are more effective there can be no doubt that at the end of the 1980s massive regional disparities existed in the UK. (*See* Data response question at the end of this chapter.)

After the 1987 election the government turned its attention to the inner cities. This policy can be traced back to 1980 when *enterprise zones* were created.

These are small areas of inner cities. The enterprise zones form 'tax free' islands within cities. These are very small areas with an average size of only 150 hectares. Firms setting up in

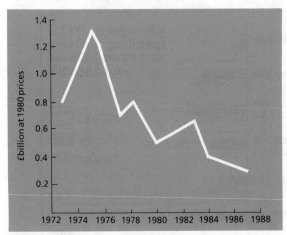

Fig. 13.2 *Expenditure by DTI on regional assistance –
constant prices*

enterprise zones were given a stream of incentives: no rates; 100 per cent capital allowances on all commercial and industrial property; no liability for development land tax; and generally less bureaucracy and fewer planning regulations.

During the 1980s the Department of the Environment created a number of Urban Development Corporations. These virtually independent bodies have freedom from many planning constraints together with tax privileges. The most famous of these is the Docklands Development Corporation which is associated with the 'yuppiefication' of London's docklands.

In March 1988 Margaret Thatcher launched Action for Cities. This was aimed at coordinating government policy on the inner cities and at encouraging private investment.

b) Legislative controls. The government can influence the location of industry by the negative method of forbidding or discouraging new building where it does not want it. Between 1947 and 1974 successive governments created a whole series of legislative controls designed to encourage firms to move to SDAs and DAs. The controls required all new industrial or office developments to first obtain Industrial Development Certificates. However in December 1981 the government suspended the regulations. This was done partly because of the government's desire to reduce the role of government

intervention in the economy and partly due to the need to facilitate development of all kinds in an effort to alleviate unemployment.

c) Direct intervention. The government can place orders for goods and services in development areas or encourage nationalised industries to do so. In addition to this it could decentralise government departments such as it did when the Inland Revenue administration was moved to Middlesbrough. The Distribution of Industry Acts of 1945 and 1950 allowed the government to build factories in development areas and lease or sell them.

The New Towns Act 1946 and the Town Development Act 1952 brought a number of new towns into existence, the first of which was Stevenage in Hertfordshire. In August 1981 the government decided to curtail the activities of new towns and eight of the New Town Corporations had to dispose of £140m of their assets.

d) Persuasion. By advertising and information, firms may be persuaded to locate in the regions. This policy is followed through both centrally and locally. The Local Employment Act of 1960 set up development councils in depressed regions. However in 1965 the whole of the UK was covered by 11 regional economic planning councils. Each of these is responsible for devising an economic strategy for its region and for publicising opportunities in the region. Adverts placed by regional planning councils and by New Town Corporations are a familiar sight in UK newspapers. The DTI provides information and advice both from its headquarters in London and from its regional offices.

As assessment of regional policy is included in Chapter 43.

Concentration of firms and industry

Location and localisation

Having examined the factors which influence the location of an industry we can turn to the measurement of the degree to which industries are localised. This is measured by *location quotients* (LQs). There are two such LQs.

a) *The specialisation LQ.* This measures the extent to which a particular region specialises in a particular industry, compared with the average specialisation for the whole nation. This is calculated as:

Specialisation LQ =

$$\frac{\text{Percentage of region X's workforce in industry Y}}{\text{Proportion of nation's workforce in industry Y}}$$

If, for example, region X is Wales and industry Y is agriculture and 4 per cent of the nation's workforce is employed in farming but 12 per cent in Wales, we arrive at:

$$\text{Specialisation LQ} = \frac{12}{4} = 3$$

In this example it means that Wales is more specialised in agriculture when compared with the country as a whole.

b) *The concentration LQ.* This measures the extent to which a particular industry is concentrated in a region compared with the proportion of all industry there. This is calculated as:

Concentration LQ =

$$\frac{\text{Proportion of industry X in region Y}}{\text{Proportion of the nation's industry in region Y}}$$

If for example, industry X is agriculture and region Y is Wales, we may obtain the following calculation:

$$\text{Concentration LQ} = \frac{28}{8} = 3 \cdot 5$$

The concentration and specialisation LQ will tend to be similar, as shown in the examples used above. Location quotients also tend to be similar for the same industries in different countries provided that the countries are at a similar stage of economic development.

Professor Sargant Florence and A. J. Wensley introduced a measure termed the *coefficient of localisation*. This measures the extent to which an industry is regionally over-concentrated. If an industry is spread absolutely evenly then the coefficient would be 0 per cent, whereas the maximum possible concentration would be 100 per cent.

The more closely we define a particular industry, the greater the location quotient or coefficient is likely to be. If, for example, we measured the coefficient of the whole engineering industry we would find that it is very low, because the industry is widespread. However if we considered a particular branch of engineering, such as steel tube fabrication, we would find it had much greater localisation.

The aggregate concentration ratio

This measures the concentration of ownership in an industry. The usual method is to take the 100 largest firms in an industry and measure the percentage of output which they account for. Thus, for example, in 1988 the 100 largest firms in manufacturing accounted for 43 per cent of output (the concentration of ownership in the UK is least in the timber and furniture industries).

Concentration is very high in the UK compared with other countries such as the USA and West Germany. Concentration of ownership, however, may not be mirrored in plant size, i.e. a monopolistic firm may nonetheless produce in small uneconomic plants.

The market concentration ratio

If we turn to look at the market for particular products this can be measured by the *five-firm market concentration* ratio. This measures the share of the market enjoyed by the five largest firms. In many UK markets such as detergents and motor vehicles, the five largest firms account for more than 90 per cent of the market. The ratios are higher in the UK than in all comparable economies. (If need not necessarily be the five-firm ratio – it could, for example, be three, four or six etc. In fact eight is often used.)

It is thus apparent that the structure of UK industry is extremely monopolistic. It is argued, however, that this is mitigated by competition from imports. This is certainly true of some **171** industries such as motor vehicles where, despite the concentration of ownership, foreign firms have been able to take over and dominate the UK market. In many other industries though, such as brewing, the nature of the industry effectively prevents import penetration.

It could be argued that in many industries monopoly control lulled firms into a false sense of security and protected inefficiency, thus making them highly vulnerable to import penetration. This is well illustrated by such industries as motor cycles, electrical goods, footwear and electronics.

Despite the enormous concentration of ownership in UK industry, the average size of plant remains small. The reason for this is that many large firms have been formed by takeovers and mergers, leaving the original structure of production unchanged.

Mergers and takeovers

Firms can become larger by:

a) *internal growth*, i.e. the acquisition of new plant, etc.;

b) *mergers*, where two firms agree to join together – this will probably involve the setting up of a *holding company* to control the organisation;

c) *takeovers*, where one firm buys out another.

Reasons for mergers and takeovers

a) *Economies of scale*. It is argued that the growth in size should lead to economies of scale. For this to happen the new business must be reorganised, otherwise the resultant situation may be less efficient than when the firms were separate (*see* full discussion of economies of scale, page 28).

b) *Market domination*. One of the most frequent motives for mergers is simply to dominate the market and thus be able to reap the advantages of monopoly power.

c) *Stability*. A merger may give the new firm stability within its markets and in its sources of supply.

d) *Diversification*. We usually associate mergers with integration and economies of scale, but many mergers have taken place to diversify a firm's interests, thus spreading its risks. BAT (British American Tobacco) has diversified into hotels, frozen foods and many other lines to protect itself against the risk of a decline in tobacco sales. A firm with interests in many different industries is known as a *conglomerate*.

e) *Asset stripping*. This occurs when a company is taken over with the object of closing all or part of it down so that its assets may be realised. This can occur when a company's real assets (land, capital equipment, etc.) have a greater value than its stock market valuation. Asset stripping has often been criticised, especially when a going concern has been closed down. In strict economic terms, however, asset stripping amounts to a more productive use of resources.

Vertical and horizontal integration

Vertical integration occurs when a firm expands *backwards* towards its sources of supply or *forwards* towards its markets. For example, an oil company which bought oil wells would be indulging in backwards integration, while if it purchased filling stations this would be forwards integration.

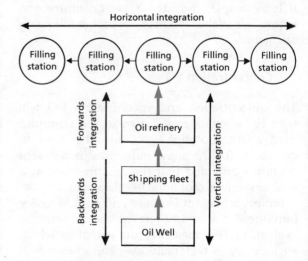

Fig. 13.3 *Vertical and horizontal integration*

Horizontal integration occurs when a firm takes over firms at a similar stage of production. For example, if an oil company which already owned a string of petrol stations were to take over another competitive chain, this would be horizontal integration. One of the most famous horizontal mergers in postwar years was that of the British Motor Company and Leyland Motors to create British Leyland (now Rover Group).

It is possible for a firm to undertake both horizontal and vertical integration. Figure 13.3 illustrates the case of an oil company which is vertically integrated from its ownership of oil wells to its control of filling stations and is horizontally integrated by controlling several chains of filling stations.

The continuance of the small business

Having examined the trend towards concentration in UK industry, we should remember that there are over 620 000 registered companies in the UK today, in addition to which there are several hundred thousand partnerships and sole traders. However, as we have seen, 43 per cent of total sales in the country are accounted for by the top 100 companies. Undoubtedly one of the reasons for this domination by large companies is economies of scale. It should be remembered, however, that many of these companies are conglomerates and may not therefore always be benefiting from economies of scale in the conventional sense. Nevertheless, despite a percentage decline in their importance in recent years, small businesses continue. This may be because there are only limited economies of scale to be gained in industries such as agriculture and plumbing, although small businesses also survive in industries where returns to scale are considerable. Some of the reasons for this are listed below.

a) 'Being one's own boss'. Entrepreneurs may accept smaller profit for the social prestige of working for themselves or the possibility of making a profit in the future.

b) *Immobility in factor markets*. Labour and other factors may be unwilling or unable to move from one occupation or area to another: for example, agricultural workers are often kept in their jobs by 'tied cottages'.

c) *Goodwill*. A small business may survive on a fund of goodwill where its customers might tolerate higher prices for a more personal service.

d) *Banding together*. Independent businesses may band together to gain the advantages of bulk-buying while still retaining their independence. This is so in the UK grocery chains such as Spar and Wavy-Line.

e) *Specialist services or products*. Businesses may provide small specialist services or products, e.g. many small car manufacturers exist making specialist sports cars.

f) *Subcontracting*. Many small businesses survive by subcontracting to larger firms. This is prevalent in the construction industry.

g) *Monopoly*. A large organisation may tolerate the existence of small businesses in an industry as a cloak for its own monopolistic practices.

Professor Galbraith in his book *Economics and the Public Purpose* suggests two more reasons. Firstly, he says: 'There are limits to the toil that can be demanded in the large firm, but the small businessman is at liberty to exploit himself and in this role he can be a severe taskmaster.' He goes on to suggest that some industries are particularly suited to this kind of discipline which 'rewards diligence and punishes sloth' and he singles out agriculture, suggesting that this is one reason why it adapts badly to socialism. The second reason he gives is that as society fulfils its more fundamental economic needs, people begin to demand aesthetic satisfaction from products, thus creating a role for the artist in the economic process.

Summary

1 The firm is the unit of ownership and control in industry. All businesses seek to maximise their profits.

2 The three main types of business are sole traders, partnerships and joint stock companies. Sole traders are the most numerous but public limited companies account for 80 per-cent of all business.

3 Location of industry is influenced by spontaneous factors such as markets and communications as well as by government policy.

4 The localisation of industry can be measured by location quotients and the concentration of ownership by concentration ratios. While localisation in the UK is similar to that in other countries, the concentration of ownership is significantly higher.

5 Takeovers and mergers are common in the UK but do not always result in economies of scale. Often they are for the purpose of monopolising the market.

6 Despite the concentration of ownership, many small businesses survive.

Questions

1 Account for the continued existence of so many small firms.

2 What are the advantages and disadvantages of sole proprietorship as a method of owning and running a business?

3 Examine and evaluate the factors which would influence a firm in the choice of a new site.

4 How could the geographical and monopolistic concentration in an industry be explained?

5 For what reason do mergers and takeovers take place? Are these in the public interest?

6 Account for the fact that despite concentration of ownership in UK industry, the average size of plant remains small.

7 Evaluate the success of government regional policy.

Data Response   The North-South Divide

Study the information in Fig. 13.4, which is taken from the *Guardian* newspaper 4 December 1987.

Answer the following questions.

1 Explain the way in which median pay rates differ from average (mean) rates.

2 For what reasons are the earnings of men higher than the earnings of women?

3 To what extent are the observed regional variations in pay a reflection of differing rates of unemployment?

4 Does regional migration tend to increase or decrease regional differences in pay?

North-South earnings gap continues to widen

By Christopher Huhne,
Economics Editor

The gap in earnings between the South-east and the rest of the country has continued to widen but most of the advantage has gone to the better off, according to the Department of Employment's annual New Earnings Survey.

The survey, the fifth and final part of which was published yesterday, shows that the discrepancy in pay is particularly marked in London where the rise in average earnings between April 1986 and April 1987 was 9.1 per cent while the average rise for the whole country (including London) was 7.7 per cent.

The rise in retail prices over the same period was 4.2 per cent, giving a real increase of 4.7 per cent in London compared with 3.4 per cent for the rest.

In a statement yesterday, the Low Pay Unit pointed out that the gap in average earnings between London and the rest of the country was now £60 and that this "pay gulf" had doubled since 1979.

The rise in average earnings between 1979 and 1987 in London was 143 per cent and 135 per cent for the whole of the South-east (including London). The lowest increase was 109 per cent in the North and the next highest after the South-east was 125 per cent in the South-west, the LPU said.

The rise in retail prices over the same period was 87.5 per cent, so that the rise in real earnings varied from 29.6 per cent in London to 11.4 per cent in the North.

However, the picture of pros-

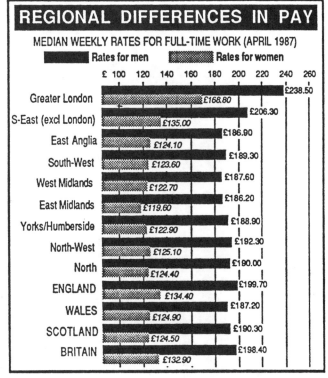

perity being concentrated in the South-east is too simple, since the cost of living has probably risen more rapidly there and the benefits of sharply rising gross earnings have been very unequal.

The gap between London and the rest is particularly pronounced at the top end of the income scale and least significant at the bottom. The highest paid 10 per cent of male Londoners earned £453.20 a week, nearly 30 per cent above the average for the highest paid 10 per cent of all Britons.

But the worst paid male Londoners in the bottom 10 per cent earned £136.9 a week, just 16 per cent above the worst paid Britons on average. It is the spectacular rewards paid to well-off Londoners that drag up the London average (mean). The gulf shown by the medians — the pay earned by someone half way between the top and bottom — is less.

London and therefore the South-east has traditionally had a higher share of the well-paid and they have been doing very well everywhere.

Fig. 13.4 *Regional differences in pay*

5   Evaluate the argument that the best way to encourage development in the regions is to cut wages in areas of high unemployment.

6   Comment on the statement that, 'Londoners are better-off than people in other parts of the UK.'

14

Competition and profits

Thou shalt not covet, but tradition
Approves all forms of competition.
  Arthur Hugh Clough, *The Latest Decalogue*

Supply

Earlier in this Part of the book we gave consider-able attention to the theory of demand. We must now turn to the other side of the market, that is to say to supply.

This part of economics is sometimes called the *theory of the firm*. The firm is the unit of supply, so that if we are able to explain the behaviour of one firm we may explain the behaviour of market supply by aggregating all firms' supply. In the same way that the market demand curve is a horizontal summation of individual demand curves, so market supply is the horizontal summation of firms' supply curves.

In Fig. 14.1 we envisage a market which is

supplied by two firms, A and B. At a price of £4 per unit firm A supplies 60 units and firm B 80 units, whereas at a price of £2 firm A would supply 20 units and firm B 30 units. If we total the amount supplied at each price we obtain the market supply, i.e. 140 units at £4 and 50 units at £2.

Profit maximisation

One of the basic assumptions on which the whole theory of business behaviour is based is that firms will seek to maximise their profits. We will first consider this and then some alternatives.

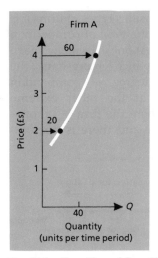 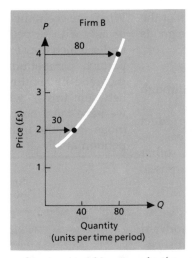 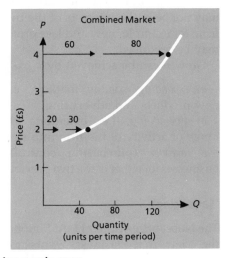

Fig. 14.1 *Firm A's and firm B's supply curves combine to make the market supply curve*

The profit maximisation hypothesis

We assume that the firm attempts to maximise its profits, i.e. it not only attempts to make a profit but attempts to make the last penny of profit possible. Although we are going to suggest some modifications to this view, no other overall explanation of the behaviour of firms has been put forward. Thus we will find that whatever type of competition we consider, profit maximisation is a unifying principle.

Market domination

This may be pursued for the purposes of profit maximisation, but this need not be so – domination of a market may also give *stability* and *security* to the firm, which might be viewed by the managers as more attractive than profit maximisation. Pursuit of market domination may lead a business to pursue a policy of *sales maximisation*. For example, a business might cut prices and accept losses for a time, with the object of driving its rivals out of business. Having achieved this it could then exploit the market.

Corporate growth

Growth means increasing power and responsibility for managers, often reflected in higher salaries. Hence growth may be achieved at the expense of profit maximisation and therefore may not be in the interests of the owners of the firm; for example, new and less profitable goods may be produced.

Growth can be achieved by:

a) expanding existing markets, e.g. through new products and advertising;

b) diversifying, i.e. extending the product range or activity of the firm into new areas;

c) takeover (purchasing control) of other businesses for either of the two previous purposes.

'Satisficing'

The Nobel prize-winner H. A. Simon put forward the view that business wants to 'satisfice', i.e. achieve certain targets for sales profits and market share which may not coincide with profit maximisation but may rather inflate boardroom egos. This can usually occur when there is a divorce between the ownership and control of a company – when the company is run by professional managers rather than entrepreneurs. Providing that *sufficient* profit is made, managers may, for example, seek to expand their right to exercise personal discretion and to obtain 'perks' such as company cars. To achieve this objective part of the organisation's profit, which could be paid out to shareholders, must be diverted and used to pay for such managerial satisfaction. Since managerial satisfaction pushes up the cost of production, and hence the price charged, it is usually associated with firms which do not operate in highly competitive industries.

It should be stated that these latter three objectives are of a controversial nature and are not accepted by all observers of firms. It is argued by some that they can all be incorporated into the single objective of profit maximisation, while others go so far as to say that, although attractive, the ideas have little or no evidence to support them. (*See* also pages 74–75.)

Types of competition

When the economist classifies types of firms it is usually with respect to the type of competition under which they exist. At one extreme we have perfect competition, which represents the theoretically optimal degree of competition between firms, while at the other extreme we have monopoly, where the firm is synonymous with the industry and there is no competition at all.

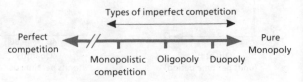

Fig. 14.2 *Types of competition*

Figure 14.2 gives a diagrammatic representation of the possibilities. We have inserted a gap in the line between perfect competition and all other types since perfect competition is only a theoretical possibility.

Perfect competition

For a state of perfect competition to exist in an industry the following conditions have to exist.

a) A large number of buyers and sellers of the commodity, so that no one firm can affect the market price through its own actions.

b) Freedom of entry and exit to the market for both buyers and sellers. The importance of this condition to the theory cannot be stressed too highly.

c) Homogeneity of product, i.e. all goods being sold have to be identical.

d) Perfect knowledge of the market on the part both of the buyers and sellers.

e) It must be possible to buy or sell any amount of the commodity at the market price.

It is obvious that all these conditions cannot exist in one market at once. There are, however, close approximations to perfect competition, e.g. the sale of wheat on the commodity market in Canada. In this situation there are thousands of sellers and ultimately millions of buyers and it is relatively easy for farmers to enter or leave the market by switching crops; as far as homogeneity is concerned, once graded, one tonne of wheat is regarded as identical with another. In addition to this, when wheat is sold on the commodity market both sides have a good knowledge of the market and it appears to the farmers that they can sell all they want at the market price even though, individually, a farmer is unable to influence it. The perfection of the market is, however, flawed by farmers banding together in cooperatives to control the supply, by widespread government intervention in agriculture and by some very large buyers in the market. For instance, in recent years the USSR has bought millions of tonnes of wheat on the North American market to make good the shortcomings in its own domestic output.

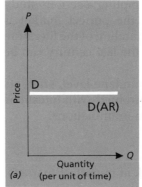 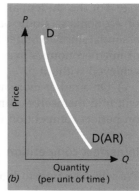

Fig. 14.3 *The demand curve under perfect competition* (*a*) **The demand curve for the individual firm's product.** (*b*) **The industry demand curve. Note: in the theory of the firm the demand curve is usually labelled AR (average revenue).**

If there were perfect competition the individual firm would *appear* to face a horizontal demand curve for its product. If it raised the price of its product it would no longer be on the demand curve and would sell nothing. Conversely, it would have no incentive to lower its prices since it appears to be able to sell any amount it likes at the market price. The organisation is thus a *price taker* and its only decision, therefore, is how much to produce (see Fig. 14.3). The price may of course change from day to day, as it does in the case of wheat, but to the farmer the demand curve always appear horizontal. The industry demand curve will remain a normal downward sloping one; indeed the world demand curve for wheat is fairly inelastic, large changes in price bringing only relatively small changes in demand.

Why study perfect competition?

If perfect competition is purely a theoretical state, the student may legitimately ask why we study it. To this we could make answer on three grounds.

a) It represents the ideal functioning of the free market system. Thus, although we cannot eliminate all imperfections in the market, we may try to minimise them, as the engineer attempts to minimise friction in the engine.

b) For the student attempting a serious study of economics, study of the perfect market is essential since no understanding of the literature of microeconomics over the last century can be achieved without it.

c) On a rather more mundane level, students will find themselves confronted with questions on perfect competition in examinations!

Imperfect competition

We will now turn to look at imperfect markets. All markets are to a greater or lesser extent imperfect. This is not an ethical judgment on the organisations which make up the markets. There is nothing morally reprehensible about being an imperfect competitor; indeed this is the 'normal' state of affairs. It could be the case, however, that firms contrive imperfections with the object of maximising their profits to the detriment of the consumer.

All imperfect competitors share the character-istic that the demand curve for their individual firm's product slopes downward, i.e. if the firm raises its prices it will not lose all its customers as it would under perfect competition. Conversely, it can sell more of the product by lowering its prices. In addition to this it can be affected by the action of its competitors. In Fig. 14.4, for example, the decrease in demand DD to D_1D_1 could have been brought about by a competitor lowering prices. If, for example, Ford were to drop the prices of their cars by 5 per cent it would probably bring about a substantial decrease in demand for Rover Group cars. This would not be so in the case of perfect competition. If, for example, Farmer Jones were to cut the price of wheat by 5 per cent it would scarcely affect the sales of the thousands of other farmers who make up the market.

It is possible to distinguish several types of imperfect competition. These distinctions rise chiefly out of different numbers of firms which make up any particular industry and the consequent differences in market behaviour in the short-run and the long-run.

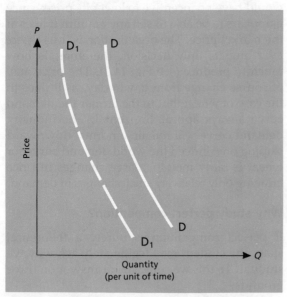

Fig. 14.4 *The demand curve for an individual firm's product under imperfect competition*
The firm has some choice over price and output, but can also be affected by competitors. The decrease in demand from DD to D_1D_1 could have been brought about by a fall in the price of a competitor's product.

Monopoly

This, literally, means a situation where there is only one seller of a commodity. This is the case in the UK with Tate and Lyle, who have a virtual monopoly of cane sugar, and Joseph Lucas with an almost complete monopoly of certain electrical components for cars. Legally speaking an organisation may be treated as a monopoly under the Fair Trading Act 1973 if it has more than 25 per cent of the market.

There are, of course, state monopolies in the UK, such as British Coal. Since, however, their economic behaviour is not usually governed by the profit-making hypothesis their behaviour is not discussed here (*see* Chapter 19).

Duopoly

Duopoly is a situation where there are only two suppliers of a commodity. In behaviour they may be classed as oligopolists and therefore do not form part of a separate analysis in this section of the book.

Oligopoly

This word, like monopoly, is derived from the Greek and means a situation where there are only a few sellers of a commodity. There are several industries in the UK dominated by a few large firms, e.g. the production of detergent is almost entirely divided between Procter & Gamble and Unilever. In some cases these firms might legally be described as monopolists rather than oligopolists.

Oligopolists might produce virtually identical products and compete with each other through prices. It is more common, however, for them to compete through advertising and *product differentiation*. In the case of detergents, for example, although the products are basically similar, there is a proliferation of brands and heavy advertising but very little price competition.

Monopolistic competition

When there are a large number of sellers producing a similar but differentiated product, then a state of monopolistic competition is said to exist. This might be the case in the supply of a commodity like shirts where essentially similar items are supplied by many different firms at widely differing prices and with a lot of product differentiation by way of colour, style and materials. Such an industry is also characterised by the frequent entry and exit of firms.

It is called monopolistic competition because, due to imperfections in the market, each organisation has a small degree of monopoly power. If, for example, Double 2 shirts can convince the public that their shirts are better than those of their competitors, then they have, as it were, created a small monopoly for their own product. The *branding* of goods is an attempt to break the *chain of substitution* by which one commodity can be substituted for another. When a consumer enters a shop and asks by brand name for a bar

Table 14.1 Different market forms

Type of competition	Number of producers and degree of product differentiation	Which industries?	Influence of the firm over prices	Marketing methods
Perfect competition	Many producers, identical products	Some agricultural products Stock exchange	None	Commodity exchanges or auctions
Imperfect competition:				
Monopoly	Single producer, no close substitutes	Electrical car components Cane sugar	Considerable	Promotional and public relations advertising
Oligopoly	Few producers with product differentiation	Detergents Cars	Considerable	Advertising Quality rivalry Administered prices
Monopolistic competition	Many producers, product differentiation	Clothing Furniture	Little	Advertising Quality and design differences Often intense price rivalry

181

of chocolate, a shirt or a tube of toothpaste, then the manufacturers have succeeded in their designs and may be able to reap the reward of their monopoly. Some advertising and branding is so successful that people use brand names without realising it, e.g. Thermos, Hoover and Vaseline. The various types of competition are summarised in Table 14.1.

It is paradoxical that under perfect competition very little competition is visible since there is no advertising and promotion of products, whereas under all types of imperfect competition rivalry between firms is only too obvious. Even monopolies advertise. Tate and Lyle, for example, not only promote their product but extol the virtues of free competition. It is a case, as Professor Galbraith wrote in *The Affluent Society*, of competition being advocated 'by those who have most successfully eliminated it'!

Profits

Normal and abnormal profits

At its simplest, profits are the difference between total revenue (*TR*) and total cost (*TC*). However, economists have a concept of *normal profit*:

Normal profit is the minimum amount of profit which is necessary to keep the firm in the industry.

It is obvious that the firm must pay for the labour it uses, pay rent for its site and pay for the capital it uses. In addition to this the entrepreneurs must be rewarded or they will not consider it worthwhile producing the product. We may thus regard some profit as a legitimate cost of the business. We therefore include this in the costs of the business; this is because if profits fall below a certain level the entrepreneur will no longer consider it worthwhile producing the good. Any profit in excess of this is termed *abnormal profit* (sometimes, excess or monopoly profit). When there is freedom of entry to the industry, as in perfect competition or mono-

polistic competition, any abnormal profit will attract new entrepreneurs into the industry. However with monopoly or oligopoly, barriers to entry exist and this abnormal profit may persist.

The concept of normal profit is an essential tool in explaining the behaviour of a firm. What the normal level of profit is may vary both from industry to industry and between firms within an industry. This may partly be explained by the concept of *opportunity cost*. For example, the level of profit which may be considered minimal for a garage in London may be different from that in Scotland where other alternatives may not be available. Despite this, no fully satisfactory explanation exists as to why the level of normal profit differs greatly from industry to industry.

Implicit and explicit costs

In arriving at a calculation of profit a firm needs to consider both explicit and implicit costs. Explicit costs are those which the firm is *contracted* to pay, such as wages, rates, electricity, etc. Implicit costs may occur when a firm *owns* some of the resources it is using. For example, suppose a firm owns the site on which it operates; the economist would argue that in addition to its wages bill, its electricity bill, etc., the firm should pay itself the market rent for the site, otherwise it is making an uneconomic use of its resources because it is conceivable that it could do better by closing down and renting the site to someone else. We are thus once again speaking of the concept of *opportunity cost*.

An example may make the point clearer. Some years ago Lyons had 'Corner House' cafés on many of the most prominent sites in London. These appeared to be making a profit. However Lyons discovered that if they were to close the cafés, dispose of the sites and invest the money gained they could make more than their present level of profit. They had been ignoring the implicit costs of their business. Having considered these costs they decided to sell-off many of these sites and London lost some of its most familiar landmarks.

Summary

1   The theory of the firm is the basis of the theory of supply, since if we are able to explain the behaviour of the firm we can then explain the operation of industry supply.

2   The theory of the firm is based upon the profit maximisation hypothesis. There are alternative explanations, such as satisficing, but none of these are completely satisfactory.

3   Perfect competition represents the ideal functioning of the market system. The two most important conditions of perfect competition are that:
   a) no individual buyer or seller can influence market price;
   b) there is freedom of entry and exit to the industry.

4   The main types of imperfect competition are monopoly, oligopoly and monopolistic competition. All firms operating under these conditions have some control over the market price.

5   Normal profit is the minimum amount of profit which is necessary to keep a firm in an industry.

Questions

1   Contrast perfect competition and monopoly as market forms.

2   In a perfectly competitive economy firms and industries are supposed to be price takers not price setters. Does this apply to you in your everyday economic dealings? How would your answer differ if you were:
   a) a business person;
   b) a member of a powerful trade union.

3   Evaluate the profit maximisation hypothesis.

4   If the government imposes a price ceiling on a product (*see* page 143) does that make the firms that sell the product price takers, regardless of whether or not they are perfect competitors? Give reasons for your answer.

5   List five products you have bought in the last week. Assuming that they were not bought from perfect competitors how did the supplier compete for your business with other rival suppliers?

6   Explain what is meant by implicit and explicit costs. How is it possible for a firm to be making an accounting 'profit' but an economic loss?

Data response   The Monopolies and Mergers Commission

Read carefully the article (on page 184) by John Kay which is taken from the *Daily Telegraph*, 7 September 1987, which is concerned with the appointment of the new chairman of the Monopolies and Mergers Commission (MMC).

Answer the following questions:

1   Name three recent cases in which the MMC has been involved. Were the MMC's findings consistent in each case?

2   Why is a monopolies commission necessary?

3   On what grounds does the MMC intervene in mergers or proposed mergers?

Playing the game with monopolies

NEXT YEAR, a businessman, Sydney Lipworth, is to take over from the more traditional judicial figure as chairman of the Monopolies and Mergers Commission.

At the same time, the Government is due to complete its own review of the future of competition policy. What, indeed, should its future be?

Anti-trust has always been a much more serious issue in the United States than here. American legislation is grounded in populist mistrust of the century-old machinations of the Rockefellers and Vanderbilts.

To possess a monopoly is to break the law and, in priniciple at least, it is no defence to demonstrate that the monopoly is the result of better products or lower costs.

The reality is somewhat less harsh, of course. But in living memory, American businessmen have been sent to prison for illegal price-fixing.

More recently, the major transatlantic airlines paid substantial sums to Laker Airways' creditors to escape court proceedings for alleged predatory activities aimed at grounding the buccaneering would-be airline tycoon.

In the last decade, however, the wings of American anti-trust enforcers have been trimmed—more as a result of the analysis of lawyers and economists than from pressure from business.

Robert Bork, whose controversial nomination to the Supreme Court is now before the Senate, has been prominent among these critics. Mr Bork's influential book is titled The Anti-Trust Paradox, and carries the subtitle of A Policy At War With Itself.

The British tradition has always been more pragmatic. There is no general legal presumption that actions which restrict competition are wrong.

Everything is to be assessed for consistency with the public interest, and there is remarkably little guidance as to what that is. People as eminent as Mr Lipworth or Sir Geoffrey le Quesne are assumed to be able to recognise it when they see it.

But they have not always found it easy. In the early 1980s, the commission found itself steadily running out of friends—in government, in the business community, or among its academic or legal critics. It suffered particularly from a series of problematic merger references.

When Standard Chartered and the Hong Kong & Shanghai Banks both attempted to take over the Royal Bank of Scotland, the commission was assailed by the Bank of England, which was determined that the management of British monetary policy should not be directed from Hong Kong, and by a Scottish lobby, who wanted it to be controlled from Edinburgh.

Then the commission was dragged into Tiny Rowland's long-running battle with House of Fraser.

And it was also used to save Sotheby's from rape by an unwelcome American suitor.

This happened not because the commission found the bid was against the public interest—it did not—but because the time taken considering its implications enabled Sotheby's to find a more congenial marriage partner.

When Charter Consolidated attempted to buy Anderson Strathclyde—another Scottish-based company—the commission itself disagreed over who would make the better job of managing it. The Government then intervened to overturn the majority recommendation and allowed the bid to go ahead, and to succeed.

The resulting storm led to the "Tebbit guidelines", which proposed that references to the Monopolies and Mergers Commission were to be based primarily on competition grounds.

Guinness's now notorious takeover for Distillers escaped reference because they agreed to sell sufficient of Distillers whisky interests to avoid significant effects on competition in the whisky market.

But this exclusive emphasis on competition itself became the subject of criticism when Paul Channon decided that since BTR and Pilkington did not compete with each other, there was no need for the commission to consider the proposed acquisition.

Competition policy is concerned with some practices which are so unlikely to be of public benefit that firms should simply be deterred from engaging in them—and the Americans are right to see that civil and even criminal penalties do this more effectively than the threat that, after prolonged inquiry, you will be told to stop.

Examples are predatory actions to put competitors out of business, or to discourage them from coming in, or agreements to fix prices.

There are others, where a process of balancing advantages and disadvantages is inevitable - the tied house system in brewing, which the commission is currently considering, is a good example of a system which inhibits competition but might have countervailing benefits.

And what of questions that raise real matters of public interest but none of competition - like BTR's absolute attempt bid for Pilkington, or the Australian attempt to acquire Allied-Lyons, the beer to teabags conglomerate, on the basis of a mountain of debt?

In the main, these issues would seem better left to the market to decide. It may not always get them right but, at least, it has to finance its own decisions and face the consequences. Better that than the adjudication of Mr Lipworth and his estimate colleagues.

John Kay

Professor of Industrial Policy at the London Business School

---

4 What advantages (if any) may monopolies confer on the consumer?
5 What means does the author support for the regulation of monopolies?
6 What was the main thrust of the 'Tebbit guidelines'?
7 How could the MMC carry out a process of 'balancing advantages and disadvantages'?
8 What alternative arrangements could be used to regulate monopolies?

15

Costs in the short-run and the long-run

Cost of production would have no effect on competitive price if it could have none on supply.

John Stuart Mill

We have seen that there are different kinds of competition, but no matter what market conditions a firm operates under its cost structures will be similar. Thus the cost structures which we investigate in this chapter apply to all types of competition, from perfect competition to monopoly.

Imperfections of competition may affect the cost structure in two ways. Firstly, monopolisation of a market may make economies of scale available to the firm which are not available to competitive firms. Secondly, the opposite may also be true, i.e. monopoly may protect inefficient cost structures. We will consider these possibilities in Chapter 18.

It is convenient to split up the costs of the business organisation in various ways because this allows us to understand its behaviour more fully. The firm itself will analyse its own cost structures in order to try and improve its performance.

We will consider costs under three main headings: *total costs*; *average costs*; and *marginal costs*.

Total costs (*TC*)

Total cost (*TC*) is the cost of all the resources necessary to produce any particular level of output.

Total cost *always rises with output*. This is because

obtaining more output must always require more input. Thus no matter what the scale of production, obtaining another unit of output must involve the input of some raw materials, no matter how small the amount, so that a greater output must always involve a greater total cost.

We can obtain a better understanding of total cost by splitting it into its two main components, fixed costs and variable costs.

Fixed costs (*FC*)

Fixed costs (*FC*) are those costs which do not alter with output in the short-run. They may also be termed indirect costs.

Fixed costs usually comprise such things as buildings and machinery. These costs will go on (and *remain constant*) whether the business is producing as much as possible or nothing at all. If a business wishes to expand beyond the capacity of its present fixed costs, then it must build or acquire new premises, capital, equipment, etc. The period of time necessary for it to do this is said to be the *long-run* period.

Variable costs (*VC*)

As a firm produces more output, so it needs more labour, raw materials, power, etc. The cost of these factors which *vary with output* is termed *variable* or *direct costs*.

Variable costs (*VC*) are those which vary with output. Variable costs are zero when output is zero and rise directly with output.

Thus, total cost comprises *fixed costs* and *variable costs*. This we can state as:

$$TC = FC + VC$$

This is illustrated in Table 15.1, where you can see that whatever the level of output, fixed costs remain constant at £116 per week. If there is no output there is no variable cost, but as output increases, so do variable costs. (Students can test their understanding of the concepts by filling in the blanks. The answers may be checked with Table 15.2.)

Table 15.1 Total costs, fixed costs and variable costs

Output, units per week, Q	Total cost, TC (£)	Fixed cost, FC (£)	Variable cost, VC (£)
0	116	116	0
1	140	116	24
2	160	116	44
3			60
4	200	116	
5	240	116	124
6	296	116	180
7			252
8	456	116	

The figures in Table 15.1 are illustrated in Fig. 15.1. Here you can see that fixed costs are constant whatever the level of ouput in the short-run. Variable costs are zero when output is zero and rise with output. The total cost curve is obtained by aggregating the *FC* and *VC* curves.

Why does the variable cost curve (and thus the total cost curve) begin to rise more rapidly at higher levels of output? The reason for this is that after a certain output, the business has passed its most efficient use of its fixed costs (buildings, etc.) and *diminishing returns* begins to set in.

Figure 15.2 illustrates the effect of a change in
186 fixed cost in the long-run. As plant size is

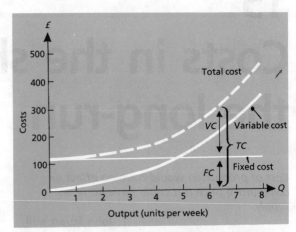

Fig. 15.1 *Total cost is fixed costs plus variable costs*

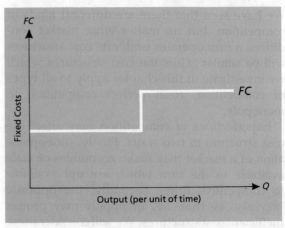

Fig. 15.2 *Fixed costs in the long-run*
The increase in fixed cost as the firm expands its capacity in the long-run causes a 'kink' in the curve.

expanded, this causes a shift from one level of total cost to another. Thus:

In the long-run all costs are variable.

Digression 1: the short-run and the long-run

We have already defined the short-run and long-run, but it is useful here to restate the definitions in terms of the costs of the firm (*see* also pages 31 and pages 134–35).

The short-run may be defined as the period during which output may be varied within the limits of the present fixed costs. It is not possible for new firms to enter the industry or for existing firms to leave it.

The long-run may be defined as the period in which all costs are variable and new firms may enter the industry or existing firms leave it.

The short-run and the long-run are *periods of supply* and refer to the ability of the business to vary its behaviour within the market. They are *not* chronological periods of time, e.g. we *cannot* say the short-run period is, say, six months.

How long the supply period is will depend upon the industry. In the motor vehicle industry, for example, it may take a very long time, e.g. 5–10 years for the business to vary its fixed costs, i.e. build a new factory or re-equip an existing one, while in the retail trade it may be possible for a business to acquire new premises in a relatively short time, e.g. six months.

Throughout most of this chapter we shall be concerned with the behaviour of costs and of businesses in the *short-run*; we will consider later how their behaviour might be modified in the *long-run*. Therefore, unless it is clearly stated otherwise, you may assume that we are talking about the short-run.

Digression 2: short-run shut-down conditions

Suppose that a business is running at a loss. Obviously in the long-run it will go out of business, but what is the best policy in the short-run? Will it make a smaller loss if it stays open so long as there is still some money coming in, or is it best to close down immediately?

The answer to this conundrum lies in the *variable costs*. So long as the revenue the business is getting in is greater than the variable cost, it is worth its while staying open in the short-run because it will make a smaller loss than it would do by closing immediately. However if the revenue it is earning from selling its product is less than its variable cost, then it will make a smaller loss by closing immediately.

Ultimately, though, in the long-run all costs must be covered if the business is to remain in the industry.

Let us consider the case of an apple grower. The cost of planting the trees and of renting the land could be regarded as fixed costs, since the farmer can only shed them by going out of business. Other costs, such as harvesting the crop and transporting it to the market, will vary with output and can therefore be described as variable costs. This being the case, it is apparent that if the price of apples were low the apple grower could not recover all the costs, but would still continue to sell apples in the short-run if variable costs could be covered. In other words, if the money from the sale is greater than the costs of picking and selling the apples, it would appear that in the short-run the grower will produce and ignore fixed costs.

Conversely, if the cost of harvesting, transport etc., were greater than sales revenue, the apple grower would be better off closing down immediately and saving the variable costs.

It is in the interests of the firm to stay in production in the short-run so long as it is recovering its variable costs.

You can check your understanding of this point by trying the Data Response question at the end of this chapter.

Average (or unit) cost (AC)

Three types of average cost

Average cost (AC) is the total cost divided by the number of units of the commodity produced.

This can be expressed as:

$$AC = \frac{\text{Total cost}}{\text{Output}} = \frac{TC}{Q}$$

As we have already seen that total costs can be divided into fixed costs and variable costs, it would follow that average cost can be divided in the same way:

$$\text{Average fixed costs} = \frac{\text{Fixed costs}}{\text{Output}}$$

$$AFC = \frac{FC}{Q}$$

and:

$$\text{Average variable costs} = \frac{\text{Variable costs}}{\text{Output}}$$

$$AVC = \frac{VC}{Q}$$

It would therefore follow that:

$$AFC + AVC = ATC \text{ (average total cost)}$$

Using the same figures as in Table 15.1, we may illustrate these various concepts. It should be apparent to the student that we can calculate all these various figures once we have the total cost schedule (see Table 15.2).

AFC declines continuously with output in the short-run as fixed costs are spread over a greater and greater number of units of output. Whether average variable cost increases or decreases depends upon the rate at which total cost is increasing. We can arrive at average total cost either by adding AFC and AVC or by dividing total cost by output. We can also verify the fact that:

$$AFC + AVC = ATC$$

For example, if the output is 5 units per week, then AVC is £24.80 while AFC is £23.20, thus giving ATC as £48.00.

Figure 15.3 shows AFC, AVC and ATC plotted graphically. You can see that AFC slopes downwards continuously and is *asymptotic* to the axis,

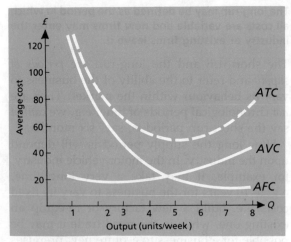

Fig. 15.3 Average costs
Average total cost is average variable cost average fixed cost.

i.e. it gets nearer and nearer to the horizontal axis but never touches it.

The average variable cost curve at first falls and later rises.

The most important curve, as far as we are concerned, is the ATC curve. This you will see is an elongated U-shape. This is always so in the short-run. ATC always starts at infinity and then falls rapidly as the fixed costs are spread over more and more units. It continues to fall until the point of optimum efficiency is reached

Table 15.2 The costs of the firm

Output, units per week, Q	Total cost, TC (£)	Fixed cost, FC (£)	Variable cost, VC (£)	Average fixed cost, FC ÷ Q = AFC (£)	Average variable cost, VC ÷ Q = AVC (£)	Average total cost, AFC + AVC = ATC (£)
0	116	116	0	∞	—	∞
1	140	116	24	116.00	24.00	140.00
2	160	116	44	58.00	22.00	80.00
3	176	116	60	38.60	20.00	58.60
4	200	116	84	29.00	21.00	50.00
5	240	116	124	23.20	24.80	48.00
6	296	116	180	19.30	30.00	49.30
7	368	116	252	16.60	36.00	52.60
8	456	116	340	14.50	42.50	57.00

(output of 5). Average costs then begin to rise as *diminishing returns* set in. Economically speaking, therefore, the best output is 5 (in our example) because here the article is being produced at the *lowest unit costs*. If output were to be any greater or any less then unit costs would rise.

The efficiency of a business can be judged by the extent to which it is managing to minimise its unit costs. This is an important point which we will return to later.

Shut-down conditions again

If we return to the section above on short-run shut-down conditions, we can re-examine the principles involved in terms of average cost. We stated the principle that the firm should continue to operate in the short-run so long as it covers its variable costs. If, for example, the variable costs of the business were £68.00 per week and output were 400 units, then the business would have to recover at least 17 pence per unit to stay in business, i.e. £68.00 ÷ 400. This we can now recognise as the average variable cost of production (AVC). Thus we can restate the short-run condition as:

The firm will continue to produce in the short-run so long as the price of the product is above AVC.

If you are in any doubt about this, then re-read this section carefully and attempt the Data Response question at the end of the chapter. It is important to understand this principle because it is a necessary component of the theory of the firm.

Average costs in the long-run

It has already been stated that the average cost curve is U-shaped in the short-run because of the law of diminishing returns. In the long-run, however, the fixed factors of production can be increased to get round this problem.

What effect does this have on costs?

If the business has already exploited all the possible *economies of scale*, then all it can do is build an additional factory which will reproduce the cost structures of the first. However if, as the market grows, the business is able to build bigger plants which exploit more economies of scale then this will have a beneficial effect upon costs.

In Fig. 15.4 SAC_A is the original short-run average cost curve of the business. As demand expands the business finds it possible to build larger plants which are able to benefit from more economies of scale. Thus it arrives at SAC_D. Eventually however this passes the optimum point and SAC_D also becomes U-shaped. SAC_M represents a repeat of the process with a larger scale of production.

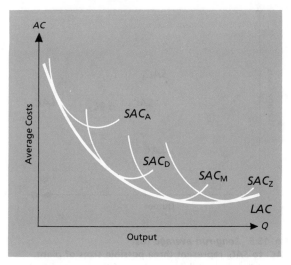

Fig. 15.4 *Smooth envelope curve*
SAC_A to SAC_Z represent an indefinite number of short-run average cost curves created as plant size is increased. *LAC* is the long-run average cost curve (smooth envelope) which is tangential to the *SAC* curves. Both *SAC* and *LAC* are U-shaped.

It is impossible, however, to go on producing more and more for less and less. This would violate the fundamental basis of economics – scarcity.

SAC_Z represents a stage where all possible economies of scale have been achieved and the business is now suffering from the long-run effects of diminishing returns and the principle of increasing costs. *LAC* therefore represents the *long-run average cost* curve for the business and you can see that this is also U-shaped. Such **189** a curve is sometimes referred to as an *envelope curve*.

The curve we have produced is known as a smooth envelope curve. It is drawn on the assumption that there are an infinite number of choices of plant size between SAC_A and SAC_D, and so on, so that we obtain a smooth transition in long-run average costs. If on the other hand there were only a limited number of choices of size of plant, this would tend to make the *LAC* curve more irregular. This is shown in Fig. 15.5.

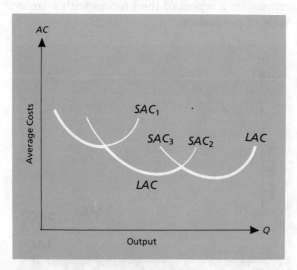

Fig. 15.5 *Long-run average cost*
SAC_1 to SAC_3 represent three possible sizes of plant. The *LAC* curve is still an envelope of these curves but is no longer smooth.

However, despite its irregular shape, you can see that the *LAC* curve still conforms to the general form of being an elongated U-shape. We can thus conclude that:

The average cost curve is U-shaped both in the short-run and the long-run.

This was the conclusion reached by Alfred Marshall and it has passed into conventional economic wisdom. However, for many large producers the average cost curve may, for all practical purposes, slope downwards continuously. This has important implications for our analysis of the behaviour of firms and

our judgement of imperfect competition. (*See* page 222.)

Marginal cost (*MC*)

Marginal cost defined

Marginal cost (*MC*) may be defined as the cost of producing one more (or less) unit of a commodity.

Like all the other costs we have considered, marginal cost may be calculated from the total cost schedule. We arrive at marginal cost by subtracting the total costs of adjacent outputs. We may illustrate this by using the same total cost figure we have used throughout this chapter. In Table 15.3 you can see that it is the cost involved in moving from one level of output to the next. The figure is therefore plotted halfway between the two outputs. Hence if we produce 6 units the total cost is £296.00, whereas if we produce 7 units, total cost rises to £368.00. The cost involved in producing unit 7 is therefore £72.00. This is shown not at 6 or 7, but halfway between.

Table 15.3 The marginal cost schedule

Output, units per week, Q	Total cost, TC (£)	Marginal cost, MC (£)
0	116	
1	140	24
2	160	20
3	176	16
4	200	24
5	240	40
6	296	56
7	368	72
8	456	88

The marginal cost curve

When we come to plot the marginal cost curve some particular problems are involved. Since the *MC* is the cost of moving *between* two levels

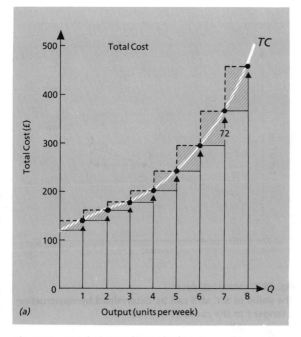

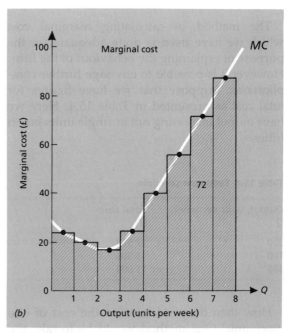

Fig. 15.6 *Total cost and marginal cost*
Marginal cost is the difference between successive levels of total cost, e.g. the cost of moving from an output of 6 units/week to 7 units/week is £72. You can see that the distance in (*a*) corresponds to the same distance in (*b*). Thus the value of the shaded areas in both diagrams is equal.

of output, it is plotted as a horizontal straight line between these outputs. Thus, in Fig. 15.6 (*b*), for example, the cost of moving from an output of 6 units per week to 7 units per week is £72·00. *MC* is therefore plotted as a horizontal line between these outputs. When this is done we end up with a graph looking like a step-ladder. If we wish to represent *MC* as a smooth curve, this can be done by joining up the midpoints of each step. This is done in Fig. 15.6 (*b*).

The step-ladder graph and the smooth curve represent two different concepts of marginal cost. The step-ladder shows that costs move in *finite* steps from one output to the next, whereas the smooth *MC* curve suggests that costs are infinitely variable between outputs. Thus we would see the marginal cost of producing 1·1 units, 1·2 units, 1·3 units and so on. The step-ladder therefore shows *discrete* data and the smooth curve *continuous* data. These conditions apply to all marginal figures. It is increasingly becoming the practice in economics texts to adopt

the discrete data approach at this level of the subject. However it is usually more convenient to adopt the continuous data approach, and this we shall do for most purposes.

The shape of the *MC* curve

You will see that the *MC* curve at first falls and then rises, presenting a similar U-shape to the *AC* curve. This is because the same principles of diminishing returns apply to marginal cost in the short-run as they do to all the other cost structures. As we shall see in subsequent chapters, the firm is almost invariably concerned with the levels of output where *MC* is rising. The student should not be surprised therefore if sometimes economic texts present *MC* as continuously upward sloping lines.

The mathematics of marginal cost

This section may be omitted without impairing your understanding of subsequent chapters. **191**

The method of calculating marginal cost which we have used is quite adequate for the purpose of explaining the behaviour of the firm. However it is possible to envisage further complications. Suppose that we have figures for total cost as presented in Table 15.4. Here we have output increasing not in single units but in fifties.

Table 15.4 Total cost schedule

Output, units per week, Q	Total cost (£)
350	12 500
400	13 500
450	15 000

How then do we determine the cost of one more unit? One method would be to take the change in total cost ($\triangle TC$) and divide it by the change in output ($\triangle Q$). Thus, using the figures in Table 15.4, if output increases from 350 to 400 per week, we would obtain the calculation:

$$MC = \frac{\triangle TC}{\triangle Q}$$

$$= \frac{£1000}{50}$$

$$= £20$$

This, however, is only an approximation because it gives the average increase per unit between 350 and 400 units per week. It would therefore be better to refer to it as the *average incremental cost (AIC)* rather than marginal cost. The figures in Table 15.4, if plotted as a graph, would give a curved line for *MC* so that its value would vary all the way from 350 units to 400 units, i.e. *MC* would be different at each level of output – 300, 301, 302, etc.

This can be better understood by considering Fig. 15.7. In measuring *MC* we have so far taken a method which depends upon comparing distance XY with distance YX₁. That is to say, if XY represents an increase in output of one unit then YX₁ is the resulting increase in total

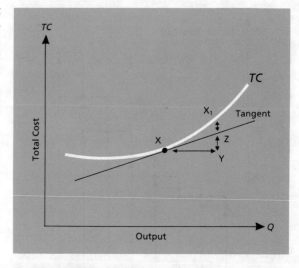

Fig. 15.7 Marginal cost
The value of *MC* at X can be determined by constructing a tangent to the curve at X. Thus:

$$MC = \frac{XY}{YZ}$$

cost, i.e. the *MC*. It would be mathematically more precise to define *MC* as the slope of the *TC* curve at any particular point, i.e.

$$MC = \frac{d(TC)}{dQ}$$

which the mathematically minded will recognise as the way of saying that:

Marginal cost is the first derivative of cost with respect to output.

That is to say it is the change in cost associated with an infinitesimally small movement along the *TC* curve. In Fig. 15.7 we can demonstrate this by the construction of a tangent to the *TC* curve at the point we wish to measure. Then the value of *MC* at point X is:

$$MC = \frac{XY}{YZ}$$

By turning our stepped *MC* curve into a smoothed-out one we are in fact making an approximation to the correct mathematical way of calculating *MC*.

Average cost and marginal cost

The relationship between *MC* and *AC*

In Fig. 15.8 we have brought together the figures for marginal cost and those for average cost. A most important point is revealed:

The marginal most curve cuts the average cost curve at the lowest point of average cost.

As you can see in Fig 15.8, this occurs at an output of 5 units per week. You can also see that *MC* cuts the lowest point of the *AVC* curve.

Why does this relationship occur? The reasons are mathematical rather than economic and the explanation is this. So long as *MC* is less than *AC*, then it will draw *AC* down towards it, but as soon as *MC* is greater than *AC* then it will pull up the *AC* curve. Thus, the *MC* curve must go through the bottom point of the *AC* curve. This applies to both the short-run and the long-run situations.

This principle applies to the relationship between any marginal and average figure. Consider the following example.

A batsman in the county cricket championship has an average score of 25 runs after 10 innings. In the next match (*marginal*) he scores 13 runs.

What happens to his average? It falls because the marginal score is below the average. In the next match he scores 18. Although his marginal score has risen, his average is still brought down because the marginal is still less than the average. However, were he to score 30 in the next match, the marginal score, now being greater than the average, would pull up the average.

The student should also note that the same principle applies to the marks or grades awarded on school or college courses!

A change in fixed cost

Suppose that a firm's fixed costs were to increase – for example, its rent might be doubled – but its variable costs were to remain unchanged. What effect would this have upon the cost structures? The answer to this question is found in Fig. 15.9. The marginal cost is not affected because marginal cost shows the change in cost associated with increasing output. Therefore:

Marginal cost is unaffected by fixed cost.

The average cost however is increased at every level of output so that the *AC* shifts upwards from AC_1 to AC_2. You will note that the *MC* curve cuts both *AC* curves at their lowest point.

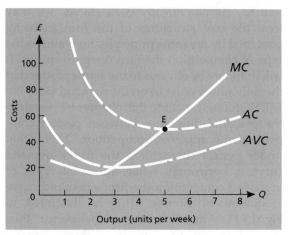

Fig. 15.8 *Marginal cost and average cost*
The *MC* curve cuts the *AC* curve at point E, which is the lowest point of average cost.

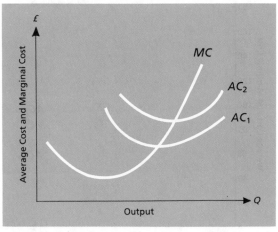

Fig. 15.9 *An increase in total costs*
If fixed costs are increased but variable costs are not, then the *MC* curve is unaffected by the *AC* curve moving upwards from AC_1 to AC_2.

Table 15.5 The effect of an increase in variable costs

Output, units per week, Q	Original total cost, TC_1 (£)	New total cost, TC_2 (£)	Original average cost, AC_1 (£)	New average cost, AC_2 (£)	Original marginal cost, MC_1 (£)	New marginal cost, MC_2 (£)
0	116	116	∞	∞		
					24	48
1	140	164	140	164		
					20	40
2	160	204	80	102		
					16	32
3	176	236	58·6	78·6		
					24	48
4	200	284	50·0	71·0		
					40	80
5	240	364	48·0	72·8		
					56	112
6	296	476	49·3	79·3		
					72	144
7	368	620	52·6	88·6		
					88	176
8	456	796	57·0	99·5		

A change in variable cost

In Table 15.5 we have doubled the level of variable cost at each level of output. As you can see this affects both the average cost and marginal cost. In Fig. 15.10 you can see that both the AC and MC curves have shifted upwards as a result of the change. The intersection of MC and AC is now *at a lower level of output*. Once again you can see that MC cuts AC at its lowest point.

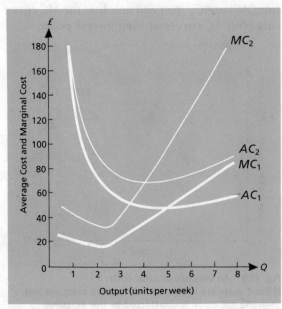

Fig. 15.10 *A change in variable costs*

As we shall see in subsequent chapters, there will be consequences for the output policy of firms as a result of these changes in cost structures.

Conclusion

We have now all but completed our examination of the costs of the firm; it only remains in the next Section of the book to demonstrate the relationship between costs and diminishing returns. As has already been stated, we may treat the cost structures of the firm as being governed by the same principles no matter what type of competition the firm operates under. It will therefore be obvious to the astute reader that the differences must lie on the demand side. We will therefore conclude this chapter by restating the essential difference between perfect competition and imperfect competition. This is that under perfect competition the firm's demand curve is horizontal, while under all types of imperfect competition the firm's demand curve is downward sloping. This is illustrated in Fig 15.11. The difference in behaviour thus stems from the relationship of these demand curves with the cost curves. Marginal revenue (MR) is explained in Chapter 17.

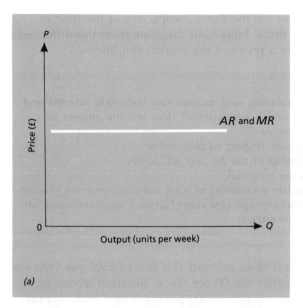

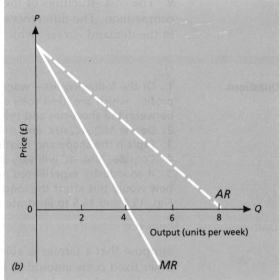

Fig. 15.11 (a) *Perfect and* (b) *imperfect competition*
The difference is that under perfect competition the firm's demand curve is horizontal while under imperfect competition it is downward sloping.

Summary

1   Total cost (*TC*) comprises fixed cost (*FC*) and variable cost (*VC*). Fixed (indirect) costs are fixed in the short-run, while variable (indirect) costs start at zero and increase with output.

2   A firm will stay in business in the short-run so long as it is recovering its variable costs. In the long-run all costs must be covered.

3   Average (unit) cost (*AC*) is total cost divided by output. It may be divided into average fixed costs (*AFC*) and average variable costs (*AVC*). Thus:

$$ATC = AFC + AVC$$

4   The *AC* curve is U-shaped in the short-run because of diminishing returns. In the long-run the *AC* curve will also be U-shaped because of diseconomies of scale and increasing costs.

5   Marginal cost (*MC*) is the cost of producing one more unit of a commodity. Mathematically it can be defined as the first derivative of cost with respect to ouput.

6   The *MC* curve is plotted in a special incremental manner.

7   The *MC* curve always intersects with the *AC* curve at the lowest point of *AC*.

8   A change in fixed cost will affect *AC* but not *MC*, whereas a change in variable cost will affect both *AC* and *MC*.

9 The cost structures of the firm are the same irrespective of the type of competition. The differences in firms' behaviour originate from the differences in the demand curves, which are a result of the market conditions.

Questions

1 Of the following list – wages, salaries, rent, power, raw materials, interest and profit – which are fixed costs and which are variable? How will the answer vary between the short-run and the long-run?

2 Define MC, AC, AFC and AVC with respect to total costs.

3 Explain the shape and relationship of the AC and MC curves.

4 Consider how AC will vary in the long-run.

5 If an industry experienced neither economies of scale nor diseconomies of scale, how would this affect the long-run average cost curve? Draw a diagram based on Figs. 15.4 and 15.5 to illustrate your answer.

Data response Short-run shut-down conditions

Suppose that a farmer is able to rent an orchard at a cost of £500 per year and other fixed costs amount to a further £50.00 per week. Itinerant labour to pick the apples can be hired at a wage of £56.00 per week and each labourer can pick 400 dozen apples per week. Other variable costs such as packaging and transport amount to 3 pence per dozen. Under these conditions:

a) What is the minimum price per dozen that the apple grower would be willing to accept in the short-run?

b) Suppose that the apple grower employs 5 workers for 5 weeks picking apples to gather the complete harvest. Assuming that all costs and productivities stay the same as stated above, what is the minimum price per dozen the apple grower will look for to remain in the industry in the long-run?

In both cases explain your answer as fully as possible. Illustrate your answers with a diagram.

16
Competitive supply

Competition means decentralised planning by many separate persons.
Friedrich August von Hayek

Having examined the cost structures of the business, we can now turn to look at how a firm's price and output policy is determined. In this chapter we consider market behaviour under conditions of perfect competition. It should be remembered that the guiding principle of the business is *profit maximisation*. We can therefore say that the firm will be in equilibrium if it is maximising its profits.

The best profit output

Output and profit in the short-run

Under perfect competition the firm is a *price taker*, i.e. it has no control over the market price. It can only sell or not sell at that price. Therefore, in trying to maximise its profits, the firm has no pricing decision to make; it can only choose the output which it thinks most advantageous. For example, in a freely competitive market a farmer could choose how much wheat to plant but could not control the price at which it would be sold when harvested.

The best profit position for any business would be where it equated the price of the product with its marginal cost (*MC*). If the cost of producing one more unit (*MC*) is less than the revenue the producer obtains for selling it, i.e. the price, then he can obviously add to his profit by producing and selling that unit. Even when *MC* is rising, so long as it is less than the price, the firm will go on producing because it is gaining

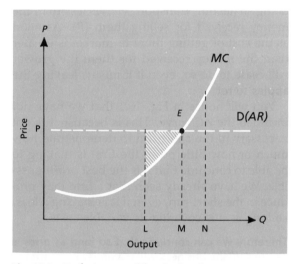

Fig. 16.1 *Perfect competition in the short-run*
The firm produces the output at which *MC* = *P*.

extra profit. It does not matter if the *extra* profit is only small, it is nevertheless an *addition to profit* and, if the firm is out to *maximise profits*, it will wish to receive this. This is illustrated in Fig. 16.1, where the most profitable output is OM. If the business produced a smaller output (OL), then the cost of producing a unit (*MC*) is less than the revenue received from selling it (*P*). The business could therefore increase its profits by expanding output. The shaded area represents the extra profit available to the producer as output expands. At point E (output OM) there is no more extra profit to be gained. If the firm were to produce a larger output (ON), then the cost of producing *that* unit (*MC*) would be greater than revenue from selling it (*P*) and the **197** producer could increase profits by contracting output back towards OM. Thus the output at which $MC = P$ is an *equilibrium position*, i.e. the one at which the firm will be happy to remain if it is allowed to.

Let us look again at our example from the last chapter where we considered the apple grower. Suppose that the orchard owner has produced a crop of apples. The grower now has to harvest them and send them to market. Since apples are highly perishable they will continue to be sent to market while the extra cost (MC) incurred in doing so (labour, transport, etc.) is less than the money received for selling them (P). As soon as the cost of getting them to market is greater than the money received for them the grower will cease to do so, even if it means leaving the apples to rot.

You will notice in Fig. 16.1 that we have not included the AC curve. This is because it is not necessary in the short-run to demonstrate how much or how little profit the firm is making to be able to conclude that it is the best profit possible. We have already seen that a firm may produce in the short-run, even if it is making a loss, so long as it is covering its variable costs.

Therefore we can conclude that so long as price is above *AVC* the business will maximise its profits or (which is the same thing) minimise its losses by producing the output at which:

$$MC = P$$

We shall see in the next chapter that under perfect competition price can be equated with marginal revenue (MR). Thus we could restate the proposition as $MC = MR$. This then becomes the profit maximisation position for all types of competition.

The long-run equilibrium

Although a business might produce at a loss in the short-run, in the long-run all costs must be covered. In order to consider the long-run situation we must bring average cost into the picture.

Before doing this it will be useful if we list some of the main points established so far. Check that you fully understand them before proceeding any further.

a) Under perfect competition there is a freedom of entry and exit to the market (*see* page 179).

b) $MC = MR$ is the profit maximisation output (*see* above).

c) MC cuts AC at the lowest point of AC (*see* page 193).

d) At below normal profit, firms will leave the industry; if profit is above normal new firms will be attracted into the industry (*see* page 182).

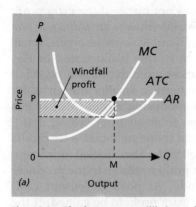
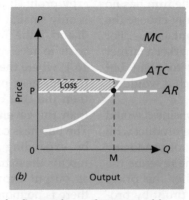
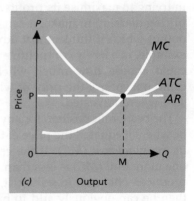

Fig. 16.2 *The long-run equilibrium of the firm under perfect competition*
(*a*) Windfall profits attract new firms to the industry. This lowers price and eliminates the abnormal profits. (*b*) The firm is making a loss and in the long-run will leave the industry. (*c*) The firm is just recovering normal profit. This is the long-run equilibrium where: *MC = P = AR = AC*

Since the *MC* curve cuts the *AC* curve at the lowest point on *AC* it follows that this intersection must occur at a level which is higher, lower or equal to price. These three possibilities are shown on Fig. 16.2. In situation (*a*) the *ATC* curve dips down below the *AR* curve and the business is making *abnormal profit*. Remember that normal profit is included in the costs of the firm. Thus any positive gap between *ATC* and *AR* must be abnormal profit. In the long-run the abnormal profit attracts new firms into the industry and the profit is competed away. Therefore (*a*) cannot be a long-run position.

Under perfect competition abnormal profit is referred to as *windfall profit*, since it is not a profit which has been contrived by the firm; it arises because the price is unexpectedly higher than anticipated. For example, if a farmer plants barley but everyone else plants oats, then the price of barley is likely to be high. The farmer will thus make windfall profits, but the high price of barley will attract farmers to that crop for the next harvest. This will lower the price and eliminate the windfall profit.

In situation (*b*) the *ATC* is at all points above *AR* and therefore there is no output at which the business can make a profit. It may remain in business in the short-run so long as price (*AR*) is above *AVC*, but in the long-run it will close down. Therefore (*b*) cannot be a long-run position either.

In situation (*c*) the *ATC* is tangential to the *AR* curve. Thus the firm exists making just normal profit but no abnormal profit. The firm may therefore continue in this position since it is not making enough profit to attract other firms to compete that profit away. Hence (*c*) is the long-run equilibrium position of the business operating under conditions of perfect competition. We may conclude, therefore, that under perfect competition the long-run equilibrium for the business is where:

$$MC = P = AC = AR$$

The average business is hardly likely to look at the process in this way. Profit maximisation is arrived at by practical knowledge of the business and by trial and error. The concepts of marginal cost, average revenue, etc., allow us to generalise the principles that are common to all businesses. Although business people may not be familiar with words like 'marginal revenue', they are nevertheless used to the practice of making small variations in output and price to achieve the best results. Thus they are using a marginal technique to maximise their profits.

The supply curve

The firm's supply curve

Having demonstrated the equilibrium of the firm we will now go on to consider the derivation of the supply curve.

It will be recalled that the supply curve shows how supply varies in response to changes in price. No matter how the *market price* changes, the *demand curve* always appears to be a horizontal line to the individual firm under perfect competition. Therefore as price goes up or down

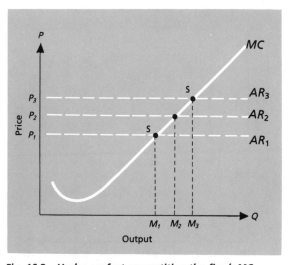

Fig. 16.3 *Under perfect competition the firm's* **MC** *curve is its supply curve*
As price rises from OP$_1$ to OP$_2$ to OP$_3$, so the firm expands output from OM$_1$ to OM$_2$ to OM$_3$, in each case equating **MC** with **P**. Thus SS is the supply curve.

199

the firm always tries to equate price with marginal cost in order to maximise its profits. In Fig. 16.3 as price increases from OP_1 to OP_2 to OP_3 the firm expands output from OM_1 to OM_2 to OM_3. This, therefore, shows how the firm varies output in response to changes in price; in other words it is a supply curve. Thus we may conclude that:

Under perfect competition the firm's *MC* curve, above *AVC*, is its supply curve.

Industry supply

If we can explain the firm's supply curve then we can explain the industry supply curve since, as we saw at the beginning of Chapter 14, the industry supply curve is the horizontal summation of individual firms' supply curves (*see* page 177).

A change in supply

Figure 16.4 illustrates a shift in the supply curve; this would be brought about by a change in the *conditions of supply*. Thus, for example, the leftward shift in the supply curve could have been

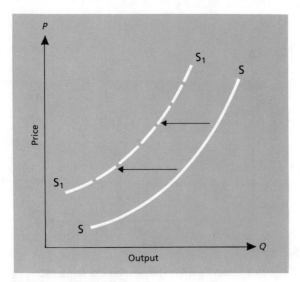

Fig. 16.4 *A change in supply*
The leftward shift of the SS curve is the result of a change in one of the conditions of supply, e.g. a rise in costs (*see* page 60)

brought about by an increase in the costs of production.

The equilibrium of the industry

The industry equilibrium occurs when the number of firms in the industry is stable and industry output is stable. As we have seen, above-normal profits will attract new firms into the industry, but the extra output produced by the firms will then depress the market price, thus squeezing out the excess profit. Conversely, if firms are making a loss then they will leave the industry. This contraction of output will cause market price to rise, thus bringing price into line with average costs. Figure 16.5 shows the relationship between industry supply and individual firm's supply. If price is OT then this attracts new firms into the industry and shifts the supply curve rightwards, whereas if price is OR then firms are leaving the industry, thus shifting the supply curve leftwards. It can be seen that the industry equilibrium price OS corresponds with the price at which the firm is just recovering normal profit.

It should not be thought that the equilibrium for the industry represents a static situation. The equilibrium may be the long-run result of a situation where different firms are constantly entering and leaving the industry, but overall the situation is stable. People also attribute other conditions to the equilibrium which are not necessary, such as identical cost structures. As we have seen, different firms may be willing to accept different levels of normal profit and therefore different levels of average cost may coexist in a long-run equilibrium situation. If this were not so, any fall in price would lead to all firms leaving the industry.

The optimality of perfect competition

The optimum allocation of resources

The importance of the idea of perfect competition is that it represents, to many economists,

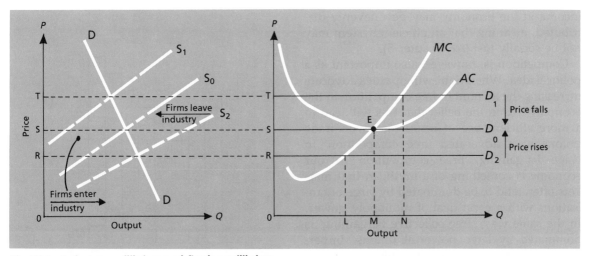

Fig. 16.5 *Industry equilibrium and firm's equilibrium*
If industry price is OT then abnormal profits attract new firms and supply increases from S_1 to S_0 and price falls
to S. If industry price is OR firms leave the industry and supply curve shifts from S_2 to S_0. Industry equilibrium is
where S_0 intersects with industry demand curve DD, corresponding to long-run equilibrium for the firm at OM.
Note: industry demand curve is downward sloping but it always appears horizontal to the firm; thus at price OT
firm's demand curve is D_1, at price OS it is D_0, and so on.

the ideal working of the free market system.
The fundamental problem of any economy, it
will be remembered, is to make the best use of
scarce resources. If we look at the model of
perfect competition we will see how it relates to
this. In its long-run equilibrium the firm is producing where $MC = AC$, i.e. at the bottom of
the average cost curve. At this point output
costs, i.e. the quantity of resources needed to
produce a unit of the commodity, are minimised.
Looking at Fig. 16.6 you can see that if the firm
produced a greater or smaller output the cost of
producing a unit would rise. In the long-run
equilibrium, therefore, the firm is making an
optimum use of its resources. If every firm in
the economy operated under these conditions it
would follow that there would be an optimum
allocation of resources and every commodity
would be produced at a minimum unit cost.
Indeed all firms would be producing to consumers' demand curves and therefore not only
would the goods be produced at a minimum
cost but they would also be the goods which
people wanted.

It has already been seen that this view of the
economy is subject to two major criticisms.

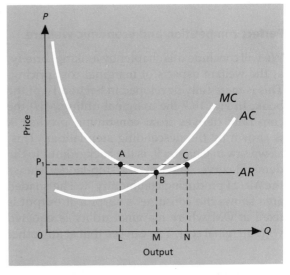

Fig. 16.6 *The optimality of perfect competition*
The long-run equilibrium is at output OM, which
corresponds to the lowest unit cost at point B on the
AC curve. At any other output, greater or smaller, the
unit cost is higher, as at points A and C on the *AC* curve.

Firstly, that the commodities which people are
willing to pay for may not be the goods which
are most useful to society, and, secondly, that **201**

income in the economy may be unevenly distributed, meaning that an efficient system may not be socially just (*see* Chapter 5).

Competition is, however, also important as a political idea. When right-wing parties advocate increasing the amount of free competition in the economy it is in the belief that this will lead to a more efficient use of resources. Even trade unions have advocated 'free competition' in wage bargaining. Free competition in our economy is something of a myth, in that markets often tend to be dominated by large organisations with a great deal of monopoly power. In the same way, 'free collective bargaining' is dominated by large powerful unions. Imperfections in the market are the rule rather than 'free and unfettered competition'. The importance of the model of perfect competition is not that it is attainable but that it gives us a measure with which to assess the imperfections of competition.

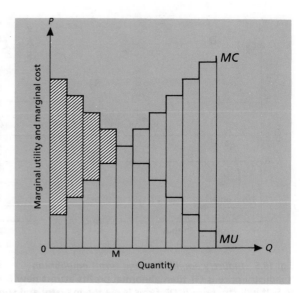

Fig. 16.7 *Welfare optimality*
This occurs where marginal utility is equated with marginal cost. The shaded area represents consumers' surplus.

Perfect competition and economic welfare

We will conclude this chapter by looking, briefly, at the welfare aspects of marginal cost pricing. This is more fully developed in Section IV of the book. In Fig. 16.7 the marginal utility (*MU*) the consumer derives from consuming product X is shown by the descending step-ladder. This, as we saw in Chapter 9, is the background to the demand curve. The upward step-ladder shows the *MC* of producing commodity X. The shaded area shows the consumer's surplus if output is fixed at OM where marginal utility is equated with marginal cost. You can see that at any other level of output the consumer's surplus would be smaller. Thus *MC* pricing represents a *welfare-maximising equilibrium* for the individual.

By the aggregation of individual *MU* and *MC* curves we could demonstrate the welfare-maximising equilibrium for the whole industry. We have touched on this rather abstract aspect of perfect competition here to encourage the student to go on to the problems considered in Section IV of the book. You will not be able to appreciate the central position which the model of competition holds in microeconomics unless you fully understand that section of the book.

Summary

1 The firm under perfect competition maximises its profits by producing the output at which *MC* = *P*.
2 In the long-run the firm's equilibrium is where *MC* = *P* = *AR* = *AC*.
3 Under perfect competition the firm's supply curve is its *MC* curve and the industry supply curve is the aggregation of individual firms' *MC* curves.
4 The equilibrium for the industry is where output is stable, the number of firms is stable and overall the industry is making normal profit.

5 An optimum allocation of resources is achieved when all firms are operating at the bottom of their *AC* curves.

6 The welfare maximising equilibrium is where the *MU*s of the consumers are equated with the *MC*s of production.

Questions

1 Discuss the relevance of perfect competition to modern market structures.

2 Explain the 'welfare connotations' of perfect competition.

3 How will a firm's long-run equilibrium differ from its short-run equilibrium under conditions of competitive supply?

4 Contrast the effects of a change in the firm's fixed costs with those of a change in its variable costs upon the equilibrium of a competitive firm.

5 The figures below give the revenue, output and costs of a firm. From this information construct the firm's short-run supply curve.

Output	0	1	2	3	4	5	6	7	8
Total revenue (£)	0	300	600	900	1 200	1 500	1 800	2 100	2 400
Total costs (£)	580	700	800	880	1 000	1 200	1 480	1 840	2 280

Explain how you established your answer.

6 A firm's *MC* curve is given by the function

$$y(MC) = 10 + 2x$$

If the firm is operating under conditions of perfect competition and the market price is 20, what will be the profit maximisation output?

Data response The Puckboat Company ━━━━━━

The following table gives the total cost schedule for Puckboat a small business making fibreglass dinghies.

Costs of the Puckboat Company

Output of dinghies per week	Total cost £
0	1 160
1	1 400
2	1 600
3	1 760
4	2 000
5	2 400
6	2 960
7	3 680
8	4 560

1 Calculate Puckboat's average and marginal cost schedules.

2 Assuming that Puckboat is able to sell any quantity of dinghies at a price of £480, construct a graph to show the firm's average cost, marginal cost and marginal revenue.

3 Determine the profit maximisation output for this firm.

4 Consider the long-run effects upon Puckboat of the following price changes, assuming that its cost structure remains unaltered.

a) Price falls to £320

b) Price increases to £640.

In both cases explain your answer as fully as possible.

5 What alternative policy strategies might Puckboat have to that of profit maximisation?

6 What extra information would Puckboat need in order to pursue each of these 'alternative policies'?

17

Price and output under imperfect competition

Like many businessmen of genius he learned that free competition was wasteful, monopoly efficient. And so he simply set about achieving that monopoly.

Mario Puzo, *The Godfather*

Having considered perfect markets we will now turn to imperfect ones. You will recall that the one key difference between the two, analytically speaking, is that the firm's demand curve under imperfect competition is downward sloping whereas under perfect competition it is horizontal. There are, as we have seen, several types of imperfect competition, but in the short-run their market behaviour is very similar so that it is only in the long-run that differences appear. In the first part of this chapter, therefore, we will deal with short-run profit maximising behaviour for imperfect competition generally and then conclude by looking at differences which appear in the long run.

Profit maximisation in the short-run

Analysis using total revenue and total cost

We can demonstrate profit maximisation most easily by simply subtracting total cost from total revenue at all levels of output. This is done in Table 17.1. Here we have used the same total cost schedule as in Chapter 15. The total revenue schedule is derived from the downward sloping demand curve for the firm's product. As you

can see, in this example, the business maximises its profits at an output of four units per week where it makes a profit of £184 per week. You will notice that this is *not* the output at which revenue is maximised; this occurs at the output of five units per week. We will see the reason for this as we work through the chapter.

Figure 17.1 presents the information from Table 17.1 in graphical form. Total profit is the gap between the total cost curve and the total revenue curve. From the graphs you can see that the firm can make abnormal profits anywhere

Table 17.1 Profit maximisation using total cost and total revenue schedules

Output, units per week, Q	Total revenue, TR (£)	Total cost, TC (£)	Total profit, TP (£)
0	0	116	−116
1	144	140	+4
2	256	160	+96
3	336	176	+160
4	384	200	+184
5	400	240	+160
6	384	296	+88
7	336	368	−32
8	256	456	−200

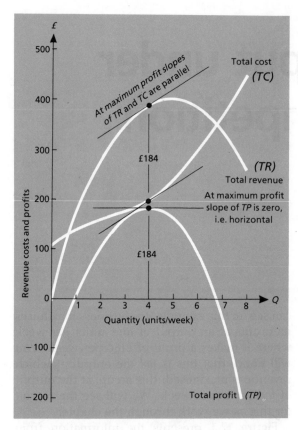

£

Total cost (TC)

At maximum profit slopes of TR and TC are parallel

£184

(TR)
Total revenue

At maximum profit slope of TP is zero, i.e. horizontal

£184

Total profit (TP)

Revenue costs and profits

Quantity (units/week)

Fig. 17.1 *Total profit can be seen as either the gap between* TR *and* TC, *or the height of the TP curve*
Note: the total profit does not occur where *TR* is at its greatest.

between the output of one unit per week up to an output of about seven units per week. While profit is increasing the *TC* and *TR* curves must be diverging, while as profit is decreasing *TC* and *TR* must be converging. Therefore, when profit is maximised the two curves will be neither diverging nor converging, i.e. they will be parallel to one another. At the same output the *TP* curve will be at its maximum and its slope will be zero, since at that point profit will be neither rising nor falling.

We will return to total cost and total revenue curves later when we consider *mark-up pricing*, but now we will turn to the more usual way of presenting profit maximisation, which is through the marginal and average cost structures.

Marginal revenue (*MR*)

In order to explain the behaviour of the firm we must introduce a new concept – marginal revenue (*MR*).

Marginal revenue is the change to total revenue from the sale of one more unit of a commodity.

Suppose for example that a firm was selling four units a week at £10 each. Then the total revenue would be £40, but, since this is imperfect competition, if it wishes to sell more it must lower its prices. Therefore, for example, selling five units a week may involve dropping the price to £9, in which case the total revenue will now be £45. Thus the change to the firm's total revenue as a result of selling one more unit is £5. This is termed the marginal revenue.

In order to sell more the imperfect competitor must, as we have seen, lower the price. If, for example, sales are 50 units per week at a price of £10 and sales are increased to 51 units by lowering the price to £9, then not only does the firm lose money on the fifty-first unit but also all the *preceding units* now all have to be priced at £9. Thus total revenue decreases from £500 to £459, giving a marginal revenue of minus £41. (For the extra £9 sales revenue gained from the fifty-first unit the firm has sacrificed £1 on the preceding 50 units; thus *MR* = (£9 − £50) = − £41.) Whether or not marginal revenue is positive or negative depends upon whether the gain in revenue from extra sales is greater or smaller than the loss on preceding units. This depends upon which part of a firm's demand curve schedule we are considering.

Table 17.2 gives a demand schedule, a total revenue schedule and, in the last column, the marginal revenue schedule. The marginal revenue can now be seen as the difference between adjacent total revenues. You can see that as price is lowered, total revenue increases until point F in the table and then begins to decrease because the increase in sales is now no longer great enough to offset the fall in price. Thus after point F marginal revenue becomes negative.

Table 17.2 Marginal revenue

	Output, Q (units/week)	Average revenue, P (£/unit)	Total revenue, P × Q (TR)	Marginal revenue, $TR_n - TR_{n-1}$ (MR)
A	0	160	0	
				144
B	1	144	144	
				112
C	2	128	256	
				80
D	3	112	336	
				48
E	4	96	384	
				16
F	5	80	400	
				−16
G	6	64	384	
				−48
H	7	48	336	
				−80
I	8	32	256	
				−112
J	9	16	144	
				−144
K	10	0	0	

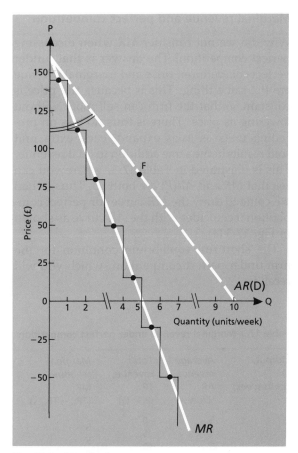

Fig. 17.2 *Marginal revenue*
The *MR* curve descends at twice the rate of the *AR* curve, bisecting the quantity axis.

Figure 17.2 presents the information for demand and marginal revenue in graphical form. Note that once again the marginal revenue curve is plotted in a special manner, as was marginal cost. The mathematical relationship between *AR* and *MR* means that the *MR* curve descends at twice the rate of the *AR* curve. Thus you can see that the *AR* curve meets the quantity axis at 10 units per week while the *MR* cuts the quantity axis at 5 units per week. This can also be seen in Table 17.2, where you can see that average revenue descends in amounts of £16, i.e. £160, £144, £128, etc., while the marginal revenue descends in amounts of £32, i.e. £144, £112, £80, etc. This relationship holds good so long as we have a linear function for *AR*, i.e. the demand curve is a straight line. If the *AR* curve is non-linear (curved) then the relationship becomes more complex. When drawing sketch graphs to illustrate examination answers the student should remember this relationship between *AR* and *MR*; a carelessly drawn graph will show the examiner that you do not appreciate the concepts involved.

Marginal revenue and elasticity

If we examine point F on the *AR* curve in Fig 17.2 we will find that it is when demand is unitary. How can we say this with such certainty? It is because *MR* is zero at that point. As we descend the demand curve towards point F then the total revenue is increasing; therefore demand must be elastic. Below point F, as price is lowered total revenue decreases and therefore demand must be inelastic. Therefore at point F total revenue must be neither rising or falling, i.e. it must be constant and thus elasticity must be unitary. You can check this by calculating E_D at F.

$$E_D = \frac{1}{5} \times \frac{80}{16} = 1$$

Thus we can conclude that:

Demand is elastic when *MR* is positive, inelastic when *MR* is negative and unitary when *MR* is zero. **207**

Marginal revenue and perfect competition

Why did we not consider *MR* when discussing perfect competition? The answer is that, under perfect competition, price and marginal revenue are the same thing. This is because the price is constant so that the firm can sell more without lowering its price. There is thus no loss on preceding units as sales expand; each extra unit sold results in the same addition to total revenue. This is illustrated in Table 17.3, where you can see that *MR* and *AR(P)* are both £5. Thus, when we come to draw the *MR* curve for perfect competition it coincides with the *AR* curve as shown in Fig. 17.3 (*a*).

The short-run equilibrium condition for the firm under perfect competition, which you will recall is:

Table 17.3 Marginal revenue under perfect competition

Output, Q (units/week)	Average revenue, AR (£/unit)	Total revenue, TR (P × Q)	Marginal revenue, MR (TRn − TRn−1)
0	5	0	
1	5	5	5
2	5	10	5
3	5	15	5
4	5	20	5
5	5	25	5

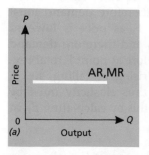

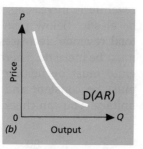

Fig. 17.3 *The marginal revenue curve*:
(*a*) **Perfect competition. *MR* and *AR* curves coincide because price is constant.**
(*b*) **The industry demand curve remains downward sloping thus the *MR* curve would look like that in Fig. 17.2.**

$$MC = P$$

can now be restated as:

$$MC = MR$$

and the long-run equilibrium as:

$$MC = MR = AC = AR$$

The short-run equilibrium of the firm: marginal analysis method

If we draw the *MR* and the *MC* curve on one graph we can see that they cross exactly at an output of four units per week. We can now state that this will be the output at which the firm will maximise its profits. How are we able to say this with such certainty? The explanation is this. While *MR* is greater than *MC* the cost of producing *another* unit of the commodity is less than the revenue to be gained from selling it, so that the business can add to its profits by producing and selling that unit. This remains true so long as *MC* is *less* than *MR*. Thus the business will increase its profits by expanding its output. However, once *MC* is *greater* than *MR*, then the cost of producing another unit is greater than the revenue to be derived from selling it and the business could, therefore, increase its profits by contracting output.

We can conclude, therefore, that:

The business will maximise its profits by producing the output at which *MR* = *MC*.

You will see that this is essentially the same analysis as for perfect competition because, although we have stated the condition for perfect competition as *MC* = *P*, we now realise that *MR* is the same as *P* under perfect competition. Thus:

***MC* = *MR* is the profit maximisation condition for all types of competition.**

Table 17.4 shows us all the information we have developed in this chapter. You can see from it that the business does indeed maximise its profits at point E on the table, i.e. at an output of four units per week, and this is where *MR* = *MC*. This is confirmed in Fig. 17.4 where we

Table 17.4 Costs, revenues and profits under imperfect competition

	Output, Q (units/week)	Average revenue, P (£/unit)	Total revenue, TR (P × Q)	Total cost, TC (£)	Total profit, TP (TR − TC)	Marginal cost, MC ($TC_n − TC_{n-1}$)	Marginal revenue, MR ($TR_n − TR_{n-1}$)	Average cost, AC (TC/Q)
A	0	160	0	116	−116			∞
						24	144	
B	1	144	144	140	+4			140
						20	112	
C	2	128	256	160	+96			80
						16	80	
D	3	112	336	176	+160			58·6
						24	48	
E	4		96	384	200	+184	MC = MR	50
						40	16	
F	5	80	400	240	+160			48
						56	−16	
G	6	64	384	296	+88			49·3
						72	−48	
H	7	48	336	368	−32			52·6
						88	−80	
I	8	32	256	456	−200			57

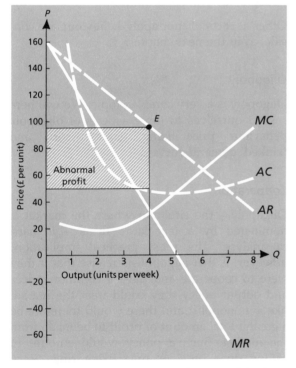

Fig. 17.4 *The equilibrium price and output of the firm under imperfect competition in the short-run*
Profit is maximised at an output of 4 units and a price of £96, i.e. where:
  MR = MC
and:
  Profit = (AR − AC) × Q = £184

see the information in Table 17.4 presented graphically.

The shaded rectangle represents abnormal profit. At an output of four units per week AR (price) is £96 and average cost is £50. The difference between the two (£46) is profit and the firm has made this profit on four units. We could express this as:

$$TP = (AR − AC) \times Q$$
$$= (£96 − £50) \times 4$$
$$= £184$$

Alternatively it could be expressed as;

$$TP = TR − TC$$
$$= (AR \times Q) − (AC \times Q)$$
$$= (96 \times 4) − (£50 \times 4)$$
$$= £184$$

The mathematically minded will realise that total profit can also be calculated by summing all MRs at the output of four and subtracting the summation of all MCs at that output, i.e.:

$$TP = \Sigma MR − \Sigma MC$$

You will recall from Chapter 14 that normal profit is included in the cost of the business. Therefore, the profit discussed above is all *abnormal profit* (also called *excess profit* or *monopoly profit*), i.e. all this profit could be eliminated **209** without forcing the business to leave the industry. How has this abnormal profit been made? The answer is by selling a restricted output at a higher price.

Under imperfect competition, in order to sell more the business must lower its prices. Therefore there must come a time when the price is so low that profit is eliminated. It is not surprising, then, that business finds its best profit position before this point. This idea is often unintentionally illustrated by bad harvests when the lack of supply forces up prices and farmers find themselves much better off, even though they are selling less produce. Abnormal profit is usually, however, considered *contrived profit* – a return to the *monopolistic* power of the business.

As a result of imperfect competition, then, consumers are paying for more products than they might, and yet this is not the most serious consequence. You will observe from Table 17.4 that at an output of four the product is being produced at a higher average cost than it might be. In our example average cost is minimised at an output of five (where AC = £48). Thus, it would seem that *imperfect competition leads to an inefficient use of resources*. This is the most important criticism of it.

Thus we can conclude that in order to maximise its profits the business restricts its output and thereby raises the price of its product. In doing so it moves backwards up its AC curve, producing fewer goods at a higher cost. The situation can only continue if other businesses are prevented from entering the market and competing for the profit. In other words, this is a *short-run* situation. What happens in the long-run will depend upon the type of imperfect market we are considering.

The long-run equilibrium

Monopoly

A monopoly is a firm which, for one reason or another, enjoys freedom from competition.

In the long-run there is no-one, therefore, to come into the market and compete for the monopolist's abnormal profit. The long-run equilibrium of the monopolist is thus like the short-run.

A monopolist may, however, choose not to maximise profits as fully as possible because of:

a) fear that the government may intervene;

b) respect for the community's welfare;

c) fear that this may attract competition from overseas. It is possible to argue that the inefficiencies fostered by monopoly were part of the explanation of why British industries, such as motor vehicles, were so vulnerable to foreign competition.

d) managerial discretion in the firm's policy. This may arise because profit maximisation may not be a survival condition.

Other aspects of monopoly behaviour are considered in the next chapter.

Oligopoly

Oligopoly is a very complex topic. We will here restrict ourselves to three aspects of oligopoly behaviour: price fixing, game theory, and 'kinked' demand curves.

Cooperation

Oligopoly – the situation where the market is dominated by a few large firms – is hard to analyse. The most practical implication, however, is that oligopolists realise that if they were to cooperate and have a common prices and output policy they could treat the market like a monopolist and there would therefore be a greater total amount of profit to be made from the market. Such a policy would amount to setting up a *cartel* or price-fixing ring. Since these are usually illegal, some industries have resorted to *information agreements* or *market sharing*; for example, the construction companies in an area might get together and take it in turns to submit the lowest tenders for contracts. Virtually all such arrangements are now illegal and the law relating to them is discussed in the next chapter.

Although agreements between organisations to exploit the market may be illegal, it is possible to see that in many oligopolistic markets price competition is avoided. If, for example, we consider the detergent market, we can see that Procter & Gamble and Unilever prefer to compete by product differentiation and advertising rather than by price-cutting wars with each other.

Game theory

The behaviour of monopolists is predictable since they have no competitors and we assume that they are out to maximise their profits. As we shall see below, monopolistic competition is also predictable since there are a sufficiently large number of competitors for us to be able to make generalisations about behaviour, as we can with perfect competition. However in oligopoly the small number of competitors makes generalisations almost impossible, since the actions of one firm may influence those of its competitors. For example, if firm A cuts its price, firm B may respond by price cutting, but it could also respond instead by increasing advertising.

Game theory attempts to analyse competition as a game played between competitors. Each firm tries to define its optimal market strategy, but is aware of the effects of its competitors' actions upon the market and tries to anticipate what the other will do. This anticipation of others' actions means that none of the firms achieves its optimal strategy nor behaves in an economically ideal manner.

The worst extreme of game theory is the *zero-sum* game. A zero-sum situation is any where the size of the pie, market, income, etc., is fixed so that the gain of one must be the loss of another. Poker, for example, is a zero-sum game where the total winnings must be exactly the same as the total losses. Oligopolists often regard competition in this manner. This has

been well explained by Lester Thurow in his book *The Zero-Sum Society*.

A 'kinked' oligopoly demand curve

One consequence of oligopoly can be that a business appears to face a 'kink' in the demand curve for its product. This arises because, although its competitors will allow it to put up the price without interference, the moment it brings its prices down below the ruling market price, they will respond by lowering their prices. Thus the elasticity of demand for the firm's product is much greater above the ruling market price than below it.

Suppose that the market for meat pies is dominated by three companies, Meaty, Beefy and Bouncy. They all sell pies at a price of about 80p per pie and choose to compete by non-price methods such as advertising or variations in flavour. Meaty however begins to pursue an independent pricing policy. It first raises its price to 85p per pie. Beefy and Bouncy are quite willing to allow it to do this because its share of the market declines and, in fact, its sales revenue decreases. Meaty therefore concludes that the demand for its product is elastic and it would be better to cut prices. Its calculations lead it to believe that if it cut the price to 70p per pie it would sell 130 000 pies per week. However as soon as it cuts its prices Beefy and Bouncy respond with similar cuts and Meaty only manages to sell 82 000 pies per week (only a third of its anticipated extra sales). Thus if we drew up a demand curve for Meaty pies it would appear to have a 'kink' in it. The 'kink' occurs at the ruling market price ($MR = MC$ for the whole market), i.e. 80p per pie in our example.

You can see this example illustrated in Fig. 17.5. It can also be seen that the effect of the 'kink' is to make the MR curve discontinuous. The effect is caused because the elasticity of demand is much greater above the ruling market price than below it. We must also consider that Beefy and Bouncy might have responded to Meaty's action in different ways, e.g. by advertising more. This **211**

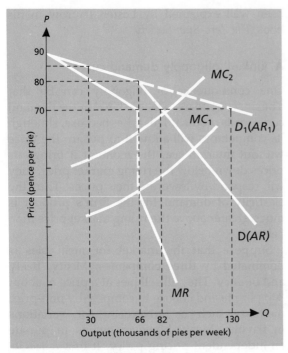

Fig. 17.5 A 'kinked' oligopoly demand curve
Meaty's original price is 80p per pie. Meaty raises the price to 85p per pie and sales fall to 30 000. Meaty calculates that if it cuts its price to 70p per pie sales will expand to 130 000 ($D_1(AR_1)$). However the cut in price causes competitors to cut prices too and therefore Meaty's sales are only 82 000. This causes a 'kink' in the demand curve and discontinuity in the MR curve.

is what makes oligopoly very difficult to analyse.

You will see from Fig. 17.5 that there is a wide latitude for the intersection of MR and MC, i.e. MC could increase significantly (from MC_1 to MC_2) but still leave the profit maximisation output and output the same. This may help to explain the rigidity of pricing which is often associated with oligopoly.

Monopolistic competition

If one business is seen to be making high profits in a situation where there are lots of competitors in an imperfect market, other businesses will be encouraged to enter that line of production and compete the profit away because there is something close to freedom of entry and exit to the market. The situation is thus similar to that of perfect competition. This is illustrated in Fig. 17.6. In (a) the average cost curve is below the average revenue curve and abnormal profits are being made. Since there is free entry to the market other businesses enter and compete their profit away. In (b), however, AC is above AR at all points; the firm is thus making a loss and will, in the long-run, leave the industry. The long-run equilibrium is therefore (c) where the AC curve is tangential to the AR curve and the business is only receiving normal profits.

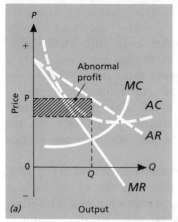

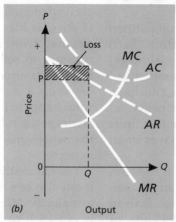

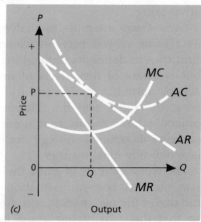

Fig. 17.6 The price and output of the firm under monopolistic competition in the long-run
(a) The existence of abnormal profits attracts new firms to the industry, which lowers the price and eliminates the profit.
(b) The firm makes a loss at any level of output and in the long-run will leave the industry.
(c) The long-run equilibrium, where the firm just recovers normal profit. AC is tangential to AR.

An example of this type of behaviour might be found in a business manufacturing shirts which might accurately predict a new fashion trend and for a short while be able to exploit its monopoly of that design of shirt. Other companies will soon be able to copy this though, and price competition between the firms will compete the excess profit away.

You will note in Fig. 17.6 (c) that, unlike perfect competition, the business does not produce at the lowest point of average cost. It is still the case, however, that it produces where $MC = MR$. Thus, even though the business is not making abnormal profits, it is still producing a restricted output at a higher unit cost. It follows that in all types of imperfect market the business organisation, in following its own interest of profit maximisation, is likely to bring about an inefficient use of resources.

We have just said that monopolistic competition and perfect competition appear to be similar. Can you pinpoint the difference? In perfect competition the firm produced where $MR = MC = AC = AR$ (see Fig. 16.2). In monopolistic competition the firm produces where $MR = MC$ and $AC = AR$ (see Fig. 17.6 (c)), but they are not the same point.

Thus, although the firm under monopolistic competition is making no abnormal profit, it is still producing *inefficiently*, i.e. at a higher average (unit) cost.

Conclusion

In this and the previous chapter we have seen that under all types of competition, and in both the short-run and the long-run, the firm always maximises its profits by producing where $MR = MC$. However an important contrast is that under perfect competition we can equate the long-run equilibrium with an optimum allocation of resources, whereas under monopolistic competition the firm always produces at below optimum capacity, thus wasting resources. Having considered the theory of the firm we will continue in the next chapter to examine various ways in which imperfect competition manifests itself in the economy.

Summary

1   Profit maximisation occurs where there is the greatest possible positive difference between total revenue and total cost.
2   Marginal revenue is the change to total revenue as a result of the sale of one more unit of a commodity.
3   Profit maximisation always occurs where marginal revenue is equal to marginal cost.
4   In the short-run any firm may make abnormal profit; the differences occur in the long-run.
5   For the monopolist organisation the long-run situation is the same as the short-run, i.e. it is free to continue making abnormal profit.
6   Oligopoly behaviour is complex and unpredictable. One explanation is founded on game theory. Another theorem suggests a 'kink' in the oligopolist's demand curve.
7   The long-run equilibrium for the monopolistic competitor occurs where AC is tangential to AR and the organisation is just recovering normal profit.
8   All types of imperfect competition result in economic inefficiency.

213

Questions

1 What alternatives exist to the profit maximisation hypothesis?
2 Explain the shape of the *TR* and *TC* curves. What relationship, if any, exists between them?
3 Explain the relationship between *MR* and elasticity of demand.
4 Demonstrate that *MR* = *MC* must always be the profit maximisation output.
5 Why does *MR* = *MC* profit maximisation occur at lower ouput than that for minimum unit cost?
6 'Profit maximisation occurs where the difference between *AC* and *AR* is at a maximum.' Discuss.
7 'The monopolist organisation will choose to produce where demand is inelastic since here it can raise its prices and thereby its profit.' Discuss.
8 What explanations exist for oligopoly behaviour?
9 Compare and constrast the long-run equilibrium of the monopolistic competitor with that of the perfect competitor.

Data response   Maximising profits

The following is hypothetical data relating to a firm operating under conditions of imperfect competition in the short-run.

Quantity q	Price p	Average cost AC
0	400	∞
10	360	350
20	320	200
30	280	146.6
40	240	125
50	200	120
60	160	123.3
70	120	131.4
80	80	142.5

1 With the aid of this data and with a diagram demonstrate that the condition

$$MR = MC$$

is the profit maximisation position for the firm.
2 If this firm is operating under conditions of monopolistic competition how will its equilibrium position alter in the long-run?

18

Aspects of monopoly

Now maple were Sam's Mon-o-po-ly;
That means it were all 'is to cut,
And nobody else 'adn't got none;
So 'e asked Noah three ha'pence a foot.
　　　　　Marriott Edgar for Stanley Holloway

Governments and monopoly

Most governments will have a policy towards monopolies. There are two reasons for this. Firstly, any government will recognise the misallocation of resources brought about by monopoly. Secondly, on the grounds of equity most governments will feel obliged to have a policy to limit monopoly profits. To some extent the government's attitude will be determined by how the monopoly arose. We will therefore first consider the sources of monopoly.

The sources of monopoly

a) Natural. This arises out of the geographical conditions of supply. For example, South Africa has an almost complete monopoly of the Western world's supply of diamonds. Another example would be Schweppes' monopoly of Malvern water.

b) Historical. A business may have a monopoly because it was first in the field and no-one else has the necessary know-how or customer goodwill. Lloyds of London's command of the insurance market is largely based on historical factors.

c) Capital size. The supply of a commodity may involve the use of such a vast amount of capital equipment that new competitors are effectively excluded from entering the market. This is the case with the chemical industry.

d) Technological. Where there are many economies of scale to be gained it may be natural and advantageous for the market to be supplied by one or a few large companies. This would apply to the motor vehicle industry.

e) Legal. The government may confer a monopoly upon a company. This may be the case when a business is granted a patent or copyright. The right to sole exploitation is given to encourage people to bring forward new ideas.

f) Public. Public corporations such as the Post Office frequently have monopolies. Most public utilities are monopolies.

g) Contrived. There is nothing much a government could or would wish to do about breaking up the monopolies discussed above. Where people discuss the evils of monopoly, however, it is not usually the above forms of monopoly they are thinking about but rather those that are deliberately contrived. Business organisations can contrive to exploit the market either by taking over, or driving out of business, the other firms in the industry (*scale monopoly*) or by entering into agreement with other business to control prices and output (*complex monopoly* – see below). It is this type of monopoly that most legislation is aimed at.

Possibilities for policy

There are three basic policies the government can adopt towards monopolies.

a) Prohibition. The formation of monopolies can be banned and existing monopolies broken up. This is basically the attitude in the USA. 'Anti-trust' legislation, as it is called, in the USA, dates back to the Sherman Act of 1890. There are still nevertheless a considerable number of monopolies in the USA. Legislation against actions 'in restraint of trade' has been more vigorously prosecuted against unions than against big business.

b) Takeover. The government can take over a monopoly and run it in the public interest. Although many industries and companies have been taken over by the government, it has not usually been done with the object of controlling a monopoly.

c) Regulation. The government can allow a monopoly to continue but pass legislation to make sure that it does not act 'against the public interest'. This is basically the attitude of the UK government.

The main legislation concerning monopolies in the UK is embodied in the Fair Trading Act 1973; this codified much previous legislation. The main agency for implementing government policy on competition is the Office of Fair Trading. Under the Fair Trading Act 1973 its Director-General must keep commercial practices in the UK under review and collect information about them so that he can discover monopoly situations and uncompetitive practices. Under the Restrictive Trade Practices Act 1976 he has a major role in the regulation of restrictive trading agreements.

Policy on monopolies

At its simplest a monopoly arises when one trading organisation supplies an entire market. This, however, is very rare and the Fair Trading Act 1973 defines a monopoly as being where one person, company or group of related companies supplies or acquires at least 25 per cent of the goods or services in question in the UK – this is a 'scale monopoly'. A 'complex monopoly' exists if at least 25 per cent of the goods or services of a particular description are supplied in the UK as a whole by two or more persons, unconnected companies or groups of companies who intentionally or otherwise conduct their affairs in such a way that they prevent, distort or restrict competition in the supply of goods or services, e.g. refusing to supply goods or services to particular customers.

Complex monopolies are far more common than scale monopolies, for there are many cases where particular industries are dominated by a small number of suppliers, each of whom holds a very large share of the market, e.g. the motor industry (four major suppliers) and detergents (two major suppliers).

The Director-General of Fair Trading may refer what he considers to be a monopoly to the Monopolies and Mergers Commission for investigation.

The main inherent dangers of a monopoly, whether a pure monopoly or the more usual scale or complex monopolies, are restriction of output, price fixing, regulation of terms supply and removal of consumers' choice and most importantly cost inefficiency. Additionally, free competition may be stifled by preventing competitors entering the market, and a monopolist may also use his monopsonic buying powers to dictate terms to suppliers. The government uses the law to forbid or regulate these practices.

Restrictive practices

The Restrictive Trade Practices Act 1976 is concerned with any agreement or arrangement between suppliers of goods or services, including recommendations made by trade associations, which restrict competition. Examples include agreements between suppliers to charge the same prices, or to divide up the market and to trade on the same terms of business. Such practices are unlawful and the object of the Act is to ensure that only such agreements, arrangements and recommendations as are in the public interest are allowed to continue. To achieve this, full details of 'registrable agreements' must be sent to the Office of Fair Trading for entry in a public register maintained by the Director-General. The Director-General then has the power to refer the practice to the Restrictive Practices Court to consider whether or not it is against the public interest. There are a number of grounds (often called 'gateways') on which the practice can be upheld as being in the public interest, e.g. the Net Book Agreement.

Under the Act the Director-General may instigate action for an injunction to restrain the continuance or repetition of the unlawful restrictive practice. A consumer directly affected by it may bring an action for damages.

The first Restrictive Trade Practices Act was passed in 1956 and by the end of 1980 3873 agreements concerning the supply of goods had been registered. A further 3211 agreements had been terminated since 1956 and 658 referred to the Court. In 1980 five organisations were found guilty of breaking previous undertakings to the Court and fines for contempt of £185 000 were imposed on four suppliers of concrete pipes and a fine of £50 000 was imposed on the British Steel Corporation.

The power given to the Director-General of Fair Trading, under the Competition Act 1980, to investigate and control the anti-competitive practices of single firms supplements the existing powers for investigation of monopolies and restrictive agreements among firms. The government's declared intention in the Act is to promote competition and efficiency in industry and commerce.

More than one company has agreed to alter its trading practices in accordance with the DGFT's suggestions rather than face an investigation by the Commission, and British Gas and British Rail have been the subject of preliminary investigations.

Although the Price Commission has now been abolished by the Act, the Secretary of State for Trade and Industry has power under the Act to investigate prices which he considers to be 'of major public concern having regard to whether the supply, or acquisition, of the goods or services in question is of general economic import-ance, or the price is of special significance to consumers'. There are no direct sanctions that can be taken in such a situation but it could be treated as an anti-competitive practice.

Resale price maintenance (RPM)

Resale price maintenance is the practice whereby manufacturers impose a fixed retail selling price on the retailers they supply. They enforce this by taking action against anyone who undercuts the price (or charges more). The enforcement of minimum selling prices by manufacturers or distributors of goods, either individually or collectively, is illegal under the Resale Prices Act 1976 unless held to be in the public interest by the Restrictive Practices Court. At present only minimum prices for books has the Court's sanction. Any person adversely affected, or the Director-General of Fair Trading, may take civil proceedings against those who seek to reimpose minimum resale prices.

Resale price maintenance poses an economic dilemma to governments. On the one hand consumers benefit, and efficient organisations are rewarded, by allowing free pricing of commodities. On the other, consumers can suffer because many small businesses will be unable to compete with large multiple retailers in price cutting and may be forced to close down or face insolvency, thereby reducing retail services to the public. A good example at the present time is the decline of independent chemists since supermarkets have been allowed to sell patent medicines. Indeed, indiscriminate promotion of competition may have the effect of operating to the detriment of the very consumers it seeks to protect.

The EEC and monopoly

Article 85 of the Treaty of Rome 1957 prohibits all agreements between business organisations, decisions by trade associations and concerted practices which may affect trade between *member states* and which have as their object or effect the prevention, restriction or distortion of competition within the EEC. Article 85 includes fixing buying and/or selling prices or other terms of business, discriminating in favour of certain business organisations, thus giving them a competitive advantage, and sharing markets. If, for example, a manufacturer appointed a sole distributor of his products in each EEC country, and each distributor agreed not to export to other EEC countries, the 'common market' would be divided into 10 separate markets and competition among member states would be effectively distorted. Article 86 declares that the abuse of a dominant position in the market structure is incompatible with the EEC objectives, e.g. imposing buying or selling prices or other trading conditions which are unfair, limit production, markets or technological development to the prejudice of consumers. Despite these provisions there is still much malpractice within the EEC; there are the occasional cases of EEC action, like that with the Distillers Company (*see below*, page 220), but many abuses remain. A later section of this chapter deals with price discrimination within the EEC.

Policy on mergers

The Fair Trading Act 1973 covers mergers involving the acquisition of gross assets of more than £15m or where a 'monopoly', i.e. 25 per cent or more of the relevant market in the UK or a substantial part of it, would be created or enhanced. Also included are situations where one company acquires the ability to control or materially influence another company without actually acquiring a controlling interest.

The Director-General of Fair Trading is responsible for keeping a watchful eye on possible mergers within the Act, but his role is only to advise the Secretary of State for Trade and Industry as to whether a reference should be made to the Monopolies and Mergers Commission; he may not make a reference directly. This contrasts with his powers relating to monopolies. The Secretary of State has power under the 1973 Act to order that the merger shall not proceed or to regulate any identified adverse effects of a merger or proposed merger, e.g. the effect on labour relations.

In 1980, for example, 182 mergers were within the Act, but only five actual references to the Commission were made. Each reference is considered on its own merits and on the criterion of the 'public interest', the latter encompassing the maintenance and promotion of competition, consumer interest, effects on employment and, in some cases, the possibility of 'asset stripping' or tax avoidance.

The Treaty of Rome makes no reference to mergers as such, but the Commission of the EEC has sought to encourage mergers which lead to improved competition throughout the Community.

The guiding principle behind UK legislation on monopolies, mergers and restrictive practices is that of 'the public interest'. Monopolies are not prohibited per se but only if they act against the public interest. The problem is that no one has defined adequately what the public interest is or established criteria for assessing it.

Pricing problems

Government policy on monopoly pricing

If a monopoly does exist and the government decides not to break it up but regulate prices in the public interest, what shall its policy on prices be? In the 'normal' monopoly situation, illustrated in Fig. 18.1, monopoly legislation could be aimed at making the monopolist produce at point F where $AC = AR$. At this point the price is OR and the output ON. All monopoly profits have been eliminated and the public is obtaining the largest output for the lowest price that is compatible with the monopolist remaining in the industry. Pure economic theory would suggest setting a price where $MC = P$, but as you can see in Fig. 18.1 this would result in the firm actually making a loss. There are also difficulties in determining MC accurately. These problems are discussed in more detail in the next chapter and also in Section IV of the book.

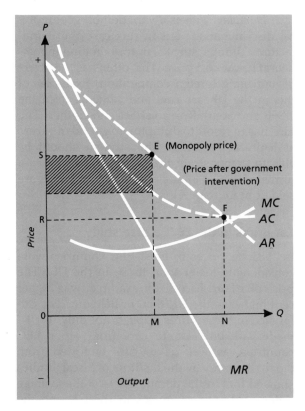

Fig. 18.1 *Government intervention in monopoly pricing*
The monopolist would choose to produce at point E, making maximum profit. Government policy aims to compel the monopolist to produce at point F where AC = AR, thus eliminating abnormal profit.

Mark-up pricing and break-even charts

Although an organisation's behaviour may be governed by concepts such as marginal revenue and marginal cost, in practice they may be very difficult to determine, especially when a large organisation is marketing a variety of products. In these circumstances they often try to base their prices on average or unit cost. To do this they must make assumptions about the future volume of sales and likely average cost at that output. This having been done, a *mark-up* of, say, 10 per cent is then added for profit. This fascinatingly simple theory seems realistic, but stops tantalisingly short of telling us why the average mark-up should be 40 per cent in one industry and 5 per cent in another.

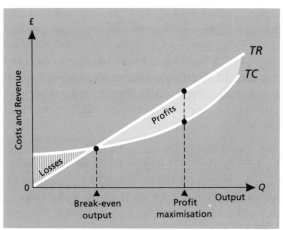

Fig. 18.2 *A break-even chart*
If the price is fixed then *TR* is a straight line. Profits or losses are the vertical distance between the two curves.

The reader should take careful note that this is the way the organisation may try to determine the right price for *itself*, but the customers may or may not be willing to pay the right price or buy the right quantity. Prices in the market are still determined by the forces of supply and demand. The monopolist organisation has great power, of course, to impose its wishes on the market. If an organisation sets its price in this manner then we can draw up a *break-even chart* to demonstrate its profits and losses. In Fig. 18.2 *TR* curve is a straight line because price is constant. *TC* is a normal total cost curve. This way of looking at profits is much closer to the accountants' view than most of the economists' ways of looking at the market.

Discriminating monopoly

Discriminating monopoly (or price discrimination) is said to exist when a business is able to charge two or more different prices for the same product.

The conditions for discriminating monopoly

Every producer knows that there are some consumers who are willing to pay more than the **219** market price for the good. The consumers are therefore in receipt of utility they are not paying for and this is known as a *consumer's surplus* (*see* page 115). A monopolist may be able to eat into this surplus by charging some consumers higher prices than others. In order for price discrimination to be worthwhile two conditions must be fulfilled.

a) The monopolist must be able to separate the two markets. This may be done geographically, by branding, or by time. The suppliers of personal services such as doctors and lawyers also often charge different prices for the same service.

b) The two or more markets thus separated must have different elasticities of demand otherwise the exercise would not be worthwhile.

Types of price discrimination

It perhaps seems unlikely that consumers would willingly pay two different prices for the same product. However this can happen if consumers are prevented from buying the cheaper product in some way, or if they are unaware that the difference exists. The main ways in which this is achieved are as follows.

a) *Geographical*. Goods are sold at different prices in different countries. This was illustrated in 1977 when the Distillers Company were ordered by the EEC to cease selling the same brand of whisky at one price in the UK and at a higher price in the rest of the EEC. (See also the example of car prices discussed below.)

b) *Branding*. Many manufacturers sell the identical product at one price under their own brand name and at a lower price branded with the name of the retailer. For example, many famous manufacturers sell some of their output more cheaply under the St Michael label of Marks and Spencer.

c) *Time*. Many public monopolies sell the same product at different prices at different times. Examples of this are off-peak electricity, weekend returns on British Rail and 'stand-by' flights by British Airways.

d) *Dumping*. This is a variation on geographical discrimination, but in this case the manufacturer 'dumps' surplus output on foreign markets at below cost price. This often has the object of damaging foreign competition. Examples of this in the UK are cars and cameras from the USSR and South Korean shoes and clothes. The EEC has to resort to dumping to get rid of excess agricultural products. The student should be able to demonstrate that dumping increases a firm's profits so long as the dumped goods are sold at more than *AVC*.

Car prices in the EEC: a case study

In 1983 car prices in most EEC countries were considerably lower than those in the UK. The price of a Ford Escort, for example, was 36 per cent higher in the UK than in Belgium. The difference in these prices applied not only to UK-made cars but also to cars from other EEC countries, as well as to cars imported from Japan. A survey by the Institute of Fiscal Studies showed that in the decade 1974–83 the average differential between prices in the UK and the rest of the EEC was never less than 10 per cent and in six of the ten years was over 19 per cent.

Despite the protestations put forward by the motor trade (differences in tax rates, exchange rates, transport costs, etc.), it is clear that there is extensive price discrimination. Motor manufacturers have discovered that the elasticity of demand for cars in the UK is substantially lower than in other EEC countries. The UK market is therefore exploited by UK, West German, French and Japanese manufacturers alike.

Table 18.1 shows the differences in prices of the top selling cars in the UK in 1983 compared with prices in Belgium and France. The prices are shown before the addition of any indirect taxes and at the exchange rates as they were in October 1983. As you can see there is often a pre-tax difference of over £1000. If prices were compared for more expensive cars such as Jaguar or Mercedes Benz the differences would run into several thousand pounds.

We, therefore, have a clear case of geographi-

Table 18.1 Prices of the ten best-selling cars in the UK compared with prices in the EEC*, 1983

Type of car	British price (£)	French price (£)	Belgian price (£)	Saving by buying cheapest (£)
Ford Escort 1·1	3362	2684	2480	882
Austin Maestro 1·6 HLS	4711	3588	3282	1429
Vauxhall Cavalier 1·3 SL	4471	3250	3323	1221
Austin Metro 1·0 L	3427	2451	2301	1126
Ford Sierra 1·6 GL	5417	3799	3902	1618
Datsun Sunny 1·5 GL	4093	3364	2854	1239
Vauxhall Astra 1·6 SR	4839	3942	3512	1327
Ford Fiesta 1·1 L	3632	2514	2557	1118
Austin Mini City E	2487	1946	1697	790
VW Polo	3209	2454	2137	1072

*All prices net of tax
Source: Bureau Européen des Unions des Consummoteurs

cal price discrimination. The English Channel has proved an effective way of separating the markets. In addition to this there is the fact that European cars are left-hand drive. This is reinforced by manufacturers being unwilling to supply right-hand drive cars and by the complications of a private individual importing a car. It should be pointed out that the practice of geographical price discrimination is illegal under the Treaty of Rome.

We will now proceed to demonstrate by the use of a hypothetical example why price discrimination benefits the manufacturer and how the marketing strategy is determined. Figure 18.3 shows the situation for a UK manufacturer. The first diagram shows the situation in the combined market (UK and EEC). Given this situation the manufacturer would maximise profits by producing where $MR = MC$. This gives an output of 25 000 cars a month at a price of £3250 giving a total revenue of £81·25 million. However, from experience the manufacturer knows that UK consumers (market B) are willing to pay more for their cars and therefore sets the price at £4000 per car, and sells 10 000 per month, thus earning £40 million in home sales. In the EEC, however, there is much more price com-

petition and the price is dropped to £3000 to compete with other manufacturers. As a result of this the company sells 15 000 cars bringing in a revenue of £45 million. Thus as a result of this price discrimination total revenue has increased by £3·75 million per month (£85 million – £81·25 million). This must all be extra profit because output, and therefore costs, are the same as in the combined market.

Figure 18.3 also shows the way in which the market strategy is determined. This is to take the level of MC at the $MC = MR$ intersection in the combined market and then equate this level of MC with the MRs in the separate markets. By then tracing this output to the demand (AR) curve the manufacturer is able to determine the best price to charge.

In practice the situation is more complicated. There are indirect taxes to consider, exchange rates and, often, many different markets. However, our analysis shows the principles underlying the practice. This applies to all types of price discrimination. Thus when one is offered cheap Awaydays by British Rail, off-peak electricity, or 'good value' by Marks and Spencer, it should be remembered that this is all part of a strategy by the producer to increase profits.

221

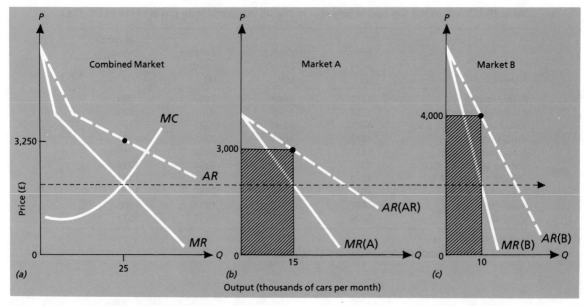

Fig. 18.3 *Discriminating monopoly*
(*a*) **Combine market.** (*b*) **Market A (exports)** (*c*) **Market B (domestic). The discriminating monopolist divides output between two markets. In the combined market it equates combined MR with MC; this would give an output of 25 000 cars at a price of £3250 per car. However by equating MR with MC in the separate markets it increases total revenue while keeping the same costs. In market A 15 000 cars are sold at £3000 (TR = £45m) and in market B the remaining 10 000 cars are sold at £4000 each (TR = £40m). This is an increase of £3.75m per month on the combined market price.**

Monopoly assessed

In this section of the chapter we will consider the advantages and disadvantages of monopoly to the economy. We will first consider two advantages, those of economies of scale and of research and development and then proceed to the disadvantages.

The flat-bottomed *AC* curve

In some industries, especially those involving a great deal of capital equipment such as chemicals and motor vehicles, it could be that the larger and more monopolistic a business organisation is the more it is able to take advantage of economies of scale. The industry is said to have a flat-bottomed average cost curve.

In Fig. 18.4 the national market for cars is 2 million per year. In our example, the production

is divided between two companies, Kruks and Toymota. Toymota has a bigger share of the market (1·1 million) and, because of the economies of scale to be gained, the long-run average cost curve (*LAC*) of the industry is downward sloping.

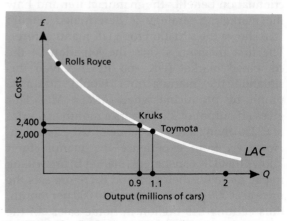

Fig. 18.4 *The flat-bottomed average cost curve*

This means that Toymota's average costs (£2000) are lower than Kruks' (£2400). In the price-conscious car market this means Toymota will sell even more cars, gaining a bigger share of the market and leaving Kruks with a smaller share and even higher costs. In this situation Kruks will eventually go out of business and Toymota will have a complete monopoly. This could be to the public's benefit if continuing economies of scale mean even cheaper cars.

The end result of such a situation, then, is monopoly or some form of oligopoly. This is very much the case in the motor industry, which is dominated by a small number of very large firms. Most medium-sized firms have tended to disappear, but companies producing a very small output of specialist and expensive cars still exist, e.g. Rolls Royce and Lotus, because they are not very concerned about unit costs.

In such an industry it would not be economic sense to break up the monopoly. Indeed it has been observed that in the UK the government has often promoted the formation of monopolies in these sorts of industry. In these circumstances the government's options are limited to either taking over the industry or regulating its prices and output. Although the choices are very clear in theory, in practice it is often very difficult to acquire enough information to judge what is happening in an industry.

Research and development

It has been argued, most notably by Schumpeter (*see* below, in Chapter 24), that it is only the monopolist or the oligopolist that can provide the large sums of money necessary to provide for expensive research and development programmes. Keen price competition can cut profit margins and leave nothing for product development. As we shall see below, it can also be argued that monopoly leads to complacency and lack of development.

Redistribution of income

Monopoly brings about a redistribution of income from the consumer to the monopolist. If the consumers are selling their own products or services in a competitive market then they will be receiving the marginal cost of doing so. The monopolist, however, receives a price above *MC* and this, therefore, represents a transfer of income above what is economically necessary. The continued existence of monopolies, therefore, further worsens the unequal distribution of income in the economy.

Allocative inefficiency

The fact that the monopolist produces at a price greater than *MC* represents a misallocation of resources. This point is fully explained in Section IV. For the moment we can simply note that monopoly power has resulted in *contrived scarcity*. This refers to the fact that, as price exceeds *MC*, extra units of output *could* be produced at a cost below that which the consumers would be prepared to pay. Thus there seems to be the potential for increasing consumer surplus and the monopolist's profit. This potential gain in welfare, however, does not take place. This is because, unless the monopolist can price discriminate, producing the extra units would cause *MR* to fall below *MC* and hence reduce the monopolist's actual profit. In short, there seems to be an underproduction of the product concerned in that not enough of the nation's resources are being allocated to its production.

Lack of the X-efficiency

X-efficiency is the term used to describe the minimisation of cost which occurs under conditions of competition. It is argued that it is a necessary corollary of profit maximisation that a firm achieves X-efficiency. However under conditions of monopoly or oligopoly the firm is protected from competition and the firm may therefore not be under pressure to be X-efficient. If this is so this will lead to an upward shift in the cost curves. Figure 18.5 shows an upward shift in the *MC* curve as a result of lack of X-efficiency, thus further worsening the adverse effects of monopoly.

223

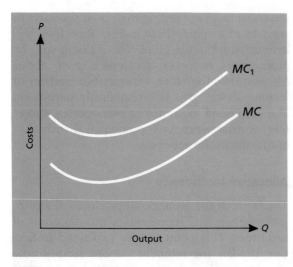

Fig. 18.5 *Increase in costs caused by X-inefficiency*

Conclusion

Economists since the time of Adam Smith have usually opposed monopoly. As we saw in Chapter 5 Adam Smith wrote:

The monopolists by keeping the market constantly understocked, by never fully supplying the effectual demand, sell their commodities much above the natural price, and raise their emoluments, whether they consist in wages or profit, greatly above their natural rate.

It should not be thought, therefore, that the modern capitalist state is the legatee of Smith; free enterprise, indeed, is the very antithesis of much that he argued for.

We have seen, however, that under certain circumstances monopoly can be both efficient and desirable. It would therefore seem sensible to say that we should take a pragmatic case study approach to the problem, weighing each situation on its merits. Against this it can be argued that full investigation of all monopoly practices would be very expensive. It must also be said that, despite the existence of much legislation on monopoly, there appears to be a general lack of effectiveness. The most cynical viewpoint on this is put forward by J. K. Galbraith who argues that the purpose of anti-monopoly legislation is so that the government can be 'seen to be doing something' about monopoly. The state, however, is too wedded to the capitalist structure to actually want to do anything about it. Thus, it is argued, monopoly legislation is a propaganda exercise.

Summary

1 Government policy on monopoly is based on the idea that they should not be 'against the public interest'. However this concept is vague and ill-defined.
2 The chief UK government agency for monopoly control is the Office of Fair Trading.
3 The EEC Treaty of Rome prohibits restrictive practices.
4 Government policy on monopoly prices could be aimed at getting the monopolist to produce where $AC = AR$, but this is impossible if there is a flat-bottomed AC curve.
5 Discriminating monopoly is a situation where a firm sells the same product at two (or more) different prices.
6 Arguments in favour of monopoly include economies of scale and support for research and development.
7 Arguments against monopoly include worsening the distribution of income, allocative inefficiency and lack of X-efficiency.

Questions

1   What is the scope for the price discrimination for the following:
   a) British Telecom;
   b) a wheat farmer;
   c) the CAP;
   d) a doctor?
2   Draw a diagram to show how dumping can increase the profits of a monopolist.
3   On page 222 we discussed flat-bottomed average cost curves. As you can see in Fig. 18.4 the *AC* curve slopes downwards continuously. Why do you think economists prefer the term flat-bottomed? (Hint: what would be the result if the curve sloped downwards for ever?)
4   What is meant by mark-up pricing? How does it work?
5   In Fig. 18.2 show the effect of:
   a) an increase in the price of the product;
   b) a rise in fixed costs.
6   Describe the main features of anti-monopoly legislation. Evaluate its success.
7   'The tragedy of monopoly is not excessive profits. There may indeed be no profits at all, the high price being frittered away in small volume and inefficient production.' Discuss.
8   Discuss the view that breaking up monopolies would increase prices by increasing costs.
9.   'While the law (of competition) may be sometimes hard for the individual, it is best for the race, because it ensures the survival of the fittest in every department. We accept and welcome, therefore, as conditions to which we much accommodate ourselves, great inequality of environment, the concentration of business, industrial and commercial, in the hands of a few, and the law of competition between these, as being not only beneficial, but essential for the future progress of the race.'

Critically evaluate this statement of Andrew Carnegie's, made in 1889.

Data response   Euro car prices ━━━━━━━━━━━━━━━━━━━━━━━━━━

Read the following article which is taken from *The Times* of 25 February 1988.

Drop in variation of Euro car prices
By Daniel Ward, Motor Industry Correspondent

New car prices in Britain are still among the highest in the EEC though the value of buying a car on the Continent and importing it to the United Kingdom is now questionable. A consumer survey shows that basic prices before value added tax and special car tax in Britain are 19 per cent higher than in Belgium where prices have been held back by government fiscal controls.

The advantage is even greater in Denmark where cripping taxation forces manufacturers to lower new car prices which are 41 per cent below the level in Britain. The survey by the Brussels-based Bureau of European Consumers' Unions says it is worth exporting a car from one EEC country to another rather than buying at home.

The pre-tax price of a Ford Fiesta is £4113 in Britain yet £2703 in Denmark before taxes of more than £5000 are heaped on to the basic price. The variation in pricing is more marked among larger cars that attract luxury taxes in many European countries. A Ford Granada 2.9 that costs £18 753 in Britain is sold for only £13 271 in Germany

225

where VAT is charged at 14 per cent and no special car tax is levied. In the Irish Republic the same car costs more than £28 000 and £36 000 in Denmark.

The AA last night advised buyers to shop around dealers in Britain for a good discount on the retail price rather than import a car. Many motorists buying new cars on the Continent through cut-price import companies had suffered problems.

The gap between prices in different countries is narrowing. Since 1981 the gap between the average Belgian and British prices has fallen from 52 per cent to 19 per cent.

The plan to create a single open market within the EEC in 1992 should help bring car prices closer together. The EEC bureaucrats are not aiming to replace every national taxation system with a single scheme but they will act to remove discrimination against certain types of vehicle.

• Sales of British cars in Japan are second only to West Germany's, and ahead of French and Italian. In 1987 sales in the highly profitable Japanese market rose from 5000 to more than 7000 as Rover, Jaguar and Rolls-Royce enjoyed success.

Answer the following questions:

1   Describe the conditions which must exist for price discrimination such as that described in the article to be both possible and worthwhile to the businesses concerned.

2   Why may differences in prices persist after the introduction of the Single European Market in 1992?

3   Examine the Chicago School view that the best protection for the consumer is competition rather than consumer legislation.

4   How do firms determine the optimum prices to sell their products at in the different markets under conditions of price discrimination?

5   What explanations could be put forward of why the gap between the average Belgium and British prices has fallen from 52% to 19% since 1981?

Additional question on the article.
Why is it so difficult for European manufactures to export cars to Japan?

19

Privatisation or nationalisation

*To secure for the workers by hand or by brain
the full fruits of their industry and the most
equitable distribution thereof that may be
possible, upon the basis of common ownership
of the means of production, distribution and
exchange, and the best obtainable system of
popular administration and control of each
industry or service.*

Clause IV of the Constitution of the
Labour Party 1918

The first 80 years of this century saw an almost
continuous widening of the frontiers of the state
in British industry from the formation of the
Port of London Authority in 1908 to the activities of the NEB in the 1970s. Since 1979 there has
been a headlong flight into privatisation. In this
chapter we will look at the arguments for and
against privatisation. We will also consider the
pricing problems of nationalised industries and
privatised ones.

Background to the debate

What is privatisation?

Undoubtedly one of the most significant trends
in economic and social policy of recent years has
been privatisation. This has not only been the
case in the UK but also in many other advanced
industrial nations. At its simplest privatisation
means the denationalisation of state controlled
industries. We are all familiar with things such
as the sale of British Gas, British Telecom and so
on. However, privatisation is much wider than

this – it also includes such things as the sale of
council houses, the sale of the assets of the New
Town Corporations and the contracting out of
local authority controlled services such as street
cleaning, etc.

At a more fundamental level we can see privatisation as a piece of social/economic engineering. It is aimed at reintroducing competition
and free market economics to the centre of the
economy. It is also aimed at changing people's
attitudes and bringing in what the Conservatives
have termed the 'enterprise culture'.

What is a nationalised industry?

In the UK nationalised industries are public corporations. These are public bodies set up by
statute to own and control the relevant activity.
Although some public corporations are referred
to as nationalised industries, strictly speaking
this is a misnomer. To be a true 'nationalised
industry' the undertaking would have to be run
directly by the government and be headed by a
minister. This, for example, used to be the case
with the GPO, but in 1969 it was reconstituted

as a public corporation, headed by a chairman, and renamed the Post Office.

Today there is no distinct legal form termed nationalised industry, but a group of public corporations are commonly referred to as such. Although termed nationalised industries for many years, it was not until 1976 that an agreed definition was published by the National Economic Development Office (NEDO). The nationalised industries were said to be those public corporations which existed mainly by *trading with the public*. The NEDO definition said that nationalised industries were those public corporations:

a) whose assets were in public ownership and vested in public corporation;

b) whose board members were *not* civil servants;

c) whose boards were appointed by a secretary of state;

d) which were primarily engaged in industrial or other trading activities.

The NEDO study concentrated on the then nine most important nationalised industries ranging from the largest, the Post Office, to the National Freight Corporation.

In addition to these there were those public corporations which are not considered nationalised industries. These include the Bank of England and the port authorities. These you will note are not engaged in trading with the public, while organisations such as the Post Office clearly are. By 1979 the state had in its ownership a share in a large number of businesses such as BP and Amersham International. Such joint ownership may be termed *mixed enterprise* (*see* page 74). Such firms did not form part of the debate on *nationalisation* because they were not monopolies and were generally seeking to maximise profit. On the other hand they were considered right for *privatisation* by a government ideologically opposed to public ownership.

The role of nationalised industries

When Margaret Thatcher came to power in 1979 the combined turnover of all public corporations amounted to £44 billion or 22·9 per cent of the gross domestic product. At the same time they employed 1 710 000 people and were responsible for 20 per cent of all investment in the economy.

This did not include other state owned assets such as the Rover Group and BP. Despite large scale privatisation the turnover of public corporations was still £46 billion in 1986 and still accounted for 10 per cent of all investment.

The development of nationalised industries

It is often thought that nationalised industries are recent developments and the creation of socialist governments. This is not entirely the case. Indeed the Post Office, which has a claim to be the oldest 'nationalised' industry, was set up in the time of Charles II.

a) The early nationalised industries. Nationalisation can be truly said to have started in the UK with the establishment of the Port of London Authority in 1908. The inter-war period saw the creation of the Central Electricity Board (1926), the British Broadcasting Corporation (1926), the London Passenger Transport Board (1933) and the British Overseas Airways Corporation (1939).

b) The Labour nationalisations of 1945–51. The major nationalisations of this period included coal, transport (road, railways and canals) and electricity generation in 1947, gas in 1948 and iron and steel in 1951. Road transport and iron and steel were subsequently denationalised by the Conservative government in 1953. The nationalisations of this period created the bulk of nationalised industries.

c) The later nationalisations. The scope of nationalisation widened in the 1960s and 1970s. Iron and steel was renationalised in 1967, and aircraft construction and shipbuilding were nationalised in 1977. The GPO ceased to be a government department in 1969 and became, as the Post Office, a public corporation. This was subsequently divided into the Post Office and British Telecommunications in 1981.

Privatising

It was said that when the Conservatives came to power Magaret Thatcher drew up a 'Household Contents List'. This is shown in Table 19.1.

Table 19.1 The Household Contents List 1979

Nationalised industries in order of turnover
  Electricity†
  British Telecom*
  British Gas*
  National Coal Board
  British Steel†
  British Aerospace*
  British Rail
  Post Office
  British Airways*
  British Shipbuilders†
  National Bus Company*
  National Freight Corporation*
  British Airports Authority*

Renamed corporations
  Britoil (BNOC)*
  Enterprise Oil*

Mixed enterprises
  British Leyland†
  Rolls Royce*
  Ferranti*
  Cable and Wireless*
  Amersham International*

    + others
* = already privatised
† = being prepared for privatisation (1988)

As you can see by 1988 a large percentage of the list had been, or was about to be, privatised. In addition to this, other state-owned assets such as the water boards were being prepared for privatisation. It was also in 1988 that the government announced that it was considering forcing local authorities to dispose of many of their assets. If undertaken this would dwarf all other privatisations since the saleable assets of local authorities were estimated at over £60 billion.

The public ownership debate

Many arguments, both of an economic and a political nature, are advanced for and against public ownership. These arguments often contradict each other. It should also be remembered that the arguments will not apply equally to each industry. We will consider both sides of the case.

Arguments in favour of nationalisation

a) Economies of scale. There are many industries which are best organised on a very large scale. A good example of this would be electricity. To have several electricity companies supplying electricity to one town would be very inefficient. The nationalisation of an industry should enable it to benefit from all the possible economies of scale and avoid *the duplication of resources.*

b) Externalities. Many industries create *negative externalities* such as pollution. It should be much easier to control these in nationalised industries than those under private ownership.

c) Capital expenditure. Some industries demand such major investment that only the government is capable of providing the funds. Such an argument was advanced to support the nationalisation of iron and steel in 1967. It might also apply to coal, railways and atomic energy. In addition to capital expenditure, some industries demand large spending on *research and development.* In the case of atomic energy and aircraft it was decided that this could only adequately be met by the government.

d) Preventing the abuse of monopoly power. Where many economies of scale are obtainable it is quite possible that, if private organisations were left to themselves, they would become monopolies. This could well be true with industries such as gas, electricity and telephones. Nationalisation can ensure that they are administered in the public interest and not just for private profit, thus gaining the benefits of large-scale production without the abuses of monopoly.

e) Control of the economy. The nationalisation of industries may enable a government to pursue its economic policies on investment, employment and prices through the operation of

229

the industries concerned. For example, it might hold down prices in the nationalised industries as a counter-inflationary measure or, alternatively, invest to create employment in depressed areas of the economy.

f) *Special pricing policies*. The fact that a nationalised industry is usually a monopoly may allow it to charge different prices to different customers. This may be for one of two reasons.

i) *Maximising revenue*. In this it would be acting no differently from a private *discriminating monopolist* (*see* Chapter 18). Examples of this can be seen when British Rail offers special fares such as Awaydays to customers, or the electricity boards charge different tariffs for electricity consumed at different times of the day.

ii) *Socially needy customers may be preferred*. A nationalised industry may offer special low rates to customers such as old-age pensioners; free bus passes for old-age pensioners might be seen as an example of this.

g) *Social benefits*. A product or service may be supplied to the public below cost price where this is considered beneficial. An example of this might be postal services supplied to the remoter parts of the country. Another example is commuter rail fares; these are effectively subsidised because if these customers switched to the roads, the inconvenience and cost would be unacceptable.

h) *Strategic reasons*. The government might find it necessary to nationalise an industry considered vital for the defence of the country. Thus, for example, the aerospace industry in the UK was nationalised to keep it in existence. The defence implications of nuclear power were also a reason for ensuring that this was a nationalised industry. Key industries of less obvious strategic significance, such as iron and steel, coal and transport, might be seen as vital to the defence of the country in times of war.

i) *Industrial relations*. It is argued that nationalisation will improve industrial relations. This would seem a hard argument to substantiate. It should be remembered, however, that many of the nationalised industries are declining industries and, therefore, problems in industrial relations are to be expected.

j) *Socialism*. A major reason for nationalisation is not based on economic considerations but is political, and is based on a commitment by the Labour Party to the ownership of the means of production. Opinions in the Labour Party vary from the pragmatic approach of Labour governments during the 1960s and 1970s to those who believe that a Labour government should nationalise the 100 largest companies in the country and renationalise privatised industries without compensation.

Arguments against nationalisation

a) *The abuse of monopoly power*. Many nationalised industries are monopolies and it could be argued that a state monopoly is more disadvantageous to the consumer than a private one. This is because there is no higher authority to protect the consumer's interests. The consumer therefore has to tolerate the lack of choice and high prices associated with monopoly, with little hope of redress, although there are normally consumer consultative bodies.

b) *Bureaucracy*. It is argued that nationalisation creates over-large and over-bureaucratic organisations which, therefore, suffer from diseconomies of scale. Evidence of this is the frequent reorganisation of nationalised industries and, often, the splitting of administration into regional boards, etc.

c) *Lack of incentive*. Although it would not be desirable for nationalised industries to maximise their profits, it could be argued that the lack of the profit motive removes the spur to efficiency which private enterprises have.

d) *The problem of declining industries*. Those industries which are faced with contracting markets, such as the railways, have a particular problem. The shrinking market forces up their unit costs. A commercial organisation would get round this by diversification. Nationalised industries, however, are prevented from doing this by the terms of the Acts which establish them. Thus they have declining business but are not allowed to branch out into anything else. Indeed, the decision of the Conservative government of 1979 to sell off the profitable sections of some of the nationalised industries, e.g. British Transport Hotels, worsened the situation for such industries by leaving them only the unprofitable parts of the industry.

e) *The corporate state.* Many people are opposed to the spread of nationalisation on political grounds. It is thought that it moves the country towards communism. Free enterprise, it is argued, is more democratic since it leaves decisions in the hands of individuals. However we probably already have a corporate state; most of the important economic decisions are today taken either by government or by large business corporations. Nevertheless it is difficult to find an example of an industry being nationalised in the UK on purely ideological grounds. Most nationalisations have either been of public utilities such as gas and electricity, where centralised planning was considered important, or of loss-making industries such as iron and steel and railways.

f) *Political interference.* The sound administration of nationalised industries is often undermined by politicians interfering in the industries' policies for short-term political gains. An example of this would be a ministerial order not to raise prices in an attempt to combat inflation. Ministers who have engaged in this type of activity are as widely varied as Edward Heath and Tony Benn.

The privatisation argument

In the short term privatisation can be seen as a way of the government raising money and thus reducing the need for taxation. But more important than this are the ideological motives which underlie the trend. At a superficial level we may view privatisation as a response to the supposed inefficiencies of nationalised industries.

More fundamental than this is the belief that the *price system* is the most efficient way to run the economy and that the price system brings about an optimum allocation of resources. The classical economists, such as Adam Smith, argued that this optimality was brought about by the 'invisible hand' of self-interest (i.e. everyone striving to maximise their own individual benifit) and was regulated by the forces of competition. Many twentieth-century economists have disagreed with this view. However, in recent years Milton Friedman and the *Chicago School* have argued for a return to classical values. According to this school of thought the market economy is essentially self-regulating and efficient. Problems in the economy such as inflation and unemployment are caused by state interference. Thus in order to have a well run economy it is essential to reduce the role of the state to a minimum so that the maximum percentage of the economy will be self-regulating.

An extension of this argument is that the state sector of the economy has 'crowded-out' private investment. During the years of high government intervention there was a high demand upon the investment funds available of which the state took a large proportion. It is argued by the free market school that the state will take investment decisions on non-economic grounds – for example, it may build coal-fired power stations to keep the miners happy – this will therefore lead to low yielding investments. It is thus necessary to reduce the role of the state as investor and leave markets to allocate capital in the most efficient manner possible. This argument also helps to explain why the Conservative government thought it necessary to keep down the size of the PSBR and therefore not compete for available funds.

It is therefore necessary to see the events of recent years not simply as the selling off of state controlled industries but a fundamental shift in the way in which the economy is organised. Initially the sale of assets could be seen as merely a change of emphasis but it is now apparent that the government is moving into the privatisation of *merit goods* such as education and *public goods* such as public health provision so that some of the basic principles which have ordered our **231** society for the last 40 years are being called into question.

The objectives of nationalised industries

The overall policy direction of an industry must come from the government. In 1948 the government laid down that industries were to meet the demand for their product at a reasonable price which would allow them to break even over a number of years. The idea of the break-even level of output is illustrated in Fig. 19.1. You will notice here the similarity to the idea of the control of monopolies dealt with in Chapter 18 (*see* page 218).

This overall equality of total revenue and total cost allowed for a large disparity between the cost of supplying any one individual and the price charged to that individual. For example, the cost of supplying a telephone to a farmer in

the Welsh mountains would obviously be higher than the cost of providing a telephone to a business in London. However the excess of cost over revenue in providing the telephone to the farmer could be met by the excess of revenue over cost in supplying the business in the cities. This *cross-subsidisation* amongst consumers was felt, by many observers, to be undesirable in that the cost to consumers did not always represent the full opportunity cost of the resources they enjoyed.

In 1961 a white paper, *The Financial and Economic Obligations of the Nationalised Industries*, was published. This placed greater restrictions on the pricing policies of nationalised industries. In particular, *financial targets* set by the government were introduced. These are expressed as a rate of return on all assets employed by the particular industry. The prevailing market conditions are taken into account in setting these financial targets; hence the required rate of return laid down by the government varies from industry to industry, as well as from year to year. Indeed, given this consideration, there is no reason why the financial target must be positive. For example, in 1979–80 the financial target for British Shipbuilders was a maximum trading loss of £100 million.

In 1967 another White Paper, *Nationalised Industries – A Review of Economic and Financial Objectives*, introduced more explicit guidelines on pricing and investment in nationalised industries. As an attempt to ensure an efficient allocation of resources, a policy of *long-run marginal cost pricing* was introduced, together with a *test discount rate* on new investment. This discount rate was intended to represent the opportunity cost of the resources diverted from the private sector by public sector investment. It was also stressed that cross-subsidisation was to be avoided and that, where appropriate, social costs and benefits estimated using the techniques of cost–benefit analysis were to be taken into account. (Cost–benefit analysis is explained in Chapter 27.)

The 1967 guidelines were clearly a reflection of the prescriptions of the *welfare economics* (*see*

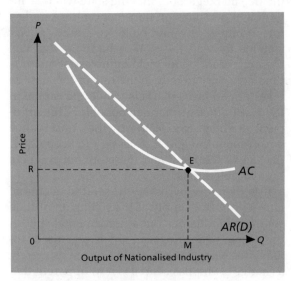

Fig. 19.1 *The break-even output*
This occurs where the *AC* curve cuts the *AR* curve at point E. Here:

$$TR = TC$$

Chapters 25–27). In order to avoid a conflict between these prescriptions and the commercial return laid down by the financial target, it was agreed that the government would take financial responsibility for non-commercial operations, e.g. in the form of specific grants or subsidies. It was often the case in practice that, despite these prescriptions, the government overrode the guidelines in pursuit of its broader macroeconomic commitments, e.g. the government applied price restraints and restrictions on investment in these industries in an effort to contain inflation.

In 1976 *A Study of UK Nationalised Industries* was published; this was a report by the National Economic Development Office (NEDO). It was a detailed and searching analysis which concentrated on the nine major nationalised industries. Some of its suggestions were:

a) the operation of nationalised industries should be removed from politics;

b) a policy council should be established to work out overall objectives for the industries.

c) measurements for the efficiency of services provided should be developed.

Before any of these policies could be acted upon there was a change of government. The Conservative government of 1979 was, of course, committed to privatisation. In the short term this meant making the nationalised industries as profitable as possible in order to make them attractive to investors. This policy was not difficult in the natural monopolies such as telecommunications and gas. However, in areas where there was competition such as in steel, profitability could only be achieved by closing down the loss making sectors of the industry.

It is important to realise that the privatised public utilities have had price constraints placed upon them. For example, British Telecom is only allowed to raise its prices by the rate of inflation minus 3 per cent. This would mean that if inflation were to fall to zero BT would have to cut its prices by 3 per cent. The government also created OFTEL, a quango, to oversee the policies of BT, OFGAS to oversee gas, and so on.

Prices and output policy of nationalised industries

Despite the wave of privatisation, with a turnover of £40 billion, the nationalised industries remain very significant. It is, therefore, worthwhile considering the problems of setting price and output in the nationalised industries. The situation for a nationalised industry is complicated by the fact that social and political factors may be at least as important as economic ones. For the economist the most fruitful policy would be one which was in some way based on costs and demand. However before we consider this we will look at several countervailing ideas.

Profit maximisation

If a policy of profit maximisation were pursued, then the behaviour of a nationalised industry could be analysed like that of a business organisation. However, many people would see it as unreasonable that an industry should be given a legal monopoly and then be allowed to charge the public as much as possible. In 1977 the Post Office made a considerable profit on telecommunications and was made to repay it to telephone users. On the other hand, as we have seen, some industries, such as electricity, were forced to raise their prices to 'fatten them up' for privatisation.

Social pricing

It could be argued that prices should be fixed at a level which everyone can afford. This would have two main effects: firstly the industry would probably make a huge loss, and secondly the price of the product would cease to have an allocating effect. This would mean that people would wish to consume much more of the product. If, for example, electricity were made free then many people might leave their lights and heating on all day. This would mean that electricity would have to be rationed in some manner. Electricity would in effect have become a public or merit good. No nationalised industry has supplied products free, but on occasions prices have been held down for social reasons, an example of this being commuter rail fares. This can be supported on economic grounds in that if commuter fares were to rise so much as to force people onto the roads, the resultant congestion would be disastrous.

Macroeconomic objectives

It could be argued that prices should be fixed to satisfy the government's economic strategy. An example of this might be prices restrained to assist a prices and incomes policy. Conversely it was argued that the large rise in gas price in 1980 was part of the government's strategy to conserve fuel resources.

The problems of marginal cost pricing

The prescriptions of modern welfare economics point to the adoption of marginal cost pricing, i.e. prices should be set at the level of marginal cost as they are in perfect competition. The optimality of marginal cost pricing was described on pages 200–2, while its welfare implications are more fully discussed in Chapters 25–27. Attractive as this idea is, it is beset with difficulties. We will now consider some of these.

The actions of competitors

Marginal cost pricing is difficult to apply where prices in the market are determined by competitors with different cost schedules. This was the case for British Steel, which faced competition from both domestic and, more importantly, overseas producers. Obviously if competitors are setting prices which are below the marginal cost which can be achieved by your own firm, it is impossible to both charge the marginal cost of production and match the price set by your competitors.

Decreasing costs

It is the case that many nationalised industries have large economies of scale which are thought

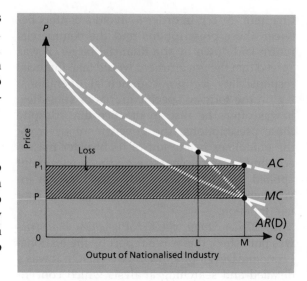

Fig. 19.2 *Marginal cost pricing and decreasing costs*
At *MC* = P the output would be OM and the price OP, but since P is below *AC* this involves the loss indicated by the shaded area.

to result in continuously decreasing average costs over the relevant range of output. This should result in a permanent financial deficit for such industries if marginal cost pricing were to be applied.

This is illustrated in Fig. 19.2. Here the marginal cost output would be OM at the price OP. This however is beyond the break-even output of OL and price of OP$_1$. This therefore results in a loss which is shown by the shaded area in the diagram. It has been argued that OM still represents the best situation and that the resultant trading deficit should be financed by taxes. However the taxes required may have disincentive effects and be a cause of allocative inefficiency.

Average incremental cost (*AIC*)

It is not always possible to identify, let alone calculate, marginal cost. Marginal cost is very much a theoretical tool. Strictly speaking it refers to infinitesimal increases in output. The concept is borrowed from mathematics where it would be known as the *first derivative of cost with respect to output.* It is hardly surprising that such highly abstract concepts cannot be directly observed in the real world. In fact this problem was recognised in the 1976 guidelines, where it was suggested that marginal cost be approximated to by using *average incremental cost*. This is calculated by dividing the change in cost resulting from a change in output by the change in output itself:

Average incremental cost (*AIC*)

$$= \frac{\text{Change in total cost}}{\text{Change in output}}$$

AIC is, of course, closer to *MC* the smaller the change in output considered (*see also* page 192).

But *AIC* does not help when it is difficult to attribute changes in cost to particular units of output. For example, in transport, vehicles are indivisible; thus although the marginal cost of transporting an extra passenger is very low, once a vehicle has begun its journey, the cost of an additional vehicle journey is high. There is obviously a problem in attributing increases in costs to individual passengers. Again in integrated systems such as in telecommunications the problem of identifying marginal cost arises. Cables are expensive to lay but relatively inexpensive to use. Also, each phone has access to equipment it may or may not use. It is thus difficult to attribute cost to users who enjoy a *potential* facility.

Theoretical problems

There are also theoretical problems. The first of these is that the *MC* pricing rule is based on the assumption that costs have been minimised. Thus the policy of *MC* pricing must be accompanied by pressure to minimise costs in public enterprises. In private firms this pressure might come from competition and the threat of insolvency or takeover, but some would argue that, although most nationalised industries do face competition in one form or another, the threat of closure is less strong in the public sector. One reason for this is that public enterprises often provide essential services. Another, often

related, reason is that where the government itself is seen as the employer, closure would arouse much political opposition. Financial targets might be seen as a substitute for the 'discipline of the market', but it is difficult to devise acceptable sanctions in the event of these targets not being met. However if costs are not minimised, *MC* pricing will not ensure a socially efficient allocation of resources.

The second theoretical problem is rather technical and comes under the heading of the *theory of second best* (*see* Chapter 27). Basically this theory demonstrates that setting price equal to marginal cost may not in fact improve efficiency if the conditions assumed in the *first optimality theorem* (*see* Chapter 25) do not hold for the rest of the economy.

An alternative: the real rate of return

We have mentioned earlier in this chapter that the government introduced a test discount rate on the new investment as an objective for nationalised industry. This was intended to reflect the opportunity cost of resources diverted from the private sector. The methods of calculating discounted returns on investments are described in Chapter 23. However if the test discount rate were applied inflexibly it would exclude much investment which is merely part of an existing system or which is necessary for reasons of safety or security.

Because of this, and the other problems discussed above, emphasis has been placed on the *financial target* and the test discount rate replaced by a required *real rate of return on assets*. Unlike the test discount rate, this is not intended to be achieved for each individual project but rather is defined as the rate of return to be achieved on new investment as a whole (the real rate of return requirement is thus separate from the financial target, which is expressed as a rate of return which takes account of existing assets and social objectives). The real rate of return was set initially at 5 per cent and was later increased to 8 per cent; it was intended to reflect real rates of return in the private sector as **235** well as broader social optimality considerations. Unlike the financial target, it does not vary from industry to industry.

In addition to this development and the change in emphasis, the nationalised industries were also asked to publish performance indicators such as labour productivity and average costs of production. These were intended to monitor efficiency in these industries and ensure that financial targets were not met simply by the exploitation of monopoly power. However no legal precautions were taken to prevent macro-economic considerations causing the government to again override the set guidelines.

Assessment and comparisons

So long as nationalisation remains a political topic it will be hard to form objective judgements about the issues. It is widely believed, for example, that all nationalised industries lose money. The problem industries were coal, shipbuilding and railways, the other nationalised industries usually being in profit. The three problem industries mentioned are in fact in trouble worldwide; it would therefore be somewhat unrealistic to expect them to boom in the UK. Comparisons of railways show that British Rail holds the dubious distinctions of being the least subsidised railway in Europe and having the highest fares. The better performance of

many foreign steel industries was the result of being heavily subsidised either directly or through artificially low energy prices. A similar situation appertains in shipbuilding. The problems of the UK industries involved are further exacerbated by protectionist policies against UK exports and by dumping on the UK market.

Table 19.2 shows the overall profits of nationalised industries from 1976–86. As you can see, as a whole they are highly profitable. Overall profits increased as the government forced price rises on such industries as gas and electricity but the aggregate profits declined as the ranks of public corporations shrank. Profitability, however, was considerably increased; even some traditional loss-makers such as steel became profitable.

Table 19.2 Gross trading surplus of public corporations in the UK after providing for depreciation and stock appreciation

Year	Profit (£m)	Year	Profit (£m)
1976	4 353	1982	9 466
1977	4 998	1983	10 157
1978	5 382	1984	8 359
1979	5 304	1985	7 345
1980	6 276	1986	8 576
1981	8 001		

Source: United Kingdom National Accounts *HMSO*

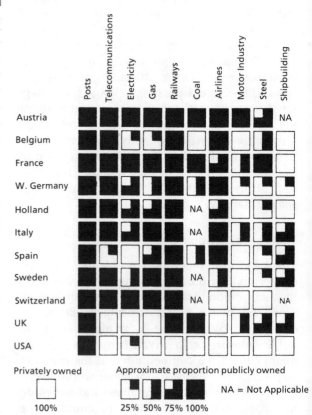

Fig. 19.3 *Public ownership in various countries 1988 Adapted from Pennant-Rea and Emmot,* **The Pocket Economist.**

It is commonly believed that nationalised industries are a phenomenon peculiar to the UK. This also is not so; most Western European countries have nationalised industries and there are some novel variations – in Sweden, for example, distilling is nationalised and in France there is a government tobacco monopoly.

Figure 19.3 illustrates the extent of public ownership in various countries. As you can see it is a widespread phenomenon throughout Europe. The caricatures of public ownership seldom fit; for example none of the banks in 'ultra-socialist' Sweden are state owned, while in 'free enterprise' France two of the three largest banks are in the public sector. You can also see that Switzerland, which has the smallest public sector of all the countries in Fig. 19.3 nonetheless has its share of state ownership.

It is true to say that the effect of the privatisations of the 1980s has been to 'move the goalposts' of the debate. That is to say that they have been undertaken in such a way as to make renationalisation very difficult. Thus the opposition has shifted its ground to espouse an ill-defined concept called the *social market*. Nonetheless for the major public utilities such as gas, water and electricity the change of ownership has made little *apparent* difference to the consumer. Also while these industries may be in private ownership, they still pose the same problems of price regulation as they did when nationalised.

Summary

1 Nationalised industries are all public corporations. They play a major role in the business of the economy.
2 The chief trend in nationalisation today is that of privatisation.
3 Many arguments, of both an economic and a political kind, can be advanced for and against nationalisation. In the end an industry should be judged by its economic efficiency and not by its ownership.
4 There have been many attempts to define the objectives of nationalised industries, but there is still no clear policy.
5 Prices and output policy presents particular problems. Economic theory would seem to suggest marginal cost pricing but this also is beset with difficulties.
6 Nationalised industries are a common feature of most European economies. The record of UK industries is no worse than that of others and in many respects is better.

Questions

1 What criteria could be used for assessing the importance of nationalised industries?
2 What argument could be advanced in favour of privatisation? Would privatisation still be valid even if it were less economically efficient?
3 Trace the development of UK government policy towards nationalised industries.
4 What arguments could be advanced for the subsidisation of rail fares?
5 Select three of the major privatised industries and compile a table to show:

   a) the number of people employed;
   b) the value of the turnover;
   c) the capital employed; and
   d) the profit and loss for each of the industries before and after privatisation.

237

6 Examine the prices and output policy of nationalised industries.

7 What do you think would be the best prices and output policy for an industry with constantly decreasing average costs?

8 Having studied Fig. 19.3, what conclusion would you draw about the pattern of public ownership in Europe and North America?

Data response   The right connections ━━━━━━━━━━━━━━━━━━━━━━━━━━━━━━━━━

Read the following article which is adapted from articles appearing in September 1987.

The right connections

The *privatisation* of electricity, one of Britain's biggest businesses, offers the unique opportunity of creating centres of employment and industry in the regions. But, so far, the debate has focused only on *the issue of competition or monopoly*.

Cecil Parkinson, the Energy Secretary, makes it clear that he wants to split the electricity industry and introduce competition.

At present the industry is split between the CEGB which generates the power and runs the National Grid and 14 area boards which distribute the power to households and run the showrooms. Lord Marshall at the CEGB is bound to resist the hiving off of the National Grid or generating to the regions. The interests of the area boards, their regions and consumers are thus in danger of taking a back seat.

The potential impact of electricity privatisation on the economies of the regions has attracted little public attention. Provincial centres such as Ipswich, Bristol, Manchester and Newcastle – where the present area boards have their headquarters – face the prospect of acquiring billion pound industries overnight.

If the option of devolution were taken it would give financial muscle to the regions as well as providing gains in efficiency in the industry itself. But will it also bring back some of the inefficiency which existed prior to nationalisation in 1948?

The answer will depend on the *regulatory regime* and the arrangements by which the area boards are able to get the supplies of electricity from the new generating authority (authorities?) via the National Grid.

The boards themselves are *natural monopolies* and will have to be regulated by the *RPI – X formula* used in the British Gas and British Telecom privatisations. The British Gas regulation has gaping loopholes and potential for inefficiency. Electricity will argue that they should not have more regulation than gas.

The privatised monoliths British Gas and Telecom are just as national i.e. London-centred as the nationalised *public corporations* they replaced. Electricity privatisation gives us a chance to do things differently.

If the chance is not taken the provinces can say goodbye to what might otherwise be the greatest decentralisation of economic power not only by Mrs Thatcher but by any British government this century.

1 Explain the words and phrases in italics in the article.

2 How, does the article suggest, would decentralisation of the electricity industry benefit the regions?

3 What arguments have been put forward for privating the electricity industry?

4 What difficulties is a regulatory body likely to have in setting the price of electricity?

5 How did the actual plans for the privatisation of electricity differ from those proposed in the article?

2

The microeconomic system

III The theory of distribution

20

The pricing of productive factors

Produce! Produce! were it but the pitifullest
infinitesimal fraction of a product, produce it in
God's name! 'Tis the utmost thou hast in thee:
out with it, then.

Thomas Carlyle

Introduction

In this section of the book we wish to examine the use of the factors of production. In this chapter we will look at the general principles governing the exploitation of resources and the factors which determine their price. In the subsequent chapters we will see how these general principles apply to each factor.

The theory of distribution

Let us return for a moment to the fundamentals of the subject. Economics must answer the 'What?', 'How?' and 'For whom?' questions in society. In this section we will be completing our explanation of the 'How?' and 'For whom?' questions. As we examine the theory of production, this will explain how and why firms use the factors of production, but in doing so it will also explain how the factor incomes – wages, rent, interest and profit – are determined. We will thus be explaining the 'For whom?' question, because it is income which will determine people's ability to buy goods. This is termed *the theory of distribution* since it attempts to explain how income is *distributed* between the factors of production.

The derived demand for the factors of production

When a firm demands a factor of production it is said to be a *derived demand*, i.e. the factor is not demanded for itself but for the use to which it can be put. If we examine the demand for such things as bread, these are wanted for *direct* consumption. If, however, a company demands labour it is because it wants to produce something which it can eventually sell. The demand for labour is thus said to be *derived* from the demand for the final product.

Marginal distribution theory

The law of variable proportions

In order to explain the factors which determine the firm's demand for a factor of production we must turn once again to the law of diminishing returns.

In the short-run the amount of certain of the factors which the firm can employ will be fixed, while it will be able to vary others. For example, a firm will have a factory of a certain size or a farm of a certain area and to this *fixed factor* the business adds *variable factors* such as labour and power. Under these circumstances the firm will be affected by the law of *diminishing returns*, i.e. as the firm adds more and more of the variable factor, e.g. labour, to a constant amount of fixed factor, e.g. land, the extra output that this creates must, after a time, become less. This means that the relationship between the amount of resources used (inputs) and the amount of goods produced (output) will vary. For this reason when considering the diminishing returns in relation to the firm it is often termed the *law of variable proportions* or the *law of non-proportional returns*.

The marginal physical product (*MPP*)

As factors of production are combined, in the *short-run* various cost structures for any firm will emerge. These are best illustrated by taking a simple example. In Table 20.1 a farmer, whose land is fixed at 10 hectares in the short-run, adds more and more units of the variable factor – labour – in order to produce a greater output of wheat. Obviously if no labour is used there will be no output. When one unit of labour is used the output of the farm works out at 8 tonnes of wheat per year. If two persons are used the output rises to 36 tonnes. The *average physical product (APP)* per person has risen from 8 tonnes

to 18 tonnes. This does not mean that the second person was more industrious than the first but rather that a 10 hectare farm was too big for one person to work and it runs more efficiently with two. The higher average product therefore applies to both workers. It may have been achieved through *specialisation* and *division of labour*, impossible when there was only one worker.

As the employer continues to employ more workers so the total output continues to rise, but eventually the rate at which it increases starts to diminish. The third worker adds 34 tonnes per year to the output, the fourth worker only 30 tonnes, the fifth adds only 20 tonnes per year, and so on. Eventually the seventh worker adds nothing more to total output, and if an eighth worker is employed total output actually falls. The amount added to the total output by each successive unit of labour is the *marginal physical product (MPP)*. If we generalise this principle we could define it as:

The *MPP* is the change to the total output resulting from the employment of one more unit of a variable factor.

These figures are illustrated graphically in Fig. 20.1. The MPP curve rises as the benefits of division of labour make the exploitation of land more efficient. Between two and three units of labour the curve reaches its highest point and then begins to decline as diminishing returns set in. At four units of labour the farm is at its most technically efficient and after this its efficiency begins to decline. This is shown by the average product curve declining. When the *APP* curve is rising the firm is benefitting from *increasing returns*. When the *APP* curve is going downwards the firm is suffering from *decreasing returns*. The diminishing returns come about because, as more labour is employed, each successive unit of labour has less of the fixed factor, land, to work with. If it were not for the law of diminishing returns we could supply all the world's food from one farm simply by adding more and more labour to it. Obviously this is not possible.

You will see that the *MPP* curve goes through

Table 20.1 Marginal physical product and average product.

Number of people employed	Output of wheat, Q (tonnes/year)	Marginal physical product, MPP (tonnes/year)	Average physical product, APP (tonnes/year)
0	0		0
1	8	8	8
2	36	24	18
3	70	34	23.3
4	100	30	25
5	120	20	24
6	130	10	21.6
7	130	0	18.5
8	120	−10	15

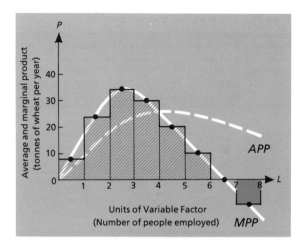

Fig. 20.1 *The marginal physical product curve*
The *MPP* shows the amount of extra output produced by each additional unit of the variable factor. Note that the *MPP* curve goes through the highest point of the *APP* curve.

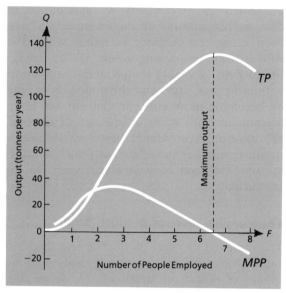

Fig. 20.2 *Marginal physical product and total product*
MPP is zero at the point where total product is maximised.

the top of the *APP* curve. This is always so. The intersection of the *APP* with the *MPP*, then, tells us when the firm is at its optimum technical efficiency (see above). The point of maximum technical efficiency, however, is not necessarily the output the firm will choose. If, for example, the product we were considering were gold then it might be worthwhile running a very inefficient mine. Eventually, however, because of diminishing returns, *MPP* may even become negative when total output falls. No business would be willing to employ more resources to get less output.

Once again, because *MPP* is a marginal figure it must be plotted in a particular way. In Fig. 20.1 the solid columns represent *discrete data* for the *MPP*. We can turn this into *continuous data* by plotting *MPP* halfway between 1 and 2 persons, halfway between 2 and 3 persons and so on. This is shown by the black dots in Fig. 20.1. These can then be joined up to give the *MPP* curve.

Output goes on increasing while *MPP* is positive. Thus in our example output is maximised when the sixth person is employed. If a seventh person is employed *MPP* becomes negative and

total output therefore falls. The relationship between *MPP* and total output is shown in Fig. 20.2.

Production and productivity

Production is the total amount of a commodity produced, whereas *productivity* is the amount of a commodity produced per unit of resources used. When a firm is improving its efficiency, productivity will be rising, i.e. if, by better management, more efficient equipment or better use of labour, the firm manages to produce the same, or a greater amount of product with a smaller amount of resources then it has increased its productivity. If on the other hand the firm produces an increase in output but only at the expense of an even greater increase in resources then, despite the increase in output, its productivity has fallen.

Productivity may be difficult to measure. One of the most common methods is to take the total output and divide it by the number of workers. Another method, used in agriculture, is to express productivity as output per hectare (see **243** discussion of productivity in agriculture in Chapter 12, page 157. In the example we have been using, productivity is rising while the *APP* is rising and falling when *APP* is falling. Productivity is vital to the economic welfare of both individual firms and the nation. It is only by becoming more efficient that we can hope to compete with other businesses or nations. We have only considered here two factors of production: other considerations, such as capital and the level of technology, are vital in productivity.

The marginal revenue product (*MRP*)

The marginal physical product is so called because it is measured in *physical* units such as tonnes of wheat or barrels of oil, depending upon what is being produced. It is more convenient, however, to express it in money terms. We can do this by examining how much money the *MPP* could have been sold for. For instance in our example, if the fourth person employed adds 30 tonnes to output and each tonne can be sold for £250 then the *marginal revenue product (MRP)* is £7500. Thus marginal revenue product can be calculated as:

$$MRP = MPP \times P$$

where P = the price of the commodity being produced. However this formula works only if the firm is producing under conditions of perfect competition, i.e. the firm can sell as much of the product as it likes without lowering the price. If, on the other hand, the firm was operating under conditions of imperfect competition then, in order to sell more, it would have to lower the price of the product. Fortunately when we studied the theory of the firm we developed a measure which told us the change in a firm's revenue as the result of the sale of one more unit of a commodity, i.e. marginal revenue (*MR*). Thus, under conditions of imperfect competition, the *MRP* would be calculated as:

$$MRP = MPP \times MR$$

244   For the sake of simplicity we will assume con-

Table 20.2 The marginal revenue product

Number of people employed	Marginal physical product, MPP (tonnes of wheat)	Price of wheat per tonne, P (£)	Marginal revenue product, MRP = MPP × P (£)
0		250	
	8		2000
1		250	
	24		6000
2		250	
	34		8500
3		250	
	30		7500
4		250	
	20		5000
5		250	
	10		2500
6		250	
	0		0
7		250	
	−10		−2500
8		250	

ditions of perfect competition for most of this chapter.

The *MRP* may be defined as the change to a firm's revenues as a result of the sale of the product of one more unit of a variable factor.

Table 20.2 gives the *MRP* based upon our example and assuming that wheat can be sold at a price of £250 per tonne.

If we plot the *MRP* schedule as a graph we find that its shape is exactly that of the *MPP*, but

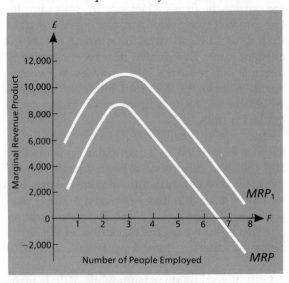

Fig. 20.3 *The marginal revenue product curve*
The shift from *MRP* to *MRP₁* could be the result of an improvement in technology or an increase in the price of the product.

the units which are used on the vertical axis have now become £s (*see* Fig. 20.3).

The firm's demand for a factor

We calculate the *MRP* in order that we may explain the quantity of a factor of production which a firm will demand. This we will find is the quantity of the factor at which its *MRP* is equal to its price. If, for example, the marginal revenue product of a unit of labour were £8500 per year and the cost of that unit of labour were £3000 per year, the business would obviously be £5500 better off as a result of employing that unit of labour. If the *MRP* of the next unit of labour fell to £7500, but the cost of it remained £3000, the firm would still employ that unit of the factor since it would be a further £4500 better off. In other words the business will go on demanding a factor of production while the *MRP* of that factor is greater than the cost of employing it.

This is best understood graphically. In Fig. 20.4 if the wage rate were £3750 per person, the best number of people for the firm to employ would be five. The cost of labour would be the area under the wage line, i.e. 5 × £3750. The shaded area, above the wage line and below the *MRP* curve, would be the money the business

would get back over and above the cost of employing the factor. The firm will always be best off by trying to obtain as much of this shaded area as possible. If, for example, the wage fell to £1250 then the firm would employ six people, but if the wage rose to £6250 it would be best off only employing four people.

The factor demand curve

From the above analysis it can be seen that:

The firm's *MRP* curve for a factor is its demand curve for that factor provided that the price of the commodity being produced remains fixed.

If we consider a fall in the price of the factor then this will have the effect of causing the firm to hire more of the variable factor. However if all other firms in the industry do the same thing this will cause a rise in output and, therefore, a fall in the price of the product. As a result the *MRP* curve will shift leftwards. In Fig. 20.5 OT represents the original price of the factor and

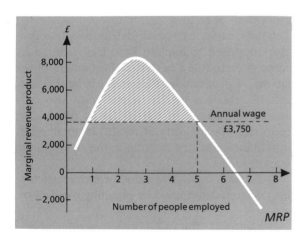

Fig. 20.4 *The marginal revenue product and wages*
The best number of workers for the firm to employ is five. This is where the marginal revenue product is equal to the wage rate.

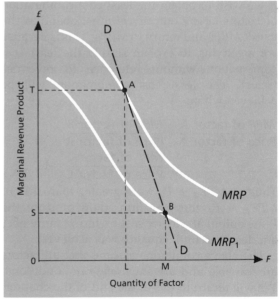

Fig. 20.5 *Derivation of the demand curve*
A fall in the price of the factor from OT to OS causes a fall in the price of the product, which shifts the *MRP* curve to *MRP₁*. The equilibrium shifts from A to B; thus AB is the demand curve for the factor.

245

the quantity of the factor employed is OL where the price of the factor coincides with the original *MRP* curve. The leftward movement of the *MRP* curve to MRP_1 shows the effect of a fall in the price of the commodity. The price of the factor is now OS and the firm employs OM units of the factor. We have thus moved from point A on curve *MRP* to B on MRP_1. If we join up these points this gives the firm's demand curve for the factor.

The best factor combination

The profit maximisation equilibrium for a firm would be when the conditions of *MRP* = price of the factor have been fulfilled for each factor. Thus it will be where:

MRP of factor A = price of factor A

and

MRP of factor B = price of factor B

and so on.

If we wish to obtain the least cost combination of factors at *any* output we must abandon the use of *MRP*s and return to *MPP*s. This is because we are trying to explain simply the least cost combination without reference to revenues (sales). The least cost combination will be achieved when:

$$\frac{MPP \text{ of factor A}}{\text{Price of factor A}} = \frac{MPP \text{ of factor B}}{\text{Price of factor B}}$$
$$= \frac{MPP \text{ of factor C}}{\text{Price of factor C}}, \text{ etc.}$$

Thus, if $MPP_B \div P_B$ were greater than that of $MPP_A \div P_A$ then the firm could produce the same output at a lower cost by hiring more of A and less of B until equality was achieved.

The above conditions assume that all factors are variable and are thus *long-run* conditions. We will return to this at the end of the chapter.

The demand and supply curves for a factor

The marginal revenue product curve gives us a normal downward sloping demand curve for factors of production, showing that more of a factor is demanded at a lower price. This is true both for the firm and for the industry. We have so far assumed that the supply curve is horizontal, i.e. that the firm could employ more of a factor without affecting its price. However if an industry wished to employ more of a factor it is likely that it would have to pay more to attract the factor from other uses. We would thus have a normal upward-sloping supply curve. Therefore we are able to analyse factor markets with the same tools of microeconomic analysis that we used for consumer goods markets.

Problems with the theory of distribution

The theory explains how the prices of factors of production are determined in competitive markets and thus how incomes are determined. However there are a number of factors which distort the allocation of incomes.

a) Non-homogeneity. The theory assumes that all units of a factor are identical. This is not true, either of the quality of a factor or the size of the units in which it is supplied.

b) Immobility. The theory assumes that factors of production can move about freely, both from industry to industry and area to area. In practice there are serious difficulties attached to the free movement of factors.

c) Inheritance. Marginal distribution theory is also supposed to explain how the national income is distributed between the owners of the factors of production. However, in addition to income, there is wealth which may also be a source of income. In the UK as in most other countries, the majority of wealth is obtained by inheritance and this is outside the operation of market forces.

d) Political–legal. The value of factors such as land is often determined by planning regulations, etc.

e) Historical. The value of factors such as land and labour is often affected by historical factors such as industrial inertia.

These criticisms notwithstanding, marginal

revenue theory is one of the best aids we have to understand the cost structures of an organisation.

Resources and costs

In this section of the chapter we will demonstrate that the principles associated with the exploitation of resources which we have just examined are consistent with the cost structures of the firm which we examined in the last section of the book.

The cost structures of the firm

So far the one cost we have been concerned with has been labour, and in our example we have assumed a wage rate of £3750 per year. Let us assume that labour costs are the only variable costs of the firm and that fixed costs (land, capital etc.) amount to £10 000 per year. This having been done, we are able to project the cost schedules shown in Table 20.3 (overleaf).

a) Variable costs. In Table 20.3 you can see that variable costs increase as the number of people employed increases. If one person is employed then variable costs are £3750; if two people are employed this becomes £7500, and so on.

b) Average costs. We calculate average costs as before by dividing total costs by output. Because the example we have been using in this chapter is based upon the number of people employed, the output increases in rather uneven amounts. Thus if two people are employed, then average costs (*ATC*) are calculated by dividing total cost by the output of 36; if three people are employed then the total cost is arrived at by dividing total costs by the output of 70, and so on. Similar calculations will produce the figures for average fixed cost (*AFC*) and average variable costs (*AVC*) shown in Table 20.3.

c) Marginal costs. It will be recalled that marginal cost is the cost of producing one more unit of commodity. However in our example here we are faced with the problem that output increases in uneven amounts as each additional unit of the variable factor is employed. We can

get round this problem, though, by taking the increase in costs as each extra unit of variable factor is employed and dividing it by the number of extra units produced. For example, if the firm employs four people rather than three, then total cost rises from £21 250 to £25 000 and the output rises from 70 to 100 tonnes. Thus we can obtain marginal cost by dividing the increase in total cost ($\triangle TC$) by the increase in output ($\triangle Q$); this gives us £3750 ÷ 30, which in turn gives the figure of £125 for marginal cost. (This method of calculating *MC* is also known as average incremental cost (*AIC*) (*see* page 192).) We have thus obtained an approximation for *MC* which is:

$$MC = \frac{\triangle TC}{\triangle Q}$$

When it comes to plotting these figures graphically we must plot the marginal cost halfway between the outputs we are considering. Thus in the figures used above, the marginal cost of £125 would be plotted halfway between the output of 70 and 100 tonnes, i.e. at 85 tonnes.

Cost curves

If we use the figures in Table 20.3 to construct average and marginal cost curves, we see that they all accord with the principles discussed in Chapter 15. Once again you can see that in Fig. 20.6 the marginal cost curve passes through the bottom of the average cost curve.

Marginal cost and price

So far we have said the firm will try to equate the marginal revenue product of a factor with the cost of that factor. The *MRP* however, depends upon the price at which the product can be sold. In Fig. 20.4 we assumed that the price of wheat was £250 per tonne and therefore we obtained an *MRP* curve by multiplying *MPP* by the price. We can then proceed to develop the cost structures of the firm based on these assumptions. In Table 20.4 we demonstrate the best profit output based on these same assump-

247

Table 20.3 The cost structures of the firm

Number of people employed	Total output of wheat, Q (tonnes/year)	Marginal physical product, MPP (tonnes/year)	Average product, APP (tonnes/year)	Fixed costs, FC (£)	Variable costs, VC (£)
0	0		0	10 000	0
		8			
1	8		8	10 000	3 750
		24			
2	36		18	10 000	7 500
		34			
3	70		23.3	10 000	11 250
		30			
4	100		25	10 000	15 000
		20			
5	120		24	10 000	18 750
		10			
6	130		21.6	10 000	22 500
		0			
7	130		18.5	10 000	26 250
		−10			
8	120		15	10 000	30 000

Table 20.4 The best profit output of the firm

Number of people employed	Output of wheat, Q (tonnes/year)	Price of wheat, P (£/tonne)	Marginal revenue product, MRP (MPP × P)	Total revenue, TR (P × Q)	Total cost, TC (FC + VC)	Total profit, TP (TR − TC)	Marginal cost, MC* (△TC/△Q)
0	0	250		0	10 000	−10 000	
			2 000				469
1	8	250		2 000	13 750	−11 750	
			6 000				156
2	36	250		9 000	17 000	− 8 500	
			8 500				110
3	70	250		17 500	21 250	− 3 750	
			7 500				125
4	100	250		25 000	25 000	0	
			5 000				188
5	120	250		30 000	28 750	1 250	
			2 500				375
6	130	250		32 500	32 500	0	
			0				∞
7	130	250		32 500	36 250	− 3 750	
			−2 500				−
8	120	250		30 000	40 000	−10 000	

* To nearest whole number.

tions about costs and price. We also include in Table 20.4 the *MC* schedule.

Having obtained the *MC* from the example we are able to use this to confirm the proposition in Chapter 16 that the best profit output for the firm is the one at which *MC* = *P*. In Fig. 20.7 you can see that this occurs at the output of 120 tonnes, this being the same output at which *MRP* is equal to the price of the variable factor.

Thus the analysis we have developed in this chapter is consistent with the analysis in Chapter 16.

As we have assumed so far in this chapter that there is perfect competition, then the price of £250 per tonne is also the marginal revenue (*MR*). This result therefore confirms the proposition that profit maximisation occurs where *MR* = *MC*.

Table 20.3 The cost structures of the firm (*contd.*)

Total costs, TC (FC + VC)	Average fixed costs, AFC* (FC/Q)	Average variable costs, AVC* (VC/Q)	Marginal costs, MC* ($\triangle$TC/$\triangle$Q)	Average cost, ATC* (TC/Q)
10 000	∞	–		∞
13 750	1 250	469	469	1 719
17 500	278	208	156	486
21 250	143	161	110	303
25 000	100	150	125	250
28 750	84	156	188	240
32 500	77	173	375	250
36 250	77	202	∞	–
40 000	–	–	–	–

* To nearest whole number.

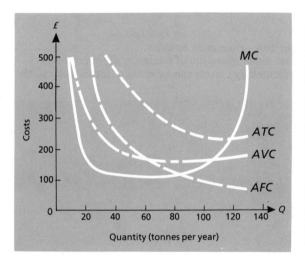

Fig. 20.6 *Cost curves of the firm*
Here:

$$ATC = AFC + AVC$$

and the marginal cost curve cuts through the lowest point of *ATC*.

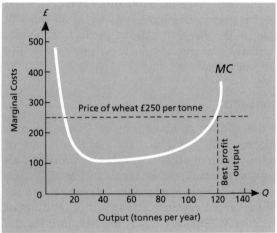

Fig. 20.7 *The best profit output*

At the output of 120 tonnes per year the firm makes a profit of £1250 per year. At this output average costs are £239·58 and, since price is £250, this gives a profit per unit of £10.42. Thus total profit is $TP = (AR - AC) \times Q = (250 - 239.58) \times 120 = £1250$, as confirmed in Table 20.4. However, it should be recalled that this is *ab-normal* profit and, therefore, in the long-run

would attract new firms into the industry. This emphasises the fact that this is a *short-run* situation.

Production in the long-run

The production function

Our example so far has mainly concerned the short-run where at least one factor of production is fixed in supply. In the long-run all costs may **249** be varied. To illustrate the principles involved we will use just two factors of production, capital and labour.

It is possible for a firm to produce the same output using different combinations of capital and labour, i.e. labour may be substituted for capital or vice versa. Figure 20.8 shows a production function for product X. You can see that the output of 69 units of X can be produced by using 6 units of capital and 1 unit of labour or 3 units of capital and 2 of labour and so on. Similarly an output of 98 units of X could be produced with various, greater, quantities of capital and labour.

If we move horizontally across the production function – for example, if we use 3 units of capital and then add successive units of labour – the gap between each successive level of output will give us the *marginal physical product* of labour. Similarly moving vertically would show the *MPP* of capital.

Isoquants

If the various combinations of factors of production which produce the same amount of output are plotted as a graph this produces an *isoquant* or *equal product curve*. In Fig. 20.9, IQ_1 plots the various combinations of capital–labour which would produce an output of 69 units of product X. Similarly IQ_2 is the isoquant for the output of 98 units of X. A rightward movement of the isoquant shows a move to a higher level of production and the use of greater quantities of factors of production.

Theoretically we can construct any number of isoquants on the graph to produce an isoquant map. The reader may notice here the similarity with indifference curves (see Chapter 9). What reason is to be found for the isoquant being a similar shape? The reason is that although capital can be substituted for labour or vice versa they are not perfect substitutes. Therefore as we substitute capital for labour, for example, it takes more and more units of capital to replace labour as capital becomes a less and less perfect substitute. In Fig. 20.9 if we move from point C to

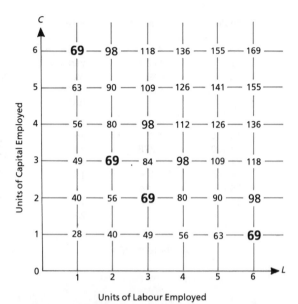

Fig. 20.8 *Production function*
This shows quantities of product X which can be produced by various combinations of labour and capital.

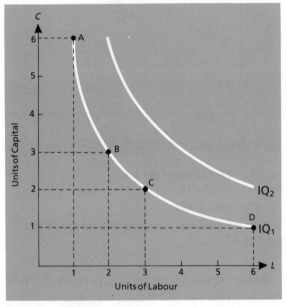

Fig. 20.9 *Isoquants*
Isoquants join the combinations of factors which would produce the same quantity of a product. IQ_1 gives the combinations which would produce 69 units of X and IQ_2 gives the combinations which would produce 98 units of X. A series of IQ curves is termed an isoquant map.

point B one unit of labour can be replaced by one unit of capital, but if we move to point A then the next unit of labour given up requires three units of capital to replace it. You can check that you understand this point by starting from point B and examining how the same thing happens in reverse as labour is substituted for capital.

The slope of the isoquant shows the substitution ratios of the factors of production.

Isocost lines

In Fig. 20.10, using the same axes, we can construct a graph to show the relative prices of the two factors of production. If, for example, capital costs £100 per unit while labour costs £150 per unit, then a line drawn from three units of capital to two units of labour would show us all the combinations of capital and labour which could be bought for a cost of £300. Similarly a line from six units of capital to four of labour would show combinations costing £600 and so on. The *isocost lines* stay parallel to each other so long as the relative prices of the two factors remain unchanged.

The slope of the isocost shows the relative prices of the factors of production.

The least cost combination

If we combine the isocosts and the isoquants on one diagram we can demonstrate how a firm could achieve the least cost combination. This occurs when an isoquant is just tangential to an isocost. For example, if we wish to produce an output of 98 units of X then the cheapest cost at which this can be achieved is £600. This is illustrated in Fig. 20.11.

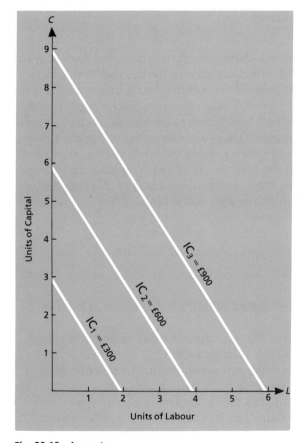

Fig. 20.10 *Isocosts*
Each isocost joins all the combinations of factors which can be bought with the same amount of money. The isocosts here are drawn on the assumption that capital costs £100 per unit and labour costs £150 per unit.

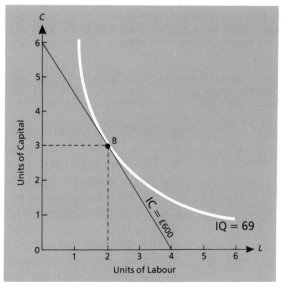

Fig. 20.11 *The least cost output*
The least cost output for the firm is at point B where the isoquant is tangential to the isocost line.

The least cost factor combination occurs where the rate of substitution is equal to the relative prices of the factors of production.

We could explain this by saying either that it is the isocost nearest to the origin which can pro-

duce an output of 98 units or, alternatively, that it is the isoquant furthest to the right which can be reached with a budget of £600.

You can confirm this by checking the cost of producing 98 units in Fig. 20.8. You will see that all other combinations result in a higher cost.

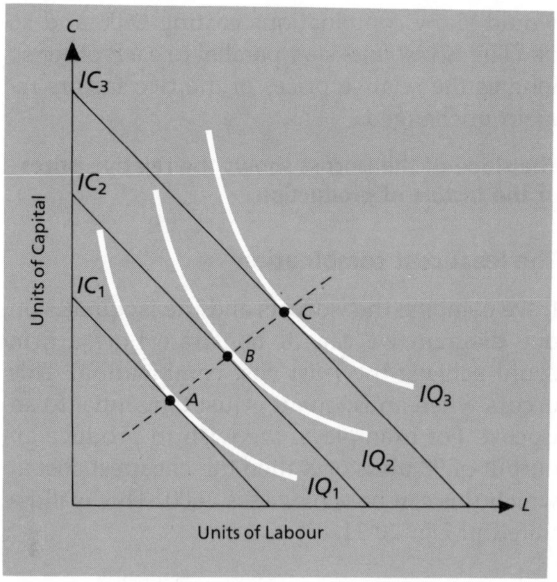

Expansion path

If we undertook the same operation as above for various levels of expenditure, then we could achieve the cost minimisation expansion path for the firm. In Fig. 20.12 this is line ABC.

Fig. 20.12 An expansion path
As total expenditure increases from IC_1 to IC_2 to IC_3 the least cost combination shifts from A to B to C. Thus this is the expansion path for the firm.

Conclusion

In this chapter we have attempted to deal with the principles governing the use of the factors of production both in the short-run and in the long-run. These principles will be applied in the following chapters to each of the factors of production. There are, however, important tie-ups with earlier parts of the book, such as the theory of the firm. To check that you have understood the implications of the ideas in this chapter you are advised to work through the questions at the end.

Summary

1   The theory of distribution is concerned with the distribution of income between the factors of production.
2   The marginal physical product is the amount added to production from the employment of one more unit of a variable factor.
3   The marginal revenue product is the change to the firm's revenue from the sale of the marginal physical product.
4   The *MRP* curve of a factor is a firm's demand curve for that factor.
5   The demand and supply of a factor can be analysed in a similar way to consumer demand and supply.
6   Marginal productivity theory can also be used to explain the cost structures of a firm.
7   An isoquant shows the various quantities of factors of production which are needed to produce the same quantity of a product.

8   An isocost shows all the combinations of a factor which can be used at a given level of cost.
9   The least cost combination for the firm is where the isoquant is tangential to the isocost, i.e. where the substitution ratio is equal to the relative prices of the factors of production.

Questions

1   The following data shows the variation in output of product X as inputs of labour are increased.

Labour	1	2	3	4	5	6
Total product	5	15	24	28	30	30

a) Calculate the marginal and average physical products.
b) Plot these on a graph.
c) Indicate on the graph over what output there is increasing returns and over what output there is diminishing returns.

2   Redraft Table 20.4 assuming that fixed costs rise to £20 000, the wage rate increases to £6000 and the price of wheat increases to £400 per tonne. Determine the best profit output for the business.

3   What shortcomings are there to marginal distribution theory as an explanation for the distribution of income.

4   Examine Fig. 20.4. If Marxists were to look at this diagram they would argue that all the shaded area is the product of labour which it is being deprived of. Do you agree? Give reasons for your answer.

5   The introduction of microprocessors should increase the *MRP* curve, thus increasing wages and employment. Reconcile this with the observed tendency of microprocessors to replace labour and create unemployment.

6   Redraw Fig. 20.11 assuming that capital increases in cost to £200 per unit. If the firm still wishes to produce 69 units of X what would now be the least cost combination and why?

7   Use the production function in Fig. 20.8 to confirm the proposition that the least cost combination is where

$$\frac{MPP \text{ of labour}}{\text{Price of labour}} = \frac{MPP \text{ of capital}}{\text{Price of capital}}$$

(Note: the answers may be slightly inaccurate due to rounding the figures to whole numbers.)

Data response   The Eversharp Pencil Company

The data in the table overleaf refers to the Eversharp Pencil Company which manufactures ballpoint pens. The company has premises and machinery which cost it £125 per week.

1   From this data calculate the marginal physical product schedule (MPP) of labour at Eversharp and plot it as a graph.

2   Suppose that Eversharp is able to sell any number of ballpoints it wishes to a distributor at a price of 5 pence each. Further suppose that Eversharp is able to employ workers at £100 per person per week. Calculate the marginal   **253**

Productivity of Eversharp

Number of people employed	Average product pens/week
0	0
1	2 500
2	2 750
3	3 500
4	4 375
5	4 500
6	4 250
7	3 785.8
8	3 187.5

revenue product (MRP) schedule and, with the aid of a graph, determine how many workers Eversharp would wish to employ.

3   Assuming that Eversharp's only variable cost is labour determine the profit maximisation output.

4   Calculate the effects of doubling the wage rate to £200. Determine the number of people that Eversharp will now wish to employ and its profit maximisation output.

5.   In question 4 it should be apparent that an increase in the wage rate would cause the business to contract both output and employment. Since the 1939–45 war real wages have risen and, for most of the period, so have output and employment. Explain how this is possible. Your answer should also consider whether marginal revenue product theory has any relevance to the very high levels of unemployment in the 1980s.

21

The determination of wages

Trade unions and wages

The demand for and supply of labour

The wage rate will be determined by the interaction of the organisation's demand for labour and the supply of labour forthcoming.

In the previous chapter we saw that an organisation's demand for a factor of production is the marginal revenue product (*MRP*) curve of that factor. The supply of labour, you will remember, is determined by such things as the size and age distribution of the population (*see* Chapter 4). Without interference from the government or trade unions the wage rate will be determined by these forces of demand and supply. This is illustrated in Fig. 21.1. The movement of the demand curve from DD to D_1D_1 could have been brought about by either an improvement in technology or a rise in the price of the product being produced. Although improving productivity is one of the most certain ways of increasing wages, there is little that trade unions can do about it. They therefore tend to work by affecting the supply of labour. (Trade unions may, of course, be involved in agreements with employers to increase productivity.)

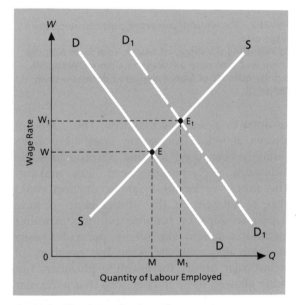

Fig. 21.1 *The determination of wage rate*
The original wage rate is OW at equilibrium E. The movement to E_1 and to a higher wage of OW_1 shows the effect of an increase in demand for labour.

Restrictive labour practices

A most effective way for trade unions to increase their members' wages is to restrict the supply of labour to a particular occupation. This can

255

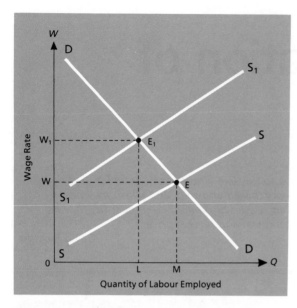

Fig. 21.2 *The effect of restrictive practices upon the wage rate*
By restricting the supply of labour from SS to S_1S_1 the union is able to raise the wage rate from OW to OW_1, but the quantity of labour employed decreases from OM to OL.

be done by *closed shop* practices. These are not always aimed at increasing wages but have certainly been used for this purpose in some industries, e.g. printing and film making. The supply of labour to an occupation could also be limited by the efforcement of long apprenticeships or training periods. Another method is *demarcation*, where particular tasks in a job may only be done by members of a particular union, for example plumbers not being allowed to do joiners' jobs in a particular factory. Demarcation or 'who does what' disputes have been a frequent cause of unrest in UK industrial relations, for example in the ship-building industry.

Figure 21.2 shows that the effect of restricting the supply of labour is to increase the wage rate from W to W_1. It also means that the quantity of labour employed declines from OM to OL. Thus, while some workers are receiving higher wages, other people are unable to obtain jobs. This kind of practice is not restricted to trade

unions; the Inns of Court run a most effective closed shop which restricts the supply of labour to the Bar, thereby keeping out many young lawyers who might like to become practising barristers. This not only has the effect of driving up barristers' fees but also contributes to the delays which bedevil the administration of justice.

Collective bargaining

Working people learned long ago that to ask the employer individually for a wage rise was a good way to lose a job. Trade unions therefore negotiate on behalf of all their members and if agreement is not reached then they may take action collectively to enforce their demands. The collective bargaining strength of a trade union varies enormously from industry to industry. Until the unsuccessful strike of 1984–5 the bargaining strength of coalminers was regarded as great because there was almost 100 per cent membership of the National Union of Mineworkers, a strong community spirit and the possibility of bringing the country to a standstill. On the other hand the bargaining strength of some workers in the UK is so poor that the government set up Wages Councils to determine minimum wage rates. However, the rising tide of unemployment in the 1980s weakened the bargaining power of most workers. Those protected by Wages Councils saw a further weakening of their position when the government set about restricting the activities of some Wages Councils and dismantling others (*see* page 144). ✳

Figure 21.3 illustrates three possibilities for collective bargaining. Which one occurs will depend upon the strength of the union. Here successful collective bargaining has raised the wage rate from OW to OW_1. As a result of this the employer would like to employ less labour (OL instead of OM); this is position A. However the strength of the union may be such that it is able to insist that the organisation retains the same number of workers as before. This is position B, where the wage rate is higher but

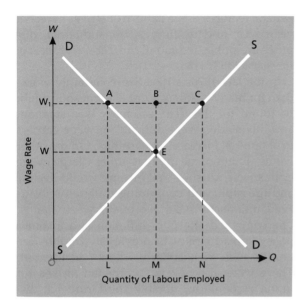

Fig. 21.3 *Collective bargaining and wages*
Collective bargaining raises the wage from the equilibrium level at OW to OW₁, thus creating a disequilibrium. The quantity of labour employed – OL, OM or ON – depends upon the bargaining power of the union.

the quantity of labour remains OM. As a result of increasing the wage rate more people would like to work for this organisation. In an extreme case the union may be able to insist that the organisation moves to position C where the wage rate is OW₁ and the quantity of labour employed is ON. If the organisation is pushed into this position it may be forced to close down since AC represents a surplus of labour which it would not choose to employ of it were not forced to.

Such *feather-bedding* and *over-manning* has occurred in a number of UK industries. One of the most notorious industries for this is newspaper printing, where these practices have contributed to the demise of a number of newspapers. The Wapping dispute when Rupert Murdoch moved the printing of his newspapers from Fleet Street to the East End was a consequence not only of the introduction of the new technology but also the desire to get round the previous restrictive practices of the unions.

Economic factors affecting bargaining strength

The ability of a trade union to raise wages will be influenced not only by its collective bargaining strength but also by several economic factors which are listed below.

a) The elasticity of demand for the final product. If the demand for the product which labour is being used to produce is highly inelastic then it will be relatively easy for the firm to pass on increased wage costs to the consumer. Conversely an elastic demand will make it difficult to pass on increased costs and, thus, make it difficult for unions to obtain wage rises.

b) The proportion of total costs which labour represents. If labour costs make up a large proportion of total costs this will tend to make it more difficult for them to obtain wage rises. On the other hand, if the labour costs are only a small proportion of the organisation's other costs and, more especially, if the worker's task is vital this will tend to make it easier to secure a wage rise. This is referred to by Professor Samuelson as 'the importance of being unimportant.'

c) The ease of factor substitution. If it is relatively easy to substitute another factor of production for labour, e.g. capital, this will mean that as unions demand more wages the business will employ fewer workers. In the UK since the 1939–45 war, rising labour costs have encouraged employers to substitute capital for labour wherever possible, e.g. the microprocessor revolution.

d) The level of profits. If an organisation is making little or no profit then the effect of a rise in wages could well be to put it out of business. Conversely, high profits would make it easier for unions to obtain higher wages and job security. In recent years high profits have had the effect of stimulating wage claims.

e) Macroeconomic influences. The influences discussed so far are all microeconomic. However, wage bargaining can be influenced by the macroeconomy. Firstly, the general state of the economy affects wage bargaining. If there is economic growth then it is easier for unions to obtain wage rises and wage earners tend to capture a larger share of national income, although the reverse is true in times of economic depression and unemployment. Secondly, inflation influences wage claims. Inflation decreases the real value of wages and, therefore, stimulates demands for higher money wages. Whether wage earners are able to keep pace with inflation depends upon their relative bargaining power. Inflation may also make it easier to obtain higher money wages if the increased costs can easily be passed on as higher prices because of the inflationary climate.

If trade union activity were successful in the national sense it would increase the proportion of the national income going to wages. Nevertheless, despite all the struggles of trade unions, this is not so. The portion of national income going to wages and salaries now is not significantly different from 40 years ago, being 65 per cent of the GNP in 1946, 67 per cent in 1961 and 64 per cent in 1986.

Industrial relations in the UK

The UK's record of industrial relations is not good. In particular the economy has been bedevilled with strikes.

The withdrawal of labour is the ultimate weapon unions possess. The word 'strike' is very emotive and many people believe that srikes have been the cause of the UK's economic difficulties. It is more likely, however, that rather than being a cause, strikes are a symptom of the UK's industrial malaise. Rather than expressing opinions it is better to examine the facts. Statistics on strikes vary greatly from year to year, but until recently you would need to look carefully to find a country with a significantly worse record than the UK. The dramatic fall in strikes meant that the number of days lost in the late 1980s was amongst the lowest in the industrialised world. However the Germans and Japanese were able to look back on 40 years of good industrial relations.

In this sections we will concentrate on the general features of the pattern of strikes in recent years. Up-to-date figures on industrial disputes are published montly in *The Department of Employment Gazette*.

In the late 1970s strikes were certainly worse than for many years. A number of reasons might be found for this. The economy was stagnant and this made it very difficult for wage earners to obtain *real* increases in earnings. On the other hand, inflation meant that unless large wage claims were satisfied real income would decline and the rapid and continuing inflation encouraged unions to make exorbitant wage claims. The combined effects of inflation and incomes policy spread strikes to previously trouble-free groups such as hospital workers and firemen. There were also several protracted strikes for union recognition, notably the Grunwick dispute. It should be remembered, however, that good industrial relations do not make good television and that we always see the very worst side of industry's troubles on our television screens.

The vast majority of strikes are for increased wages. *Sympathetic strikes*, i.e. one union striking to support another, and *political strikes* are very uncommon in the UK. There was an exception to this in the years 1971–4 when many unions took action against the Industrial Relations Act 1971. In 1979, 28 million days were lost through strikes. The total was the highest since the general strike of 1926, and it was partly the result of opposition to the Labour government's pay policy in what became known as the 'winter of discontent' (1978–9). However a far greater number of days were lost in the autumn of 1979 because of the series of weekly one-day and two-day strikes called in the entire engineering industry. In the early 1980s the number of days lost through strikes fell rapidly. This may be at least partly attributed to rising unemployment.

When the Conservative government was elected in 1979 one of its chief aims was to counter the power of the unions. Legally this was done through the Employment Acts of 1980 and 1982 and the Trade Union Act 1984. The government saw these as redressing the balance after the privileges given to the unions by the Labour governments in the 1970s.

The 1980 Act made available public funds for secret ballots for such things as electing officers, calling or ending a strike or amending union rules. The Act also gave the Secretary of State wide-ranging power to issue codes of practice 'for the purpose of improving industrial relations'. The 1982 Act, among other things, provided for regular reviews of closed-shop agreements by secret ballot, brought legal immunities for trade unions into line with those of individuals and restricted the meaning of lawful disputes to those between workers and their employers, i.e. it made sympathetic strikes illegal.

The 1984 Trade Union Act made strike action lawful only if sanctioned by a secret ballot of members and it also placed strict limitations on actions such as secondary picketing. This Act also required that every voting member of a union's principal executive committee be (re)elected by ballot at least every five years.

Opinions differ as to whether this bout of legislation was an outright attack on trade unions or a much needed attempt to introduce sanity into industrial relations.

Whatever the motives it did not immediately produce industrial peace. The 1984–5 miners' strike was one of the most protracted and bitter in British labour history. It ended with the defeat of the miners and the splitting of the NUM.

By the late 1980s the incidence of strikes in the UK was exceptionally low. This did not necessarily mean that there was harmony in industrial relations. There continued to be long and bitter disputes such as those in education and at Wapping.

The government argued that its intentions were to sweep away restrictive practices and allow free determination of wages. In this way it was hoped that industry would be able to compete successfully with countries such as Japan and Germany. Either coincidentally or as a result of government policy the economy passed through a huge economic depression. It was this as much as legislation which broke the grip

of unions. By 1988 the government was able to boast of a record of a low level of strikes, increasing productivity and economic growth. On the other hand it could be argued that much of the UK's manufacturing base lay in ruins. By 1988 industrial production had only just returned to the 1979 level.

Monopoly and monopsony in labour markets

Most labour markets are subject to imperfections. These may be both on the demand side (employers) or the supply side (employees). We have considered the supply side monopoly above, i.e. that a trade union may act as a monopoly supplier of labour. If the trade union restricts the supply of labour as described on page 256 above, then the union is behaving in a classic monopolist fashion. However, as we have seen, unions may also act to protect jobs, thus departing from typical monopoly behaviour.

Employment and the monopolist

If a firm is the monopoly supplier of a product, then, as the monopolist sells more of the product, it will have to lower the price of the product. Thus the MRP for labour is determined by the formula

$$MRP = MPP \times MR$$

rather than

$$MRP = MPP \times P$$

This is illustrated in Fig. 21.4. Thus curve MRP represents the firm's demand curve for labour as it would be under perfect competition and MRP_1 as it is under monopoly. We have here assumed that the wage rate remains constant. Thus we can see that the monopolist will choose to employ OL units of labour rather than OM as it would under conditions of competitive supply.

Under conditions of monopoly the employer will tend to restrict the employment of a factor.

259

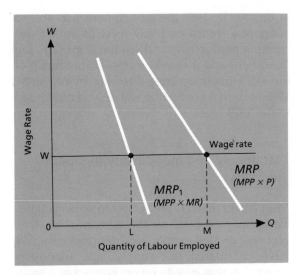

Fig.21.4 *Employment and the monopolist*
Under perfect competition the business would employ
OM units of labour, but under monopoly:

$$MRP = MPP \times MR$$

and therefore the monopolist restricts employment to
OL.

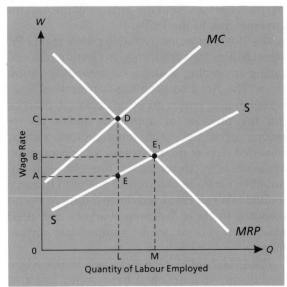

Fig. 21.5 *Wages and the monopolist*
The profit maximisation equilibrium is where *MC* =
MRP, i.e. employment of OL, but the business is only
obliged to pay a wage of OA. This compares with the
competitive wage of OB and employment of OM. Thus
both wages and employment are lower under
monopsony.

This restriction of employment in the labour
market is associated with the monopolist's restriction of supply of consumer goods. Both
therefore distort the optimum allocation of
resources (*see* Chapter 18).

Wages and the monopsonist

A monopsony exists when there is only one
buyer of a commodity. This may exist in labour
markets; for example, British Coal is the sole
employer of miners and British Rail of train
drivers. Under these conditions the employer
may influence the wage rate. In Fig. 21.5 SS
shows the supply curve for labour. Under normal competitive conditions the equilibrium
would, therefore, occur where the *MRP* (demand)
curve for labour intersects with the supply curve
(point E_1), i.e. at a wage rate of OB and a quantity
of OM. However, if the monopsonist is a profit
maximiser it will wish to equate the *MC* of the
factor with the *MRP*. This gives an equilibrium
point D. To attract this quantity of labour (OL)

this monopsonist must only pay a wage of OA.
Thus, the wage is less than that in the competitive market by the amount of AB and the quantity of labour employed is reduced by the
amount LM. These conditions could apply to
the monopsonic purchase of any factor, not just
labour. Thus we can conclude that:

**The monopsonist will tend to employ less of a
factor and pay a lower price than in competitive
markets.**

This imperfection therefore also creates a distortion in the allocation of resources (*see* below,
Chapter 25, discussion of Pareto optimality).

The situation may be further complicated if
the monopsonist employer is bargaining with a
monopolist union because under these circumstances the union may be able to prevent the
employer moving to position E on the graph.
Under these circumstances the income rep-

resented by area ACDE becomes a zone of bargaining between employer and union.

The supply of labour

Total supply and industry supply

The total supply of labour is primarily determined by non-economic factors such as the size of the population and its age and sex distribution (*see* Chapter 4). It may also be influenced by institutional factors such as the school leaving age and social attitudes to such things as women working. In general, therefore, the total supply of labour is highly inelastic, although that is not to say that it may not be varied by exceptional circumstances, as was seen in the 1939–45 war when many women went out to work.

However if we consider an industry or a single firm there is a great deal more elasticity of supply, since offering higher wages will attract workers from other industries. The elasticity of supply will be greater the longer the period of time considered, as people have more opportunity to respond to differentials by retraining, etc.

The leisure preference

The supply of labour is also influenced by the length of the working week. Here we encounter the factor known as the *leisure preference*. As real wages have risen over this century people have taken the opportunity not only to consume increased quantities of goods and services, but also to reduce the length of the working week. They have, therefore, consumed part of the income as increased leisure.

The possibilities for the individual confronted with a rise in the wage rate are illustrated in Fig. 21.6. In the original situation the wage rate is £1.25 per hour. The various possibilities for the worker are, therefore, represented by the budget line TA. At T the worker enjoys 24 hours' leisure but no income, while at A the worker has an income of £30 per day but has

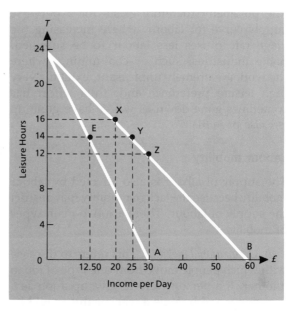

Fig. 21.6 *The leisure preference*
The increase in wages from £1.25/hour to £2.50/hour moves the budget line outwards from TA to TB. Originally the worker supplied 10 hours of work per day (point E). As a result of the increase in pay the worker may move to position X, Y or Z.

to work 24 hours to earn it. Suppose that the worker chooses point E working 10 hours a day, i.e. 14 hours of leisure, and an income of £12.50. Now suppose that the wage rate doubles to £2.50 per hour, so that the worker's budget line is now TB. As a result of this, three possibilities confront the worker. Firstly the worker may continue to work the same number of hours and therefore moves to point Y, so that income now increases to £25 per day. Secondly the worker could choose to take some of the increase in more leisure and some as more income; for example, at point X income would rise to £20 per day and the working day decrease to 8 hours. The third possibility is that, in response to the higher wage rate, longer hours are worked; for example, at point Z the working day has increased to 12 hours and therefore the wage to £30.

Historically what seems to have happened is that workers have moved towards the position represented by X, i.e. a shorter working week. **261**

The possibility therefore exists for a perverse supply curve for labour, where increasing the wage rate causes less labour to be supplied. Some industries, such as coal-mining, where the work is extremely unpleasant, exhibit a very high leisure preference and, thus, effort has sometimes gone down as wages have gone up (*see also* page 61).

Labour mobility

The supply of labour is also affected by labour mobility because the lack of mobility may restrict the supply of labour. There are two main types of mobility.

a) Occupational mobility. This refers to the ease with which people move from one type of job to another. If a person were to give up a job as a coal-miner and become a teacher this would be an example of occupational mobility. This type of mobility is likely to be influenced by the amount of training required for a job, the reluctance of workers to change jobs, the restrictions on job entry placed by unions and professional associations and by the age of the person concerned.

b) Geographical mobility. This refers to the ease with which people move from a job in one area to a similar job in another area. This is restricted by the unwillingness of people to leave the social ties they may have in an area, by the difficulty of finding housing, the reluctance to disturb their children's education, the cost of moving and the lack of information about opportunities elsewhere in the economy. Surprisingly, geographical mobility tends to decrease as unemployment rises as people become unwilling to risk a new job in an unknown area.

Both types of mobility tend to be low in the UK compared with a country like the USA. A higher level of mobility would both reduce the level of unemployment and also the differentials between wages.

Differentials and disequilibriums

Wage differentials

In 1987 the typical general medical practitioner received an income of £32 000 pa while the typical agricultural worker received less than £7000 pa. Similarly, at the same time the highest paid 1 per cent of the population received 6.2 per cent of incomes whilst the lowest paid 10 per cent received only 2.8 per cent of incomes. Some of the reasons for these differences are listed below.

a) Non-homogeneity. Differences may exist in the work force by way of natural abilities such as strength, intelligence and skill and also because of training and education.

b) Non-monetary rewards. Workers may receive benefits in addition to their wages, e.g. company cars, cheap loans and mortgages, and payments in kind such as free coal in the case of coal-miners. People may also be willing to work for the non-monetary rewards of a job such as social prestige or pleasant working conditions. This last factor may also work in reverse, with people having to be rewarded for working in unpleasant or hazardous occupations.

c) Ignorance. People may simply be unaware of the opportunities which exist elsewhere.

d) Barriers to mobility. As discussed above, barriers may exist to the geographical and occupational mobility of labour, either from the unwillingness of people to move from area to area or because of the restrictions placed on entry to certain jobs.

e) Geographical considerations. Certain areas are considered more desirable to live in than others. The so-called 'sunrise industries' such as computer software have tended to concentrate in areas which are considered geographically desirable. This, however, increases house prices, etc., and therefore higher wages may be necessary.

f) Vocationalism. Certain jobs such as nursing or teaching are thought to give *non-pecuniary advantages* to the worker by way of job satisfaction and therefore workers may tolerate lower wages.

Having considered all these problems many economists would maintain that jobs and incomes are still determined by the *principle of net advantage*, i.e. people will still choose their job and move job so as to achieve the greatest net advantage having considered both the pecuniary and non-pecuniary advantages of jobs.

Disequilibriums in the labour markets

It may be surprising that excess demand can exist in a labour market when there is general unemployment or that excess supply can exist when there is generally full employment. However this is so and a number of factors which may account for this are listed below.

a) Non-competing groups. Since labour is a heterogeneous factor, excess supply in one sector may not influence another; for example, it is quite possible to have an excess supply of history teachers whilst experiencing a shortage of mathematics teachers.

b) Rigidity of wages. Although it may be possible to increase wages it is very hard to decrease them. Thus successful union pressure may raise wages, creating excess supply, but union bargaining strength may prevent employers from shedding labour (*see* Fig. 21.3).

c) Internal promotions. In many occupations people are recruited relatively young and untrained and then gain specialist training. It thus becomes very difficult for someone outside to compete for the higher grades in such jobs; for example, it would be very unlikely that a person might switch into a senior post in education or local government if their experience is outside the industry, whatever their qualifications may be.

d) Information costs. Seeking a new job or a new employee imposes costs on both the employee and the employer. The more senior the post, the more important these costs will tend to become. This point is developed below in search theory.

Search theory

This modern theory of labour markets maintains that both employers and employees will 'search' for the best bargain in the labour market. According to this theory the traditional marginal productivity approach ignores the cost of pay bargaining, information collection and labour mobility.

To the employer the cost of the search may include advertisements for suitable employees, interviewing costs and the costs of doing without the required labour in the interim period. The costs are likely to rise with seniority of the post. For the potential employee there is the *opportunity cost* of the search, i.e. doing without income until the right job has been found. High levels of unemployment may discourage the worker in the search.

Thus differentials in incomes may be partly explained by the problems of job search (*see also* page 328).

Summary

1 Trade unions attempt to affect wage rates both by restricting supply and by collective bargaining.
2 Factors which affect the bargaining strength of unions are elasticity of demand for the final product, the ease of factor substitution and the proportion of total cost which labour represents.
3 A monopolist is likely to restrict employment of a factor and a monopsonist is likely to restrict both employment and payment.

4   The supply of labour as a whole is determined by non-economic factors. The supply of labour is also influenced by leisure preferences and labour mobility.

5   The differentials which exist between wages are much greater than can be explained by marginal productivity theory.

6   Disequilibriums frequently occur in labour markets irrespective of the overall employment situation.

Questions

1   Examine the factors which influence a trade union's ability to raise wages.

2   Discuss the factors which account for the differentials in wage rates.

3   'If unions succeed in raising real wages this will lead to less employment and ultimately a smaller total of wages.' Evaluate this statement. (Hint: remember elasticity of demand, page 144.)

4   Discuss the view that minimum wage legislation leads to more unemployment and a smaller total payment of wages.

5   Analyse the demand-side influences which might limit wages and employment.

6   To what extent do you think that the government should interfere in collective bargaining?

7   Evaluate the success of equal pay legislation in raising women's wages.

8   Identify and explain an example of:
   a) excess supply;
   b) excess demand in labour markets.

9   To what extent do you consider unemployment to be an inevitable consequence of the introduction of the new technology?

10   Refer to Fig. 20.3 and Fig. 20.4. Demonstrate that if the wage were to be set equivalent to the highest level of average product there would be no product left to pay land, capital or profit.

Data response   Employment and unemployment

Study Fig. 21.7. This illustrates data relating to employment and unemployment in the UK.

Answer the following questions:

1   Say what is meant by the term *the working population*. What was the size of the UK working population in:
   a) 1970?
   b) 1985?

2   Explain the observed changes in the UK's employed labour force.

3   Between 1982 and 1986 it appeared that both employment and unemployment were increasing. How is this possible?

4   What impact did the rise in the level of unemployment have upon real wages? Explain your answer.

5   How did the rise in the level of unemployment affect trade union bargaining power?

6   To what extent is the size of the employed labour force an indicator of the level of economic activity in a country?

7   What effect are changes in the total supply of labour likely to have upon wages and employment?

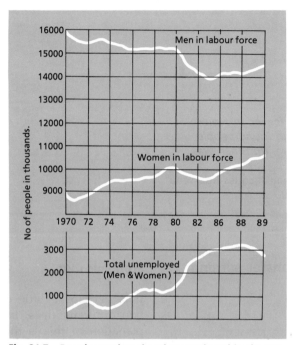

Fig. 21.7 *People employed and unemployed in the UK*

22

Rent

*The first man who, having fenced in a piece of
land, said, 'This is mine', and found people
naive enough to believe him, that man was
the founder of civil society.*

Jean Jacques Rousseau

Economic rent and transfer earnings

Definitions of rent

The term rent has a wide usage in the
economy. People speak of renting a car or
renting a house. Economists, however, use
the word in a much more specific fashion.
There are in fact two concepts of rent which
are in current use in economics.

a) Rent. This is the payment made for the use
of *land* as defined in the economic sense. In
practice, however, land is frequently 'mixed up'
with other factors of production and it is difficult to ascertain precisely how much is being
paid for the land and how much is being paid
for the capital bound up with it.

b) Economic rent. This is the payment made to
any factor of production over and above that
which is necessary to keep the factor in its
present use; for example, a soccer star may earn
£500 per week because his special skills are in
great demand. If his skills were not in great
demand it is possible that he would be willing to
work as a footballer for £100 per week, for there
is little else he can do, in which case £400 of the
£500 is a kind of *producer's surplus* or *rent of
ability,* for it is not necessary to keep his skills in
their present use. This payment can therefore
be described as an *economic rent.*

Economic rent

It is perhaps a little confusing that we have
two different ideas, both called rent. The explanation of this is that the idea of economic
rent, which we now apply to any factor of production, was an idea which was first put forward by David Ricardo with respect to land and
it was only later applied to other factors.

In developing the idea Ricardo made two
assumptions, firstly that the supply of land is
fixed, and secondly that land has only one use
and that is growing food. If this were the case,
the supply curve for land would be a vertical
straight line as in Fig. 22.1.

The demand for land, or any other factor, is a
derived demand, for it is demanded, not for
itself, but for what can be produced with it. In
Ricardo's time the demand for land was very
high because Napoleon's Continental System
had cut off European grain from the UK market.
The result of this was that the landlords were
able to charge very high rents for the land on
which to grow grain. Ricardo argued that this
did not create more land, so that landlords
were receiving more money but not supplying
anything more. Conversely, the demand for
land might fall, in which case the rents would
decrease but the supply of land would not.
From this Ricardo concluded that rent fulfilled
no purpose and was a *producer's surplus.*

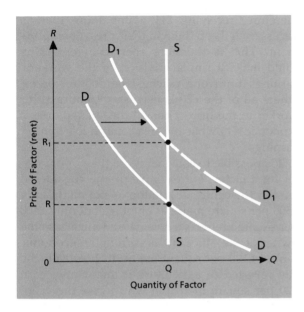

Fig. 22.1 *Economic rent*
All factor earnings are economic rent because, whatever happens to the price, the quantity supplied remains the same.

Although Ricardo's assumptions are subject to criticism, he did manage to construct the theoretical extreme of the supply of a factor of production. In Fig. 22.1 you see that the supply curve is vertical and that, therefore, the factor earning is determined by the demand curve. The increase in demand from DD to D_1D_1 increases the price but not the quantity of land. Thoretically demand could decrease until the price (rent) were zero without the quantity supplied decreasing. Thus all the earnings made by this factor are over and above that which is necessary to keep it in its present use and are therefore *economic rent*.

Ricardo also argued that rent was *barren* since, however high rent was, it produced no more of the factor. To some extent this is true, but high rents do have the function of making us exploit scarce resources more sensibly. For example, when land was very cheap in the USA it was ruthlessly exploited. This resulted in the 'dust bowl'. High rents for land mean that farmers are anxious to preserve the fertility of land and look after it carefully.

Since the time of Ricardo his view of rent has been modified in two major ways.

a) It is now acknowledged that the supply of land is only fixed in the global sense. There is not a single market for land but different markets for building land, agricultural land, etc. Thus in practice changes in the price of land for one use cause land to shift from use to use, thus creating some elasticity of supply.

b) We now apply the idea of economic rent to any factor of production. Thus we can repeat our definition that:

Economic rent is the payment made to *any* factor of production over and above that which is necessary to keep it in its present use.

Transfer earnings

In practice if a factor's earnings decline there comes a time when that factor will transfer to some other use.

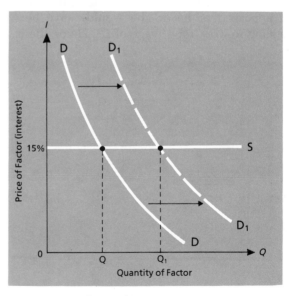

Fig. 22.2 *Transfer earnings*
All factor earnings are transfer earnings because, whatever the demand, the same price must be paid for the factor. If, for example, the firm offered less than 15 per cent for capital then the capital would all transfer to another use.

The payment which is necessary to keep a factor in its present use is described as transfer earnings.

If we assume that a firm is borrowing money and it is able to borrow all it wishes at 15 per cent but the bank is not willing to lend any at lower rates, then we could represent the supply curve for capital as a horizontal straight line. In this case the whole of the 15 per cent interest payment could be regarded as being necessary to prevent capital transferring to another use. It is, thus, all transfer earnings. This is illustrated in Fig. 22.2.

Separating economic rent and transfer earnings

The cases of pure economic rent and pure transfer earnings present the theoretical extremes of the concepts; in practice most factor earnings are a composite of the two. In Fig. 22.3 the firm requires a workforce of 500. In order to attract this many workers it must pay a wage of £20 a day. If we consider the 200th worker, however, it appears that he or she would, have been willing to work for a wage of £9. He or she is,

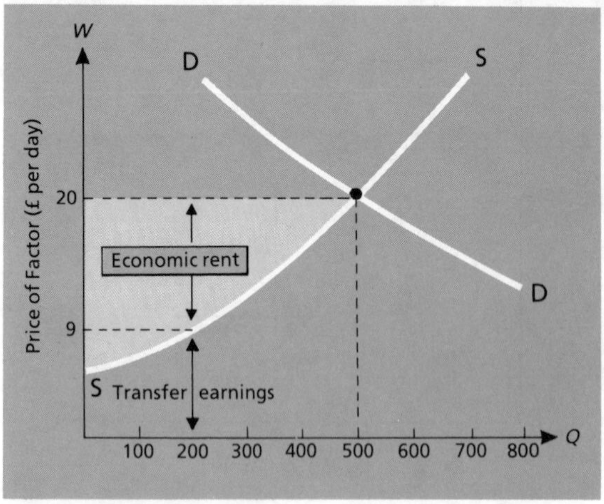

Fig. 22.3 *Factor earnings*
A composite of economic rent and transfer earnings. The wage is £20 and therefore the 200th worker's pay is £9 of transfer earnings and £11 of economic rent. The shaded area represents the economic rent of the entire workforce.

therefore, receiving £11 a day more than is necessary to keep them in their present employment. This is therefore economic rent. One could make a similar division of the workers' earnings until one reaches the 500th worker, where all of the £20 is necessary to attract this worker to the firm. Thus all the shaded area is economic rent while the area beneath it is transfer earnings.

It is possible to consider more than one transfer for a factor. For example, if one considered land in the centre of London, a site might earn £500 per square metre as an office but only £400 per square metre as a cinema, in which case the owner of the office site is earning an economic rent of £100 per square metre. If, however, the site reverted to agriculture it might only earn £20 per square metre, in which case the economic rent would be £480. Thus we can say that:

The division of any factor earning between economic rent and transfer earnings depends upon the transfer being considered.

Rent and profits

It is now possible to see the exact correspondence between the concepts of rent and profits. It may be recalled that we defined normal profit as that amount of profit which is necessary to keep a firm in the industry (page 182). This we may now align with our definition of transfer earnings. Similarly we defined abnormal profit as any profit in excess of normal profit just as we have defined eocnomic rent as any payment made to a factor over and above transfer earnings.

Quasi-rent

Whether or not a particular portion of a factor earning is considered to be economic rent or transfer earnings may sometimes depend upon the period of time we are considering. If one considers a machine that is recovering £500 a year above its operating cost, then in the short-run we could consider this as an economic rent since it is £500 more than is necessary to keep capital in its present use. However in the long-run the machine must recover not only its operating cost but also its replacement cost if capital is going to remain in that use. If, for example, the replacement cost of this machine were £500 per year then, in the long-run, all the machine's earnings become transfer earnings.

Those earnings which are economic rent in the short-run but transfer earnings in the long-run are correctly termed quasi-rent.

The problem of rent incomes

The problem

Ever since Ricardo described rent as a surplus, people have been concerned with the potential social injustice of this. If we start from the proposition that land is fixed in supply then we may view the problem as one in which, as more and more people and capital, etc., are added to the fixed factor, there is an ever-increasing demand for land and, therefore, ever-increasing rents. As a result, more and more of the national product will accrue to the owners of the land but nothing more will be supplied in return for it. This forms an important plank of Marxist philosophy and is still a live policy issue today, with many left-wing politicians believing that land should be nationalised.

Henry George (1839–97)

Henry George has the distinction of writing the single most popular book ever written on economics, *Our Land and Land Policy*. George's central thesis was that poverty is caused by the monopolisation of land by the few who expropriate the product of working people. The solution, he suggested, was that rent should be confiscated by the government through a *single tax* on land. According to George no other taxes would be necessary.

The idea of the single tax was debated by famous economists such as Alfred Marshall and J. B. Clark. They concluded that the tax would have less adverse effects upon the allocation of resources than other taxes but the idea had three major shortcomings.

a) The tax would be unjust because, as we have explained, rent can be earned by other factors of production even though they would escape the tax.

b) The tax would not produce enough revenue to replace all other taxes.

c) The tax would be impossible to administer since, in practice, it is often impossible to separate land from other factors such as capital.

George himself died in 1897 during a campaign to become mayor of New York. However an active Henry George Society still exists to promote his ideas, proving the enduring popularity of fiscal ideas suggesting that all the taxes in the country should be paid by someone else.

Economic rent and taxes

It could be argued that economic rent is the subject of tax today, since high incomes are hit by higher income tax. Thus, for example, the soccer star who is earning £100 000 a year, most of which the economist would describe as an economic rent, is likely to find a good proportion of it appropriated by the government in taxes. There have, however, been specific attempts to tax economic rent, such as the Labour government's Development Land Tax Act 1976, which was an attempt to tax profit made through the development (change of use) of land. The problem remains that of identifying rent and separating it from the other factor rewards for tax purposes.

The other alternative would be to nationalise land. The problem with this solution is that of destroying the price mechanism as a means of allocating scarce resources. Would a government be able to allocate land between different uses as efficiently as the market system?

Summary

1 Rent is the payment made to land.
2 Transfer earnings are the payment made to keep a factor in its present use and economic rent is any payment made in excess of this.
3 The amount of economic rent and the amount of transfer earnings in any factor payment depends upon the transfer being considered.
4 The earnings which are economic rent in the short-run, but transfer earnings in the long-run, are correctly termed quasi-rent.
5 Because rent has been described as 'barren surplus' it has often been the target for taxation schemes.

Questions

1 Explain why the rents in the City of London can be as high as £500 per m² but may only be this much per square hectare for agricultural land in Lancashire.
2 Discuss the effect of a 50 per cent tax on all rent incomes from land in the UK. How would the effect differ if this tax were only imposed in Greater London?
3 Account for the fact that property values may be twice as high in Enterprise Zones as in immediately adjacent property.
4 Distinguish economic rent from transfer earnings.
5 Discuss the relationship between elasticity of supply of a factor and economic rent.

Data response   Nuts to a dated system

Read the following letter which was written to the *Gardian* newspaper in 1987. It is concerned with a proposal for a Site Valuation Rating (SVR), i.e. rating (taxing) land according to its site value rather than according to the value of buildings on it as was the case with the existing system. Under a system of SVR an acre of land would be taxed according to its position whether or not it had buildings on it. This would discourage the practice of leaving land, or buildings, idle to avoid rates.

An article in the paper the previous week had suggested that advocates of SVR were unrealistic members of the 'nuts and sandals' brigade. The correspondent writes to say that Winston Churchill had once favoured SVR and he could hardly be described as a 'hippie'.

Ultimately is was not to be SVR, or any kind of rating, which was to be introduced, but rather the Community Charge (Poll Tax).

Nuts to a dated system
Sir, – Would Winston Churchill have been a member of the 'nuts and sandals' fraternity had he still been alive? I doubt it, nor for that matter, are many of today's supporters of Site Value Rating. In 1907 at the Drury Lane Theatre, Covent Garden, Winston Churchill called for 'Valuation of the land, rural and urban, at a fair market value of the land, apart from buildings and improvement of all kinds.' He went on to say: 'The present land system hampers, hobbles and restricts industry . . . a reform of our rating system . . . would be followed by an upward movement in the material welfare of the nation.'

The present day Covent Garden is a success story.

This came about because the score or so bomb sites which had lain derelict since the war, were brought into use by a GLC armed with statutory powers – including finance, compulsory purchase, and the creation of a local Action Area Plan. Without such a plan, the spurring onto the market of these bomb sites, which would have been the result of SVR, would have led to a Victorian jumble. Therefore, a plan which initiates a balanced environment of work, living, welfare and leisure, is absolutely necessary to give SVR a coherent and rational basis.

If the present government is serious about ending the inner-city crisis before it explodes, SVR is needed along with Action Area Plans drawn up by the LA's and the neighbourhood community. Initial funding from the government, with which the pumps are primed, makes private capital begin to flow, as Covent Garden shows.

Alan Spence
Labour Land Campaign.

Answer the following questions:

1   Why, according to the author, were bomb sites left undeveloped for so long although they stood in the centre of London?

2   Assess SVR as a method of taxing economic rent.

3   Adam Smith laid down four *canons of taxation*. How well do you consider that the traditional rating system, the SVR proposal in the article and the Community Charge meet those canons? What are the properties of a good tax in a modern society?

23

Capital and interest

We have heard it said that five per cent is the natural interest of money.
Thomas Babington Macaulay

Capital and capital formation

Types and forms of capital

When the economist uses the expression capital, it usually refers to the stock of *capital (or producer) goods*. As we saw in Chapter 3, the definition of a capital good arises not out of its intrinsic nature but out of the use to which it is put. For example, if we consider a commodity such as a potato, to the household it is a consumer good but if used by the farmer to plant for next year's crop then it is capital because it is being used in the production of further wealth. Similarly a can of beans is a consumer good once it reaches the shopping basket but it is a producer good while still on the shelves of the supermarket since it is then still part of the capital of the business. There are some goods, such as oil tankers or tractors, which are invariably capital goods; this is because they are only used for the purpose of supplying other goods and services.

The term capital is also used to describe the legal forms by which wealth is owned. Thus, for example, the real capital of Ford UK is the factories, etc., it possesses; these are owned by shareholders and their shares represent the legal, or financial, claim upon that capital. Thus the term capital is used in two senses, either to describe capital goods or to describe financial resources. In this latter sense one may distinguish between invested finance (share capital in the case of a company) and the loaned finance

(loan capital) of a firm. This is the way most people think of capital. These two legal forms tell us the way in which the organisation is owned and controlled.

It is important to realise that capital goods are real wealth, while shares, debentures, money, etc., are not wealth but a legal claim upon it. This distinction may not be important to the individual but it is vital to the economy as a whole. If these paper forms of capital were real wealth then the country could solve all its economic difficulties by printing more of them.

Capital formation

As we have already seen, capital goods are not necessarily different from consumer goods but, rather, are used for a different purpose. If, for example, we have a stock of potatoes then we can consume them all or consume some and then plant the others. In this way one hopes to have more potatoes next year. In the same way, an organisation is faced with the choice of distributing all its profits or *ploughing them back* into the business in the hope that this will enable them to make even more profit in the future. This is the old familiar idea of 'no jam today for more jam tomorrow'. In other words capital is *formed* by doing without now and using the resources so freed to create more wealth in the future.

Capital is formed by forgoing current consumption and diverting these resources to the production of future wealth.

Figure 23.1 shows the possible effects of capital formation on growth. Line C shows the growth of consumption in an economy over a 50 year period with 15 per cent of income devoted to capital formation. At point K a change in the consumption pattern occurs and 20 per cent of income is now devoted to capital formation. Thus consumption is reduced to 80 per cent of income, i.e. people have a lower material standard of living. However this creates a new consumption path (C_1) which has more rapid growth than before. At point L in year 20 consumption has now reached the level it would have been had not the extra capitalisation taken place. After this point line C_1 is above C, showing that a higher standard of living has been achieved. Thus the economy on path C_1 is able to reach point N, which is unobtainable for the economy on path C. The shaded area to the left of point L represents the extra current consumption forgone in order to obtain path C_1. The shaded area to the right of point L shows the extra consumption made possible.

International comparisons

The thing which separates the rich nations of the world from the poor is the possession of capital. Since capital is formed by going without now to produce more for the future, it is relatively easy for the richer nations to become even richer since they can forgo current consumption of some goods and still have a high standard of living. However if a very poor country is living near subsistence level it is impossible for them to depress living standards to form capital since this would result in mass starvation. Imagine an economy which is so poor that everyone must spend all their time working in the fields to produce sufficient food just to keep them alive. Under these circumstances it will be impossible for the population to turn aside from agriculture to build roads or factories which might increase their living standards, since they will have nothing to live on while they do so. It is very difficult indeed for poor nations to break out of this cycle of poverty.

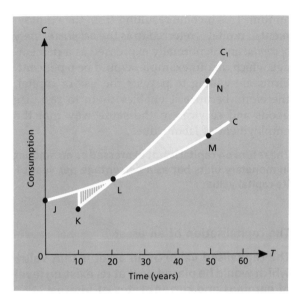

Fig. 23.1 *Capital formation*
Growth path C_1 shows the result of increased capital formation at point K.

(*See* page 630.)

Even for a country such as the UK it is important to realise that we cannot hope to keep pace with our competitors while we are devoting less to capital formation than they. For example, in 1985 the UK devoted only 17 per cent of GDP to investment while Japan devoted 28 per cent. The disparity is even greater if one considers this as investment per head – in 1985 investment per head was $1438 in the UK but $3164 in Japan. We may compare these figures with those of India, where investment was 25 per cent of GDP although this amounted to only $70 per head.

The net productivity of capital

As with any other factors of production, a firm employs capital for the product which it creates. Imagine that the owner of a barren hillside in Scotland invests £100 000 of capital by planting and growing trees on it. The trees take 25 years to grow, at the end of which time they are sold for £250 000. Thus in return for the investment the forester has received £150 000 or £6000 per annum. This income resulting from the employment of capital is referred to as the *net productivity of capital* and is normally expressed as a percentage which, in our example, would be 6 per cent. Firms are willing to pay for the use of capital, therefore, because it enables them to produce goods and services in the same way that the employment of labour does.

The return on capital is not expressed as an amount in monetary units but as a percentage per year of its capital value.

The capitalisation of an asset

The capitalised value of an asset is that value which would be placed on it at its existing level of earnings and current rates of interest.

The thing which determines the capital value of an asset is the income it produces. Suppose, for example, we have an asset which gives a fixed income per year of £500 forever and that the prevailing rate of interest is 5 per cent. Then the *present value* (V) can be calculated from the formula:

$$V = \frac{A}{i}$$

where A = amount of permanent receipt, e.g. £500, and, i = interest rate (in decimal terms), e.g. 0·05.

Thus in our example we would obtain the result:

$$V = \frac{£500}{0·05}$$

$$V = £10\ 000$$

If the interest rate were 10 per cent and A remained £500, this would give a value of £5000, whereas an interest rate of 2½ per cent would give a value of £20 000. In other words:

The value of an asset and the rate of interest are inversely proportional to one another.

The marginal efficiency of capital

Marginal efficiency of capital (*MEC*)

As we have seen, the output attributable to capital is referred to as the net productivity. This behaves in the same way as the returns to other factors; thus we see the same pattern of *APP* and *MPP*. Once again with capital the terminology is a little different because we are measuring the output as a percentage rate of return. When the *MPP* is measured in this way we obtain a figure known as the marginal efficiency of capital (*MEC*).

The marginal efficiency of capital is the rate of return on the last unit of capital employed.

Figure 23.2 shows an *MEC* curve. This is arrived at by plotting the return from each additional unit of capital. The *MEC* curve relates the rate of return to the desired *stock* of capital at any particular time. (It does *not* refer to the flow of investment over time. This is a macroeconomic concept which is dealt with in Part Three. See marginal efficiency of investment (*MEI*, page 361).

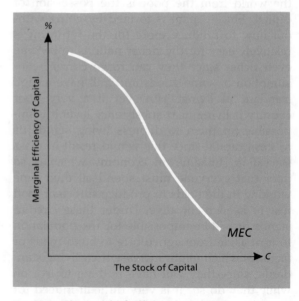

Fig. 23.2 *The marginal efficiency of capital*

Capital deepening and widening

The *MEC* curve is drawn on the usual assumption of *ceteris paribus*. If we continue with the assumption we can then explain the meaning of *capital deepening* and *capital widening*.

a) Capital deepening. This refers to the accumulation of more capital in relation to the other factors of production. If, for example, a firm acquires more capital so that each worker has twice as much capital to work with, this would be an example of capital deepening.

b) Capital widening. This refers to the accumulation of more capital without changing the proportions of factors of production. If, for example, a firm was to build a second factory which duplicated the system in its first factory, this would be an example of capital widening. Capital widening can only take place if there are unemployed resources in the economy.

It is capital deepening which accounts for the downward slope of the *MEC* curve. If we assume that technology is constant, as more and more capital is combined with a constant amount of other factors, then diminishing returns must be experienced.

MEC and the rate of interest

We measure the productivity of capital as a percentage rate so that we can compare it with the rate of interest which is the price of borrowing capital. If we combine the two together we can explain the size of the capital stock at any particular time. If the *MEC* is greater than the rate of interest then firms will expand the stock of capital. In Fig. 23.3 the rate of interest is 10 per cent. If the existing stock of capital is OL then the stock of capital would be expanded to OM where the *MEC* is equated with the rate of interest (*i*). Conversely, if the stock of capital is ON then the tendency would be to contract the stock to OM. Thus the optimum stock of capital is where:

$$MEC = i$$

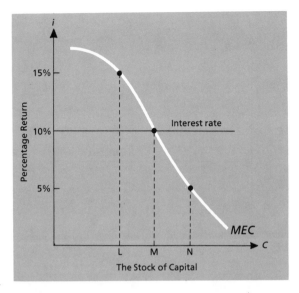

Fig. 23.3 *The marginal efficiency of capital and the rate of interest*
If the *MEC* is 15 per cent then the stock of capital will be expanded, whereas if the *MEC* is 5 per cent the stock of capital will be contracted.

You should be able to recognise this as a variation on the $MRP = P$ statement of Chapter 20 (*see* page 245). We could also examine the effect of changes in the rate of interest. *Ceteris paribus*, a fall in the rate of interest should cause the stock of capital to be expanded and a rise in the rate of interest should cause the stock to be contracted. *Thus the MEC curve could be described as the demand curve for capital*. Again you should be able to see how this fits in with the analysis in Chapter 20. It is only the terminology which is slightly different.

The *MEC* and technology

An improvement in technology within a firm would have the effect of shifting its *MEC* curve upwards as shown in Fig. 23.4. As you can see, if the rate of interest is 10 per cent then the shift of the *MEC* causes the stock of capital to expand. *Ceteris paribus*, the firm would be substituting capital for other factors.

If we turn to the effect of improvements in technology in the whole economy and look at **275**

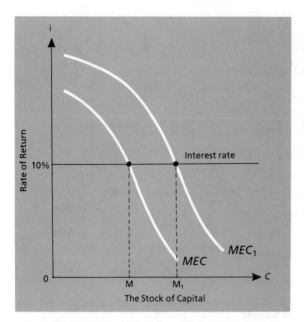

Fig. 23.4 *Interest, the marginal efficiency of capital and technology*
An increase in the level of technology causes the stock of capital to be expanded from OM to OM₁.

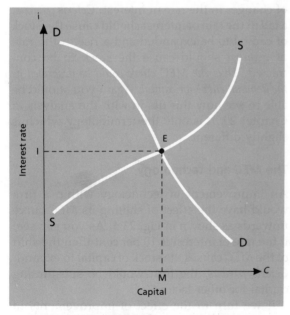

Fig. 23.5 *The determination of the rate of interest*

the history of technology over this century, then obviously there have been tremendous improvements, and this should have had the effect of increasing the rate of interest. This is because improvements in technology improve the productivity of capital, i.e. a more efficient machine produces more and can therefore command a higher income. However, despite periodic fluctuations in the interest rate, it has not shown a significant increase. This is because the accumulation of greater stocks of capital has offset the rise in the *MEC* caused by improvements in technology. Conversely we could say that the accumulation of a greater stock of capital over the century should have caused a decline in the interest rate, but this has been prevented by the increase in *MEC*.

The interest rate

The determination of the interest rate

We have already argued that the firm's demand curve for capital will be downward sloping. If we were to aggregate all the individual demand curves we would produce a downward sloping market demand curve for capital. We have taken the supply curve as being horizontal, although we could argue that the total supply curve of capital will be upward sloping, since a higher rate of interest will encourage people to save more. Thus we can present the rate of interest as a price formed by the intersection of the demand and supply curves in the normal way. This is illustrated in Fig. 23.5.

This is the neo-classical theory of the interest rate. A fuller discussion is to be found in Chapter 36, when we also consider monetary theories of the rate of interest.

The real rate of interest

One way of looking at the rate of interest is to say that it is the payment made to the lenders to compensate them for doing without their capital

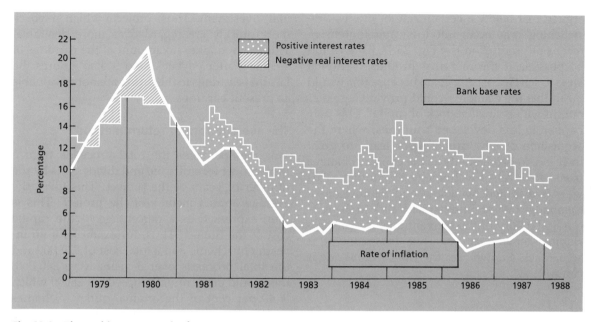

Fig. 23.6 *The real interest rate in the UK*
The real interest rate is the vertical distance between the two graphs. Negative real rates of interest occur when the rate of inflation is greater than the nominal rate of interest.

for a time. At the end of the period of the loan they receive the repayment of the capital as well as the interest. If there has been inflation, this will have decreased the value of the capital, so in order to obtain the *real rate of interest* we need to subtract from it the rate of inflation.

The real rate of interest is the difference (+ or −) between the nominal rate of interest and the rate of inflation.

Figure 23.6 shows the real rate of interest in recent years. As you can see in the early and mid-1970s the rate was negative. High nominal rates were often accompanied by negative real rates. In the 1980s the nominal rate declined but real rates increased substantially.

Reswitching

If the rate of interest falls then firms will 'switch' to more capital-intensive methods of production. This is the implication of the normal downward-sloping demand curve. However Joan Robinson and Nicholas Kaldor of Cambridge (UK) have

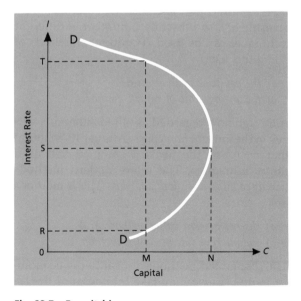

Fig. 23.7 *Reswitching*
As the interest rate falls from OT to OS, so the demand for capital expands from OM to ON. However as the interest rate falls even further the economy 'reswitches' to less capital-intensive methods, so that at interest rate OR the demand for capital is the same as it was at OT.

argued that below a certain rate of interest 're-switching' may occur into less capital-intensive means of production (*see* Fig. 23.7). This would be possible if the marginal product of capital were to start increasing again because this would mean that the economy could provide a greater output with a smaller stock of capital. This may happen in less developed countries, where the acquisition of new capital stock leads to great increases in productivity as the country changes from one level of technology to another. This view is disputed by Solow and Samuelson of Cambridge (Massachusetts) who stick to the neo-classical theory of the conventional downward-sloping demand curve. This disagreement is sometimes known as the 'two Cambridges controversy'.

Appraising investments

Different techniques

When a firm comes to decide whether or not an investment is worthwhile, a number of different techniques can be used. Traditional methods of doing this use:

a) *the pay-back method*; and
b) *the average rate of return method*.

Although now regarded as old fashioned, a survey in the journal *Economics* (August 1978) found that over half the firms it sampled still used these techniques. The more modern methods use *discounted cash flow analysis*. These methods are:

a) *the net present value method*; and
b) *the internal rate of return method*.

The discounted methods appeal to the economist more because they take into account the *opportunity cost* of the use of capital funds.

The pay-back method

This method appraises projects by considering the length of time required to pay back the orig-inal investment. Thus, projects which payback more quickly are regarded as more desirable. This method takes no account of the earnings of a project after payback, and it also ignores the fact that earnings in the future are not as valuable as present earnings.

The average rate of return method

This method takes the total proceeds from a project over its entire life and divides this by the number of years of the project. This gives the average annual income of the project. This is then expressed as a percentage of the capital cost of the project. Thus, for example, if an investment scheme had a total cost of £20 000 and the total proceeds over 5 years were £40 000, this would give annual proceeds of £8000 which is 40 per cent of the original outlay. Schemes with higher average rates of return are presumed to be more desirable. Not only is this method complicated by the depreciation of capital but also it can only be used to compare projects of identical lifespans.

Discounted cash flow

Discounted cash flow is a method of appraising the value of an asset based upon the idea that the value depends upon when the income from it is to be received. It is always better to receive money now rather than in the future. For

Table 23.1 Amounts of money invested needed to produce £100

Net present value invested today	Today	Produces			
		1 year from today	2 years from today	3 years from today	4 years etc from today
£100·00 →£100		£100	£100	£100	£100
£ 90·91					
£ 82·64					
£ 75.13					
£ 68.30					
etc					

Rate of discount = 10%

example, £100 received now would produce £110 in a year's time if invested at 10 per cent, £121 in two years' time, £133.1 in three years, and so on. Conversely we could discount the present value of money by asking what amount of money today would be necessary to produce say £100 in 1 year's time, 2 years' time, and so on. To do this we discount money by the rate of interest. Thus, for example, if £90.91 were invested at 10 per cent this would be worth £100 in 1 year's time, whereas £82.64 invested would be worth £100 in 2 years' time, and so on. This is illustrated in Table 23.1.

Present discounted value (*PDV*)

It is possible therefore to discount the future earnings of a project. If, for example, a scheme produces an income of £2000 per year for five years and we assume an interest rate of 10 per cent, then we could discover its *present discounted value (PDV)* as follows:

$$\begin{array}{ccc} \text{Year 1} & \text{Year 2} & \text{Year 3} \end{array}$$
$$PDV = £1818.18 + £1652.89 + £1502.63 +$$

$$\begin{array}{cc} \text{Year 4} & \text{Year 5} \end{array}$$
$$£1366.03 + £1241.84$$

$$PDV = £7581.57$$

This compares with the undiscounted earnings of:

$$5 \times £2000 = £10\ 000$$

The discounted values for each year can be found by looking them up in tables. However, they may also be calculated from the formula:

$$PDV = \frac{A}{(1 + i)^t}$$

where A = amount of earnings per year, i = the rate of interest and t = number of years of the project.

Thus in our example above we would obtain the calculation:

$$PDV = \frac{£2000}{(1 + 0.1)} + \frac{£2000}{(1 + 0.1)^2} + \frac{£2000}{(1 + 0.1)^3}$$
$$+ \frac{£2000}{(1 + 0.1)^4} + \frac{£2000}{(1 + 0.1)^5}$$

This produces the value shown in the text above and therefore gives us:

$$PDV = £7581.57$$

Net present value method

Having obtained the present discounted value we can arrive at the net present value by subtracting from it the initial cost of the investment. Suppose that the scheme we have considered above had an original cost of £5000, then:

$$\begin{aligned} \text{Net present value} &= £7581.57 - £5000 \\ &= £2581.57 \end{aligned}$$

The result is positive which indicates that it is a profitable investment.

The internal rate of return method

This method seeks to find the rate of interest that will discount the proceeds from the project to the original cost.

If the internal rate of return is greater than the rate of interest paid for borrowing money, then the scheme is worthwhile. If in our example the capital cost were £5000 while the proceeds of the scheme were £2000 a year over five years, a rate of 28·5 per cent would discount this flow of proceeds to £5012. If we subtract this total from the initial cost of £5000 we obtain an answer of almost exactly zero. Thus 28·5 per cent is the internal rate of return. If this rate is higher than the rate of interest then the project is profitable.

Financing the firm

Sources of finance

As we have seen, capital is formed through forgoing current consumption. Thus the source of capital funds is the savings of both private individuals and firms. We may divide the sources of **279** funds into *internal* and *external*. Internal funds are those generated by the firm itself whilst external funds are those obtained outside the firm. Internal finance (or ploughed back projects) is generally the most important source of funds to firms, although it has declined in importance in recent years. The sources of external finance are listed below.

a) The capital market. The firm can raise money by selling shares (equity) on the capital market or by the sale of debentures (fixed interest securities). The shares or debentures might be purchased by private individuals, pension funds, insurance companies or unit trusts. Table 23.2 shows the distribution of the ownership of shares between these various people and institutions. You will note the declining importance of the individual investor (*see also* page 359). The distribution of figures shows the remarkable rise in the importance of pension funds and insurance companies. However, this survey of ownership covers only those companies listed on the London Stock Exchange. The newly formed Unlisted Securities Market has been a big magnet for the private investor.

It may at first seem surprising that there has not been a more dramatic growth in the shareholding of private investors as a result of the government's privatisation programme during the 1980s. Several reasons can be advanced to explain this. Firstly the table shows *percentage* of shares owned. Most of the new shareholders from privatisation had very small holdings (e.g. £500) which made very little difference to the overall picture. Secondly the institutions such as insurance companies took major shareholdings in the privatised companies. Thirdly many of the new small shareholders promptly resold their shares to make a capital gain.

These comments notwithstanding the 1980s saw a dramatic increase in the *number* of private shareholders. At the end of the 1970s it was estimated that only 6 per cent of the population were shareholders whereas by the end of the 1980s estimates suggested that this had risen to between 14 and 19 per cent.

Table 23.2 The ownership of company shares in the UK (percentages)

	1963	1975	1981	1987
Private individuals	62	37	28	29
Insurance companies	11	16	20	22
Pension funds	7	17	27	28
Trusts	9	15	10	11
Overseas investors	5	6	4	6
Other	6	9	11	4
	100	100	100	100

Source: London Stock Exchange

b) Banks. UK banks do not buy shares in companies (such shares that they do own are usually limited to those of their subsidiaries). In other countries such as West Germany and the USA, banks are significant shareholders. In the UK banks finance firms by giving loans or overdrafts. They are thus really helping to finance the working, or circulating, capital of the firm.

c) The government. During the 1970s the government became a significant shareholder in a number of firms, the shares being held by the National Enterprise Board. In the early 1980s the government was concerned to reduce the role of the government in industrial finance. However some government finance is still important such as regional grants and subsidies; the farming industry, for example, is heavily dependent upon government finance.

d) Trade credit. A traditional method of finance is simply to delay the payment of bills, thus in effect obtaining an interest-free loan. The granting of trade credit in this manner is an important sales technique to many firms.

Shares and debentures

As we have seen, companies may raise capital by the sale of shares or debentures. While both result in the same thing – finance for the company – there are a number of differences between them. Primarily, debentures are loan capital which acknowledge and secure loans to the company, while shares are evidence of part ownership of the company and part investment in it. Thus debenture-holders are a company's creditors while shareholders are its members. Debentures normally provide for repayment and they are usually secured by a mortgage over the property of the company; a shareholder's investment is only completely repaid if and when the company is wound up while solvent. Consequently, the latter involves greater *risk*. An important commercial difference is that dividends on shares can only be paid out of profits and therefore presuppose a profitable year's trading, but the interest on debentures may be paid out of capital. Hence, a debenture-holder receives payment for the loan, irrespective of whether the company makes a profit or a loss.

Debentures are usually issued to raise temporary finance up to the limit specified in the company's articles of association. Debentures may be either *redeemable* or *irredeemable*. The former are repayable at or after a specified date and they are usually issued when the need for finance is temporary or when interest rates are high and likely to fall. Conversely, the latter are not repayable until the company is wound up or it defaults on the payment of interest due. They will usually be issued when longer-term finance is required or when interest rates are low and likely to rise.

Many companies will also have overdrafts with their banks and these accommodate fluctuations in their 'cash flow'. The amount and duration of the overdraft will depend largely upon the reputation of the company. The directors of small companies often give their personal guarantee as security for the debt to the bank.

Types of shares

There are two main types of share and they are distinguishable according to the voting rights and rights to receive dividends and repayment of capital which their holders enjoy.

a) *Preference shares*. The holders of preference shares receive a dividend in priority to other

shareholders, but it is usually only a fixed-rate dividend. Preference shares are presumed to be cumulative, i.e. if in any one year the dividend cannot be paid it is carried forward and added to the dividend for the following year, and so on. In many cases preference shareholders are also entitled to repayment of capital in priority to other shareholders should the company be wound up.

Preference shares do not normally give voting rights and their holders are not entitled to share in the surplus profits of the company unless they hold *participating* preference shares.

b) *Ordinary shares*. The precise rights of ordinary shareholders depend on a company's articles of association, but normally they are entitled to attend and vote at meetings and to receive a variable dividend according to, and from, the profits remaining after the preference shareholders have received their dividend. If the company is wound up they are entitled to share in the surplus assets after all debts have been discharged and shareholders repaid. Ordinary shares are the risk-bearing shares because they have the greatest potential for either profit or loss.

Capital gearing

As you have seen there are different types of both shares and loans. The make-up of the company's financial resources we refer to as its *capital structure*. The proportion of loan capital to share capital in a company is referred to as the *capital gearing* of the company. If there is a small proportion of share capital to loan capital, the capital is said to be *high geared* because a small number of ordinary shares (giving voting rights) controls a large amount of capital. Conversely, if the company's capital is mainly shares, with only a small proportion of loan capital, it is said to be *low geared*. Generally speaking it is to the company's advantage to have at least some of its capital as loan capital since this gives two benefits.

a) *Reduced tax burden*. Since debt interest can **281**

be claimed against corporation tax this will reduce the amount of tax the company has to pay.

b) *Increased growth*. Because the company retains more of its earnings it will require a smaller cash sum to pay the *rate* of dividend on each share. This could result in more money being available for ploughing back into the company or it could be used to pay a higher dividend on each share. In the case of a successful gearing operation this can lead to spectacular results. The National Freight Corporation (NFC) which was privatised in 1981 was financed by a very high geared operation. As a result of the success of the NFC its shareholders saw a 35-fold increase in the value of their shares in seven years.

However it may be dangerous for a firm to have too large a proportion of loan stock if business is poor, since the interest on it *must* be paid, whereas with shares the firm can always reduce the dividend.

Calculating the return

To the economist the return on capital is interest, which is the return for lending money where *no risk* is involved. However, many investments involve risk and therefore the factor earnings will be a composite of both interest and profits. The person who buys shares is therefore both a capitalist and an entrepreneur.

Interest and dividends

Debentures have a fixed rate of interest, i.e. in return for a loan of £100 the debenture-holder will receive a guaranteed rate of interest. Some shares, e.g. preference shares, may have a stated income on them, but by and large their income will depend upon the *dividend* declared by the company. When the company has paid all its costs, including taxes, and after it has retained some profits to finance growth, it distributes the rest of its earnings as a dividend on the par (or face) value of each share. If a share is bought

on the Stock Exchange it will almost certainly be at a price other than its par value, e.g. a £1 share may be bought for £2. This, however, will not affect its earning capacity. If, for example, the company has declared a 10 per cent (or 10p) dividend per share then it is 10p that the owner of the share will receive. Since the investor paid £2 for it, the effective return is not 10 per cent but 5 per cent. This principle also applies to the return on debentures.

To the owner of the share, however, the important thing will be the effective earning of the share. Shareholders may obtain benefit from shares in two ways: firstly, from the *dividends* declared by the company; secondly, they could gain benefit by selling the share for more than they paid for it. Since dividends vary from share to share and the price of a particular share may vary from day to day, various methods of expressing the share's earnings or potential earnings have been devised. This is so that the shares of one company may more easily be compared with the shares of a different company. The different ways of expressing this are considered below.

Yield

This gives a simple measure of the return to capital expressed as a percentage of the share's current market price. If, for example, a company declared that it would pay a dividend of 15 per cent on each £1 share in the company, but the current market price of each £1 share is £2.50, then the yield is not 15 per cent but 6 per cent. This can be worked out in the following manner:

$$\text{Yield} = \frac{\text{Par value} \times \text{Dividend}}{\text{Market price of share}}$$

In our example:

$$\text{Yield} = \frac{1 \cdot 00 \times 15}{2 \cdot 50} = 6\%$$

Price/earnings (P/E) ratio

The yield of a share may not be a good guide to its earning capacity. The P/E ratio is the relationship between the market price of the share and total earnings, i.e. all profit, not just the declared dividend. The P/E ratio can be expressed as:

$$P/E = \frac{\text{Market price of share}}{\text{Earnings}}$$

If the company has a share capital of £100 000 and its total profits or earnings are £50 000, then its earnings are 50 per cent or 0·50. If the market price of the shares is £2·50 then the P/E ratio will be:

$$P/E = \frac{2.50}{0.50} = 5$$

This is a ratio, not a percentage.

Dividend cover

Since 1973 the complexities of corporation tax have made the calculation of the P/E ratio somewhat problematic. A new measure of the earnings of shares has arisen and that is dividend cover. This relates the net after-tax profits of the company to the declared dividend. If, for example, the profits of the company were £50 000 after tax had been paid, and £20 000 were distributed in dividends, then the dividend cover would be 2·5.

There are thus several ways of looking at the earnings of a company. Anyone contemplating the purchase of shares in a company should take care to look at the financial position of the company in as many different ways as possible.

The Stock Exchange

The Stock Exchange is not involved with the issue of shares; it is only concerned with the sale and transfer of 'secondhand' shares. Thus when shares are bought on the Stock Exchange they do not bring money to the company concerned but to the shareholder who has sold them. The Stock Exchange is important to the new issue market, however, since the ease with which shares can be resold encourages people to invest as they know they can easily turn their shares back to cash. In addition, market makers

may be members of the Stock Exchange and may sell the new shares they have recently acquired to other brokers on the Exchange.

In Stock Exchange jargon, those who speculate on rising markets are termed *bulls*, those who speculate on a falling market are termed *bears*, and those who speculate on new issues are called *stags*.

The 27 October 1986 saw significant changes in the Stock Exchange. Collectively these changes were known as the 'Big Bang'. The Stock Exchange changes were part of wider developments affecting financial institutions generally. The changes encompassed both the regulation of the Stock Exchange and the introduction of new technology. As far as the operation of the Stock Exchange the most important changes were:

a) *Dual capacity dealing*. Before October 1986 there was strict division between *jobbers*, who had no contact with the public, and *brokers* who dealt with the the public and made deals with the jobbers. After 1986 a member of the Exchange could undertake both jobs. This raised the problem of a possible conflict of interest. For example, a member of the Exchange might be *making a market* in a company's shares, i.e. buying and selling the shares, producing research information on the company etc., while on the other hand, in their other capacity, be buying shares for customers who are members of the public. You could argue that such an Exchange member might not give unbiased advice to clients.

b) *Abolition of fixed commissions*. From 1912 onwards there was a fixed commission on all dealings. That is to say, whatever member of the Exchange a member of the public dealt with they would be charged the same percentage commission on all sales and purchases. This practice was abolished in October 1986. It was argued that this would lead to greater competition and lower commissions but on the other hand it was also argued that brokers might charge higher commissions to certain customers. This latter criticism was borne out when many **283** brokers began to impose minimum fees on deals for small customers.

c) *The ownership of firms.* Up to 1986 stock-broking firms had to owned by members of the Exchange. After this date it became possible for firms to be owned by outside businesses. This meant, in effect, that companies such as banks were able to take over stockbroking firms, thereby giving their customers direct access to the Exchange. As examples of this, Credit Suisse acquired Buckmaster & Moore, while Barclays acquired the jobbers Wedd Durlacher Mordaunt as well as the brokers de Zoete & Bevan.

Other changes came about as a result of the new technology. Instead of dealing face-to-face with each other firms were able to gain their information through electronic systems. *Topic* and *Talisman* were already in existence. October 1986 saw the introduction of *SEAQ* (the Stock Exchange Automated Quotation System). This is a composite screen network which shows the latest prices on a range of over 3 500 domestic and international securities. These changes were, in themselves, sufficient to bring about the death of the 'floor' in a matter of months. However, members were still required to deal with each other via telephones but the introduction of the *TAURUS* system at the end of the 1980s meant that deals could be done directly on the screen.

In addition to the Stock Exchange there is now the USM (the Unlisted Securities Market) which deals in the securities of companies too small to be quoted on the Exchange. Also established in 1986 was the *third tier* of dealings in even smaller companies.

Regulation and deregulation

The changes which have come about in the stock market were, in fact, introduced by the Stock Exchange itself. They were a result of the *Parkinson – Goodison* accord whereby the Stock Exchange agreed to reform itself rather than have reform imposed on it by the government. It was the Conservative government's (1979) intention to increase competition and to deregulate as many sectors of the economy as possible. However, the government also recognised the need to protect the interests of investors. It was with this in mind that the *Financial Services Act 1986* was passed. This established a regulatory framework, not only for the Stock Exchange but for all sectors of the financial services industry. The various bodies, such as FIMBRA, are made up chiefly of representatives of the various sectors of the industry. Thus the guiding principle is essentially one of self-regulation.

With the need to report to regulatory bodies and stricter rules on the sale of services many people in the industry thought that the new regime was one of greater regulation rather than less. At the end of the 1980s it remained to be seen whether or not the new system would prove satisfactory for both the industry and the consumer.

The crash in the market in October 1987 illustrated the dangers involved in stock market dealings. Commenting on the Stock Exchange, Keynes said: 'When the capital development of a country becomes a byproduct of the activities of a casino, the job is likely to be ill done.' Many people do indeed criticise the Stock Exchange for the speculation which goes on there, arguing that the changes in the price of shares often have little to do with the *real* economy. On the other hand, supporters of the Stock Exchange would claim that speculation *decreases* the fluctuations in the prices of shares. It is argued that if the price of a share is rising then investors will speculate on its falling, thus decreasing the magnitude of the rise. Conversely if a share's price is falling, investors will speculate on its rising.

Summary

1   Capital goods are those used in the production of further wealth. Financial capital is the paper claims upon the wealth of the country.
2   The marginal efficiency of capital (*MEC*) is the rate of return on the last unit of capital employed. The *MEC* relates the stock of capital to the rate of interest.
3   The rate of interest is the cost of borrowing capital or the reward recovered for lending it. The real rate of interest is obtained by subtracting the rate of inflation from the rate of interest.
4   There are a number of techniques for appraising investment projects. Economists tend to favour discounting techniques because these take account of opportunity cost. Two of these techniques are the net present value method and the internal rate of return method.
5   Companies raise finance by selling shares and by taking loans. The relationship between share capital and loan capital is known as capital gearing.
6   There are a number of methods of assessing the return on a share. These include the yield, the P/E ratio and the dividend cover.
7   The Stock Exchange is not directly involved in the raising of new capital but is important to it because it provides a way of selling shares once they have been bought.

Questions

1   What is the capitalised value of a bond with a permanent income of £500 per year if the interest rate is 15 per cent?
2   A project has an initial capital cost of £100 000 and gives an income of £30 000 over a five year period, whilst the rate of interest is 15 per cent.
   a) What is the present net value of the project?
   b) Calculate the internal rate of return for the project.
3   Explain the difference between capital deepening and capital widening.
4   State the advantages to a company of having its capital structure high-geared.
5   Umoco plc has a nominal share capital of £500 000. This is made up of £350 000 £1 preference shares which have a fixed maximum dividend of 8 per cent. There are also 150 000 £1 ordinary shares. Umoco plc makes a profit of £125 000 all of which is distributed to shareholders.
   a) What is the dividend per share in pence which each ordinary share would receive?
   b) If the current market price of Umoco's ordinary shares is £3·00, what is the yield on each ordinary share?
6   Suppose that a country's gross capital formation during 1987 is $30·2 billion but capital consumption amounts to 42 per cent of this. In 1988 the gross capital formation is only 92 per cent of the 1987 figure whilst capital consumption rises to 46 per cent. What is the net output of capital in 1988 in dollars?
7   Assess the importance of the Stock Exchange in the raising of finance for companies.

285

Data response Savings, investment and growth

Study the figures in table 23.3. The figures in the last column are for *resource balance*. This is the difference between exports and imports expressed as a percentage of GDP.

Table 23.3 Investment savings and growth

Country	GDP/capital 1985 ($)	Gross domestic investment as % of GDP 1965	Gross domestic investment as % of GDP 1985	Gross domestic saving as % of GDP 1965	Gross domestic saving as % of GDP 1985	Average annual growth rate GDP/capita 1965–85 (%)	Average annual growth of GDP 1980–85	Resource balance 1965	Resource balance 1985
Mozambique	160	n/a	7	n/a	−3	n/a	−9.6	n/a	−10
India	270	18	25	14	21	1·7	5·2	−2	−3
Ghana	380	18	9	8	7	−2·2	−0·7	−10	−2
Nigeria	800	19	10	17	14	2·2	−3·4	−2	4
Uruguay	1 650	11	8	18	12	1·4	−3·9	7	4
South Korea	2 150	15	30	7	31	6·6	7·9	−8	1
Greece	3 550	26	21	15	9	3·6	1·0	−11	−12
UK	8 460	20	17	19	18	1·6	2·0	−1	1
West Germany	10 940	28	20	29	24	2·7	1·3	0·4	4
Japan	11 300	32	28	33	32	4·7	3·8	1	4
Sweden	11 890	27	19	26	21	1·8	2·0	−1	2
USA	16 690	20	19	21	16	1·7	2·5	1	−3
United Arab Emirates	19 270	n/a	31	n/a	59	n/a	−2·8	n/a	28

n/a = not available.
Source: IBRD

Using these figures and any other information which you may have attempt to answer the following questions:

1 What connection does there appear to be between the rate of investment and the rate of growth?

2 You will note that for several of the countries in the Table the rate of domestic savings is less than the rate of domestic investment. How is this possible?

3 What are the possible consequences of the rate of savings being higher than the rate of investment?

4 For several countries in the Table growth performance was worse in the last five years shown than over the period as a whole. Comment as fully as possible on the reasons for this.

24

Enterprise and profit

Entrepreneurial profit ... is the expression of the value of what the entrepreneur contributes to production in exactly the same sense that wages are the value expression of what the worker 'produces'. It is not a profit of exploitation any more than are wages.

Joseph Schumpeter

Enterprise

The importance of enterprise

Labour, capital and natural resources do not naturally form themselves into a wealth-making combination. Someone must make the decisions – not only *what* to produce but also *how* and *when* to produce. The people who undertake this task are providing a very special service because they must, in so doing, take a *risk*. In this chapter we discuss the nature of this risk and the consequence of taking it both successfully and unsuccessfully. Economists term this decision-taking and organisational factor *enterprise* and the person who supplies it is the *entrepreneur*.

Some economists have doubted the existence of this separate factor of production – enterprise – and argued that it is just a special form of labour. However if we do away with the idea we will still have to explain how economic decisions get taken. Having said this, we will find that, as with other factors such as land, it is difficult to identify pure enterprise because it is usually mixed up with other factors. For example, the person who invests in a company by buying shares will be acting as both entrepreneur and capitalist and the reward received will be a mixture of profit and interest.

The role of the entrepreneur

The traditional view of the entrepreneur was as owner-manager of a company. Today the capitalist might be a group of people (shareholders) who have lent money to the business but may have never visited it; alternatively the capital could just have easily come from the banks, from the government or from entrepreneurs themselves. The entrepreneur's function, however, is to *organise* the business. In order to produce goods and services it is necessary for someone to take a risk by producing in *anticipation of demand*, i.e. since it takes time to produce goods the entrepreneur must predict what the demand is going to be when the goods are produced. Entrepreneurs differ from the other people involved in the business in that the amount of money they make is *uncertain*. The workers, the capitalists and the landlord will all have to be paid an agreed *contractual amount* if the business is not to go into liquidation. There is no way in which one can contract to make a profit, and if the entrepreneur is unlucky or unwise he or she will be left with not a profit but a loss.

In organising production entrepreneurs carry out three main functions.

a) They buy or hire the resources, labour, raw materials, etc., which the business requires.

b) They combine the resources in such a way that goods are produced at the lowest cost.

c) They sell the products of the business in the most advantageous way possible.

We assume that the entrepreneurs will always try to maximise the profits of the business and also that they will act in a rational and sensible manner. These assumptions were discussed more fully in Section II of the book.

The role of profit

Since goods must be produced in anticipation of demand, it is essential that someone takes the risk of doing this. In a mixed economy many production decisions are taken by the government, but there are still many more taken by private persons. Entrepreneurs do not act from a sense of public duty but out of a desire to make profit. Adam Smith argued that the 'invisible hand' of self-interest guided the economy to the best possible use of its resources. This was because, to produce profitably, the business would not only have to produce the goods which people wanted but also the business would have to produce them at minimum cost in order to compete with its rivals. Profit acts not only as an incentive to encourage businesses to produce but it also acts as an indicator. If, for example, profits are high in one particular line of business, this indicates that people want more of that good and encourages more firms to produce it. Also if one firm in an industry is making more profit than another this could indicate that its methods are more efficient, and the other firms will therefore have to emulate this greater efficiency or go out of business.

Schumpeter saw profit and economic development inextricably bound up with each other: 'Without development there is no profit, without profit no development. For the capitalist system it must be added that without profit there would be no accumulation of wealth.'

Thus profit acts as an *incentive* to firms to encourage them to take risks, as a *measure of efficiency* and as a *spur* to the introduction of new products and processes.

Joseph Alois Schumpeter (1883–1950)

We shall have cause to mention Joseph Schumpeter several times in this chapter. Schumpeter was an Austrian who fled to the USA in 1939, where he made his name as professor of economics at Harvard University. He is perhaps best known for his writing on monopolies. His most famous book, *Capitalism, Socialism and Democracy*, was published in 1942, and looked forward to the end of economic growth and capitalism. Despite being one of the most original thinkers of the 20th century he has never attracted the following of other famous economists such as Keynes, with whom he shared his year of birth.

The entrepreneurial function

In a small firm it is easy to identify the entrepreneur; this may not be so in a large firm. While the board of directors may be the most obvious risk-taker, many of the senior and middle management may have to take decisions which in a small firm would be considered the job of the entrepreneur. In a large firm, therefore, the *entrepreneurial function* may be spread amongst many people and be hard to identify. It may also be the case that when a large company is run entirely by managers and not by profit earners they may be less interested in maximising profits and more interested in such things as growth of the company and security. They may therefore act more as risk-avoiders than risk-takers.

When a company is in a monopoly position the profits it earns may owe more to its dominance in the market than to any risk taken.

Schumpeter foresaw a day when economic progress may have proceeded so far that the entrepreneurial functions become redundant. What would be the result of this?

A more or less stationary state would ensue. Capitalism being essentially an evolutionary process, would become atrophic. There would be nothing left for entrepreneurs to do. They would find themselves in much the same situation as generals would in a society perfectly sure of permanent peace. Profit, and along with profits the rate of interest, would converge toward zero. The bourgeois strata that live on profits and interest would tend to disappear. The management of industry and trade would become a matter of current consumption, and the personnel would unavoidably acquire the characteristics of a bureacracy. Socialism of a very sober type would automatically come into being. Human energy would turn away from business. Other than economic pursuits would attract the brains and provide the adventure.

It should perhaps be pointed out that Keynes had a similar view of the future free from most economic wants when he wrote of the 'Economic possibilities for our grandchildren' in his *Essays on Persuasion*.

Achieving the best factor mix

It is the job of the entrepreneur to achieve the optimum combination of factors of production, i.e. to achieve the desired output for the least cost in relation to the demand for the commodity. We examined the principles underlying this in Chapter 20 (*see* pages 249–252). This is essentially an economic problem rather than a technological one. One can produce a technically superb product such as a Rolls Royce car and still go bankrupt. It is an economic problem because the supply, and hence the prices, of resources differ greatly from place to place. An English farmer who tried to grow wheat in a manner which is successful in Canada would rapidly come to grief, since in Canada land is plentiful and cheap whereas farming in the UK depends upon getting as much as possible out of a limited area. This simple but fundamental point is commonly misunderstood. Many projects in less developed countries have come to grief because they have copied the techniques of advanced countries. If, for example, a heavily capitalised synthetic fibre plant were to be built in India this would throw many people in the textile industry out of work. If labour is cheap and plentiful it is better to use a process which exploits that. Many people laugh at pictures of the Chinese building reservoirs by moving earth in wicker baskets, but if labour is cheap and plentiful and capital equipment expensive and imported, then wicker baskets are the better way. This will give work and wages to the workers while an imported earth-moving plant would make them unemployed.

There is no blueprint for the running of a firm because each commercial situation is unique. Two farms side by side will have to be run differently, just as two chemist shops in the same high street will have to be run differently. Therefore in every situation the entrepreneur has to work out that combination of resources which is economically correct. If they do it successfully they will be rewarded with profit – unsuccessfully and they will make a loss. Since they are responsible for production decisions you can see that entrepreneurs are one of the most vital cogs in the economic system.

Different views of profit

The accountant's and the economist's views contrasted

To the accountant profit is essentially a residual figure, i.e. the money which is left over after all the expenses have been paid. Even so, one might talk of profits before tax or after tax, distributed or undistributed. In the last chapter, for example, we saw that there is a difference between profit and dividends. To understand these figures fully requires a working knowledge of accounts and is beyond the scope of this book. We may say, however, that there are many judgmental elements at work in accounts. Accountancy is often regarded as an exact study but in arriving at a figure for profit the accountant will have to exercise judgment in *estimating* many figures in the accounts; for example, estimates will have to be made in arriving at figures for the value of stock, debts and assets q.v. the writing-off of Third World debts by many banks in 1987. These calculations are made all the more difficult today when the accountant must also estimate the effects of inflation. It is therefore possible for a company to have a healthy-looking balance sheet but be near to insolvency, or to appear to be making virtually no profit at all but be very sound.

It is possible that a firm owns some of the resources it uses; for example, it may have the freehold on its premises. In these circumstances it is essential to its effective running that these are costed and accounted for as if they were rented. This point is developed below.

It is possible for a business to make an accounting profit but an economic loss. This is perhaps best explained by taking a simple example. Imagine the case of a self employed solicitor who works in premises he or she owns. At the end of the year he or she finds they have made £20 000 above the running costs of the practice and therefore regard this as profit. The economist, however, will always enquire about the *opportunity cost*, i.e. what else could have been done with their resources of capital, labour, etc. We may find on examination that the solicitor could have rented the building out for £4000 per annum, that the capital involved would have earned £2000 interest if invested elsewhere and that he or she could have earned £16 000 working as a solicitor for the local council. Under these circumstances he or she could be £2000 per annum better off as a result of closing down their practice and placing their resources elsewhere.

As we saw in the previous section of the book, economists also have a view of the *normal profit* for a firm. You may recall that normal profit is that amount of profit which is just sufficient to keep a firm in an industry, i.e. even though a firm may be making a profit in accounting terms, if this is very small the entrepreneur will not consider it worthwhile and will close down. The amount of profit which is considered normal will vary from industry to industry and area to area. Since this profit is necessary to keep the firm in business, economists regard this as a legitimate cost of the business. Any profit in excess of normal profit is *abnormal* or *super-normal profit*.

The sources of profit in a firm is an area where there are many different views. We will now go on to consider some of these.

Profits and the returns to other factors

As we saw above in our example of the solicitor, much of what is commonly called profit is in fact the *implicit cost* of other factors of production. Thus, for example, the owners of a corner shop might say they have made £15 000 profit but in fact £5000 is payment for their own labour, £2000 is rent for the shop which they own, and so on. This principle can apply to any size of organisation (*see also* page 182).

The return to innovation

Schumpeter's view was that profit is the reward for bringing new products or processes to the market. This has a special name – *innovation*. Innovation is the application of invention to industry. It is often the innovators who are remembered rather than the inventors, e.g. James Watt, George Stephenson and Guglielmo Marconi were all people who made a commercial success of already existing inventions. If someone is *enterprising* enough to bring in a new product or process and it is successful then they will for a time make a large profit. This will disappear after a while when competitors copy the process.

Recognising the importance of innovation the state rewards the entrepreneur with a limited legal monopoly of it in the form of a patent. There are of course often many more unsuccessful inventors and innovators than successful ones.

Risks, uncertainty and profit

Frank H. Knight in his book *Risk, Uncertainty and Profit*, published in 1921, said that profit is the reward for a risk successfully taken. Profits therefore arise because the future is uncertain. This would certainly include the innovator's profit because this can be viewed as the reward for the risk of bringing in a new product.

To a certain extent all the factors of production

may earn a profit from uncertainty. For example, when a young person decides to train as a lawyer he or she is taking a risk that society will later wish to buy their services. The person who trains as an engineer runs the risk that they might be replaced by an automated machine. We saw in the previous chapter how the payment made to a debenture in a risky business contains an element of profit. In all these cases if the risk is successfully taken then the person receives a reward, if unsuccessful a loss. In other words profit can be both positive and negative.

We might distinguish between:

a) a speculative risk, where a broker or similar person buys shares, bonds or commodities in expectation of a favourable change in their price;

b) an economic risk, where an entrepreneur anticipates the demand for goods and services and supplies the product to the market.

Businesses do not, of course, go around looking for 'risky' products. In fact they tend to try and avoid risk as much as possible. Indeed, many risks may be avoided by *insurance*, but so long as uncertainty remains in the world, someone, be it the entrepreneur or the state, will have to assume the risk of supplying goods to the market.

Monopoly profits

Where a company has reached a dominant position in the market, it may reap a rich reward without taking very much risk. However it is not only entrepreneurs who might benefit from monopoly power. A trade union might use its monopoly power in a wage market to obtain a greater reward for its members. Similarly, any factor which is earning an *economic rent* could be regarded as making a monopoly profit (*see* page 268).

We should distinguish, however, between the situation where a monopolist deliberately *contrives a scarcity* to drive up the price of the product and a situation where the scarcity occurs naturally.

Economists almost universally condemn monopoly profits because they cause a distortion in the allocation of resources. Schumpeter however disagreed with this view. He maintained that monopolies, with their economies of scale and ability to innovate, are the handmaids of economic growth.

The government and profits

The problem

Profits present special problems of control to the government. Although profits are a relatively small share of GDP (17 per cent in the UK in 1986), the government may have particular reasons for wishing to control them.

a) *Equity.* In times when the government may be urging restraint upon other factor incomes such as wages, it may find it expedient also to control profits.

b) *Monopoly profits.* Since monopoly profits are usually regarded as undesirable, the government may feel bound to do something about these.

It is arguable that control of profits is more desirable from the point of view of social justice than on straight economic grounds. It has been calculated that monopoly profits may account for as little as 2 per cent of GDP, so that redistribution of this would do little for other factor incomes. If we went along with Schumpeter's view, the taxing of monopoly profits may be positively harmful because it may restrict the innovative potential of monopolies on whom, he argues, rests the burden of technological change. It should be stated that this view is highly contentious. The Conservative government of 1983, which was highly sympathetic to capitalists, nonetheless found it necessary to bring in special measures to control the monopoly profits of the pharmaceutical companies.

The control of profits

If a government decides to restrict profits there are two main ways by which it might do this. **291**

a) Price controls. By forcibly holding down the price which a firm wishes to charge, the government can reduce or eliminate profit. There are two circumstances in which this might be the appropriate policy. Firstly, the government might wish to do this as part of an incomes policy. To enlist the cooperation of trade unions in any incomes policy it will be necessary to have price restraint. Secondly, irrespective of prevailing economic conditions, price control is one of the best ways of dealing with monopoly profit. Taxing monopoly profits does not alleviate the misallocation of resources involved in prices and output policy of the monopolist (*see* page 218).

b) Taxation. The government has a number of fiscal weapons which it uses, depending upon how the profits arise and how they are paid. The earnings of a company are taxed by *corporation tax.* However the firm will usually incur less tax if it ploughs profits back into the business rather than distributing it. On distribution the profit may also become subject to *personal income tax.* Profits which are made from the sale of shares, commodities, property, etc., are taxed by *capital gains tax.* The rate of tax may be much higher if it is a short-term capital gain rather than a long-term gain.

If we regard taxation as a method of dealing with abnormal profit we face the problem of identifying the amount of normal and abnormal profit in the profits of any particular company. This is difficult because, as we have seen, the rates of normal profit may differ significantly from one industry to another.

In the case mentioned above where the government took measures to deal with the monopoly profits in the pharmaceutical industry, it did two things simultaneously. Firstly, it restricted the price charged for certain drugs. This it was able to do both as government and as *monopsonic* buyer. Secondly it imposed a system of generic prescribing on doctors. This latter point is worthy of note since it points to the significance of *ignorance* as a source of monopoly profit and hence of inefficiency and misallocation of resources. This arose because doctors were continuing to prescribe drugs by their trade names, e.g. Valium when the patents had long run-out and a perfect substitute existed at a third of the price. In their defence the pharmaceutical companies used Schumpeter's argument that high profits were necessary to finance research and development.

The consequences of profit control

The control and taxation of profit presents problems to any government. Although price controls may be appropriate to a monopoly, and may be politically expedient, elsewhere they run the risk of forcing the firm into a loss and so driving it out of business. Since profits are the return to enterprise, high profits could be regarded as the reward to a very successful business. By removing this profit the government will take away the incentive for firms to seek new opportunities and to take new risks. Under these circumstances the removal of profits could have a disastrous effect upon the economy. Alternatively, the firm may find it possible to pass taxes on to consumers by way of higher prices, in which case the object of the government will have been defeated. If the business is an exporter, high taxation may have the effect of making its products uncompetitive abroad.

Another problem of company taxation is that it encourages what Keynes termed 'the double-bluff of capitalism'. This is where companies are not taxed on the profits which they plough back because capitalisation will be to the advantage of the economy. The ploughing back of profits will, however, lay the foundation for even larger profits in the future. Undistributed profits also improve the *dividend cover*, thus forcing up the price of shares and making capital gains for their owners.

Conclusion

Ricardo believed that profits would decline whilst wages are fixed at a subsistence level.

The quote from him which begins Chapter 21 continues: 'The natural price of labour is that price which is necessary to enable the labourers, one with another, to subsist and perpetuate their race, without either increase or diminution' Thus wages are fixed whilst increased demand for land, because of population growth, forces up rents, therefore contracting profits. Marx also believed that profits must eventually decline, squeezed in the dialectic of materialism. We have also seen in this chapter that Schumpeter believed profit would disappear in the long-run and the economy would stagnate.

None of these gloomy prophecies seem to have come true as yet. However, when we regard the present state of our economy, we can see that there has probably never been a greater need to resolve the question of whether or not to expect continuous increases in employment, growth and profits.

Summary

1   Enterprise is the vital decision-making factor in the production process, deciding what, how and when to produce and when to take a risk by producing in anticipation of demand.
2   Profits fulfil a vital allocative function in the economy, redistributing resources from one use to another, rewarding efficiency and punishing inefficiency.
3   As with the other factors of production, it is very difficult to isolate pure enterprise.
4   The job of the entrepreneur involves achieving the best mix of the factors of production, i.e. the one which gives the desired output for the lowest cost.
5   The accountant's and the economist's view of profit differ. The economist has a view of normal profit which is counted as a cost of the business. This is not so in accountancy.
6   Profits may be the return to enterprise and innovation, to risk or to monopoly.
7   The control of profits presents particular difficulties for the government. On the grounds of equity, profit must be controlled but controlling profit may stifle enterprise.

Questions

1   What is meant by 'implicit' factor earnings? Compare this with other concepts of profits.
2   Discuss the arguments for and against taxing 'excess' profits.
3   In 1986 UK farmers earned a gross income of £5·5 billion. Part of this went to cover explicit costs of £4·5 billion, leaving farmers with net income of £1·5 billion. Would that net income be best thought of as wages, rent, interest or profit? Give reasons for your answer.
4   A teacher spent several months of her spare time writing a book for which she subsequently received £1000 in royalties. She argues that, since her only costs were paper and typewriter ribbon, nearly all the £1000 could be regarded as profit. Do you agree? Give reasons for your answer.
5   Explain the difference between invention and innovation. What innovations or inventions were the following responsible for:

a) Charles Babbage

b) Sir Henry Bessemer

c) Christopher Cockerell.

6 The role of the entrepreneur and of risk-taking is fundamental to a capitalist society. However if we consider a communist state there appear to be no entrepreneurs. Is it therefore true to say that there are no economic risks in a communist state? If there are risks, who takes them and who benefits (or loses) from them?

7 Assess the importance of profit as an allocative mechanism in the capitalist system.

Data response   Why the age of the inventor is over ━━━━━━━━━━━━━━

Read the following article which was printed in the *Guardian* newspaper 4 March 1988.

Why the age of the inventor is over

Peter Large
Technology Editor

THE INVENTOR is dead. Long live the pure scientist. That, according to a first-division futurologist, is one of the already established strands of post-industrial change.

Professor Daniel Bell, of Harvard, listed the evidence in a lecture at Salford University yesterday.

All the major industries of the industrial age — steel, electricity, the phone, even aviation — were created by 'talented tinkerers', who were clever with equipment but knew little, or cared less, about the science behind their ideas.

Alexander Graham Bell, one of the inventors of the phone, was a speech teacher who wanted to transmit amplified voice by wire to help the deaf.

Thomas Edison, who invented the long-lasting filament for the light bulb, the phonograph, and the motion picture, was a mathematical illiterate.

Marconi invented radio communication while knowing little about scientific work on radio waves.

And Bessemer, whose inventions led to stronger steel, knew equally little of what had been discovered about the properties of metal.

But the developments that underpin the post-industrial economy stem from science.

Einstein's work was the starting point for opto-electronics; Bohr's model of the hydrogen atom, constructed in 1912, was the key to today's solid-state physics and therefore to the microchip; Alan Turing's mathematical work in the 30s created computer science.

On the basis of that evidence, Bell gets dogmatic. Theory now precedes artifice, he says. The inventor 'disappears from the horizon'.

There will always be innovation and new products, but fundamental innovation in theoretical knowledge — not just in physics but in biology or cognitive psychology — becomes 'the new principle of innovation in society'.

So much for the UK Government's reduction in investment in pure science. On other fronts, too, Bell's conclusions are a refutation of most of the industrial-age thinking of Thatcherism. What he says about today's need for deeper education investment, about obsolete economics, about the logic of devolving more government power to local units, is not merely orthodox post-industrial thinking; it's what many nations are actually doing.

Bell's aphorism here is: 'The national state has become too small for the big problems of life,' and too big for the small problems.' Today's politics, he says, are increasingly ineffective in dealing with the tidal waves of the international economy. 'Coordination through economic summitry is only a charade.'

Equally, when political decisions are concentrated in a bureaucratic centre, the nation state is too big 'for the diversity and initiative of the varied local and regional units under its control'.

Post-industrial society, Bell says, is not a projection of existing trends. It is a new principle of social organisation, just as the industrial age replaced an agrarian way of life.

The change to activities based on information-processing and automation of production is producing a social way of life that becomes a 'game between people'. The old service jobs of the industrial age were auxiliary to industry — transport, real estate, utilities. The new ones are 'human' services — health, social services, professional help, analysis, design, programming.

Classical economics saw services as inherently unproductive. But education and health services contribute to the increased skills and strengths of a population.

Answer the following questions:

1   What reasons does the Professor Bell give for saying that the inventor now 'disappears from the horizon'?

2   What is meant by the term the 'post-industrial society'?

3   What is the role of invention and innovation in the creation of profit?

4   If Professor Bell's arguments are correct on the nature of research and its impact on post-industrial society, what are the implications for government policy towards profits, companies and the economy?

2

The microeconomic system

IV The market assessed: welfare economics

25

An introduction to welfare economics

The key insight of Adam Smith's Wealth of Nations *is misleadingly simple: if an exchange between two parties is voluntary, it will not take place unless both believe they will benefit from it. Most economic fallacies derive from the neglect of this simple insight, from the tendency to assume that there is a fixed pie, that one party can gain only at the expense of another.*

Milton Friedman

Introduction: what is welfare economics about?

It is becoming increasingly accepted that economists are inevitably led to examine the questions of what ought to be done by the very nature of the problems they study. Economics is concerned with the problems of choice in the face of scarcity; it is thus natural to ask the question 'What would be the best use of existing resources?' (Making the best use of existing resources is of course what is meant by 'economising'!)

The notion of 'best' can only be defined subjectively of course. I might take it to mean that I have everything and you have nothing; you of course might define it differently. However it would seem absurd for the economist to reply 'I can offer no suggestions as to what might be considered the best allocation of resources; it's not my job to consider such questions.' It seems sensible to many that persons trained in the techniques of making choices should also consider what might be meant by the best use of resources.

It is important, however, that the economist makes clear exactly what value judgments have been made and how economic decisions would be altered if different value judgments were made. In this way the economist can clarify the thinking of the final decision-maker without claiming a monopoly knowledge of what is morally right or wrong.

Welfare economists study both positive and normative questions. The notion of 'best' in economics involves considerations of both efficiency and equity.

The Pareto criterion

Production efficiency

To the welfare economist the term efficiency has a precise meaning, which was first formulated by Vilfredo Pareto (1848–1923).

'Pareto optimality' requires that it must not be possible to change the existing allocation of resources in such a way that someone is made better off and no one is worse off.

This criterion is intended to guard against wasting opportunities, to squeeze more utility for some people out of existing resources at no expense in terms of lost utility to others. We can illustrate this efficiency aspect of Pareto optimality by referring back to the concept of an economy's *production function*.

In Fig. 25.1 we assume that, because of a misallocation of resources, e.g. land best suited to growing wheat is being used for barley production and vice versa, the economy is producing at point A in the diagram. Further assume that consumers always desire more of both wheat and barley, i.e. 'goods are good'. Now what can be said about point A in terms of the Pareto criterion? Clearly point A is not Pareto optimal, for, by changing the allocation of resources, it would be possible to have:

a) more wheat and no less barley;
b) more of both wheat and barley;
c) more barley and no less wheat.

These three possibilities are shown in Fig. 25.1. A move to anywhere in the shaded area

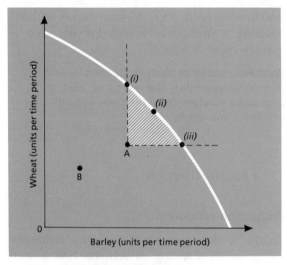

would improve optimality. If, then, it is possible to have either more of one good and no less of any other, or more of all goods, then it follows that it must be possible to distribute this extra output in such a way that all consumers are made better off or some consumers are made better off without other consumers being made worse off. If this is done it is said that a *'Pareto improvement'* has been made. The student should now be able to explain why a movement from B to A in the diagram also represents a Pareto improvement.

Product-mix efficiency

It is tempting for the student to think that points on the production boundary represent Pareto optimal resource allocations. This is not necessarily the case. Although such points do indicate that production is efficient, this does not ensure that the *product mix* is Pareto efficient. Product-mix efficiency requires that it would not be possible to change the existing combination of outputs in such a way that someone is made better off and no one is worse off (or, of course, everybody made better off). In fact at most points on the production boundary this possibility will arise. Take for example the point in our wheat/barley example where the production possibility boundary crosses the horizontal axis, i.e. where the economy is producing nothing but barley. It seems most unlikely that consumers as a whole would not be prepared to sacrifice any of this barley in order to obtain wheat. If consumers are prepared to make this sacrifice then overall welfare, in the Pareto sense, could be increased by moving along the production boundary, sacrificing barley output in order to increase the output of wheat. The potential for such a Pareto improvement will in fact exist whenever consumers as a whole are prepared to accept, in return for the sacrifice of one unit of one good, an amount of another good which is less than that amount which the economy can in fact provide for that sacrifice.

For example, suppose that consumers as a

300   **Fig. 25.1**   *The Pareto criterion*

group are prepared to sacrifice one unit of barley in order to obtain three units of wheat, but that the economy's production possibility boundary is such that decreasing the output of barley by one unit would allow the output of wheat to increase by four units. It would thus be possible to use three of the four extra units of wheat to compensate consumers for their loss of barley and use the remaining unit of wheat to raise overall welfare, i.e. to bring about a Pareto improvement. Only when changes in the product mix can just compensate consumers, and no more, is it no longer worthwhile making further changes to the output mix. This could also be expressed by saying that it is no longer worthwhile moving further along the production possibility frontier. We will then have reached the Pareto efficient product-mix.

Consumption efficiency

We must now ensure that the Pareto criterion for consumption efficiency is satisfied before we can identify this point on the production boundary as representing a Pareto optimal allocation of resources. As might be expected, efficient consumption requires that it should not be possible to redistribute the consumption of a given product-mix in such a way that someone is made better off and no one worse off. Take, for example, the situation where one consumer has all the wheat that has been produced and another has all the barley that has been produced. It seems most unlikely that the utility of both consumers could not be increased by trading with each other, i.e. the first consumer trades some wheat for barley and the second consumer trades some barley for wheat. In fact the potential for a Pareto improvement will exist whenever the rate at which one consumer is prepared to exchange one good for another differs from the rate at which another consumer is prepared to exchange the two goods (*see also* Chapter 37 on comparative costs). For example, suppose consumer A is prepared to accept one unit of wheat in return for the sacrifice of two units of

barley (obviously to consumer A one unit of wheat has a value, in terms of utility, equal to that of two units of barley) and that consumer B is prepared to exchange two units of wheat for one unit of barley. We can summerise this information as follows:

	Willing to trade	*For*
Consumer A	1 unit of wheat	2 units of barley
Consumer B	2 units of wheat	1 unit of barley

By examining this table we can see that consumer A has a relative preference for wheat and, hence, consumer B has a relative preference for barley. Not surprisingly then we can demonstrate that each consumer can gain, in terms of utility, by trading with the other. Suppose consumer A exchanges one unit of barley for one unit of wheat; this means, of course, that consumer B has exchanged one unit of wheat for one unit of barley. We can summarise this information as follows:

	Wheat	*Barley*
Consumer A	+ 1 unit	− 1 unit
Consumer B	− 1 unit	+ 1 unit

Now we can see that although consumer A would have been prepared to sacrifice up to two units of barley for one unit of wheat (as this would leave the level of utility unchanged), in fact only one unit of barley had to be sacrificed. Similarly, consumer B would have been prepared to sacrifice up to two units of wheat for the one unit of barley, but has only to give up one unit of wheat. As each consumer has had to sacrifice less than the amount that would have left their level of utility unchanged, it follows that each consumer has gained, i.e. their utility increased, through the trade.

As we might expect, consumption can only be Pareto efficient if the rates at which consumers are *just* prepared to sacrifice one good for another are the same. For example, if consumer A values an extra unit of wheat equally to a unit of barley, i.e. they both yield an equal amount of utility to consumer A, and consumer B also values an extra unit of barley equally to a unit of wheat, then trade between the consumers **301** would be pointless. This is because an exchange of one unit of wheat for one unit of barley would leave the level of utility for each consumer unchanged.

Efficiency and the free market

The price mechanism and Pareto optimality

We now turn to the important question of whether the allocation of resources as determined by a free market is Pareto efficient. The answer is no, unless highly unrealistic assumptions are made. Nevertheless, economic theory has demonstrated that under these assumptions (the first of which is that perfect competition exists in all markets!) the price mechanism would act to automatically bring about a Pareto efficient allocation of resources, i.e.:

Under certain conditions, which are not met in the real world, a price mechanism will automatically bring about efficient production and consumption and an efficient product-mix – in short a Pareto optimal allocation of resources.

The student should now be justified in asking: 'If Pareto optimality does not exist in the real world, nor will it ever be likely to exist, what is the point of studying it?' The answer is quite simply that unless we are aware of the conditions necessary for Pareto efficiency we will not be able to identify deviations from these conditions. Hence this unrealistic model can, at least, provide an analytical point of departure for discussing reality.

The conditions for Pareto optimality

The conditions under which a free market economy, functioning via the price mechanism, would produce a Pareto optimal allocation of recources, are summarised in the *first optimality theorem* of modern welfare economics:

If, in all markets, there is perfect competition, no externalities and no market failure connected with uncertainty, then the resulting allocation of resources will be Pareto optimal.

(*See* Chapter 26 for discussion of externalities such as pollution.)

Needless to say, the situation described by this theorem is not even an approximate description of reality. Nevertheless it represents a benchmark to which real-world situations can be compared.

A formal proof of the first optimality theorem is beyond the scope of this book, but we have learned enough economics to grasp in an intuitive way why the conditions stated in it will produce Pareto efficiency. Turning first to the question of *efficient production*, we will accept that the assumption of perfect competition in all markets is sufficient to ensure this result. We can rationalise this as follows: the model of perfect competition assumes that all firms are profit maximisers, that all producers have perfect knowledge of production techniques and factor prices, and that all factors of production are perfectly mobile; therefore firms will choose the least-cost methods of production. In short, firms will hire those factors which are relatively most productive and use the smallest possible quantity of these factors to produce any given output, thereby ensuring that, for any given level of resources, overall output is maximised, i.e. the economy is operating on its production possibility frontier.

Consumption and market prices

It can also be shown that the conditions listed in the first optimality theorem are sufficient to bring about *efficient consumption*. It should be apparent from our earlier discussions of perfect competition that in an economy in which all markets are perfect all consumers will face a common set of product prices. This will mean that all consumers will be maximising utility, subject to the same set of price ratios. These price ratios set the rate at which, in effect, one product can be traded for another in the market, i.e. the rate at which one product must be forgone in order to purchase another. For our purpose it is useful to think of these price ratios as representing, to a consumer, the rate at which another consumer is prepared to trade one good for another. Now we know, from our previous discussion of the conditions necessary for efficient consumption, that a consumer can gain through trading with another consumer if the rate at which they are just prepared to sacrifice one good for another differs from the rate at which the other consumer is prepared to exchange one good for another.

Consumers will adjust their consumption patterns until the rate at which they are just prepared to exchange one good for another is equal to the rate, set by market prices, at which they are forced to forgo one good in order to purchase another.

As this latter rate is set by market prices which are common to all consumers, this ensures that, in equilibrium, the rates at which all consumers are just prepared to sacrifice one good for another are the same. This is the condition which is necessary for efficient consumption. (*See also* concept of equi-marginal utilities, page 108.)

Market equilibrium

Indifference curve analysis can also be used to demonstrate the result that perfect competition can bring about efficient consumption. However we turn in the next section of this chapter to the question of an efficient *product-mix*, i.e. the question of which levels of output, of goods and services, constitute a Pareto efficient output. We will assume in what follows that the conditions stated in the first optimality theorem still hold, i.e. perfect competition, no externalities and no relevant forms of ignorance. Hence in locating the efficient product-mix we will automatically be assuming that the conditions for efficient production and consumption are satisfied. This will mean that in identifying the efficient output-mix we will have also located the level of product outputs corresponding to a Pareto-efficient allocation of resources. This will also

represent an equilibrium of the economy as a whole as there will be no remaining possibilities for mutual gain through trade between firms and factors, consumers and other consumers, nor between firms and consumers.

Pareto efficiency and perfect markets

Social marginal benefit (*SMB*)

It can be shown that the conditions of the first optimality theorem in a free market economy will automatically bring about a Pareto-efficient (sometimes known as a 'socially efficient') allocation of resources. The first of these conditions is that there must be perfect competition in all markets. If this condition is satisfied (plus the two other conditions which we will examine below), then we can give the following interpretations to our familiar demand and supply curves.

We know that under the conditions of perfect competition all consumers are faced with the same price for a product. We also know that consumers will continue to purchase extra units of this product so long as they place a higher monetary value on these units than the price they actually have to pay (this is the concept of consumer surplus, *see* Chapter 9). They will thus consume extra units of the product up to point at which the monetary valuation they place on the marginal unit of consumption is equal to its price (*see* Fig. 25.2).

When consumers are in equilibrium, then the price of a product will reflect its marginal valuation by consumers (in monetary units). As this price is common to all consumers, all consumers will attach the same monetary valuation to their marginal unit of consumption. We will call this monetary valuation the *social marginal benefit* (*SMB*) of the marginal unit of output of the product concerned. The demand curve for a product, of course, shows how much of the product will be demanded at any market price. Hence by reading off the market price at a

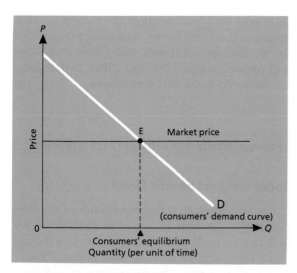

Fig. 25.2 *Marginal valuation of a product*
Point E is where the consumer's marginal valuation of
the product is equal to the price of the product.

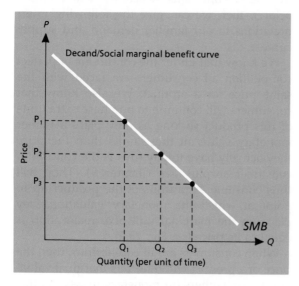

Fig. 25.3 *The social marginal benefit curve*

specific output, the demand curve automatically
shows the *social marginal valuation* of the product
at any level of output (*see* Fig. 25.3).

We can see that at an output of Q_1 the social
marginal benefit, i.e. consumer valuation of the
last unit sold, of the product is equal to P_1. At
Q_2 *SMB* is equal to P_2, and so on. As might be
expected, the demand curve for the product

shows that the *SMB* of an extra unit falls as
output increases.

The significance of marginal cost pricing

We now turn to the interpretation of the supply
curve under the conditions of perfect competition. Recall that firms in perfect competition
will produce up to the level of output at which
marginal cost is equal to price. Hence, reading
up from the quantity axis, the supply curve tells
us what the marginal cost of production is at
any level of output (*see* Fig. 25.4).

We can see that at Q_1 the marginal cost of
production must be equal to P_1. What, however,
is the significance of marginal cost for our analysis under these conditions? It can be shown that,
under the assumptions we have made, marginal
cost will measure the valuation by consumers of
the alternative products forgone by increasing
the output of the product concerned by one unit.
We can rationalise this somewhat surprising
result as follows. Recall that in perfect competition the factors of production are free to transfer from one industry to another. Now marginal
cost measures the payment to the factor services
(including the payment to the entrepreneurial
element) needed to produce the last unit of

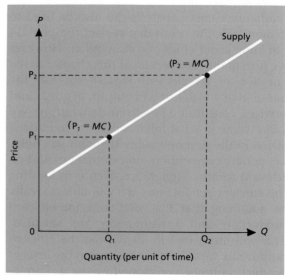

Fig. 25.4 *The supply curve is the marginal cost curve*

output. The cost of these extra factors, at the margin, must be just sufficient to induce these factors of production away from their best alternative employment. In short the payment to these extra factors will equal the opportunity cost to these factors of forgoing their best alternative employment in another industry, i.e. the factors' transfer earnings. Hence if factors are perfectly mobile (if they are not it complicates the analysis) they must be paid, at the margin, the amount they could earn in their best alternative employment. However the amount these extra factors could earn in an alternative industry will be equal to the amount that consumers would pay for the alternative products that would be produced by these factors, i.e. the valuation by consumers of the alternative products forgone. Hence we have the result that, under the conditions cited:

The marginal cost in one industry measures the valuation by consumers (in monetary terms) of the alternative products that are forgone by increasing the output of that industry by one unit. We call this valuation of alternatives forgone the 'social marginal cost' (*SMC*) of increasing output in the industry by one unit.

We can write this as:

$$MC = \begin{array}{l} \text{Payment to} \\ \text{extra factors} \\ \text{required} \end{array} = \begin{array}{l} \text{What these factors} \\ \text{could have earned} \\ \text{in an alternative} \\ \text{industry} \end{array}$$

$$= \begin{array}{l} \text{Consumers} \\ \text{valuation of} \\ \text{alternative} \\ \text{products forgone} \end{array}$$

$$= SMC$$

We know that the supply curve of an industry under perfect competition is represented by the marginal cost of that industry at any level of output. However this marginal cost in turn measures the value to consumers of the alternative forgone, i.e. the *SMC*. We thus have the result that, under the conditions we have assumed, the supply curve represents the social marginal cost of increasing the level of output by one unit (*see* Fig. 25.5).

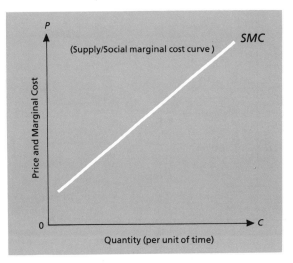

Fig. 25.5 *The social marginal cost curve*

The welfare significance of market equilibrium in a perfect market

The equilibrium price

From the previous section of this chapter we have derived the following results.

a) The price that consumers will pay for the last unit of output of a product is equal to the marginal valuation by consumers of the product concerned. This is known as the social marginal benefit of this unit of output and is shown by the demand curve for the product.

b) Marginal cost reflects what the factors used to produce the last unit of output could earn in their best alternative employment. These earnings in turn reflect the valuation by consumers of these alternative uses of factors. Hence marginal cost measures the valuation by consumers of the best alternative products forgone by increasing production by one unit. This valuation is called the social marginal cost and, because firms will produce where price equals marginal cost, this is shown by the supply curve of the product.

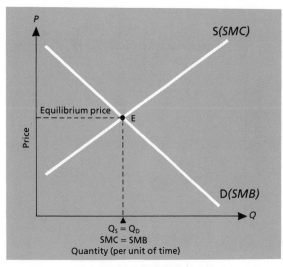

Fig. 25.6 *The socially efficient price*
This occurs where consumers' valuation of the best alternatives forgone by producing an extra unit (*SMC*) is equal to consumers' valuation of an extra unit of the commodity (*SMB*).

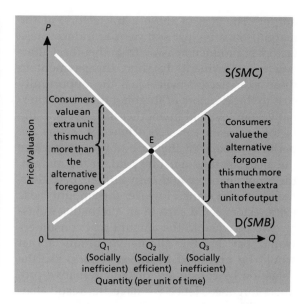

Fig. 25.7 *The social efficiency of the equilibrium price*

We can now draw the important conclusion:

When the market for a product is in equilibrium the last unit of a product bought is valued equally by consumers to the best alternative forgone by its production.

This is illustrated in Fig. 25.6.

The Pareto- or socially-efficient level of output

It is now fairly easy to see why an equilibrium of output at which $SMC = SMB$ corresponds to a Pareto-efficient allocation of resources. We need only consider the points either side of the equilibrium level of output.

In Fig. 25.7 we can see that at Q_1 consumers value an extra unit of output more than the alternative that would be forgone by its production. (Recall that if all consumers are in equilibrium they all have consumed the product up to the point at which their valuation of the last unit consumed is equal to the market price. As this price is common to all consumers, they all attach the same monetary valuation to the last unit of the product they consume.) The

actual gain in welfare available to consumers and hence society from the production of an extra unit at Q_1 is given, in monetary units, by $SMB - SMC$, i.e. the vertical distance between the demand and supply curve. The overall loss in welfare associated with the output Q_1 can therefore be calculated, in monetary units, by summing the vertical distance between the supply and demand curve for all extra units up to the point at which the level of output is socially efficient. Thus the loss of welfare to society associated with the output being at Q_1 rather than the socially-efficient output of Q_2 can be represented by a *welfare loss triangle* (*see* Fig. 25.8).

Welfare loss triangles

It can be seen that under the assumptions of the *first optimality theorem*, whenever actual output is below the market equilibrium the overall welfare of consumers could be increased by increasing the output of the product, i.e. there exists the potential for a Pareto improvement.

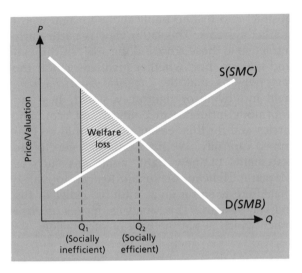

Fig. 25.8 *Welfare loss at outputs below the equilibrium*

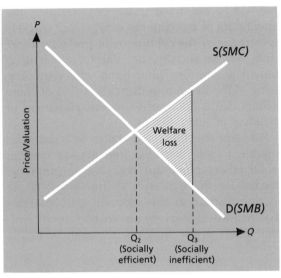

Fig. 25.9 *Welfare loss at outputs above the equilibrium*

Under the assumptions of the first optimality theorem outputs below the market equilibrium are associated with a 'welfare loss' and hence a socially-inefficient allocation of resources.

Conversely, at Q_3 (*see* Fig. 25.9), consumers value the alternative forgone by producing an extra unit more than they value that extra unit of output. There is therefore a welfare loss, as consumers would have preferred the alternative now forgone. The welfare loss associated with the production of this marginal unit can be measured in monetary units by the vertical distance between the demand and supply curve, i.e. $SMC - SMB$. As the overall welfare of consumers could be increased by *decreasing* the output of the product and diverting resources towards alternative employment, it is clear that at outputs above the market equilibrium a potential Pareto improvement exists. The overall welfare loss associated with the output Q_3 can be calculated by summing the vertical distance between the demand and supply curves for all units of output from Q_3 down to Q_2. Hence the loss of welfare to society associated with output being at Q_3 rather than the socially efficient output of Q_2 can again be represented by a welfare loss triangle. This is illustrated in Fig. 25.9.

Under the assumptions of the first optimality theorem, outputs above the market equilibrium are associated with a 'welfare loss' and hence a socially-inefficient allocation of resources.

The 'invisible hand' theorem

The only point at which it is impossible to change the allocation of resources so as to raise overall welfare, i.e. bring about a Pareto improvement, is Q_2, the level of output which would be arrived at through the operation of market forces. At this point want and scarcity are brought into balance and the gain, in monetary units, to consumers from the last unit of output is exactly matched by the cost in terms of alternative output forgone. Before this point all consumers would be prepared to sacrifice the alternative output for more of the product so that all consumers can be made better off through increasing output. After this point all consumers would be prepared to sacrifice their last units of the product in order to obtain the alternative output forgone. Hence all consumers could be made better off by reducing output of the product and increasing the alternative output.

This result, that (subject to certain conditions **307**

that will be examined in the next chapter) the equilibrium of an economy in which all markets operate under the conditions of perfect competition will be socially, i.e. Pareto, efficient, is known as the 'invisible hand' theorem. The name of the theorem reflects the belief of some writers that it is a more rigorous statement of the ideas of Adam Smith.

For some this theorem is taken as a powerful argument in favour of a free market system, while others point out that the assumptions needed for the efficiency of free markets are so unrealistic that the theorem demonstrates that real-world markets are socially inefficient. Still others argue that the theorem is totally abstract and has no implications for real-world market systems. This latter view is particularly attractive to those who find the analysis difficult and tedious, but, whether justified or not, the fact remains that the *'invisible hand' theorem*, held intuitively or rigorously stated, has had enormous influence in political and economic circles and for this reason alone should be examined carefully. We have only to listen to the statements of 'new right' politicians such as Margaret Thatcher or Ronald Reagan to realise that there is still a great intuitive belief in the market system. This analysis makes explicit much which lies at the base of such beliefs.

Summary

1 Welfare economics is concerned with both positive and normative questions. The notion of *best* considers both efficiency and equity.

2 Pareto optimality requires that it must not be possible to change the allocation of resources in such a way that someone is made better off and no one worse off.

3 Pareto-efficient consumption occurs if the rates at which consumers are just prepared to sacrifice one good for another are the same.

4 Under certain rigorously stated conditions Pareto optimality in both production and consumption may be brought about by the price mechanism.

5 *The first optimality theorem* states that if in all markets there is perfect competition, no externalities and no market failure connected with uncertainty, then the resulting allocation of resources is Pareto optimal.

6 The social marginal benefit (*SMB*) is the monetary valuation of the marginal unit of consumption.

7 Social marginal cost (*SMC*) in one industry measures the valuation by consumers of the alternatives forgone by increasing the output of that industry by one unit.

8 Under the conditions stated, where the demand (*SMB*) curve intersects with the supply (*SMC*) curve, the resulting equilibrium price is Pareto optimal. Any other level of output involves a welfare loss.

9 When these conditions are met in all markets then society is achieving an optimum allocation of resources. This is known as the 'invisible hand' theorem.

Questions

1   Discuss the statement 'Because of their special training economists are in a better position than politicians to decide which economic policies should be implemented.'

2   'Economists are agreed on the answers to positive questions; it is over normative issues that they disagree.' True or false?

3   Examine Fig. 25.10 and rank points A, B, C, D and E in terms of Pareto optimality. Is a complete ranking possible? If not why not?

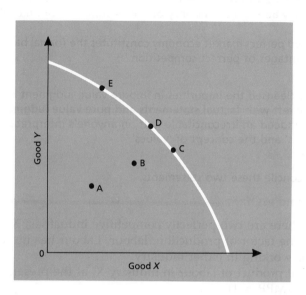

Fig. 25.10

4   Assume that an economy consists of three consumers and two industries. The production function is such that, at present output levels, an increase in the output of barley of four units requires a reduction in the output of wheat of one unit. The rates at which the consumers are prepared to exchange wheat for barley are given by the following table:

Consumer A is prepared to sacrifice 1 unit of wheat for 5 units of barley
Consumer B is prepared to sacrifice 1 unit of wheat for 3 units of barley
Consumer C is prepared to sacrifice 1 unit of wheat for 1 unit of barley

Demonstrate that this does not represent a Pareto-efficient product-mix.

5   Assume that an economy has a fixed weekly output of milk and coal. This economy also has two groups of consumers, type A and type B. With the present distribution of output between consumers, group A consumers would be indifferent between a choice of 1 litre of milk and 5 kg of coal. Group B consumers, on the other hand, would be indifferent between a choice of 5 litres of milk and 1 kg of coal. Demonstrate that consumption is not Pareto efficient.

6   Assume that utility can be measured and that you have the following information about the utility schedules of two consumers:

	1 tonne barley	1 tonne wheat
Crusoe	2 utils	10 utils
Friday	10 utils	2 utils

What would be the rate at which each consumer would just be prepared to sacrifice one good for another? What are your conclusions regarding the efficiency of the situation represented in the table? Show how trade between the two consumers can increase overall utility.

7 Assume that you are given the following information about a two-good, two-consumer economy. An increase in the production of oats of 1 tonne necessarily requires a reduction in the output of rye of 2 tonnes. If each consumer traded 1 tonne of oats for 2 tonnes of rye their levels of satisfaction would be unaltered. What can you say about the efficiency of the existing allocation of resources in this economy?

8 'This so-called perfect market economy constitutes the formal basis for propositions about the advantages of perfect competition.'

P. Bohm

'Once we have cleansed the impurities in impure value judgment by a rational debate, we are left with factual statements and pure value judgment between which there is indeed an irreconcilable gulf on anyone's interpretation of the concept of 'facts' and the concept of 'values'.'

M. Blaug

Attempt to reconcile these two statements.

Data response **Prices output and welfare** ━━━━━━━━━━━━━━━━━━━

Assume that there are two perfectly competitive industries, X and Y, and there is only one factor of production, labour. Labour has no non-monetary preference for working in either industry.

The marginal product of labour in industry X, at the present level of output, is one (MPP = 1).

1 If the wage in industry X is £100, what is the marginal cost (MC) in industry X?

2 The marginal product of labour in industry Y is two (MPP = 2) and the price of a unit of Y is £5. Assuming equilibrium, show that the MC of industry X measures the valuation by consumers of the number of units of Y forgone by increasing the output of industry X by one unit.

(*Remember that in perfect competition the wage equals the labour's marginal product multiplied by price.*)

3 Using the above information explain why the equilibrium is said to be socially efficient.

4 Demonstrate how the equilibrium would be likely to change if there were an increase in the price of product X.

5 Explain the loss of welfare if the production of product X involved the output of negative externalities.

26
Market failure

In attempting to answer the question 'Could it be true?', we learn a good deal about why it might not be true.

K. J. Arrow and F. H. Hahn

In the last chapter we demonstrated that under certain conditions an economy that has perfect competition in all markets has equilibrium positions that are socially (or Pareto) efficient. The conditions necessary for this outcome were summarised in the first optimality theorem of modern welfare economics. We can thus gain insight into why social efficiency is not achieved in real-life markets by examining the implications of deviations from the conditions assumed in this theorem.

Imperfect competition

Welfare loss under imperfect competition

A profit maximising firm, operating under the conditions of monopoly or monopolistic competition, produces and sells the volume of output at which marginal cost and marginal revenue are equal. Equilibrium will thus occur with marginal cost being less than the market price. From the arguments of the last chapter this implies social inefficiency, i.e. a loss of welfare to society. This is illustrated in Fig. 26.1 where the shaded area represents the welfare loss to society, with the firm producing output Q_1 rather than Q_2.

Cost inefficiencies

So far we have looked only at the loss of social welfare caused by price exceeding marginal

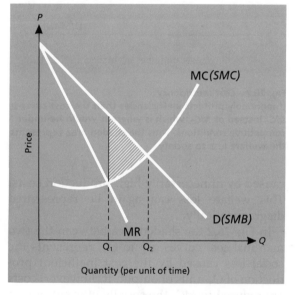

Fig. 26.1 *Welfare loss under imperfect competition* Q_1 is the profit maximising output, while Q_2 is the socially efficient output. The shaded area represents the welfare loss at the profit maximisation equilibrium.

cost. However the lack of competition might also result in cost inefficiency. Firms which are, for various reasons, insulated from competition might have the potential to make very large profits and thus are not forced to minimise costs in order to match the prices of their competitors. In such situations firms have more discretion as to the objectives they pursue, for example, they may pursue managerial objectives (*see* Chapter 14). To the extent that costs are not minimised, this will result in a second kind of efficiency loss **311**

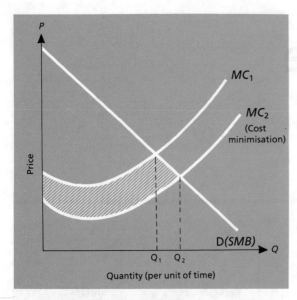

Fig. 26.2 *Cost inefficiency*
If monopoly protects inefficiencies then the cost curve is MC_1 instead of MC_2, which is where it would be under competitive conditions. Thus the shaded area represents the welfare loss to society.

caused by unnecessarily high production costs. This welfare loss can again be represented diagrammatically.

In Fig. 26.2 the shaded area between the two marginal cost curves, up to Q_1, represents the social loss caused by the cost inefficient production of Q_1 units of output. If, however, costs are reduced to MC_2 the socially efficient output becomes Q_2. Thus the shaded triangle between Q_1 and Q_2 would also be available as part of the total welfare gain to society. The whole of the shaded area therefore represents the welfare loss to society from the wasteful method of production.

Some, admittedly inconclusive, empirical evidence has suggested that the welfare loss from cost inefficiency monopolies is far greater than that caused by under-production. This has led some observers to state that under-production due to monopoly pricing policy is of no practical significance. However it has been pointed out by other observers that even a small welfare loss in the present will accumu-

late into a large long-term welfare loss if left uncorrected. It should also be pointed out that policies designed to decrease monopoly power through increased competition will tend to reduce both types of inefficiency.

Externalities

What are externalities?

Externalities are said to exist when the action of producers or consumers affect not only themselves but also third parties, other than through the normal workings of the price mechanism.

This is likely to result in social inefficiency because individuals normally only consider the private costs (the cost incurred by themselves) of their decisions. They largely ignore, or are unaware of, the wider social costs (the full opportunity cost to society) and benefits of their actions. External effects can be either positive or negative. For example, if one person is cured of a contagious disease this obviously gives benefit to others; hence the external effect is said to be positive. On the other hand airports near residential areas are likely to have negative external effects.

We can categorise these 'spill-over' effects under four headings.

a) Production on consumption. A negative example of this would be the adverse effects of pollution on recreational areas. A positive externality could result from the warm water discharge from many industrial cooling processes making rivers more attractive to bathers.

b) Production on production. A negative externality would result if the release of industrial waste into rivers decreased the catch of commercial fishermen. An important positive externality in this category is that arising from the utilising of non-patented inventions. As inventors would receive no payment for their efforts this suggests that under laissez-faire too little would be spent on research and development.

c) Consumption on production. Negative externalities might arise from the careless discarding of packaging on farm land. Alternatively, congestion caused by private motorists will increase the transportation costs of many firms. Positive externalities in this category are in principle possible, but in practice of little significance.

d) Consumption on consumption. Negative externalities include the unwelcome noise from radios and the congestion caused to other private road users of using one's own car. Positive externalities include neighbours enjoying the sight of each other's gardens and the fact that other people's possession of a telephone increases the utility of one's own telephone. A rather controversial negative externality in this category is that of envy (*see* page 24, conspicuous consumption). It is argued that status-orientated consumption by one consumer is likely to reduce the utility of others. However it might conversely be argued that the copying of others' consumption is due to the information provided by this consumption. This latter argument suggests a positive rather than a negative externality, i.e. people are receiving free information.

It should be noted that the same spill-over effect can simultaneously have both positive and negative effects; for example, the smoke from oil refineries is beneficial to the cultivation of citrus fruits, but it can also be considered as undesirable pollution.

Pecuniary 'external effects'

Pecuniary 'external effects' are the effect of prices in one sector of the economy upon other sectors of the economy.

As we have seen, prices are determined by the interaction of all the economic 'units', i.e. producers and consumers, in the economy. Hence the act of demanding or supplying these units by one group will affect the prices faced by other groups. Although such changes can cause a redistribution of welfare among such units, they are not a cause of social inefficiency. This is because such effects work *within* the price mechanism; they are not external to it and are therefore not ignored by profit or utility maximising decision-makers. For example, if firms in one industry increase their demand for a particular factor of production, this is likely to raise the price of this factor of production. It is not a case of market inefficiency because it is the normal working of the price mechanism; the increased price of the factor of production merely reflects the fact that it is scarce in relation to the demand for the products it produces. Such price increases provide an incentive for producers to economise in their use of this factor and conveys to the consumers the fact that to have more of one product they must, as a group, have less of another. It is exactly this type of consideration that brought about the efficient balance between wants and scarcity outlined in the previous chapter.

In view of the confusion between pecuniary externalities and true spill-over effects, it might be better to call the former 'price effects'. However, in a world of imperfect information, pecuniary effects do have an importance as regards efficiency. For example, suppose that one entrepreneur found an ideal but remote location for a hydroelectric dam, but also finds, however, that it would be uneconomical to transmit power to where it is in demand and decides not to go ahead with the project. Further suppose that a separate entrepreneur surveys the same area and finds that it is rich in deposits of bauxite (the ore from which aluminium is extracted). Aluminium smelting requires vast amounts of power, so this entrepreneur also decides not to go ahead with this project. It might thus be the case that if both projects were to go ahead the first entrepreneur would be able to sell electricity at a high enough price to make the dam profitable and the second entrepreneur would be able to buy electricity from the first entrepreneur at a low enough price to make the smelting of aluminium profitable. The essential point to realise here is that it is not the pecuniary effects themselves that are the cause of market failure; indeed they work in exactly the **313** direction required. It is the *lack of information* and hence coordination between the entrepreneurs that results in inefficiency. We will return to the problem of market failure caused by incomplete information later in this chapter.

Cases of externalities

Case 1: pollution

Consider the soap industry which, in a free market, would discharge waste products into the air and rivers. This is because owners of soap factories, if they are profit maximisers, will consider only their private costs and ignore the wider social costs of their activities. Indeed, if competition was fierce they might be unable to incur the cost of purification or non-polluting disposal of their waste products and still match the price of their competitors. Where such negative externalities are present the price mechanism is likely to fail in bringing about a socially efficient allocation of resources. This is because the cost to society in terms of the deterioration of the environment is unpriced by the price mechanism. Private profit-makers are given the use of the environment free of charge. It is in this sense that such spill-over effects are external to the price mechanism. The cost to society of the use of this resource is not reflected in the private costs of the individual using it. Individuals are thus 'invited' to destroy these resources at zero price. There is no incentive provided by the price mechanism to economise on the use of the environment and hence the price mechanism fails to bring about an efficient balance between the wants of society as a whole and the use of the scarce resources available to it.

Using the analysis we have developed we can again represent the welfare loss resulting from negative externalities in the form of a diagram. This is illustrated in Fig. 26.3. It is assumed in the diagram that the soap industry is perfectly competitive. The supply curve of the industry is

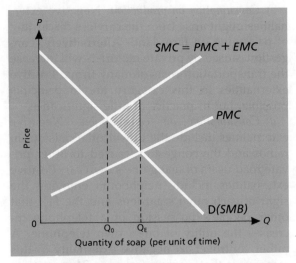

Fig. 26.3 *Negative externalities*
Q_E represents the profit-maximising equilibrium when firms in the industry are able to ignore external marginal costs (*EMC*). The socially efficient output is Q_O. Thus the shaded area represents the welfare loss to society at the profit-maximising equilibrium.

thus the horizontal summation of the marginal cost curves of all the firms in the industry. This curve is represented by the private marginal cost curve (*PMC*) in the diagram. As firms in perfect competition will equate *MC* to price, the free market equilibrium output of the industry is thus Q_E. The social marginal cost curve represents the full opportunity cost to society of an extra unit of soap production. *SMC* lies above *PMC* as *SMC* includes not only the cost to society in terms of forgone alternative marketed products, i.e. *PMC*, but also the loss to society in terms of the deterioration of the environment, i.e. the external marginal cost (*EMC*). *EMC* represents the loss in value corresponding to what consumers would have been prepared to pay to avoid this loss in utility from the environment associated with extra units of soap production. It can be seen that *SMB* equals *SMC* at Q_O units of output.

Thus in terms of social efficiency, as we have defined it above, there is an over-supply of soap. By summing the excess *SMC* over *SMB* for the units between Q_O and Q_E we again arrive at a monetary measure of the welfare loss to society, i.e. the shaded triangle in the diagram.

Case 2: congestion

These negative externalities often arise from the provision of free access to public facilities such as roads, shopping centres, museums, etc. The individual will consider their opportunity costs in making use of such free-access facilities but will not consider the fact that they will get in the way of other users. For example, motorists will decide whether or not to take a journey on the basis of their valuation of the benefits from the journey and their valuation of the alternatives forgone in terms of time and money for petrol. They will not consider, however, the additional cost imposed on others due to increased con-·gestion. The reader should now be able to draw a similar diagram to Fig. 26.3 which demonstrates that road congestion will tend to be above the socially optimal level.

We will now use the example of road use to examine more closely why a divergence between private and social costs leads to Pareto inefficiency. This analysis will introduce the important notion of *compensation*. In Fig. 26.4 we have a similar diagram to that in **case 1** above. Marked on the diagram, however, is a level of road use (Q_X) between the equilibrium and the socially efficient level of road use.

In the diagram it is assumed that the only beneficiaries are the motorists themselves; hence *PMB* equals *SMB*. In contrast, *social marginal cost* (*SMC*) is the addition of private costs, e.g. time, petrol and wear and tear, and the various externalities at the margin, e.g. pollution, congestion and the threat to the safety of others. At Q_X the marginal negative externality is equal to b, but the motorists' valuation of the marginal unit of road travel, over and above their valuation of the forgone alternatives, is only equal to a. Hence those suffering from the externality may be prepared, in principle, to compensate a motorist for the loss of his unit of travel and still enjoy an increase in welfare equal to $b - a$. Such Pareto improvements could

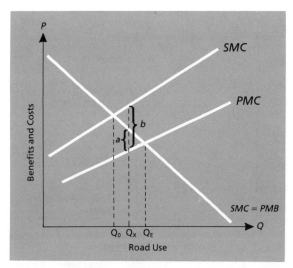

Fig. 26.4 *Negative externalities*
Q_O = socially efficient level of road use. Q_E = equilibrium level of road use. Q_X = an alternative (but still socially inefficient) level of road use compared to Q_E. a = excess of private benefit over private cost at Q_X. b = external marginal cost at Q_X.

continue until Q_O is reached. The readers should now satisfy themselves that at levels of road use below Q_O motorists could compensate those who suffer from the negative externalities and still enjoy a net increase in welfare. As we shall see, 'compensation tests' have been used to evaluate the desirability of proposed projects.

Case 3: positive externalities

The same framework as above can be used to analyse the welfare losses associated with positive externalities; for example, those arising from medical care, attractive front gardens, telephone installations and inventions and innovations which can be copied without charge. We could proceed by representing social costs as being less than private costs. It is conceptually easier, however, to represent the positive externality by an upward shift of the marginal benefit curve. This indicates that the benefits of consumption include not only the benefits to the purchaser but also the benefits to those enjoying the positive spillover effects of this consumption.

315

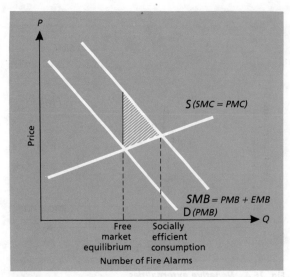

Fig. 26.5 *Positive externalities*
The existence of external marginal benefit (*EMB*) shifts the *SMB* curve to the right. The free-market equilibrium is below the socially efficient level of consumption. The shaded area shows the welfare loss brought about by under-production.

We have adopted this procedure in Fig. 26.5. Here the upward shift in the *SMB* curve represents the valuation of other residents of having their neighbour's property protected by fire alarms. It can be seen that when positive externalities exist there is a tendency for under-production of the product in question, i.e. the socially efficient output is greater than the equilibrium output that would occur in an 'uncorrected' free market.

Public goods

Definition of public goods

We have already mentioned public goods in Chapter 6. We will now define them more precisely.

Public goods are defined as products where, for any given output, consumption by additional consumers does not reduce the quantity consumed by existing consumers.

Although it is difficult to think of many pure public goods, the following are examples where there is a large element of 'collective consumption': defence, broadcasts, law and order, uncongested roads, parks, swimming pools, museums and bridges. These contrast sharply with the purely private goods such as chocolate bars, where consumption by one person rules out the consumption of that chocolate bar by another person.

A pure public good has the characteristics of *non-rivalry* in consumption, as discussed in the previous paragraph, and *non-excludability*. Defence and lighthouses are the usual examples; the amount of consumption to existing beneficiaries is not reduced by an additional consumer, nor is it possible to exclude from these benefits those consumers who have not contributed towards the cost. As we shall see, these properties suggest that not only is it impossible to charge for the consumption of public goods, it is also undesirable. These considerations obviously make public goods unsuitable for provision through the price mechanism.

The *SMB* curve of public goods

Because the same unit of a *public* or *collective* good can be consumed by more than one consumer, the social marginal benefit of such products is thus the vertical summation of all the individual consumers' private marginal benefits. As we shall see in the next chapter, the estimation of these benefits poses difficult problems. However we shall ignore these problems for now and assume that we can draw individual demand curves which measure the true willingness to pay of each individual consumer. This is shown in Fig. 26.6.

The socially efficient output of public goods

The socially efficient output will have been reached when the aggregate valuation of the last unit is equal to the valuation of the best alternative forgone by its production. This is shown in Fig. 26.7, where the socially efficient

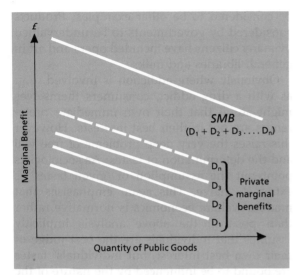

Fig. 26.6 *The social marginal benefit curve of a public good*

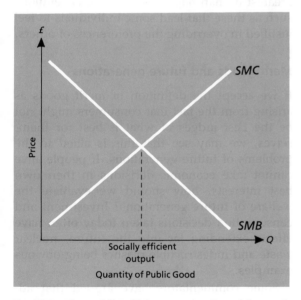

Fig. 26.7 *The socially efficient output of a public good*

output of a public good is where the *SMC* curve cuts the *SMB* curve. The problem here, however, lies in calculating *SMB*; as we shall see in the next chapter, the *SMC* = *SMB* condition seems to raise insuperable problems.

Imperfect knowledge

We now drop the last of the conditions assumed in the first optimality theorem, that of perfect information. Lack of information is probably the most apparent cause of market failure to consumers. We have all, no doubt, experienced frustration from our less than perfect knowledge of the prices on offer, the qualities and range of commodities on offer and our weakness in resisting persuasive advertising. As workers we also are forced to make decisions based on incomplete information regarding, for example, the wage rates on offer in an area, the jobs available in other areas, or even other countries, and the career prospects in rival firms. When it comes to the decisions to invest in human capital, i.e. in education and training, the problems become even more acute. How are we to know our aptitude for a particular career? What exactly are the best qualifications? How are we to know how future economic changes will affect the prospects from various careers? Producers face similar information problems concerning available supply prices for labour, raw materials and capital. They too face uncertainty when it comes to deciding on investment projects, e.g. will technological change make present processes unprofitable and hence obsolete? What will be the most profitable lines of production in the future? What are the most effective production methods? Do rival firms have information not possessed by one's own firm?

It is the cost of information which causes many economic decisions to be less than optimal, thus resulting in social inefficiency. Information gathering involves inputs of resources and time. In principle it is an easy matter to define the optimum level of 'search'. Search should continue up until the point at which the marginal benefit from search is equal to the marginal cost. However there is a logical problem here; how can the benefit from extra search be calculated unless the content of the resulting information is known? But if the content of the **317** piece of information is known, then there is no need to search for it! As with public goods the application of the $SMC = SMB$ condition raises more problems than it solves.

Merit goods

Problems of definition

We have so far defined merit goods as:

Those products or services which are not distributed through the price system but on the basis of merit or need.

The concept of merit goods is somewhat controversial and is often confused with *information* and *externality* problems. Thus health care is often given as an example of a merit good. It is argued the consumers will not know in advance if they are going to need expensive health treatment and thus might under-invest in health insurance; as we have seen this can be analysed in terms of a lack of information. Alternatively, it is argued that health care benefits people other than just the recipient, and should therefore be subsidised. This analysis is essentially correct but is simply an application of the analysis above concerning positive externalities.

The essential reasons why health care and other products might be thought of as merit goods is the consideration that fully informed consumers might not be the best judge of what is best for themselves.

This of course immediately begs the question 'Who is the best judge?' It is thus best to state that merit goods arise from a divergence between the values of society (as expressed through government) and the values of individuals. Hence smokers might be fully informed of the health risks to themselves yet society might feel obliged to act in a paternalistic manner by discouraging this activity through taxation. Tobacco, in this case, would be an example of a 'de-merit' good; drugs and pornography might

be considered to be other examples. Products considered by governments to be undervalued by many citizens have included opera and art in general, libraries and milk.

Obviously where addiction is involved, e.g. as with a drug addict, consumers themselves might admit that their own immediate preferences are not in their best interests. However this raises the very deep problems of free will and the determination of tastes. As sociologists point out the assumption of 'given tastes' is extremely naive. This again emphasises that modern welfare economics is normative rather than positive; the above analysis implicitly assumes that individuals are the best judge of their own best interest, but individuals' tastes are bound to be influenced by the nature of the society in which they live. How then can they be sure that the present goals, both of themselves and society, are those that will lead to the greatest human happiness? It is considerations such as these that lead some individuals to feel justified in overriding the preferences of others.

Merit goods and future generations

If we accept the definition of merit goods as arising from the fact that consumers might not be the best judges of what is best for themselves, we may see that this is allied to the problems of future generations. If people alive cannot take economic decisions in their own best interests, how should we evaluate the welfare of future generations? Investment and consumption decisions taken today often have effects extending far into the future, nuclear waste and indestructible plastics being obvious examples.

Some commentators have argued that advancing technology and economic growth will mean improved living standards. Hence economic decisions should be weighted in favour of existing generations. Other observers argue that pollution, the depletion of non-renewable resources and rapid world population growth will lead to crises. Hence economic decisions should be weighted in favour of the future rather than the present. The essential point for the analysis outlined in the previous chapter is that future generations, like animals and the destitute, have no money votes. Hence their preferences are ignored by the price mechanism. Society then might decide that policies which protect the interests of future generations are desirable, as the wishes of these generations cannot be directly reflected by their own 'money votes' or laws in the present.

Conclusion

In this chapter we have outlined the reasons why free markets will not, in practice, result in Pareto optimality. Our conclusion must thus

be that it is impossible for a laissez-faire market economy to attain a state of social efficiency. Hopefully, however, in attempting to answer the question 'Could it be true?', we have increased our understanding of why it is not. In the next chapter we will examine how our analysis might be used to design policies intended to help real economies reach an efficient state. However we will also note arguments which claim that the first optimality theorem does not provide a fruitful point of departure when it comes to policy formation. We will additionally examine the concept of 'the maximisation of social welfare'; as we shall see this is a broader concept than social efficiency in that the former includes considerations of equity as well as efficiency.

Summary

1   The restriction of output involved in profit maximisation under imperfect competition brings about a welfare loss to society.

2   If monopolistic practices protect inefficient cost structures this also involves a welfare loss.

3   Externalities exist when the actions of producers or consumers affect third parties other than through the price mechanism.

4   Where changes in prices in one market influence other sectors of the economy this is said to be an external pecuniary effect, perhaps better described as a 'price effect'.

5   Public goods are those where, at any given output, consumption by additional consumers does not reduce the quantity consumed by existing consumers. An example of this would be defence.

6   The socially efficient output of public goods is where the SMB curve intersects the SMC curve, but this is very difficult to determine.

7   Imperfect knowledge is a major source of inefficiency in markets, both for consumers and producers.

8   Merit goods are normally defined as those distributed on the grounds of merit or need rather than by price. However the essential reason why goods such as health care are thought of as merit goods is the consideration that fully informed consumers might not be the best judge of what is best for themselves.

9   Because of the problems caused by such things as externalities, ignorance and merit goods it is impossible for a fully laissez-faire economy to be socially efficient.

Questions

1 Study Fig. 26.1 and then demonstrate that if $Q_2 - Q_1$ units were to be sold at a price equal to MC at output Q_2, while Q_1 are sold at the original price, then there would be a gain in welfare to both consumers and monopolists.

2 Demonstrate that if the monopolists were able to practise perfect price discrimination there would be no loss of welfare through inefficiency, i.e. output of the goods would be socially efficient (assume profit maximising behaviour). Explain why this situation might be held to conflict with equity considerations.

3 Assume straight line demand curves and profit maximising behaviour. Draw a diagram which indicates that the social loss of monopoly will be smaller the greater the competition from potential new entrants to the industry and from the producers of other goods.

4 Assume that a monopolist equates MR and MC but does not minimise production costs. Draw a diagram indicating the total welfare loss to society resulting from inefficiency. To what extent is it possible to reconcile the two assumptions made at the beginning of this exercise?

5 We saw in Chapter 18 that a monopolist might be able to achieve lower production costs than if the industry were more competitive. Discuss the relative merits of these two situations.

6 Classify the following in terms of positive, negative, and pecuniary externalities.

a) Smoke from a soap factory.
b) One firm in an industry sets up a training school for its workers.
c) A mine owner installs a powerful pump which lowers the water table in the area.
d) Smith makes a right turn on a busy road and causes a traffic jam.
e) A school leaver decides to go to university.
f) Miss Smith wears a mini-skirt.
g) A crop disease increases the price of bread.
h) Fred hits Bill.
i) A reduction in the cost of producing colour televisions decreases cinema attendance.
j) The Labour Party wins the election.

7 Suppose that Fig. 26.4 represents the costs and benefits associated with flights from a particular airport. Show that if the airport authority were given the criterion 'Allow the flight if the gainers could compensate the losers,' the socially efficient number of flights would take place.

Would you think that this criterion is desirable if:

a) compensation is actually paid;
b) compensation is not paid?

8 Discuss the view that not enough attention is given to the interest of future generations in taking economic decisions today. Give examples both for and against this argument.

Data response Profit maximisation and welfare ▬▬▬▬▬▬▬

A firm which charges a single price to all its customers faces the following cost and revenue schedules:

Output	(units)	0	2	4	6	8	10	12	14	16	18	20	per week
Revenue	(£s)	0	18	32	42	48	50	48	42	32	18	0	per week
Cost	(£s)	0	12	23	33	42	50	57	63	68	72	75	per week

a) Using graph paper, draw the demand curve faced by the firm.

b) On the same graph locate and indicate the equilibrium output if the firm is a profit maximiser.

c) Indicate the equilibrium output of an output maximising firm (ignore possible advertising campaigns and note that costs must be covered).

d) Do either of the above two outputs you have indicated represent a socially efficient allocation of resources? Explain your answer in not more than two paragraphs.

e) *With reference to the above* evaluate the statement: 'Private enterprise is always efficient, for unless a firm makes a profit it is forced out of business.'

27
Microeconomic policy

Would you really tax General Motors for selling unsafe cars? Isn't that selling the right to destroy human life? The economist thought for a moment and replied, Surely, it is better than giving that right free of charge.

W. J. Baumol and W. E. Oates

Government intervention in markets

Given the analysis of the previous two chapters, it is a simple matter to demonstrate that if the allocation of resources is already Pareto optimal, i.e. there is no imperfect competition, externalities nor uncertainty, then government intervention in the form of subsidies, taxation and tariffs will actually cause inefficiency of resource allocation.

Subsidies

Figure 27.1 illustrates the effect of a subsidy. The subsidy causes a welfare loss because it 'artificially' lowers price below marginal cost, i.e. the market price no longer reflects the 'true' or social cost of extra units of the product concerned. Consumers are thus 'fooled' into thinking that the opportunity cost of the extra units is less than it actually is. They therefore 'over-consume' the product, unaware that in doing so they are diverting resources away from the production of other goods which they would have actually preferred.

Indirect taxes: import duties

In Fig. 27.2 we show the effect of a customs tariff on imported goods. For simplicity, we assume in the diagram that the supply of the

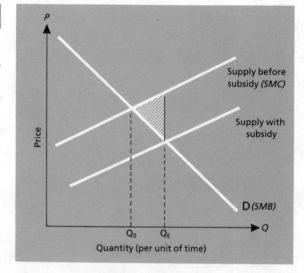

Fig. 27.1 *The effect of a subsidy*
Q_O is the socially efficient output, where $SMC = SMB$. Q_E is the market equilibrium after the subsidy. The shaded area represents the welfare loss caused by the subsidy.

product from the rest of the world (S_W) is perfectly elastic. Hence, before the imposition of the tariff consumers bought Q_4 of the product concerned at price OH. At this price domestic producers are able to sell Q_1. After this level of output their costs would not enable them to match the price of imports from the rest of the world; $Q_4 - Q_1$ is thus imported. Note that the

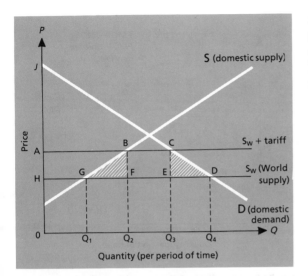

Fig. 27.2 *The effect of an import tariff*
The shaded triangles represent the 'deadweight' loss to society of imposing a tariff.

total *consumer surplus* in this situation is represented by the triangle JDH.

A tariff of AH is now imposed on each unit of the product imported. The supply curve from the rest of the world to the domestic market thus shifts up to S_W + tariff. Consumers now purchase Q_3. Of this Q_2 is supplied by domestic producers, leaving $Q_3 - Q_2$ to be imported. Note that consumers' surplus has now decreased to JCA.

It is important to realise that not all of the area ACDH represents a *welfare loss* to society as a whole. Part of the consumer surplus (ABGH) has been transferred to producers as an increase in *producer surplus*. Similarly the area BCEF is not lost to society but transferred from being a consumer surplus to being a tariff revenue to the government. This tariff revenue could thus be given back to the community by the government. This leaves the shaded triangles GBF and ECD. It is these triangles which represent the 'deadweight loss' caused by the tariff. The explanation for the loss represented by GBF is that before the tariff $Q_2 - Q_1$ only cost society Q_1GFQ_2. After the tariff $Q_2 - Q_1$ is produced by domestic producers at a cost of Q_1GBQ_2 (recall that in perfect competition the supply curve represents the

marginal cost of the industry). BGF thus represents the extra cost of domestic production in excess of the previous cost of importing $Q_2 - Q_1$. ECD is lost to society in the same way that any indirect tax might cause a loss of welfare. The price to consumers after the imposition of the tariff, i.e. OA, no longer represents the actual cost to society of obtaining extra units of the product. Thus consumers reduce their consumption by $Q_4 - Q_3$, even though they value these units more than the opportunity cost to society of obtaining them.

Other considerations

a) Administration costs. We should also note that taxes, subsidies, etc., will require civil servants and other administrative costs. The use of such resources will impose welfare losses on society in addition to those outlined above.

b) Market correction. In the real world government policy does not act upon an otherwise perfect economy. Microeconomic policy can have three goals: correction of *market failure*; *paternalism*; and the *pursuit of equity*. Below we examine some of the major forms of intervention.

Policy and imperfect competition

We have examined the arguments for and against monopolies and restricted competition in Chapter 18. The main advantages listed were possible *economies of scale, increased funds* and *incentives for research and development*. The possible disadvantages are the likelihood of *undesirable redistribution of income towards producers, allocative inefficiency* caused by price exceeding marginal cost, and *cost inefficiency*. These conflicting considerations led to the conclusion that a pragmatic, case-study approach might be desirable. Against such a solution are the disadvantages of administration costs and the possibility that the policy might lack effectiveness.

Perhaps the most worrying consideration for the policymaker is the possibility that increased allocative efficiency, through greater competition in the present, might have adverse long-term effects. This argument assumes that restricted competition caused by the market dominance of large monopolies is actually favourable to economic growth (*see* page 222). It might be that it is the expectation of large profits from future monopoly positions that provides the incentive for companies to undertake research in order to introduce new goods and cheaper methods of production. Conversely, firms facing strong competition might be forced to concentrate only on short-term survival and might in any case lack the necessary funds for extensive and financially risky research. This latter point is particularly important as the internal funds of firms (ploughed-back profits) are an important source of research and investment funds.

Nationalised industries

One obvious approach towards monopoly policy is nationalisation. There are many, however, who believe (despite the lack of conclusive evidence), that cost inefficiency is inevitable in nationalised industries. This suggests that nationalisation is not a complete remedy. Whatever is the case, the policy towards nationalised industries, and their actual behaviour, has important implications for the overall efficiency of resource allocation. Having worked through this chapter the student should re-read Chapter 19 on nationalised industries for a full discussion of the problem.

Externalities: a case for intervention?

We saw in the last chapter that, when there are negative externalities associated with production, there will tend to be an *over-supply* of the product in question. We now consider six forms of market 'correction'.

Fees and subsidies

The government might force the firm to pay a fee (indirect tax) on each unit of output, the amount of the fee corresponding to the *external marginal cost*. Similarly, appropriate subsidies

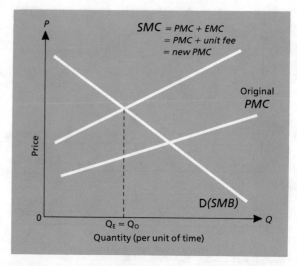

Fig. 27.3 *The effect of the imposition of a fee (tax) to counteract negative externalities*
The imposition of the fee moves the equilibrium to the socially efficient level where SMC = SMB.

could be given to generators of positive externalities. In either case the intention would be to bring private costs and benefits in line with social costs and benefits so as to prevent allocative inefficiency.

Figure 27.3 illustrates a case of a negative externality caused by pollution. A fee charged on each unit of production has the same effect as an increase in the costs of production. If this fee accurately reflects the external marginal cost the firm is now in effect having to pay for the use of the environment. The externality has then, in a sense, been *internalised* and is thus now taken account of by profit maximising firms.

As can be seen in the diagram, the market equilibrium (Q_E) after the imposition of the fee will now correspond to the socially efficient level of output Q_O. It is important that the fee be flexible so that it can be varied with changes in *EMC*. This is because there are long-term benefits from a fee which is effectively charged on the pollution, rather than a tax placed on the product itself. If the fee is seen as payment for the use of the environment, then there will be a substitution effect away from using this, now costed, factor of production and towards other factors, e.g. pollution-reducing devices. Moreover there will be an incentive for research directed towards economising on the use of the environment.

Regulation

Where a negative externality exists firms could be prohibited by law from producing more than the socially efficient output. If it is the quantity of the product itself, however, that is regulated there will be no incentive for firms to reduce the level of pollution associated with each level of production. A more efficient form of quota would therefore be one which placed a legal maximum on the amount of pollution that the firm can produce.

A total ban on the product

Figure 27.4 compares the welfare loss caused by the externalities of producing a product with the welfare loss brought about by banning the product. If the free market or profit maximising output (Q_E) is compared with the socially

efficient output (Q_O), it can be seen that there is an associated welfare loss equal to the area of the shaded triangle marked A. Conversely if a zero output is compared with the socially efficient output then the welfare loss would be equal to the area of the shaded triangle marked B. This indicates that banning the polluting product might involve a greater welfare loss than not attempting to control pollution at all.

A total ban on pollution

If producers find it impossible to eliminate pollution from their production process, then a ban on pollution will in effect be the same as the previous case in which the product itself was banned. The banning of pollution rather than the product might cause producers to discover or adopt methods of eliminating the pollution, but if the total costs of the required modifications are greater than the amount which the consumers would be prepared to pay to get rid of the pollution, then the result might be a loss of welfare rather than a gain. This is because the resource costs will have outweighed the benefits from the reduction in pollution.

Nationalisation

This option has already been examined. Briefly we could argue that firms with associated externalities could be taken into public ownership and their output controlled to take account of social costs and benefits. Some commentators would argue that this is likely to lead to cost inefficiency.

A bargaining solution

An important hypothesis of modern welfare economics is known as the *Coase theorem*. Put very simply, this theorem states that:

If there are no transaction costs and no restrictions on contracts, then there is no problem of externality as any misallocation of resources is put right by bargaining among the parties concerned.

We saw the possibility of this in the last chapter

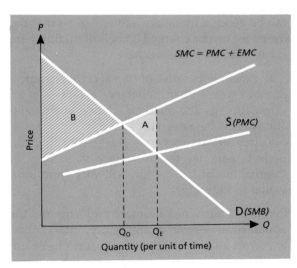

Fig. 27.4 *A total ban on a product*
Q_E represents the free-market equilibrium and Q_O the socially efficient output: thus the shaded area A represents the welfare loss. A total ban on the product would reduce output to zero and thus the shaded area B would now represent the welfare loss.

325

when discussing the negative externality caused by congestion (*see* page 315). You will recall that at levels of road use below the point of social efficiency, motorists could compensate those who suffer from the negative externalities and still enjoy a net increase in welfare from an extra unit of car travel. Similarly, at levels of road use above the socially efficient point, those suffering from the associated externalities could compensate motorists for the loss of their marginal journey and still enjoy a net increase in welfare. In each of these cases the level of road use would be adjusted to the socially efficient level by the gainers compensating those that would have otherwise have lost welfare. The surprising prediction of the Coase theorem is thus that no matter what the legal position, regarding who must compensate whom, the output after bargaining will be socially efficient. This consideration, that if *SMB* is not equal to *SMC* then potential gainers can compensate potential losers and still enjoy a net increase in welfare, is the basis of what is known as *cost–benefit analysis* and is examined in more detail at the end of this chapter.

A digression: the Coase theorem in practice

An interesting example of the Coase theorem in operation has been provided by Cheung (S. N. S. Cheung, 'The fable of the bees: an economic investigation', *Journal of Law and Economics*, vol. 16, April 1973). Economists in the past have often used the example of bees and orchards as a demonstration of positive externalities. Bees, it is pointed out, pollinate fruit trees which provides benefits for fruit growers. Bee-keepers also benefit in that the fruit trees provide nectar for their bees. This appears to be a clear case of positive externalities as bee-keepers cannot enforce property rights (they cannot, for example, order their bees to stay out of the orchard) and thus collect a price for the services of the bees. Similarly, orchard owners have no legal right to insist on a price for the nectar extracted from their trees. As these benefits are not directly reflected in the normal workings of the price mechanism, our theory suggests that under-production of both honey and fruit would result. Cheung in fact discovered that it was often the case that fruit growers would pay bee-keepers for their pollination of trees which gave little suitable nectar. Conversely, bee-keepers often paid orchard owners for the privilege of grazing their bees on those fruit trees providing better-quality nectar. Moreover, Cheung calculated that the fees paid were consistent with the theoretical prediction of what would be appropriate.

We must now ask, however, why externalities such as pollution and congestion are not *internalised* through such bargaining. The answer is that where the parties involved are numerous and/or difficult to identify, the transaction and administration costs of such bargaining procedures are likely to outweigh the benefits. Thus bargaining solutions are usually relevant to small groups only.

Problems of measurement

In designing a policy to deal with externalities it is obviously important that the external effects can be given a monetary value, e.g. so that the *correct* fee can be charged on pollution. But there are two major problems here.

a) Precisely because of its nature, consumers do not express their monetary valuations of an externality in the market. Hence such valuations must be assessed.

b) In contrast to goods freely consumed in perfect markets, the monetary valuations of externalities at the margin will vary from individual to individual.

Because of such measurement problems and the administrative costs of any policy, intervention to correct all externalities would seem to be unjustified. However in many cases the external effect will be of such magnitude that even inexact and/or costly intervention may be preferable to none.

As we shall see, cost–benefit analysis (CBA) does attempt to place monetary values on the external effects of various economic activities. For example, in a CBA of the Victoria underground railway in London it was concluded that, although the line would run at a financial loss, the social benefits in terms of reduced road traffic congestion justified its subsidisation.

Practical problems of providing public goods

Free riding

The provision of pure public goods cannot be left to the market as *non-excludability* makes it impossible to charge for their use. The problem is known as *free riding*, i.e. because all consumers automatically benefit from the provision of public goods, they withhold payment hoping to enjoy the benefits of free charge.

Problems of calculating the *SMC*s and *SMB*s

In the last chapter we saw that the theoretical solution was simple; public goods should be provided up until the point at which *SMC* equals *SMB*. In practice, though, not only is there the practical problem of calculating *SMC*, which we have already discussed, but there is also the problem of calculating *SMB*. You will recall that *SMB* for a public good is the vertical summation of the *PMB*s of consumers. Suppose that a government attempts to achieve an efficient volume of production of a public good and therefore asks consumers how much they would be willing to pay for marginal increases in the production of the public good in question, i.e. the *PMC* of consumers.

If consumers realise that an increase in production will have less than proportionate effects upon their tax bills, they are likely to exaggerate their willingness to pay, e.g. motorists might exaggerate their demand for better roads if they know that all taxpayers, including non-motorists, will share the final bill. Conversely, if consumers are told that they will have to pay in accordance

with their expressed willingness to pay, they are likely to understate their true willingness to pay. This is because, if they are each one of many consumers, they know that their declared demand will have little effect upon the final provision of the public good, but, under the circumstances given to them, it will determine how much they personally have to pay. In understating their true demand they are hoping to enjoy the public good at a *price* below that of their actual valuation. In both cases declared willingness to pay will differ from actual *PMB*; hence the government's estimate of *SMB* will not reflect the *true* level of demand.

Non-excludability and non-rivalry

Although *non-excludability* is important, the element of *non-rivalry* is more common. Hence there are few cases where collective goods *must* be provided at zero cost; for example, tolls on roads and bridges could be charged and they would thus provide information as to the true willingness to pay. The disadvantage here is that welfare economics suggests that no charge should be made for goods collectively consumed; i.e. where consumption by one person does not prevent the consumption of the same unit by others. The argument is that, although there is a cost in providing extra units of the public or collective good, there is no cost involved in supplying additional consumers with those units of the public good already in existence. Hence the marginal cost of providing the existing units of public good to a consumer is zero. Our condition for social efficiency, in the absence of externalities – *P* equals *MC* – thus suggests that no charge should be made to consumers.

We can illustrate the above argument by considering a bridge, for the use of which a toll is charged. This toll will deter some potential users from crossing the bridge and will thus result in a loss of welfare, i.e. these persons *could* have used the bridge at no cost to anyone else. Fig. 27.5 illustrates the loss in welfare involved.

This raises the obvious problem of how the provision of public or collective goods in general **327**

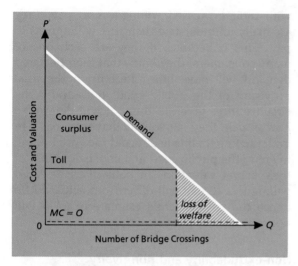

Fig. 27.5 *The effect of a toll on the level of welfare from a public good with a marginal cost of zero*

should be financed. The efficiency aspects of government taxation and borrowing must thus also be taken into account. For example, taxation can have disincentive effects on work, and investment and borrowing might 'crowd out' more valued investments by diverting finance from the private sector.

Policy towards merit goods

Although the concept of merit goods is rather subtle, the policy implications are clear. The state can subsidise products thought to be 'good for you', e.g. Shakespearian productions, and, conversely, tax or ban those thought to be 'bad for you', e.g. drugs, tobacco, gambling and pornography.

Imperfect information

Providing information

As suggested in the previous chapter, the problem of uncertainty is ubiquitous. To a certain extent the free market can itself overcome this problem. For example, as consumers are often

ignorant of the range and qualities of goods

available, it might be possible to increase their welfare by supplying them with this information. However consumers will be willing to pay for such information; hence the price mechanism will provide incentives for the collection and sale of such information. *Exchange and Mart, Car Buyers' Magazine* and *Which?* are examples of publications which sell information.

Many forms of ignorance may not be corrected at all by the price mechanism. For example, a tobacco manufacturer is unlikely to spend millions of pounds on an anti-smoking campaign! Indeed, many governments have felt it necessary to pass laws concerning misleading and, sometimes, merely *persuasive* advertising. Governments can also increase the flow of information by setting up or subsidising consumer associations, introducing compulsory labelling, standardisation of products, providing information about potential employees and vacancies through Job Centres and disseminating information about investment opportunities, e.g. through regional development boards. The government can also respond to what it sees as imperfections in the finance market caused by uncertainty, e.g. by providing funds for projects through the British Technology Group. Governments can also take steps to lessen the incentive to provide incorrect information and lessen its effects on consumers, e.g. by passing consumer protection legislation.

Search theory again

The determination of the socially efficient level of information raises problems which seem extremely difficult to resolve. The heart of these problems is that the optimal level of search and research cannot be determined unless the expected returns can be specified. However in most cases this will be impossible as the information sought is, by defination, unknown. In short, the assumption of perfect information about information would make the idea of search nonsensical, but without this assumption we cannot apply our conventional condition for efficiency, i.e. $SMC = SMB$, as SMB cannot be known.

What the economist can point out, however, is that information gathering involves costs in terms of both time and resources. It is therefore most unlikely that complete information would, in the real world, be efficient, e.g. for the consumer complete information would almost certainly imply that the marginal costs of search have exceeded the marginal benefits. The conclusion must be that complete information is not optimal as the marginal costs of obtaining this information would almost certainly be greater than its marginal benefit.

This is an extremely important conclusion. It suggests, for example, that firms which seek to maximise profits in the real world will not in fact obtain the whole of potential profit. Instead such firms will collect information up until the point at which they estimate that the costs of further search would outweigh the benefits. They will thus base their estimates of the profit maximising price, etc., on incomplete information. It follows that actual profits are likely to be less than the potential profits that could have been obtained if information were more complete.

Excludability and information

The economist can also point out that information often has the characteristics of a public good. Hence free riding could lead to too little being spent on research and development in a laissez-faire economy. *Excludability* might be possible in some cases, e.g. patent laws, but then the *non-rival* aspect of information seems to be an argument against charging for the use of information. In addition some observers feel that the patenting of an invention can block further technical progress, e.g. some economic historians have suggested that James Watt, by patenting his steam engine (he did not if fact invent the first such device), did more to retard the development of industry than to advance it. There would thus seem to be a strong case for government intervention in the provision of information, e.g. subsidies or government sponsored research, even though the precise level at which the production of information is socially efficient is difficult to identify.

The theory of second best

Up until now we have considered only situations in which the conditions necessary for Pareto optimality are violated one at a time. We have assumed that the conditions stated in the first optimality theorem hold in all other respects and in all other markets. We then identify the policy, at least in principle, which would bring about a 'first best solution'. However in situations where there is more than one imperfection (i.e the real world!) the theory of 'second best' is relevant. For example, suppose a government decides to 'correct' a negative externality produced by a private good which is produced by a monopolist. The theory of first best could prescribe imposing a tax equal to EMC, but this could bring about the result shown in Fig. 27.6.

As can be seen in the diagram, the effect of the tax might be to move the equilibrium further

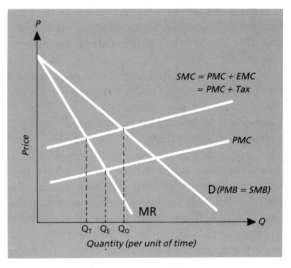

Fig. 27.6 *The theory of 'second best'*
The profit maximising-equilibrium before tax is Q_E. The desired equilibrium is Q_O, but the imposition of a tax equal to the *EMC* moves the equilibrium in the opposite direction to Q_T.

away from the socially efficient output rather than having the intended effect. Similarly it can be shown that, in the absence of externalities, setting price equal to marginal cost in one market will only be socially efficient if all other prices are set equal to their respective marginal costs. This has an important implication for the application of marginal cost pricing in the nationalised industries. Here the policymaker would probably be wrong in assuming an equality between MC and price in the private sector. As the private sector is characterised by oligopoly and monopoly, it is probably the case that private sector prices in general exceed marginal cost. The theory of second best suggests that prices in the nationalised industries should thus also be set above MC as 'over'-consumption and -production of the products of nationalised industries would result if prices were to be set equal to marginal cost in these circumstances. For example, if prices in the private sector are on average 8 per cent higher than MC, then this margin should also be included in nationalised industries' prices so as to produce a 'correct balance' of resource allocation between the private and public sectors of the economy.

When the theory of second best was first put forward by Lipsey and Lancaster, it was implied that this rendered the application of modern welfare economics to the real world a hopeless task. It was argued that the information needed about the economy in order to apply the theory of second best it prohibitively vast. This of course, if true, would be an important result.

However others have questioned this view. They argue that much more is known about real economies than when the theory of second best was first formulated and that this makes the computation of second best solutions more feasible. They therefore argue that it is important to continue the development and refining of the pure theory of welfare economics in the hope that the necessary information might one day be known. Whatever the truth of the matter, it does seem to be the case that modern welfare economics has, through its rigour, provided penetrating insights into the successes and failures of market economies. As Samuelson has put it:

Even if perfect competition were a poorer descriptive tool than it is, students of economies would still want to study it intensively and master its principles. This is so for a reason unconnected with mere description. The competitive model is extremely important in providing a benchmark to appraise the 'efficiency' of an economic system. Russians, Chinese, Indians, as well as the Swiss, need to study its analytical principles.

The maximisation of social welfare

Pareto and equity

So far we have examined only the efficiency aspects of market economies. However social welfare involves considerations of the best allocation of resources *and* the best distribution of products among the members of society. It is desirable of course that, other things being constant, the configuration of the economy is efficient, but we must also ask the question 'Is it fair?' The Pareto criterion is inapplicable to such questions. For example, suppose that society consisted only of the very rich and the very poor; there is nothing in the Pareto criterion which suggests that a redistribution of income should take place. As long as a redistribution of income would *necessarily* reduce the welfare of the rich, the existing situation would be Pareto efficient, but to any policymaker the concept of social welfare will involve both efficiency *and* equity considerations. It should be clear that questions of equity can only be answered by reference to normative criteria, i.e. subjectively.

Changes in social welfare

From the above it is clear that the desirability of any economic changes does not depend on efficiency alone and, that in presenting an appraisal of such changes, the economist should include the equity aspects as well as the efficiency aspects. In practice these considerations often conflict, e.g. subsidies might be used to protect jobs in low-productivity coal mines even though the total value of the nation's output could be increased by closing these mines and allowing the price mechanism to reallocate the freed resources to other industries. Hence, although regional policy (*see* Chapter 13) may be used to offset imperfections and frictions to the workings of the price mechanism, it is also often justified in terms of equity improvements, even if this involves a potential loss of efficiency.

The reader might be wondering how the two criteria conflict in such circumstances. Surely a Pareto improvement implies no-one has lost, even though someone has gained? The answer is that, unfortunately, most economic changes in the real world do hurt someone. And even if it were theoretically possible for the gainers to compensate the losers and still be better off themselves, this is rarely done in practice. If then we were only willing to undertake projects if an actual Pareto improvement results, we would be unable to appraise the desirability of most important potential economic changes.

To compare situations which involve some people gaining at the expense of others we need what is known as a *social welfare function*. Such a function must necessarily involve the subjective considerations of the policymaker. In an economy of just two consumers a social welfare function would have the following form:

Change in social welfare	=	Change in consumer A's utility	×	The social weighting of consumer A's utility	+
		Change in consumer B's utility	×	The social weighting of consumer B's utility	

Social weighting

The social weights must be determined subjectively by the policymaker. There is nothing in economic theory to suggest what these weights

should be. They depend, ultimately, on the policymaker's own subjective judgment. Indeed, the advantage of formulating a social welfare function is that *it forces policymakers to identify and declare exactly the value judgments they have made*. It should also be realised that changes in consumers' utility cannot be directly measured; utility is an abstract theoretical tool. Here the techniques of cost–benefit analysis must be used in order to estimate the changes in utility in terms of monetary units. This, basically, involves measuring how much the potential gainers from a project would be prepared to pay to bring about the proposed change and, conversely, how much money the potential losers would require to compensate them for the proposed change. These values can then be thought of as the equivalent increase in income to the gainers from the project and the equivalent decrease in income to the losers. The social welfare function could then be used to appraise the desirability of the project by taking the equivalent changes in income and multiplying them by their respective social weights. Table 27.1 shows a hypothetical example of this.

Table 27.1 An example of the social weighting of a project

Person	Equivalent change in income	Social weighting	Contribution to social welfare
A (rich)	+£400	$\frac{1}{2}$	+£200
B (poor)	−£100	$2\frac{1}{2}$	−£250
Net change in social welfare			−£ 50

Given the weights in Table 27.1, we can see that although a potential Pareto improvement is possible, in that A could compensate B and still enjoy a net increase in welfare, in the absence of such compensation *the project is deemed by the policymaker to be undesirable*. Obviously if the rich did actually compensate the poor the project would pass the test. Hence Pareto improvements can be considered as a special case where all the changes in utility are positive (or at least non-negative).

Altering the distribution of wealth and income

The problem

From our discussion of social welfare we can see that even if the allocation of resources were socially efficient in the Pareto sense, a government is likely to intervene to change the distribution of income and/or wealth in the pursuit of equity and/or justice. However the policymaker should take into account the fact that the imposition of taxes is, in itself, likely to lead to efficiency losses. For example, taxes on commodities will cause a divergence between SMC and SMB and, hence, as we have seen, will cause a loss of potential welfare. On the other hand, taxes on income will mean that workers will receive less than the value of their marginal product. Many economists believe that this will have significant net disincentive effects. It should be noted that the latter point is controversial (*see below*). Nevertheless governments might want to take account of the possibility of a trade-off between equality and national income.

The Laffer curve

There is the possibility, pointed out by Professor Art Laffer of the USA, that increasing tax rates might, because of disincentive effects, actually lower tax revenue. Laffer based his argument on the logic that tax revenue would be zero if tax rates were either zero or 100 per cent. If they were zero then obviously no tax would be collected; if they were 100 per cent all of one's income would be taken in tax and hence there would be no incentive to work and no income to tax. As tax revenue is positive between these two extremes, Laffer concluded that there must be a tax rate at which tax revenue is maximised.

In fact Michael Beenstock of the London Business School has estimated a 'Laffer curve' for the UK. His results are summarised in Fig. 27.7.

Tax revenue and GDP

Beenstock's estimates suggest that a peak in tax revenue would be reached at an average tax rate of around 60 per cent; only those with an overriding passion for equality would be prepared to squeeze out the last drops of potential tax revenue. This is because, due to the rounded top of the Laffer curve, these last drops are at the expense of comparatively large increases in the average tax rate. As Beenstock went on to demonstrate, these tax increases are likely to have adverse effects on GDP. Hence the policymaker is likely to decide that once a certain level of tax has been reached further gains in equity are more than offset by losses in efficiency. Beenstock summarised his finding in a chart similar to that in Fig. 27.8.

The chart should be read as follows. Starting at the top of the curve, it can be seen that increasing tax revenue has an adverse effect on GDP. Tax revenue can be increased, however, until point A is reached. Point A thus corresponds to the peak of the Laffer curve. Points below A are inefficient since the same tax revenue is possible but with a lower GDP.

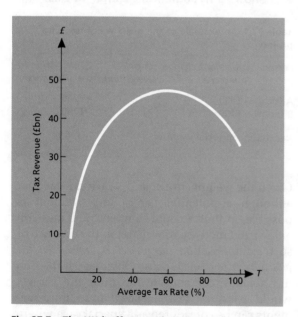

Fig. 27.7 *The UK 'Laffer curve', 1977*
Based on Michael Beenstock, 'Taxation and incentives in the UK', Lloyd's Bank Review, Oct. 1979

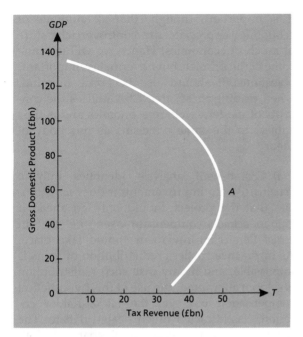

Fig. 27.8 Estimated trade-off between tax revenue and GDP in the UK, 1977
Based on Michael Beenstock, op. cit.

It cannot be stressed too strongly that Beenstock's results are highly speculative and have been criticised by other writers. In particular, as Beenstock himself points out, the evidence about disincentive effects (or income versus substitution effects) is not conclusive. Nevertheless the above has illustrated important possibilities and principles that policymakers should be aware of. (*See* pages 557–561.)

Cost–benefit analysis

Definition

This branch of economics is the result of the practical application of modern welfare economics to public sector decision-making. Put simply, it attempts to evaluate the social costs and benefits of proposed investment projects as a guide when deciding upon the desirability of these projects. Cost–benefit analysis (CBA) differs from ordinary investment appraisal in that the latter considers only private costs and benefits. In short, it is intended to enable the decision-maker to choose between alternative projects on the basis of their potential contribution to social welfare.

E. J. Mishan, perhaps the leading authority on CBA, has summarised CBA concisely as follows:

It transpires that the realisation of practically all proposed cost–benefit criteria . . . implies a concept of social betterment that amounts to a potential Pareto improvement. The project in question, to be considered as economically feasible, must, that is, be capable of producing an excess of benefits such that everyone in society could, by costless redistribution of the gains, be made better off.

The Hicks–Kaldor criterion

Recall that in our example of the application of a social welfare function (*see* page 331) the benefits of £400 were received wholly by the rich and the costs of £100 were borne solely by the poor. Nevertheless, given the criteria outlined by Mishan, the project would pass the test of CBA, i.e. the gainers could *in principle* compensate the losers and still enjoy a net increase in welfare. This test of the potential for a Pareto improvement is known as the *Hicks–Kaldor criterion*.

The major difficulty in attempting CBA stems from the fact that, in a world where imperfect competition, externalities and ignorance abound, market price will not reflect the true social costs and benefits. The cost–benefit analysis thus estimates *shadow prices*. These are imputed prices which are intended to reflect more faithfully the true social costs and benefits of a project. For example, the value of the time saved by an individual following an improvement in transport facilities is often approximated using that person's average hourly wage. The Roskill Commission used the depreciation in house prices around Gatwick Airport in estimating the likely value of the negative externality that would be caused by a third London airport.

Cost–benefit analysis: an example

Cost–benefit techniques have been used for many purposes but particularly in town planning and transport. A recent and fairly typical example is the cost–benefit study commissioned by the Covent Garden Market Authority. This study attempted to ascertain whether the relocation, at Nine Elms, Vauxhall, of the London horticultural wholesale market formerly at Covent Garden, had proved worthwhile. The results of the study are summarised in Table 27.2. The researchers estimated the net return on the capital investment involved at 16 per cent. As this rate exceeded that commonly required and received for most public enterprises, the researchers concluded that the move had been worthwhile.

Table 27.2 Study of costs and benefits of relocating Covent Garden

Operational costs and benefits	Net benefits (£000 per annum)
Labour and machinery use	200
Saving of waiting time:	
Delivery vehicles	500
Wholesalers' collection vehicles	100
Retailers (various aspects)	500
Reduction of wastage and pilferage	1420
Administration and maintenance	nil
Traffic flow	no estimate
Value of land released at Covent Garden	3000
Total	£5720

Source: J. H. Kirk and M. J. Sloyan, 'Cost-benefit study of the new Covent Garden market', Public Administration, Spring, 1978, pp 35–49, reprinted in L. Wagner (ed.), Readings in Applied Microeconomies, *2nd Edition*, OUP, 1981

Criticisms of cost–benefit analysis and welfare economics

There are many criticisms of this field of economics, some of which are extremely technical.

It is important, though, that all students of economics appreciate the controversial nature of much of economics. Hence we will examine some of the simpler, but nevertheless important, objections. It should also be borne in mind, when reading these, that CBA utilises the concepts of modern welfare economics and is thus subject to the same criticisms as this body of theory.

a) Cost–benefit analysis identifies only a *potential* Pareto improvement; it does *not* stipulate that the project should only go ahead if gainers *actually* compensate losers, i.e. that an *actual* Pareto improvement should take place. As in practice costless redistribution of gains is impossible, and in any case such redistribution is seldom attempted, the use of this hypothetical compensation test, i.e. the Hicks–Kaldor criterion, has attracted much heated debate. The details of this debate are somewhat technical. Suffice it to say that the majority opinion appears to be that the Hicks–Kaldor criterion does not sufficiently incorporate considerations of equity. For example, when discussing social welfare functions, we saw that although a potential Pareto improvement might be identified, consideration of the actual consequences of the project might lead to it being rejected on grounds of equity. The problem in the social welfare function approach lies in agreeing on the social weighting to be given to the gains and losses of the different income groups. Another method, used by the Roskill Commission, is simply to supplement the hypothetical compensation test with a separate list of the gains and losses as they would accrue to different income groups. This then, in effect, simply leaves open the question of the social weighting to be given.

b) The money values placed on intangibles such as the 'value' of the environment are extremely speculative. We have already noted the formidable problems which arise when attempting to estimate risk, measure the demand for public goods and account for the welfare of future generations. Many observers have complained that the methods used are often 'artificial', arbitrary and provide no means of cross-checking.

c) CBA often involves estimates of consumer surplus, but it can be shown that, unless extremely unlikely assumptions are made, conventional measures of consumer surplus will be inaccurate. A simple example of this is the commonly used assumption that demand curves are linear, i.e. straight lines. Since this is extremely unlikely, considerable inaccuracy results when changes in consumer surplus are estimated following large price changes. Indeed, one authority on CBA, I. M. D. Little, has gone so far as to suggest that consumer surplus is 'a totally useless theoretical toy'.

d) Welfare economics is ultimately normative and this led early on to criticisms from *positivists* who felt that normative issues should not be the concern of the economists.

e) Some writers have reacted against the abstract nature of welfare economics. Often this simply reflects the lack of understanding of the observer; they fail to realise that *all* theory is abstract, including one's own! However it can be meant in a deeper sense; sometimes it reflects the view that welfare economics (and indeed general equilibrium analysis in general) has shifted the emphasis in economics towards the formalisation of purely logical problems and away from the production of testable theories of actual economic behaviour. This should be taken seriously, but it should also be noted that ultimately theory is indispensable to analysis and it is thus desirable that the theory be refined and developed in readiness for a time when it might be possible to apply it. In any case, pure theory does not prohibit other forms of research and perhaps too often its *critics are guilty of wishing to replace analysis with mere description*. At a still deeper level, many radical economists argue that the 'liberal' assumptions of welfare economics obscure the more important questions of the formation of tastes and the nature and origins of prevailing culture.

f) Some economists feel that welfare economics concentrates on relatively insignificant welfare losses and ignores the far more important losses caused by cost inefficiency, e.g. in complacent monopolies (sometimes known as the 'X-inefficiency') and the loss of welfare caused by unemployment. This may be a valid criticism if the social returns to the development of welfare economics have been less than the social costs! However it hardly seems fair to criticise a body of theory simply because it does not provide answers to all the questions one would like answered.

The Austrian School

More recently a school of thought known as the 'Austrian School' has been increasingly used as a theoretical basis for the support of free market capitalism. The term 'Austrian' refers to the School's beginnings in Vienna rather than to the nationality of its modern followers. This school of thought differs in important respects from the modern 'neo-classical' welfare economics that we have been examining in the rest of this section. We are using the term 'neo-classical' here as referring to that economic analysis which is based on utility or profit maximising equilibriums under perfectly competitive conditions. The two schools both stem from the 'marginalist' revolution in economic theory in the 1870s, and thus they have much in common. An example of this is that they both place an emphasis on explaining economic phenomena in terms of the choices made by utility maximising individuals. However, the Austrian School has come to be distinguished by its insistence that markets can only work effectively in the complete absence of government 'interference' or of restrictions on the choices of buyers and sellers.

Austrian economics is also distinguished from neo-classical economics in that it gives far less stress to the concept of equilibrium. The neo-classical welfare economics which we have looked at is based on the conditions which hold in equilibrium, whereas the Austrian school stresses the desirable welfare effects produced by the *dynamic* competitive processes which are generated by market forces within free market *capitalism*. For Austrian economists it is the process of learning and discovery which is made possible by free market systems that is the major source of economic welfare. Indeed, for many Austrian economists economic welfare is increased through time by allowing firms to compete for monopoly power. According to this perspective, prospective monopoly profit is the spur necessary to induce firms to undertake risky and expensive innovations designed to capture or maintain a monopoly position. The welfare gains to consumers from the 'gales of creative destruction', generated as firms compete for tenuous monopoly positions, are seen as far outweighing any static welfare losses arising from deviations of price from cost at the margin.

Conclusion

Welfare economics is a difficult and controversial area of modern economics. The concepts on which it is based are suspect and the conditions it assumes are so far removed from actual real-world conditions that it is of limited use to policy-makers. Nevertheless, it has, through CBA and the public sector, had serious applications. The reason it is worth studying is that it deals with a central and inevitable question arising from microeconomics, i.e. 'What is meant by the *best* allocation and distribution of resources and what is the relationship between this ideal and actual economic systems?' This question stems directly from the economic problem of scarcity and choice and it thus seems ridiculous for economists to reply 'I've never really thought about it.' If nothing else, not only has modern welfare economics forced us to state exactly what we mean by such terms as *efficiency* and to state clearly the value judgments we are making, but it has also identified and illustrated many of the formidable problems in attempting to use economic theory to make the world a 'better place'.

Summary

1 Government intervention in markets by way of indirect taxes or subsidies is likely to lead to a welfare loss.

2 Externalities can be either positive or negative. They may be counter-balanced either by fees (taxes) or subsidies. Most other ways of dealing with externalities lead to a loss of welfare.

3 The Coase theorem maintains that under certain conditions misallocation of resources will be corrected by bargaining between the parties concerned.

4 There are almost insurmountable problems in determining the most welfare-efficient output of public goods.

5 Imperfect knowledge remains a major source of inefficiency in resource allocation.

6 The theory of second-best applies when more than one of the conditions for Pareto optimality breaks down.

7 There is nothing in Pareto optimality which suggests that redistribution of income should take place, but the modern welfare economist will be concerned with considerations of equity as well as efficiency.

8 It has been argued that attempts to redistribute income and wealth bring about disincentives as well as inefficiency. However this is a very vexed area of theory.

9   Cost–benefit analysis attempts to evaluate projects in terms of their total costs and benefits to society, for example, by considering externalities as well as other costs.

10   Welfare economics with all its faults remains the only tool we have for analysing these problems. If we were to throw it overboard because of its many shortcomings there is no comparable theory to put in its place.

Questions

1   If subsidies cause a welfare loss, defend the decision to subsidise school meals.

2   Assuming a socially efficient allocation of resources, explain why a tax placed on a commodity will lead to a loss of potential welfare. Illustrate your answer with a diagram.

3   Assume an economy with perfect competition in all markets, no externalities and no uncertainty. You are given the following data regarding a product which is produced domestically but which can also be imported:

Price per unit (£)	5	4·5	4	3·5	3	2·5	2	1·5	1
Domestic demand (units)	0	20	40	60	80	100	120	140	160
Domestic supply (units)	160	140	120	100	80	60	40	20	0

World supply is perfectly elastic at a price of £2 per unit. Calculate the welfare loss to society of a tariff placed on imports of 50p per unit.

4   Can it be proved that the banning of abortion is Pareto inefficient? Explain your answer.

5   Show how a subsidy might be used to correct for *under-production* in the case of a product which has external benefits.

6   Under what circumstances would the socially efficient level of pollution be zero?

7   Figure 27.9 shows a teenager's benefit from his stereo system and a neighbour's disbenefit from the teenager's use of the said stereo system. Ignoring the costs involved in running the stereo system, show that bargaining between the teenager and the neighbour could, at least in principle, result in a socially efficient level of stereo system use. Is the final outcome affected by the allocation of compensation rights, i.e. who must compensate whom?

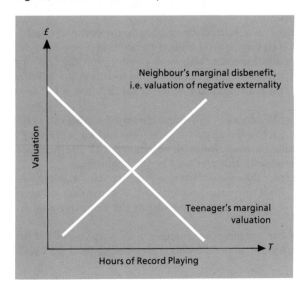

Fig. 27.9

8 *a*) Study the figures in Table 27.1 on page 331. Show that a different set of social weights could lead to a positive value for the net change in social welfare.

b) Does a positive value for the net change in social welfare *prove* that the project should go ahead?

c) Show, using the social weights given in Table 27.1, that appropriate compensation paid by A to B could result in the proposed project passing the test of desirability.

d) On what grounds might a proposed project be rejected even though all the estimated equivalent changes in income are positive?

9 Why would you expect a 'lump-sum poll tax', i.e. a fixed amount of tax which must be paid by everyone regardless of their income, to have no disincentive effects? What objections are likely to be raised against such a form of taxation?

10 'An unaided price mechanism ensures the best use of resources.' Discuss.

11 What are the arguments for and against using toll gates as a means of controlling traffic flow?

12 Discuss the view that welfare economics has demonstrated that free markets do not maximise social welfare but is of no use to the policymaker.

13 When might the existence of an externality call for government intervention?

Data response   No peace at Stansted ━━━━━━━━━━━━━━━━━━━━━━━━━━━━━━━

Read the following article carefully. It is condensed from an article in the *Herts and Essex Argus* of August 1987.

No peace at Stansted

By J R S Hawesbad

Industry Correspondent

The elaborate ceremony last week signalled the arrival of London's newest major airport. The 'topping out' ceremony was performed by Paul Channon the Transport Secretary. This ended over 30 years of argument over the site of London's third airport.

The huge expansion of Stansted which is likely to cost a total of around £800 million, answers the immediate problem by providing capacity up to 1995. But already the debate has begun, even before Stansted is half built, over where to site London's next airport.

Local opinion in the Herts and Essex region remains deeply divided on the pros and cons of the scheme.

Before any of the new construction had begun the cost of the public enquiry headed by Graham Eyre QC ran into several million pounds. Mrs Sue Forsyth, one of the leading objectors reiterated her protests last week pointing out the loss of amenity that will be caused by the expansion of the airport. Added to this is the fall in value of houses near to the site. The arrival of more traffic looks set to cause a bonanza for double-glazing salesmen.

Local estate agents, however, are not so gloomy. John Steven of Keith Stephen Ltd said the immediate impact of the airport had been to add an average of 15 per cent to house prices in surrounding areas. 'And with an estimated 10 000 more houses needed because of the airport' he added, 'this can only be the beginning'.

Positive support for the new airport also came from the Harlow Chamber of Commerce. Mr Alan Plater, the chairman, pointed to the expansion of employment which the development would bring. 'Our slogan during the campaign said it all. '*Jobs before garden parties*'.

Interviewed at the 'topping out' ceremony Mr N Payne of the BAA said that, 'By the year 2000 there are going to be 114 million air passengers at the London airport compared with today's 57 million. If we don't handle them then they will go to Schipol or Paris. The whole British economy will be the loser.'

One of the other oppenents still protesting at the expansion, Malcolm Bowler of the Green Party, put forward the environmental case. 'This is a crazy use of resources. There are tens of thousands of houses standing empty in the north of England and people crying out for jobs. The third airport should have gone to Manchester.'

The residents of Herts and Essex are going to have to live with the consequences of Stansted – good and bad. What seems tragic is that the whole process of selection is starting again as demand already outstrips supply for airport capacity. Isn't there a better way of arriving at a decision than the whole costly and tedious business of planning enquiries which seem to please no one?

Using the siting of Stansted airport as an example, evaluate the role of welfare economics and cost–benefit analysis as methods of determining the maximisation of social welfare in public policy decisions.

In your answer you should address yourself to the following points:

a) What is meant by social welfare?

b) Distinguish private costs from social costs.

c) Who will pay the social costs of Stansted?

d) What is meant by cost–benefit analysis?

e) What kind of alternative perspectives about the use of scarce resources are presented to planning enquiries?

f) What kind of economic analysis can you use to illustrate your answer?

3

Macroeconomics
V The determination of national income

28

The macroeconomy

Though Say's law is not an identity, his blundering exposition has led a long series of writers to believe that it is one.

Joseph A. Schumpeter

We are all Keynesians now.

Milton Friedman

The nature of the macroeconomy

In macroeconomics we are concerned with the behaviour of broad aggregates in the economy, e.g. the total level of investment or the volume of employment. To explain this we shall develop a model of the functioning of the economy. In microeconomic theory we are concerned with such things as the determination of the relative wage rates in particular industries, whereas in macroeconomics we are concerned with the general level of wages in the economy. Similarly a microeconomic view could be used to explain the determination of the relative prices of products, i.e. the price of one product in terms of other products, whereas in macroeconomics we are concerned with the general level of all prices in the economy.

We have already seen that there are some contrasts between the micro and macro views. In order to understand them more fully we must examine the components of the macroeconomy. Whilst doing this we must bear in mind that the micro and macro models are not entirely compatible. As Professor Lipsey says:

The student should beware of the essentialist belief that there is one true model and that debates between two theories should be settled according to which theory best approximates to the true model. Different theories and models may be best for different uses.

A classical view of the economy

Most microeconomic theory revolves around the idea of self-regulating markets. The forces of demand and supply reconcile the disparate aims of producers and consumers through the medium of prices. The equilibrium price clears the market, so that there are no unplanned additions to stocks (excess supply) and also no consumers planning to buy at present prices but unable to find a seller (excess demand). It is possible to view the whole economy as being governed by relative prices. This microeconomic view, in which all markets clear, is the *general equilibrium theory* which we met in Chapter 5.

At the beginning of the 19th century the French economist Jean-Baptiste Say (1767–1832) put forward the view that the free enterprise economy will automatically reach an equilibrium where there is no unemployment and no inflation. Any unemployment or inflation which exists can be only a temporary phenomenon. For example, Say argued that if there were unemployment then there would be an excess supply of labour; this would cause wages to fall and therefore employers would be more willing to employ labour; therefore unemployment would be cured. Most classical economists subscribed to this view.

A Keynesian view

The idea of a self-regulating economy became increasingly untenable during the 1930s when there was continuous chronic unemployment. The classical view was overturned by Keynes.

343

He argued that equilibrium in the economy was determined by *aggregate* demand and *aggregate* supply. Because these aggregates do not necessarily work in the same way as demand and supply in microeconomics, Keynes argued that it was possible for the economy to be in equilibrium when there was either unemployment or inflation. According to Keynes the coincidence of the equilibrium level of national income with full employment was a matter of chance. Say had argued, for example, that lower wages would create more demand for labour. Conversely Keynes said that, since wages are the largest component of aggregate demand, lower wages would lead to a lower demand for goods. In the face of this falling demand firms would further reduce their demand for labour. Thus employment and production are pushed into a downward spiral.

Thus the equilibrium which results from aggregate demand and supply is *not a market-clearing equilibrium*, i.e. it is possible for there to be unemployed resources, unplanned stocks of goods, or conversely, excess demand in the form of inflation, Keynes therefore argued that since the economy is not self-regulating it is necessary for the government to intervene to ensure a satisfactory level of national income. The failure of Keynesian policies in the 1970s lead some economists to advocate a return to market centred policies. Much of the policy of the Thatcher government was guided by this. We may call such economics the New Classical School or neo-classicists.

Before we can evaluate these arguments it is necessary that we first explain them more fully.

The circular flow of national income

Goods and money

In Chapter 7 we saw that there were two sides to the national product – national income and national expenditure. We thus established that:

$$Y = C + I + G + (X - M)$$

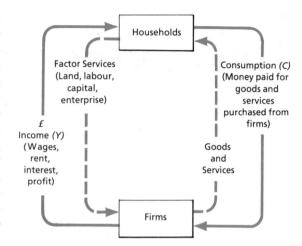

Fig. 28.1 *The flow of goods and money between households and firms*

We now wish to examine these components of national income more closely.

Figure 28.1 recapitulates the basic elements of the circular flow of income. Firms produce goods and services: households buy them. These components are thus identified not by who they are but by what they do, i.e. firms *produce* while households *consume*.

In our simple view of the economy the households own all the factors of production. Thus, in order to produce, the firms must hire *factor services* from households. On the other hand households buy goods from firms in return for which they pay money. The money received by households is termed income (*Y*) and the money spent by households is termed consumption (*C*).

You can see in Fig. 28.1 that goods and factor services flow one way round the diagram while money flows the other way. The flow of money and goods are said to be *counter-cyclical* to one another. Since there is always a counter-cyclical flow it is convenient to simplify our future diagrams by leaving out the flow of goods and to just show money flows. We shall also use abbreviations wherever possible.

Withdrawals and injections

If the value of consumption (*C*) were to equal

the value of income (Y) it would appear that there would be no tendency for the level of Y to change, in which case our economy could be said to be in equilibrium. However there are various factors which cause money to be withdrawn, or to 'leak', from the system and conversely there are also injections into it.

A withdrawal (W) is any part of income that is not passed on within the circular flow.

Savings are an example of a withdrawal. Savings may be undertaken by either households or by firms not distributing all their profits but retaining some to finance future development.

An injection (J) is an addition to the circular flow of income which does not come from the expenditure of domestic households.

The most obvious example of an injection is exports because the income of the firm selling them comes not from domestic households but from overseas. Less obviously, if a firm produces investment (or capital) goods and sells them to another firm this is an injection because the circular flow has been increased, even though this increase is not a result of extra spending by households.

The effect of an increase in withdrawals, other things being constant, is to reduce the circular flow of income, whereas an increase of injections will increase it. If the total of withdrawals is greater than that of injections then national income will contract. This is because the *planned* expenditure of the economy is insufficient to take up all the goods and services which the firms had *planned* to produce. Firms will therefore be faced with mounting stocks of unsold goods (inventories) and will, therefore, cut back on their output, thereby reducing the income of households. (Remember: the costs of the firm are the income of the households.)

Conversely, if injections are greater than withdrawals then the *planned* expenditure will be greater than the *planned* output of firms. Firms will therefore expand output and thereby raise the level of households' income.

If the total of all withdrawals (W) is equal to the total of injections (J) there will be no tendency for the level of national income to change and it is said to be in *equilibrium*. Thus the equilibrium condition for the economy is:

$$W = J$$

You will also have noticed an emphasis in this section on the word *planned*. Another way of stating the equilibrium would be to say that it occurs when the planned expenditure is equal to the planned output.

Components of national income

We have so far examined the nature of the circular flow and also the general effect of injections and withdrawals upon that flow. In this section we wish to describe and define the various injections and withdrawals which constitute the components of national income and to construct a simple model of the economy.

Savings and investment

The simplest model of the economy would be one in which there was no government and no foreign trade. This is referred to as *a closed economy with no government intervention*. Such an economy has only one sector, the private (i.e. households and firms), one withdrawal (savings) and one injection (investment). This is illustrated in Fig. 28.2.

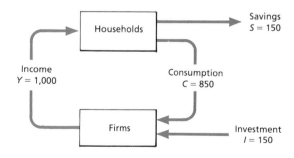

Fig. 28.2 *Savings and investment*
Because the amount of withdrawals ($S = 150$) is equal to the amount of injections ($I = 150$) there is no tendency for the level of income (Y) to change. The economy is said to be in equilibrium.

Savings (S) is defined as income not spent.

Savings might be undertaken by either house-holds or firms. With households, savings is simply a part of their income which they have not consumed. For firms, savings would consist of profits not distributed to shareholders. For the sake of simplicity in drawing the diagram we shall represent all savings as being under-taken by households.

Investment (I) is any addition to the real capital stock of the nation.

Investment therefore consists of the purchase of new capital equipment, the construction of new buildings and any additions to stocks. It is important to understand that investment is con-cerned with *real* capital goods and not with paper claims upon them. For example, the purchase of shares on a stock exchange is *not* investment, as used in this sense, because all that has happened is that the ownership of pieces of paper has changed but there has been no 'real' effect upon the economy.

In Fig. 28.2 a value has been put upon savings and investment and you can see that they are equal to each other. This economy is therefore in equilibrium because injections are equal to withdrawals.

Planned and actual values

What people plan to do and what actually happens may be two different things. Con-sider what would happen if people suddenly started to save much more; this would mean that spending on consumption would fall. Firms would therefore be left with increased stocks of unsold goods. Stocks, it will be re-membered, are capital goods and therefore investment. Thus, as savings go up, so does investment. Therefore *actual* savings equal *actual* investment. Conversely, if people save less then more must have been spent on con-sumption. Firms' stocks of unsold goods will therefore have gone down. Thus once again actual savings equal actual investment.

This we can demonstrate in the following

manner. Income is made up of spending on consumer goods and spending on investment goods, which we can write as:

$$Y = C + I$$

However, income received is divided between consumption and saving. This we can write as:

$$Y = C + S$$

Since both $C + S$ and $C + I$ are equal to Y, it must follow that:

$$C + I = C + S$$

C is common to both sides of the equation so that if we cancel it out we get:

$$I = S$$

It would therefore appear that actual savings will equal actual investment. However there is nothing to prevent the plans of savers and in-vestors from differing (savings and investment are different activities carried out by different people and for different motives). There must therefore be something at work which frustrates their plans. The thing which frustrates plans is the lack of supply or demand. In this model of the economy changes in factor incomes cause changes in the plans of consumers and pro-ducers until the two sets of plans are compatible.

If people planned to save more than actual investment then incomes would fall because withdrawals are greater than injections. This fall in income would continue until people are no longer able to afford to save more than is invested. Conversely, if planned investment was greater than saving then incomes would rise. The rise in income would bring about more saving so that saving would once again equal investment.

Therefore we can conclude that for an equi-librium to exist it is necessary for:

Planned savings = Planned investment

The open economy

An economy which takes part in international trade, as all do, is described as an open economy.

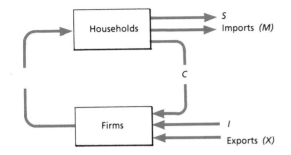

Fig. 28.3 *The open economy*
Imports (*M*) are a withdrawal from the circular flow and exports (*X*) an injection.

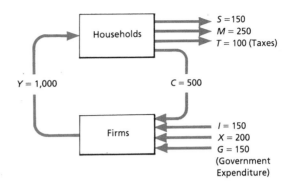

Fig. 28.4 *The complete model of the economy*
Taxes (*T*) are a withdrawal and government expenditure (*G*) an injection. This model of the economy is in equilibrium because the total of all withdrawal (*S* + *M* + *T*) is equal to the total of all injections (*I* + *X* + *G*).

The sale and purchase of goods and services overseas introduces two more components into our model. Imports (*M*) are a leakage because the money paid for them goes out of the economy and, conversely, exports (*X*) are an injection because people overseas are now creating income for domestic households and firms. Figure 28.3 shows foreign trade incorporated into our circular flow model. We have simplified matters by showing all imports being bought by households and all exports creating income for firms.

If imports are greater than exports then the economy is said to have a *trade deficit* and, other things being equal, this will cause the level of national income to fall. Conversely, if exports are greater than imports there is a *trade surplus* and, other things being equal, this will cause the level of national income to rise.

The government and the circular flow

Governments, both local and central, influence the circular flow of income. Taxes (*T*) are a withdrawal from the circular flow whereas government expenditure (*G*) is an injection. Once again in Fig. 28.4 we have reduced each to a single flow. Taxes might be levied on personal incomes, on expenditure or upon firms, but it is easier to show them as simply being paid by households. This will not destroy the validity of the model.

Earlier in this chapter we stated Keynes's view that the government should intervene in

the economy to regulate the level of economic activity. Keynes suggested that this should be done by varying the amount of government expenditure and taxes. Directing the economy in this manner is termed *fiscal policy*. If, for example, there was a deficiency of demand in the economy so that there was unemployment, the government could increase the level of aggregate demand by running a *budget deficit*, i.e. it could spend more than it collected in taxes. Conversely, if the government wanted to reduce the level of national income it could withdraw more from the economy in taxes than it put in by way of government expenditure. This would be termed a *budget surplus*.

The equilibrium of national income

We have now completed our simple model of the macroeconomy. You can see in Fig. 28.4 that there are three withdrawals (*W*) consisting of:

$$W = S + M + T$$

and three injections (*J*) consisting of:

$$J = I + X + G$$

The figures used in Fig. 28.4 indicate that the model is in equilibrium because withdrawals are equal to injections. As you can see it is not necessary for each withdrawal to be equal to its corresponding injection for an equilibrium to

347

exist, only that the total of all withdrawals is equal to the total of all injections. Thus the equilibrium occurs when:

$$S + M + T = I + X + G$$

or:

$$W = J$$

This model of the economy is developed in subsequent chapters.

It is worth restating that there is nothing necessarily desirable about an equilibrium level of national income. What we have tried to demonstrate is that there are equilibrium forces in an economy which push it towards a certain level of income. The significance of this is that our living standards, employment and well-being depend upon the level of national income. Hence the factors which determine its size are of great significance.

Summary

1 Macroeconomics deals with the broad aggregates in the economy such as employment and inflation.
2 Micro- and macroeconomics give us contrasting views of the economy.
3 The circular flow of national income is affected by injections and withdrawals. A withdrawal is any part of the income that is not passed on within the circular flow, whereas an injection is an addition to the circular flow which does not come from the expenditure of domestic households.
4 An equilibrium level of income is reached where withdrawals are equal to injections and where planned expenditure is equal to planned output.
5 Savings (S), imports (M) and taxes (T) are all withdrawals, whereas investments (I), exports (X) and government expenditure (G) are all injections.
6 An equilibrium level of an income is reached where:

$$S + M + T = I + X + G$$

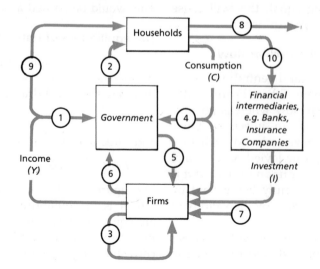

Questions

1 What is meant by the circular flow of income?

2 Distinguish between microeconomics and macroeconomics.

3 How would you fit unemployed workers into the circular flow diagram.

4 Study Fig. 28.5 which presents a more complex picture of the circular flow. Then try and match the following items with the numbered flow which best illustrates it.

a) Government payment of civil servants' salaries.

b) A UK householder's purchase of a Volkswagen.

c) Old-age pensioners' deposits in a building society.

d) A UK firm's sale of goods to a West African firm.

e) Income tax.

f) The government's purchase of arms from a munitions firm.

g) Disposable income.

h) A firm ploughs back profit by purchasing new equipment.

i) VAT.

j) Corporation tax.

Which of the above items are:

a) withdrawals;

b) injections;

c) neither?

5 Discuss the view that savings must always equal investment.

6 In a closed economy with no government intervention $C = 2 + 0.8Y$ and investment is constant at 50 units at all levels of income. What will be the equilibrium level of national income?

Data response The circular flow and national accounts ▬▬▬▬▬▬▬▬▬▬▬

The following data relates to the UK economy in 19xx.

	£ m
Consumers' expenditure	65 389
General government final consumption	23 118
Gross domestic fixed capital formation	21 035
Value of physical increase in stocks and work in progress	−1 354
Export of goods and services	27 007
Imports of goods and services	29 004
Taxes on expenditure	14 036
Subsidies	3 686

1 Construct a circular flow diagram to incorporate all these items.

2 Determine total domestic expenditure (TDE).

3 Determine gross domestic product (GDP) at factor cost.

4 Explain why, if taxes on expenditure are taken account of in this method of compilation of the national product, taxes on income are not.

5 If, as the National Accounts demonstrate national income, product and expenditure are always equal, how is it possible for the size of the national product to increase or decrease?

29

Consumption, savings and investment

The individual serves the industrial system not by supplying it with savings and the resulting capital, he serves it by consuming its product.
J. K. Galbraith

We have no more right to consume happiness without producing it than to consume wealth without producing it.
G. B. Shaw, *Candida*

Income and consumption

Consumers' expenditure (C) in the UK makes up the largest part of national expenditure, being 60 per cent of GDP at market prices (1985). This compares with 65 per cent in the USA and France. In West Germany and Japan the figures are lower, being 57 and 58 per cent respectively. Consumption is therefore the most important determinant of the level of national income. Conversely we shall see that the main determinant of consumption is the level of income. There is, therefore, a 'feedback mechanism' between the two.

Components of consumption

As the country has become wealthier over the years, people have been able to afford a wider range of goods and services and need to spend a smaller proportion of their expenditure on necessities. In 1938 food accounted for 30 per cent of all consumer spending, whereas in 1987 it was only 16.7 per cent. Spending upon durable goods such as furniture and cars, however, increased from 4·6 to 21·8 per cent over the same period. Thus although more is spent on more and better food it represents a smaller proportion of total expenditure. The amount spent on non-durables such as food remains much more con-

stant than that on durables such as cars. It is possible to see changes of demand of up to 25 per cent in a month for cars, whereas this is virtually inconceivable for food. (*See* page 426.)

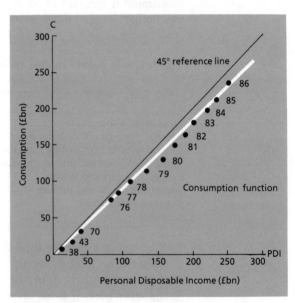

Fig. 29.1 *The consumption function*
This shows the amount of personal disposable income spent (consumed) in the UK in various years from 1938 to 1986. Most years are on or near the line of best fit. Note the dip in consumption in 1979 and 1980. The relationship between consumption and income is termed the consumption function.

The consumption function

As income increases, so does consumption. The proportion of income devoted to consumption, however, may decrease as income increases. Thus, although a greater amount would be consumed at higher levels of income, this would represent a smaller percentage of income. Figure 29.1 shows the amount of personal disposable income which has actually been consumed from 1938 to 1986. The 45° line on the diagram shows what would happen if all income were consumed. The line of best fit shows that the proportion of income consumed has gradually fallen over the years but remains reasonably stable from year to year. The relationship between consumption and income is referred to as the *consumption function*.

To advance the theory of national income a little further we will use a simplified version of the consumption function based on hypothetical data. We will, for the present, ignore foreign trade and government intervention. The figures in Table 29.1 show consumption increasing with income. What is not consumed must be saved and therefore we can calculate savings as:

$$S = Y - C$$

You can see that at very low levels of income consumption is actually greater than income so

that savings is a negative figure which is termed *dissaving*.

We can plot these figures graphically to obtain a picture similar to Fig. 29.1 National income (*Y*) is placed on the horizontal axis, whilst the amount of money devoted to the various components of national income, such as consumption and savings, is plotted on the vertical axis. This axis, therefore, measures *expenditure* (*E*). The 45° line shows all the points of equality between the two axes; hence mathematically its value may be said to be $E = Y$.

Figure 29.2 is constructed from the figures used in Table 29.1. The consumption function

Table 29.1 A consumption function

	National income, Y (£bn)	Planned consumption, C (£bn)	Planned savings, S (£bn)
A	0	30	−30
B	30	50	−20
C	60	70	−10
D	90	90	0
E	120	110	10
F	150	130	20
G	180	150	30
H	210	170	40
I	240	190	50
J	270	210	60
K	300	230	70

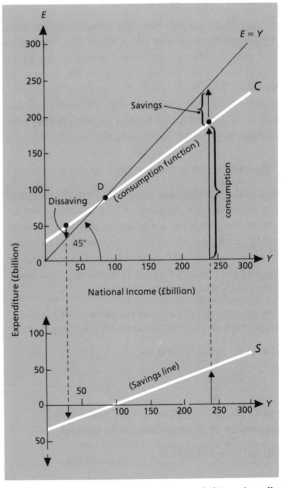

Fig. 29.2 *The consumption function and the savings line* **351**

(C) passes through the 45° line at the level of income (£90bn) at which savings are zero. To the right of this point saving is positive while it is negative at lower levels of income.

We can use the same figures to construct a graph to show savings. Now where dissaving occurs the graph is below the horizontal axis. It cuts the axis at £90bn where savings are zero and rises above the axis as savings become positive. In the upper graph savings (or dissaving) can be seen as the vertical distance between the consumption function and the 45° line, whilst in the lower graph it is the distance above or below the horizontal axis.

Autonomous consumption

In Fig. 29.2 you can see that when income was zero consumption was still £30bn. This indicates that people plan to consume some quantity of goods and services regardless of their level of income. This is termed, by some economists, *autonomous consumption*. In Fig. 29.3 you can see that it is equal to the height at which the consumption function intersects the vertical axis.

Propensities to consume and to save

If we take the amount saved and consumed and express them as proportions of income, we arrive at the propensities to consume and to save. In Fig. 29.4 you see that, of 100 units of income, 10 are saved and 90 are consumed. Thus 9/10 of income is consumed. This is termed the average propensity to consume (APC).

The average propensity to consume (APC) is the proportion of income devoted to consumption.

The APC is calculated as:

$$APC = \frac{C}{Y}$$

The average propensity to save (APS) is the proportion of income devoted to savings.

The APS is calculated as:

$$APS = \frac{S}{Y}$$

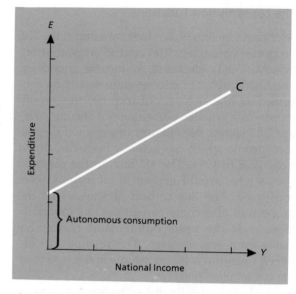

Fig. 29.3 **Autonomous consumption**

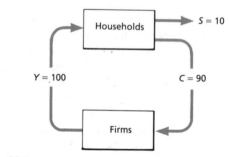

Fig. 29.4

In the example used in Fig. 29.4 the APS is therefore 1/10. It therefore follows that:

$$APC + APS = 1$$

This is always so since 1, here, represents the whole of income, and the whole of income is either consumed or saved.

If national income were to increase, then a proportion of this increase would, similarly, be saved and the rest consumed. In Fig. 29.5 you can see that Y has been increased by 10 units and, of these 10 units, 4 have been saved and 6 consumed. You will note that a smaller proportion of the additional income is consumed. We assume that the proportion of income

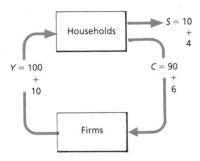

Fig. 29.5

devoted to consumption decreases as income increases (*see* page 350).

The marginal propensity to consume (*MPC*) is the proportion of any addition to income that is devoted to consumption.

The *MPC* may be calculated as the increase in consumption divided by the increase in income.

$$MPC = \frac{\triangle C}{\triangle Y}$$

In the example used in Fig. 29.5 it would be:

$$MPC = \frac{6}{10}$$

The marginal propensity to save (*MPS*) is the proportion of any addition to income that is devoted to savings.

This could therefore be calculated as:

$$MPS = \frac{\triangle S}{\triangle Y}$$

In our example it would be:

$$MPS = \frac{4}{10}$$

It also follows that

$$MPC + MPS = 1$$

because, here, I represents the whole of the addition to income. In the theoretical model we assume that the *APC* is greater than the *MPC*. This is because a greater proportion of income is consumed at lower levels of income.

The *APC*, the *MPC* and the consumption function

Table 29.2 shows the value of the *APC* and *MPC* for various points on a consumption function. As you can see, the *MPC* remains constant as *Y* rises whilst the *APC* declines. This occurs wherever a consumption function is a straight line, as it is in this case. This may be confirmed by examining Fig. 29.6, which is drawn from these figures.

The *MPC* shows what happens to consumption as income rises. It can therefore be calculated as the slope of the consumption function between any two points. Since the slope of the consumption function is constant, the value of the *MPC* is constant in this example. Examine the slope of the *C* line between points H and I and you will find that income increases by £30bn whilst consumption increases by £20bn.

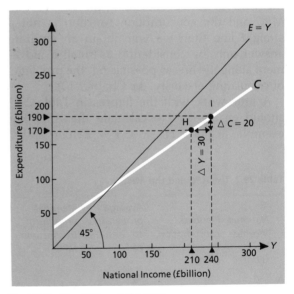

Fig. 29.6 *The* APC *and the* MPC
The *APC* can be calculated from any point on the *C* line, e.g. at point H:

$$APC = \frac{170}{210}$$

whereas the *MPC* is the slope of the line between two points, e.g. between points H and I:

$$MPC = \frac{20}{30}$$

353

Therefore we have:

$$MPC = \frac{\triangle C}{\triangle Y}$$

$$MPC = \frac{20}{30}$$

$$MPC = 0.66$$

The value of the *APC* can be taken from any point on the line. For example at point H:

$$APC = \frac{C}{Y}$$

$$= \frac{170}{210}$$

$$= 0.81$$

We can therefore conclude that the coordinates at any point on a consumption function will give us the value of the *APC*, while the slope between any two points will give the value of the *MPC*. If we are calculating the value of the *MPC* and the consumption function is not a straight line then we will obtain an accurate answer only by considering as small a movement along the line as possible (cf. the problems of calculating elasticity, *see* Chapter 10).

A little work with the figures in Table 29.2 should enable you to calculate the *APS*. For example, at point H, since $Y = £210bn$ and C

$= £170bn$, S must be £40bn. Therefore:

$$APS = \frac{40}{210}$$

$$= 0.19$$

Since we know the value of the *APC* to be 0.81 at this point we are able to confirm that:

$$APS + APC = 1$$

This remains true even when the *APC* is greater than 1 because under these circumstances the value of the *APS* becomes negative. It should also be reasonably simple for you to confirm from Table 29.2 that:

$$MPC + MPS = 1$$

Determinants of consumption

We have already seen that in our model the most important determinant of consumption is the level of income. However, there are other theories and factors which modify this view. Two of the most important are the *permanent income hypothesis* and the *life cycle hypothesis*.

The permanent and life cycle hypotheses

The hypothesis is that people, in the short-run, have a concept of their *permanent income level*. If their income were to suddenly increase (or decrease) they would, in the short-run, go on spending roughly the same amount because they regard the change as only temporary. Thus a sectoral analysis of household incomes would reveal much greater variations in short-term than in long-term propensities to consume.

The permanent income hypothesis is primarily associated with Milton Friedman. An alternative formulation is that of the *life-cycle hypothesis* formulated by Professors Modigliani, Ando and Brumberg. In the life-cycle hypothesis households are supposed to formulate their expenditure plans in relationship to their expected lifetimes' earnings.

Both formulations attempt to explain the observed variation of actual expenditure patterns

Table 29.2 The APC and the MPC

	National income, Y (£bn)	Planned consumption, C (£bn)	Average propensity to consume, APC	Marginal propensity to consume MPC
A	0	30	∞	
B	30	50	1.67	0.66
C	60	70	1.16	0.66
D	90	90	1.0	0.66
E	120	110	0.92	0.66
F	150	130	0.87	0.66
G	180	150	0.84	0.66
H	210	170	0.81	0.66
I	240	190	0.79	0.66
J	270	210	0.78	0.66
K	300	230	0.77	0.66

from the predicted pattern if expenditure was entirely determined by disposable income levels. Modern econometric models of the economy usually divide consumption (C) into two components C_1 and C_2, where C_1 is dependent upon the level of disposable income while C_2 is not.

When we consider these theories it brings into question our original proposition that APC declines as income rises. We can now see, and observation confirms this, that consumption and savings may be subject to considerable fluctuation, at least in the short-run. However, regarded in the long-run, there is greater stability.

Other determinants

a) *The distribution of income*. Income remains very unequally distributed and different income groups have different MPCs. Understandably the MPC of lower income groups tends to be much higher than that of the very rich. A movement to a more even distribution of income should therefore lead to a higher MPC for the economy as a whole.

b) *Consumers' expectations*. Consumers' spending now is influenced by their expectations of the future. Three main factors we might mention are their expectations of inflation, unemployment and income. The evidence for this is considered after we have discussed savings in more detail (*see* page 357).

c) *Cost and availability of credit*. Since many goods, especially consumer durables, are bought with the aid of hire purchase or other forms of credit, the terms on which these are available and their cost must have an effect upon the level of consumer demand.

d) *Wealth and savings*. Since purchases can be made not only out of current income but also from assets and savings of consumers, the quantity of these can influence consumption. For example, those with savings may be more willing to maintain their level of consumption in the face of falling income. It is also argued that those with a cushion of savings are more willing to spend a greater proportion of their income. This would conflict with the Marxist view of

consumption which argues that low-income groups (wage earners) spend most or all of their income whilst high-income groups (capitalists) spend a very small proportion and plough the rest back into capital accumulation.

Shifts and movements

If the level of national income increases then we would expect to see a movement *along* the consumption function to a higher level of consumption. Thus a change in the level of income need have no effect upon the MPC. However if one of the determinants of consumption changes, such as the availability of credit, this might be expected to lead to a change to a new level of consumption at the *same* level of income, so that we will have *shifted* to a new consumption function above or below the old one. We will also have moved to a different propensity to consume.

Savings

Savings is money not spent; it is a withdrawal from the circular flow of income. The most usual formulation of savings is that it is the proportion of personal disposable income that is not consumed. Thus savings is seen as being only undertaken by households. However, as stated in the previous chapter, saving might be undertaken by firms and even by the government. For most of this section of the chapter we will concentrate on household savings; indeed it is the usual pattern for firms and government to be dissavers (borrowers) rather than savers. (*See* page 358 for other sectors of economy).

Savings, income and consumption

We have examined the determinants of consumption and discovered that the most significant factor is the level of income. Since saving is defined as income not spent we have, therefore, considered the most significant influence upon savings. It would follow, therefore, that as income increases savings will increase both as a total figure and as a proportion of income. If you refer back to Fig. 29.1 you can see that this is indeed so. The reason for the rapid increase in savings in the 1970s and the early 1980s is considered below (*see* page 357).

Hoarding

Since savings is money taken out of the circular flow of income it decreases the level of Y. However, since most savings are deposited with financial intermediaries (banks, insurance companies, etc.) they are therefore made available to the economy and it is possible, for example, for firms to borrow these savings and use them for investment. Indeed, it is essential that households do save so that funds are available for investment. However, if savings are not placed with financial intermediaries but *hoarded*, this has a deleterious effect upon the economy. If, for example, people put their savings 'under the mattress', then this purchasing power is lost to the economy and cannot be used until the money reappears.

Hoarding is a problem of insignificant dimensions in the UK economy. However it does present a problem in some less developed economies because of either mistrust or the simple lack of well-developed banking and insurance facilities.

Motives for saving

Given the income to do so, there are many reasons why people do save. The motives are, primarily, *non-economic*, i.e. people are not saving in order to make themselves richer but for other motives. The motives also are often not closely related to current economic circumstances, although high rates of inflation or unemployment will alter people's saving habits.

Some of the most important motives are listed below.

a) Deferred purchase. This is saving up to buy something in the future such as a car, a house or a holiday.

b) Contractual obligations. The most significant

form of contractual saving is assurance premiums. Contractual savings form a very significant share of all personal savings.

c) Precautionary motives. Most people will, if they can, put some money by for a rainy day.

d) Habits and customs. Some people and societies save more than others out of habit. This will therefore be an important determinant of savings.

e) Age. People tend to save and dissave at different times of their life. For example, many young people will be borrowing for house purchase while older people will be saving for their retirement.

Saving may also be significantly affected by *taxation policy* towards savings. If, for example, people are able to gain tax relief on assurance premiums this will encourage them to save. *Expectations* of the future economic situation can also be a significant factor.

Savings and the rate of interest

The view of the classical economists was that the amount of saving was determined by the rate of interest, i.e. a rise in the rate of interest would call forth more savings. However, as we have just seen, there are many non-economic reasons for savings. This was well demonstrated during the 1970s when, in many years, the real interest rate was negative but people saved significantly more. The real interest rate is arrived at by subtracting the rate of inflation from the rate of interest. Thus, if, for example, the interest rate was 10 per cent and inflation was running at 15 per cent, the real rate of interest would be −5 per cent; anyone who saved £100 would, at the end of the year, have purchasing power equal to only £95 in real terms. (*See* page 277.)

This is not to say that interest rates have no effect. High rates of interest may encourage savings while low rates will discourage them. It would appear, however, that other motives such as deferred purchase are more important. Differences in rates of interest between financial institutions, however, have a significant effect upon the type of savings which take place.

The savings ratio

A common measure of the amount of savings taking place is the *savings ratio*. This is the amount of savings expressed as a percentage of personal disposable income (PDI). It is thus very similar to *APS* except that it is expressed as a percentage. In 1980 the savings ratio in the UK was 14·2 per cent which would give an *APS* of 0·142. This was the highest figure to that date.

During the depression of the 1930s the savings ratio was very low as people had to draw on their savings to get by. In the USA in the same period the savings ratio was actually negative. During the 1939–45 war the savings ratio shot up as people were encouraged to lend to the government to help the war effort. After the war the ratio returned to a more normal 4–5 per cent. During the 1960s the ratio gradually rose to 9·3 per cent in 1970. From 1973 onwards the ratio began a rapid rise to 14·2 per cent in 1980. However, by 1986 it had fallen back to 9·1 per cent.

This rise in the savings ratio in the UK during the 1970s is in need of some explanation. It may appear entirely consistent with the rapid rise in income during the 1970s, but this was mainly a rise in *nominal* income attributable to high rates of inflation. Apart from the early years of the decade real income was growing very slowly and in some years actually fell. We must also consider that high rates of inflation might be expected to discourage thrift since inflation devalues savings. Both these factors therefore argue *against* a rise in the savings ratio.

How then do we account for the observed increase in the savings ratio and decline in the *APC*? The following are given as possible reasons.

a) The volatility of incomes made people uncertain about their future incomes and therefore inclined to save more.

b) Unemployment also made people uncertain and more likely to increase their precautionary savings. Unspent redundancy money may also have increased savings.

c) Inflation also had an effect by increasing uncertainty. Because inflation devalues savings many people were led to save more to ensure that they had sufficient stocks of money wealth. This may, for example, have had an important effect upon contractual savings. Consider the example of people taking out endowment policies in 1975, when inflation was running at over 25 per cent. If they anticipated high rates of inflation in the future they might have been led to greatly increase the size of the policies in order to safeguard their future. (*See also*: permanent income hypothesis, page 354).

Savings ratios differ considerably from country to country. In 1986, while the savings ratio in the UK was 9·1 per cent, in the USA it was only 4·5 per cent whilst in Japan it was 17·5 per cent. These differences, which are a result of the different structures and habits in the economy, result in considerable variation in the way industry is financed.

Discretionary and contractual savings

Personal savings may be divided into contractual savings and discretionary savings. Contractual savings are those where a person contracts to save a certain amount per month. The most significant forms of contractual savings are life assurance and superannuation and pension schemes. Discretionary savings are all other forms of savings where people are not obligated to save a specific amount. The most significant forms of discretionary savings are building society deposits, bank deposits and lending to the government.

Figure 29.7 traces the development of savings in the UK in recent years. The diagram shows a growth in saving in the early 1970s, then a very rapid growth in the late 1970s and subsequently a relative decline in the 1980s. It should be apparent from Fig. 29.7 that contractual savings are a much more stable and predictable figure than discretionary savings. Thus rapid changes in savings are caused by large changes in discretionary savings.

357

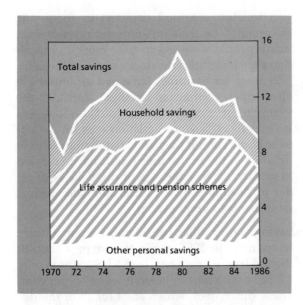

Fig. 29.7 *Discretionary and contractual savings in the UK* Contractual saving is that done through life assurance and pension funds. Discretionary saving is household savings and other personal savings. *Source*: Social Trends, *CSO*

Other sectors of the economy

It is possible for sectors of the economy other than households to save; companies, for example, can save by not distributing all their profits. If we take the saving of each sector and subtract from it capital formation (investment) we arrive at a figure for the *financial surplus or deficit* for

Table 29.3 The financial surplus or deficit of sectors of the UK economy, 1986

Sector	£m
Personal sector	4 681
Industrial and commercial companies	6 439
Monetary sector	2 472
Other financial institutions	1 156
Public corporations	1 195
Central government	−8 448
Local authorities	−1 515
Total	5 980
Net investment abroad	+980
less Residual error	6 960

that sector. It is often the case that a large surplus in the personal sector is balanced by deficits in the other sectors. Overall the total of the surpluses will exactly match that of the deficits. This may be confirmed by the figures in Table 29.3. The figure for the overseas sector is described in the Blue Book as 'net investment abroad'; this is equivalent to the current account balance in the balance of payments, except that the sign must be changed. Hence in 1986 the current deficit was −£980m.

Investment

Investment is an important component and determinant of the level of national income. When we use the term investment in this context it refers exclusively to the acquisition of new physical capital such as buildings and machines. It is in this sense that we can describe investment as an addition, or an injection, to the circular flow of income. 'Investment' on the stock exchange, or in government bonds, is not investment as the term is used in macroeconomics because it only involves the transfer of ownership of pieces of paper.

Types of investment

Investment is not a homogeneous mass; it consists of many different types of things. The different types of investment have differing effects upon the economy; for example, the building of a new oil terminal and the building of an old people's home will have very different consequences, though both are investment.

a) *Stocks (or inventories).* Net additions to the physical stocks of materials and goods held by businesses are counted as investment. They are the most volatile component of investment, being subject to change in response to changes or expected changes in the level of national income. It is possible for the change in stocks to be either positive or negative.

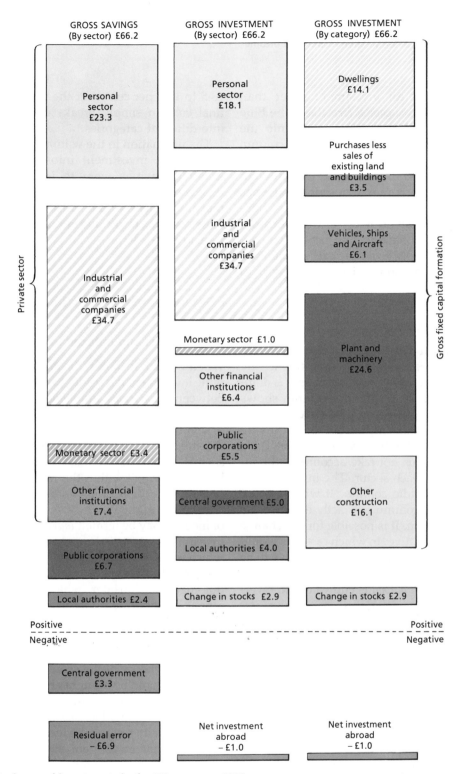

GROSS SAVINGS
(By sector) £66.2

GROSS INVESTMENT
(By sector) £66.2

GROSS INVESTMENT
(By category) £66.2

Private sector

Personal
sector
£23.3

Industrial
and
commercial
companies
£34.7

Monetary sector £3.4

Other financial
institutions
£7.4

Public corporations
£6.7

Local authorities £2.4

Personal
sector
£18.1

industrial
and
commercial
companies
£34.7

Monetary sector £1.0

Other financial
institutions
£6.4

Public
corporations
£5.5

Central government £5.0

Local authorities £4.0

Change in stocks £2.9

Dwellings
£14.1

Purchases less
sales of
existing land
and buildings
£3.5

Vehicles, Ships
and Aircraft
£6.1

Plant and
machinery
£24.6

Other
construction
£16.1

Change in stocks £2.9

Gross fixed capital formation

Positive

Negative

Positive

Negative

Central government
£3.3

Residual error
– £6.9

Net investment
abroad
– £1.0

Net investment
abroad
– £1.0

Fig. 29.8 *Savings and investments in the UK economy, 1986*
**Gross savings are equal to gross fixed capital formation together with the value of the physical increase or
decrease in stocks. Each column (+) and (–) totals £66.2bn. All figures in the diagram are in £bn. Note that the
figure for net investment abroad is equivalent to the current account balance of the balance of payments (see page
358).**

b) Fixed capital. All investment other than stocks is termed *fixed capital formation*. The Blue Book divides fixed capital formation into the five categories shown in the right-hand column of Fig. 29.8. As you can see, construction of housing is included in investment even though it might be more accurate to describe houses as consumer durables. As was explained in Chapter 7, much investment is to replace worn out capital. We would have to subtract capital consumption from gross fixed capital formation to give us the net addition to fixed capital stock of the country.

Savings and investment

As was explained in the previous chapter, *realised* saving will always equal *realised* investment. The equality between these two components is demonstrated in Fig. 29.8. The first column shows the gross saving carried on by different sectors of the economy. This differs from the net saving figures (shown as the financial surplus in Table 29.3) in that it does not take account of the investment within each sector. The investment is shown in the middle column. It will be noted that the savings column is exactly equal to the investment column. It is possible for the change in stocks to be negative. In which case this would be referred to as *destocking* and would have to be subtracted from the total for investment. The item *net investment abroad* is equivalent to Oversea's sector's financial deficit or surplus (*see* Table 29.3).

As you can see, most savings come from the personal sector (households) and from the industrial and commercial sector (firms). When we turn to the investment column it can be seen that the private sector (households and firms) is also responsible for the bulk of investment. In 1980 public corporations accounted for 17 per cent of all investment but by 1986 this had dropped to only 8·3 per cent. This was mainly a result of the government's privatisation programme. Despite the government's attempts to reduce their role in the economy, the central and local government share of investment only fell from

13·5 to 11·2 per cent over the same period. The final column simply breaks down investment into different categories.

The fluctuation in the volume of stocks brings saving and investment into equality. If, for example, savings were to increase suddenly then consumption would fall. This would mean that investment would be rising to keep pace with savings. If you are not sure of this point re-read page 346.

Determinants of investment

Autonomous and induced investment

When we turn to look at the factors which determine investment it is useful to make a distinction between *autonomous* and *induced* investment.

When we were looking at the determinants of savings we saw that an increase in the level of income was quite likely to *induce* an increase in saving. Thus the saving had been brought about by a variable (Y) within the model of the economy we are developing. Similarly investment which is brought about by changes in the level of income may be termed *induced investment*, i.e. investment which is brought about by a factor which is *endogenous* to (within) the theory. However, much investment is not brought about in this manner. Consider, what might happen to a new invention, e.g. 3D television. It is quite likely that firms would go ahead and invest in such a development but there need have been no prior change in income or any other variable within our theory of the economy. Thus the investment would be brought about by something outside or *exogenous* to the system. Such investment may be termed *autonomous*.

We normally reserve the term induced investment for that investment associated with the *accelerator principle*, i.e. the relationship between investment and the *rate of change of aggregate demand*. All other types of investment may be termed autonomous. In practice one may be very hard to disentangle from the other.

Investment and the rate of interest

A detailed discussion of individual investment decisions and the rate of interest is included in Chapter 23. Here we are concerned with the relationship between the rate of interest and the aggregate level of investment within the economy.

It seems reasonable to assume that firms make the decision to invest on the expectation of making a gain. This we may contrast with the decision to save where, as we saw earlier in the chapter, households will save even if it involves economic loss. Most decisions to invest involve borrowing money and there should therefore be some relationship between the cost of borrowing and the amount of investment taking place.

There is a relationship between the rate of interest and the capital *stock* which people will wish to hold. This is illustrated in Fig. 29.9, which shows an *MEC* (marginal efficiency of capital) curve. The *MEC* relates the desired stock of capital to the rate of return (yield) an additional unit of capital will produce. The yield is related to the rate of interest. Suppose, for example, that a capital project were to yield 10

per cent; if the rate of interest were 12 per cent investors would not be interested in it. However, were interest to fall to 8 per cent, investors might wish to invest. The capital stock they desire would have increased. (*See also* page 275).

Marginal efficiency of investment

While the *MEC* shows the relationship between the rate of interest and the *desired* stock of capital, the marginal efficiency of investment (*MEI*) shows the relationship between the rate of interest and the *actual rate* of investment per year. Thus *MEC* is concerned with a *stock* while *MEI* is concerned with a *flow*. There will be important differences between the capital stock people desire and the capital investment that takes place. This is because there are physical constraints upon the construction of capital.

Figure 29.10 shows two possibilities for *MEI*. With both we show the effect of dropping the interest rate from 14 per cent to 7·5 per cent. If the curve is relatively flat (*MEI₂*) then the rate of investment increases substantially from £18bn to £30bn, but if the curve is steep (*MEI₁*) then there is only a small response and the rate of in-

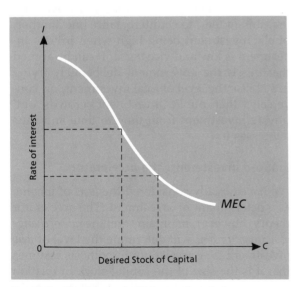

Fig. 29.9 *The marginal efficiency of capital*
A fall in the rate of interest increases the size of the desired stock of capital.

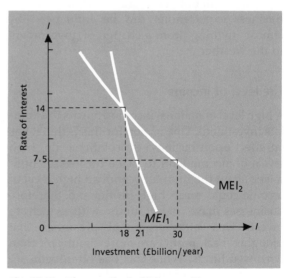

Fig. 29.10 *The marginal efficiency of investment*
A fall in the rate of interest brings about more investment; how much more depends on the slope of the *MEI* line.

361

vestment increases from £18bn to £21bn. The *MEI* could be said to show the *interest elasticity of investment*.

It would be theoretically possible for the *MEI* line to be vertical, in which case there would be no relationship between investment and the rate of interest. This would be a very extreme view; most economists today believe that there is a relationship, even if it is difficult to plot. There are, however, other factors to consider.

Business expectations

The classical view of investment was that if a scheme yielded 11 per cent and interest was 10 per cent, then investment would take place. However we cannot see into the future to be able to judge the profitability of a scheme with such accuracy, nor can we tell whether or not circumstances will change. Because investment decisions take time to accomplish, there must be a great deal of uncertainty about them. Thus what *businesses expect* to happen in the future is very important. If they are pessimistic about the future, low rates of interest will not encourage them to borrow, whereas if they are optimistic, high rates will not necessarily discourage them. Business expectations can be influenced by almost anything, from a change of government to the weather.

The level of income

A high level of national income appears to stimulate investment. One reason for this is that it has an effect upon business expectations, i.e. high levels of income tend to make businesses optimistic about the future. Secondly a high level of income could mean high profits and therefore businesses have more funds with which to invest. This latter argument presumes that ploughed-back profits are more significant than borrowed funds. While this has often been so, in recent years borrowed funds have assumed increasing importance.

There is much disagreement about whether or not the level of income determines the level of investment. Many economists would reverse the causality of the relationship and say that high levels of investment *cause* high levels of income. Whichever way round it is, high levels of income are certainly associated with high levels of investment.

The government and investment

The government has a very significant effect upon investment, both indirectly through its policies and directly as the largest investor in the economy. Investment decisions by businesses are influenced by government taxation policies, which may give incentives to investments, and by monetary policy, which plays a significant role in determining interest rates.

The government and the public corporations account for over 21 per cent of all the gross fixed capital formation in the country. It is important to realise that criteria for investment which the government uses may often be non-economic, i.e. they may not be interested in maximising profits but may be guided by other motives. The building of schools, hospitals, roads and old people's homes all provide examples of this type of investment.

There is evidence that public and private investment tend to counterbalance one another, public investment being high when private investment is low and vice versa. It can be argued that this is the government deliberately trying to stabilise the level of total investment, or, conversely, that public investment 'crowds out' private investment from time to time and thus depresses it.

Induced investment: the accelerator

We have already considered the *level* of income as a determinant of investment. The accelerator theory, however, maintains that the *rate of change of national income* will determine the level of *new* investment. The accelerator hypothesis assumes that it is the size of the capital stock in relation to national income that is the object of decision making. In its simplest form the accelerator hypothesis assumes that firms seek to maintain a constant capital to output ratio. Investment is thus reduced to behaviour which seeks to change the capital–output ratio if it is not at the desired level.

The capital stock of the nation is several times greater than national income (*see* page 87). We may say, therefore, that it takes several £s of capital to produce £1 of output. For example, say that it takes £3 of capital to produce £1 of output (i.e. the capital–output ratio is 1:3). If total demand in the economy were to rise then, in order to meet the new demand, £3 of capital equipment would have to be built to meet each £1 of new demand. Conversely, if national income were to fall investment could possibly fall to zero if the capital stock is greater than that desired for that particular level of income.

The accelerator hypothesis predicts that it is the rate of change of income rather than its level which determines investment.

In the appendix to this chapter several possible offsetting factors are discussed which make the

accelerator effect a matter of some dispute amongst economists. Nevertheless, although not invented by Keynes himself, the hypothesis accords with his view that the aggregate demand of the private sector is subject to fluctuations which can have a destabilising effect on the economy (*see* pages 364–366).

Postscript on investment

There are important theoretical differences between Keynes, and the classical economists, and the monetarists and neo-classicists about interest, investment and income. We cannot go into these fully until we have had a closer look at income determination and monetary theory. We may simply note here that the classicists placed a much greater importance on the rate of interest than we do today. As you have seen in this section of the chapter, we have argued that investment might also be determined by factors as diverse as government policy and the weather.

Summary

1 The consumption function is the relationship between consumption and income. Generally speaking the proportion of income consumed declines as income rises.

2 The *APS* and *APC* show the proportions of income which are devoted to savings and consumption respectively. The *MPS* and *MPC* show the proportions of any increase in income which are devoted to savings and consumption.

3 A rise in income will bring about a movement along the *C* line while a change in the other determinants of consumption will cause a shift to a new *C* line.

4 Saving is a withdrawal from the circular flow of income. It is related to the level of *Y* and is motivated by a number of non-economic factors such as habit and age. There is no clearly-defined relationship between *S* and the rate of interest; people will save even when real interest is negative. Savings may be divided into contractual and discretionary. Contractual savings are the more stable.

5 Savings may be undertaken by any sector of the economy. Overall there is a balance between the financial deficits and surpluses of the various sectors.

6 Investment is an injection to the circular flow of income and consists of

363

additions to real physical stock of capital. There is an equality between realised savings and realised investment.

7 Autonomous investment is determined by exogenous factors such as business expectations. Induced investment is brought about by the rate of change of Y.

Questions

1 What reasons can be advanced to explain the observed variations in the propensity to consume in Fig. 29.1? How do you think this diagram would differ if there were no inflation?

2 Does the information contained in Fig. 29.7 support the permanent income hypothesis? Give reasons for your answer.

3 We have spoken of induced and autonomous investment. How far would it be true to speak of induced and autonomous savings?

4 Consider Fig. 29.10. What would be the significance of a vertical *MEI* curve?

5 Prepare a table to compare the percentage of GDP devoted to gross fixed capital formation of four different countries with which you are familiar, e.g. the UK, the USA, Nigeria and Malaysia. Suggest reasons for the observed differences.

6 Examine the role of interest in determining savings and investment.

7 What factors determine investment in a modern economy?

8 In a closed economy with no government intervention:

$$C = 50 + 0{\cdot}85Y$$

Autonomous investment is constant at 60 units. Induced investment is $I = 0{\cdot}05Y$ for all levels of Y. At what level of Y will $S = I$? Suppose that autonomous investment were to increase to 80 units. At what level of Y would $S = I$?

Appendix: the accelerator

A model of the accelerator

To explain the working of the accelerator we will use the model of a very simplified economy. In this economy the initial capital stock is valued at £200m. When fully employed, this stock is just adequate to produce the £100m of goods which constitute the aggregate demand (Y) in the economy for a year, i.e. there is a capital–output ratio of 2:1, which means that a capital stock of £2 is necessary to produce a flow of output of £1. The capital in this economy has a life of five years and is replaced evenly so that a replacement investment of £40m per year is needed to maintain the capital stock.

Aggregate demand (Y)	Capital stock required
£100m	£200m

Investment required	
Replacement	Net
£40m	0

Suppose now that aggregate demand were to rise by 20 per cent to £120m. This would mean that to meet this demand a capital stock of £240m is required. If demand were to be met the following year it would mean that the economy's demand for capital will now be £80m, i.e. £40m for replacement and £40m to meet the new demand. We can summarise it thus:

Aggregate demand (Y)	Capital required
£120m	£240m

Investment required	
Replacement	Net
£40m	£40m

Thus between the first and second year a rise of 20 per cent in aggregate demand has brought about a 100 per cent rise in investment demand. This is an illustration of the accelerator principle.

The accelerator (a) is concerned with new (or net) investment demand. In our example £40m of the new investment is necessary to meet a rise in Y of £20m. This is because it takes £2 of capital equipment to produce £1 of output per year. From this we can derive a formula for the accelerator effect which is:

$$I_N = a \cdot \triangle Y$$

I_N is the new investment, a is the accelerator co-efficient (the capital–output ratio, in this case 2) and $\triangle Y$ is the change in income. Thus in our example we have:

$$I_N = 2 \times \text{£20m}$$
$$= \text{£40m}$$

To explain the accelerator more fully we need to follow our example through several time periods. This is done in Table 29.4.

Years 1 and 2 in Table 29.4 recapitulate our example. Now assume that in year 3 demand rises to £130m. The capital stock required is now £260m. Therefore there will be a demand for £20m of extra capital but the total demand for capital will have *fallen*. The capital demand is now £40m for replacement and £20m for new capital. The £40m of extra capital last year will not need replacing for a further five years. Therefore, although aggregate demand is still rising, capital demand has fallen. This is because when the *rate of increase* of aggregate demand

Table 29.4 A model of the economy (capital–output ratio = 2, capital is replaced over a five-year period)

Year Y (£m)	Aggregate demand, (£m)	Capital stock required (£m)	Replacement	Investment (£m) Net	Total
(1)	(2)	(3)	(4)	(5)	(6)
1	100	200	40	–	40
2	120	240	40	40	80
3	130	260	40	20	60
4	140	280	40	20	60
5	120	240	–	–	–
6	120	240	40	–	40

falls, the absolute level of induced investment will decline. You can confirm this by applying the formula.

Further implications of the principle can be observed between years 3 and 4, where the demand for capital is constant because the rate of increase is the same as between years 2 and 3 (remember the increase is $\triangle Y$ not $\triangle Y/Y$). Between years 4 and 5 aggregate demand drops from £140m to £120m and the capital stock required, therefore, decreases from £280m to £240m. What new investment is required?

If we apply the formula we get:

$$I_N = 2 \times (-\text{£20m})$$
$$= -\text{£40m}$$

There is therefore no need to replace the £40m of capital stock which has worn out. In this case it has therefore completely eliminated the need for replacement investment.

Finally in year 6 demand has stabilised at £120m. The formula predicts that there will be no demand for new capital. However it is necessary to replace the £40m of capital stock which will have worn out.

The accelerator (a) links the rate of change of aggregate demand to the level of new investment demand.

Factors modifying the accelerator

When we look for evidence of the accelerator in the economy we do indeed find that fluctuations in the level of investment demand are significantly greater than those in aggregate demand. But:

a) they are much smaller fluctuations than those predicted by the theory;

b) it is very difficult to demonstrate any mathematical relationship between the two.

This does not necessarily mean that the theory is therefore wrong. It could be that a number of factors modify the accelerator and, therefore, mask the effect. Some of these are listed below.

a) *Businesses learn from experience.* This means that they are unlikely to double their capacity on

365

the strength of one year's orders. Conversely, if demand is dropping, they might be willing to increase their inventories against a rise in demand in subsequent years.

b) Capital–output ratios. These are not as constant as suggested by our example. If demand rose it might be possible to obtain more output from the existing capital stock by varying other factors of production. For example, the workforce might undertake shift work or overtime to meet the extra demand.

c) Depreciation. The replacement of the capital stock may be a function of factors other than time. In our example it was assumed that capital wore out after five years. If there was an increase in demand it might be possible to continue using old capital equipment after it was planned to scrap it. Often the period over which capital is depreciated is an accounting convenience and does not correspond to the physical life of the capital. Conversely, capital may be obselete before it has physically depreciated.

d) Other investment. It should be recalled that the accelerator only applies to net or 'new' in-

vestment resulting from changes in Y. There are other forms of investment such as replacement investment and investment in new techniques.

e) Time lag. New capacity cannot be created immediately after a rise in demand, since plant and machinery take time to build. Also the time lags will vary depending on the nature of the capital we are considering. We are thus concerned with a *distributed time lag*. Thus much more sophisticated mathematics will be needed to measure the effects.

f) Capacity. The operation of the accelerator depends upon the economy being at or near full capacity, otherwise the new demand would be coped with by existing plants expanding their output. However, in apparent contradiction to this, there must be surplus resources (labour, land, etc.) with which to construct the capital equipment.

All these factors make it very difficult for us to observe the accelerator effect in any simple manner.

Questions on the accelerator

1 Draw up a table to show the annual percentage change in GDP and the annual percentage in gross fixed capital formation and net capital formation for each year in the last decade. Use this as information to argue a case for the existence of the accelerator.

2 Reconstruct Table 29.4 assuming that the capital–output ratio is now 3:1 (columns (1) and (2) will be unchanged).

Data response **What determines consumption?**

Study the figures in Table 29.5 relating to income, savings and inflation in the UK. The income figures refer to *personal disposable income*, i.e. the income of individuals after allowing for deduction of income tax and National Insurance contributions. The saving referred to is that of the personal sector.

1 Using graph paper, construct a consumption function for the UK economy based on this data.

2 Determine the marginal propensity to consume (MPC) and the average propensity to save (APS) for the years:
1976
1980
1986.
Explain how you arrived at your answers.

Table 29.5 Income, savings and inflation in the UK.

Year	Personal disposable income. £m	Savings £m	Consumer price percentage change from previous year %
1976	86 229	10 356	16·5
1977	96 862	10 105	15·8
1978	113 462	13 439	8·3
1979	136 046	17 685	13·4
1980	160 297	22 827	18·0
1981	176 132	23 105	11·9
1982	190 938	23 339	8·6
1983	205 096	22 028	4·6
1984	220 711	24 799	5·0
1985	238 418	24 698	6·1
1986	257 512	23 345	3·4

Source: National Accounts *HMSO* and Economic Outlook *OECD*

3   How would you account for the observed variations in the size of the APC?

4   What theories have been advanced to explain the determination of the level of consumption in an economy?

The determination of the equilibrium level of national income

equilibri|um *n.* (*pl.* ~ **a** *or* ~ **ums**). state of balance (lit. or fig.); mental state of uncertainty or equanimity; **stable, unstable, neutral,** ~ **um** (in which body when disturbed tends to return to equilibrium, to move farther from equilibrium, or has neither tendency).
The Concise Oxford Dictionary

Who knows when some slight shock, disturbing the delicate balance between social order and thirsty aspiration, shall send the skyscrapers in our cities tumbling.

Richard Wright

We have already described, in general terms, how equilibrium is reached in the level of national income. In this chapter we examine the determination of the equilibrium in more detail and also see how changes occur in that equilibrium. It is once again worth stating that the equilibrium level of national income is not necessarily the desirable level of national income but it is extremely significant in that the welfare of everyone is affected by changes in the equilibrium level.

A model of the economy

Assumptions

The economy is an extremely complex entity. Therefore, in order to advance our understanding and to make the construction of our model more straightforward, we will make general simplifying assumptions. Having dev-

eloped a better understanding of the economy we will then drop these assumptions.

a) Potential national income. Although there is a gradual upward trend in national income we assume that at any time there is a fixed level of *potential national income* which corresponds to the full employment of all resources; this is given the symbol Y_F. Thus the level of actual national income Y may be less than but no greater than Y_F. If everyone in the economy were to start working overtime it would be possible to exceed the level of Y_F.

b) Unemployment. We assume that there is some unemployment of all factors of production. Thus it is possible to increase the level of Y by bringing these into employment.

c) Constant prices. For most of the time it is convenient to assume that there is no inflation (or deflation). In this way the changes in income which we are looking at are changes in real income.

d) Technology. We also assume that there are no significant changes in the level of technology such as would significantly alter the relationship between inputs and outputs.

What is Y?

We use Y as an abbreviation for national income. However this could denote aggregate demand or output or income. Where the distinction is significant we can accomplish it by suffixing another letter. As we have just seen Y_F could be used to denote the full employment level of Y. There is also the problem of which measure of national income Y corresponds to, whether it is GNP or NNP. In a mainly theoretical chapter like this the distinction is of little significance. However we take it that:

$$Y = GNP$$

The reason for adopting this is that it is upon the GNP that significant aggregates such as employment depend, rather than upon the NNP. Some major economists however, such as Samuelson, adopt Y as a measure of NNP.

Investment

For the first part of this chapter we will make the assumption that investment is constant. There are two reasons for doing this.

a) It is a simplifying assumption which will make the construction of our model more straightforward.

b) Investment, as we have seen, is divided between autonomous and induced. Autonomous investment is determined by factors outside the model we are developing. Thus it is logical to regard it as exogenously determined. Induced investment will only be brought about when the economy is at full employment and we have already made the assumption that there are unemployed resources; thus there will be no induced investment.

Therefore in Fig. 30.1 investment I is represented as a horizontal straight line at £50bn, determined by exogenous factors.

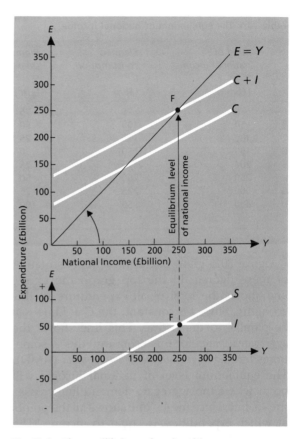

Fig. 30.1 *The equilibrium of national income*

The equilibrium

Table 30.1 presents the data for a hypothetical economy in which there is no government intervention and no foreign trade. An equilibrium will be reached in this economy when planned savings are equal to investment. As can be seen from Table 30.1, this will occur at line F when national income is £250bn. Another way of looking at the equilibrium would be to say that it will occur when total expenditure (E) in the economy is equal to total income (Y). Total expenditure in this economy has two components; spending on consumer goods (C); and spending on investment goods (I). Thus total expenditure is $C + I$. In Table 30.1 it can be seen that total expenditure is equal to income at the level of £250bn, therefore confirming this as the equilibrium level of income.

369

Table 30.1 The equilibrium of national income

	Level of national income, Y (£bn)	Planned consumption, C (£bn)	Planned savings, S (£bn)	Autonomous investment, I (£bn)	Total expenditure, C+I=E (£bn)	Tendency of income to:
A	0	75	−75	50	125	
B	50	100	−50	50	150	
C	100	125	−25	50	175	Expand
D	150	150	0	50	200	
E	200	175	25	50	225	
F	250	200	50	50	250	Equilibrium
G	300	225	75	50	275	
H	350	250	100	50	300	Contract

Figure 30.1 gives a graphical representation of these figures. In the top graph the $C + I$ line shows the total of all expenditure in this economy. Since I is constant, the $C + I$ line will be parallel to the C line. This line shows the *aggregate demand* for this economy; this is sometimes termed *aggregate monetary demand* (AMD). The equilibrium level of national income will occur where the aggregate demand line crosses the 45° line, since the 45° line shows all the points at which expenditure is equal to income. The lower graph demonstrates the relationship of savings and investment. It can be seen that the equilibrium level of national income corresponds to the point at which $S = I$. Thus the graph demonstrates, once again, that $S = I$ is the equilibrium condition for the economy.

The nature of the equilibrium is illustrated in Fig. 30.2. Here, if the level of Y were below the equilibrium, e.g. OL, then I would exceed S by AR. Thus injections would be greater than withdrawals and Y would rise. Conversely if Y were to be ON then S would exceed I by TG, so that withdrawals would now be greater than injections and Y would fall.

It is worth reiterating that there is nothing necessarily desirable about the equilibrium level of national income. In Fig. 30.2 it could be that the level of Y which is necessary to maintain full employment is ON but the equilibrium level is less than this and there will, therefore, be unemployment.

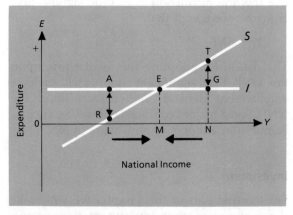

Fig. 30.2 *The reasons for equilibrium*
At income level OL, *I* > *S* and therefore *Y* tends to rise. At income level ON, *S* > *I* and therefore *Y* tends to fall. Therefore OM is the equilibrium level of *Y*, where *S* = *I*.

The multiplier

The multiplier defined

Having considered the determination of the equilibrium level of Y, we will now proceed to look at changes in the equilibrium. In Fig. 30.3 we show the effect of an increase in the level of autonomous investment. Investment has increased by £50bn from I to I_1 and this has had the effect of raising the level of national income by £100bn. Thus £50bn of extra investment has

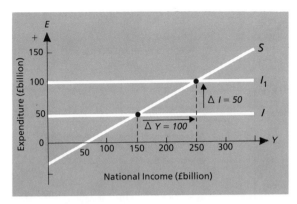

Fig. 30.3 *The multiplier*
An increase in investment of £50bn has increased the equilibrium level of national income by £100bn.

brought about £100bn of extra income. This is an operation of the *multiplier principle*. The numerical value of the change is known as *the multiplier (K)*. In our example the multiplier would be:

$$K = \frac{\triangle Y}{\triangle I}$$

$$= \frac{100}{50}$$

$$= 2$$

In this case the multiplier is 2. This means that every extra £1 of investment that is injected into the economy will lead to a rise in national income of £2. This effect can also work downwards so that if there were a decrease in investment this would cause a multiple decrease in national income.

The multiplier principle is that a change in the level of injections (or withdrawals) brings about a relatively greater change in the level of national income.

The operation of the multiplier

The operation of the multiplier can be explained by taking a simple example. If a firm decides to construct a new building costing £1000, then the income of builders and the suppliers of the raw materials will rise by £1000. However the process

Table 30.2 A simple example of the multiplier at work

	Increase in income, $\triangle Y$ (£)	Increase in consumption, $\triangle C$ (£)	Increase in savings, $\triangle S$ (£)
1st Recipients	1000	666.67	333.33
	+	+	+
2nd Recipients	666.67	444.44	222.23
	+	+	+
3rd Recipients	444.44	296.30	148.14
	+	+	+
4th Recipients	296.30	197.53	98.77
	+	+	+
5th Recipients	197.53	131.69	65.84
	+	+	+
	.	.	.
	.	.	.
	.	.	.
Total	$\triangle Y$=£3000	$\triangle C$=£2000	$\triangle S$=£1000

does not stop there. If we assume that the recipients of the £1000 have a marginal propensity to consume of $\frac{2}{3}$, then they will spend £666.67 and save the rest. This spending creates extra income for another group of people. If we assume that they also have an *MPC* of $\frac{2}{3}$ then they will spend £444.44 of the £666.67 and save the rest. This process will continue, with each new round of spending being $\frac{2}{3}$ of the previous round. Thus a long chain of extra income, extra consumption and extra saving is set up (see Table 30.2).

The process will come to a halt when the additions to savings total £1000. This is because the change in savings ($\triangle S$) is now equal to the original change in investment ($\triangle I$) and, therefore, the economy is returned to equilibrium because $S = I$ once again. At this point the additions to income total £3000. Thus £1000 extra investment has created a £3000 rise in income; therefore, in this case, the value of the multiplier is 3.

Temporary and permanent changes

In order for the change in the equilibrium level of national income to be permanent it is necessary that the increase in investment is also permanent. **371**

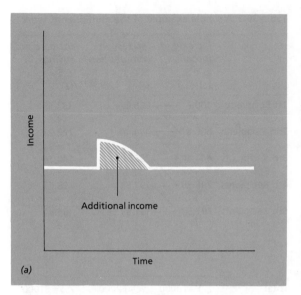

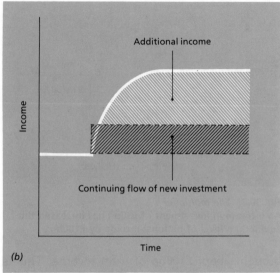

Fig. 30.4 *Effects of investment*
(*a*) **The effect of a single act of investment of £1000.** (*b*) **The shift to a higher equilibrium level of income caused by a continuous flow of new investment of £1000. Here the value of the multiplier is 3.**

If in our example (see Table 30.2) the £1000 of investment were an isolated example then it would create a 'bulge' in national income of £3000 and then the equilibrium would return to its previous level. On the other hand if £1000 of investment were undertaken in each time period then this would cause a permanent increase in the equilibrium level of national income of £3000. This is illustrated in Fig. 30.4.

The multiplier formula

The size of the multiplier is governed by the *MPC*. In our example we saw that additions to income were generated in the following series:

$$\triangle Y = £1000 + £666.67 + £444.44 + £296.30, \text{ etc.}$$

because the *MPC* was $\frac{2}{3}$ and therefore $\frac{2}{3}$ of all income received was passed on to create income for someone else. However if the *MPC* were larger, say $\frac{9}{10}$, then the same increase in investment would yield

$$\triangle Y = £1000 + £900 + £810 + £729, \text{ etc.}$$

If we followed each series we would find that each successive round of extra income would get smaller and smaller but never quite reach zero. Fortunately such a series is well known in mathematics and is termed an infinite geometric progression. Its value is given by the formula:

$$\frac{1}{1-r}$$

where *r* is the value of the common ratio. In the case of the multiplier the common ratio is the *MPC* so that we obtain:

$$K = \frac{1}{1 - MPC}$$

If, therefore, the *MPC* were $\frac{2}{3}$ we would obtain

$$K = \frac{1}{1 - \frac{2}{3}}$$

$$= 3$$

whereas if the value of the *MPC* were $\frac{9}{10}$ then we would obtain:

372

$$K = \frac{1}{1 - \frac{9}{10}}$$

$$= 10$$

The larger the *MPC* the larger the multiplier will be.

If in fact the *MPC* were to be 1 then the value of the multiplier would be infinity. However if everything were consumed there could be no investment anyway, so this is only a theoretical possibility.

Because of its mathematical derivation it is usual to express the formula as:

$$K = \frac{1}{1 - MPC}$$

but since we know that

$$MPC + MPS = 1$$

we could also write the formula as

$$K = \frac{1}{MPS}$$

It is also possible to substitute *s* for *MPS* so that we would write the formula as:

$$K = \frac{1}{s}$$

Thus if we know the value of the *MPS* we can predict the effect of a change in investment upon national income. The effect will be the change in investment multiplied by *K*, which we can write as:

$$\triangle Y = K . \triangle I$$

or as:

$$\triangle Y = \frac{1}{s} . \triangle I$$

Other multipliers

The theory of the multiplier was developed in the midst of the depression of the 1930s by Richard (later Lord) Kahn. In fact it is from his name that the abbreviation is derived. However the multiplier Kahn wrote about in 1931 was an *employment multiplier*. Kahn observed the

millions of unemployed and suggested that if more people were employed they would spend their wages, thus creating new jobs for other people, and so on. Keynes later developed the *investment multiplier* which placed the emphasis on spending rather than on jobs. It is this investment multiplier which we have been considering. Keynes' emphasis on investment, to the exclusion of other injections and withdrawals, led his followers to greatly over-estimate the size of the multiplier. Subsequently other multipliers, such as the foreign trade and the government multiplier, have been incorporated into the theory and thus have reduced the overall size of the multiplier effect. We will consider these when we have looked at the other sectors of the economy in more detail.

Non-autonomous investment

What would be the effect upon the multiplier if we dropped the assumption that investment is autonomous? Suppose that investment were to increase with income. This would mean that an increase in investment would cause income to rise and this in turn would cause investment to rise. This, therefore, would magnify the multiplier effect. This is illustrated in Fig. 30.5. In diagram (*a*) investment is autonomous and a rise in investment causes the equilibrium level of Y to rise from OA to OB, whereas in diagram (*b*) a shift of the same magnitude in the investment line causes the equilibrium to rise from OA to OC.

Modifying factors

There are a number of factors which prevent the multiplier working out as precisely as has been suggested in our examples so far.

a) Personal disposable income. We have stated that the size of the multiplier is determined by the *MPC*. However the *MPC* is calculated from PDI, but before extra spending in the economy can become PDI it is first received by firms, who may retain part of it for reserves or for depreciation and will also pay part of it in tax. **373**

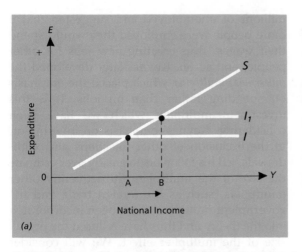

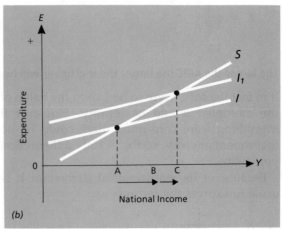

Fig. 30.5 *The multiplier and non-autonomous investment*
If investment is constant (*a*) then the increase in *I* increases *Y* from OA to OB. However, if investment increases with income (*b*) then the same increase in *I* increases *Y* from OA to OC.

Therefore this tends to diminish the size of the multiplier.

b) Type of investment. Different types of investment will have different multiplier effects. For example, extra defence spending will have a different effect from spending on house building because the *MPCs* of the recipients will vary. In addition to this, some types of increased investment spending will create a more favourable economic climate, thus bringing about more investment, as was suggested in Fig. 30.5 (*b*).

c) Time lags. The time taken for the multiplier to work out through the various 'rounds' of spending may vary. Time lags are discussed later in this chapter (see page 376).

The paradox of thrift

In the previous section we considered the effects of shifts in the investment schedule. We will now consider what happens if there is increased thriftiness (saving) in the economy. Thriftiness is usually regarded as desirable. However changes in the propensity to save can have unusual consequences.

In Fig. 30.6 the effect of an increase in savings is to shift the savings line from *S* to *S*$_1$, so the

Fig. 30.6 *The paradox of thrift*
Increased savings cause the equilibrium level of national income to fall.

equilibrium changes from R to R$_1$. The effect of increased saving is, therefore, to *decrease* the equilibrium level of national income. This comes about because if, at a given level of income, people save more, they will automatically consume less. Therefore there is less demand for goods and services. Since most incomes are derived directly or indirectly from the production and sale of goods and services, it follows that

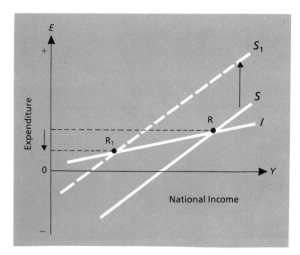

Fig. 30.7 *The paradox of thrift*
Increased savings eventually lead to less being saved.

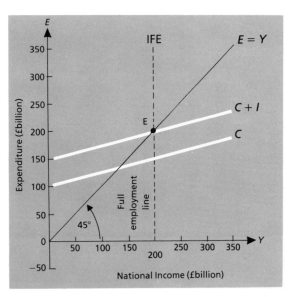

Fig. 30.8 *The full employment line*
Here the equilibrium level of national income coincides with the full employment line. However, this need not be so.

there will be less income. This is what brings about the paradox of thrift.

The paradox can be further developed if we dispense with the assumption that investment is autonomous. Let us now assume that investment increases with income so that the investment line now slopes upwards from left to right. In Fig. 30.7 we again consider the effect of an upward shift in the savings line. Here the paradox is fully illustrated in that not only does increased saving bring about a lower level of income and investment but it also leads, ultimately, *to less being saved*. This effect comes about because there is a lesser ability to save at lower levels of income. People's *planned* increased saving has been frustrated by the fall in income which it occasions. It can also be seen from Figs. 30.6 and 30.7 that there is a multiplier effect (downwards) from the change in savings.

The paradox of thrift is that an increase in the level of planned savings may bring about a fall in the level of savings.

The effect of increased thriftiness also depends upon the state of the economy. In times of inflation an increase in savings might reduce the inflationary pressure in the economy and therefore be a desirable thing. If, however, we have

an economic depression, with lots of unemployment, an increase in thriftiness could be quite disastrous, taking us into a vicious deflationary spiral. It would appear, therefore, that if we 'tighten our belts' in times of economic depression, the depression is likely to be made even worse. As Keynes wrote in 1931: 'Whenever you save five shillings you put a man out of work for a day.'

Inflationary and deflationary gaps

At any particular time there is a level of national income (Y_F) which, if attained, will be sufficient to keep all resources in the economy fully employed. In Fig 30.8 this is represented by the vertical line, FE, which we may term the *full employment line*. In this diagram the equilibrium level of national income (£200bn) corresponds with the full employment level. It has already been stressed, however, that the equilibrium level of national income may be fortuitous.

375

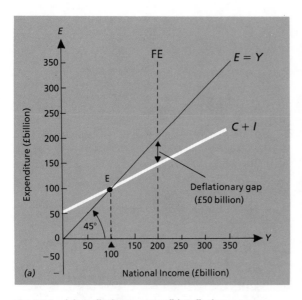

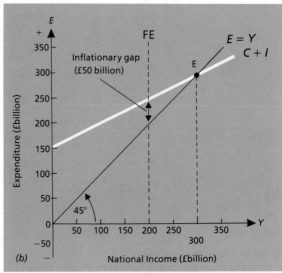

Fig. 30.9 (a) *Deflationary gap.* (b) *Inflationary gap*

If there is insufficient demand in the economy the equilibrium will occur at a lower level of income and to the left of the FE line. This is illustrated in Fig. 30.9 (*a*). Here you can see that the equilibrium level of national income is £100bn and there is therefore severe unemployment in the economy. The distance between the 45° line and the *C* + *I* line at the full employment level of national income is referred to as the *deflationary gap*. In order for unemployment to be eliminated, the *C* + *I* line must be moved up by £50bn. Why would extra spending of £50bn raise national income by £100bn? The answer is that in this case the multiplier is 2.

In Fig. 30.9 (*b*) the equilibrium level of national income appears to be to the right of the FE line at £300bn. This is because people are trying to buy more goods and services than can be produced when all resources are fully employed. There is 'too much money chasing too few goods'. The result is that the excess demand pulls up prices and there is inflation. The excess demand for goods and services is being met in money terms but not real terms. The vertical distance between the *C* + *I* line and the 45° line at the full employment level of national income is termed the *inflationary gap*. In this case it would

be necessary to lower the *C* + *I* line by £50bn to eliminate inflation. Again note that, because of the multiplier, cutting demand by £50bn causes income to decline by £100bn.

This is the Keynesian or 'demand pull' view of inflation. There is, however, much argument about the causes of inflation and these are more fully discussed in Chapter 42.

Time lags and stock changes

Savings and investment in national income accounts

We have been able to demonstrate in previous chapters that *realised* savings will always equal *realised* investment. In this chapter we have been mainly concerned with what happens if investment is greater than savings or vice versa. How do we reconcile these two viewpoints?

The truth of the statement (realised *S* = realised *I*) we have been able to demonstrate from national accounts. However this, in part, arises from the method by which national income accounts are compiled.

Let us say, for example, that we started from a position where $S = I$ and then investment rises by £10bn. How would we deal with this in terms of national income accounts? The only way in which an increased demand for investment goods could be met immediately would be by a fall in the stocks (inventories) of such goods. Therefore, as far as the national income accounts are concerned, *disinvestment* is taking place to the exact extent of the rise in investment. Thus I will still equal S. The same analysis would continue to say that the sale of these stocks would create no income for households (since they are already manufactured). Thus firms would be in receipt of £10bn which they would not have to spend on factor services and this would appear as money not spent, i.e. savings.

Thus we find that $S = I$ because they are two ways of measuring the same thing as far as national income accounts are concerned. This is because the accounts are essentially concentrating on one point of the circular flow, i.e. the value of the ouput of firms. The other values, expenditure and income, are adjusted to be consistent with the value of output. However, what we are concerned with when we are examining the determination of national income is the various different parts of the flow and how one gives rise to the other.

Time periods in national income

It is obvious that a time element must enter into the determination of national income. We can explain the effect of time on national income by dividing it into periods. How long the period is need not concern us here – it might be a week or a month. We will simply assume that what happens in one time period affects what happens in the next. It will aid our understanding if we return to the circular flow diagram with which we began our study of national income.

Suppose that we start with consumers' expenditure and investment expenditure. This is used to purchase goods and services from firms. Thus as we have already seen it will constitute the value of national income or output. We may write this as:

$$Y = C + I$$

which is the national income accounts way of looking at it. However we may now view this as happening in one time period (t) and the payment of households for the use of their factor services as happening in the subsequent period ($t+1$). Thus the value of national income/output in period 1 we may now write as:

$$Y_t = C_t + I_t$$

This gives rise to the income of households (Y_H) in period 2. This we may write as:

$$Y_{H_{t+1}} = C_t + I_t$$

This is illustrated in Fig. 30.10. The righthand side of the diagram shows what happens to households' income ($Y_{H_{t+1}}$). It is divided between consumption and savings. This we can write as:

$$Y_{H_{t+1}} = C_{t+1} + S_{t+1}$$

The total of this consumer spending in period 2, together with investment in period 2, constitutes national income/output for this period. The national output in period 2 goes on to become households' income for period 3 ($Y_{H_{t+2}}$) and so on. Thus the equilibrium which may exist between the two sides of national income, i.e national income and national expenditure, is a *post-factum equilibrium*, i.e. an equilibrium when considered over time. Thus we can say that income in one period is the result of output in the previous period.

Time lags in output

We have thus assumed that households' income lags one period behind output. However this also assumes that output can adjust instantaneously to changes in demand. If, for example, aggregate demand were to rise by 10 per cent we have so far assumed that output could rise by that amount *in the same time period*. This **377**

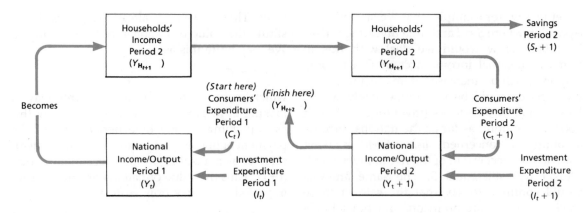

Fig. 30.10 *Households' income and consumer expenditure and investment*
Households' income (Y_H) in period 2 is the result of consumers' expenditure and investment in the previous period:

$$Y_{H_{t+1}} = C_t + I_t$$

Households' income is divided between consumption and savings:

$$Y_{H_{t+1}} = C_{t+1} + S_{t+1}$$

Consumption expenditure and investment in period 2 become households' income in period 3:

$$Y_{H_{t+2}} = C_{t+1} + I_{t+1}$$

would therefore leave firms' stocks of goods unchanged.

However, as we have already argued, it would be reasonable to assume that any change in demand might be met by changing the firms' stocks of goods (or inventories). If, for example, demand were to rise, business could meet this by depleting their stocks. Output would take some time to adjust to the change in demand. How long the time lag would be would depend upon a wide number of factors such as raw material availability, business confidence, etc. To examine the effect of a time lag in output we will make the simplest assumption possible, which is that changes in output (Y) lag one period behind changes in aggregate demand ($C + I$).

An example of such an economy is given in Fig. 30.11. Time periods 1 and 2 describe an economy in equilibrium, behaving as described in the previous section, i.e. the value of output (Y) in period 1 becomes the value of households' income (Y_H) in period 2. We then go on to see the effect of an increase in investment in period 3 if there is a one-period lag in output. You can see that in period 3 the rise in autonomous investment from £40bn to £80bn is met by depleting stocks. Thus I_1 is −£40bn. The effect of this is therefore to leave the value of output (Y) unchanged in period 3. This also means, therefore, that the value of households' income (Y_H) is unchanged in period 4. Now in period 4 output responds to the change in demand in period 3. Thus autonomous investment is £80bn and there is no change in stocks, so that output (Y) now rises and, since the *MPC* is constant at 0·8, consumption therefore increases to £192bn. Thus aggregate demand ($C + I$) rises by £32bn in period 5, which is met by depleting stocks by this amount. The effect of this is to leave output (Y) unchanged at £240bn. Households' income (Y_H) is therefore unchanged in period 6, but output responds to the rise in $C + I$ in the previous period. Hence Y now rises to £272bn, and so on.

The introduction of time lags into the model in no way influences the determination of the equilibrium level. As you can see in Fig. 30.11, the ultimate equilibrium level of Y is £400bn, which is what it would be with or without time lags. However the existence of time lags in the

Time Period	1	2	3	4	5	6	7		n	
Households' income (the value of last period's national output) ($Y = Y_{t-1}$)	200	200	200	200	240	240	272		400	Y_H
Savings ($S = 0.2Y_H$)	40	40	40	40	48	48	54.4		80	S
Consumption ($C = 0.8Y_H$)	160	160	160	160	192	192	217.6		320	C
Autonomous Investment (I)	40	40	80	80	80	80	80		80	I
Change in stocks (I_1) (Last period's $C + I$ minus this period's $C + I$) ($I_1 = [C_{t-1} + I_{t-1}] - [C_t + I_t]$)	0	0	−40	0	−32	0	25.6		0	I_1
National Income (the value of this period's output) ($Y = C + I + I_1$)	200	200	200	240	240	272	272		400	Y

Fig. 30.11 *The effects of a one-period time lag in output on the operation of the multiplier (all figures in £bn)*

circular flow means that the path from one equilibrium to another becomes very uneven.

Conclusion

In this chapter we have examined the determination of national income with reference to savings and investment. We have yet to discuss how the government and foreign trade influence income determination. However when we examine these sectors we will find that all withdrawals act upon income in the same way as savings, and all injections in the same manner as investment. Thus we have developed a theory which is all but complete.

There are several reasons why we have adopted this savings-and-investment-only approach. Firstly, it simplifies discussion of income determination. Secondly, it lays emphasis upon the Keynesian origins of this analysis and its subsequent enshrinement in many major textbooks. Lastly, but not least, if you are preparing for an examination you will often find questions and problems based upon the model used in this chapter.

Summary

1 Equilibrium is reached in the economy when aggregate demand is equal to income. Graphically this is where the $C + I$ line crosses the 45° line. It is also the level of income at which $S = I$.

2 Any change in spending results in a larger change in the level of Y as a result of the multiplier effect.

3 The size of the multiplier is determined by the MPC and can be calculated from the formula:

379

$$K = \frac{1}{1 - MPC}$$

4   The paradox of thrift is that, *ceteris paribus*, a rise in the propensity to save causes income to decline and hence, ultimately, less saving.

5   At any particular time there is a level of Y which, if attained, would mean the full employment of all resources. The existence of an equilibrium at any other level of Y creates either an inflationary or deflationary gap.

6   There is a periodicity in the determination of national income such that output (Y) in one period creates the income (Y_H) in the next period. The periodicity may be complicated by the existence of time lags in the economy.

7   In explaining the determination of national income in relation to savings and investment we are also explaining the mechanism by which other injections and withdrawals will influence income.

Questions

1   Explain as clearly as possible the basic theory of income determination developed in this chapter.

2   Give a brief:
   a) commonsense;
   b) arithmetical;
   c) graphical
explanation of the multiplier.

3   Distinguish between the individual and the community viewpoints on the desirability of thrift.

4   Compare the operation of the multiplier and the accelerator principles. In what sense are they incompatible?

5   Redraft Fig. 30.11 assuming that there is no time lag in output.

6   What policies would you advocate to eliminate:
   a) an inflationary gap;
   b) a deflationary gap?

7   If

$$C = 40 + \tfrac{2}{3}Y$$

and investment is constant at $I = 50$, can you confirm that $Y = 270$ when the economy is in equilibrium? Increase I by 1 and confirm that Y increases by 3. What is the value of the multiplier and why?

Data response   Plotting the equilibrium

Complete the following table for a hypothetical economy (all figures £bn). Assume that the consumption function is a straight line and that investment is constant at all levels of income.

Y	C	S	I	APC	MPC
0	25		25		
100	100				
200					
300					
400					
500					

a) From this data, draw a graph of the consumption function and of aggregate demand. Underneath this graph draw another to show savings and investment. Demonstrate the relationship between the two graphs.

b) What is the equilibrium level of national income? Show it clearly on the graph. 200

c) Now assume that I increases by £25bn. What will be the new equilibrium level of national income? 300

d) Explain the principle that is at work in moving from the first to the second equilibrium.

e) This is a model of a closed economy with no government intervention. What would be the situation if these assumptions were dropped.

31

Modelling the economy

Nature has . . . some sort of arithmetical-geometrical coordinate system, because nature has all kinds of models. What we experience of nature is in models, and all of nature's models are so beautiful. It struck me that nature's system must be a real beauty, because in chemistry we find that the associations are always in beautiful whole numbers – there are no fractions.

Richard Buckminster Fuller

If in other sciences we should arrive at certainty without doubt and truth without error, it behoves us to place the foundations of knowledge in mathematics.

Roger Bacon

It is now possible to complete our building of the model of the economy by including the government sector and foreign trade. In this chapter we shall examine them in so far as they affect the theory of income determination. Descriptive treatments of government fiscal policy and of foreign trade are dealt with in later chapters. At the end of this chapter we will have built a *relatively* simple model of the economy and there are suggestions for how to turn this into a computer operated model.

The government sector

Government spending (G)

The spending of central and local government can be grouped under three headings:

a) current spending on goods and services;
b) investment spending;
c) transfer payments.

It is only the first two of these categories which can be classed as *injections* to the circular flow of income. They may be grouped together and abbreviated to G. *Transfer payments* such as old-age pensions are not included since they are not payments for factor services. In fact transfer payments will appear as part of consumption (C). Transfer payments may affect the national income if they cause a change in the *MPC*. This is significant if one realises that transfer payments constitute about 39 per cent of government expenditure in the UK, whereas 20 years ago they accounted for only 29 per cent. This is partly because of a rise in the number of people requiring help, due to an increase in the old-age population and the drastic rise in unemployment. It is also due to a shift in policy in favour of this type of payment. For example, over the same period, old-age pensions have risen by 40 per cent more than average incomes.

The size of government expenditure is determined by public policy. We therefore regard it as *autonomous* for the purposes of our model building. Aggregate demand in the economy now consists of:

$$Y = C + I + G$$

Taxes (T)

Taxes are a withdrawal from the circular flow. All the main forms of tax are levied either upon incomes or upon spending. Thus, although the tax rates may be determined by the government, the amount of tax paid will depend upon the circular flow. Therefore taxes are a function of income and are an endogenous variable. If, for example, there were a 15 per cent tax on all incomes, then we could write:

$$T_Y = 0.15Y$$

This would leave us with disposable income (Y_D). Previously, although we have distinguished between income and disposable income, they have been the same amount since all income was passed on. Now, because of income taxes, disposable income is smaller than national income.

Taxes on consumer spending could be expressed as a proportion of disposable income, after we have netted out the effect of subsidies. Thus if, for example, taxes on spending constituted 20 per cent of disposable income we could write:

$$T_C = 0.2Y_D$$

Thus the total for all taxes would be:

$$T = 0.15Y + (0.85Y \times 0.2)$$

Equilibrium in the closed economy

We can incorporate the government sector into a graphical analysis of national income determination. Injections into the economy will be:

$$I + G$$

and withdrawals will be:

$$S + T$$

and therefore equilibrium will be where:

$$I + G = S + T$$

as in Fig. 31.1. Here we can see both investment and government spending represented as horizontal straight lines since both are autonomous. On the other hand both savings and taxation are functions of income. We therefore show them as increasing with income. Equilibrium is therefore where the two lines cross, i.e. where injections equal withdrawals.

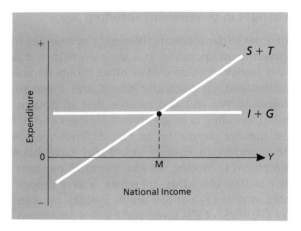

Fig. 31.1 *Equilibrium in the closed economy*
This occurs where:

$$S + T = I + G$$

The $I + G$ line is horizontal since both are autonomous, whereas both S and T rise with Y.

Multiplier effects

A change in either government spending or taxation will have a multiplier effect. Previously we have seen that the size of the multiplier will be determined by the marginal propensity to save:

$$K = \frac{1}{MPS} \text{ or } \frac{1}{s}$$

However we must now consider that there is another withdrawal, taxation, to be taken into account. We now find that the value of the multiplier is:

$$K = \frac{1}{s + t}$$

where s is the *marginal propensity to save* and t is the *marginal rate of taxation*. If, for example, the MPS were 0.15 and the marginal rate of taxation were 0.25 then the value of the multiplier would be:

$$K = \frac{1}{0.15 + 0.25}$$

$$= 2.5$$

383

Changes in government spending

In order to demonstrate the effects of changes in government spending in a simple manner it is necessary to assume that all other things remain unchanged, in particular that s and t remain constant. We will also assume that all government spending is on goods and services and not on transfer payments. In Fig. 31.2 (a) we see an economy in equilibrium. Taxes have been simplified to income tax which is at 15 per cent. If Y is 1000 units this, therefore, leaves disposable income (Y_D) at 850 units. Twenty per cent (or 170 units) of Y is saved and the rest consumed. All these flows can be expressed as proportions of Y or Y_D. Investment and government spending are autonomous constants.

In Fig. 31.2 (b) government spending has been increased by 80 units to 180. The resultant change in Y will be determined by the size of the multiplier.

$$K = \frac{1}{s + t}$$

Savings are 0·2 of disposable income, which is 0·85 of total income, whilst taxation is 0·15 of total income. Thus we have:

$$K = \frac{1}{(0\cdot85 \times 0\cdot2) + 0\cdot15}$$
$$= \frac{1}{0\cdot17 + 0\cdot15}$$
$$= \frac{1}{0\cdot32}$$
$$= 3\cdot125$$

Each extra unit of government spending will therefore be multiplied 3·125 times. Therefore:

$$\Delta Y = K \times \Delta G$$
$$= 3\cdot125 \times 80$$
$$= 250$$

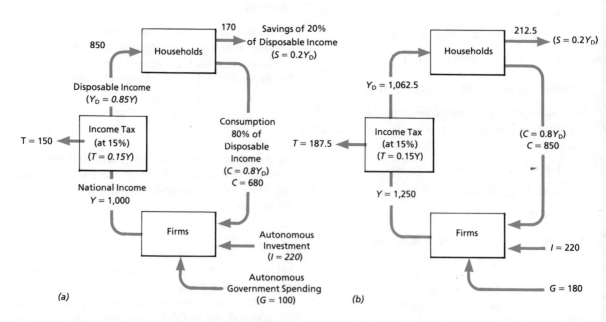

Fig. 31.2 *The effect of changes in government spending*
(a) The economy is in equilibrium. The value of the multiplier is determined by the size of the withdrawals functions:

$$K = \frac{1}{0.32} = 3.125$$

(b) The effect of an extra 80 units of government spending is shown. We now have an equilibrium Y of 1250 units.

Therefore the level of national income will rise by 250 units to 1250. This is illustrated in Fig. 31.2 (*b*). The other variables in the model will all change as a result of the change in Y, although they remain constant as proportions of Y. Investment is unchanged since it is autonomous.

It is worthy of note that, although the government increased its spending from 100 to 180, this caused Y to rise and therefore more taxes to be collected. Thus the size of the budget surplus (previously 50 units) has actually only *decreased* from 50 units to 7·5 units.

Changes in taxation

The effects of a change in taxation are slightly more complex because not only will a change in taxes alter the quantity of withdrawals, it will also alter the size of the withdrawals function and hence the value of the multiplier.

We may illustrate the effect of a change in

taxation by considering the equilibrium condition. For equilibrium it is necessary that:

$$I + G = S + T$$

In Fig. 31.3 I and G are autonomous constants, so therefore we can say:

$$220 + 100 = S + T$$

In Fig. 31.3 (*a*) the economy is in equilibrium where:

$$320 = (0.85Y \times 0.2) + 0.15Y$$
$$= 0.17Y + 0.15Y$$
$$= 0.32Y$$
$$Y = 1000$$

Let us now consider the effect if income tax were to be increased to 25 per cent. If I and G remain constant then the new equilibrium must be where:

$$320 = S + T$$

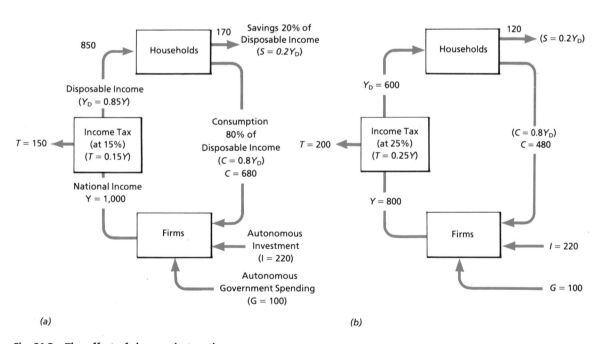

(a)   *(b)*

Fig. 31.3 *The effect of changes in taxation*
(*a*) The economy is in equilibrium. (*b*) We see the effect of increasing the rate of income tax to 25 per cent. This now means that the value of all withdrawals in the economy is increased to $W = 0.4$. Since injections are an autonomous constant at $J = 320$, and in equilibrium injections must equal withdrawals, then if withdrawals are 320 units and withdrawals are 0.4Y, Y must equal 800 units.

Savings will still be 0·2 of disposable income (Y_D), which is now 0·75 of Y, while T will be 0·25Y. Therefore the new equilibrium condition is that:

$$320 = (0·75Y \times 0·2) + 0·25Y$$
$$= 0·15Y + 0·25Y$$
$$= 0·4Y$$
$$Y = 800$$

You can confirm this by looking at the figures in Fig. 31.3 (b). Are you able to say what the value of the multiplier is in Fig. 31.3 (b)?

The balanced budget multiplier hypothesis

It can be argued that the effect of exactly equal aggregate changes in taxes and government expenditure ($T = G$) is such that, because of multiplier effects, a new equilibrium will be reached when national income has risen by the amount of the original change in government expenditure ($\triangle Y = \triangle G$).

Suppose that we have an economy with a constant propensity to withdraw ($s + t$) of 0·2. Now suppose the government increases its purchases of goods and services by £1000 and increases income tax by £1000. The effect of the increased spending sets up a multiplier sequence, the value of which will be:

$$\triangle Y = \triangle C \times \frac{1}{s + t}$$

where $\triangle C$ = the value of the extra purchase of goods and services by government and $s + t$ (the propensity to withdraw) remains constant at 0·2. We would therefore obtain:

$$\triangle Y = £1000 \times \frac{1}{0·2}$$

$$= £5000$$

However, when we consider the effect of increased taxation we must consider that 0·2 of £1000 would have been withdrawn from the circular flow anyway and that therefore the value of the multiplier will be:

$$\triangle Y = \triangle C \times \frac{1}{s + t}$$

$$\triangle Y = - £800 \times \frac{1}{0·2}$$

$$= - £4000$$

Therefore the combined effect of these changes is:

$$\triangle Y = £5000 - £4000$$
$$= £1000$$

We can therefore see that the change in income is equal to the original change in government expenditure.

The effect does not work out as simply as suggested here, but it is important to realise that an apparently balanced budget does not have a neutral effect upon the economy.

Modifying factors

The balanced budget hypothesis and the other calculations we have looked at in this section are all subject to modification when we come to compute their actual value in the economy. Some of the factors which cause these modifications are listed below.

a) Different MPCs. Different sectors of the community (the very rich, old-age pensioners, etc) will have different propensities to consume. Thus the type of taxes and the type of government expenditure undertaken will have differing effects. For example, increased taxes will make little difference to the consumption expenditure of the rich but will significantly affect the spending of the poor (this point is further developed on page 562).

b) Progressive taxes. Because of the progressive nature of taxation, any rise in income will tend to increase the proportion paid in tax and vice versa. This therefore modifies the multiplier.

c) Inflation. Inflation and the resulting fiscal drag tend to decrease the size of the multiplier.

d) Transfer payments. Money spent on transfer payments is usually not treated as part of G. However, since most transfer payments are made to lower-income groups and since lower-income groups have high MPCs, the effect of increased transfer payments is to increase the value of the *MPC* and therefore the value of the multiplier.

Foreign trade: the open economy

The inclusion of foreign trade will allow us to complete our model of the economy. As explained in Chapter 28, imports (*M*) are a withdrawal from the circular flow and exports (*X*) are an injection.

Exports (*X*)

The demand for exports is determined by a large number of factors such as the state of world trade, restrictions on trade and exchange rates. However for the purposes of our model we will assume that *exports are autonomous*, since none of these factors is linked directly to the level of national income.

Imports (*M*)

When we consider the demand for imports we can see that in the main it is determined by the level of *Y*. If, for example, output is rising, it follows that imports of raw materials, etc., must also rise. We can also see that a fairly constant proportion of consumer demand is met by imports. Thus a rise in *Y* should cause a rise in *M*. This is not so when we consider exports; there is no reason why, as output rises, a constant proportion of it will be exported.

The propensity to import

In the same way that we were able to calculate propensities to save, we may calculate propensities to import.

The proportion of income which is devoted to imports is termed the average propensity to import and may be calculated as:

$$APM = \frac{M}{Y}$$

The proportion of any addition to income which is devoted to imports is termed the marginal propensity to import and may be calculated as:

$$MPM = \frac{\triangle M}{\triangle Y}$$

The foreign trade multiplier

Having calculated the *MPM* we are able to determine the value of the foreign trade multiplier as:

$$K = \frac{1}{MPM}$$

However it is more usual to consider this as part of the combined multiplier which takes account of all withdrawals from the economy.

Equilibrium and the multiplier

Equilibrium in the open economy

An equilibrium is reached when total withdrawals are equal to total injections. As was explained in Chapter 28, this is where:

$$I + G + X = S + T + M$$

which we may abbreviate to:

$$J = W$$

It was also explained earlier that it is not necessary for each withdrawal to equal its respective injection, only that the value of all injections equal the total of all withdrawals. It therefore follows that if there is any disturbance in the equilibrium the necessary condition for the return to equilibrium is that:

$$\triangle J = \triangle W$$

We can demonstrate the equilibrium graphically by using either aggregate expenditure and income or injections and withdrawals. This is done in Fig. 31.4. The top graph shows that aggregate demand (the total of all expenditure in the economy) is now

$$E = C + I + G + (X - M)$$

The last part of the expression (*X* − *M*) is placed in brackets to draw attention to the fact that **387**

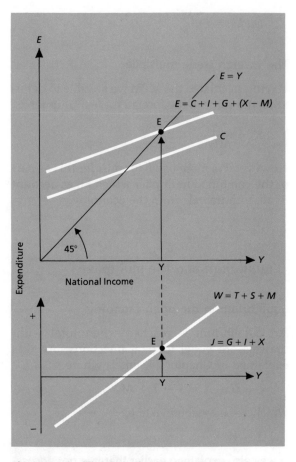

Fig. 31.4 *Equilibrium in the open economy*
This is where total expenditure (C + I + G + (X – M)) is equal to income (Y) and where withdrawals are equal to injections (W = J).

the net figure from foreign trade can be either positive or negative (it is inconceivable in an economy that the other figures such as G should be negative). A trade surplus would move the E line upwards whilst a trade deficit would move it downwards. The equilibrium occurs where this total expenditure line crosses the 45° line, i.e. where expenditure is equal to income. From the lower graph it can be seen that this is also the level of income at which:

$$W = J$$

The J line remains horizontal because all three

injections have been assumed to be autonomous, i.e. independent of Y.

The combined multiplier

Figure 31.5 illustrates that there will be a multiplier effect from any movement of the J line. Here we can see that an increase from J to J_1 has brought about an increase in income of Y to Y_1. Clearly $\triangle Y$ is considerably greater than $\triangle J$ and we can therefore express the value of the multiplier for the entire economy as:

$$K = \frac{\triangle Y}{\triangle J}$$

The size of the multiplier will be determined by the magnitude of withdrawals from the circular flow. We can calculate the multiplier as:

$$K = \frac{1}{w}$$

where w is the marginal propensity to withdraw.

To determine w we must total all the other propensities to withdraw, i.e.

$$K = \frac{1}{s + t + m}$$

If for example the marginal propensity to save (s) were 0·10, the marginal rate of taxation (t) were 0·15 and the marginal propensity of import (m) were 0·25 then we would have:

$$K = \frac{1}{0·10 + 0·15 + 0·25}$$

$$= \frac{1}{0·5}$$

$$= 2$$

In fact this is the value of the multiplier shown in Fig. 31.5. You should also be able to see from Fig. 31.5 that there can also be a multiplier effect from a change in the W line as well as in the J line.

There are therefore several ways in which we might formulate the effect of any multiplier change.

$$\triangle Y = K . \triangle J$$

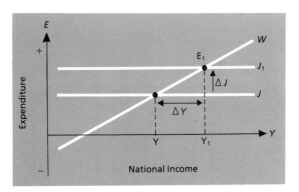

Fig. 31.5 *The combined multiplier*
The effect of an increase in injections from J to
J_1 is to increase the level of income from Y to Y_1. Thus
the value of the multiplier is

$$K = \frac{\triangle Y}{\triangle J}$$

would give the effect of a change in injections, while

$$\triangle Y = K \cdot \triangle W$$

would give the effect of a change in withdrawals. Both changes in withdrawals and injections make themselves felt as changes in spending (C). Thus we could encompass both the above formulations and write:

$$\triangle Y = K \cdot \triangle C$$

where $\triangle C$ is the result of a change in consumption resulting from a change in either injections or withdrawals.

Remember that the multiplier effect can operate either upwards or downwards.

The multiplier: an algebraic approach

The reader who has followed the explanation so far and has a little knowledge of algebra may like to consider the following algebraic derivation of the multiplier formula. Readers who are terrified of algebra may omit this passage without impairing their understanding.

The value of the multiplier effect, as we have seen, is:

$$\triangle Y = K \cdot \triangle J \qquad (1)$$

We also know that in equilibrium we will have:

$$W = J \qquad (2)$$

If there is any disturbance of the equilibrium the necessary condition for return to equilibrium is:

$$\triangle W = \triangle J \qquad (3)$$

Let us suppose, therefore, that J increases by some amount. This will increase the level of income and therefore increase the level of withdrawals, which are all determined by income. The size of this increase will be:

$$\triangle W = w \cdot \triangle Y \qquad (4)$$

Since to return to equilibrium we must have the change in injections equal to the change in withdrawals, we must have (substituting (4) into (3)):

$$w \cdot \triangle Y = \triangle J \qquad (5)$$

If we divide both sides by w we will obtain:

$$\triangle Y = \frac{1}{w} \cdot \triangle J \qquad (6)$$

If we substitute the letter K for $\frac{1}{w}$ we will obtain:

$$\triangle Y = K \cdot \triangle J \qquad (1)$$

This will be recognised as the expression which we started with. Since both (1) and (6) are equal to $\triangle Y$ we may substitute (1) into (6) and obtain:

$$K \cdot \triangle J = \frac{1}{w} \cdot \triangle J \qquad (7)$$

Since $\triangle J$ is common to both sides we may cancel it and obtain:

$$K = \frac{1}{w} \qquad (8)$$

which is immediately recognisable as the multiplier.

The value of the UK multiplier

The value of the multiplier can be arrived at by considering the change in withdrawals from one year to the next. If we divide this by the change in GDP this will give us the marginal propensity to withdraw (w).

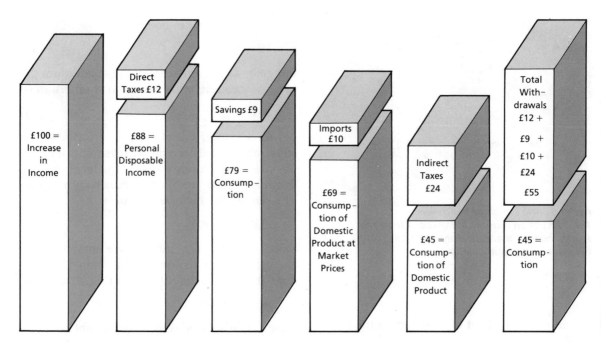

Fig. 31.6 *Withdrawals from the UK economy, 1985–86*
For every £100 of additional income, £55 was withdrawn from the circular flow. The value of the multiplier is thus:

$$K = 1 = \frac{1.82}{0.55} \text{ (approx.)}$$

$$w = \frac{\triangle W}{\triangle GDP}$$

We can then state the value of the multiplier as:

$$K = \frac{1}{w}$$

Figure 31.6 shows the approximate value of the various withdrawals for the year 1985–6.

It can be seen from Fig. 31.6 that, overall, £55 out of each additional £100 was withdrawn from the circular flow. This therefore gives a value of:

$$w = 0{\cdot}55$$

Thus a multiplier of:

$$K = \frac{1}{0{\cdot}55}$$

$$= 1{\cdot}82 \text{ (approx.)}$$

Quite significant changes can come about in the individual withdrawals. Remember that we are here concerned with how the *additions* are distributed. Therefore, there can be quite dramatic changes in the value of MPM, MPS or the MPT from year to year. For instance, in the year we have considered (1985–86) savings in the personal sector actually *declined* which would therefore give a negative value for MPS. (The MPS we used in the example actually refers to the whole economy and not just to PDI.) However, overall the marginal propensity to withdraw remains relatively stable as increases in one withdrawal are compensated for by decreases in another.

Note Actual values used in this example as calculated from the 'Blue Book' are $s = 0.0869$, $t = 0.3565$ and $m = 0.1043$. These give a value of $K = 1.8256$.

Internal and external changes

When we looked at the balanced budget multiplier we saw that equal changes in G and T might not have equal effects upon the circular flow. Since, however, in the closed economy we knew the value of the various withdrawals, it was possible to predict these effects. Now that we have included foreign trade in the circular flow the effects of changes in the components are less certain because we cannot be sure of the propensities to withdraw of our trading partners. The problem is further complicated by such things as movements in exchange rates. Some propositions are considered below:

a) *Changes in G or I*. A rise in G or I would cause an increase in Y. Any increase in Y would cause more to be imported, whilst exports would remain unchanged, since they are autonomous. Thus the balance of payments situation would have *worsened*. A fall in G or I should have the opposite effect and *improve the* balance of payments by *reducing income*.

b) *Changes in X*. If exports increase this will cause Y to rise until total withdrawals equal total injections. However only part of the withdrawals will be imports. Therefore a rise in exports should improve the balance of payments. Conversely a fall in exports would worsen the situation.

c) *Feedback effects*. These are said to occur when a nation's overseas trade is significant enough to affect world trade. Since as we are about to argue that the results are mathematically uncertain, we will digress from our abstract treatment and use a practical example. The large OPEC oil price rises of 1978 could be likened to a massive increase in their exports. This, however, had the effect of pushing their trading partners into deficit, these deficits reduced their income and they, therefore, had to curtail imports. Eventually the fall in imports was sufficient (coupled with the rise in imports in OPEC countries brought about by increased income) to push the OPEC countries into deficit.

The existence of feedback effects makes it difficult to predict the long-term effects of changes in imports and exports. This is especially so for a nation like the UK which is very dependent upon overseas trade. The effect of changes in exports and imports will depend upon the relative propensities to withdraw in the trading countries.

National income accounts reconsidered

We started our study of macroeconomics (Chapter 7) with a look at national income accounts. Having built up a model of the economy it will be useful to check it against the actual economy. It can be seen from Fig. 31.7 that our model most closely approximates with the national expenditure method of calculating national income. The model is quite simple because national income accounts are concerned with accounting in one time period (usually a year). Thus, although income is a flow with respect to time, we can represent all withdrawals or injections as simple aggregates without being concerned at the sequence of them. If we consider items (1) to (7) in Fig. 31.7 we arrive at a total for Y which in this case is the GDP. This is our familiar equation of:

$$Y = C + I + G + (X - M)$$

The figures for 1986 are shown in Table 31.1 on page 392. You can see the correspondence with

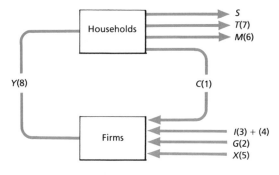

Fig. 31.7 A model of national income
The numbers in brackets correspond to the items in
Table 31.1

Table 31.1 National income accounts, expenditure method, 1986

Category of expenditure	£m
(1) Consumers' expenditure (C)	234 167
(2) General government final consumption (G)	79 423
(3) Gross domestic fixed capital formation (I)	64 227
(4) Value of physical increase in stocks and work in progress (I)	551
(5) Exports of goods and services (X)	97 835
(6) Less imports of goods and services (M)	−101 308
Gross domestic product (GDP) at market prices	374 895
Factor cost adjustments:	
(7) Less taxes on expenditure (T)	62 273
Subsidies	6 467
(8) Gross domestic product (GDP) at factor cost (Y)	319 089

Fig. 31.7 (by referring back to Chapter 7 you can see what adjustments need to be made to arrive at GNP and NNP).

As was explained previously, since the national income is always expressed in terms of production value, i.e. at 'firms' in the circular flow, it must always be the case that output = expenditure = income. However, when we consider the determination of national income we become concerned with the order in which things happen within the model.

simple macroeconomic model. Readers should make themselves thoroughly familiar with this before progressing to a higher level of study. We will now go on to consider the practical problems raised by such things as inflation and exchange rates. It should also be stated that the theory of how the economy functions is extremely contentious. So far we have presented an orthodox post-Keynesian view of the economy. We must also go on to see the modifications which monetarist ideas have made to our understanding of the economy.

Conclusion

We have now concluded our construction of a

Summary

1 The economy is in equilibrium when withdrawals (W) are equal to injections (J).

2 Both changes in government activity and foreign trade will have multiplier effects upon the economy.

3 Because of multiplier effects, equal changes in government spending and taxes do not have equal effects upon the economy.

4 The value of the various components within the circular flow will tend to change as the level of income changes. For example, a rise in income increases the proportion of income paid in taxes.

5 The value of the combined multiplier is:

$$K = \frac{1}{s + t + m}$$

$$= \frac{1}{w}$$

6   The external position of the economy (the balance of payments) may be affected by changes in any of the components of the circular flow.

7   Feedback effects occur when a nation's foreign trade is sufficiently large as to affect the national income of its trading partners (the rest of the world).

8   The model of the economy developed over the last few chapters can be most closely equated with the *national income expenditure method* of calculating the national income.

Questions

1   Explain why a given change in government spending may have a greater effect upon the economy than the same change in taxation.

2   Throughout this chapter we have regarded government expenditure as autonomous. To what extent is the government free to determine its expenditure and to what extent is this determined by the economic situation?

3   Suppose that the proportion of disposable income which is consumed is 85 per cent and that disposable income is 80 per cent of total income. Imports account for 20 per cent of disposable income and there is an expenditure tax of 10 per cent on all forms of consumer spending. What is the value of the multiplier?

4   If in Fig. 31.2 government expenditure were increased from 100 units to 200 units, what would be the new equilibrium level of income? If in Fig. 31.3 income tax were decreased to 20 per cent instead of 25 per cent, what would be the new equilibrium level of national income and what would be the value of the multiplier?

5   Why does inflation tend to decrease the size of the multiplier?

6   Explain what is meant by feedback in foreign trade? Does it follow that a rise in exports is always beneficial to a country's balance of payments?

7   If injections rise with income instead of being autonomous then we must modify the multiplier formula to:

$$K = \frac{1}{w - j};$$

where j is the marginal propensity to inject. Demonstrate that if injections are autonomous and $C = 0.5Y - 200$ then $K = 2$, whereas if $j = 0.1Y$ and $C = 0.5Y - 200$ then $K = 2.5$.

   If $C = 0.5Y - 200$ and $J = 300$ then $Y = 1000$, and also if $J = 200 + 0.1Y$ and $C = 0.5Y - 200$ then $Y = 1000$. Contrast the effect of a rise in J of 100 units in both these situations to show that in the first case the equilibrium of Y will be 1200 whereas in the second case it will be 1250 units.

Appendix: a computer model

We have so far used modelling as a method of understanding the economy, but these days models of the economy are used in determining government and business policy. There are today dozens of macroeconomic models of the economy operated by computers. In the UK the

393

Treasury model is perhaps the most important. Others include the St James Group, the Cambridge Economic Policy Group and the Item models. In the USA models include the US Department of Commerce, the Modigliani, FRB–MIT–Penn, and the Chase-Manhattan Bank models. Such models are used primarily for forecasting and for assessing different policy alternatives.

Models are built by assessing the statistical data on the various components of national income and adopting values based on past experience. The model we have used has, of course, been very much simplified; a model such as the Treasury one would use dozens of multiple correlation equations. However, anyone with access to a microcomputer can construct a model of the economy, either simple or complex. Figure 31.8 gives a starting point. Here we have broken down some of the flows; for example, we see that there are three forms of tax, income tax, VAT and corporation tax. Government spending, exports and investment are still assumed to be autonomous in this model. The values given do not correspond

exactly to the actual values in the UK economy, although the value of the multiplier for this model is very close to the UK one (see page 390).

Before proceeding with the last part of this chapter you should make sure you have clearly understood pages 377–79 on the significance of time periods in the circular flow. In Fig. 31.8 national output in one period gives rise to national income in the next period. Thus the order in which things happen becomes very important and will affect the equilibrium level of national income.

We can now proceed to Fig. 31.9 which gives a computer program developed from Fig. 31.8. Here we have now made almost everything a dependent variable except for government expenditure. A function has also been added for an interest rate relationship between savings and investment. With a little effort it should be possible for anyone with a knowledge of BASIC to operate this model. The program is well within the capacity of any 16K RAM computer.

At the outset the value of GNP = 200 is inputted; with the values given in lines 40 and 50, this gives a value for GNP which is below the desired full employment equilibrium of 250. You can change either of the government expenditure inputs, the rates of tax and the rate of interest to achieve the desired equilibrium level. Overshooting the desired level causes inflation which is assumed to be undesirable.

This in fact is a program which has been very much condensed from a larger program which gives more detailed information on all aspects of the model. There are two reasons for condensing it; firstly to save space and secondly to make the program more machine non-specific. It is perhaps a little bit naughty to build in an interest rate function but it does make the problem more interesting. Exports have also been slightly randomised in line 300 to the extent of about 0·5 per cent of their total which is calculated from industry income. The program stops when two successive values of GNP are equal, i.e. equilibrium has been reached.

1 The expression @ % = &20209 is peculiar

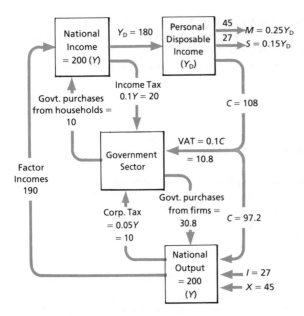

Fig. 31.8 *A model of the economy*

```
>L.
      10CLS:PRINT''''
      20@%= %20209:Tax=0.1:EQUILIBRIUM=FALSE
      30Intr=0.15:Imports=30:Vat=0.15:Savingtotal=1:Ctax=0.05
      40Xport=30:Govexp1=20:Govexp2=30
      50 PRINTTAB(0,0);:INPUT"GNP"GNP:CLS:PRINT''''
      60 PRINTTAB(5);"GNP"TAB(14);"Intr"TAB(22);"Savings"TAB(32);"PDI"
      70REPEAT
      80PROCcalc
      90PRINTGNP,Intr,Savings,PDI
     100G$=GET$
     110UNTIL EQULIBRIUM=TRUE
     120PRINT"EQUILIBRIUM REACHED"
     130END
     140DEFPROCcalc
     150Tax1=GNP*Tax
     160PDI=GNP-Tax1
     170Savings=Intr*.3*PDI+(0.1*PDI)
     180Cspend=PDI-(Imports+Savings)
     190Vat1=Vat*Cspend
     200Cspend1=Cspend-Vat1
     210Savingtotal=Savingtotal+Savings
     220Investment=0.97*Savingtotal
     230Savingtotal=Savingtotal-Investment
     240IndusInc=Cspend1+Xport+Govexp2+Investment
     250Corptax=Ctax*IndusInc
     260Indusexp=IndusInc-Ctax
     270GNP2=Govexp1+Indusexp
     280Intr=Intr-((Savings-(.135*GNP))/200)
     290Imports=0.25*PDI
     300Xport=0.22*IndusInc+(RND(1)*IndusInc*0.001)
     310IF INT(GNP2)=INT(GNP) EQUILIBRIUM=TRUE
     320GNP=GNP2
     330ENDPROC
```

Fig. 31.9 *Computer program based on Fig. 31.8*
Intr = interest rate; Ctax = corporation tax.

to the BBC microcomputer. It sets the tab positions and restricts the output to two decimal places.

2 The REPEAT/UNTIL loop can be replaced by FOR/NEXT loop.

3 The PROCcalc can be replaced by a subroutine.

4 All variables have long names merely to ease readability. These can be shortened.

If you are successful with this model you can then proceed to build up more sophisticated ones based upon actual national income data.

Questions on the model

1 Determine the value of the multiplier in Fig. 31.8.

2 Using the model in Fig. 31.8, confirm proposition (*a*) on page 391 by demonstrating the effect of an increase in the level of autonomous investment of 28·2 units. Confirm that the balance of payments will now be −11·25 units.

3 Similarly confirm proposition (*b*) on page 391 by demonstrating the effect of an increase in X of 5·64 units. Confirm that the balance of payments will now be +3·39 units.

4 If Fig. 31.8 both government expenditure and taxation are increased by 10 units but the propensity to withdraw remains constant. Confirm that the new equilibrium level of Y will be 210.

5 Confirm that if in Fig. 31.8 the rate of VAT is lowered to 5 per cent the new equilibrium level of Y will be 210·05 units.

6 If you have managed to operate the computer model illustrated in Fig. 31.9, work through the questions above and give reasons for the observed differences between the two sets of answers.

The algebra of equilibrium

Suppose that there is a closed economy with no government intervention. In this economy consumption (C) is always three quarters of disposable income. Investment is assumed to be exogenous.

1   Calculate the equilibrium level of national income if investment is £50bn.

2   Explain what would happen if investment expenditure were to increase to £75bn.

3   Suppose with investment remaining constant at £50bn, direct taxation of 20 per cent of all incomes is introduced. If planned government expenditure is £30bn what will the equilibrium level of national income be?

4   Now suppose that the economy is opened up to international trade and that, as a result of this, one sixth of total consumption is spent on imports. Exports are constant at £40bn. What will be the equilibrium level of national income and what is the value of the multiplier?

An extra task for the adventurous.

5   Suppose we drop the assumption that injections are exogenously determined and instead assume that there is a propensity to inject of $j = 0.1Y$. What is now the equilibrium level of national income and the value of the multiplier?

32

Fluctuations in the level of economic activity

No the earth doesn't get drunk
The earth doesn't turn askew
It pushes its little car regularly
Its four seasons
Rain, snow, hail, fairweather
           Jacques Prevert, *Song in the Blood*

It is apparent that there are fluctuations in the level of economic activity. At one time we may have prosperity and economic growth whereas at another we may have heavy unemployment and falling production. Many people believe that, like the weather, these ups and down are inevitable. One 19th century economist, Stanley Jevons, went so far as to attribute variations in the economy to sunspot activity. It is the intention of this chapter to show that variations in economic activity have very real and tangible causes which, if we understand them, we should be able to control.

The trade cycle

Different cycles

The level of economic activity (trade) is subject to fluctuations. However if we use the term 'cycle' we are implying that there is something regular about the pattern. Several different cycles have been described and these are considered below

a) *The classical trade cycle.* In the 19th century there appeared to be fairly regular fluctuations of boom and slump in the UK economy (and

those of many other countries). They appeared to take about 8–10 years from boom to boom. We will consider this cycle in more detail later.

b) *The Kuznets cycle.* This is named after Simon Kuznets, the Nobel prizewinner who first commented on this cycle in the 1930s. It refers to a cycle of activity in building construction and allied industries which is said to take from 15 to 25 years.

c) *The Kondratieff cycle.* This is named after the Russian economist W. D. Kondratieff and was also developed by Joseph Schumpeter. These two economists claimed that, in addition to the 10-year cycle, there is a major long-period cycle which takes some 50 or 60 years to complete.

d) *The business cycle.* For much of the time since the 1939–45 war most advanced economies have suffered minor fluctuations of economic activity lasting approximately 4 to 5 years. The pattern is usually referred to as the *business cycle.*

e) *The inventory cycle.* There appears to be a very short-duration cycle of 2 to 4 years which is associated with stocking and destocking in industry. These changes in investment bring about changes in the level of income.

Economic activity

We have spoken of fluctuations in the level of **397**

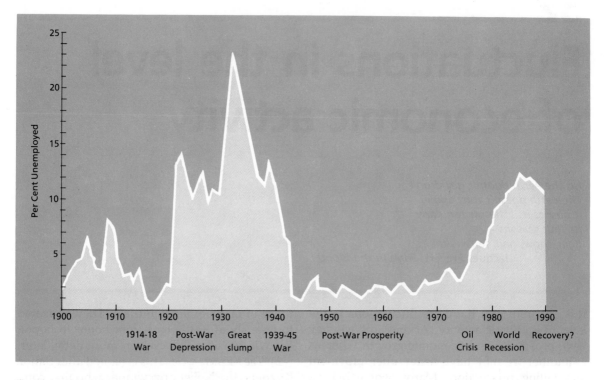

Fig. 32.1 *Unemployment in the UK in the 20th century*

economic activity but this is in itself a difficult thing to quantify. In order to do it we have to amalgamate several measures such as the change in the real GDP, the change in volume of retail sales and so on. However we can take an easy way out and use the inverse measure which the level of unemployment gives us, i.e. we can assume when unemployment is high economic activity is low and vice versa. Thus a graph of unemployment over the years would give us a mirror image of economic fluctuations.

Figure 32.1 shows the percentage of the working population unemployed in the UK for each year this century. As you can see it does not present convincing evidence for any of the cycles mentioned above. On the other hand we can detect traces of all of them. The first years of the century show the last years of the classical trade cycle. Economic activity was naturally very high (and therefore unemployment low) during the 1914–18 war years. Almost immediately

after the war the UK plunged into depression, although there were ups and downs within this. In 1929 the economy was overtaken by the great slump which originated in the USA, and this brought in a period of unprecedented depression. The severity may be gathered by realising that in 1941 unemployment was still 6 per cent despite two years of war. After the 1939–45 war there was a period of unprecedented prosperity, with a series of minor fluctuations lasting 4 to 5 years. The late 1970s saw unemployment climbing rapidly to reach 1.2 million by 1979. In the early 1980s the UK and world economy were in recession. Employment in the UK was particularly badly hit reaching 3.2 million by 1985. Despite recovery in the economy, unemployment remained stubbornly high, still being 2.3 million in 1988.

It is unsettling to consider the possibility of the Kondratieff cycle. The 20-year slump of the inter-war years followed by 30 years of post-war prosperity would give us a 50-year sweep with the plunge into recession in the late 1970s being the start of another 20 years of depression.

Phases of the trade cycle

Before proceeding further it will be useful to consider some of the terminology associated with the trade cycle and also to examine the characteristics of the four phases of the cycle. Figure 32.2 gives an illustration of the classical trade cycle.

a) Slump. A slump can also be termed a *depression.* In a slump we expect to find heavy unemployment, deflation and a low level of demand and capital utilisation. Profits will be low, as will business confidence. The point at which a slump '*bottoms out*' and the economy begins to recover may be termed the '*lower turning point*'. This is shown as points B in Fig. 32.2.

b) Recovery. The *upswing* of the trade cycle is characterised by expanding production, the replacement of old machinery, rising consumers' expenditure, increasing profits and buoyant business expectations. We would also expect to find some increase in prices.

c) Boom. Expectations are high, profits are high and prices will be rising rapidly. Investment will also be high but labour will be in short supply and production bottlenecks will be reached. The point at which the boom begins to turn into recession is termed the '*upper turning point*', and this is shown as points A in Fig. 32.2.

d) Recession. The *downswing* of the trade cycle will be characterised by falling consumption, decreasing profits and expectations and rising stocks of unsold goods. Firms will become unprofitable and some will go into liquidation. Unemployment will be rising and inflation falling.

The business cycle

The prosperity of the 1950s and 1960s made it somewhat unfashionable to talk of trade cycles. Instead the economy seemed to be experiencing short-period limited fluctuations in the level of economic activity. These have been generally termed the *business cycle*. It has already been stated that it is necessary to combine several measures to give a true picture of economic activity. The measure used by the UK government comprises the three different measures of GDP at constant prices, the index of the volume of retail sales, the index of production industries and the CBI index of firms working below capacity, as well as changes in stocks of materials. These are combined into one *composite index*. The upper turning point of the cycle is termed the *peak* and the lower turning point the *trough*. Figure 32.3 illustrates the business cycle for the years 1968–87.

As you can see that in the 1960s the period from peak to peak was around 4 to 5 years. The gentle undulations of the 1960s give way to more violent oscillations in the 1970s. The swift climb out of the trough of February 1972 was brought about by the expansionist policy of the Heath government. The long recovery from the trough of August 1975 culminated in a peak in May 1979 which almost exactly coincided with the fall of the Labour government. In the 1980s you can see that the pattern was altered somewhat. The whole cycle was deepened with the economy in profound depression, especially in the manufacturing industries. The cycle then failed to return to the peaks of earlier years. This measure of the trade cycle does not include a measure of unemployment; otherwise the troughs might be much deeper because of the

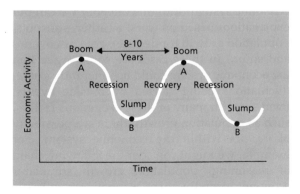

Fig. 32.2 *Phases of the trade cycle*

399

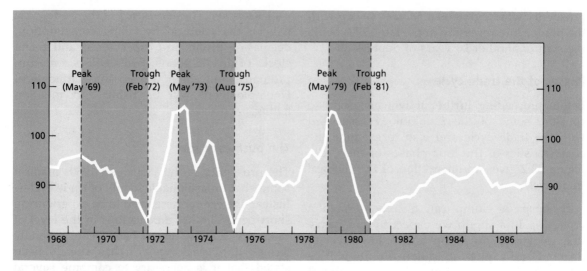

Fig. 32.3 *The business cycle in the UK based on coincident indicators*
January 1980 = 100
Source: CSO, Economic Trends, *HMSO*

persistent rise in unemployment in the 1970s and 1980s (unemployment is in fact included in lagging indicators – see page 403).

Explanations of the trade cycle

We have spent much of this section of the book explaining equilibrium forces within the economy, but in this chapter we have been saying that the capitalist system is not inherently stable and is subject to fluctuations. Why is this?

A basket of explanations

We are faced with an embarrassment of explanations. Monetarists such as Friedman put the cycle down to fluctuations in the money supply, while Schumpeter and Hansen attribute the cycle to bouts of technical innovation. Some theories blame the cycle on under-consumption while at the other extreme Hayek and Mises attribute it to over-investment. The psychological theory, as expounded by Pigou and Bagehot, attributes the cycle to bouts of optimism and pessimism amongst consumers and producers.

We have already mentioned Jevons' theory that the cycle is caused by sunspot activity. Finally we might mention the theory of the Polish economist Kalecki who attributed the cycle to periodic 'political' attempts to squeeze inflation out of the economic system.

Internal and external theories

We might classify theories by dividing them into internal (endogenous) or external (exogenous) theories. The external theories are those which find the cause of the cycle outside the economic system. Into this category we can put explanations based on wars, weather, sunspots, population growth (or decline), gold discoveries and so on. In these cases we could argue that the economic system could be inherently stable, fluctuations being caused by outside events. Even so, with many of these exogenous factors, such as population growth, there is a possibility of *feedback* within the economic system. For example, we might consider the following chain of reasoning: population growth stimulates economic growth; then economic growth encourages population growth; and so on.

Internal theories maintain that the causes of the cycle are within the economy itself. Many economists today would argue for a combination of internal and external causes. For example, the recent advances in microprocessor technology (external) have given rise to unemployment in some industries. However, this will be made greater or smaller by the effect of internal factors such as goverment policy, business optimism, etc.

Having noted that cycles may have external causes we will go on to consider three internal theories:

a) the political theory;

b) the multiplier–accelerator interaction theory associated with Samuelson; and

c) the inventory cycle.

Political cycles

Governments undoubtedly have a great effect upon the determination of national income. We could therefore argue that expansions or contractions in government expenditure and taxation will bring about fluctuations in economic activity. The monetarists, for example, argue that fluctuations are brought about by changes in the rate of growth of the money supply as the result of government policies. Since it would be unreasonable to assume that governments deliberately set out to destabilise the economy, if we are to accept political theory, we would have to argue that politicians will inevitably blunder when trying to run the economy. Such a view has a long history in economics, from Adam Smith through to Friedman and Hayek.

Michael Kalecki, a Polish economist of the inter-war years, argued that instability is inevitable in a democratic state. In an attempt to eliminate unemployment governments increase aggregate demand, which leads in turn to inflation. In order to counter inflation governments therefore deflate the economy, which causes unemployment. Unemployment, however, is politically unacceptable and therefore governments are forced to expand the economy again, and so on. This is an appealing expla-

nation of the stop–go policies of the post-war years in the UK.

The multiplier–accelerator cycle

We can consider this in three stages: firstly why upswings and downswings in the cycle tend to be cumulative; secondly why floors and ceilings exist in the cycle; and thirdly why there are turning points in the cycle.

a) *Cumulative movements.* We have already seen that any change in consumption expenditure will be increased by the multiplier. If in a depression, for example, expenditure were to rise a little the multiplier would magnify this, thus creating more income and jobs for others. Conversely, in a downswing any small drop in investment spending will be increased by the multiplier.

The accelerator will also enter the picture. If productive capacity is low then any small rise in consumption will call forth more investment. For example, if the capital/output ratio is 3:1 then each £1 rise in consumers' expenditure will bring about £3 of extra investment. However, as we have seen (see page 364), any small fall in consumers' expenditure is likely to lead to investment levels dropping towards zero. Many economists believe that the volatility of investment is a key factor in the business cycle.

If, as we have just described, a small drop in consumption causes a large fall in investment, then this fall in investment, via the multiplier, will cause a greater fall in national income, and so on. This interaction of the multiplier and the accelerator tends to suggest that any small movement will become magnified into a major swing. To explain why such a movement, upwards or downwards, does not go on forever we must introduce the idea of floors and ceilings.

b) *Floors and ceilings.* Let us consider what is happening in an upswing. The economy may expand rapidly whilst there are unemployed resources, However, as we approach full employment, bottlenecks occur. This therefore tends to stop or rapidly reduce the speed of expansion. Conversely, when we consider **401** downward movements it is possible to see that gross investment could fall to zero. However, this would have the effect to reducing income, and as income falls so does savings. If saving is reduced to zero it is theoretically impossible for income to decline any further. We are therefore at the absolute floor of economic activity. In terms of our national income graphs this is the level of income at which the consumption function crosses the 45° line.

In practice we do not reach this floor since some investment is always taking place. Some industries, which we might term 'depression-proof', continue to invest even in the depths of depression. These are usually associated with the necessities of life such as food and clothing.

The floors and ceiling approach gives a reasonable explanation of the behaviour of the economy in the 1950s and 1960s. It does not, however, tell us why some floors tend to be lower than others, as in the depression that commenced in 1979.

c) *Turning points.* Why, having reached a floor or ceiling, does the economy not remain there? Why is it that there are turning points in the business cycle? Consider the example of the accelerator which we used on page 364. The main features of the example are shown in Table 32.1.

Table 32.1 The accelerator at work

Year	Aggregate demand, Y (£m)	Total investment, I (£m)
1	100	40
2	120	80
3	130	60
4	140	60
5	120	0
6	120	40

From year 1 to year 2 we see a rise of 20 per cent in Y, causing a rise of 100 per cent in I. This is consistent with our view of cumulative upward movements. Observe what happens, however, in year 3; as a result of the increase in Y slowing down, total investment declines. We can now

see this as a turning point in the business cycle because this drop in investment will be magnified by the multiplier and the economy will have commenced a cumulative downward movement. As aggregate demand declines between years 4 and 5 we can see that investment is wiped out altogether.

Let us now consider what might happen at the floor. Suppose that no investment were taking place at all. Eventually some firms would be faced with having to undertake some replacement investment or going out of business. If just a few firms invest, then this would be taken up by the multiplier and we will have the beginning of a cumulative upward movement. In year 5 in Table 32.1 we can see that even replacement investment is not taking place because the fall in Y means that a smaller capital stock is required and this takes care of replacement I. However in year 6, with Y stabilised, we need 40 units of replacement I, which could be the beginning of an upward movement. (Note that the increase in investment shown in year 6 is *not* attributable to the accelerator since it is replacement investment; the accelerator is only concerned with new investment.)

Thus if we consider the interaction of the accelerator and the multiplier we have a theoretical construct which can explain cyclical fluctuations. However, it is doubtful if it is in itself sufficient to explain the observed fluctuations in the economy. Other factors must also play a part.

The inventory cycle

There is a wide fluctuation in the purchase of stocks of goods. This fluctuation is usually known by its US name – the inventory cycle. It is in some ways similar to the accelerator but differs because the accelerator is concerned with the demand for new capital equipment while the inventory cycle is concerned with the stocks of goods held by producers and retailers.

To illustrate this cycle let us suppose that there is some change in the economy; for example, there might be a drop in the level of demand for consumer goods. Shops whose level of stocks (inventories) is usually determined by the size of demand will now find that their stocks increase as sales fall. They will therefore cut back their orders of stocks severely, or even stop them altogether, until they have reached their desired stock level. This fall in orders will be transmitted back down the chain from wholesalers to manufacturers. They will ultimately have to cut production and so reduce the level of national income.

However, once retailers have reached their desired stock level they will increase their orders to match the level of sales. This increase is again passed back down the line so that manufacturers expand output and national income rises so that demand rises. Retailers will now expand their stocks faster than sales (remember there is a desired level of stocks and sales and therefore if demand is higher stocks must be higher). This increase will be passed back down the line to producers. Once the desired level of stocks is reached orders will fall off. This is again transmitted down the line to producers; income declines so therefore demand declines and retailers' stocks thus begin to rise, and we are back at the beginning of another cycle.

A recent trend which may modify the inventory cycle is the 'just-in-time' principle. This is the tendency of many retailers and manufacturers to hold very few (or no) stocks. For example, in Ford assembly plants parts are delivered from component manufacturers direct to the production line 'just-in-time' to be used. Similarly, many chain stores now have daily deliveries of goods direct to their shelves and have dispensed with the old stock-rooms.

Forecasting the cycle

It would obviously be of great use to businesses and to the government to be able to forecast the future. No way has yet been found of doing this with continuous accuracy though. We might liken economists' success in forecasting the economic future with that of meteorologists forecasting tomorrow's weather; they are usually accurate but can often be wrong, sometimes spectacularly so. However it would appear that economists are more likely to make accurate predictions than the man in the street, just as meteorologists are more likely to forecast the weather correctly.

Those interested in predicting the future train of events have to take careful note of present trends of things such as GDP, the volume of retail sales, the level of unemployment, changes in stocks, and so on. Also available are various surveys of business intentions and opinions of the future, the most famous of which is the CBI survey. With such information a model can be constructed and predictions made, as was explained in the previous chapter.

However, in addition to forecasting with models, we may be able to predict trends from changes in the statistics we are monitoring, just as meteorologists may be able to predict weather from changes in barometric pressure.

Economic indicators

As we have stated repeatedly, changes in the economy do not happen simultaneously; there is always a sequence to events. Therefore, if we know that some things always take place before others, a careful watch on these events can help us to forecast the future. If, for example, we note that profits usually rise *before* a peak in the business cycle then an observed rise in profits may be a clue to a coming revival in trade.

There are a number of statistical series which are thought to be significant in measuring the business cycle; these are termed *economic indicators*. Those which generally react ahead of the economic trend are known as *leading indicators*, while those which do not react until after changes in the business cycle have occurred are called *lagging indicators*. Those which are actually thought to trace the cycle itself are termed *coincident indicators*. In the UK these indicators are published quarterly by the Central Statistical Office in the journal *Economic Trends*.

There are four series.

403

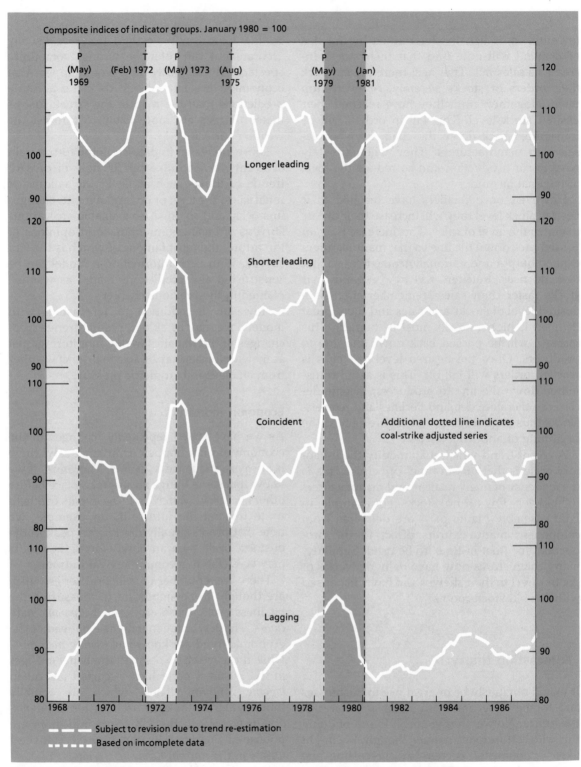

Composite indices of indicator groups. January 1980 = 100

P (May) 1969   T (Feb) 1972   P (May) 1973   T (Aug) 1975   P (May) 1979   T (Jan) 1981

Longer leading

Shorter leading

Coincident

Additional dotted line indicates coal-strike adjusted series

Lagging

Subject to revision due to trend re-estimation

Based on imcomplete data

404   Fig. 32.4   *Indicators of the business cycle in the UK*   *Source*: CSO, Economic Trends, *HMSO*

a) *Longer leading indicators.* These are series which point to turns in activity 12 months or more in advance. They consist of such things as housing starts, the FT 500 share index, the interest rate on 3 month prime bank bills and the CBI survey of business optimism.

b) *Shorter leading indicators.* These indicate changes in activity about 6 months in advance. Included in these are new car registrations, gross trading profits and the credit extended by finance houses.

c) *Coincident indicators.* Changes in such things as the real GDP and the volume of retail sales are termed coincident indicators because they form the basis of the business cycle itself (the full list of coincident indicators is given on page 399).

d) *Lagging indicators.* These confirm turning points in activity usually about 12 months after they have happened. Included in these are unemployment and investment in plant and machinery.

We have described the coincident indicators as the business cycle itself. However all the indicators, leading, lagging and coincident, form part of the business cycle. The reader who has followed the reasoning on time lags in the economic system will realise that we are speaking of a *distributed time lag* as opposed to a *discrete one.*

Composite indicators

Obviously any one indicator could be misleading. However if we have a series of six leading indicators and five point to an upturn in activity then we may take this as a reasonably good omen for the business cycle. In fact, in order to achieve this, the CSO combines the various components into a composite index for each of the four groups.

Figure 32.4 shows the four composite indices for the UK economy for the period 1968–87 The coincident series, which we may regard as the business cycle, is the same as that shown in Fig. 32.3.

A careful examination of the four graphs should allow you to come to an assessment of their efficiency. If, for example, we consider the peak of May 1973, it can be seen that the longer leading index was peaking about 14 months before this, just after the trough of February 1972, while the shorter series peaked in January 1973. The lagging series, however, kept on rising right until January 1975.

As you can see from Fig. 32.4 the situation in the 1980s was more confused. The indices could show a cyclical peak in economic activity in early 1985 followed by a mild trough in early 1986. However, the decline in the indices during 1985, before their renewed growth, was less marked than previous cyclical movements, especially those of the 1970s. The most recent years shown in Fig. 32.4 would be subject to revision as more information became available.

Conclusion

We have seen in this chapter that the economy is subject to fluctuations in activity. The chapter has also advanced some of the theories for the causes of this. In the final section we have even suggested that we may be able to predict accurately the business cycle. What we do not appear to be able to do is eliminate it. This may either be because our understanding of its causes is faulty or because the weapons at our disposal are inadequate.

Discussion of the business cycle in economics textbooks has tended to be limited. One of the reasons for this was that it was thought that post-war Keynesian demand-management policies had eradicated all but minor fluctuations. The late 1970s and early 1980s, however, saw economic dislocation rising to heights unknown since the 1930s and we must, therefore, again address ourselves to the problem which many thought had gone for good.

A discussion of the problems of the management of the economy must wait till Chapter 41, when we have developed a fuller understanding of the problems involved.

405

Summary

1   Several different trade cycles have been described. Each one refers to fluctuations of various magnitudes and periodicities in the level of economic activity.

2   There are four phases to the traditional cycle: slump; recovery; boom; and recession. Different economic characteristics are associated with each phase.

3   There are many different explanations of the trade cycle. We may classify the theories as external or internal theories, but these may interact (feedback) with one another.

4   The interaction of the multiplier and the accelerator provides an explanation for a self-perpetuating cycle.

5   The inventory cycle refers to the fluctuations brought about by changes in stock levels.

6   The cycle is traced and may even be predicted by the behaviour of economic indicators.

Questions

1   Marx predicted crises of ever-increasing magnitude in capitalist countries. To what extent to you think that the business cycle in the twentieth century supports this view?

2   Which would you expect to rise first in the upswing of a business cycle, consumption or investment? Which would be the first to decline near the peak of the cycle? Explain why.

3   Discuss the view that ups and downs in the business cycle are less important than trends in unemployment, economic growth and prices.

4   To what extent can the interaction of the multiplier and accelerator principles explain the business cycle?

5   Examine Figs. 32.3 and 32.4 and then assess the extent to which the observed fluctuations can be attributed to external influences.

6   From official statistics plot the following for the past decade:
   a) gross fixed capital formation;
   b) real GDP;
   c) unemployment;
   d) job vacancies.
Then assess which of these gives the best measure of the business cycle and explain why.

Data response   The business cycle

Study the information contained in the graphs in Fig. 32.5 which are taken from the OECD *Economic Outlook*.

Answer the following questions:

1   a) Which of the various measures shown are indicators of the business cycle and to which series do they belong (leading, lagging etc.)?

   b) Explain how it is possible for total retail sales to increase by (approximately) 30 per cent over this period (graph 2) but for output to increase by only (approximately) 15 per cent. What other information would be useful in answering this question?

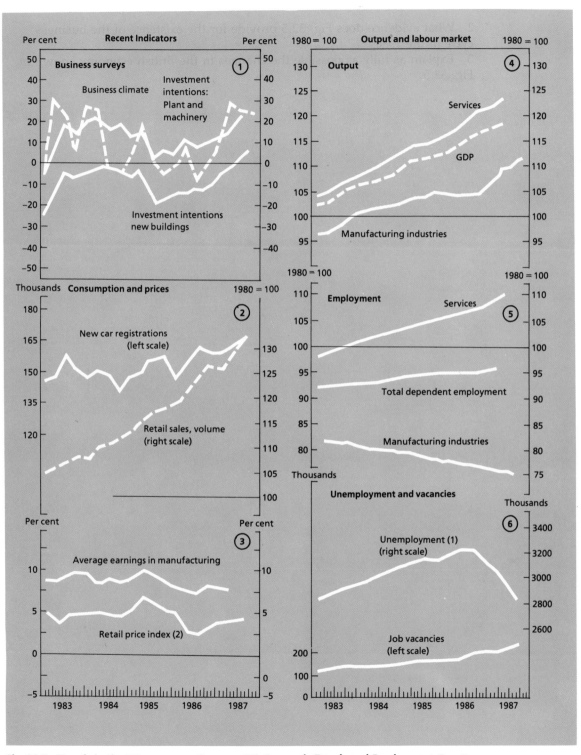

Fig. 32.5 *Trends in the UK economy* *Sources*: CBI, Economic Trends and Employment Gazette

2   What evidence does Fig. 32.5 provide for the existence of the business cycle in the 1980s?

3   Explain as fully as possible the changes in the British economy shown in Fig. 32.5.

3

Macroeconomics
VI Monetary theory and practice

33

Money and prices

A feast is made for laughter and wine maketh merry but money answereth all things.
Ecclesiastes 10:19

Money is a good servant but a bad master.
Oxford Dictionary of English Proverbs

Introduction

Monetary economics

In this section of the book we will concern ourselves with money. We will look at monetary theory, at institutions which are concerned with the creation and transmission of money and at the monetary policy of the government. Together these subjects constitute the branch of the subject known as *monetary economics*. Not only is monetary economics an important branch of the subject, it is one of the most controversial areas of modern economics.

In this chapter we shall explain the nature and functions of money in a modern society, as well as the concept of the price level.

The importance of money

'Money', said Geoffrey Crowther, 'is a veil' thrown over the working of the economic system. Money may indeed obscure some of the workings of the 'real economy' but it also facilitates its working. It would be impossible for a complex society to function without money. However money does more than facilitate the working of the economy; it may also be a powerful influence upon the real economic variables such as consumption, investment, foreign trade and employment. Monetary economics has much to tell us about how changes in the demand, supply and price of money influence the economy.

The development of money

The origins of money

The word money derives from the Latin *moneta* – the first Roman coinage was minted at the temple of Juno Moneta in 344 BC. Before coinage, various objects such as cattle, pigs' teeth and cowrie shells had been used as money. Such forms of money are termed *commodity money* and they are not confined to ancient societies; for example, when the currency collapsed in Germany in 1945, commodity money in the form of cigarettes and coffee took its place.

For most of its history money has taken the form of coins made of precious metal. The money, thus, had *intrinsic value*. Many of the units of modern money recall their origin in amounts of precious metal; for example, the pound sterling was originally the Roman pound (twelve ounces) of silver. Hence the symbol £ derives from the letter L standing for *libra*, the Latin for a pound. Similarly, dollars were originally 1-ounce pieces of silver (the origin of the $ symbol is obscure; it probably derives from the figure 8 on old Spanish 'pieces of eight', which had the same value as a dollar).

From coins to banknotes

Both paper money and modern banking practice originated from the activities of goldsmiths. Goldsmiths used to accept deposits of gold coins and precious objects for safe keeping, 411 in return for which a receipt would be issued which was, in effect, a *promissory note*. As time went by these notes began to be passed around in settlement of debts, acting as bank notes do today. Goldsmiths also discovered that they did not need to keep all the gold they had on deposit in their vaults because, at any particular time, only a small percentage of their customers would want their gold back. Thus they discovered that they could lend out, say, 90 per cent of their deposits, keeping only 10 per cent to meet the demands of their depositors. This relationship of cash (assets) retained to total deposits (liabilities) is known as the *cash ratio*.

Let us now consider what happened to the gold which the goldsmith re-lent. This was used by borrowers to pay bills and the recipient would then re-deposit it with the same or another goldsmith. This goldsmith issued a promissory note for the deposit and then re-lent 90 per cent of the new deposit of gold. The process would then be repeated with the re-deposit of more gold and the writing of more promissory notes. The limit to this process was that the goldsmiths always had to keep, say, 10 per cent of their assets in gold. This would mean that if the goldsmiths kept to a 10 per cent ratio, each £1 of gold could secure a further £9 in promissory notes. Thus, the banker, for this is what the goldsmith had become by this time, could be said to have created money or, more properly, created credit, because the expansion of the money supply came from the loans which the banker had made at interest.

The completion of this process came in the 1680s when Francis Childs became the first banker to print banknotes. Today the process of credit creation lies at the heart of our money supply. Originally the gold had intrinsic value and the paper money was issued on the faith in the bank. Any currency issued that was not fully backed by gold was called a *fiduciary issue*. Today banks create credit in the form of deposits against the security of Bank of England notes in the same manner that the old banks created banknotes on the security of gold. Today, however, it can be seen that the whole edifice of money rests on confidence in the banking system since all notes are now fiduciary issue. The creation of credit is kept under control by the Bank of England since it issues the banknotes and insists upon the banks maintaining specific ratios of assets to liabilities.

Credit creation

A single-bank system

Let us imagine there is only one bank, not a small bank, but a large bank with which everyone in the country does business. This bank has initial deposits of £10 000 in cash so that its balance sheet would be:

Liabilities (£)		Assets (£)	
Deposits	10 000	Cash	10 000

The bank knows from experience, however, that only a tenth of its deposits will be demanded in cash at any particular time and so it is able to lend out £9000 at interest. The people who borrow this spend it. The shopkeepers, etc., who receive this money then put it into the bank and the bank finds that the £9000 it has lent out has been re-deposited. This could be described as a created deposit. It is then able to repeat this process, lending out nine-tenths of this £9000 and retaining £900. The £8100 it has lent out will find its way back to the bank again, whereupon it can once more lend out nine-tenths, and so on. This is illustrated in Table 33.1.

Thus at the end of the process, with total cash of £10 000 in the system and a cash ratio of 10 per cent, the bank is able to make loans amounting to £90 000. Although so many more deposits have been created, you will see that everything balances out because the bank still has the necessary one-tenth of its assets in cash to meet its liabilities. You can also see that each horizontal line in Table 33.1 balances assets against liabilities and, therefore, at no stage are accounting principles infringed. The bank's balance sheet at the end of the process would appear as:

Table 33.1 Deposit creation in a single-bank system with a 10 per cent cash ratio

	Liabilities (£) (Deposits)	Loans and advances		Assets (£) Cash retained	
Initial deposit	10 000	1st Loan	9 000	$\frac{1}{10}$ of deposit retained	1 000
1st Re-deposit	9 000	2nd Loan	8 100	$\frac{1}{10}$ of re-deposit retained	900
2n Re-deposit	8 100	3rd Loan	7 290	$\frac{1}{10}$ of re-deposit retained	810
3rd Re-deposit	7 290	4th Loan	6 521	$\frac{1}{10}$ of re-deposit retained	729

Created deposits (bracket on left)

The maximum possible creation of deposits occurs when

Liabilities =	£100 000	Assets =	£90 000	+	£10 000

Liabilities (£)		Assets (£)	
Initial deposits	10 000	Cash	10 000
Created deposits	90 000	Loans and advances	90 000
	£100 000		£100 000

Note: the bank itself cannot distinguish between its initial deposits and created deposits.

The bank multiplier

The limit to credit creation in this manner is the cash ratio – here it is 10 per cent. This we can express in the formula:

$$D = \frac{1}{r} \times C$$

where D is the amount of bank deposits, r is the cash ratio and C is the cash held by banks. Thus, in our example we would get:

$$D = \frac{1}{0\cdot1} \times £10\ 000$$
$$= £100\ 000$$

The value of the expression $1/r$ is known as the *bank* or *credit creation multiplier*. It shows the relationship between the cash (or reserve assets) retained against total liabilities. If, as here, the cash ratio is 10 per cent, then the bank multiplier would be 10; however if the cash ratio were dropped to 5 per cent the multiplier would be 20, whereas if it were raised to 20 per cent it would be only 5.

The effect of any additional deposit of cash into the system upon the level of deposits can be given by the formula:

$$\triangle D = \frac{1}{r} \times \triangle C$$

where $\triangle D$ is the effect upon total deposits as the result of a change in cash deposits, $\triangle C$. Note also that there would be a comparable multiple contraction in deposits if cash were lost from the system.

A multi-bank system

If we consider a system in which there are many banks, credit creation will go on in the same manner except that money which is loaned out may find its way into a bank other than the one who made it. This is illustrated below, where we assume that there are two banks in the system. Here we have raised the cash ratio to 12·5 per cent, partly to guard against the possibility of deposits being lost to the other bank(s) or leaking out of the banking system altogether. The initial £10 000 of deposits is divided equally between the two banks, and with a cash ratio of 12·5 per cent they are able to create deposits of seven times this amount:

Bank X

Liabilities (£)		Assets (£)	
Initial deposits	5 000	Cash	5 000
Created deposits	35 000	Loans and advances	35 000
	£40 000		£40 000

Bank Y

Liabilities (£)		Assets (£)	
Initial deposits	5 000	Cash	5 000
Created deposits	35 000	Loans and advances	35 000
	£40 000		£40 000

Thus, the initial £10 000 is used to support £80 000 of liabilities.

Note: it is not possible for a bank to lend out eight times its deposits. The multiple expansion comes about because of the *re-deposit* of money which has been borrowed.

Modern ratios

The cash ratio was abolished in the UK in 1971 and was replaced by a 12·5 per cent *reserve assets ratio*, although the clearing banks were expected to keep 1·5 per cent of their assets in cash at the Bank of England. In August 1981 the *reserve assets ratio* was abolished. From this date all *banks* were required to keep the equivalent of 0·5 per cent of their eligible liabilities in cash at the Bank of England. This is held in *non-operational accounts*, i.e. the banks may not use this cash. The object of these non-operational, non-interest bearing accounts is to supply the Bank with funds. In addition to this money, banks will have to keep cash at the Bank for the purpose of settling inter-bank indebtedness (clearing).

Although there is no cash or reserve assets ratio, banks need to keep a minimum level of cash and liquid assets, i.e. assets that can quickly be turned into cash in order to meet their obligations on a day-to-day basis. The Bank has laid down guidelines for banks to assess the proportion of liquid assets which they need. The asset cover varies according to the kind of deposits (liabilities) the bank has accepted. Thus it is not possible, at present, to state this as a simple ratio. The composition of banks' assets and liabilities is discussed in detail in the next chapter.

The functions and attributes of money

We have not as yet defined money. So far we have suggested that coins, banknotes and bank deposits are money. Whether an asset is regarded as money or not depends not so much on what it is but upon what it does.

Money can be defined as anything which is readily acceptable in settlement of a debt.

Thus we have a functional definition of money. As Hanson says, 'money is what money does'. For any asset to be considered as money it must fulfil the four functions discussed below. The different forms of money do not all fulfil the functions equally well.

The functions of money

a) *Medium of exchange*. Money facilitates the exchange of goods and services in the economy. Workers accept money for their wages because they know that money can be *exchanged* for all the different things they will need.

If there were not money, then exchange would have to take place by barter. For barter to be possible there must be a *double coincidence of wants*. For example, if you have chickens but wish to acquire shoes then you must find someone who has shoes which they wish to exchange for chickens. The difficulties of barter will limit the possibilities of exchange and thus inhibit the growth of an economy. This situation was summed up by the classical economists when they said that, rather than a coincidence of wants, there was likely to be a want of coincidence.

b) *Unit of account.* Money is a means by which we can measure the disparate things which make up the economy. Thus, barrels of oil, suits of clothes, visits to the cinema, houses and furniture can all be given a common measure which allows us to compare them and to aggregate their value.

It could be argued that there are many things which cannot be given a price. For example, you might possess mementoes of your family or friends which you value highly but which the economist would say were economically worthless. At this stage you might be tempted to agree with Oscar Wilde and say, 'What is a cynic? A man who knows the price of everything and the value of nothing.' The economist, however, is commenting on the exchange value of things within the economy, not the sentimental value which a person may put upon their possessions.

c) *Store of value.* For a variety of reasons, people may wish to put aside some of their current income and save it for the future. Money presents the most useful way of doing this. If, for example, a person were saving for their old age, it would be impossible to put to one side all the physical things – food, clothing, fuel, etc. – which they would require, apart from the fact that their needs may change. Money, however, allows them to buy anything they require.

In times of inflation the value of money is eroded and people may turn to real assets such as property. The value of physical assets is, however, also uncertain, in addition to which they may deteriorate physically, which money will not.

d) *Standard of deferred payment.* Many contracts involve future payment, e.g. hire purchase,

mortgages and long-term construction works. Any contract with a time element in it would be very difficult if there were not a commonly agreed means of payment. The future being uncertain, creditors know that all their economic needs can be satisfied with money.

Inflation and the functions of money

Inflation adversely affects the functions of money but it does not affect them all equally. Inflation would have to become very rapid before money became unacceptable as a medium of exchange; for example, when the rate of inflation in the UK was above 20 per cent in the 1970s, shopkeepers showed no disinclination to accept money. Even in the hyperinflation in Germany in 1923, money was still used.

The unit of account function is affected by inflation since it becomes more difficult to compare values over time. For example, we may know that the GDP increased from £44·1 billion in 1970 to £319·1 billion in 1986 but how much of this was real increase and how much due to inflation? It requires statistical manipulation to *deflate* the figures and separate the *real* change from the *nominal* (see page 88). In fact, in the figures used above, the nominal increase of 624 per cent in GDP is reduced to only 34·4 per cent when the effects of inflation have been discounted.

The effect of inflation on the store of value function should be to discourage savings, since the savings will be devalued. This would be especially so when real rates of interest are negative, as they were in several years in the 1970s. However, as we have seen, the effect of inflation was to increase savings (see page 357) as people were forced to put more on one side *because* money was being devalued and they believed that they would require higher *real* reserves in the future. Inflation did, however, encourage people to search for substitute methods of preserving the value of their assets, such as purchasing gold, property or even works of art. In order to encourage people to save in times of inflation, the government **415** introduced index-linked financial assets such as 'granny bonds'.

Inflation also effects the standard of deferred payment function. Businesses, for example, may be unwilling to become creditors over long periods of time when they fear a decline in the value of money. Alternatively, special clauses may have to be written into contracts to take account of inflation. On the other side of the coin, people will become more willing to borrow money when they believe that the real burden of the debt will be reduced by inflation.

Inflation may also have an international effect upon the currency. High rates of inflation will make the currency less acceptable internationally and therefore cause adverse effects upon the exchange rate.

The attributes of money

We have seen that money fulfils four functions and also that many different things have functioned as money. Here we will consider what attributes, or characteristics, an asset should have to function as money.

a) *Acceptability*. The most important attribute of money is that it is readily acceptable.

b) *Durability*. Money should not wear out quickly. This is a problem which may affect paper money and to a lesser extent coins. The chief form of money in a modern society, which is bank deposits, suffers no physical depreciation whatsoever as it only exists as numbers on a page or digits in a computer.

c) *Homogeneity*. It is desirable that money should be uniform. Imagine, for example, that a country's money stock consisted of £1 gold coins, but that some coins contained 1 gram of gold and others 2 grams. What would happen? People would hoard the 2 gram coins but trade with the 1 gram coins. Thus, part of the money supply would disappear. This is an illustration of Gresham's law, that 'bad money drives out good'. Most forms of commodity money will suffer from Gresham's law.

d) *Divisibility*. Another of the disadvantages of commodity money, such as camels' or pigs'

teeth, is that they cannot be divided into smaller units. Modern notes and coins allow us to arrive at almost any permutation of divisibility.

e) *Portability*. Commodity money and even coins suffer from the disadvantage that may be difficult to transport. A modern bank deposit however may be transmitted electronically from one place to another.

f) *Stability of value*. It is highly desirable that money should retain its value. In the past this was achieved by tying monetary value to something which was in relatively stable supply, such as gold. It is one of the most serious defects of modern money that it may be affected by inflation. The hyperinflation in Germany in 1923, for example, made the mark worthless.

g) *Difficult to counterfeit*. Once a society uses money which has only exchange value and not intrinsic value, it is essential that the possibilities for fraud and counterfeit be kept to a minimum.

A cashless society?

In today's society we are seeing ever more sophisticated ways of ways of paying for goods and services. Following cheques we have seen the arrival of direct debits, standing orders and credit cards. The late 1980s brought the introduction of EFTPOS (Electronic Funds Transfer at Point Of Sale). Under this system a customer presents the shop with a card which is fed into a machine which automatically debits the amount of the sale from the customer's bank account. It is possible to envisage a future in which there is no need for cash. However, cash retains an enormous resilience; 90 per cent of all transactions are in cash so that, although they account for only a small percentage of the total *value* of sales, it is unlikely that cash will be replaced for minor day-to-day transactions such as for slot machines, bus fares, etc. In addition to this the UK remains a very 'unbanked' nation with only about 65 per cent of the population having bank accounts. This may change in the 1990s as building societies (with whom many of the non-banked have accounts) start to offer more banking services such as credit cards and EFTPOS cards.

Thus, although it seems unlikely that we shall see the end of cash, it may well be possible that the cheque system will go into decline as people switch to the use of clever pieces of plastic of one kind or another.

Measuring the money supply

As we have seen, the vast majority of the number of transactions take place in cash, but in terms of the amount of money spent the most significant form of money is bank deposits. People have deposits of money in a bank which are only fractionally backed by cash but they are quite happy to write and accept cheques which transfer the ownership of these deposits from one person to another. It is not the cheques which are money. We could print more or less cheques without making any difference to the money supply. The money supply is the bank deposits. Thus, when we come to try to measure the stock of money in a country, we will find that it is made up of cash and bank deposits. However, since there are several types of bank deposits, we find that there are several measures of the money stock.

M1, M2, M3 and money base

There was much interest in the money supply during the 1980s by the Conservative government which originally placed great faith in monetarism. (Monetarists place a great deal of emphasis on control of the money supply – see Chapter 36). Changes in the financial world and the effort to try to find a 'true' measure of the money supply lead to several different measures of the money stock being introduced. In 1987 the Bank of England introduced new definitions of the broader definitions of the money stock. M1 closely accords with our definition of money and it consists of *notes, coins and sight deposits*. A sight deposit is any bank deposit which can be turned into cash without interest penalty. In the UK, therefore, sight deposits are principally current (cheque) accounts. The 1980s saw a growth of interest-bearing cheque accounts. This was a result of the growing competition between banks and building societies for deposits.

The M3 measure takes account of virtually all bank accounts. Thus, if we add to the M1 measure UK private-sector sterling time deposits we obtain a measure known as M3. In the UK many people have bank deposits in other currencies. If we add to M3 *private sector holdings of other currencies* we obtain the M3c *money stock* figure. These measures are shown in Table 33.2. M3 corresponds to the old measure *sterling M3* (£M3) and M3c to the previous measure M3, the c standing for (foreign) currencies. In 1981 (revised in 1987) the Bank of England introduced the M2 measure of the money stock. This is intended to measure all the money in the economy which is immediately available for

Table 33.2 Money stock M1, M2, M3, M3c
4th Quarter 1987

Money stock	£m
1 Notes and coins in circulation with the public	14 149
UK private-sector sterling sight deposits	
2 Non-interest bearing	31 642
3 Interest bearing	46 504
4 **M1** (1 + 2 + 3)	92 295
5 UK private sector sterling time deposits	93 816
6 **M3** (4 + 5)	186 111
7 UK private sector deposits in other currencies	30 256
8 **M3c** (6 + 7)	216 367
9 UK private sector sterling retail interest-bearing deposits with banks (parts of 3 + 5)	47 233
10 UK private sector retail shares and deposits with building societies	93 164
11 National Savings Bank Ordinary accounts	1 655
M2 (1 + 2 + 9 + 10 + 11)	187 843

Source: Bank of England Quarterly Bulletin

transactions purposes (see page 468). You can see in Table 33.2 that it contains the *retail* deposits of both the banks and the building societies. The inclusion of building society deposits reflects the growing similarity of banks and building societies. The factors determining the growth of the money stock are discussed in Chapter 34.

Definitions of the money stock have tended to become wider and wider (see M5 below) but a much narrower definition was introduced in 1982. This is termed *money base* (M0). This consists only of notes and coins and the monetary sector's deposits with the Bank of England. There have been criticisms of M0 as a measure of money stock, suggesting that it is subject to too many distortions. Another suggestion has been that a measure entitled Nib–M1 should be introduced. This would consist of notes and coins plus non-interest bearing deposits with banks.

Table 33.3   M0 the wide monetary base (December 1987. Seasonally unadjusted)

Money stock	£m
Notes and coins in circulation outside the Bank of England	16 447
Bankers' operational deposits with the Banking Department	186
M0 (wide monetary base)	16 633

Source: Bank of England Quarterly Bulletin

M4 and M5

Since time deposits are included in the M3 definition it can be argued that there is no logical reason to exclude similar building society deposits. The first attempt to do this was the *private sector liquidity* (PSL) definitions which were introduced in 1979. In the 1987 redefinitions, building society retail deposits were incorporated in the new measure M4. This definition also reflects the growing similarity between banks and building societies. The widest definition of the money stock is M5. This consists of M4 plus

Table 33.4   Money stock M4 and M5 (4th Quarter 1987)

Money stock	£m
1 **M3**	186 111
2 UK private sector holdings of building society shares, deposits and CDs	133 241
less 3 Building society holdings of M3	15 005
4 **M4** (1 + 2 − 3)	304 347
5 Holdings of money market instruments by UK private sector excluding building societies	4 595
6 National Savings deposits and certain securities	10 643
7 **M5** (4 + 5 + 6)	319 585

Source: Bank of England Quarterly Bulletin

near money assets such as bills of exchange and other *money market instruments*. It also includes some National Savings deposits.

Two economists, Gurley and Shaw, have suggested that in the wider definitions of the money supply the various components should be weighted according to their liquidity. Thus, for example, notes and coins would be given a greater importance, while building society deposits would be given a smaller weighting, and so on. Fig. 33.1 shows the relationship between the various definitions we have discussed. The reader may well ask which is the correct definition. The answer is that the various measures reflect different concepts of money and different definitions may be useful for different purposes. For example, the Nib M1 definition corresponds with the Keynesian view of money while the M4 definition might be said to be equivalent to the monetarist definition of money being anything which is the '*temporary abode of purchasing power*.' (See also Goodhart's Law, page 581.)

Legal tender

Legal tender is anything which *must* be accepted in settlement of a debt. In the UK, Bank of

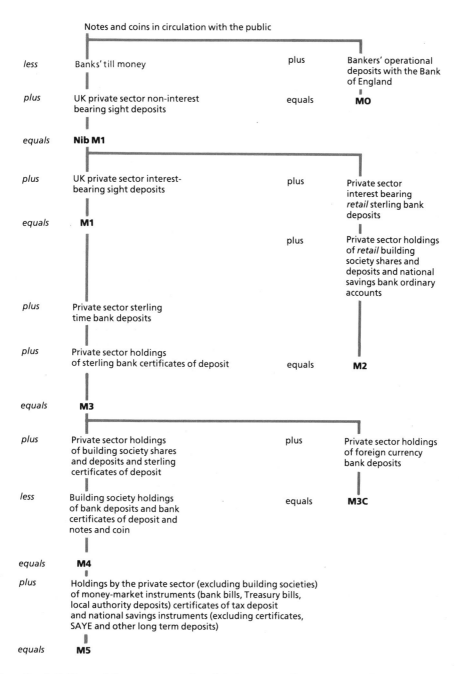

Fig. 33.1 *How the definitions of the money supply relate to one another*

England notes have been legal tender since 1833. The notes which are issued by Scottish and Northern Ireland banks are also legal tender. Royal Mint coins are also legal tender, but the law places limits on the quantities of coin which a creditor is forced to accept. Thus, for example, a creditor can refuse to accept payment of a £1000 debt entirely in 1p coins.

The form of money which the state has decreed to be legal tender may also be termed *fiat money*. In the UK this means notes and coins. Notes and coins may also be termed *representative money*; this is because their nominal value exceeds the value of the metal or paper of which they are made. Bank deposits are not legal tender. This is essential, otherwise a bank could repay a depositor by giving him another deposit at the same bank. Nevertheless, although bank deposits are not legal tender, because of their greater security and convenience they are often more acceptable than cash in settlement of a debt.

Quasi-money and near money

There are some assets which have some of the attributes of money and fulfil some of its functions, but not well enough to be considered money. Such assets may be termed *quasi-money*. For example, a postal order may be used as a medium of exchange and perhaps also as a store of value, but its usefulness as such is limited and we would say that it is a form of quasi-money. Other examples would be book tokens and luncheon vouchers.

Near money is any asset which can quickly be turned into money. This consists of things such as Treasury bills, certificates of deposit and local authority bills. Near money assets provide *liquidity* for banks. They also comprise the main instruments which are dealt with in the *money markets*.

The quantity equation of money

The equation of exchange

Whatever measure of the money stock we take, it is immediately apparent that none of them equates with the measure of the GDP. All are significantly smaller. This is hardly surprising since each unit of the money supply may be used several times during a year. The number of times that a unit of currency changes hands in a

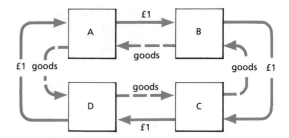

Fig. 33.2 *Velocity of circulation*

given time period (a year) is referred to as the velocity of circulation (V).

Consider Fig. 33.2. Here we see a simple economy made up of four individuals, A, B, C and D. As in a real economy, each makes their living by selling goods and services to others. Thus, B is producing the goods which A wants, A is producing the goods which D wants, and so on. In each case the value of the goods concerned is £1. Therefore the total value of all the goods exchanged is £4. However it would only be necessary to have a money stock (M) of £1 because A could pay this to B who in turn uses it to pay C and so on. Thus the value of the total income generated is £4.

This is because income is a *flow* of money with respect to time, while the amount of money is a *stock*. An analogy might be a central heating system; the amount of water in the system is the stock, which is constantly being circulated around. The quantity of water passing through any particular part of the system is the flow. The stock may remain constant while the flow becomes greater, or smaller, as the system is speeded up or slowed down. Similarly, the amount of money in an economy does not solely depend upon the stock of money but also upon how quickly it is used. The quantity of money is calculated as the stock of money (M) multiplied by the velocity of circulation (V):

Quantity of money = M × V

In the above example this would be £1 × 4 = £4. It is possible to arrive at the same figure by taking the *general price level* (P), in our example £1, and multiplying it by the number of final transactions

(Y), in our example 4. This would give the same figure £4. Thus we can derive the formula:

$$M \times V = P \times T$$

This is sometimes known as the *quantity equation* or, more properly, the *equation of exchange*. It was first developed by the American economist Irving Fisher.

The velocity of circulation

Let us consider another simplified economy. Suppose that the following is a summary of all the final transactions in one time period.

2 shirts sold at £10	£20
6 pairs of shoes sold at £5	30
10 loaves sold at £1	10
2 coats sold at £20	40
Total value of all transactions	£100

If we assume that the money stock is £25 we can then determine the values of the other components in the quantity equation:

$$M \times V = P \times Y$$

This would give:

$$£25 \times 4 = £5 \times 20$$

As we have already seen in the real economy, it is possible to measure the money stock (M1 or M3) and we can also measure the general price level and the number of transactions. The velocity of circulation however can only be determined from the formula.

If we have a measure of the money stock, for example M1, then in order to calculate V we need to know the value of $P \times Y$. This is fairly straightforward since the value of all final transactions in the economy will be the GDP (at market prices). We can therefore determine V by rearranging the quantity formula thus:

$$M \times V = P \times Y$$

which can be written as:

$$M \times V = GDP$$

and therefore:

$$V = \frac{GDP}{M}$$

If we used M1 as the money stock, then the value of V in the UK in 1986 could be shown as:

$$V = \frac{£374\ 895m.}{£\ 75\ 230m.}$$

Therefore, the velocity of circulation of sterling M1 in 1986 was:

$$V = 4 \cdot 983$$

An equation or an identity?

As we have explained it, the quantity formula is not an equation but an identity, i.e. the two sides of the formula are two different ways of saying the same thing. Thus we should really write:

$$M \times V \equiv P \times Y$$

The formula is more usually stated as:

$$MV \equiv PT$$

where T is the number of transactions. This is the form in which it was put forward by Fisher. However, *transactions* in this case would mean all transactions including those of intermediate products. As you will recall GDP is, essentially, a measure of all the *final goods* produced in the economy and it is therefore more convenient for our purposes to consider only the output of final products (see page 81). We shall, therefore, use $P \times Y$ rather than $P \times T$. By using this measure we may conveniently arrive at a measure of V.

A fuller discussion of the formula is left to pages 465–67. At the moment an important lesson can be learned if we realise that the quantity of money is not synonymous with the money stock, but rather is determined by what is done with the money stock.

The concept of the general price level

Purchasing power

As we have seen, money is a unit of account and as such we can use it to measure the value of goods and services in the economy. We must now consider how we measure the value of money.

The value of money is determined by its *purchasing power*. Even when a country is on a gold standard, it is still possible for the value of money to change. The relative prices of goods and services are always changing but this may not imply any change in the value of money. However, if there is a rise in the general level of prices, so that the value of money *declines*, we have *inflation*. Conversely, if the general level of prices were to fall, so that the value of money *increased*, we would be experiencing *deflation*.

Although an accurate measure of changes in purchasing power over long periods is virtually impossible, Fig. 33.3 gives a general idea of what has happened to the value of the pound this century. As you can see, in 1987 it would take £1 to purchase what would have cost only 2·5 pence in 1900 or, put another way, prices rose 40 fold over this period. However, Fig. 33.3 also shows the *deflation* of the inter-war period when the value of money increased by some 70 per cent between 1920 and 1935.

Measures of the price level

A measure of the general price level is arrived at by monitoring the price of many individual commodities and combining them together in one *index* number. By then looking at the rise or fall in the index we are able to see how prices change and consequently how the value of money alters. In the UK, two indicators of annual

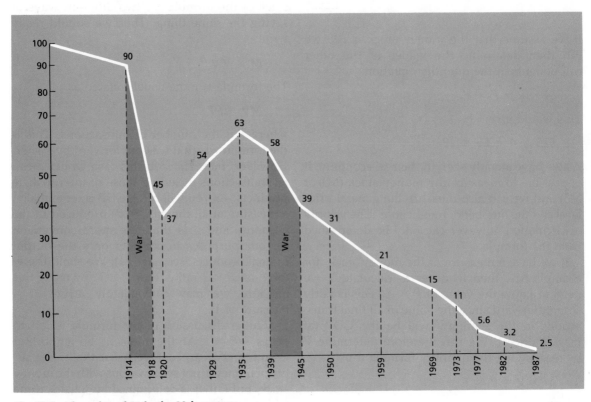

Fig. 33.3 *The value of £1 in the 20th century*

changes in the level of *consumer prices* are the *general index of retail prices* (RPI) and the *consumers' expenditure deflator* (CED) which is derived from the national income accounts. The RPI is the best known indicator and we will concentrate on this. In addition to measures of consumer prices, numerous other price indexes exist. These include the wholesale prices index, export prices index, agricultural prices index, pensioner prices index and the taxes and prices index (TPI).

The index of retail prices (RPI)

The construction of an index number was discussed on page 15. The RPI since 1974 is shown in Table 33.5. The base for the index was 15 January 1974 = 100. Since the table shows annual averages, the overall figure for 1974 is therefore greater than 100 at 108·5. In 1987 there was a major restructuring of the index and the new base became 13 January 1987 = 100.

Table 33.5 General index of retail prices in the UK 1974–1987

Year		Index
1974		108·5
1975		134·8
1976		157·1
1977		182·0
1978		197·1
1979		223·5
1980	Annual averages	263·7
1981		295·0
1982		320·4
1983		335·1
1984		351·8
1985		373·2
1986		385·9
1987 Jan 13		394·5
1987 Jan 13		100·0

Source: Monthly Digest of Statistics, *HMSO*

To compile an index which gives an accurate reflection of the change in all retail prices is obviously a difficult and complex task. In constructing the index three questions must necessarily be answered.

1 *Who?* Who is the index thought to be relevant to? In the case of the RPI it is supposed to reflect price changes for the vast mass of the population but it is not relevant for those on very high or very low incomes.

2 *What?* We must also make decisions as to which goods are to be included. In fact over 130 000 separate price quotations on a specified Tuesday near the middle of each month. Commodities sampled are divided into 14 main groups and 85 sub-groups.

3 *Weight?* The many different commodities must be allotted an importance, or weight, in the index. A 10 per cent rise in the price of bread would have a very different effect upon the average household from the effect of the same percentage rise in the price of cars. (The weighting of an index is discussed on page 15.)

Problems associated with the RPI

Having compiled the index, there are problems associated with the interpretation of the figures.

a) *Time factor*. Because the compilation of the series has been varied from time to time, and because the weighting has changed significantly, comparisons of prices over many years is difficult. This is well illustrated by the change in the value of weights in Table 33.6 (see page 425).

b) *High rates of inflation*. If the RPI increases from 100 to 103, it is obvious that prices have risen 3 per cent. However, high rates of inflation quickly make it difficult to see annual rates of inflation. For example, from 1979 to 1980 the RPI increased from 223·5 to 263·7. Some minor mathematics is necessary to see that this is an annual rate of inflation of 18 per cent. This has meant that in recent years it has become common practice to express prices as *x* per cent higher than 12 months previously rather than giving the index number.

High rates of inflation have also encouraged the projection of monthly rates into annual rates. Thus, if inflation were to be 1·5 per cent for the last month, we could argue that if inflation were to continue at this rate for 12 months, then prices **423** would be 19·6 per cent higher. (The answer is not 18 per cent because we have to use the compound interest formula. Similarly, if prices rose by 5 per cent a month then this would give an annual rate of inflation of 79·6 per cent, not 60 per cent.)

c) *Quality changes.* As time goes by the quality of products will change, either improving or worsening, but this will not be reflected in the index. For example, television sets are now generally much better than they were some years ago, but only the change in their price will appear in the index.

d) *Taxes and benefits.* Changes in indirect taxes such as VAT will be shown in the RPI since they affect prices; changes in direct taxes, however, will not affect the index. Similarly, government price subsidies will influence the index whereas changes in social security benefits will not. Indeed it was partly these limitations which led to the introduction of the TPI.

e) *Minorities.* While giving a generally good impression of how prices have changed for the mass of the population, the RPI will not be a good guide to how the cost of living has changed for groups whose spending patterns differ greatly from the norm. As examples of such groups we can mention the very rich, the very poor and those with large families.

f) *Political implications.* Because it is the most widely recognised measure of prices, the RPI has also acquired a political dimension, being quoted, for example, by employers and unions in wage negotiations. The index linking of some financial assets and of pensions has also made the RPI of great significance. Attempts to overcome some of these shortcomings we have considered have led to the introduction of the TPI (taxes and prices index), as well as special indexes for pensioner households.

The development of the RPI

The first index of prices compiled by the UK government was the *cost of living index*. This was introduced in 1914 and continued until 1947. It was designed to measure the costs of maintaining

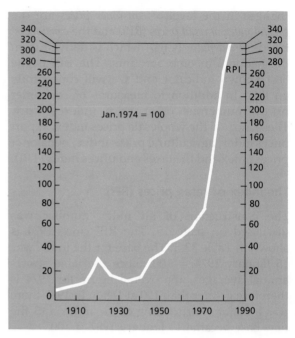

Fig. 33.4 *Composite index of retail prices in the UK in the 20th century*

living standards of working-class households. From 1947 to 1956 the *interim index of retail prices* was similarly angled towards lower-income households. In 1956 the *index of retail prices* was introduced which was supposed to reflect changes in prices for the average household.

In 1962 the general index of retail prices (RPI) was introduced. The next major revision of this was in 1974. There is a need to change the index from time to time, partly because with inflation the index number becomes so large, and partly because the composition of the 'basket' of goods in the index changes so greatly. For example, goods such as video cassette recorders were not even in existence when the index of 1974 was compiled.

Although it is difficult to make meaningful comparisons of prices over long periods of time because the weighting changes so much, we have attempted to do so in Fig. 33.4. This shows a composite index of prices for this century based on 1974. It has been compiled from the various indexes described above. It demonstrates the

Table 33.6 Weights used in calculating in UK retail prices index 1914–1987

	1914	1947	1956	1974	1987
I Food	600	348	350	253	167
II Catering	—	—	—	51	46
III Alcoholic drink	—	217	71	70	76
IV Tobacco	—		80	43	38
V Housing[i]	160	88	87	124	157
VI Fuel and light	80	65	55	52	61
VII Household goods[ii]	40	71	66	64	73
VIII Household services	—	79	58	54	44
IX Clothing and footwear	120	97	106	91	74
X Personal goods and services[iii]	—	35	59	63	38
XI Motoring expenditure	—	—	68	135	127
XII Fares and other travel costs	—	—			22
XIII Leisure goods	—	—	—	—	47
XIV Leisure services	—	—	—	—	30
Total of weights	1000	1000	1000	1000	1000

(i) 1914 and 1947 figures refer only to rent and rates
(ii) 1914 figure refers to all other categories of goods
(iii) Prior to 1987 this includes goods in categories XIII and XIV

Sources: British Labour Statistics: Historical Abstract *and* Employment Gazette

enormous extent of inflation in recent years. The reader may like to compare the increase in prices in Fig. 33.4 with the decrease in the purchasing power of the pound shown in Fig. 33.3

The weighting of the RPI

The weights for the indexes mentioned above are given in Table 33.6. A profound change has come over the measurement since the first *cost of living index* in 1914. This was very much a measure of the cost of staying alive and therefore concentrated on the essentials. It was thus of relevance only to those on low incomes. The present RPI is specifically *not* a cost of living index but a method of measuring changes in all retail prices.

Each set of weights totals 1000. The size of the weight given to each group reflects its relative importance. In the case of the present RPI, the weighting is based on the family expenditure survey (FES) and is revised each January. Thus in 1987 the food groups had a weight of 167; we

could therefore consider it as being of 16·7 per cent importance in the index.

As incomes have increased one might have expected to see a decline in the importance of essentials. This is indeed reflected in the decline of the food weight from 350 in 1956 to 167 in 1987. However when we look at some of the other categories such as housing and fuel, we see that they have increased. This is because of the disproportionate rise in the price of these commodities. You will see that the weight for motoring costs has also increased. In this case it is due to the vastly increased car ownership over the period.

Despite the increase in the weights in some categories, the general tendency has been for the range of products included in the index to increase. It was this expanding pattern of household expenditure which prompted the 1987 revision. Several new categories of expenditure were added such as leisure goods and leisure services. Fig. 33.5 gives a detailed breakdown of the 1987 index. You will see if you look at the diagram that house prices are *not* in

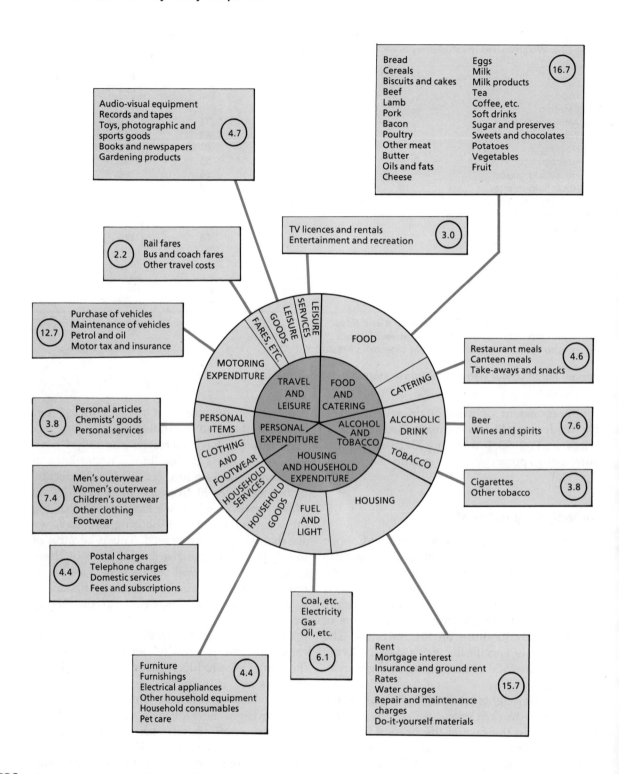

Bread **Cereals** **Biscuits and cakes** **Beef** **Lamb** **Pork** **Bacon** **Poultry** **Other meat** **Butter** **Oils and fats** **Cheese** **Eggs** **Milk** **Milk products** **Tea** **Coffee, etc.** **Soft drinks** **Sugar and preserves** **Sweets and chocolates** **Potatoes** **Vegetables** **Fruit** — 16.7

Audio-visual equipment
Records and tapes
Toys, photographic and sports goods
Books and newspapers
Gardening products — 4.7

Rail fares
Bus and coach fares
Other travel costs — 2.2

TV licences and rentals
Entertainment and recreation — 3.0

Purchase of vehicles
Maintenance of vehicles
Petrol and oil
Motor tax and insurance — 12.7

Restaurant meals
Canteen meals
Take-aways and snacks — 4.6

Personal articles
Chemists' goods
Personal services — 3.8

Beer
Wines and spirits — 7.6

Men's outerwear
Women's outerwear
Children's outerwear
Other clothing
Footwear — 7.4

Cigarettes
Other tobacco — 3.8

Postal charges
Telephone charges
Domestic services
Fees and subscriptions — 4.4

Coal, etc.
Electricity
Gas
Oil, etc. — 6.1

Rent
Mortgage interest
Insurance and ground rent
Rates
Water charges
Repair and maintenance charges
Do-it-yourself materials — 15.7

Furniture
Furnishings
Electrical appliances
Other household equipment
Household consumables
Pet care — 4.4

426 *Fig. 33.5 Structure of the Retail Prices Index in 1987*

the index. Instead there is merely an allowance for the cost of borrowing money for house purchase. This meant that in 1987 the index estimated an average mortgage interest payment across all households in the nation of £7 per week! You may find, therefore, that if you commence house purchase, your pattern of expenditure is significantly different from that in the index.

The RPI and CED compared

The consumers' expenditure deflator (CED) is arrived at by comparing the national account estimates of total 'consumers' expenditure' at current prices with these revalued at constant prices. The CED is thus a byproduct of the national account calculations. It aims to cover the personal expenditure of the whole population and this includes those sections of the population where expenditure is excluded from the RPI calculations. These categories are expenditure by those in institutions (hotels, army barracks, etc.) those on national insurance pensions and those on over two and a half times the national average income. All business and government expenditure is excluded. This therefore produces an index which does not reflect price change in precisely the same way as the RPI. (There are several other 'deflators' such as the government expenditure deflator.) RPI and the CED are compared in Table 33.7.

Table 33.7 The UK index of retail prices and the consumers' expenditure deflator compared (1980 = 100)

Year	RPI	CED
1976	59·6	60·4
1977	69·0	69·4
1978	74·8	75·8
1979	84·8	86·1
1980	100·0	100·0
1981	111·9	111·4
1982	121·5	121·1
1983	127·1	127·2
1984	133·4	133·2
1985	141·5	140·1
1986	146·3	145·2

Sources: National Accounts *and* Annual Abstract of Statistics

Table 33.8 The first TPI published in the UK in August 1979

Income in July 1978 (£)	Increase in gross income up to July 1979 in order to maintain net spending power (%)
2,000	14·9
3,000	14·0
4,000	13·1
5,000	12·5
6,000	12·1
8,000	11·8
Overall TPI increase	13·2

The taxes and prices index (TPI)

In 1979 the government introduced the TPI (see Table 33.8). It did this because it believed that changes in the RPI would not give an accurate view of changes in purchasing power because of the government reduction of direct taxes. The TPI is designed to show the increase in gross income (before tax) needed in order to maintain the same level of *real net income* after taking account of changes in both prices and tax rates and allowances. Alternatively we might describe it as the index formed by averaging changes in taxes including social security contributions and changes in the prices of goods and services.

Looking at Table 33.8 we can see that, for example, a person with an income of £3000 per annum would have needed an increase in their gross salary of 14·0 per cent to maintain the same net spending power a year later. The overall TPI was 13·2 per cent which compared with an RPI increase for the same period of 15·5 per cent.

Table 33.9 compares RPI and TPI increases over recent years. These are each presented as year-on-year changes.

International comparisons

The previous section of this chapter has shown that inflation in the UK has been very severe. Inflation, **427** however, is an international phenomenon. Figure 33.6 traces the purchasing power of the UK, German and US currencies over this century.

Table 33.9 Changes in the RPI and TPI

| Year | Percentage increase on previous July | |
	RPI	TPI
1975	26·3	31·7
1976	12·9	13·8
1977	17·6	16·4
1978	7·8	1·9
1979	15·6	13·2
1980	16·9	18·5
1981	10·9	14·3
1982	8·7	9·6
1983	4·2	3·1
1984	4·5	3·3
1985	6·9	6·3
1986	2·4	0·4

Source: Annual Abstract of Statistics

Table 33.10 Rates of inflation for selected countries, 1965–85

| | Average annual rate of inflation (%) | |
	1965–80	1980–85
West Germany	5·1	3·2
Switzerland	5·3	4·5
USA	6·1	5·3
Canada	7·4	6·3
UK	11·2	6·4
India	7·4	6·8
Sweden	8·0	8·6
Australia	8·8	9·1
France	8·0	9·5
Nigeria	14·5	11·4
Italy	11·2	14·2
Israel	25·2	195·3
Argentina	78·5	342·8

In each case it can be seen that the decline in value is comparable. The German mark, however, has had a remarkable history. The

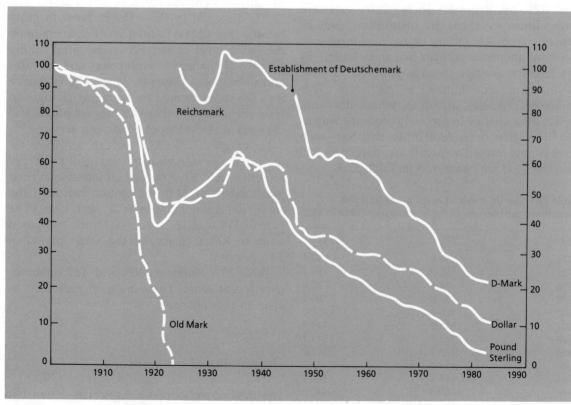

Fig. 33.6 *The purchasing power of various currencies in the 20th century compared*

hyperinflation of 1923 ended with an exchange rate of 534 910 marks = $1. At this time the price of a loaf of bread in Berlin was 201 000 000 000 marks. The currency was re-established in November 1923 but collapsed again after the 1939–45 war. Although there was not the hyperinflation of 1923, marks became almost totally unacceptable and cigarettes and coffee became the money of the country. In 1947 the currency was re-established as the Deutschemark, since when it has been one of the world's soundest currencies.

Table 33.10 shows the average rates of inflation for selected countries from the 1960s to the 1980s. The general pattern during the 1970s was of a rising trend of inflation worldwide. During the 1980s many nations strove to reduce their rates of inflation. In this the UK was moderately successful as you can see from Table 33.10. Some countries such as Argentina continued to experience runaway rates of inflation. With an average annual rate of 342.8 per cent in Argentina this meant that an item which cost $1000 in 1980 would cost $473 330 in 1985!

Summary

1   Monetary economics is concerned with the nature and functions of money, as well as with how the supply and price of money can influence the main macroeconomic variables.

2   Modern money can be traced back to the goldsmiths of the late middle ages.

3   The majority of the money supply is bank deposits. Banks are able to create credit. The limit on their ability to do so is the cash (or reserve assets) ratio.

4   Money has four main functions: medium of exchange; unit of account; store of value; standard of deferred payment. In order to function as money an asset must have a number of characteristics, or attributes, such as acceptability, divisibility, homogeneity and portability.

5   There are several different measures of the money stock such as M1, M3 and M5.

6   The equation of exchange $M \times V = P \times T$ demonstrates that the 'quantity' of money in the economy is determined not only by the size of the money stock but also by the velocity of circulation.

7   As money values goods and services, so the price of goods and services are used to give a value to money. Changes in the value of money can be seen as changes in its purchasing power or the converse, which is changes in the price level.

8   The price level is measured with index numbers, the most well known of which is the RPI. There are many problems associated with the compilation of the RPI. Other measures exist such as the CED and the TPI.

9   Inflation is worldwide. Over the last two decades the UK's rate of inflation has been amongst the highest of developed nations, but much higher rates of inflation have been experienced in LDCs such as Argentina.

Questions   1   Discuss the suitability of the following to function as money:
   a) gold;

429

b) caviar;
c) diamonds;
d) copper; and
e) cattle.

2 Examine the extent to which bank deposits possess the attributes of money.

3 Explain how inflation will affect the functions of money.

4 The following is the balance sheet of a monopoly bank. It is obliged not to let its cash ratio fall below 10 per cent.

Liabilities (£)		Assets (£)	
Deposits	1000	Cash	250
		Loans and advances	750
	£1000		£1000

a) If the bank wishes to do as much business as possible, illustrate the effect this will have on the balance sheet.

b) How would the answer to (a) differ if the cash ratio were $12\frac{1}{2}$ per cent?

5 Distinguish between a change in relative prices and an inflationary change in prices.

6 Assuming that there is to be continuing inflation, what measures might people take to protect themselves from its effects?

7 Explain the difficulties which are associated with the interpretation of changes in the RPI.

8 Describe what is meant by the weighting of an index.

9 The following information about four married couples was obtained in December 1988.

	Family			
	A	B	C	D
Ages of parents	35 & 32	36 & 28	60 & 58	45 & 43
Total income	£10 000	£22 000	£25 000	£60 000
Ages of children	2, 5 & 10	—	32 & 28	8, 12 & 15
Residence	Rented		Owner-occupiers	
Change in cost of living over previous 12 months	9%	2%	5%	0%

Give possible reasons why the change in the cost of living varied so much between those families.

10 'If the GDP rises by $8\frac{1}{2}$ per cent and the general price level by $4\frac{3}{4}$ per cent while V is constant, then M must grow by $13\frac{1}{4}$ per cent.' Explain.

11 Consider the following information about a hypothetical economy: the money stock (M) = £30 million; the velocity of circulation (V) = 4; and the number of transactions is 20 million per year.

a) What is the general price level (P)?

b) If the stock of money were to increase to £40 million but the velocity of circulation (V) and the number of transactions (T) were to remain constant, what would be the new price level (P)?

c) If in the original situation the velocity of circulation were to rise to $V = 6$ and the number of transactions were to rise to $T = 25$ million, what would the new general level of prices be?

Data response   Telling result of the property boom ━━━━━━━━━━━━━━━━━━

The following article is taken from the *Daily Telegraph* of Saturday 21 May 1988. It was in the City Comment column.

Telling result of the property boom

The British property boom has already destroyed civilised dinner conversation. Now it is threatening to destroy our faith in the Retail Prices Index as a fair measure of inflation.

Yesterday saw disturbing figures showing the RPI rising at an annual rate of 3.9 p.c. in the year to April. If it was recast to include the cost of buying a house, rather than the cost of money borrowed to do so, it would show real cause for alarm.

Tim Congdon at Shearson Lehman Hutton has stripped out the RPI components for rent and mortgage interest payments, and substituted the Building Societies Association figure of a 26.4 p.c. rise in price in the year to March. His answer is an inflation rate of 7.3 p.c. This is statistically dubious, but the result is telling.

The chart (page 432) shows one way of looking at what has happened to house prices in the last decade. The market value of housing in private ownership has risen from slightly more than the value of what Britain produces in a year to getting on for twice that figure.

The pause in 1982 is probably a statistical quirk; the figures are calculated from the average value of houses where building society mortgages were granted, and in that year, the banks came in, specifically aiming for the biggest borrowers.

Some rise is justified; improving homes is a disease among home-owners, all the billions spent on DIY and double glazing add value to the property. More homes have basic amenities, and items like central heating, once luxuries, are now commonplace.

There are more houses in the sector. Thanks to council house sales and new construction, the privately-owned housing stock has risen by a tenth in the decade.

Similar factors are at work in shares, whose value has risen much faster than either national output or houses, as the chart shows. The market value of shares has been boosted by privatisations, new issues and capital raising from existing companies.

The biggest factor has been management regaining control in an environment of quiescent inflation. Both the quality and quantity of profits has improved, and shares have been re-rated as a result. A study out on Monday from Greenwell Montagu shows that this process has some way to go yet, and that 5 p.c. a year productivity growth can be sustained.

It is hard to be as confident about further gains in house prices. We have reached the stage where buyers are encouraged to be reckless, believing that further rises will bail them out if the payments get too much. Should they be mistaken there will be no soft landings.

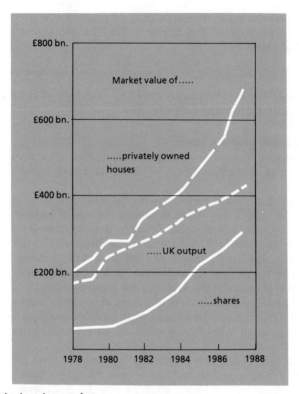

Fig. 33.7 *Boom in the housing market*

Answer the following questions:

1 Describe how the Index of Retail Prices (RPI) is compiled.

2 Explain as fully as possible why housing presents special problems in the RPI. Put forward arguments for and against including the price of houses in the index.

3 In paragraph four of the article there is reference to 'the value of what Britain produces in a year'. What is meant by this? The same paragraph also says that the value of the housing stock has risen by nearly twice as much as the value of national output (see chart). What does this imply for the standard of living in the country?

4 What factors do you consider caused the rise in house prices? Explain the pause in the rise in house prices around 1982 referred to in paragraph five.

5 What significance, if any, does the rise in share prices over the period considered have?

6 Explain the significance of rising productivity for changes in the RPI.

7 In what way may the rise in house prices have an impact upon the wider measures of the money stock such as M3?

34

The banking system

A power has grown up in the government greater than the people themselves consisting of many and various and powerful interests combined into one mass, and held together by the cohesive power of the vast surplus in the banks.

John Cauldwell Calhoun

Introduction

In this chapter we will examine the operation of those institutions which make up the *monetary sector* of the economy. We will also examine the money markets and the capital market. All the institutions involved may be termed financial intermediaries.

Financial intermediaries

These are the institutions which channel funds from lenders to borrowers. Among the institutions which are termed financial intermediaries are banks, building societies, finance houses (hire purchase companies), insurance companies, pension funds and investment trusts. It is usual to distinguish between the *banking sector* and the other *non-bank financial institutions*. The reason for this is because, as we saw in the previous chapter, the liabilities of banks form part of the money supply whereas those of the other institutions usually do not.

It is important to realise that financial intermediaries are more than go-betweens. They do not just act like employment agencies, placing one lot of people in touch with another – other more important functions are involved. This situation was summarised by the Wilson Committee in 1976 as follows:

When a financial institution intermediates it not only passes funds from lenders to borrowers, it usually changes their terms and conditions. By aggregating small amounts of funds obtained from each of a large number of savers it is able to on-lend in larger packets, and often to transform *risk* and *maturity* characteristics.

As well as the *go-between* function of financial intermediation, we now have two others, namely *maturity transformation* and *risk transformation*. To illustrate this let us take an example. People deposit money in their current accounts which the bank promises to repay on demand – it then lends the money to a customer for, say, three years. Maturity transformation has taken place. But if you were to lend your money directly to a friend to buy a new car you would be taking a great risk. However, by taking many such risks and by knowledge of its business the bank greatly reduces the risk. This is risk transformation.

These processes are achieved through the bank's correct structuring of its balance sheet (this is considered below, pages 436–440).

Banks and their functions

Types of bank

When we look around the UK and the world we discover many different types of bank. Some of the differences may be attributable to legislation, such as the Glass – Steagall Act in the USA which forbids commercial banks from being investment banks. Similarly in the USA restrictions on the number of branches a bank may have has resulted in the *unit banking* system with no fewer than 14 500 separate banks. In the UK, on the other hand, commercial banking is dominated by the 'big four' which, between them, have over 11 000 branches. In general we might divide banks by the type of business they undertake. *Primary banks* are those which are mainly concerned with the transmission of money, i.e. clearing cheques, paying standing orders and so on. This obviously includes the high street banks such as Barclays and Lloyds; less obviously it also includes the discount houses (see below). *Secondary banks* are those which are mainly involved in dealing with other financial intermediaries and providing services other than the transmission of money. A good example is the merchant banks.

a) *Central banks*. These are usually owned and operated by governments and their most significant functions are in controlling the currency and in implementing monetary policy. They do not generally trade with individuals. Their operations are considered in the next chapter.

b) *Commercial banks*. These are the profit-motivated banks involved in high-street banking activities. In the UK this means the London clearing banks and the Scottish and Northern Irish banks. Many foreign commercial banks now have offices in the UK but they are usually concerned with major commercial types of lending. UK banks also operate extensively overseas; the Barclays Group, for example, operates in more than 75 countries.

c) *Savings banks*. Originally designed to encourage the small saver, and often non-profit making, these banks have become very significant in some countries. In West Germany, for example, the *Sparkassen* now account for 35 per cent of all deposits and have their own clearing system. In the UK savings banks are represented by the National Savings Bank (NSB) which is fairly insignificant in terms of its total deposits although, via the Post Office network, it has more branches than the rest of the banks put together (about 20 000).

d) *Cooperative banks and credit unions*. These institutions are much more important in the USA and Europe than in the UK. They are generally small and usually have been established by a group of individuals with a common interest, such as farmers. In France, however, a union of these cooperatives, *Credit Agricole*, is now one of the largest banks in the world. The Cooperative Bank in the UK, although established by the cooperative movement, operates more like an ordinary commercial bank.

e) *Building societies*. Many countries possess specialist institutions to assist home buyers and they often enjoy special privileges from the state. Building societies in the UK and savings and loan associations (S & Ls) in the USA have developed to such an extent as to rival the commercial banks. In Germany, however, the *Hypothekenbanken* and *Bausparkassen* are relatively small. We have spoken of financial intermediaries as transforming short-term deposits into long-term loans. In the case of building societies we have reached the extreme of this situation as they may grant mortgages for up to 30 years while accepting deposits for as little as seven days or less.

f) *Merchant banks*. With merchant banks we have reached the wholesalers in banking. It is often said that commercial banks live on their deposits while merchant banks live on their wits. They act more like banking brokers putting those with large sums of money to lend in touch with borrowers and by offering a wide range of financial advice to companies and even to governments.

g) *Discount houses*. Peculiar to UK banking, the discount houses make their living by discounting bills of exchange with funds mainly borrowed from the commercial banks.

We will now consider the operation of these various institutions in more detail.

Commercial banks

The functions of commercial banks

The most significant function which the commercial bank fulfils is that of *credit creation*, as described in the previous chapter. The bank itself, however, would not see it in this light as it is not able to distinguish £1 within its deposits from another. It would see its role as accepting money on deposit and then loaning the money out at interest. The commercial banks must compete with other financial intermediaries such as building societies, both in attracting deposits and in making loans.

The *transmission of money* is also a vital function of banks. Customers with current accounts may write *cheques* to pay their creditors. In the UK and the USA payment by cheque is the most common form of payment after cash. In Europe cheques are less significant because the 'giro' system of payment, run by the banks and post offices, is more popular. Banks also offer other methods of transmitting money such as *standing orders*, *direct debits* and now EFTPOS. In the UK the major *credit cards* are also run by the banks; they are not only a method of making a payment but also a method of obtaining credit. We can also include *travellers' cheques* as a method of transmitting money.

Banks also offer *advisory services* to their customers, usually charging for these services. The sort of advisory services which are offered are trusteeship, foreign exchange, insurance, broking, investment management and taxation. Since the Big Bang the banks are also now able to offer their customers stockbroking services.

Clearing

In order for payments to be made by cheque it is necessary to have some system of *clearing* the cheques. There used to be separate clearing for Scotland but since 1985 all clearing in Britain has been handled by the Committee of London and Scottish Banks. Clearing takes place at the Clearing House which is at 10 Lombard Street in London. This consists of the following bank groups: Bank of Scotland, Barclays, Lloyds, Midland, National Westminster, Royal Bank of Scotland, Standard Chartered, and the TSB. Some banks which are not full members, such as the Coop Bank, have associate status and can clear their own cheques while any other banks have to make arrangements with one of the clearers to clear on their behalf.

If a person draws a cheque on their bank and pays it to someone who has an account at the same bank then the clearing can be accomplished without going through the Clearing House. This is known as *interbank* or *head office clearing*.

If, on the other hand, a payment by cheque involves two different banks then the Clearing House becomes involved. This is perhaps best explained by following a cheque through the system. Suppose that Miss Smith draws a cheque on her account with Barclays at their Sheffield branch and gives it to Mr Jones who has an account with the Midland at their Nottingham branch. When Mr Jones has paid in the cheque at the Nottingham branch of the Midland, it is sent with all their similar cheques to the Midland's clearing department at head office. Midland then total all the cheques drawn on Barclays and the other banks. The cheques are then taken to the Clearing House where they are handed to representatives of the other clearing banks, who in turn hand bundles of cheques to the Midland. It is then possible to arrive at a figure for the net indebtedness of one clearing bank with the other. This means that instead of hundreds of thousands of separate payments being made by Barclays to Midland, and vice versa, one payment will settle their accounts. The banks settle their indebtedness to one another by transferring money which they keep in their accounts with the Banking Department of the Bank of England. Thus, at the end of each day their debts have been settled by changes in the book-keeping entries at the Bank of England.

Meanwhile Miss Smith's cheque has been returned to Barclays' head office along with all the others that have been exchanged. Details

435

are then fed into the bank's computer so that the accounts may be debited the next day. Provided that Miss Smith's account is in order her account at the Sheffield branch will then be debited.

This process will normally take about three working days. Sometimes in excess of 5 million cheques are cleared daily. This system has been speeded up by the introduction of CHAPS (Clearing Houses Automated Payments System). In addition to this, the banks have introduced an electronic method for the clearing of standing orders and direct debit; this is known as bankers' automated clearing services (BACS) and is the largest system of its kind in the world.

The balance sheet of the clearing banks

One of the best ways to understand the business of a commercial bank is to study its balance sheet. Table 34.1 gives the combined balance sheet for the London and Scottish clearing banks. One difference which we observe from a normal balance sheet is that there is no sign of the banks' capital nor of their real physical assets such as premises. This balance sheet concentrates on the business of the banks in accepting deposits and making loans. (Numbers after the following headings refer to items in Table 34.1.)

The banks' liabilities (1)

The banks' liabilities are the deposits which they have accepted. These are held in a number of different types of account, the most significant of these being *current accounts* and *deposit accounts*. Banks also raise substantial deposits on the money markets. It used to be the case that deposit accounts earned interest whereas current (cheque) accounts did not. However, in recent years there has been a decline in the importance of traditional current accounts. In order to attract business away from building societies the banks have introduced such things as high-interest cheque accounts. The important distinction

these days is between *sight deposits* and *time deposits*. A sight deposit is any deposit which can be withdrawn on demand without interest penalty. With time deposits notice of withdrawal (e.g. 7 days) is necessary if the depositor wishes

Table 34.1 Balances of the Committee of London and Scottish Banks Groups as at end-April 1988

	£m	£m
LIABILITIES (1):		
Sterling deposits of which:		192 986
Sight	81 642	
Time	111 344	
Foreign currency deposits		64 060
Total deposits		257 046
Other liabilities		48 586
TOTAL LIABILITIES		**305 632**
of which eligible liabilities (2)	149 895	
ASSETS (3)		
Sterling:		
Cash (4) and balances with the Bank of England:		
Cash ratio deposits (5)	631	
Other balances (6)	2 120	2 751
Market loans (7):		
Discount houses (8)	5 819	
Other UK monetary sector (9)	26 982	
Certificates of deposit (10)	5 568	
Local authorities (11)	1 035	
Other	6 738	46 142
Bills:		
Treasury bills (12)	130	
Other bills (13)	5 247	5 377
Special deposits with the Bank of England (14)		nil
Investments:		
British government stocks (15)	5 524	
Other	5 354	10 878
Advances (16)		142 996
Other sterling assets		18 899
Foreign currencies:		
Market loans		49 894
Bills		306
Advances		20 632
Other		7 757
TOTAL ASSETS		**£305 632**

Source: CLSB Statistical Unit

to receive all the interest they are entitled to. The greater the period of notice that is needed the greater the interest the depositor is likely to receive. Large depositors, such as companies, may place money on deposit for periods of three months or more. When this happens it is likely to be by way of special arrangements such as certificates of deposit (CDs). (See below item 10.) In 1988 the clearing banks had over £14 billion of deposits in the form of CDs. You can also see in Table 34.1 that deposits of foreign currency are very important to the British banks.

The distinction between sight and time deposits is important for the various measures of the money supply. For example, sight deposits, being more liquid, are included in the narrower definition, M1, while time deposits are not. (See Table 33.2, page 417.)

Eligible liabilities (2)

Since the banks' liabilities (deposits) form a major portion of the money supply it is understandable that the monetary authorities will wish to supervise them. Since 1981 the bank of England's supervision has applied not only to banks but to the whole of the *monetary sector*. The portion of the banks' liabilities which form the basis of control are termed *eligible liabilities*, and are those which are of most relevance to the size of the money stock. They comprise, in broad terms, sterling deposit liabilities, excluding deposits having an original maturity over two years, plus any sterling resources obtained by switching foreign currencies into sterling. The banks are then allowed to offset certain of their interbank and money market transactions against their eligible liabilities. In the balance sheet shown in Table 34.1, 49 per cent of the clearing banks' total liabilities were classified as eligible liabilities. Having been defined, these liabilities then form the basis for the various ratios of assets which the banks may be required to maintain.

The clearing banks' assets (3)

In the previous chapter we spoke of a cash ratio which banks maintain. In fact the situation is more complex, with banks possessing a whole spectrum of assets from cash, which is the most liquid, to highly illiquid assets such as mortgages that they have made. In Table 34.1 we divide the banks' assets into those which are primarily designed to protect liquidity, i.e. those in the balance sheet down to *bills*, and those which are primarily earning assets, i.e. all the items from *investment* onwards.

Banking business is a conflict between *profitability* and *liquidity*. To earn profits, banks would like to lend as much money as possible at as high a rate of interest as possible. On the other hand they must always be able to meet a depositor's demand for money. Although most business these days is carried out by cheque, the bank must always be prepared to meet depositors' demands for notes and coins.

When we examine the banks' assets we find that they have different maturity dates; for example, a bank may have loaned money to another bank overnight, while, at the other extreme, it may have granted mortgages which are repayable over 25 years. These days, therefore, the Bank of England, rather than laying down a simple ratio, insists that the banks hold ratios of assets which are appropriate to the type of liabilities it has accepted.

Thus, for example, if a bank has accepted overnight deposits of cash from the money market which are likely to be entirely withdrawn the next day, it is appropriate that these should be 100 per cent covered by highly liquid assets. If, on the other hand, banks have accepted deposits which they will not have to repay for one year a 5 per cent cover might be appropriate.

The assets cover which a bank requires will therefore depend upon the type of deposits it has accepted. It is no longer possible to state it as a simple ratio; it will differ from bank to bank and from time to time. The clearing banks whose activities are relatively stable might well have a predictable ratio but this will differ from other members of the monetary sector.

a) Coins and notes (4). These are reserves of cash kept by the banks, sometimes referred to as

Till Money. Since 1971 there has been no requirement to keep a specific percentage. In the case of the clearing banks the amount of cash they require is predictable and is a very small portion of their assets. All banks will wish to keep their holdings of cash to a minimum since they earn no interest. The banks' holdings of cash are not included in the Bank of England's calculations of banks' liquidity.

b) *Cash ratio deposits (5).* All members of the monetary sector are required to keep 0.5 per cent of their eligible liabilities in cash at the Bank of England. These deposits are kept in non-operational, non-interest bearing accounts, i.e. the banks and other members of the monetary sector may not use this money, its purpose being to supply the Bank of England with funds rather than for control purposes or for liquidity.

c) *Other balances (6).* In addition to the cash-ratio deposits the banks keep *operational deposits* at the Bank for the purpose of *clearing* their debts to each other, as described above. No ratio is laid down by the Bank for these deposits.

In Table 34.1 the total of coins and notes and the banks' balances with the Bank of England is equivalent to 1.8 per cent of the banks' eligible liabilities but only 0.9 per cent of their total liabilities.

d) *Market loans (7).* The market referred to is the *London money market* which is discussed in detail later in this chapter. The loans consist of money lent for periods from one day up to three months. All banks must agree to keep an average of 5 per cent of their eligible liabilities with certain sectors of the money market and never less than $2\frac{1}{2}$ per cent with the discount houses.

e) *Discount market (8).* This is money lent to members of the London Discount Market Association (LDMA) at *call* or *short notice.* Money lent at call is lent for a day at a time while money lent at short notice is lent for periods up to 14 days. Money lent overnight usually commands a lower rate of interest than that lent for a week, but overnight rates can be very high if the whole market is short of money.

After cash these loans are the banks' most liquid assets and will be called in if the banks are short of cash. These loans also form a vital part of the system of money control.

f) *Other UK monetary sector (9).* Banks will make and receive short-term loans from other banks and members of the monetary sector to even out their cash flows.

g) *Certificates of deposit (CDs) (10).* If a customer is prepared to make a deposit of cash for a fixed period of time, say three months, they will receive a higher rate of interest than in a deposit account. However the holder may want the money back before then. The best of both worlds can be enjoyed if the customer accepts a *certificate of deposit.* This is a written promise by the bank to repay the loan at a stated date. The certificate is negotiable, i.e. it can be sold on the money market should the customer require the cash before that date. CDs issued by a bank will, of course, form part of its liabilities, but banks also hold CDs issued by other banks as investments and it is these we see on the assets side of the balance sheet.

Dollar CDs were first introduced in the USA in the early 1960s and were introduced on the London market by US banks in 1966. CDs are now also denominated in sterling and other currencies. They are only available for very large deposits.

h) *Local authority loans (11).* These are loans made through the money market to local authorities who are now major borrowers. In addition to local authorities, banks may also make short-term loans to companies.

i) *UK Treasury bills (12).* The Bank of England sells Treasury bills weekly (see below, page 443). These are bought in the first instance by the discount houses. The bills have a life of 91 days and they are often acquired by banks from the discount houses when they have five or six weeks left to maturity.

j) *Other bills (13).* These are commercial *bills of exchange* issued by companies to finance trade and acquired by the banks on the money market. In the early 1960s commercial bills were almost extinct and it was Treasury bills that were important in the bills section of the banks' balance sheet. You can see that commercial bills are now more important; they have staged a comeback in the rapid expansion of the money markets over the last two decades.

The primary function of the assets so far discussed is to give liquidity; the remaining items fulfil different functions.

k) Special deposits (14). If the Bank of England wishes to control banks' lending it is empowered to call for them all to make *special deposits* of cash with it. The bank usually calls for them in amounts equivalent to 0.5 per cent or 1 per cent of banks' liabilities. You can see from Table 34.1 that at this particular time the Bank was holding no special deposits. In addition to this the Bank used to call for supplementary deposits from individual banks if their deposits increased too rapidly. This so-called 'corset' scheme was abandoned in 1980.

l) British government stocks (15). When the term investment is used in banks' balance sheets it refers to their ownership of government stock. The government borrows money by issuing interest-bearing bonds such as Exchequer stock or Treasury stock. These are mainly fixed-interest bearing, although there are now some which are index linked. Government stocks are termed 'gilts' (gilt-edged). As you can see the banks hold a considerable amount of UK and other government stocks. The banks will always ensure that they maintain a *maturing portfolio* of bills, stocks, loans, etc., i.e. that a quantity of these mature each week so that the bank has the option of liquidating its asset or re-investing.

m) Advances (16). The chief earning assets of the banks are the advances they make to customers. These take the form of overdrafts and loans. The lowest rate at which a bank is willing to make loans (prime rate) could be as little as 1 per cent above base rate, but this is offered only to favoured customers; others may pay 8 or 10 per cent above base. In recent years the clearing banks have made big inroads in the mortgage market, in 1988 accounting for over 25 per cent of all new mortagages. The rate of interest on mortgages usually stays close to base rate.

Liquidity ratios

In the previous chapter we saw that it was necessary for banks to maintain a cash ratio. Today, instead of a cash ratio, the Bank of England requires that banks and other institutions in the monetary sector keep a certain proportion of their assets in a prescribed form. There are two main reasons for this.

a) In order to ensure the stability of the system. The 'fringe' banking crisis of 1973 which necessitated the 'lifeboat' operation and more recently the failure of Johnson Matthey Bankers in 1984 emphasised the point that it is still possible for banks to go 'bust'.

b) It allows the Bank of England to control the credit creation of banks and thus, the money supply.

Until 1971 the clearing banks were required to keep a *cash ratio* of 8 per cent and a 28 per cent *liquid assets ratio.* In 1971, as part of the competition and credit control regulations, these were replaced by the 12.5 per cent *reserve assets ratio.* Since 1981 there has been no stated ratio and the liquidity ratio which is required of a bank will depend upon the type of business it undertakes. The Bank of England nevertheless still requires banks to maintain appropriate ratios and its control now extends to all institutions in the monetary sector.

The present *integrated* approach to banks' balance sheets does not closely define which assets are acceptable, as the old ratios did. However the assets which the Bank of England is willing to accept as providing adequate liquidity for banks are very similar to the old reserve assets. These are:

a) balances with the Bank of England;
b) money at call with the LDMA;
c) UK Treasury bills;
d) local authority and other bills eligible for rediscount at the Bank of England;
e) UK government stocks with less than one year to maturity.

The cash which banks require is now a very **439**

small and predictable proportion of their assets and it is therefore today of little significance. However banks must always have an adequate proportion of their assets in highly liquid form. Under the old reserve assets ratio, the items above had to be at least 12.5 per cent of the banks' eligible liabilities, but for *prudential* reasons banks may require more liquidity than this. At present typical ratios for clearing banks are in the range of 9–12 per cent.

Limits to credit creation by banks

The limits to banks' ability to create credit may be summarised as follows.

a) Liquidity ratios. As we have seen above, the Bank of England lays down liquidity requirements, in addition to which banks will have their own prudential reasons for maintaining ratios.

b) Other banks. If one clearing bank pursued a significantly more expansionist policy of credit creation than all the others, then it follows that it would quickly come to grief. This is because a majority of the extra deposits it created would be re-deposited with other clearers. The expansionist bank would therefore find itself continually in debt to the other clearers, thus rapidly exhausting its balances at the Bank of England. It would then be forced to reduce its lending to replenish its reserves. Conversely, an over-cautious policy of credit creation would decrease the profitability of the bank.

c) The supply of collateral security. A majority of bank lending is in the form of *secured loans*, i.e. the bank has to take something in return, such as a mortgage on a property, an assurance policy or a bill of exchange, as security in case the loan is not repaid. The supply of such assets will therefore influence a bank's ability to make loans. In particular the supply of money market instruments such as Treasury bills and CDs will greatly influence banks' liquidity. The Bank of England is able to manipulate the supply of such instruments as Treasury bills and government stocks to control banks' credit creation.

d) The monetary authorities. Central banks and governments have a variety of weapons at their disposal for influencing bank lending. These are discussed in detail in the next chapter.

The regulation of banking

Banking in the UK has, historically, been subject to little statutory control. Indeed it is possible to argue that until the 1979 Act the last previous major legislative change had been the Bank Charter Act of 1844. The reasons for bringing in the 1979 Bank Act were the secondary banking crisis of 1973, the influx of many foreign banks to London and the need to comply with an EEC directive that all member states must have a system of authorising banks by December 1979.

The Banking Act 1979

The Act became law on 1 October 1979, along with the Credit Unions Act. However it was to be a further two years before its three major provisions were implemented. Subsequently this Act was amended by the Banking Act 1987 but the 1979 Act is still the substantive legislation on the recognition of banks.

a) The licensing of banks. All deposit-taking institutions had to be licensed by the Bank of England. These fell into two main categories, *banks* and *licensed deposit-takers* (LDTs). To be licensed as a bank an institution had to have considerable funds and offer a wide range of banking services or a highly specialised banking service. In addition to this, several other stringent criteria had to be met. Deposit-taking institutions which did not offer a wide range of services were allowed to operate as LDTs. The Bank of England has the power to revoke a licence or the recognition as a bank, or to grant only a conditional licence.

b) The banking names and advertisement. Before the Act any money-changing institution could call itself a bank. Since the Act only recognised banks and other named institutions may use the title bank or banker. The named institutions include the Bank of England, the National Savings Bank and National Girobank. Thus many institutions which had been calling themselves banks had to drop the title. One such organisation was the People's Bank, a Bradford-based institution which only gained recognition as an LDT. The Bank of England also has powers to regulate the form and content of any advertisement inviting the making of deposits.

Foreign institutions which are not recognised as banks may use the title if that is the name they operate under in their home territory and so long as the title is accompanied by an indication that the institution is formed under the law of that territory. Most of the major foreign banks in London are in fact recognised by the Bank, and in many cases their bills are eligible for discount at the Bank, e.g. the Chase Manhattan Bank, Credit Suisse and Mitsubishi Bank.

c) *The deposit protection scheme.* This part of the Act was a response to the secondary banking crisis of 1973. The aim of the scheme was to give protection to small depositors in the event of a bank failure. The scheme is similar to the Federal Deposit Insurance Corporation (FDIC) in the USA. It is administered by the Deposit Protection Board which consists of representatives of the contributory institutions. The Governor of the Bank of England is chairman. The Board administers the Deposit Protection Fund, to which all banks and LDTs must contribute. No contributor's initial payment may be less than £5000, and each institution must contribute the equivalent of 0.3 per cent of its deposit base, subject to a maximum payment of £300 000.

In the event of an institution becoming insolvent the fund will pay the depositors an amount equal to three-quarters of the deposit up to the maximum of the first £10 000 of any deposit. This is rather less generous than the FDIC, which repays all deposits up to the first $100 000.

Monetary control provisions 1981

The present regulations governing the activities of banks came into effect on 20 August 1981;

they are set out in the Bank of England paper *Monetary Control. – Provisions.* Previously the activities of banks were regulated through the *Competition and Credit Control* regulations of 1971. The main provisions of the 1981 regulations were as follows.

a) Each institution in the *monetary sector* was required to keep 0.5 per cent of its *eligible liabilities* in a non-operational account at the Bank of England.

b) A new 'monetary sector', somewhat broader than the old 'banking sector', was defined. It included:

i) all recognised banks and LDTs;

ii) National Girobank;

iii) those banks in the Channel Islands and Isle of Man which comply with the Bank's regulations;

iv) Trustee Savings Banks (TSBs) (now privatised);

v) the Banking Department of the Bank of England.

c) Eligible liabilities were to be calculated in an integrated uniform manner for all institutions (see above, page 437).

d) The special deposit scheme was retained.

e) The list of institutions whose acceptances (of bills of exchange) were eligible for discount at the Bank was widened.

f) The *reserve assets ratio* was abolished.

g) The Bank of England discontinued the regular 'posting' of the *minimum lending rate* (MLR). Instead the Bank now indicates to the market what it believes the rates should be.

The objectives of these regulations were to extend the Bank's control over a wide range of institutions, to make that control more effective and also to bring UK banking practice more in line with that of other European banks.

The Banking Act 1987

The failure of Johnson Matthey Bankers in 1984 demonstrated that there was a need for closer supervision of the banking system. The Banking **441**

Act 1987 provides for the regulation and supervision of banks in the UK. Deposit-taking by banks is regulated and supervised by the Bank of England and by a committee set up by the Bank known as the Board of Banking Supervision.

The Act laid down that in order to be recognised as a bank by the Bank of England an institution must have at least £5 million paid-up capital. Other financial institutions with at least £1 million paid-up capital may be allowed to provide financial services and accept deposits, but cannot use the word 'bank' in their business name.

The Building Societies Act 1986

This Act lifted some of the restrictions on building society activities; they were, for example, allowed to offer unsecured personal loans, although the Act limited the amount of these. The Act also allowed building societies to issue cheque books and cheque guarantee cards. Also included in the Act were provisions by which the building societies could abandon their Friendly Society status and become Plcs.

This Act may, therefore, be seen as part of the process by which banks, building societies and other financial institutions are coming to compete with each other. It is possible to imagine that, within a few years, customers will see banks and building societies as genuine alternatives to each other for all financial services. We might also, in the near future, see the takeover of a building society by a foreign bank and greater variation in the services offered in the high street which have long been dominated by the oligopolistic practices of the banks.

Supervision and regulation

The financial system in the UK continues to change rapidly. The 1980s saw increasing competition in the world of financial services but at the same time new systems of regulation were put into place. We may summarise these as follows:

a) Commercial banking remains under the supervision of the Bank of England and is regulated by the Banking Acts.

b) Building societies are regulated by the Building Societies Act and are outside the supervision of the Bank of England. Now that banks and building societies are becoming more alike and building society deposits are within some definitions of the money supply, it seems only a matter of time before a more unified pattern of supervision is established.

c) Under the terms of the Financial Services Act 1986 investment activity is supervised by The Securities and Investments Board and various Self Regulating Organisations (SROs). Banks must belong to an appropriate SRO if they wish to conduct investment business. (See page 284.)

Money markets

The classical and parallel markets

The expression 'money markets' is used to refer to those institutions and individuals who are engaged in the borrowing and lending of large sums of money for short periods of time. Most money market transactions are concerned with the sale and purchase of *near money* assets such as bills of exchange and certificates of deposit. Most advanced countries have a money market, but they are most developed in the major banking capitals of the world such as London, New York, Tokyo and Zurich.

In London the money market is geographically very concentrated, all the participants being within a short distance of Lombard Street, although the scope of the market is worldwide through its telephone and telex links.

The *classical money market* is the expression used to describe dealings between the Bank of England, the clearing banks and the discount houses. Traditionally the banks have lent money at call or short notice to the discount houses which they, in turn, have lent out by buying Treasury bills from the Bank of England or by purchasing other first-class bills of exchange. In recent years many new activities have been undertaken on the money market and these are referred to as the *parallel markets*. These include the following.

a) The local authorities market. Local authorities borrow money by issuing bills and bonds which are traded on the money market. They may also place funds when they have a surplus.

b) Finance houses. These institutions, which are involved in hire purchase, obtain some of the funds from the money market.

c) Companies. Large industrial and commercial companies both borrow and place money on the market. If a company lends money to another through the market this is known as an *inter-company deposit*. Companies will also make large deposits with banks in return for a *certificate of deposit*, and these are also traded on the market.

d) Eurocurrencies. The market began as the eurodollar market, which referred to the holding of US dollars in European banks. Today a euro-currency is any holding of currency in a financial institution which is not denominated in the national currency; for example, if a UK bank has holdings of Deutschemarks, then this becomes a eurocurrency. The market extends beyond Europe to take in other financial centres such as Tokyo. The main centre of the eurocurrency market is London. Today this market is huge and extremely important. It was one of the chief ways that the OPEC surpluses were recycled in the 1970s, with the OPEC nations placing billions of dollars on deposit. The very large sums held on short-term deposit are a potential source of disequilibrium to a nation, because this so-called 'hot money' may move quickly from nation to nation in search of better interest rates or in anticipation of the change in value of a currency.

Significance of the money market

The money markets are the place where money is 'wholesaled'. As such the supply of money and the interest rate are of significance to the whole economy. It is also used by the central bank to make its monetary policy effective.

Since the abandonment of MLR in 1981, money market indicators have acquired a new signifi-cance; for example, the three-month interbank interest rate (the rate at which banks are willing to lend to each other) is now carefully monitored.

Negotiable instruments

Banknotes, cheques, bills of exchange and cer-tificates of deposit are all *negotiable instruments*, i.e. documents which can be readily exchanged. Ownership of the asset passes simply with their delivery. Such negotiability is vital to money market dealings. Life would be very difficult if, for example, each time a Treasury bill changed hands solicitors had to be called in and the change of ownership recorded. Many assets which are not negotiable, such as government bonds, are also traded on the money market and can also be used as collateral security.

Discount houses and discounting

A group of institutions make up the London Discount Market Association (LDMA). They are termed discount houses because their original business was concerned with the discounting of bills of exchange and Treasury bills. Discounting a bill is a method of lending money. We can illus-trate the process by considering Treasury bills.

Each week the Bank of England, on behalf of the government, offers Treasury bills for sale. The essentials of a Treasury bill are shown in Fig. 34.1. They are a method of borrowing and consti-tute part of the national debt. A Treasury bill is a promise by the government to pay a specific sum, e.g. £100 000, 91 days (three months) after the date it is issued.

A discount house might offer to buy the £100 000 bill for, say, £97 500, in which case it will cost the government £2500 to borrow £97 500 for 91 days. This is equivalent to an annual rate of interest of just over 10 per cent. However the rate on bills of exchange is expressed not as an interest rate but as a *discount rate*. Using the figures above the calculation of a discount rate can be illustrated as:

443

Fig. 34.1 *A Treasury Bill*
(The design of Treasury bill is Crown copyright and is reproduced here at less than actual size, with the permission of the Controller of Her Majesty's Stationery Office and Gerrard and National Plc.)

$$\frac{£2500}{£100\,000} \times \frac{100}{1} \times \frac{365}{91} = 10\%$$

Thus we arrive at a discount rate of 10 per cent, whereas the true interest rate, or yield, will be higher, in this case 10.28 per cent. If interest rates are falling this will cause discount houses to tender at a higher price. Conversely, if interest rates rise the price the government can expect will obviously fall since the price of the bill and the rate of interest are inversely proportional to one another.

Commercial bills of exchange are discounted in a similar manner. Commercial bills are a method by which a business can borrow money for a short period at advantageous rates. Often they will be to finance a particular transaction, as in the bill illustrated in Fig. 34.2. The bill illustrated has been *accepted*, i.e. guaranteed, by a *recognised* bank and is therefore eligible for discount at the Bank of England. Such *first-class bills* of exchange command the *finest* rates of interest on the money market.

The discount houses and the banks

The discount houses obtain their funds by borrowing money from banks at call or short notice. The rate of interest which they pay is a slightly lower rate than they charge for discounting bills, and in this manner they make their profits. Traditionally the banks have been pleased with this arrangement and have ensured the continued existence of discount houses by not tendering for Treasury bills themselves. The advantage to the banks is that they are lending money for only 24 hours at a time instead of 91 days, thereby giving them an asset almost as liquid as cash but earning some interest. If a bank calls in money from a discount house it is usually to settle an interbank debt. The discount house is then usually able to reborrow the money from the creditor bank.

If the Bank of England is restricting the supply of money then it is possible that all the banks will be calling in money from the discount houses. In this situation, if the discount houses cannot

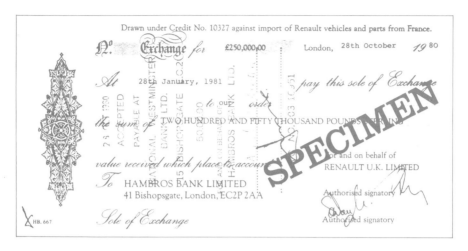

Drawn under Credit No. 10327 against import of Renault vehicles and parts from France.

Nᵒ. *Exchange for* £250,000.00   London, 28th October *19* 80

At 28th January, 1981 *pay this sole of Exchange*

to our order

the sum of TWO HUNDRED AND FIFTY THOUSAND POUNDS STERLING

SPECIMEN

value received which place to account *or and on behalf of*
RENAULT U.K. LIMITED

To HAMBROS BANK LIMITED
41 Bishopsgate, London, EC2P 2AA

Authorised signatory

Authorised signatory

HB. 667   *Sole of Exchange*

Fig. 34.2 *An eligible bank bill*
(Reproduced by kind permission of Gerrard and National Plc, Tate and Lyle Plc and National Westminster Bank Plc.)

find the money anywhere else, they can in the *last resort* borrow from the Bank of England. The Bank of England does this by *re-discounting* the eligible bills of exchange which the discount houses have. The rate at which the Bank is willing to re-discount is very important, because all other rates move in sympathy with it. The rate is always higher than the Treasury bill rate; the discount houses will, therefore, lose money if they are forced to re-discount with the Bank. Thus, in the event of the Bank restricting the money supply, it is the discount houses which get into difficulties first, therefore providing the banks with a shield, or cushion, against government monetary policy. This is another reason why the banks support the discount houses.

The monetary control provisions of 1981 laid down that the banks must keep a minimum of 4 per cent of their eligible liabilities with the LDMA. This was done to ensure the continuance of discount houses. The big banks have, however, objected to this because it has often meant that they have been forced to place money with the discount houses at disadvantageous rates. This requirement was reduced in 1983 (see above, page 438).

Table 34.2 shows rates of interest at 11 June 1988. Here you can see that the discount houses could borrow from the banks at 7·6 per cent up-

wards. The table also shows the interest rate on some other significant money market transactions.

Table 34.2 Selected UK interest rates at 11 June 1988

Money market rate	%
Clearing banks' deposit rate	1.8
Call money	7.6
Eurodollars (3 months)	7.7
Clearing banks' base rate	8.5
Treasury bill rate	8.2
Fine trade bills (3 months)	7.8
Clearing banks' overdrafts	11–15

Merchant banks

Merchant banks are so called because they were originally merchants. However, over the course of time they found it more profitable to become involved in the financial aspects of trade rather than the trade itself. Many institutions claim the title of merchant bank; indeed some of the clearing banks have set up merchant banking subsidiaries. Usually, however, we limit the term to the 16 members of the *Accepting Houses Committee*. This includes such institutions as Hambros, Schroders, Lazards and Barings.

Accepting is a process whereby the accepting house guarantees the redemption of a commercial bill of exchange in the case of default by the

445

company which issued the bill. For this they charge a commission. A bill which has been accepted by a London accepting house becomes a 'fine' bill or *first-class bill of exchange*. This makes it much easier to sell on the money market, where it will also command the lowest or 'finest', discount rate. The bill will also be eligible for re-discount at the Bank of England. In order to be able to guarantee bills in this way, accepting houses have to make it their business to know everyone else's business. A merchant banker will therefore specialise in certain areas of business or in particular areas of the world (companies from all over the world raise money on the London money market); Hambros, for example, specialise in Scandinavian and Canadian business. The regional specialisations often reflect the merchant origins of the bank.

In addition to accepting, merchant banks undertake many other functions. They might undertake to raise capital for their clients or invest in the company themselves. They act as agents in takeover bids and in the issue of new shares. In recent years many merchant banks have become involved in unit trusts and investment trusts. However merchant banks do not involve themselves in high-street banking activities.

The capital market

The capital market is concerned with the provision of longer-term finance – anything from bank loans to investment in permanent capital in the form of the purchase of shares. Unlike the money market, the capital market is very widespread. Some of the participants in this market are as follows.

a) Commercial banks. These are important in providing short- and medium-term loans to industry. In the UK, however, it is most unusual for commercial banks to invest in industry by taking shares or debentures, unlike the USA and West Germany where this is common practice.

b) *Merchant banks*. These banks participate in the capital market by assisting companies in the

issue of new shares and also by direct investment in industry.

c) *Insurance companies and pension funds*. Over recent years the institutional investors have become more and more important, so that today the insurance companies and pension funds own almost half the shares in public companies.

d) *Investment trusts*. There are joint stock companies whose business is investment in other companies. Shares are bought in the normal way and the funds thus raised are used to buy shares in other companies.

e) *Unit trusts*. Although unit trusts also invest in other companies they are not normal companies. Unit trusts are supervised by the Department of Trade and Industry and are controlled by boards of trustees. They attract small investors who buy units in the trust which can be redeemed if the investor so wishes.

f) *Government-sponsored institutions*. Two government-sponsored organisations were created in 1945, the Industrial and Commercial Finance Corporation and the Finance Corporation for Industry. In 1973 a merger of the two corporations was proposed and in 1975 Finance for Industry Ltd (FFI) was formed; this is now called Investors in Industry (3is). Its shareholders are the clearing banks (85 per cent) and the Bank of England. Investors in Industry has access to funds of over £1 billion and is intended to give medium-term assistance to industry.

g) *Consortium banks*. A relative newcomer to the money and capital markets, consortium banks may be defined as banks which are owned by other banks but in which no one bank has a shareholding of more than 50 per cent and in which at least one bank is an overseas bank. The first consortium bank, which was called the Midland and International Bank Ltd, was formed in 1964. The multinational nature of most of these banks stresses the international nature of finance these days.

h) *Private individuals*. The trend for many years has been the decline in the importance of the private individual as an investor. The privatisations of the 1980s did not significantly alter this trend. There are, of course, a few, very wealthy private individuals who are important investors.

    i) *Self finance.* One of the most important

sources of finance to industry is ploughed back profits. (See also discussion in Chapter 23.)

Summary

1   Financial intermediaries are institutions which channel funds between different sectors of the economy.

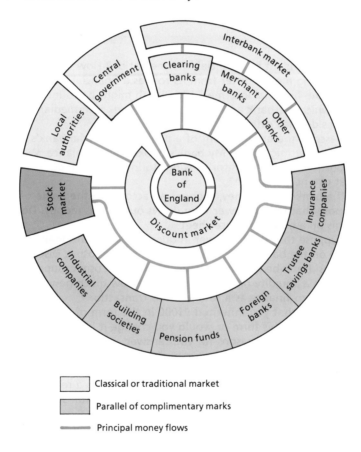

Classical or traditional market

Parallel of complimentary marks

Principal money flows

Fig. 34.3 *The main participants in the UK financial markets*

2   The many different types of bank can be grouped under the two headings, primary and secondary banks. Primary banks operate in the high street and deal with the general public, whilst secondary banks deal in very large amounts of money with other banking institutions.

3   The main functions of commercial banks are the creation of credit, the transmission of money and the provision of advisory services to customers.

4 The study of commercial banks' balance sheets explains how their business is conducted.

5 Banks are regulated by statute and by the central bank in the UK. Two recent changes are the monetary control provisions of 1981 and the Banking Act 1987.

6 Money markets are those institutions and arrangements which are concerned with the borrowing and lending of money on a very large scale for very short periods of time (overnight to three months).

7 The capital market is concerned with the provision of capital for industry, commerce and the government. The market is very widespread and provides capital for periods over three months to permanent.

Questions

1 What is meant by financial intermediation? How do a bank's activities in transmitting money differ from its role as a financial intermediary?

2 List the financial intermediaries which might be found in a typical high street. State which are bank and which are non-bank intermediaries. What types of services do they offer?

3 Describe the arrangement of a typical commercial bank's balance sheet.

4 A banker might say: 'My bank's books always balance. We simply lend a proportion of my depositor's savings to investors. We do not create money.' To what extent is this true?

5 If a bank lends money, it opens an account in the name of the borrower. Suppose that the borrower then draws out all this money. Demonstrate the effect of this on a bank's balance sheet.

6 Suppose that the borrower in question 5 uses this loan by drawing a cheque of £1000 on the bank (Lloyds) to buy goods from Cosmic Discount who bank with Barclays. Describe how money will be paid to Cosmic. Suppose that Barclays maintain a liquidity ratio of 20 per cent. How much new lending or investment will it be able to finance as a result of this transaction?

7 Imagine that you inherited £1000 in the form of gold coins. Would you keep the inheritance in this form or would you change it into money and place it on deposit with a bank? Give reasons for your answer.

8 Describe the limitations on a bank's ability to create credit.

9 Assess the importance of the money market.

10 Suppose that in Fig. 34.1 the Treasury bill has a redemption value of £250 000. Suppose that on 8 May, when it has still had the full 91 days to run, £222 500 was offered for it. What is the discount rate? Examine Fig. 34.2 and suppose that the going discount rate for such bills was 9.5 per cent. If the bill had 36 days left to go before redemption what price would be offered for it?

11 Assess the advantages and disadvantages of the capital market being dominated by large institutions.

Data response   Balancing the books

Table 34.3 gives all the figures which are necessary for the presentation of Midwest Bank Plc's balance sheet. Midwest is a recognised bank and its business is in sterling. The distribution of its assets is in accordance with Monetary-control Provisions of 1981.

Table 34.3 Midwest Bank PLC
[Recognised as a bank by the Bank of England]
Items in the balance sheet as at 1 April 1989

	£m
Advances	14 367
Other bills*	602
Coins and notes	451
Money at call and short notice*	650
Certificates of deposit*	729
Loans to UK banks*	531
Investments	3 732
Operational balances with the Bank of England*	563
Government stocks with less than one year to maturity*	206
UK Treasury bills*	326
Sight deposits	9 922
Local authority bills*	279
Time deposits	12 628
Non-operational deposits with the Bank of England	114

1 Present these figures as a balance sheet laid out in the conventional manner for a bank and determine the overall balance for Midwest Plc.

2 If the whole of the items marked * in Table 34.3 are regarded as liquid assets for control purposes, determine the liquidity ratio on which Midwest is operating.

3 Outline the factors which determine the distribution of a bank's assets and liabilities.

4 Examine the consequences of there being a significant decrease in the required liquidity ratio.

5 To what extent does the balance sheet of Midwest differ from that of a typical clearing bank?

35

Central banking and monetary policy

Central banking

Introduction

Every country in the world has a central bank,
the oldest in the world being that of Sweden
(1668). The Bank of England was founded in
1694, while in the USA the Federal Reserve did
not come into existence until 1913. The Bank
of England was founded by a group of businessmen headed by a Scotsman William Paterson.
In return for a loan to the Crown of £1.2 million
the Bank acquired several privileges. This began
its close association with the UK government
which culminated in its nationalisation in 1946.
Few central banks are really independent of
government although the Federal Reserve of the
USA and the West German Bundesbank are
rather more independent than most.

An important step in the development of the
Bank of England was the Bank Charter Act of
1844. This divided the Bank into two departments, the Issue Department, responsible for
the issue of notes, and the Banking Department,
which is responsible for all the Bank's other
activities. The Act also set in motion the process
by which the Bank was to become the sole issuer
of notes in England and Wales.

Functions of central banks

Central banks are important to the working
of the monetary system. Amongst their most
important functions are the following.

a) Government's banker. Governments pay
their revenues into the central bank and pay
their bills with cheques drawn on it. The fees
which the bank changes for this are an important
source of revenue to the bank.

b) Banker's bank. As explained in the previous
chapter, commercial banks keep balances with
the central bank. This is both a method of controlling banks and also the way by which inter-
bank indebtedness can be settled.

c) Lender of last resort. The central bank stands
ready to support commercial banks should they
get into difficulties.

d) Banking supervision. Central banks usually
have a major role to play in the policing of the
banking system. In some countries this responsibility is shared with other authorities;
for example, in the USA the Federal Reserve is
supported by the Comptroller of Currency and
by the Federal Deposit Insurance Corporation
(FDIC).

e) Note issue. In most countries of the world
the central bank is responsible for the issue of

banknotes. This is not so everywhere. In the USA, for example, the currency is issued by the government.

f) *Operating monetary policy*. It is usually the central bank which operates government monetary policy.

The balance sheet of the Bank of England

In the same manner that the operations of commercial banks can be understood through their balance sheet, so can those of a central bank. Table 35.1 shows the balance sheet of the Bank of England as at 30 December 1987. The Bank *return*, as it is termed, has been published weekly since 1844. Since this date the balance sheet has been in two portions, the Issue Department and the Banking Department. (Numbers after the following headings refer to items in Table 35.1.)

The Issue Department

a) *Notes in circulation (1)*. This item illustrates the Bank's function as the sole *issuer of notes* in England and Wales. There are two monetary authorities in the UK, since coins are issued by the Crown through the Royal Mint, now based at Llantrisant in Wales. Although coins are very important, until 1983 they only formed a minor proportion of the cash in circulation; however at this date the Royal Mint began to issue £1 coins, thus modifying the Bank's role.

The Scottish and Northern Irish banks also issue notes, but beyond a total of £4.3 million these must all be fully backed by Bank of England notes and they, therefore, have little effect on the volume of notes in circulation.

b) *Notes in Banking Department (2)*. These are notes which have been printed by the Issue Department and sold to the Banking Department where they are kept ready for distribution to the banks. Thus we also find this item in the balance sheet of the Banking Department. Since the two departments are separate, Bank of England notes are a liability to the Issue Department but an asset to the Banking Department.

c) *Government securities (3)*. All banknotes these days are fiduciary issue and the backing for the currency is government securities. Effectively the backing for the currency is that it is both readily acceptable and it is legal tender.

d) *Other securities (4)*. These consist of securities other than those issued by the UK govern-

Table 35.1 Balance Sheet of the Bank of England as at 30 December 1987

Liabilities	£m	Assets	£m
Issue Department			
Notes in circulation (1)	14 548	Government securities (3)	9 161
Notes in Banking Department (2)	12	Other (4)	5 399
	14 560		14 560
Banking Department			
Public deposits (5)	109	Government securities (9)	638
Special deposits (6)	–	Advances and other accounts (10)	815
Bankers' deposits (7)	1 086	Premises, equipment and other securities (11)	1 664
Reserves and other accounts (8)	1 934	Notes and coin (2)	12
	3 129		3 129

Source: Bank of England Quarterly Bulletin.

ment. This item also includes the government debt dating back to the foundation of the Bank in 1694. Coins bought from the Royal Mint, but not yet put into circulation, are also included in this item. Also in this item are the eligible bills purchased by the Bank in order to even out flows in the money markets.

The liabilities of the Banking Department

a) *Public deposits (5)*. These are the UK government's deposits at the Bank and represent the Bank's function as the *government's banker*. The figure is perhaps surprisingly small; this is because the Bank, on behalf of the government, balances its revenues and expenditures through the sale and purchase of Treasury bills. This item also includes the dividend accounts of the Commissioners of the National Debt, illustrating the Bank's function as the *manager of the national debt*.

b) *Special deposits (6)*. The existence of this item illustrates the Bank's function as the *operator of government monetary policy*. (*See* page 457.)

c) *Banker's deposits (7)*. These are the deposits of the *monetary sector* which are equivalent to 0·5 per cent of their eligible liabilities plus the balances they keep for operating the clearing system. This item demonstrates the Bank's role as *bankers' bank*.

d) *Reserves and other accounts (8)*. This item consists of undistributed profits and the accounts of persons and institutions with the Bank. These fall into three categories: the Bank's employees; private customers who had accounts at the Bank in 1946; and institutions having special need to bank with the Bank, e.g. foreign banks. This illustrates that the Bank also functions as an *ordinary bank*. Most central banks do not operate as commercial banks; some however, such as the *Banque de France*, compete for ordinary business in the high street with commercial banks.

The assets of the Banking Department

a) *Government securities (9)*. Like the Issue Department, the main assets of the Banking Department are UK government securities.

b) *Advances and other accounts (10)*. This item consists mainly of loans which the Bank has made to institutions such as discount houses. This illustrates the Bank's function as *lender of last resort*. By always being prepared to lend money, the Bank ensures that the banking system never becomes insolvent. This was described in the previous chapter.

c) *Premises, equipment and other securities (11)*. Like any other business the Bank possesses real assets. As well as its well-known Threadneedle Street site in London, the Bank also has seven branches in other cities, e.g. Birmingham and Bristol.

d) *Notes and coins (2)*. The Bank is responsible for supplying the banks with the new banknotes and coins which they require.

Other functions of the Bank of England

There are several functions of the Bank of England which are not apparent from its balance sheet. Firstly, since 1946 it has had the responsibility for 'disposing of the means of foreign payment in the national interest', i.e. all *foreign exchange transactions* are monitored by the Bank. This function is not so important since the abolition of exchange controls in 1979. However, the Bank operates the *Exchange Equalisation Account*. This is a fund, established in 1932, the purpose of which is to buy and sell currency on the foreign exchange market with the object of stabilising the exchange rate. This function is equally important whether there is a fixed or floating exchange rate. The Bank also *sells stock* on behalf of the government. It advises the government on the issue of new securities, it converts and funds existing government debt, it publishes prospectuses for any new government issues and it deals with the applications for them and apportions the issue. It also *manages the servicing of the national debt*, i.e. the payment of interest on behalf of the government. The Bank is also responsible for giving the government general *advice on the monetary system*; it publishes large quantities of *statistical information* on the monetary system, along with studies of various sectors of the economy. (Conscientious students should acquaint themselves with the *Bank of England Quarterly Bulletin* in which much of this information is contained.) The effect of the Banking Act and the monetary control-provisions has been greatly to widen the scope of the statistics which the Bank publishes.

Finally an important function of the Bank is to *represent the government* in relations with foreign central banks and also in various international institutions such as the Bank for International Settlement (BIS) and the International Monetary Fund (IMF).

The development of monetary policy

Monetary policy is the direction of the economy through the supply of and price of money. In most countries, as in the UK, the operation of monetary policy is undertaken by the central bank.

Early changes

It used to be believed that changes in the rate of interest (the price of money) determined the volume of investment in the economy. Thus lowering the rate of interest would stimulate the economy while raising it would contract the economy. Up to the time of the 1914–18 war, monetary policy consisted of little more than minor changes in bank rate. The question of variations of the money supply hardly arose since the UK was on the gold standard.

During the 1930s the relationship between investment and interest was challenged by Keynes. Certainly, events seemed to support him as interest rates were very low but investment was also very low. This Keynes explained as the *liquidity trap*. Thus when Keynes's view became the economic orthodoxy after 1945 it was believed that the connection between interest rates and the level of economic activity was weak and the government relied upon fiscal policy as the principal method of directing the economy. (See discussion in Chapter 36.)

Thus, in the immediate post-war years, active monetary policy was severely curtailed. Interest rates were held at a low level for a number of reasons.

a) There was a large supply of savings which had been undertaken during the war. The continuance of rationing and the lack of consumer goods limited the ability of people to use their savings.

b) The government needed to borrow large sums of money for its economic programmes and was therefore inclined to keep down the cost of borrowing.

c) Allowing the interest rate to rise would automatically devalue the price of existing securities and the government believed that this would be unfair to those who had purchased these securities during the war.

d) The socialist government believed that fiscal policy and direct intervention were better and more equitable ways of directing the economy than monetary policy.

Monetary policy in the 1950s and 1960s

Monetary policy was revived in the 1950s, as is evidenced by the rise in bank rate over the decade. It came to be believed that raising interest rates would 'lock-up' investment funds in financial institutions. This was because a large proportion of their assets were in government securities and a rise in interest rates would decrease their value, thus making institutions unwilling to sell them because they would make a loss. Thus the orthodox view at this time was that putting up rates would 'choke off' investment and was therefore useful in restricting the economy. However lowering interest rates would not, of itself, be sufficient to stimulate the economy.

The Radcliffe Report (Committee on the Working of the Monetary System, 1959), endorsing the view that the control of overall liquidity was more important than control of the money supply, said:

We advocate measures to strike more directly and **453**

rapidly at the liquidity of spenders. We regard a combination of control of capital issues, bank advances and consumer credit as being most likely to serve this purpose.

The Report was subsequently criticised for its lack of attention to control of the money supply. The Report argued that any contrived changes in the money supply (M) were as likely as not to be offset by changes in the velocity of circulation (V). The view was also challenged by monetarists in later years. (See page 465).

The Radcliffe Report's conclusions formed the basis of government monetary policy until the early 1970s. In particular it was believed that monetary policy should be concerned with the *fine tuning* of the economy, while its overall direction was a matter for fiscal policy.

The rise of monetarist ideas

The Competition and Credit Control regulations of 1971 (CCC) were an important change in policy. From this date interest rates were supposed to be left free to be determined by market forces. Competition was to be encouraged by such measures as the abolition of the syndicated bid for Treasury bills and the abandonment of the clearing banks' cartel on interest rates. The CCC changes also abandoned the old 28 per cent liquid assets ratio in favour of a 12½ per cent reserve assets ratio. This resulted in an unprecedented rise in the money supply which was one of the major causes of inflation in subsequent years.

Economists in the UK and the USA, especially the leader of the monetarist school, Milton Friedman, were convinced that the only way to control inflation was through control of the money supply (M). The increasing severity of inflation and the apparent inability of traditional fiscal and incomes policy methods to deal with it won many people over to the monetarist school. In particular the IMF was convinced of the need to control M. Thus when the UK was forced to apply for a major loan in 1976 it was only granted it on the condition that the money supply be controlled. The accession of

monetarist ideas to dominance in monetary policy can be seen to date from 1976.

In 1979 a Conservative government was elected which placed control of the money supply at the centre of its policies. In 1980 the government adopted a *Medium Term Financial Strategy* (MTFS). This set down diminishing targets for the growth of the money supply so as to squeeze inflation out of the system. In most years the target rates were exceeded while, at the same time, measures of the money supply were changed and redefined. In October 1985 the MTFS was largely abandoned when the most favoured target, £M3, was suspended. By 1988 the only measure of money supply for which targets remained was MO. Despite these changes the Conservative government continued to see control of the money supply and of interest rates as central to its policies. (See also discussion of money supply pages 578–80 and of MTFS page 581.)

The stages of monetary policy

The five stages of policy

The Bank of England has a number of *weapons* or *instruments* of monetary policy at its disposal, for example, it may lower interest rates in order to stimulate the economy. However, policies do not take effect immediately and there are several steps, or stages, along the way. These we may list as follows:

a) *Instruments (or weapons) of policy* which include, for example, open market operations and special deposits, which are used to implement policy. It will take some time for these to act upon:

b) *Operating policy targets* such as the liquidity of banks. These in turn will affect such things as the growth of money stock which are termed:

c) *Intermediate targets*. They are termed 'intermediate' because they are not the actual objective of policy but are important steps along the way. For example, restricting the money supply may be seen as essential in achieving the overall policy objective of controlling inflation. To do this they must affect:

d) Aggregate demand. This is the actual level of national income as measured by GDP, NNP etc. The control of which leads directly to:

e) Overall policy objectives. This is the ultimate goal of policy such as the promotion of economic growth or the control of inflation.

Intermediate targets

The central link in the chain is intermediate targets. In choosing the best or most appropriate target, the monetary authorities are constrained by two major considerations. First, which target it is *possible* to control, i.e. it is no good selecting a target which is impossible to influence. Perhaps, we should say that some targets are more influenceable than others! Second, which intermediate target is thought to most influence the desired ultimate policy objective. Here there is considerable disagreement. Monetarists, for example, would argue that changes in interest rates have a significant influence on economic growth, while Keynesians would argue that the effect would be slight.

There are said to be five intermediate targets:

a) *The money stock;*
b) *The volume of credit;*
c) *Interest rates;*
d) *The exchange rate;*
e) *The level of expenditure in the economy.*

It is possible for expenditure to be considered an intermediate target as well as stage four of monetary policy.

The weapons of monetary policy

Monetary policy is aimed at controlling the supply and price of money. However, elementary economics tells us that government cannot do both simultaneously, i.e. it can fix the interest rate but it will then be committed to creating a money supply which is appropriate to that rate, *or* it can control the money supply and leave market forces to determine the interest rate.

With the exception of M0 whichever definition of the money supply we take (M1, M3, etc.), the major component of it is bank deposits. Thus monetary policy must be aimed at influencing the volume of bank deposits. The ability of banks to create deposits is determined by the ratio of liquid assets which they maintain. If, for example, banks keep to a 12½ per cent liquid (or reserve) asset ratio, then because we have a *bank multiplier* of 8, each reduction of £1 in banks' liquid assets would cause a further reduction of £7 in their deposits. Much of monetary policy is therefore aimed at influencing the supply of liquid assets.

In order to effect its monetary policy the Bank of England uses a number of methods. These *weapons* of policy are considered below.

The issue of notes and coins

Theoretically the Bank could influence the volume of money by expanding or contracting the supply of cash. In practice it is very difficult for the Bank not to supply the cash which banks are demanding, so that it is not a viable method of restricting supply. The reverse may not be true, however, for expanding the issue of cash could well expand the money supply. Indeed, many people would argue that the over-printing of banknotes, i.e. sale of government securities to the Bank's Issue Department, was one of the causes of inflation in the mid-1970s. Table 35.2 traces the growth of the fiduciary issue in recent years (this is now modified by the introduction of £1 coins).

The quantity of cash is now such a small proportion of the money supply that we might, in the words of the Radcliffe Report, regard it as the 'small change' of the monetary system. However the introduction of a new, much tighter, definiton of the money supply, termed money base (M0), consisting only of cash and banks' balances with the Bank of England, has meant that the supply of cash has assumed more importance. You can see from Table 35.2 that the growth of the fiduciary issue and, hence, of M0 was quite stable in the 1980s. This stability was **455**

Table 35.2 The growth of the UK fiduciary issue

Years to end 2nd quarter	Fiduciary issue (£m)	Percentage increase over preceding year
1972	4 052	–
1973	4 545	12·2
1974	5 109	12·4
1975	5 902	15·5
1976	6 674	13·1
1977	7 314	9·6
1978	8 512	16·4
1979	9 305	9·3
1980	9 798	5·3
1981	10 256	4·6
1982	10 566	3·0
1983	11 500	8·8
1984	12 167	5·8
1985	12 717	4·5
1986	13 359	5·0
1987	14 149	5·9

Source: Bank of England Quarterly Bulletin

one of the reasons which recommended it to the government as a target for control. However, the credit boom of the late 1980s demonstrated that controlling the monetary base does not necessarily control spending in the economy.

Liquidity ratios

In 1981 the bank abandoned the reserve assets ratio. The only stated ratios now are the 0.45 per cent of eligible liabilities which the monetary sector must keep with the Bank and the 6 per cent which had to be kept with the money market (this was reduced to 5 per cent in 1983 at the insistence of the clearing banks). However, as we have seen above (page 439), although there is no overall liquid assets ratio, banks are still required to order their assets in particular ways. Since the Bank of England is able to influence the supply of liquid assets, it is therefore still able to influence bank lending. The Bank has stated that it regards these funds and in addition to this money which the banks voluntarily retain with it for clearing purposes as 'the fulcrum for money market management'.

Interest rates

By lowering interest rates the Bank of England could hope to encourage economic activity by decreasing the cost of borrowing, while, conversely, raising interest rates should discourage borrowing. Most of the weapons of monetary policy will indirectly affect interest rates, but the Bank has a direct influence upon interest rates because, as lender of last resort, it guarantees the solvency of the financial system. Thus the rate at which the Bank is willing to lend is crucial. Great importance used to be attached to the Bank Rate but this was abandoned in 1972 in favour of minimum lending rate (MLR), which was supposed to be determined by a formula geared to the Treasury bill rate, thus placing greater reliance on market forces. The announcement (or 'posting') of MLR was suspended in 1981.

The Bank now works within an unpublished band of rates. Important money market rates such as the Treasury bill rate will stay close to the Bank's lending rate. This is because the Bank's rate is kept above Treasury bill rate, so that discount houses would lose money if they are forced to borrow. Thus all market rates tend to move in sympathy with the Bank of England's rates; clearing banks' base rate for example is always at, or near, the Bank's rate.

Open-market operations

These are the sale or purchase of securities by the Bank on the open market with the intention of influencing the volume of money in circulation and the rate of interest. Operations are undertaken in the market on the Bank's behalf by one of the smaller discount houses, Secombe, Marshall and Campion. The selling of bills or bonds should reduce the volume of money and increase interest rates, whilst the repurchase of, or reduction in sales of, government securities should increase the volume of money and decrease interest rates.

In order to explain the effects of open-market operations it is necessary to explain their effect upon the balance sheets of commercial banks. Let us consider a bank whose assets and liabilities are arranged in the following manner

Bank X before open-market sales

Liabilities (£)		Assets (£)	
Deposits	100 000	Liquid assets	
		(10% ratio)	10 000
		Securities	40 000
		Advances	50 000
	£100 000		£100 000

You will note that Bank X has a liquid asset ratio of 10 per cent. Let us now assume that the Bank of England *sells* securities, £1000 of which are bought by the depositors of Bank X. The customers pay for these by cheques drawn on Bank X and the Bank of England collects this money by deducting it from Bank X's balance at the Bank. Thus after open-market sales, the Bank X's balance sheet will be as follows:

Bank X after open-market sales

Liabilities (£)		Assets (£)	
Deposits	99 000	Liquid assets	
		(9.09% ratio)	9 000
		Securities	40 000
		Advances	50 000
	£99 000		£99 000

The Bank of England's actions will have immediate (or primary) effects by reducing the amount of money in circulation by the amount of open-market sales and may also increase the interest rate if increased sales depress the price of securities. However the most important effects of open-market operations are the secondary effects which come about as a result of Bank X's need to maintain its liquidity ratio. In order to restore its ratio the bank is forced to sell off securities, thus further reducing their price and thereby raising the rate of interest, and by reducing its advances, which may involve both making advances harder to obtain and more expensive.

Students are often puzzled as to why selling securities does not increase increase the banks' reserves of cash. The supply of cash is effectively under the control of the monetary authorities so that as the banks sell securities these are paid

for by customers running down their deposits. And after all banks cannot deposit money in themselves!

Final position of Bank X

Liabilities (£)		Assets (£)	
Deposits	90 000	Liquid assets	
		(10% ratio)	9 000
		Securities	36 000
		Advances	45 000
	£90 000		£90 000

The final position of Bank X's balance sheet shows that in order to restore its liquidity ratio it has been forced to reduce its balance sheet to £90 000. Thus £1000 of open-market operations have reduced the volume of money in circulation by £10 000. The magnitude of the effect is determined by the bank multiplier. If, for example, Bank X worked to a 20 per cent ratio, then there would only be a five-fold effect.

We have demonstrated here the effect of open-market sales. If the bank were to buy securities it would have exactly the opposite effect.

Funding

This is the conversion of short-term government debt into longer-term debt. This will not only reduce liquidity but also, if the Bank of England is replacing securities which could be counted as liquid assets by securities which cannot, it could bring about the multiple contraction of deposits described above. In recent years the government has been concerned to borrow money in a way which would not increase banks' supplies of liquid assets and has therefore created more longer-term non-negotiable securities such as 'granny bonds'.

Special directives and special deposits

Since its nationalisation in 1946 the Bank of England has had the power to call for special deposits and to make special directives. However, these powers were not used until after the Radcliffe Report. If the Bank calls upon the **457** members of the monetary sector to make a deposit of a certain percentage of their liabilities in cash at the Bank, and stipulates that these may not be counted as liquid assets, then this brings about a multiple contraction of their lending in the same way as open-market operations, the difference being that it is more certain and less expensive. The power to call for special deposits was specifically retained in the monetary control provisions of 1981. Despite retaining the power to call for special deposits the monetary authorities avoided the use of them during the 1980s.

The Bank of England has issued special directives on both how much banks should lend (quantitative) and to whom they should lend (qualitative). However, since the competition and credit control changes of 1971 it has ceased to make quantitative directives and makes only qualitative ones.

In 1973 a new scheme came into operation termed *special supplementary deposits* which was nicknamed 'the corset'. By this scheme, if banks expanded their *interest-bearing eligible liabilities* (IBELS) too quickly they automatically had to make special deposits of cash with the Bank. This scheme was abandoned in 1980.

Moral suasion

For many years the Bank of England was able to hold considerable sway over the banking system by simply making its wishes known. The last two decades, however, have seen such a battery of legislative and administrative controls introduced that moral suasion is no longer considered a major weapon of policy. The method of policy is still used in the USA where it is known as 'the jawbone'.

Problems of monetary policy

We have discussed the weapon of monetary policy but there are many doubts about their efficacy. These can be broadly classified into two groups. Firstly there are conceptual problems concerning the ability of monetary policy to influence the economy, as for instance the doubts about the ability of lower interest rates to stimulate investment (*see also* Chapter 36). Secondly there are the more mechanistic problems which may prevent the weapons from being effective, as for example the existence of excess liquidity in the system preventing open-market operations from being effective.

Some of these problems are discussed below.

Interest rate policy

It has already been suggested that decreasing the interest rate may not encourage investment but that raising the interest rate tends to lock up liquidity in the financial system. Businesses, however, might still be willing to borrow at a relatively high rate of interest if they are sufficiently confident. This is because most investment decisions are *non-marginal*, i.e. the entrepreneur will be anticipating a sufficiently great return on investment that small changes in the interest rate are unlikely to make a potentially profitable scheme unprofitable. We may also consider the converse of this and reason that small falls in the interest rate are unlikely to turn unprofitable schemes into worth-while ones.

In considering the effect of interest rates we must also take account of the effect of time on investment decisions; the longer the term of an investment project the greater the proportion of total cost interest will represent. We can illustrate this by an analogy with the individual consumer by asking which borrowing would be most influenced by a rise in the interest rate, borrowing to buy a car or to buy a house? Obviously it is the house purchase, the long-term scheme.

Having mentioned house purchase we have touched on another problem and that is that governments may be unwilling to put up interest rates because, as so many voters are homebuyers, this is extremely unpopular.

There are other factors which make governments unwilling to face high interest rates. With a large national debt to service, raising interest rates increases their own expenditure. Similarly, with so many foreign deposits in the UK monetary sector, each percentage rise in interest rates means a drain of foreign currency on the balance of payments.

Despite these reservations the 'normal' rate of interest has risen greatly over recent years. This may be partly attributed to inflation, but in a number of years in the 1970s interest rates did not keep pace with inflation so that the economy experienced negative 'real' rates of interest (see page 277). In these circumstances it was understandable that people were still willing to borrow despite high nominal rates of interest. When, in the 1980s, interest rates remained high but the world economy was depressed, the effects were felt most keenly in less developed countries with their huge burdens of overseas debt to service. (See the discussion of the effects of interest rates upon the economy in the following chapter.)

Liquidity and the multiple contraction of deposits

Many of the weapons of monetary policy depend upon limiting liquidity, which has a multiple effect upon banks' deposits through their liquidity ratios. If, however, banks keep surplus liquidity this will protect them against such measures as open-market operations and special deposits. The more liquid the assets which banks possess, the less they will be affected by policy changes; for example, an increase in the interest rate from 9 to 10 per cent would reduce the value of securities with three months to run by less than 0·25 per cent, while long-dated stock would have its value cut by anything up to 15 per cent.

The efficacy of open-market sales is also affected by who purchases the securities. In order for open-market sales to be effective it is necessary that sales be to the general public. If the securities are bought by the banks they will have little effect upon their liquidity since most of them count as liquid assets. This problem was especially acute when governments were forced to borrow large amounts in the late 1970s and early 1980s. As banks acquired government securities they used them as a base to expand deposits. Thus, rather than controlling the money supply, sales of securities provided the springboard for its expansion. To counter this effect the monetary authorities adopted the practice of selling more government debt to UK non-bank holders than was necessary to cover the PSBR. The object of doing so was to moderate the effects of rising bank lending on M3. This practice is known as *overfunding*.

The velocity of circulation

Theoretically it is possible for decreases in the money stock (*M*) to be offset by rises in the velocity of circulation (*V*). This is, however, a controversial topic and it is considered in the next chapter.

Other problems

Funding may be effective in controlling liquidity and we have already mentioned the government's attempts to increase the sale of non-negotiable securities. However it is expensive, since the rate of interest on long-term debt is usually much higher than on short-term debt. Considerable funding of the debt might therefore have the undesirable consequence of increasing long-term interest rates.

When we consider special deposits and special directives we discover that these can be simple, cheap, effective and quick acting. However in recent years governments have tried to avoid using them because they tend to damage the relationship between the central bank and the commercial banks. They also have the effect of distorting market forces, so government policy now tends to concentrate upon manipulating market forces rather than imposing its will directly on the system. The distorting effect of direct controls was well illustrated when the 'corset' was abolished in 1980. The immediate result was a surge in the money supply as banks, who had been keeping assets in Eurocurrencies switched them back to sterling.

Conclusion

The role of monetary policy has been the subject of much controversy in recent years. People expected monetary policy to accomplish tasks which it was never designed to do. In the best of all possible worlds the job of the central bank would be simply to maintain the system with small adjustments here and there. Monetary policy, however, has often been viewed as a way in which overall management of the economy could be achieved. In addition to this burden, monetary policy has had to cope with the unprecedented problems such as inflation, recession, the oil crises, etc. For the UK there is also an extra dimension to the problem, for London is a world banking centre and the central bank must therefore contend not only with domestic economic problems but also with those of much of the world as well.

Summary

1 Most central banks act as the government's banker, the banks' bank, lender of last resort, issuer of notes as well as supervising the banking system and operating monetary policy.
2 The Bank of England's balance sheet illustrates most of its major functions. It is divided into two sections, Issue Department and Banking Department.
3 The Bank has other functions such as managing the national debt and running the Exchange Equalisation Account.
4 Interest rate used to be thought of as the most important aspect of monetary policy, but during the Radcliffe era interest rates were thought to have only an indirect effect upon the economy. In recent years there has been much more emphasis on controlling the money supply.
5 The weapons of monetary policy may be listed as the issue of notes, changing liquidity ratios, variations in interest rates, open-market operations, funding, special deposits and directives and moral suasion.
6 There are many problems associated with the operating of monetary policy. In particular interest rates do not appear to have a strong correlation with investment, and excess liquidity in the system may frustrate the Bank's ability to influence the money supply.
7 Monetary policy is now at the centre of government policy and economic debate.

Questions
1 List the functions of central banks.
2 Describe the operations of the Bank of England.
3 Examine the weapons of monetary policy.
4 In what ways may the government's budget deficit (or surplus) be linked to the money supply?
5 What factors may limit the efficacy of variations in interest rates as a weapon of policy?

6 What conditions are necessary for open-market operations to be effective?

7 Consider the usefulness of the government's adoption of M0 as an objective of policy.

Data response **Defining the money supply** ━━━━━━━━━━━━━━━━━━━━━

The following is the conclusion of an article in the May 1987 *Bank of England Quarterly Bulletin*. The article was entitled *Measures of Broad Money* and explained the reasons for the introduction of the new measures of the money stock such as M4 and M5.

The inescapable conclusion is that there can be no unique definition of broad money. Any choice of dividing line between those financial assets included in, and those excluded from broad money is to a degree arbitrary, and is likely over time to be invalidated by developments in the financial system. The *velocity of the chosen aggregate* would accordingly suffer the same unpredictability as has beset that of £M3 and, to a lesser extent, of M4 and M5. Moreover, as has been pointed out in successive restatements of the *MTFS* in recent years, broad money is largely interest bearing, so its growth cannot be relied upon to respond quickly to changes in interest rates. It follows that the problems encountered in using £M3 as the basis for targeting broad money cannot be eliminated simply by adopting some other definition. Nevertheless, the authorities have found *broader aggregates* useful in seeking to make assessments of monetary conditions. For example, the behaviour of broader aggregates including building society liabilities has provided valuable additional information at times when short-run movements in £M3 have been dominated by the switching of funds between building societies and banks, and by the *portfolio behaviour* of the societies themselves.

The Bank proposes to reflect this approach to the interpretation of movements in broad money by providing in future releases of monthly monetary statistics, the same range of information on the behaviour, the components and the counterparts of M4 and M5 as has hitherto been provided for £M3.

1 Explain the terms in italics.

2 Why is it difficult to arrive at a definition of what constitutes money?

3 What measures may the monetary authorities use to control and influence the various measures of the money stock?

4 Explain the reasons for including building society deposits in the definitions of money stock.

5 What was the government's response in the late 1980s to the difficulties of targeting the growth of broad money?

6 The article states 'broad money is largely interest bearing and so its growth cannot be relied upon to respond quickly to changes in interest rates'. Explain why this is so. How might Keynesian and monetarist views on this point diverge?

36

Monetary analysis and income analysis

The central issue that is debated these days in connection with macroeconomics is the doctrine of monetarism.

Paul A. Samuelson

The age of Sado-Monetarism has begun, in the corridors of power they are naming the money supply after motorways M1 and M2 and M3, to try to map its mysteries better.

Malcolm Bradbury, *Rates of Exchange.*

In Sections V and VI of the book we have examined the determination of national income and monetary economics. We have treated them in a fairly neutral manner. However we have been considering an area of economics over which there are fundamental theoretical disagreements. In this chapter we will review some of these disagreements. There are, of course, as many views on economics as there are economists. Possibly more! It is therefore necessary for us to generalise. We will look on the one hand at those views which we may term Keynesian (and neo Keynesian) and on the other at the views of monetarists and other neo-classicists.

Monetarists and Keynesians

What are monetarists?

One thing that monetarists are not is new; they are simply a modern variation of the *neo-classical* school which dominated economics from the 1870s to the Keynesian revolution of the late 1930s and 40s. Monetarists share the same essential 'vision' as the neo-classical school, that is they reject theories of macro demand deficiencies and emphasise the efficiency of free markets, for instance, they believe that market forces act

quickly to eliminate unemployment. Monetarists are new only in the sense that their theory is more sophisticated than that of their ancestors and that their doctrine has reasserted itself after a long period following 1945 in which Keynesians dominated both economics and economic policy. The modern term 'monetarist' derives from the debate of the 1960s and 1970s concerning the role of money in determining aggregate demand.

Keynesian views of money

Keynes had argued that, in times of deep depression, monetary policy might be totally ineffective as a means of stimulating aggregate demand. By the time of the Radcliffe Report in 1959 most Keynesian economists held the view that there was no causal link between the quantity of money and aggregate demand. They argued, for example, that if an attempt was made to expand the money supply at a time when people in general did not want to spend, then either the money would be held in 'idle' money balances or banks would find it impossible to create new loans. Equally the Radcliffe Report had stated:

We cannot find any reason for supposing or any experience in monetary history indicating that there is any limit to the velocity of circulation.

Hence, it seemed that a given quantity of money could support almost any level of aggregate demand. (See below page 465.)

Some Keynesians, such as Kaldor, accepted that there might be a correlation between nominal national income and the money supply but argued this merely reflected the fact that the money supply adjusted passively to peoples' desire to spend, i.e. that the money supply adjusted to national income and not *vice versa*. In short Keynesian economists, for one reason or another, had come to the conclusion that manipulating the money supply was ineffective as a means of demand management and hence monetary policy should be set in relation to other objectives (see Chapter 41). Keynesian economists therefore emphasised fiscal policy rather than monetary policy as the means of implementing the demand management they believed necessary, for this reason they were known as 'Fiscalists' in the USA.

The rise of monetarism

The rise (or re-emergence) of monetarism within mainstream economics dates largely from Milton Friedman's 1956 restatement of the 'quantity theory of money'. Friedman argued that the demand for money depended in a stable and predictable manner on several major economic variables. Thus if the money supply was expanded people would not simply wish to hold the extra money in 'idle' money balances, i.e. if they were in equilibrium before the increase then they were already holding money balances to suit their requirements, and thus after the increase they would have money balances surplus to their requirements. These excess money balances would therefore be spent and hence aggregate demand rise. Similarly, if the money supply were reduced people would want to replenish their holdings of money by reducing their spending. Thus Friedman challenged the Keynesian assertion that 'money does not matter', he argued that the supply of money *does* affect the amount spent in an economy, thus the word 'monetarist' was coined.

The rise of monetarism in political circles accelerated as Keynesian economics seemed unable to explain or cure the seemingly contradictory problems of rising unemployment and inflation. On the one hand higher unemployment seemed to call for Keynesian reflation, but on the other hand rising inflation seemed to call for Keynesian deflation. The resulting disillusionment with Keynesian demand management was summed up in the now famous quote by James Callaghan the Labour Party Prime Minister in 1976:

We used to think that you could just spend your way out of a recession and increase employment by cutting taxes and boosting government spending. I tell you, in all candour, that that option on longer exists; and insofar as it ever did exist, it only worked by injecting bigger doses of inflation into the economy followed by higher levels of unemployment as the next step. That is the history of the past twenty years.

Not only did monetarists seek to explain contemporary problems; they reinterpreted historical ones. Milton Friedman and Anna Schwartz in their book, *A Monetary History of the United States, 1867–1960* argued that the depression of 1930 was caused by a massive contraction of the money supply and not by lack of investment as Keynes had argued. They also maintained that post-war inflation was caused by *over-expansion* of the money supply. They coined the famous assertion of monetarism that 'inflation is always and everywhere a monetary phenomenon'. At first, to many economists whose perceptions had been set by Keynesian ideas, it seemed that the Keynesian/monetarist debate was merely about whether fiscal or monetary policy was the more effective tool of demand management. But by the mid-seventies the debate had moved onto more profound matters as monetarists presented a more fundamental challenge to Keynesian orthodoxy.

Keynesianism v. monetarism

Keynes had argued that the volatility of expectations meant that aggregate demand was subject to large fluctuations, this in turn caused

463

large fluctuations in the level of output and employment. The central political belief of Keynesians is therefore that it is necessary for governments to intervene and manage the level of demand in the economy in order to maintain full employment. As the Keynesian/monetarist debate progressed monetarists sought to resurrect the pre-Keynesian orthodoxy that market economies are inherently stable (in the absence of major unexpected fluctuations in the money supply). Because of this belief in the stability of free market economies they asserted that active demand management is unnecessary and indeed likely to be harmful (see Chapter 44). The political right then adopted monetarism as an intellectual underpinning for its wish to return to a *laissez-faire* approach to economic policy in which economic outcomes are left to be determined by the free play of market forces. This was especially attractive to those on the right, such as Margaret Thatcher and Keith Joseph, who interpreted the expansion of the role of government as 'back door socialism'.

There have been several developments in the debate since the seventies, many of these (such as the *adaptive* versus *rational expectations debate* and the role of *supply side economics*) are examined in this book. (see Chapter 42). But the central questions at the core of the debate, and which dominate the political discussion of economic policy, remain unchanged. The first question is the extent to which market forces in a free market economy do, or do not, ensure desirable outcomes (see also Section 4). The second question is the extent to which any government is able to correct for any failings of free market capitalism.

Money and national income

The 'Classical' Dichotomy

The Classical Dichotomy provides a useful starting point for examining the technicalities of the Keynesian/monetarist debate. There is a prob-

lem, however, with the term 'Classical'. Keynes had lumped together all previous economists (with the exception of Malthus) under the title 'Classical'. But many economists see the neo-classical or marginalist revolution of the 1870s as a watershed in the development of economic thought. Whether we wish to use the the term *classical* or *neo-classical* the dichotomy referred to is central to the perspective of monetarists:

The Classical Dichotomy states that nominal prices are determined by the quantity of money but that the quantity of money has no effect on real things.

Nominal prices are prices in terms of the number of units of money that goods and services sell for, or factors of production are bought for. Hence we can speak of nominal (or money) prices, nominal wage rates and nominal income. Movements in the price 'level' record changes in these nominal prices. In contrast, 'relative' prices are the price of one thing in terms of another. For example, if an egg costs 10p and a loaf 20p then the relative price of a loaf in terms of eggs is 2. If the price level were to rise by 100% (i.e. if all nominal prices doubled) then relative prices would remain unchanged. The nominal price of an egg would now be 20p, and the nominal price of a loaf would now be 40p, but the relative price of a loaf in terms of eggs would still be 2.

It should now be clear that if *all* prices were to increase by the same proportion then all relative prices would be unchanged. For example, suppose your money wage (the nominal price of your labour) has doubled, but at the same time the nominal price of everything that you buy has also doubled. You would soon realise that you are no better off than before. In this situation the money wage has doubled but the real wage, i.e. the price of labour relative to goods and services, has remained unchanged. Indeed, put like this, it is not apparent that anything *real* has changed. This is indeed the gist of the Classical Dichotomy; if an increase in the money supply merely increases all nominal prices proportionately, then all real variables such as relative prices, output, the goods and services earned in return for work, the level of employment/

unemployment, the level of investment etc. would be unaffected. It is in this sense that Geoffrey Crowther described money as a veil thrown over the workings of the real economy.

To develop further our understanding of the debate we must now turn to the technicalities involved. Firstly we shall examine the debate concerning the link between the money supply and aggregate demand. Secondly, we shall examine the debate concerning what actually determines the level of real variables, such as output and employment, and how stable these variables are likely to be.

Money as a determinant of aggregate demand

The effectiveness of monetary policy as a determinant of the level of aggregate demand in the economy depends upon the nature of both the demand for and the supply of money. Most attention and research, however, has focussed on the demand for money. Before we turn to this relatively modern concept, however, it is instructive to trace its development starting with Irving Fisher's 'quantity equation' which we introduced earlier.

You will recall that Fisher's equation of exchange is:

$$M \times V \equiv P \times T$$

The symbol '≡' denotes that this is an identity, i.e. something which is true by definition. For example, the statement 'All men who have never married are bachelors' is hardly the basis for further research! Similarly Fisher's equation simply says that 'the amount spent is equal to the amount received' in effect this is another way of representing the national income identity that we saw in Chapter 33. The early quantity theorists, however, made three assumptions which turned the identity into a theory of the determination of the price level. They argued that the quantity of money (M) is 'exogenously' set (e.g. by the amount of gold mined or the quantity of notes printed) and that V and T are constant. If these assumptions are made it follows mechanically that, say, a doubling of

the money supply must be associated with a doubling of the price level. Therefore we are back to the Classical Dichotomy and the assertion of the quantity theorists that the price level varies in direct proportion to changes in the quantity of money leaving real variables unchanged.

a) The velocity of circulation. Let us now concentrate on what determines V, i.e. the velocity of circulation of money. Later we shall return to the question of whether *M* is exogenously determined and also to the question of whether T is constant.

If *M* can be set by the monetary authorities and if we can predict V then it is easy to calculate the level of expenditure that would be 'caused' by any level of *M*. For example, if V is fixed at 3 then a money stock of £50m would be associated with a total level of spending of £150m, whereas a money stock of £100m would give rise to expenditure of £300m, and so on. The early quantity theorists saw the determination of V in rather mechanical terms. They argued that any given level of spending in the economy would require a certain amount of money to finance it.

In much the same way as an engine running at a higher speed requires the oil within it to circulate at a faster rate to avoid friction reducing its speed, so a higher level of spending in the economy would require a given money stock to circulate faster so that money is always at hand for those desiring to make transactions. But the quantity theorists argued that the rate at which money can circulate around the economy is determined by the payments practices which prevail and the current structure of the economy. For example, if people are paid monthly rather than weekly they must keep more money 'idle', to be spent later in the month, and hence the rate at which the money stock can circulate is reduced. It was argued that factors such as payment practises and the degree of vertical integration changed only slowly. Hence, at any one time the velocity of circulation of money could be considered a constant and thus a higher level of spending *would* require a larger money stock to sustain it.

b) *The role of* T. If V is a constant then the money value of transactions ($P \times T$) will vary in direct proportion to the quantity of money in the economy (M). We have explained earlier that 'T' refers to *all* transactions in the economy and thus includes the purchases of intermediate goods and purely financial transactions. We are more interested, however, in the level of output of the economy. Hence it is more convenient to confine our definition of transactions to only those involving the sale of final goods and services. For direct proportionality of the money value of output to the quantity of money we thus require the further assumption that the number of transactions is directly related to the volume of output. We can thus write the quantity equation as:

$$M \times V = P \times Y$$

Where Y is the level of output (real income), P is the price level of final goods and services. In this equation V becomes the 'income-velocity of circulation'. If, therefore, V and Y are constants then the *nominal* level of income ($P \times Y$; or money GDP) will vary in direct proportion to M.

The Cambridge Approach and the demand for money

In the crude manner in which the quantity theory was formulated by Fisher money appears as a technical input to spending, i.e. a certain quantity is required per unit of spending. There is no indication that the velocity of circulation might be affected by the decisions of people themselves to hold money. But the more people tend to want to keep their wealth in liquid form (e.g. cash and chequeing/current/sight accounts) rather than time deposits or longer term loans, the smaller the proportion of the existing stock of money that can be lent out by the financial institutions to be spent by borrowers. Thus the more people wish to hold reserves of liquidity in money balances the lower will tend to be the velocity of circulation of money.

In the 1920s the notion of the demand for money was reintroduced as an explicit argu-

ment in the quantity theory. This approach was developed by the Cambridge economists Pigou and Marshall, hence their formulation became known as the Cambridge equation. In their formulation the demand for money was written as:

$$Md = k \times P \times Y$$

This states that the demand for money (Md) is some proportion (k) of money income ($P \times Y$). Once we introduce the notion of a demand for money we can write the equilibrium condition for the economy as

$$M = Md$$

This states that for equilibrium the quantity of money demanded (Md) must be equal to the quantity of money in the economy (M). For example if M exceeded Md then there would be more money in existence than people wish to hold in their money balances. This would cause people with excess money balances to attempt to reduce them. For the economy as a whole, of course, the total level of money balances cannot be reduced. But the attempts to reduce excess money balances will lead to an increase in expenditure. This increase in expenditure will in turn increase the level of money income. Now, if the demand for money is some fraction of money income, the rise in money income will cause the increase in the demand for money that is required to restore equilibrium.

From the above we can now see that in equilibrium:

$$M = Md = k \times P \times Y$$

or

$$M = k \times P \times Y$$

By a simple rearrangement of this equilibrium result we have the Cambridge equation:

$$M \times 1/k = P \times Y$$

This looks very much like Fisher's crude representation of the quantity theory except that 1/k has taken the place of V. Indeed, if k is constant (i.e. the demand for money is a constant fraction of money income) it produces exactly the same proportionate relation between M and money income as Fisher's equation of exchange. That is, if k is constant and

$$V = 1/k$$

then V is also constant. For example, if k = 1/5 then V = 5, thus a money stock of £100m would imply an equilibrium level of money income of

$$£100m \times 5 = £500m$$

If k were to change to say k = 1/3, then V = 3 and the same money stock would imply an equilibrium level of money income of only

$$£100m \times 3 = £300m$$

This result also makes intuitive sense; it says that velocity of circulation of money is inversely related to the demand for money. Hence if (ceteris paribus) the demand for money should rise then people will attempt to increase their holding of money balances. As more money is held rather than passed on the rate at which money circulates in the economy falls. The fall in V in turn is seen in a fall in money income, until the fall in the level of money income reduces the demand for money back in line with the existing stock of money.

The Cambridge equation thus differs from the crude quantity theory in that it allows for the velocity of circulation to be affected by peoples' desire for money. By introducing a role for human behaviour it is less mechanical than Fisher's version. Indeed, the early Cambridge school did explore the possibility that the demand for money (and hence the velocity of circulation) might be influenced by factors other than purely the level of money income. If this is the case, then a change in these other factors could 'disturb' the relationship between a given money stock and the level of money income making the level of money income for any quantity of money less predictable.

For example, perhaps a fall in interest rates reduces the opportunity cost of holding money vis á vis investing it in, say, a building society to be lent out and spent on property. Such a change in interest rates might have explained the rise in the proportion of money income that people wanted to hold in 'idle' money balances in our example above when k rose from 1/5 to 1/3. If then an increase in the quantity of money is accompanied by a fall in interest rates the resulting rise in the demand for money as a proportion of money income might cause the velocity of circulation to fall. This could offset the rise in the quantity of money thereby leaving money income unaltered. In short, a rise in M might cause V to fall such that there is no increase in aggregate demand and hence no increase in money income ($P \times Y$).

In fact the early Cambridge school, as with the earlier quantity theorists, placed most emphasis on money as a means of making transactions. Thus the role of other factors was usually ignored and k was treated as more or less constant. As we have seen, if k is constant the Cambridge equation simply reproduces the crude quantity theory assertion that the price level is directly proportionate to the stock of money. It was left for Keynes, the most famous of all Cambridge economists, to develop the notion of a demand for money other than as a means of making transactions.

Liquidity preference

Belief in the quantity theory of money and the Classical dichotomy was challenged by the traumatic depression of the interwar years. As unemployment soared it no longer seemed possible to argue that free market capitalist economies are inherently stable; the failure of financial institutions cast doubt on the monetary authority's ability to control the money supply and large fluctuations in aggregate demand suggested that the velocity of circulation of money was highly volatile. We have yet to examine the exogeneity of the money supply (M) and the stability of output (Y), but here we are concerned with the instability of V. Keynes argued in *The General Theory of Employment, Interest and Money* **467**

(1936) that V can be unstable as money shifts in and out of 'idle' money balances reflecting changes in peoples' liquidity preference.

Unlike his predecessors, who focussed upon money as a medium of exchange held only for *transactions* purposes, Keynes emphasised money as a *store of wealth*. Holding one's wealth in bonds, shares or real assets can be risky as the value of such assets can fluctuate widely, but this risk can be avoided by holding money instead. Thus in addition to money's usefulness for transactions purposes its quality of relatively certain purchasing power means that money will also be held for its own sake. Thus, Keynes argued that a wave of pessimism concerning real world prospects could precipitate a 'retreat into liquidity' as people sought to increase their holdings of money. This increase in money holding would lower the velocity of circulation of money and thus aggregate demand would fall bringing about the recession which everyone had feared!

Portfolio balance

If we examine the wealth (or assets) of a person or society in general, we could arrange them in a spectrum of liquidity from most liquid to least liquid, the most liquid being cash and the least liquid being real physical assets such as buildings. People will attempt to find a balance in their holding of assets which they think most advantageous. Holding of money (cash and bank deposits) gives *certainty* and *convenience*. On the other hand, the person holding money is forgoing the earning or interest that could be gained by putting this money into bonds and equities. If money is put into earning assets then, although *income is gained*, certainty and convenience are sacrificed and *risk is increased*. This is illustrated in Fig. 36.1

Each individual will try to structure his or her assets to give maximum satisfaction. A selection of financial assets can be termed a 'portfolio' and hence the distribution of assets within the portfolio is called *portfolio balance*.

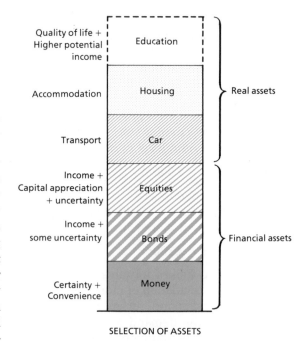

SELECTION OF ASSETS

Fig. 36.1 *Portfolio balance*
People distribute their assets between money, financial assets such as bonds and real assets such as housing in a way which they consider maximises their utility. Friedman included in the portfolio investment in human capital such as education.

Keynesian theory of the demand for money

Keynes argued that there are three motives for holding money; the transactions, precautionary and speculative motives.

1) *Transactions motive*. This motive closely corresponds to the notion of money held by the quantity theorists. People hold cash and money in bank accounts simply to carry on the everyday business of life – to pay the gas bill, to buy petrol, to spend on groceries and so on. Since people are usually paid weekly or monthly but spend money daily (i.e. their monetary receipts and expenditures are not perfectly synchronised) they therefore have to hold a proportion of their income as money rather than in more illiquid assets. This gives a pattern as shown in Fig. 36.2, where the peaks in the money balance are caused by monthly salary inputs and the downward

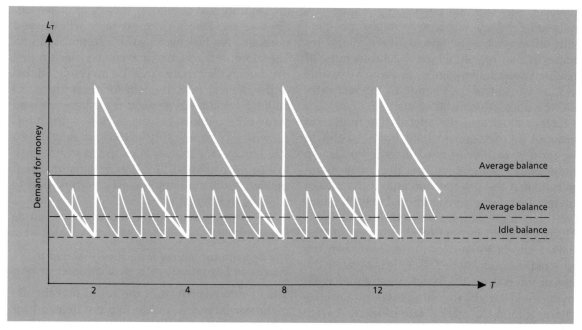

Fig. 36.2 *Transactions demand for money*
Every fourth week there is an injection of salary. This runs out over the month as bills are paid. This gives an average balance (demand for money). If not all of the salary is spent, but is retained in the bank account, then this gives a level for the idle balance. The dotted line shows what would happen if a person was paid weekly instead of monthly. The demand for money is smaller but the velocity of circulation is greater.

slope of the curve shows money being spent over the month.

If the troughs are above zero then there is an amount of idle money held in hand.

The lower jagged line shows what happens if a person is paid weekly. We can see there is a quicker turnover of money but the overall demand for money is smaller. There is thus a higher velocity of circulation. This type of regular pattern of income and payments is one of the reasons that the quantity theorists believed that the velocity of circulation of money is stable.

What determines the size of transactions demand for money? Keynes thought that it would be determined by the level of money income. Indeed, it is clear from our discussion of the transactions motive that this will tend to be the case. It has been demonstrated since (from stock control theory) that such transactions balances are also likely to be economised on when interest rates rise.

2) *The precautionary motive*. People hold money to guard against unexpected eventualities – the car breaking down, a period of illness, a large electricity bill, and so on. It seems reasonable to suppose that the higher the level of income the larger will be the size of precautionary balances. The reason for this is that the rich need higher precautionary balances; if, for example, you are running several cars and a large house, then the unexpected bills are likely to be larger, thus demanding a larger precautionary stock of money. Again it is likely that a rise in interest rates might cause people to economise somewhat on precautionary balances. But because of the similarity with the transactions motive the two are often lumped together.

3) *The speculative motive*. By emphasising this motive Keynes broke with the quantity theorists' view of money. The quantity theorists did not think that people will want to hold money for itself but only for transactions purposes. Keynes, **469**

however, believed that people might speculate by holding money, just as they might speculate with other assets. The speculative demand for money is that money which is held in hope of making a speculative gain, or to avoid a possible loss, as a result of the change in interest rates and the price of financial assets.

Keynes illustrated the speculative motive in terms of the decision to hold one's wealth in the form of cash or in fixed income bonds. To understand his argument it is necessary to appreciate that the price of bonds and the rate of interest are inversely proportional to each other. Consider, for example, a fixed income bond which yields an income of £5 per year. If the market rate of interest is 10 per cent then the price of the bond will be £50. This is because the rate of interest on the bond must equal what savers could earn by investing their money elsewhere. If then the market rate of interest were to fall to 2½ per cent, then the price of that same bond would rise to £200.

Keynes believed that investors had some notion of the *normal rate of interest*. If the current rate of interest was below this then people would *speculate* by holding cash, anticipating that interest rates would rise and hence bond prices fall. Hence, the lower the interest rates the more people would expect the prices of bonds to fall and thus the more people would hold cash rather than bonds in their wealth portfolios. Thus, low interest rates are associated with a high speculative demand for money. Conversely then, if the rate of interest was high, people would buy bonds because their price would be low and therefore their rate of earning high. Such bond holders would also stand to make a capital gain if, as might be expected, the interest rate falls and bond prices increase. Thus a high rate of interest is associated with a low demand for money.

Modern Keynesians, such as Tobin, tend to generalise risk to a wider range of assets than just bonds. Basically they argue that holding money is an insurance against the risk associated with other financial assets. If the interest rate increases then the cost of this insurance, i.e. the opportunity cost of holding money, is increased. Thus an increase in interest rates will cause a portfolio readjustment away from liquidity. Therefore they too arrive at the conclusion that the demand for money will be inversely related to the interest rate. Indeed, for the purpose of holding wealth Keynesians regard money and many other financial assets as close substitutes. As with any commodity with close substitutes, the demand for money is expected to be sensitive to price changes, i.e. Keynesians hold that the demand for money is elastic with respect to changes in interest rates.

We can summarise the above discussion as follows:

The demand for money is positively related to income and negatively related to the interest rate

Thus we have arrived at the result that the demand for money is rather like the demand for any normal good; if we put the price of holding money (i.e. the interest rate) on the vertical axis we have a demand curve that slopes downward and which shifts to the right as income increases. What we should emphasise, however, is that, in Keynesian theory expectations play a large part. This means that the relationship between the demand for money and observable variables such as income and the interest rate is likely at any time to become unstable. For example, pessimistic views on the future prices of financial assets and the yield to investment in general could cause a large increase in the demand for money associated with previous levels of income and the interest rate.

Monetarist theory of the demand for money

In common with modern Keynesians, monetarists also take a portfolio adjustment approach to money. Again individuals are seen to have a choice of different ways in which to hold their wealth. Again these assets will have varying liquidity as well as other advantages and disadvantages. Thus individuals weigh up the various costs and benefits associated with each asset and arrange their portfolios such that their utility is maximised. But the monetarist concept of a wealth portfolio is much broader than that of Keynesians. Monetarists hold that the relevant portfolio includes not just financial assets but also physical goods. Thus an increase in the money supply which disturbs the equilibrium of wealth holders by making their portfolios 'too liquid' is just as likely to spill over into physical investment assets and durable consumption goods as into financial assets.

Monetarists, as did the earlier quantity theorists, concentrate on the convenience of money as a medium of exchange. Thus, unlike Keynesians, they believe that there is a dividing line in the portfolio between money and all other assets. Therefore they do not regard money and other financial assets as close substitutes. Monetarists would state this condition in the following form:

Money is a substitute for all assets alike, real and financial, rather than a close substitute for only a small range of financial assets.

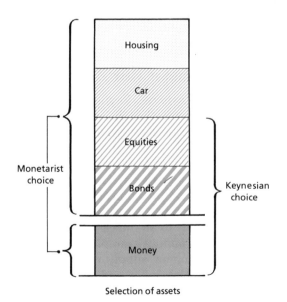

Fig. 36.3 *Different views of portfolio balance*
Monetarists see portfolio balance as choice between money and all other assets, but Keynesians see money and financial assets as close substitutes.

As money is not regarded as having close substitutes the demand for money is expected, in contrast to the Keynesian view, to be inelastic with respect to the rate of interest. In addition, monetarists do not include as a determinant of money demand any variable which is likely to be volatile. Thus, again in contrast to the Keynesian view, the demand for money has a fairly stable and predictable relationship to its determinants.

Monetary transmission mechanisms

The transmission mechanisms in a car transmit the power of the engine to the wheels. But how is an increase in the money supply transmitted into increased aggregate demand? We have already touched upon this in our discussion of portfolio adjustments. As would be expected from that discussion monetarists and Keynesians differ as to the mechanisms involved and the strength of the links between variables. What makes it more difficult for the author of a textbook is that there is not complete unanimity within each school of thought and that there are many complex 'feedback' effects to consider. The presentation here seeks to elucidate the differences which have generated most debate and also serves as a useful introduction to more 'advanced' IS/LM presentations (e.g. see *Modern Macroeconomics* by Parkin & Bade).

The Keynesian transmission mechanism

Figure 36.4 represents in diagrammatic form the stages in the Keynesian view of the transmission mechanism. In part (*a*) of Fig. 36.4 we see that there has been an increase in the supply of money (M_{S1} to M_{S2}). At the previous equilibrium rate of interest (r_1) there is now an excess supply of money. Banks thus seek to expand their loans by offering lower rates of interest, or people with excess liquidity in their wealth portfolios will seek to purchase other financial assets and in so doing drive up the price of these assets **471**

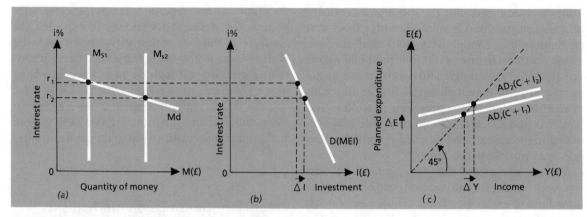

Fig. 36.4 *A Keynesian monetary transmission mechanism*
An increase in the money supply in (*a*) causes a relatively small fall in the rate of interest. This causes a relatively small increase in investment (△ *I*) in (*b*). This increase in investment leads to a small increase in income (*Y*) in (*c*).

thus reducing interest rates. In short, interest rates will fall to the new equilibrium indicated by r_2. In part (*b*) we can see that the fall in the rate of interest will cause an extension of the demand for investment, i.e. the level of the investment will increase by $\triangle I$. Part (*c*) is the familiar '45° degree diagram'. The increase in the level of investment has increased income by $\triangle Y$, i.e. the increase in the money supply has finally led to an increase in aggregate demand.

There are several important points to note about this transmission mechanism:

1) The link between changes in the money supply and aggregate demand is indirect as it operates only through the effect of money on the interest rates prevailing in financial markets.
2) Keynesians believe the demand for money to be interest elastic. Thus much of the impact of an increased money supply is absorbed because falls in the interest rate cause people to readily increase their holdings of 'idle' money balances.
3) To the extent that interest rates do fall a little, the effect on investment and hence aggregate demand are slight. This is because Keynesians believe the *interest elasticity of the demand* for investment to be low.
4) Both the demand for money and the de-

mand for investment are likely to be highly volatile in the face of changes in expectations.

In short, Keynesians believe that the link between changes in the money supply and changes in aggregate demand are extremely tenuous; not only are the links weak, they are unstable. Therefore they prefer the more direct manipulation of spending and hence aggregate demand through fiscal measures.

An extreme Keynesian view

Some so-called 'extreme Keynesians', notably Kaldor, take a somewhat different tack. They deny money *any* causal role as a determinant of aggregate demand. Instead they argue that the money supply responds in an entirely *passive* manner to accommodate any increase in the desire to spend, i.e. the direction of causation flows from an autonomous increase in the desire to consume or invest to an increase in the money supply. Kaldor's famous example was the sharp increase in the money supply which occurs in the months of November and December. He teased those that ascribed a causal role to money by asking whether it was this increase in the money supply that caused increased consumer spending in the run up to Christmas! Of course what actually happens is that the monetary

472

authorities *anticipate* the increase in spending and therefore expand the money supply so that consumers and traders will have sufficient cash for their transactions.

Kaldor's point should not be dismissed lightly. We have seen that quasi and near money can perform to some extent the functions of money. It is also the case that attempts since 1976 to control the money supply within pre-set target bands of growth were often unsuccessful and have now been largely abandoned (see Section 8). Part of the argument is that banks have access to reserve assets that cannot be directly controlled by central banks and that restrictions on such banks tend merely to cause 'disintermediation' or the diversion of business to 'fringe' banks or Eurocurrency markets not covered by such regulations. Others stress that, historically, central banks have acted to accommodate the stock of money to changes in the needs for trade by giving their *supportive responsibilities* priority over their *control duties*. This latter argument explains why many Keynesians are not impressed by the historical evidence presented by Friedman and Schwartz of a correlation between nominal income and the money supply.

But the nature of money itself might make it difficult to control. Essentially money is based on faith, e.g. we accept bank deposits as payment because it is believed that we could exchange them for cash. But equally any promissory note that one has faith in might be accepted as payment. The granting of credit is often extremely informal between regular trading partners. Credit arrangements can be extended by any large business that feels the advantages in attracting custom outweigh occasional defaults. Indeed, extreme Keynesians do not think that the elasticity of substitution between money and its close substitutes is sufficiently small and stable to substantiate a distinction.

Whether they take the view that expansion of the money supply has a weak and unpredictable effect on aggregate demand, or that money is an entirely passive variable which is for practical purposes impossible to control, it is clear that such Keynesians would not emphasise monetary policy as a means of demand management.

The monetarist transmission mechanism

Figure 36.5 represents in diagrammatic form the monetarist view of the transmission mechanism:

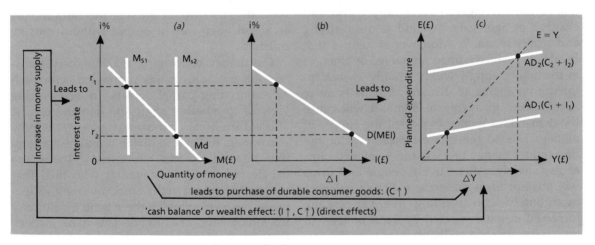

Fig. 36.5 *A monetarist monetary transmission mechanism*
An increase in the money supply causes a large fall in interest rates in (*a*). This in turn causes a large increase in investment (△ *I*) in diagram (*b*). This increase in investment brings about a large increase in money national income (△ *Y*) in diagram (*c*). Money national income is also boosted by the fall in interest rates causing people to buy more consumer durables. Aggregate demand is also boosted by the 'cash balance' effect. Notice the difference in slopes of the demand for money and investment schedules compared with the Keynesian view in Fig. 36.4.

Again there are several important points to note

1) The links between the money supply and aggregate demand include not only *indirect effects* but also, through the *cash balance effect* of portfolio adjustment, *direct effects*. Moreover, not only does the fall in interest rates prevailing in financial markets cause an increase in business investment it also causes consumers to increase their 'investment' in durable goods.

2) The demand for money is *interest inelastic*. Thus large reductions in the interest rate can occur before excess money balances become absorbed by an extension of people's desire to hold money. (Indeed, most of the increase in the demand for money will come from the resulting increase in income. For simplicity such feedback effects are ignored.)

3) Not only is the fall in interest rates from r_1 to r_2 likely to be substantial, it is also assumed that the *interest elasticity of investment* is high.

4) Monetarists consider the demand for investment and, in particular, the demand for money to have a relatively stable relationship to several major economic variables such as consumption.

In short then, monetarists believe that the link between changes in the money supply and changes in aggregate demand is very strong and relatively stable. Moreover it follows that fiscal policy which is unaccompanied by changes in the money supply will have only a weak influence on aggregate demand. This is because any increase in aggregate demand will cause the demand for money to exceed the supply of money. Due to the interest *inelasticity* of the demand for money this will cause interest rates to rise sharply. Alternatively people and firms will attempt to increase their money balances by cutting back on spending. In either case the increased demand injected by fiscal policy will tend to be offset by reductions in consumption and investment. Thus monetarists believe that the effect of increased government spending is to 'crowd-out' the private sector rather than to increase aggregate demand.

Unlike the crude quantity theorists, mon-

etarists do not believe that V is always constant. If this were true then their assumption that the money supply can be exogenously set by the monetary authorities would imply that aggregate demand in the economy could be controlled with great precision. Instead, monetarists argue that the lags and the strength of links in the transmission mechanisms are uncertain in the short run. Hence, policies attempting to 'fine-tune' the economy will in practice tend to have destabilising effects (see also Chapter 44.)

In place of the crude quantity theorists' assertion that V is always constant, monetarists argue that there is a fairly stable demand for money function which will be deviated from in the processes of adjustment but which will tend to re-establish itself as a new equilibrium is reached. Thus, despite significant short term fluctuations, the velocity of circulation will tend to change only slowly over the long term. Hence monetarists argue that active or 'discretionary' stabilisation policies should not be attempted but rather a 'fixed throttle' non-discretionary monetary expansion regime should be adopted and then observed by all governments. Ideally, the money supply should be set to grow roughly in line with the normal rate of growth of the economy, this would provide the extra money to absorb increases in output without causing inflation.

The debate concerning the monetary transmission mechanism has proceeded with each side conceding partial defeats. In terms of the view as to whether aggregate demand can be affected by fiscal or monetary policy it is now much more difficult to divide economists neatly into Keynesians and monetarists. Today the debate is between monetarists who hold that the level of output in the economy is self adjusting to the level at which there is no involuntary unemployment and Keynesians who believe that the level of aggregate demand must be managed by governments so as to produce full employment. It is to this more profound distinction that we now turn.

The determination of aggregrate real income

The nature of the debate

If the only difference between Keynesians and monetarists were that the former advocated fiscal policy to iron out fluctuations while the latter advocated monetary policy, then the debate would concern mere technicalities of policy rather than a fundamental difference of political vision. But it is this difference of vision concerning the nature of capitalist economies and the proper role of government that is at the heart of mainstream political debate today.

To use a medical analogy, Keynesians (except radical post-Keynesians; see Chapter 47) view the free market capitalist economy as an organism which works well when healthy but, from time to time, is prone to chronic illness. But it is believed that these illnesses can be cured if governments apply the correct treatments. Monetarists/neoclassicists especially admire the workings of free markets but they differ from Keynesians in that they believe the organism seldom suffers from malfunctions. From time to time capitalism might catch a chill but this will be cured by the system's own strong recuperative powers. Indeed, the only thing which is likely to turn a chill into serious ill health is the misguided prescription of Keynesian doctors! (For example, when attempts are made to preserve declining industries instead of allowing market forces to replace them in time with the growth industries of the future.)

As we have seen, Keynesians take the view that, when left unattended, fluctuations in aggregate demand are likely to destabilise the economy. Monetarists differ in that they believe that if the money supply is not allowed to fluctuate then fluctuations in aggregate demand will be slight. But of yet greater importance is the monetarist notion that real variables such as output and employment are resilient to fluctuations of aggregate demand.

Although both schools might say that an increase in aggregate demand will lead to an increase in income, Keynesians are likely to be referring to an increase in *real* income (i.e. output) while the monetarist is referring to an increase in *nominal* income only (i.e. a rise in the price level with no change in output). This is because Keynesians believe that (at less than full employment) increases in aggregate demand will result in an increase in output and employment. Conversely monetarists believe the economy is always, more or less, at an equilibrium at which there is no involuntary unemployment; the level of employment and hence the supply of output is determined more or less independently of aggregate demand. Hence, in the monetarist's view increases in aggregate demand are not met by an increased supply as all those who wish to work are already working as much as they wish to. It follows that increasing aggregate demand will result only in inflation:

Keynesians believe that aggregate output and thus employment are demand determined; monetarists believe that such 'real' aggregate variables are supply determined.

Aggregate supply

The notion that real variables are supply determined is easy to explain to anyone who has understood the microeconomic sections of this book. This is because monetarists believe that aggregate output and employment are determined by the same market forces that operate in individual competitive markets. Indeed, in such neoclassical analysis there is no clear distinction between micro and macroeconomics. Whereas Keynes warned that those who extended micro analysis to analyse macro variables were guilty of a 'fallacy of composition' (e.g. see his explanation of the 'paradox of thrift' page 374), monetarists tend to view aggregate variables as only the sum of many millions of individually made 'micro' decisions. In particular they dismiss the Keynesian notion of an 'irrational' wave of pessimism being a self fulfilling prophecy leading to recession.

To understand how the level of employment, **475**

and hence output, is determined in the monetarist view we need only refer back to the neoclassical 'marginal distribution theory' of Chapter 20. In that chapter we saw how a firm in perfect competition in both its product and factor markets would be maximising its profits when:

Wage = Marginal Revenue Product

Before moving on we should remind ourselves that both sides of this equality are in money terms, i.e. 'wage' refers to money (nominal) wage and 'marginal revenue product' refers to marginal physical product multiplied by money (nominal) price:

$$W = MPP \times P$$

As we have seen, monetarists emphasise that real things are determined by real things. The above equality can be interpreted in real terms simply by dividing through by nominal price:

$$W/P = MPP$$

W/P can be thought of as the real wage, i.e. the actual purchasing power of the worker's money wage. There is an *aggregation problem* here in that

P refers to a particular product's price whereas the wage of the worker will be spent on many products. Thus to see how much the money wage could purchase in general terms we would have to divide it by some composite index of the price level (see for example the construction of the RPI in Chapter 33). It makes it easier to 'strip away the veil of money to reveal the real workings of the economy' if we assume that there is only one product which we will simply call 'output'. Thus we assume that workers are paid in output and that firms employ workers to produce output. Therefore if the money wage is divided by the price of output we have the real wage in terms of units of output. Marginal physical product, of course, is already measured in real terms, i.e. units of output.

We can now interpret the equilibrium of the firm in real terms. In Fig. 36.6 we represent the equilibrium of a perfectly competitive firm in monetary terms in part (a) and in real terms in part (b). In part (a) the employer will employ all workers up to L_E as each of these workers adds more money to revenue ($MPP \times P$) than they add to costs (W). In part (b) the same level of

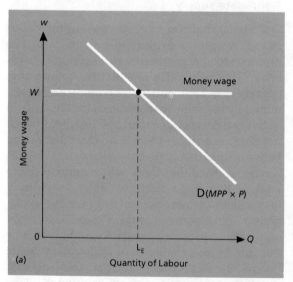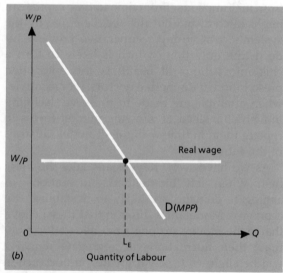

Fig. 36.6 *The same equilibrium (L_E) expressed in monetary and real terms*
Diagram (a) shows the equilibrium of the perfectly competitive firm in money terms. This occurs where the MRP ($MPP \times p$) is equal to the wage rate. This equates with a quantity of labour employed of L_E. By dividing through by the price (p) we see the same equilibrium expressed in real terms.

employment results as each worker up to L_E adds more to output (*MPP*) than the output they receive (*W/P*).

A numerical example will demonstrate the equivalance of part (*a*) and part (*b*) in Fig. 36.6. Recall that in the short run the *MPP* depends only upon the number of workers employed by the firm and that, as employment increases *MPP* falls due to the law of diminishing marginal returns. Let us suppose that at L_E *MPP* = 5 units of output. If *W* = £10 and *P* = £2 then at L_E we have:

$$W = MPP \times P = 5 \times £2 = £10$$

or

$$W/P = MPP = 5 \text{ units of output.}$$

Hence the same profit maximising equilibrium condition can be expressed in both real and monetary terms. Monetarists extend this micro analysis of equilibrium to the economy as a whole. In doing this they make use of the notion of an *aggregate production function*. Thus it is assumed that at any one time there is a fixed stock of capital in the economy as a whole. As total employment increases the MPP of labour therefore falls according to some aggregate version of the law of diminishing returns. It has to be said that the idea of a capital stock and aggregate production function raises logical problems that are complex but which cast doubt on the consistency of neoclassical theory. Nevertheless, as with other schools of thought, we brush aside these problems to present the monetarist/neoclassical view as simply as possible.

In Fig. 36.7 we have extended marginal distribution theory to the economy as a whole. The demand curve for labour is the *MPP* of labour and slopes downward according to the law of diminishing returns. As we are now looking at the economy as a whole the supply of labour is upward sloping indicating that higher wages will attract more people into the labour force (in fact the analysis is not significantly altered if the supply of labour is vertical or even slightly backward bending). We should note that everything in the diagram is in real terms, i.e. *MPP* is

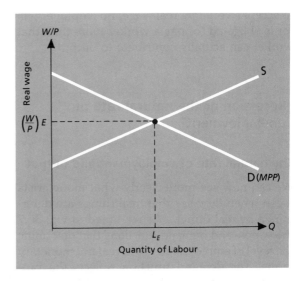

Fig. 36.7 *Equilibrium in the labour market as a whole* The demand curve for labour is the *MPP* curve. The supply curve represents the supply of labour for the whole economy. Equilibrium occurs where the real wage (*W/P*)$_E$ is equal to *MPP*.

measured in units of output and the supply of labour is determined by the real wage. The equilibrium of the labour market occurs at the level of employment L_E where the real wage (*W/P*)$_E$ is equal to *MPP*.

It is instructive to examine the nature of the equilbrium in Fig. 36.7. Firstly, we can note that if the nominal prices *W* and *P* are increased by the same proportion, the real wage, and hence the equilibrium, is unchanged, i.e. $W/P = 2 \times W/2 \times P = 3 \times W/3 \times P$ etc. This assumes that workers are not fooled by increasing money wages into offering more labour than before even though the real wage has not changed, in short there is no 'money illusion'. Secondly, we should note that at L_E the demand for labour equals the supply of labour, i.e. anyone who wants to work at the equilibrium wage rate is able to find a job and thus there is no involuntary unemployment. Thirdly, we should note that the economy is actually composed of many such labour markets each of which has its own clearing real wage. Thus if a worker's *MPP* is very low they will only find work if they are willing **477** to accept a very low real wage; no employer will (or is obligated to) pay a worker more than that worker can actually contribute to output.

Recession or the natural rate of unemployment?

The natural rate of employment and output

We can now see more clearly what monetarists mean when they say that 'real things are determined by real things'. As we noted in Fig. 36.7 the supply and demand functions that determine the level of employment are in real not monetary terms. The demand function reflects the productivity of labour when combined with the existing capital stock. The supply of labour reflects 'human nature', i.e. the amount of labour that people are willing to offer in return for any given real wage. Hence, far from the level of employment being the government's responsibility as is the implication of Keynesian theory, in monetarism the level of employment is not within the government's control to increase. The government cannot wave a magic wand to make people willing to work longer at the same real wage, nor would it be meaningful for the government to pass laws stating that the *MPP* of labour when combined with the actual capital stock is higher than it actually is. In short, within monetarist/neoclassical theory, insisting that the government should 'do something about unemployment' is rather like demanding that the government command the natural elements such as the amount of rainfall!

Indeed, it is in their use of the term 'natural' that the political vision of the monetarists is most evident:

Monetarists use the term the 'natural rate of employment' to summarise their belief that the operation of market forces, if not obstructed by government or powerful institutions, will quickly produce an equilibrium in which everybody is doing the best they can save by infringement of the rights of others.

This equilibrium is thus brought about by contracts between employers and employees which are voluntarily entered into because they confer mutual benefit.

For example, in Fig. 36.7, at levels of employment *below* L_E the worker is willing to work for a real wage which is below his or her *MPP* when his or her labour is combined with the employer's stock of capital. Thus in real terms the employer can pay the worker less output than is added to total output by employing that worker. But in fact both employer and employee gain in that the equilibrium wage that the employer must pay to attract the worker is $(W/P)_E$. $(W/P)_E$ is above the real wage the worker requires as compensation for his or her loss of leisure, hence the worker gains. But equally, $(W/P)_E$ is below the amount added to the employer's total output (i.e. below *MPP*), hence the employer gains a 'surplus output', or in monetary terms, *profit*, by employing the worker.

This situation continues until the level of employment L_E is reached. After this point the *MPP* of labour is below the real wage required to compensate the extra workers for their loss of leisure and hence there is no opportunity for a mutually beneficial contract of employment. L_E is thus the 'natural rate' of employment. It also follows that for any given capital stock L_E level of employment must also imply a definite level of output (this is the concept of a short run production function where output can only be increased by increasing the input of labour). Thus we can state:

Monetarists believe that, in the short run, the equilibrium of the labour market also sets the level of output or aggregate supply.

The level of output determined by the natural rate of employment can thus be called the natural rate of output. Obviously it is not a constant but will increase through time with the growth of the capital stock.

Because the natural rate of employment is the result of mutually beneficial agreements, there will be a strong tendency for it to reassert itself if disturbed. For example, if (for some unspecified reason) the real wage is above $(W/P)_E$ there will be an excess supply of labour. As long as the the real wage is above $(W/P)_E$ there will be more people looking for work than employers wish to employ. But such involuntary unemployment will only be transitory. Monetarists argue that, as in any other market, an excess supply will cause a downward pressure on price. In this case it will be unemployed labour competing with the employed that will lower real wages. Hence involuntary unemployment is eradicated when the real wage falls to $(W/P)_E$ and the supply of labour once again matches the demand. Equally, a real wage below $(W/P)_E$ would cause an excess demand for labour and hence a rise in the real wage back to $(W/P)_E$.

The neutrality of money

We are now in a position to present the Classical Dichotomy in diagrammatic form. In Fig. 36.8 the lower part of the diagram represents equilibrium in the labour market where L_N is the natural rate of employment. The initial money wage is W_1 and the initial price level is P_1. Thus the real wage which clears the labour market is W_1/P_1. The upper part of Fig. 36.8 represents equilibrium in the goods or product market. Although the composition of aggregate output is determined by the interaction of demand and supply in individual markets, the arrow indicates that the level of *aggregate* output is set by the equilibrium of the labour market.

AD_1 represents the initial level of aggregate demand in the goods sector or product market(s). Note that, in accordance with monetarist views of the monetary transmission mechanism, AD_1 corresponds to a specific supply of money, i.e. M_1. According to monetarist theory the aggregate demand curve is downward sloping as lower levels of nominal prices mean a larger *real* money supply. We can see that a nominal money supply of M_1 implies an equilibrium nominal price level in the product market of P_1. Hence, initially the real money supply is M_1/P_1. As the nominal money supply is exogenously set by the monetary authorities and the demand for

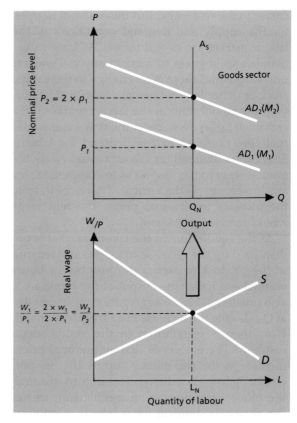

Fig. 36.8 *The classical dichotomy and the neutrality of money*
A doubling of the money supply causes the money wage and the price level to double but leaves the equilibrium in the real economy unchanged.

money is stable there will be no change to the economy's equilibrium unless something real changes, e.g. if changes in the capital stock increase *MPP* or people's willingness to work somehow alters.

Now let us suppose that, perhaps in an attempt to increase employment and output, the government doubles the money supply. At the original price level of P_1 the real money supply will thus have also doubled. The effect, as shown in Fig. 36.8, will be to shift aggregate demand from AD_1 to AD_2. This will cause excess demand which in turn will cause product prices to rise. If money wages were to remain at W_1 these increases in product prices would cause a de- **479** crease in the real wage. But this will not happen for the supply and demand conditions in the labour market are in real terms. As long as the people's willingness to work at any *real* wage is unchanged and there is no change in the capital stock or technology to change the *MPP* of labour, then the equilibrium in the labour market must remain at L_N. A decrease in the real wage would therefore cause an excess demand for labour. This excess demand for labour would cause the money wage to increase so as to compensate for any increase in product prices. Therefore despite the increase in nominal prices the real wage would remain unchanged.

As the equilibrium in the labour market is undisturbed by the increase in aggregate demand in the product market(s) the number of hours worked and hence the output of the economy is also unaltered. Hence aggregate supply remains at Q_N despite the increase in aggregate demand. How then is equilibrium in the goods sector restored? The answer is that as nominal prices increase so the real money supply (i.e. its purchasing power) is reduced. This in turn, through the monetary transmission mechanism, causes the aggregate demand for products to contract until it is again equal to aggregate supply at Q_N.

It should be clear that once nominal prices have doubled the real money supply is the same as it was before, i.e.:

$$\frac{M_1}{P_1} = \frac{2 \times M_1}{2 \times P_1} = \frac{M_2}{P_2}$$

Equally if product prices and money wages have doubled the real wage will be as it was before. Thus once nominal prices have doubled all things real are as they were before. The only difference is that the nominal price level has doubled. In short, attempts to increase employment and output through increasing aggregate demand will only result in inflation. Readers should now check their understanding by working back through the analysis on the assumption that the money supply is reduced once again to M_1.

The above analysis provides a theoretical underpinning for the Classical Dichotomy:

The Classical Dichotomy states that real and monetary things are separate, hence money plays a 'neutral' role in the economy in that an increase in the money supply merely causes an equiproportionate increase in the price level leaving real things unaltered.

Keynesian recession or the natural rate of unemployment?

Monetarist theory implies that involuntary unemployment can exist only so long as it takes for the labour market to clear. As monetarism is based on the assumption of strong competitive forces this should not take too long. Indeed for many Keynesians (often called 'neo-Keynesians') and monetarists the supposed speed of this adjustment is what distinguishes the two schools of thought.

Neo-Keynesians believe that persistent unemployment *can* be caused by the real wage being too high. If this were so there would be more people looking for jobs than there were jobs being offered. Thus some people would be involuntary unemployed. Unlike monetarists these Keynesians believe that money wages are 'downwardly sticky' for institutional reasons. For example, workers are likely to resist a cut in money wages for fear of losing ground relative to other workers (erosion of 'relativities' or 'differentials' as union leaders often put it). Nevertheless, a decrease in the real wage brought about by product price inflation might be acceptable in that all workers are affected equally. Neo-Keynesians thus recommend that the necessary reduction in real wages can be speeded up by increasing aggregate demand in the economy until full employment is reached. Monetarists reject this account of things as it smacks of 'money illusion' and hence 'irrationality'.

Some 'extreme' Keynesians believe that the adjustment of prices plays a very minor role in the overall operation of the economy. They point out that the implicit assumption of perfect competition is hard to reconcile with the widespread existence of monopoly and oligopolistic power of both firms and organised labour. They argue

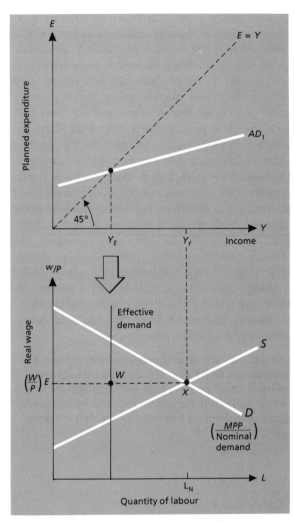

Fig. 36.9 *Keynesian Recession: demand deficiency*
In the upper part of the diagram a demand deficiency causes the equilibrium level of national income (Y_E) to be below the full employment equilibrium (Y_f). In the lower part of the diagram this imposes a quantity constraint on the labour market. At wage level ($W/P)_E$ *WX* amount of labour remains unemployed.

that in such a world quantities rather than prices are likely to adjust to changes in aggregate demand. Thus if there is a shortage of demand firms will cut back on output and labour without lowering prices or attempting to offer lower money wages. Thus although nominal prices and the real wage might be consistent with that

needed for full employment the economy becomes 'stuck' in recession.

Fig. 36.9 demonstrates a Keynesian recession brought about by lack of demand rather than incorrect prices. The top part of the diagram illustrates the equilibrium of aggregate demand in the economy. As can be seen from the lower part of the diagram this level of demand is insufficient to purchase the volume of output that would be produced at full employment. The arrow pointing downwards from Y_E indicates that this level of aggregate demand imposes a quantity constraint on the labour market. The nominal demand for labour as shown is again the *MPP* of labour. This shows how much labour it would be profitable to employ if it were *possible to sell* all the output so produced. It can be seen that at a real wage of $(W/P)_E$ the level of employment that would occur if the labour market cleared could be reached were there sufficient demand in the economy. But it would not be profitable to employ all this labour, at whatever real wage, if the output cannot be sold. Thus the *effective* demand for labour is constrained by the level of demand for products. Therefore *WX* amount of labour remains unemployed even though these people wish to work at the going wage rate and it would be profitable to employ them at this wage if their output could be sold. It should be clear that a cut in wages will not decrease unemployment in Fig. 36.9. It will never be profitable for firms to employ more labour unless the level of demand for products is expanded. Indeed, if a reduction in wages acts to decrease the demand for products it will shift the quantity constraint in the labour market further away from L$_N$. Thus such a recession, if it existed, would not go away by itself. Rather, such Keynesian theorists argue, goverment intervention to increase aggregate demand is essential.

Keynesian economists can thus account for persistent unemployment in terms of *real wages being stuck too high* or a *general lack of demand* in the economy. To this they can add *frictional* unemployment caused by people moving from one job to another and *structural* unemployment caused by a mismatch of labour and jobs in terms of either location or skills (see also Chapter 43).

Voluntary and involuntary unemployment

How then can monetarists account for the persistent high unemployment of the 1980s? As we have seen, in terms of involuntary unemployment this is difficult. Some monetarists do emphasise the role of unions in preventing real wage adjustment and lowering labour productivity. But more purist monetarists do not accept that unions can so bend market forces as to contribute significantly to unemployment. Thus such monetarists make much of the distinction between *involuntary* and *voluntary* unemployment. In short they believe that persistent unemployment must be voluntary. Two prominent monetarists Minford and Peel argued thus:

The general point is that, on our assumptions, the economy behaves in a way that reflects people's choices, given the framework imposed on them by laws and other government intervention. There is no 'slack' in this system, in other words, unless government itself has created it. Unemployment, for example, is voluntary. If a man loses his job owing to a surprise shift in demand against his firm, he then chooses whether to work elsewhere probably at lower net-of-tax wages (and with the costs of moving) or to take social security benefits. Wages go to a level at which demand for labour equals the supply, given these benefits.

Monetarists thus argue that even at the natural rate of employment, where there is overall equilibrium in the labour market, there will be those that remain voluntarily unemployed. For example, at anyone time there will be a flow of people through the unemployment register who are searching for better jobs. These people will search until the marginal cost of their search is equal to their expected marginal gain. They are voluntarily unemployed in that they are refusing the job offers already found in order to search for better jobs.

Monetarists point out that the unemployed person might not see themselves as voluntarily unemployed. For example, unskilled persons or those whose skills are no longer in demand can only expect to be offered jobs where low pay reflects their low market value. Such persons may well curse 'the system' or their own bad luck, but the monetarist argues that they are only worth a low wage and must thus accept the charity of the state or move house and/or retrain. Keynesians would argue that this is a harsh attitude but the monetarist would reply that attempting to eliminate such unemployment by demand measures will only result in inflation. For the monetarist the only way to reduce the 'natural rate of unemployment' in an economy is through *supply side measures* such as skills training, reducing social security payments, lessening the disincentives present by taxation, facilitating the easier flow of finance to firms, removing restrictive practices etc.

The natural rate of unemployment is defined by monetarists to be that level of unemployment which is consistent with overall equilibrium in the labour market. It cannot be reduced by increasing aggregate demand but only by making markets work better.

Conclusion

Monetarism appeared in the 1950s as a part of a technical debate concerning the importance of money to the functioning of the economy. It soon developed into a revival of the neoclassical school of 'macroeconomics' which Keynes had all but beaten into submission. By the 1980s it had gained (regained) political ascendancy. This had led to a profound shift in economic policy from measures designed to influence demand to measures designed to improve the functioning of the supply side of the economy. These policies are examined in greater length in Section 8.

Summary

1   Keynesian and post-Keynesian economics had down-graded the importance of money in the determination of national income. Monetarism represents a return to the pre-Keynesian orthodoxy of the (neo-)classicists.

2   The Classical Dichotomy states that nominal prices are determined by the quantity of money but the quantity of money has no effect on real things.

3   In the quantity equation of money ($MV = PT$) monetarists argue for the stability of both V and T. This therefore establishes a firm link between the money supply (M) and the general price level (P).

4   In the Cambridge equation ($M \times 1/k = P \times Y$) the expression 1/k replaces the velocity of circulation. The symbol k is the proportion of nominal income which is demanded in money.

5   The theory of portfolio balance is concerned with the way in which people distribute their assets between money, financial assets and real assets.

6   The Keynesian view of the demand for money distinguishes three motives for demanding money:

   a) transactions
   b) precautionary
   c) speculative

The first two are directly linked to income while the third is inversely proportionate to the rate of interest.

7   Monetarists argue that there is a dividing line in the portfolio between money and other assets thus there is only a weak link between the demand for money and the rate of interest.

8   The Keynesian view of the transmission mechanism is that increases in the money supply have weak indirect effects upon national income as falls in the interest rate lead to small increases in investment because the demand for money is interest elastic and the demand for investment is interest inelastic.

9   Monetarists argue for strong links between the money supply and national income through both direct and strong indirect effects. However, such effect only act upon money nominal income and not real national income.

10   Monetarists argue that the economy is essentially self-regulating while Keynesians maintain that periodic periods of imbalance are possible.

11   Keynesians have tended to focus on the demand side of the economy while monetarists and neo-classicists have stressed the importance of the *supply side*.

12   Neo-classicists have argued for the existence of a *natural level of employment* in the economy. It follows from this that such unemployment as exists is either temporary or voluntary.

13   Keynesian economists account for unemployment in terms of lack of demand or real wages being 'stuck' too high. To which can be added frictional and structural unemployment.

14   The political ascendancy of neo-classical views has led to profound shifts in policy designed to improve the functioning of the supply side of the economy.

483

Questions

1 What factors determine the demand for money in a modern society?

2 Contrast the effect of an increase in the money supply upon a Keynesian and a monetarist model of the economy:

a) in the short-run;

b) in the long-run.

3 What is meant by the theory of portfolio balance?

4 Examine the effects of increasing numbers of employees being switched from weekly to monthly payment upon the demand for money and the velocity of circulation.

5 What effect upon the equilibrium level of national income would there be if the government were to lower interest rates?

6 Contrast the quantity equation of money with the Cambridge equation.

7 Describe the mechanism by which Keynes said increasing the money supply would lead to an increase in real GDP.

8 What is meant by the 'money illusion'?

9 Evaluate the importance of the concept of the 'natural level of unemployment' in the neo-classical view of the economy.

10 Nobody doubts that monetarism will stop inflation if it is practised long enough and hard enough. At some point high interest rates stop all economic activity as well as inflation. But the price is very high, not equally distributed across the population and not endurable in a democracy. Lester Thurow. *The Economist*. 23 January 1982.

Critically evaluate Thurow's statement in the light of the last fifteen years of government economic policy.

Data response People are not like bananas – whatever the Chancellor says. ━━━━

Read the following article written by the *Guardian's* Christopher Huhne in November 1984.

Answer the following questions:

1 What is the 'real wage debate' referred to in paragraph two. With the aid of marginal distribution theory explain how it is possible for real wages to rise without increasing unemployment.

2 What arguments does the article put forward for the rise in unemployment in the 1970s and 1980s?

3 Do you agree with the argument that cutting real wages creates more jobs? Give reasons for your answer.

4 What effect is increasing the money supply (*M*) likely to have upon employment?

5 Examine 'supply side' measures that might be taken to reduce unemployment.

People are not like bananas —
whatever the Chancellor says

If you thought you had already heard everything the Chancellor had to say about people pricing themselves out of jobs, you are in for a surprise. Tuesday's speech in the House of Commons was only another shot in what promises to be a long and increasingly subtle campaign of jawboning about wages.

The first question is whether the Chancellor is right that wage changes cause job gains or losses. This 'real wage debate' is still one of the most contentious in economics, and one which is bedevilled by jargon. The second question is whether his proposed wage restraint is at all practicable without direct measures such as incomes policy.

For this first time, Mr Lawson quantified the effects of restraint on jobs, saying that each percentage point change in the average level of real earnings — gross pay before tax but after inflation — would in time change employment by ½ to 1 per cent, or by 150 000 to 200 000 jobs.

He went on to point out that this need not imply pay cuts. The beneficial effects on jobs would happen if pay merely rose in line with prices, rather than at 3 per cent or so more than prices during the last few years. Gross pay would clearly be lower than it would otherwise be, but not lower in absolute terms. We would forgo real wage increases. On this view, three successive years of such restraint would create a cumulative 1½ million jobs.

In one of the most interesting passages, Mr Lawson tried to reassure anyone afraid of pay cuts that keeping gross pay flat, after allowing for inflation, could still mean rising spending power for the average worker.

The solution to this apparent paradox is the tax wedge: 'take home pay should gradually increase as taxation is reduced.' This is a far cry from the simple plea for wage cuts. Indeed, it looks rather like Mr Denis Healey's attempts to bargain tax cuts for moderation over wage increases.

There is also of course, another tax wedge between gross pay and the costs of an employee to a firm — namely, National Insurance contributions. The Chancellor did not mention this, but he could cut real wages on this definition — by cutting employers NICs. Gross pay and take home pay would not be affected.

So the way that most economists talk about real wages — as the cost of labour to firms — is not the way most people think about their real wages — or what they have left in their pockets. There are, nevertheless, considerable problems with the simple way in which the Chancellor asserted that changes in real gross pay cause changes in jobs.

Real earnings, after all, nearly doubled between 1946 and 1970 but the unemployment rate was exactly the same in both years. The reason why people did not 'price themselves out of jobs' in the post-war period was because output per person — productivity — rose broadly in line with earnings, thus keeping labour costs to employers for each unit of output fairly stable.

There is a definition of real wages which allows for this, called 'real unit labour costs' and sometimes the 'real product wage.' But, the link between real product wages and jobs since 1980 does not look strong. Only the United States has behaved as the theory would suggest. In other countries, both real wages and employment have fallen, or both have risen.

This, though, is not conclusive. Monetarists can point out that in Britain, rising pay forced companies to boost productivity. This in turn lowered the real product wage, which responded to the rise in wage costs in the first instance. It can merely show what happens after the event, not what caused it.

However, Keynesians can reply that it is simply incredible to argue that it was only the rise in real gross pay between 1980 and 1981 which caused the rise in unemployment. The Government's anti-inflationary policies depressing demand were more important. Indeed, the rise in real pay costs to employers was actually aggravated by the Government's pressure on demand and prices (because profits and prices were squeezed, pay after allowing for prices rose). So once again, another definition of real wages — real gross pay — merely responded to other developments — tight government policy.

In each case, there may indeed be a link between real wages and jobs which can be observed using sophisticated statistical techniques, but the link alone does not imply that

it is always a change in real wages which is the prime mover in a chain of events. Real wage changes can in turn be caused by other factors — notably government policy.

Thus, econometric work at the LSE's Centre for Labour Economics implies that much of the unemployment created between 1973 and 1979 was indeed due to excessive real wage growth, while most of the unemployment created since must be blamed on depressed demand.

The next crucial question is whether real wage cuts can create jobs in the future. This also depends on how they happen, and what else happens at the same time.

If demand stays stable while real earnings are cut, employment should rise. So a cut in labour taxes should stimulate jobs. A pay cut might work if increased profits meant increased investment, or extra markets abroad.

But, as Keynes pointed out in the famous Chapter 19 of the General Theory, it is not obvious that demand does stay stable if wages — and hence probably consumption — fall. A fall in the price of bananas boosts demand for them, because banana producers are an insignificant part of the whole economy. But people are not like bananas. There are too many of us to ignore knock-on effects from lower earnings on spending.

Nor is it obvious that some of the factors which might offset weaker consumption — such as increased competitiveness boosting exports — work for the world as a whole. Interplanetary trade is still in its infancy. So an increase in demand may be necessary on these grounds too.

Ultimately, the question of whether real wage cuts can create jobs in the future, like the question of whether real wage rises have destroyed jobs in the past, is an empirical one, and it would be well worthwhile the NEDO or the House of Commons Treasury Committee's probing hard at the evidence in which the Chancellor proclaims such faith.

Even if it were unequivocally proven that a pay cut created jobs, the Government would still face the thorniest problem of all — how to do it. It is rather easy to cut taxes or increase public spending to boost demand, but it is not at all easy to persuade people to take pay cuts — or even to forgo pay increases.

Pay, after all, rose steadily

485

throughout the thirties in real terms despite record unemployment and record ministerial jawboning about wages. The first snag is that the punishment — unemployment — does not hit the people taking the pay rises. The second snag is that no individual or group of workers can see that their own behaviour can make much difference.

Self-interest rules. Everybody's first priority is to go for a high pay rise while everyone else takes a low one, and helps the unemployed. That way, you get your money and salve your conscience. The second preference might be to exercise mutual restraint, while the third is for everyone to scramble for high pay for fear of being left behind. The dilemma is that the pursuit of the first option automatically entails the third.

Mutual restraint requires mutual guarantees, and collective sanctions of some kind to assure everyone that everybody else will play fair. One option is for the TUC to run an incomes policy with teeth, like expulsion. Another is the inflation tax on recalcitrant groups. What we need is multilateral disarmament in the labour market, because unilateralism does not work. Sadly, tax cuts on their own are not likely to alter the reality of this social trap. Intervention is also required.

3
Macroeconomics
VII International economics

37

The gains of international trade

Free trade is not a principle, it is an expedient.
Benjamin Disraeli

Our interest will be to throw open the doors of commerce, and to knock off its shackles giving freedom to all persons for the rent of whatever they may choose to bring into our ports, and asking the same in theirs.
Thomas Jefferson

We have so far limited ourselves to an examination of economics at a national level. However we live in an increasingly international world. Nations trade more and more with each other; in the words of Marshall McLuhan, 'interdependence recreates the world in the image of a global village'.

In this section of the book we examine the economics of international trade; the accounting of international trade which is summarised in the balance of payments and the monetary aspects of trade which determine exchange rates. Finally we need to consider the major world institutions which are concerned with trade, such as the IMF.

One of the major problems we have to deal with in studying international trade is the *bias of nationalism*. 'The notion dies hard', said Lord Harlech, 'that in some sort of way exports are patriotic but imports are immoral'. Many people believe it is best to buy the products of their own country; we are all familiar with slogans like 'buy British'. However, it makes no more sense to 'buy British' than it does to 'buy Lancastrian'. It does not occur to us in our private lives to feel threatened because we are dependent upon others for our food and clothing, but many people feel threatened by imports.

The bias of economic nationalism often obscures the benefits of specialisation which appear self-evident within the national economy. It is necessary, therefore, to examine the theory of the gains from trade – the *theory of comparative advantage* – and to see how international trade leads to what J.S. Mill described as 'a more efficient employment of the productive forces of the world'.

The theory of comparative advantage

David Ricardo (1772–1823)

Men and nations have traded since the time of the Phoenicians, but for the most of this time they provided for most of their needs out of the local economy. Trade was for such things as spices, wines and precious metals. However, by the 19th century the UK had embarked upon the course which would see her export her products all over the world in return, not for luxuries, but for her basic food and raw materials. It was at this time (1817) that, in his book *Principles of Political Economy*, Ricardo explained his *theory of comparative advantage* (sometimes called the theory of comparative costs). It is this theory, as

489

subsequently modified by another great classical economist, John Stuart Mill, which is still the foundation of our theory of international trade today.

Absolute advantage and comparative advantage

One of the most fundamental reasons for trade is the diversity of conditions between different countries. For example, the UK can produce cars more cheaply than West African countries, but West African countries produce cocoa more cheaply than the UK. In these circumstances the UK is said to have an *absolute advantage* in cars and West African countries an absolute advantage in cocoa. If the West Africans want cars and the UK wants cocoa it is obviously to their mutual advantage to trade. However trade depends not upon *absolute advantage* but upon *comparative advantage*; as Professor Samuelson says, 'it is not so immediately obvious, but it is no less true that international trade is mutually profitable even when one of the two can produce *every commodity* more cheaply'.

Consider the example of a town which has only one doctor but the doctor is also the best typist in town. Should he or she be a doctor or a typist? Obviously the *comparative advantage* is greatest in the medical field and the fortunate individual should concentrate on that. If a typist has to be employed, the doctor will be better off because he or she can concentrate on supplying a relatively rarer skill, the town will be better off because it gets more services of the doctor and a job will be created for the typist that is employed. So it is with international trade; a country should specialise not at what it is *absolutely* best at but at what it is *relatively* best at.

Comparative advantage: a model

Production possibilities

Ricardo illustrated his theory by considering trade between two countries, the UK and Portugal, and two products, wine and cloth. We will use two hypothetical countries, Richland and Poorland.

Richland has a population of 10 million and Poorland of 20 million. In Richland a day's labour will produce either 20 units of food or 18 units of clothing, whereas in Poorland a day's labour will only produce either 10 units of food or 4 units of clothing. It is apparent, therefore, that Richland has an *absolute advantage* in the production of both commodities.

If the two countries do not trade, then they must produce both food and clothing for themselves, dividing their labour between the two commodities. Poorland's production possibilities are summarised in Table 37.1. Thus if all resources were devoted to producing food, then 200 million units could be produced, but no clothing. At the other extreme, 80 million units of clothing could be produced but no food. The Poorlanders must therefore choose some combination between those extremes. Say, for example, that the Poorlanders choose possibility D, producing 50 million units of food and 60 million units of clothing. These production possibilities can be represented graphically. Figure 37.1 shows that Poorland can obtain any combination of food or clothing along line AE, such as point D, or any combination within it such as U.

The slope of the line shows the *opportunity cost* of food in terms of clothing; each 4 units of clothing given up will secure 10 units of food or vice versa. Thus we have a *domestic trading ratio* of 4:10. Position D_1 shows a better situation for Poorland, where it would be consuming both

Table 37.1 Poorland's production possibilities

Possibility	Food (million units)	Clothing (million units)
A	200	0
B	150	20
C	100	40
D	50	60
E	0	80

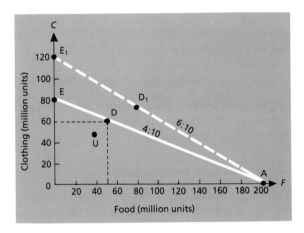

Fig. 37.1 *Poorland's production possibilities*
The line AE shows Poorland's production possibilities before trade, i.e. any combination of food and clothing along line AE or within it. This represents a domestic ration of 4:10. Line AE₁ shows possibilities not attainable at present and a better trading ratio of 6:10.

more food and clothing, but this is unattainable at the moment.

We can now construct a similar table and graph to show Richland's production possibilities. As you can see in Table 37.2, if Richland devoted all its resources to producing food then 200 million units could be produced (possibility A) while at the other extreme if all resources were devoted to clothing production then 180 million units could be produced (possibility K).

Table 37:2 Richland's production possibilities

Possibility	Food (million units)	Clothing (million units)
A	200	0
B	180	18
C	160	36
D	140	54
E	120	72
F	100	90
G	80	108
H	60	126
I	40	144
J	20	162
K	0	180

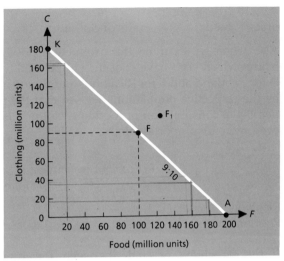

Fig. 37.2 *Richland's production possibilities*
AK is the production possibility line. At point F Richland is producing and consuming 90 million units of clothing and 100 million units of food. Point F₁ shows a position where both more food and clothing would be consumed but which is at present unattainable.

If there is no international trade, then Richland must produce all its own food and clothing. One of the possible combinations must be chosen, for example possibility F which is 100 million units of food and 90 million units of clothing. This is illustrated in Fig. 37.2. You can see from Table 37.2 and Fig. 37.2 that the domestic trading ratio of food for clothing is 20 units of food given up gains 18 units of clothing. To make comparison with Poorland easier, instead of writing this as 20:18 we could express it as 10:9.

The opening up of trade

It might appear that there is little possibility of trade between the two nations.

In Richland
1 day's labour will produce
either
20   or   18
units of food   units of clothing

In Poorland
1 day's labour will produce
either

491

10   or   4
units of food   units of clothing

Also when we examine the production possibilities which each have chosen, i.e. possibility D for Poorland and F for Richland, and divide it by the respective populations we see that their per capita consumption of food and clothing is even more disproportionate.

| | Per capita consumption of | |
	Food	Clothing
Richland	10.0	9.0
Poorland	2.5	3.0

If the possibility of trade between the two countries arises we can imagine the arguments which might be advanced against it in the two countries. In Richland it would be:

It is highly dangerous for us to trade with Poorland because the low wages of people there will enable producers to undercut our products by using cheap labour.

while in Poorland they would say:

If we trade with Richland we shall surely be swamped by the productive might of that country.

However let us examine what is likely to happen if trade does begin between the two countries.

In Poorland 10 units of food can be exchanged for 4 units of clothing, but the same 10 units of food in Richland can be exchanged for 9 units of clothing. The Poorlanders therefore find that they can clothe themselves better by selling food to Richland rather than producing clothes themselves.

In Richland 10 units of food can be acquired at the cost of 9 units of clothing but in Poorland 10 units of food only cost 4 units of clothing. The Richlanders therefore find it more advantageous to produce clothing and export it to Poorland in exchange for food.

Thus it can be seen that although Richland has an absolute advantage in both commodities it is to its advantage to specialise in the commodity in which it has the greatest comparative

advantage (clothing) and trade this for the other commodity. Similarly Poorland has a comparative advantage in food and is better off specialising in producing this and trading it for clothing. We can draw from this the general principle that:

International trade is always beneficial whenever there is a difference in the opportunity cost ratios between two countries.

An international trading ratio

If trading is opened up between the two countries the two domestic trading ratios will be replaced by one international ratio. In our example, since the domestic ratios are 10:9 and 10:4, the international ratio must be somewhere between them. When Ricardo explained the theory he did not say how the ratio could be determined; he merely stated that any ratio which lay between the two domestic ratios could be beneficial to both countries involved. Followers of Ricardo argued, wrongly, that the international ratio would lie halfway between the domestic ratios. It was John Stuart Mill who explained that the ratio would be determined by the forces of demand and supply in international markets. This is known as the *law of reciprocal demand*.

We cannot determine the ratio unless we have all the demand and supply information for both countries. Therefore in order to proceed with an example we will simply assume an international ratio of 10:6. With the ratio of 10:6 we can demonstrate the advantage of trade to both countries. In Richland, 10 units of food previously cost 9 units of clothing but now it only costs 6 units, whereas in Poorland, 10 units of food bought only 4 units of clothing but with international trade they now buy 6. It is therefore to Richland's advantage to specialise in clothing and trade for food and for Poorland to specialise in food and trade for clothing.

The position after specialisation and trade

Let us assume that, once trade has begun, Richland specialises completely in the production of clothing and so produces 180 million units but no food at all. Similarly Poorland specialises entirely in food production and therefore produces 200 million units. If you turn back to Fig. 37.1 you can see how Poorland's prospects have changed. It is now at A and if it were to trade all its food for clothing at the improved ratio of 10:6 it could obtain 120 million units instead of 80 million.

In order to complete the example we must make some assumption about the quantity of exports and imports. Let us suppose that Poorland exports 120 million units of food. If each 10 units of food buys 6 units of clothing then Poorland will be able to exchange its exports for 72 million units of clothing. Thus, before specialisation and trade Poorland consumed 50 million units of food and 60 million units of clothing. After specialisation and trade it is now able to consume 80 million units of food and 72 million units of clothing. Thus its position has clearly improved. Figure 37.3 illustrates Poorland's position after trade.

Richland's position has similarly improved. It has specialised in clothing, producing 180 million units. Of these, 72 million have been exported, leaving it with 108 million units. The 72 million units of exports have earned it 120 million units of food, whereas before it consumed only 100 million units. Its position has therefore clearly improved. If you turn back to Fig. 37.2 you will see that Richland is now at point F_1, a previously unattainable position.

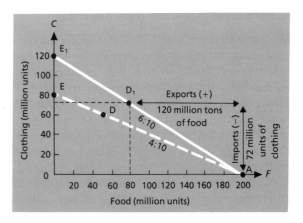

Fig. 37.3 *Poorland after specialisation and trade*
By exporting food and importing clothing Poorland is able to attain position D_1 previous unattainable.

Thus it can be seen that as a result of specialisation and trade both Richland and Poorland are better off. Not only that, but the total world production of both commodities has risen. These findings are summarised in Table 37.3.

Look again at the Table on page 49 showing you the consumption per capita of both products in the two countries. You should now be able to determine that, after trade, the per capita consumption of *both products in both countries has risen*. For example, in Poorland consumption of food rises to 4 units per capita and clothing to 3.6. What are the figures for Richland?

Table 37.3 Richland and Poorland before and after trade

Country	Trading ratio, food/ clothing	Clothing output	Clothing consumption	Clothing exports (+) or imports (−)	Food output	Food consumption	Food exports (+) or imports (−)
Situation before specialisation and trade:							
Richland	10:9	90	90	0	100	100	0
Poorland	10:4	60	60	0	50	50	0
Situation after specialisation and trade:							
Richland	10:6	180	108	+72	0	120	−120
Poorland	10:6	0	72	−72	200	80	+120
World gain from specialisation and trade:							
Total	—	30	30	—	50	50	—

Long-term versus short-term benefits

We have demonstrated that the levels of consumption and production increase as a result of international trade so that we can argue that in the long-run everyone benefits from trade. However in the short- and medium-term we must consider the fortunes of those who work in industries without comparative advantage. In our example agriculture in Richland contracted as food was bought more cheaply in Poorland. This was to the advantage of the average Richland consumer, but the contraction of agriculture involved farmers going bankrupt and agricultural labourers losing their jobs.

This was indeed what happened in the UK in the late 19th century as the UK imported cheap food from the USA, Australia and Europe. As a result of this, agriculture in the UK experienced the 'great depression'. In the long-term, however, it was also to the advantage of those in agriculture since it was better to enjoy high wages in a factory than low wages on a farm. At the present time the UK is going through great changes and many industries which traditionally had an advantage find that they have lost this advantage to new producers in the Far East. Many arguments have been put forward in favour of protecting the UK's traditional industries against foreign competition. In the short-term this may protect some jobs but in the long-term protecting such industries will depress the living standard of everyone.

Comparative advantage and exchange rates

The overall theory of exchange rates is considered in a subsequent chapter, but we will here briefly consider the relationship between comparative advantage and exchange rates. Most international trade is not the swopping of one lot of goods for another but buying and selling through the medium of money and the exchange rate. Let us return to our Richland/Poorland example and

Domestic price of food and clothing (assuming the same domestic trading ratios as in the text)	Import prices at various exchange rates		
	Exchange rate 1 $1 = £1	Exchange rate 2 $3 = £1	Exchange rate 3 $5 = £1
Price of clothing in Richland = £1.11	£5.00	£1.67	£1.00
Price of food in Richland = £1.00	£2.00	£0.66	£0.40
Price of clothing in Poorland = $5.00	$1.11	$3.33	$5.55
Price of food in Poorland = $2.00	$1.00	$3.00	$5.00

☐ Import price higher than domestic price
No trade

▨ Import prices are lower than domestic prices in both countries
Trade will take place

▨ Import price lower than domestic price but exports too expensive
No trade

Fig. 37.4 Comparative advantage and exchange rates

assume that in Poorland food costs $2.00 a unit and clothing $5.00 a unit. These prices maintain the original domestic trading ratio of 10:4. Similarly we will assume that in Richland, food costs £1.00 a unit and clothing £1.11, thus retaining the ratio of 10:9.

If the exchange rate is such that in Richland imported goods are cheaper than domestically produced ones, then the Richlanders will buy them. Consider Fig. 37.4. Here it can be seen if the exchange rate is $1 = £1 then no trade will take place because in Richland the price of imported goods is higher than that of domestically produced ones. Conversely, if the exchange rate were $5 = £1 then although imports would be cheap in Richland no trade would be possible because Richland exports are too expensive for Poorlanders. However if the exchange rate is $3 = £1 Richlanders will buy Poorland food, because it is cheaper than the domestic price, and, similarly, Poorlanders will buy Richland clothing because it is cheaper. Trade is therefore possible. In our example trade is possible so long as the exchange lies between the limits $2 = £1 and $4.50 = £1.

It is disadvantageous to a country to have its exchange rate set incorrectly. An exchange rate set too high (overvalued) will cause a trade deficit, while if the rate is fixed too low (undervalued) consumers at home suffer although exporters may benefit. Governments are often tempted to manipulate exchange rates in the hope of benefiting trade. Although this may bring some short-term benefit it cannot alter the basic opportunity cost ratios on which international trade is based.

Extending the theory

In explaining the theory we have utilised a model with only two countries and two commodities. In practice the pattern of trade is much more complex than this. We must therefore consider a number of factors which bring about this complexity.

Many countries

The theory of comparative advantage will work better as more countries are brought into the example. This is because, not only does international trade require a comparative advantage but it also depends upon countries wanting the goods which another country produces. In Fig. 37.5 you can see that trade is possible between the four countries but would not be possible between two or even three. The UK wishes to import from Canada but Canada does not want the UK's exports, and so on. *Multilateral trade* allows for the international offsetting of debts from one country to another and so makes greater trade possible. In effect the UK pays for Canadian wheat with exports of machinery to Nigeria which in turn pays for these with exports of oil to the West Indies.

The greater the number of countries involved in trade the greater will be the opportunities for trade. It is for this reason that economists tend to favour multilateral trade agreements but oppose bilateral ones.

Many commodities

Harberler in his book *Theory of International Trade* demonstrated that when many commodities are introduced into the theory they can be arranged in order of comparative advantage. Figure 37.6 gives an illustration of this. The UK will tend to specialise in the commodities in the righthand side of the diagram. As we move to the left so comparative advantage passes to the UK's trading partners. The extent to which a country is able to specialise in producing a commodity in which it has a comparative advantage will depend upon the strength of international demand for that commodity. For example, the greater is the demand for, say, chemicals, the more the UK will be able to specialise in producing these and the less it will need to produce other products in which it lacks advantage, such as wheat.

It will be obvious to the reader that although the UK has no comparative advantage in wheat,

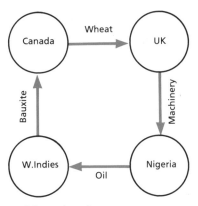

Fig. 37.5 *Multilateral trade*

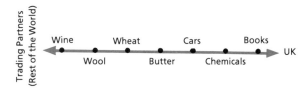

Fig. 37.6 *International trade and comparative advantage* **495**

it is still produced in the UK. This leads us to an important modification of the theory of comparative cost:

Specialisation is never complete.

Some wheat, and even wine, can be produced in the UK because there are some resources that are uniquely well suited to that product. Thus some of a product can be produced even though the country as a whole has no comparative advantage in it. Total specialisation may also be prevented by the *principle of increasing costs* (see below).

Factor price equalisation

The idea was put forward by the economist Eli Hekscher, later refined by Bertil Ohlin, that international trade would bring the prices of factors of production closer together. We might illustrate this *factor price equalisation hypothesis* by considering the example of Europe and the USA in the 19th century. In the early 19th century rents were very high in Europe because land was scarce and consequently food was also expensive. Wages on the other hand were low because people were plentiful. In the USA land was practically free. In the second half of the century improvements in transport allowed the USA to exploit its cheap land by exporting cheap food to Europe while Europe utilised its labour by exporting manufactured goods to the USA. Consequently rents fell and wages rose in Europe and in the USA land became a valuable property. Thus the effect of international trade was to bring factor prices and commodity prices closer to each other. The effect of moving goods from country to country is a substitute for moving the factors of production themselves.

Again we might note that international trade does not benefit every single person. Those that own the factors which are in very short supply have their incomes diminished as international trade lowers high factor prices and raises low ones. However factor prices never completely equalise because national markets are protected by such things as transport costs and tariffs (see below).

Economies of scale: decreasing costs

As a country specialises in the production of a particular commodity it could benefit from economies of scale. In our model so far we have assumed a *constant cost case*, i.e. the production possibility line is a straight line, indicating that the rate of exchange (food for clothing) is the same at all levels of output. Thus in Richland each time resources are switched from food to clothing production 9 units of clothing are gained for 10 of food. It could be, however, that, as Richland specialises in clothing production, economies of scale reduce the cost of a unit of clothing.

This is illustrated in Fig. 37.7. Here the production possibility line is *convex* to the origin, illustrating decreasing costs. Originally Richland produced 90 million units of clothing at point F. It then specialises in clothing production and plans to move to position I (144 million units) but because of economies of scale it is able to produce more with the same amount of re-

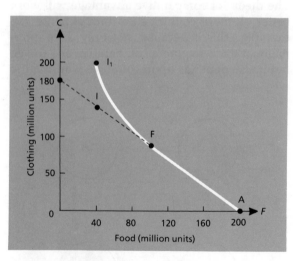

Fig. 37.7 *Decreasing costs*
Richland starts from F and specialises in clothing, but experiences economies of scale so that instead of producing at point I (144 million units) it produces at point I₁ (200 million units).

sources. Thus, it arrives at point I_1 (200 million units).

If an industry does experience decreasing costs as it specialises, then this will increase the benefits of international trade. This was said to be one of the main reasons why the UK joined the EEC. The possibilities of achieving economies of scale could be a reason for specialisation and trade even when no comparative advantage exists.

Differences in tastes: a reason for trade

Let us assume that Richland and Poorland can produce fish and meat equally successfully. Let us also assume that the Richlanders have no taste for fish but like meat, whereas the situation is the reverse in Poorland. The result will be that, if there is no trade, the fishing industry in Richland will languish, fish will be very cheap and meat expensive. The converse will be the case in Poorland. However if trade takes place between them, Poorland will buy fish cheaply from Richland and Richland cheap meat from Poorland. This will reduce the cost of meat in Richland and of fish in Poorland, while the income of fishermen in Richland and of farmers in Poorland will go up. Thus trade will have proved beneficial to both countries even though no comparative advantage existed. (Note: we are here witnessing another example of factor price equalisation.)

The UK fishing industry has benefited from this principle for many years, catching herrings which are not at all popular in the UK and selling them at a good price in Scandinavia.

Increased competition

By bringing more producers into the market, international trade increases competition and, thereby, economic efficiency, and domestic monopolies may be broken down by foreign competition. The greater efficiency encouraged by competition also benefits consumers by offering them a *wider choice*.

Limitations of comparative advantage

There are a number of factors which prevent us from benefiting fully from comparative advantage. Some arise 'naturally' out of the economic situation, e.g. transport costs; others, however, are artificially imposed, e.g. customs duties. We will consider the more important of these limitations.

Obstacles to trade

There are a great many obstacles to trade which arise out of political considerations.

1) *Tariffs and quotas*. Tariffs are taxes placed on imports. They may either have the objective of raising revenue or protecting industries. Which they accomplish will be determined by the elasticity of demand for imports. Quotas are a quantitative restriction on the amount of imports. Where restrictions successfully keep out imports they have the effect of protecting inefficient home producers. This means that although people employed in that industry may benefit, consumers generally are condemned to paying higher prices for goods.

2) *Political frontiers*. Political frontiers can also be economic frontiers, as in the case between the Western world and the Communist bloc. Trade is further hindered by language differences and differing legal systems.

3) *Currencies*. Foreign trade involves exchanging currency. This in itself is a barrier, but it is often added to by restrictions placed on currency exchange by governments.

4) *Disguised barriers*. Governments may be able to discriminate in favour of home producers by such things as health and safety regulations. The Japanese safety requirements for cars are designed to favour Japanese methods of construction. In 1982 the UK imposed special health regulations on poultry which had the effect of keeping out European imports. In the same year the French insisted that all video recorders entering France had to be processed by an obscure customs post in the centre of France, thus effectively limiting imports.

497

5) *Trade diversion*. Before leaving obstacles to trade we must consider the phenomenon of *trade diversion*. This refers to the distortion of the pattern of world trade by tariffs and other artificial obstacles to trade. Suppose, for example, we consider three countries, West Germany, France and Japan. The first two have free trade because they are in the EEC but have a common external tariff to keep out non-EEC electrical goods. Both West Germany and Japan produce video recorders but the West German ones are more expensive. Without tariffs both West Germany and France would import from Japan, but the effect of the tariff is that France now buys West German videos even though they are more expensive to make. Thus the pattern of trade is distorted and French consumers suffer, as do Japanese exporters.

The creation of large trading blocs such as the EEC introduces considerable trade diversion into the pattern of world trade. The effects of the abolition of tariff barriers between countries can be observed from the application of the Single European Act in 1992.

Transport costs

Although a country may have a comparative advantage, this will be of little use if it is offset by high transport costs. Transport costs have a great influence upon the pattern of UK farming. UK farmers tend to produce products, such as milk or fresh vegetables, in which they are naturally protected by high transport costs.

Factor immobility

In order for a country to benefit from comparative advantage it is necessary for it to contract those industries in which it is at a disadvantage and expand those in which it has an advantage. This will involve wages, prices and employment falling in the declining industry. The fact that prices seem to go up easily but are very difficult to bring down is referred to as the *downward inflexibility of prices* or, more memorably, the 'sticky-upwardness' of prices. This will form part

of a general resistance to change from those in the declining industry. We need only look at the recent problems in some UK industries such as coal to appreciate this. Such inflexibility may prevent an economy from benefiting fully from comparative advantage.

Increasing costs

Earlier in the chapter we considered the possibility that specialisation might produce decreasing costs. There is, on the other hand, the possibility that specialisation could lead to increasing costs. This could come about as the expansion of an industry drove up the price of labour and other factors, or it could occur as an industry expanded into less and less appropriate resources. This is illustrated in Fig. 37.8. Here, starting from point F, forgoing the production of 60 million units of food at the constant cost ratio of 10:9 should have been expected to gain Richland a further 54 units of clothing, thus moving it to point I. However, because of increasing costs, it has arrived at point I_1, a much lower level of production.

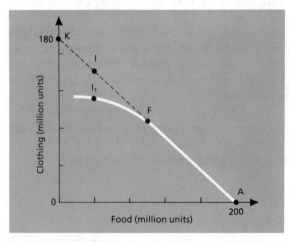

Fig. 37.8 *Increasing costs*
As Richland moves from point F it arrives not at point I but at I_1. If point I_1 is less than an output of 126 million units of clothing it would not be in Richland's interest to specialise this far because, at 126 million units of clothing, 60 million units of food given up have gained only 36 million units of clothing, a rate equal to the international trading ration of 10:6.

The principle of increasing costs also helps to explain why specialisation is not complete in international trade. If a country experiences increasing costs as it specialises then its domestic trading ratio is worsening. It would therefore stop specialising at the point where its domestic ratio became worse than the international ratio, since at that point it would become more advantageous to import the product in which it was specialising. For example, in Fig. 37.8, as Richland specialises in clothing production and moves from point F towards point I, it expects that each 10 units of food given up will gain it 9 units of clothing, but, because the production possibility line bends inwards, the rate deteriorates. Thus 10 units of food gains it only 8 of clothing and then 7 and so on. Once the rate has deteriorated to 10:6 (the international trading ratio) it would then be better to trade for clothing rather than produce more.

Other problems

Specialisation itself can create problems if there is a change in demand. For example, it could be argued that in the UK Lancashire over-specialised in cotton production so that when demand changed the whole area was plunged into depression. In recent years the dangers of *over-specialisation* were illustrated by the over-dependence of the West Midlands in the UK on car production.

This problem also points to a shortcoming of the theory of comparative advantage, which is that it is *static*. The theory does not explain how comparative advantage arises in the first place, nor how it changes. The history of recent years illustrates only too well that comparative advantage can change; many Western nations which enjoyed an advantage in manufacturing have lost it to nations in the Far East.

Protectionism considered

Adam Smith's *Wealth of Nations* was designed to show the adverse effects of restrictions on trade.

The majority of economists since his time have favoured free trade. However the depression in the world economy in the late 1970s and early 1980s led to the revival of the protection lobby. Many prominent economists such as Professor Wynne Godley of Cambridge have argued the need to protect the home market. The UK, however, has remained one of the most free markets in the world. Elsewhere protectionism is rife, not only through the use of tariffs but also through the subtler forms of economic nationalism. The UK has entered the EEC which, while freeing trade between members, has erected tariff barriers to the rest of the world.

Many arguments are advanced in favour of protectionism. Some of the arguments are sounder than others, but all forms of protection suffer from the disadvantage that they may invite retaliation from trading partners. We will consider the more significant arguments more fully.

Cheap labour

It is often argued that the economy must be protected from imports which are produced with cheap, or 'sweated', labour (see page 492). This argument is basically unsound because it is contrary to the whole principle of comparative advantage. It would not only ensure that wages are kept low in the exporting country but it would protect inefficient practices at home, in the long-run depressing domestic living standards.

Dumping

If goods are sold on a foreign market below their cost of production this is referred to as dumping. This may be undertaken either by a foreign monopolist, using high profits at home to subsidise exports, or by foreign governments subsidising exports for political or strategic reasons. (Dumping is also discussed on page 220). It is quite legitimate and necessary for a country to protect its industries from this type of unfair competition.

Infant industries

If a country is establishing an industry it may be **499**

necessary to protect it from competition temporarily until it reaches levels of production and costs which will allow it to compete with established industries elsewhere. This argument was advanced to support the protection of the European video cassette recorder industry. The problem is that protected industries tend to become dependent upon the protection.

Unemployment and immobile factors

Imports may aggravate domestic unemployment and protection could be a way of alleviating this. As we have already noted factors are immobile and protection could allow a country time to reallocate factors of production in a more efficient manner. However, in the long-run, such protection cannot be justified since it will protect inefficiency and ultimately depress the living standards of a nation.

Balance of payments

Perhaps the most immediate reason for bringing in protection is a balance of payments deficit. A package of measures was brought in by the UK government in 1966 for this reason. They included exchange controls, an import surcharge and an import deposit scheme. Again this argument can only be justified in the short-run, especially as it also invites retaliation from other countries.

Strategic reasons

Two world wars taught the UK the danger of being over-reliant on imports. For political or strategic reasons a country may not wish to be dependent upon imports and so may protect a home industry even if it is inefficient. Many countries maintain munitions industries for strategic reasons. In the UK, for example, the aerospace industry has received substantial 'protection' in the form of government money.

Similarly the EEC is committed to protecting agriculture.

Bargaining

Even when a country can see no economic benefit in protection it may find it useful to have tariffs and restrictions as bargaining gambits in negotiating better terms with other nations.

Revenue

Customs duties are one of the oldest sources of government revenue. It should be remembered, however, that a tax on imports cannot both keep out imports and at the same time raise money. The effect of customs duties will depend upon the elasticity of demand for imports. If the demand is inelastic the tax will indeed make money for the government but will also add to domestic inflation. Where demand is elastic the government could increase its revenues by cutting the tax; this was confirmed as long ago as 1844 when Sir Robert Peel cut import duties. (The analysis of this is the same as that for any other indirect tax; see pages 146–48.)

Conclusion

We have endeavoured to show that the economic arguments are overwhelmingly in favour of a pattern of free world trade. However, in conclusion, we might note three qualifications upon this. Firstly, the pattern of world trade which has grown up has not always reflected comparative advantage; it has all so often depended upon historical accident or upon the possesion of surplus resources. Secondly, tariffs and other forms of protection have significantly modified the pattern of trade. Thirdly, even where the country is committed to free trade and it has comparative advantage, it may be unwise to follow such a policy in a world of protectionism.

Summary

1   The bias of nationalism often prejudices our views on international trade.
2   The theory of comparative advantage explains that international trade is worthwhile and beneficial to both parties wherever there is any difference in their respective opportunity cost ratios.
3   The theory may be extended to include many countries and many commodities and comparative advantage may be improved by such things as decreasing costs.
4   There are many obstacles to free trade such as tariffs, quotas, exchange control and economic nationalism.
5   Comparative advantage is diminished by such things as transport costs, increasing costs and factor immobility.
6   Comparative cost ratios help to explain the determination of exchange rates.
7   Many arguments are advanced to support protectionism but few are valid in the long-run.

Questions

1   List the commodities in which you think the UK (or another country with which you are familiar) is at a:
  a) competitive advantage;
  b) disadvantage.
(Note: do not confuse absolute advantage with comparative advantage.)
2   Explain, in an essay, the benefits of specialisation and trade according to the principle of comparative advantage. Illustrate your answer by means of a numerical example.
3   In an essay, evaluate the arguments for and against free trade.
4   Construct a graph similar to Fig. 37.3 (see page 493) to show Richlands's position after specialisation and trade. (Hint: in Fig. 37.2 point F_1 is Richland's position after deciding to trade.)
5   To what extent does the EEC benefit from comparative advantage?
6   To what extent are exchange rates a result of the differing opportunity cost ratios between nations?
7   Explain what you think the effect of the Single European Act will have on the pattern of the UK's trade.

Data response   Comparative advantage

Consider the following production possibilities.

Country	Labour input (days)	Output of Wine (litres)	Olive oil (litres)
France	5	200	150
Greece	5	100	120

a) Which country has an absolute advantage in production?

b) Does comparative advantage exist? If so explain which country has advantage in which product.

c) Define the limits of possible international trading ratios within which the two countries might trade. (Hint: what are the domestic trading ratios in each country?)

d) Explain how the international trading ratio will be determined.

e) In what ways may Greece's membership of the EEC have affected its trade with France?

f) Wine costs 10 francs a litre and olive oil 13.3 francs a litre in France whereas in Greece wine costs 120 drachma a litre and olive oil 100 drachma. Determine the limits of the exchange rate of the franc with the drachma between which trade will be worthwhile for the two countries.

38

The balance of payments

'We've got cedars from Lebanon due at the sawmill in Oslo to be turned into shingles for the builder in Cape Cod. C.O.D. And then there's the peas.'
'Peas?'
'That are on the high seas. We've got boatloads of peas that are on the high seas from Atlanta to Holland to pay for the tulips that were shipped to Geneva to pay for the cheeses that must go to Vienna. M.I.F.'
'M.I.F.?'
'Money in Front. The Hapsburgs are shaky.'
'Milo.'
'And don't forget the galvanised zinc in the warehouse at Flint.'

Joseph Heller, *Catch 22*

The pattern of the UK's overseas trade

The importance of international trade

There are few other nations in the world as dependent upon foreign trade as the UK. The UK depends upon imports for almost half its food requirements and for most of the raw materials needed by its industries. Equally, the continued well-being of the economy depends upon exporting a large proportion of the national product each year. In 1986, imports were equivalent to 31·7 per cent of the GDP while exports were 29·4 per cent. The growth of exports and imports is closely linked to the growth of GDP as Table 38.1 shows. This tendency for an economy to become more international as it becomes wealthier is not confined to the UK; there is a similar pattern in most industrial countries.

International trade is a vital component of national income as we can see from the identity:

$$Y = C + I + G + (X - M)$$

A trade deficit has a depressing effect upon the level of income and employment whereas a surplus will boost income. The UK economy suffers from the structural problem that, as the economy expands, it tends to draw in raw materials which are necessary for manufacturing industries. However, it often happens that, before these can be turned into exports, the flow of imports

Table 38.1 GDP and international trade in the UK

	Index of GDP (1980 = 100)	Exports as % of GDP	Imports as % of GDP
1965	73·6	18·8	22·4
1971	85·7	23·8	25·9
1975	92·6	25·1	26·7
1980	100·0	30·1	29·0
1985	109·5	32·6	32·7
1986	112·4	29·4	31·7

Source: National Income and Expenditure, *HMSO*

has caused a balance of payments crisis which necessitates contractionary policies to rectify the imbalance.

In recent years a disturbing trend has been the tendency for the expanding economy to draw in manufactured goods which the domestic economy is failing to produce. In 1983, for the first time since the Industrial Revolution, the UK imported more manufactured goods than it exported. After that date the imbalance in manufactured goods continued to deteriorate.

The components of trade

Table 38.2 summarises the main categories of products which are traded. The near equality in distribution between the different types of imports and exports emphasises the changing pattern of UK trade.

The traditional pattern has been for the UK to import raw materials and export manufactured goods but, increasingly, the UK is importing manufactured goods. In addition to trade in goods, which is termed 'visible' trade, there is trade in 'invisibles', i.e. services. For most of the last 100 or so years, the UK has had a deficit on visible trade which has been made up by a surplus on invisible earnings. However, whilst invisibles have become increasingly important, the UK has also enjoyed an improved position on visible trade due to North Sea oil, which has both added to exports and reduced the need for imports. The years 1980–82 saw surpluses on visible trade which were due both to the impact of North Sea oil and the depressed state of the economy which restrained imports. However, after 1982 visible trade swung back into deficit. A record visible trade deficit of £8463 million was recorded in 1986. This was principally due to the increasing imbalance in the export and import of manufactured goods.

The changing nature of the UK's trade

The traditional view of the UK is as 'the workshop of the world', i.e. importing raw materials and exporting manufactured goods. This picture is changing rapidly because of:

Table 38.2 UK exports and imports by value, 1986

	Value of exports		Value of imports	
	£m	%	£m	%
Food beverages and tobacco	5 439	7·5	9 230	11·4
Basic materials	2 058	2·8	4 416	5·4
Oil	8 221	11·3	4 165	5·1
Other fuels and lubricants	462	0·6	1 829	2·2
Semi-manufactured goods	20 946	28·8	21 524	26·5
Finished manufactured goods	33 540	46·0	38 453	47·3
Miscellaneous	2 176	3·0	1 689	2·1
	£72 843	100·0	£81 306	100·0

Source: *CSO*, Balance of Payments, *HMSO*

a) exports of North Sea oil have once more turned the UK into an exporter of primary products;

b) growing reliance on tertiary industries such as tourism.

The growing tendency is for the UK to import dear and export cheap, i.e. to import high value, low bulk products but to export low value, high bulk products.

We might express this relationship as a *trade value–weight coefficient* thus:

Trade value-weight coefficient =

$$\frac{\text{Average value of 1 tonne of exports}}{\text{Average value of 1 tonne of imports}}$$

If the value were to be 1·0 then the average value of a tonne of exports would be equal to a tonne of imports. A value less than 1·0 would mean that exports were, in general, less valuable per tonne than imports. In the early 1970s the UK's coefficient stood at just over 0·6, but by 1986 it had decreased to 0·5. Meanwhile West Germany's coefficient had risen from 1·0 to 1·2.

The direction of trade

In Table 38.3 you can see that nearly 70 per cent of the UK's overseas trade is with ten countries.

Table 38.3 The UK's ten leading trading partners (by value) 1985 and 1971

Country Position (in order of importance in UK's trade)	International trade 1985 Imports (CIF) £m	%	Exports (FOB) £m	%	Trade 1971 Imports %	Exports %	Position
1. West Germany*	12 601	14·7	8 947	11·4	6·6	5·8	2
2. USA	9 919	11·7	11 498	14·7	11·1	11·9	1
3. France*	6 632	7·8	7 751	9·9	4·5	4·3	6
4. Netherlands*	6 550	7·7	7 344	9·4	5·2	4·5	5
5. Italy*	4 293	5·0	3 466	4·4	2·9	2·7	12
6. Belgium/Luxembourg*	4 016	4·7	3 347	4·3	2·3	3·7	10
7. Ireland*	2 816	3·3	3 642	4·6	5·2	5·5	3
8. Norway	4 367	5·2	1 140	1·5	1·9	2·0	16
9. Sweden	2 465	2·9	3 006	3·8	4·1	4·2	7
10. Japan	4 117	4·9	1 012	1·3	1·7	2·0	21
Total of these ten	£57 776	67·9	£51 153	65·3	45·5	46·6	
Total of all visible trade	£87 789	100·0	£78 331	100·0	£9980	£9290	

* Members of EEC
Source: Annual Abstract of Statistics *HMSO*

Despite the growing concentration of trade illustrated by these figures, the UK continues to have a more worldwide pattern of trade than almost any other nation. Traditionally, the UK drew her imports of raw materials from the Commonwealth and Empire to whom, in return, she exported her manufactures. Since 1945 there has been a growing dependence on North America and Europe. This trend was quite apparent before the UK joined the EEC and, indeed, was one of the reasons why it was essential for the UK to join. Since joining the EEC, the UK has become much more dependent upon EEC trade. In the year before the UK entered the EEC around 27 per cent of visible trade was with the community but by 1986 this had increased to 50 per cent. This is well illustrated by considering the position of one of the UK's traditional trading partners, Canada. In 1967 Canada was the second most important nation in the UK's overseas trade; by 1976 it was ninth and in 1986 it was fourteenth. Japan joined the list of the UK's top ten trading partners only in 1985. This may seem a little surprising considering the vast quantities of cars and electronic equipment imported from there. However, the list measures both imports *and* exports and as you can see from Table 38.3 there is a large deficit in the UK's balance of trade with Japan. Japan sells four times as much to the UK as it buys from it. This imbalance is, at least in part, due to the excessive protective measures which the Japanese use to guard their home market.

You will see in Table 38.3 the abbreviations FOB after exports and CIF after imports. These stand *for free on board* and *cost, insurance and freight*. The figures are valued in this way because it gives the value of exports and imports at the point they enter or leave the country.

Table 38.4 illustrates the proportion of UK exports and imports going to different parts of the world. The majority of growth in value between 1971 and 1986 is accounted for by inflation; whereas the *value* of exports has risen by 481 per cent in this time the *volume* has only risen by 41 per cent. Similarly, while the *value* of imports has risen by 465 per cent, the volume has risen by 61 per cent.

The terms of trade

The 'terms of trade' is a measure of the relative prices of imports and exports. It is calculated by taking the index of export prices and dividing it

Table 38.4 Geographical Analysis of UK's Visible Trade 1971 and 1986

Area	1971				1986			
	Exports £m	%	Imports £m	%	Exports £m	%	Imports £m	%
European Community[1]	2536	28·0	2720	30·0	34 792	48·0	43 174	53·0
Other Western Europe	1450	16·0	1470	17·0	7 197	10·0	11 366	14·0
North America	1422	16·0	1585	18·0	12 171	17·0	9 368	11·0
Other developing countries	1085	12·0	851	10·0	3 656	5·0	6 319	8·0
Oil exporting countries	584	6·0	802	9·0	5 501	7·0	1 619	2·0
Rest of world	1966	22·0	1425	16·0	9 526	13·0	9 459	12·0
Total	£9043	100·0	£8853	100·0	£72 843	100·0	£81 306	100·0

[1] Figures relate to all eleven countries
Source: Balance of Payments HMSO

by the index of import prices. The import index is compiled from a sample of the prices of 200 commodities while the export index samples 250.

The present index of the terms of trade is based on 1980. If we discover that in 1976 the index of export prices was 60.8 while that of imports was 70.9 then we can calculate the terms of trade as:

$$\frac{\text{Terms of trade}}{\text{index}} = \frac{\text{Index of export prices}}{\text{Index of import prices}} \times \frac{100}{1}$$

$$= \frac{60\cdot8}{70\cdot9} \times \frac{100}{1}$$

$$= 85\cdot7$$

If the index increases this is said to be a *favourable* movement in the terms of trade, whilst when it falls it is termed *unfavourable*. A favourable movement in the terms of trade means that a given quantity of exports will buy more imports. The word favourable may, however, be misleading; a relative rise in the price of exports will only be beneficial if the demand for exports is inelastic (see below page 511).

In the mid 1970s the index was low because of the rise in oil and other commodity prices and because of the fall in the value of sterling. The recovery in the late 1970s is attributable to the recovery in the exchange rate of sterling. During the 1980s, despite great changes in the volume and direction of trade, the terms of trade remained relatively stable.

The balance of payments

We have so far considered the export and import of goods and services. However there are many other international transactions. These are brought together in the balance of payments.

The balance of payments is an account of all the transactions of everyone living and working in the UK with the rest of the world.

If a person normally resident in the UK sells goods or services to someone abroad, this creates an inflow (+) of pounds, while anyone in the UK buying goods or services abroad creates

Table 38.5 The UK's terms of trade

	1976	1977	1978	1979	1980	1981	1982	1983	1984	1985	1986
Exports (FOB)	60·8	72·0	79·1	87·6	100·0	108·8	116·2	125·7	136·0	143·5	136·6
Imports (CIF)	70·9	82·1	85·2	90·9	100·0	108·2	116·7	127·5	139·7	145·2	134·0
Terms of trade	85·7	87·7	92·7	96·4	100·0	100·5	99·6	98·6	97·4	98·8	101·9

Table 38.6 Balance of payments of the UK 1986

Current account	£m
Visible trade:	
Exports (f.o.b.)	72 843
Imports (f.o.b.)	81 306
Visible balance ('balance of trade')	−8 463
Invisibles:	
Services	
General government	−1 399
Private sector and public corporations:	
Sea transport	−937
Civil aviation	−449
Travel	−646
Financial and other services	8 421
Interest profits and dividends	
General government	−908
Private sector and public corporations	5 594
Transfers	
General government	−2 235
Private sector	42
Invisibles balance	7 483
Current balance (1)	−980
Transactions in external assets and liabilities	
Investment overseas by UK residents	−34 256
Investment in the UK by overseas residents	+13 622
Net foreign currency transactions by UK banks	+10 494
Net sterling transactions of UK banks	−343
Official reserves (addition to (−), drawings on (+))	−2 891
Other	+2 627
Net transactions in assets and liabilities (2)	−10 747
Balancing item (3)	11 727

Source: CSO, Balance of Payments, *HMSO*

an outflow (−), while if a foreigner invests in the UK, e.g. if a US company takes over a UK company, then an inflow (+) of currency is created. Not so obviously, if the UK reduces its reserves of foreign currency, this is recorded as a credit (+), as is the receipt of loans from abroad, while, conversely, increasing the reserves of foreign currency or making a loan is shown as a debit (−). When all these transactions are recorded we arrive at a balance of payments statement as in Table 38.6.

Items in the account

The format of the balance of payments account was revised in 1986, eliminating the section of the account which was termed *official financing*. We will follow the new format. The numbers against the following headings refer to items in Table 38.6.

a) *Current account (1)*. This has two main components: *visible trade*, which is the export and import of goods (from which we get the balance **507** of trade); and *invisible trade*, which is chiefly the sale and purchase of services. The balance of trade is often confused with the balance of payments. In Table 38.6 you can see that the balance of trade is only a part of the balance of payments, albeit an important part. It is therefore possible to have a deficit on the balance of trade but a surplus on the balance of payments, or vice versa. The traditional pattern for the UK is to have a deficit on the balance of trade made up by a surplus on invisibles. One of the disturbing trends in the current account involves the growing propensity to import manufactured goods discussed above and the decline in the relative size of the invisible surplus.

b) *Transactions in external assets and liabilities.* (2). This involves the movement of capital (money) rather than goods and services, i.e. it is concerned with international loans and investment. It includes such items as:

i) UK investment overseas;

ii) overseas investment in the UK;

iii) borrowing and lending overseas by UK banks;

iv) changes in official reserves;

v) other items such as government loans to foreign countries

Item (*iv*), the changes in official reserves, refers to the increases or decreases in the reserves of gold and foreign currency held by the Bank of England. Increases in the reserves are shown as a minus (−) and drawings on (running down the reserves) as a plus (+). If this point is not clear remember that the balance of payments is recorded in £s, and, therefore, if the reserves of foreign currency increase this must be because foreigners have bought £s. This being the case £s must have left the country and hence we show this as a minus (−). Conversely if the Bank of England runs down the reserves (sells foreign currency) it will be obtaining £s in return and hence there is a flow of £s into the country (+).

The transactions in external assets and liabilities part of the account is often a deficit. Its importance has grown in recent years, as has its instability. This instability is caused by large movements of short-term capital. This so-called 'hot money' tends to move about in search of better interest rates or expectations of changes in the value of currencies. It should also be remembered that the UK is the major exporter of capital. By this we mean that Britons invest in companies and property overseas to a greater extent than foreigners invest in the UK. In the short-term, therefore, this creates an outflow. However, we should recall that, in the longer term, money will flow back into the country by way of interest, profits and dividends on the current account. The UK is, in fact, one of the world's largest creditor nations (see page 515).

Prior to the 1986 changes in format there used to be a separate section of the account termed *official financing*. In this section were the changes in official reserves and borrowing and lending to such official bodies as the IMF. It used to be said that the overall deficit or surplus on this section was needed to balance the overall deficit or surplus on the rest of the account. The reason for discontinuing this section was that it had become dwarfed by the transactions in the private sector so that it was unrealistic to speak of official financing balancing the books. There is, of course, still massive government intervention from-time-to-time but other measures are needed such as changes in interest rates.

c) *The balancing item* (3). This item is necessary to allow for statistical errors in the compilation of the account. It can be either positive or negative. Old accounts are often adjusted in the light of better information and, for this reason, the size of the balancing item may be made smaller. For example, this item was particularly large in 1986 at £11 727 million, but this would be reduced as the statistical errors were eliminated.

Types of imbalance

It is often said that the balance of payments always balances'. This is indeed true, both in the short-term and the long-term. In the short-term a balance is achieved through changes in official reserves. In the long-term we can also demonstrate that a balance will be arrived at because,

Table 38.7 Problems and solutions with balance of payments

Causes of problem	Suggested remedies
Deficit problems:	
Problem 1:	
a) Inflationary pressures, exports low because prices too high, e.g. UK 1975–6.	a) Increase productivity to lower prices and increase exports.
b) Interest rates low and therefore 'hot' money flows out to earn high interest elsewhere.	b) Tight fiscal policy and dear money policy to deflate economy; also higher interest rates attract 'hot money'.
Problem 2:	
a) Currency overvalued, therefore export low despite unemployment in the domestic economy, e.g. UK 1981.	a) Depreciate or devalue the currency if import/export elasticities are favourable.
b) Capital outflow because of investment overseas or too much government expenditure overseas.	b) Stop or reduce drain, e.g. by exchange control regulations on investment.
Surplus problems:	
Problem 3:	
a) Spare capacity in the economy, prices relatively low, exports high, e.g. West Germany 1982.	a) Easy fiscal and cheap money policies, with low taxes and higher government expenditure, boost internal economy while lower interest rates reduce inflow of 'hot money'.
b) Interest rates high, 'hot' money flows in to earn high interest.	
Problem 4:	
a) Currency overvalued, embarrassment to trading partners, exports artificially cheap while imports dear, domestic living standards restricted, e.g. Japan 1983.	a) Appreciate or revalue currency; this will reduce exports and increase imports if Marshall–Lerner conditions fulfilled.
	b) Increase capital expenditure overseas or increase foreign aid.

if there is any deficit on current account, this must be matched by a surplus on investment and other capital transactions or else by a surplus in future years. The fact that a balance must eventually be achieved may, however, obscure the fact that a disequilibrium exists in the short-term. A short-term disequilibrium need not cause major problems as it may be conveniently dealt with by a change in reserves or by borrowing or lending. A long-term or fundamental disequilibrium exists when there is a persistent tendency for outflows of trade and capital to be significantly greater or smaller than the corresponding inflows.

The correct policy for a fundamental disequilibrium will depend upon its *size, cause* and upon the *exchange rate policy* which the government is pursuing. Obviously the size of a deficit or surplus will affect its significance, but it will also be influenced by which items in the account are affected; for example, a persistent deficit on capital items might be expected to cause inflows of interest, profits and dividends in future years and, therefore, pose little problem. Even with the current account, imbalances with different items may call for different remedies. In this connection we must also consider the state of the domestic economy. Table 38.7 summarises some of the possible combinations of problems. A deficit on the balance of payments might be accompanied by either a high or a low level of domestic activity. The required solutions would obviously be very different; for example, if an external deficit was accompanied by heavy unemployment domestically, a solution which aimed at further depressing the level of economic activity would hardly be ideal. Similarly, when we consider the possibility of a surplus on

509

the balance of payments, this too could be accompanied by either a high or low level of domestic economic activity.

The type of exchange rate policy to which a country is committed will also influence the situation. When, as was the case with the UK up to 1972, the country is committed to *fixed exchange rates*, this limits the options. Under these circumstances the UK was often obliged to subordinate internal policy, such as the pursuit of economic growth, to the external objective of maintaining the exchange rate. However the adoption of a floating exchange rate has still not entirely freed internal policy from external constraints.

The problems of a surplus

Why worry?

It might not be immediately obvious that a surplus presents problems. However there are a number of reasons why it might.

a) De-industrialisation. The UK's experience of surplus in the late 1970s and early 1980s has demonstrated that a surplus can lead to undesirable domestic consequences. The oil surpluses were used to finance industrial imports, thus leading to a rundown of the economy. The surpluses also attracted 'hot' money which led to an over-valuation of the currency, which in turn decreased the competitiveness of exports. This syndrome is sometimes known as the 'Dutch disease' after the experience of the Netherlands following the exploitation of North Sea gas in the 1950s.

b) Feedback effects. Since it is the case that overall the international payments of all nations must balance, it must also be the case that whilst one economy is in surplus, others must be in deficit. A persistent surplus may, therefore, embarrass one's trading partners and force them to place restrictions on imports which are to the detriment of world trade. The activities of a country's

trading partners in getting rid of their deficits may well decrease the demand for the surplus country's exports, thus 'feeding-back' the effect of a deficit to the surplus country.

c) Inflationary consequences. Both Keynesian and monetarist analysis of a balance of payments surplus points to possible inflationary consequences. In Keynesian analysis demand-pull inflation will be caused if the economy is at, or near, full employment since a surplus is an *injection* into the economy. Monetarists argue that a surplus increase the money supply unless exchange rates are freely floating. This argument is considered in more detail below (see page 512).

d) Depression of domestic living standards. A country running a considerable balance of payments surplus is, in fact, keeping down the standard of living of its citizens. This is because the reserves of foreign currency built up by the surplus could be turned into goods and services for the population without any cost in resources to the economy.

Curing a surplus

A surplus might be reduced or eliminated by inflating the economy and/or revaluing the currency. Inflating the economy will tend to increase the demand for imports especially if the economy is at full employment. Revaluing the currency will reduce the price of imports and increase the price of exports thus tending to eliminate the surplus.

Japan had huge current account surpluses during the 1980s. This was partly a result of the superb productivity of Japanese industry but it was also due to protective measures. Under these circumstances the surplus could be reduced by getting rid of the protectionist measures.

A current account surplus is often eliminated by an outflow of funds on the capital account. This balances the books but, of course, creates further *inflow* of funds on the current account in future years.

It would also be possible for a nation to reduce its surplus by increasing overseas aid.

Deficit problems

Types of policy

The correct measures to remedy a deficit will depend upon its cause and also upon the exchange rate regime. A *short-term deficit* might be dealt with by *running down reserves* or by *borrowing*. Another short-term measure might be to *raise interest rates* to encourage the inflow of money. When there is a more *fundamental payments deficit* other measures will have to be taken.

We can divide measures to rectify a deficit into two main categories.

a) Expenditure reducing. These are measures such as *domestic deflation* which aim to rectify the deficit by cutting expenditure.

b) Expenditure switching. This refers to measures such as *import controls*, designed to switch expenditure from imports to domestically produced goods.

The two types of measures need not be regarded as alternatives but rather as *complements*; for example, a government might reduce expenditure to create spare capacity in the economy prior to creating extra demand through expenditure-switching policies.

Deflation

The demand for imports could be restrained (*expenditure-reducing*) by restricting the total level of demand in the country through fiscal and monetary policies. It might appear that this is a very indirect method. However, there are three reasons why it might be adopted. Firstly, the country may wish to maintain a *fixed exchange rate* policy. Secondly, protective measures such as import controls may *conflict with a nation's treaty obligations* such as GATT and the Treaty of Rome. Thirdly, protective measures also invite *retaliation*. These reasons explain why in the period 1947–72 deflation was the UK's chief method of rectifying a payment deficit. The recurring need to deflate the economy formed part of the so-called 'stop–go cycle'.

Using deflation to rectify a deficit is subordinating the needs of the domestic economy to the external need to maintain exchange rates. The cost of such a policy may be high in terms of unemployment.

Deflation might have a secondary expenditure-switching effect if domestic rates of inflation are reduced below those of the nation's trading partners, thus giving it a price advantage.

Protection

The various methods of protecting the home market from foreign competition were discussed on page 497). We may note here that they are aimed at *expenditure switching*. It should also be remembered that protective measures do little or nothing about the underlying causes of the deficit but attempt to cure it by simply cutting off imports. Recent years have seen a rising tide of protectionism in world trade.

If tariffs are used to restrict imports, then their efficacy will be determined by the elasticity of demand for imports. For tariffs to reduce expenditure, it is necessary for demand to be elastic.

Devaluation or depreciation

If a nation operating a fixed exchange rate drops the external price of its currency, as the UK did in 1967 when the exchange rate changed from £1 = \$2·80 to £1 = \$2·40, this is referred to as *devaluation*. If a country has a 'floating' exchange rate and it allows the external value of its currency to decrease, this is referred to as *depreciation*. Both of these actions have the same effect, i.e. exports will now appear cheaper to foreigners while imports will appear more expensive to domestic consumers. These measures are thus *expenditure switching*. In order to assess devaluation or depreciation as a method, we need to consider the elasticities of demand for imports and exports.

The Marshall–Lerner criterion

A. P. Lerner in his book *Economics of Control* applied Alfred Marshall's ideas on elasticity to **511** foreign trade. It is clear that devaluation will increase total earnings from exports only if demand for exports is elastic and, similarly, expenditure on imports will only be reduced by devaluation if demand for imports is elastic. However the question arises as to how the relative elasticities of demand affect the balance of payments position. The Marshall–Lerner criterion states that devaluation will only improve the balance of payments if the *sum of the elasticities of demand for exports and imports is greater than unity*. Conversely, a payment surplus would be reduced by *revaluation* if the same criterion was fulfilled.

The J-curve

It has frequently been observed that measures taken to rectify a balance of payments deficit have often led to an immediate deterioration in the payments position followed by a subsequent recovery. If we plot this on a graph we obtain the J-curve effect illustrated in Fig. 38.1. Why should this occur?

a) *Crises of confidence.* Measures taken to rectify a deficit may have the initial effect of creating

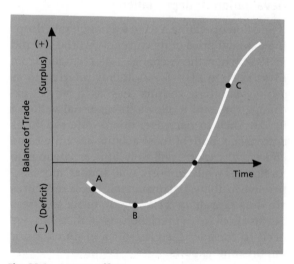

Fig. 38.1 *J-curve effect*
In response to a trade deficit at point A the government depreciates the currency. Initially this causes a further deterioration to point B before moving the balance of trade into surplus (point C).

anxiety, thus leading to an outflow of money which initially leads to a deterioration in the payments position before the (hoped for) recovery.

b) *Insufficient capacity.* If the economy is at, or near, capacity then expenditure-switching policies are unlikely to be successful immediately until capacity can be increased.

The existence of the J-curve effect is an argument for taking expenditure-reducing measures preparatory to taking expenditure-switching measures.

The absorption approach

The Keynesian approach to the balance of payments would look on it in terms of whether aggregate demand is sufficient to *absorb* national output. We write the equilibrium condition for the economy as:

$$Y = C + I + G + (X - M)$$

We can rewrite this as:

$$X - M = Y - (C + I + G)$$

The lefthand side of the equation $(X - M)$ shows the overall payments deficit or surplus. On the other side the expression $C + I + G$ may be recognisable to the reader as the figure for total domestic expenditure (TDE) (see page 84), and we have also identified Y with GDP. Thus we could say that the balance of payments will be in deficit if total domestic expenditure (TDE) is greater than national income (GDP).

From this we can argue that devaluation or depreciation of the currency will only be successful if TDE *does not absorb* the whole of GDP. For this condition to be fulfilled there must be spare capacity in the economy, otherwise output will not be able to rise to meet the increased demand for exports.

We must now consider the income effect that any depreciation of the currency might have. Any increase in value of exports which is induced will, via the *multiplier*, create an increase in national income which will in turn create more demand for imports. Thus, even if there is spare capacity in the economy, absorption will reduce the effect of any depreciation.

The absorption approach underlines the necessity to have spare capacity in the economy before attempting a depreciation of the currency, demonstrating that it may be necessary to undertake expenditure-reducing policies before expenditure-switching depreciation. The need to combat inflationary pressure created by rising import prices may also argue for the necessity to control factor incomes, for example by incomes policy.

This Keynesian approach to the balance of payments concentrates on the current account.

Capital problems

Where the deficit problems occur on the capital account different policy measures may be called for. The government needs to take action to stem the outflow of capital and/or to stimulate the inflow of capital. In the short-term capital inflows can be encouraged by raising interest-rates. However this is expensive and is also potentially dangerous if inflation is depreciating the external value of the currency and calling forth even higher interest rates.

Exchange control is a method by which capital flows may be regulated. Many countries have restrictions on the exchange of currency for investment purposes. The UK, however, abolished all exchange controls in 1979 and considerably increased the outflow of capital thereby. The outflow of capital creates inflows on current account in future years. However, when it occurs at a time when the economy is depressed, as it did in the UK during the early 1980s, it can be argued that it has very bad effects. Firstly it may starve the domestic economy of funds and secondly it is being used to develop the economies of competitors. Thus in future years the economy may have a deficit from importing goods which its own capital has produced.

A monetarist view

The effect of a payments deficit or surplus will depend upon the type of exchange rate policy being pursued. If a country is on a fixed exchange rate, a surplus will cause an expansion of the money supply because the government will be forced to buy up its currency on foreign exchange markets to prevent the exchange rate rising. A deficit would have the opposite effect. However, with a floating exchange rate any imbalance would be adjusted by appreciation or depreciation of the currency. Since monetarists place great emphasis in the control of the money supply, it is easy to see why they favour floating exchange rates.

However, it would be more strictly monetarist if we approach the payments position from the point of view of how changes in the money supply affect the balance of payments. The monetarist view is that the balance of payments is a monetary problem. The economy will be in equilibrium if the total demand for money (L) is equal to the total supply (M). The supply of money, however, is the result of that which is created domestically plus any net inflow resulting from a payments surplus or minus any outflow resulting from a deficit. According to this view, a too-rapid increase of the money supply will cause a payments deficit because the supply of money will exceed the demand because some of this money will be used to buy imports. Thus if a country wishes to maintain its payments in equilibrium it must control its money supply. Therefore a monetarist prescription for a stable balance of payments situation would be one in which there is a regime of floating exchange rates coupled with tight control of the money supply.

Stages of development of the balance of payments

Professor Samuelson has identified four stages in the development of the USA's balance of payments, from *young debtor nation to mature creditor nation*. It would be impossible to simplify all nations' balance of payments in this manner. However we may learn something of the way the world conducts its business by looking at **513**

Table 38.8 Balance of payments of selected countries 1985

	Low income		Lower middle-income		Upper-middle income			High-income oil exporters	Industrial market economies		Non-reporting
	Ghana	Pakistan	Nigeria	Jamaica	Brazil	Malaysia	Korea	Saudi Arabia	UK	Japan	USSR
Export of goods ($m)	617	2740	12 567	538	25 637	15 282	30 283	27 403	101 096	175 858	87 201
(of which primary products*) (%)	(95)	(37)	(99·0)	(88·0)	(59·0)	(73·0)	(9·0)	(98·0)	(32·0)	(2·0)	(N/A)
Import of goods ($m)	727	5890	8 877	1124	14 346	12 302	31 129	23 697	109 110	130 488	82 596
(of which primary products*) (%)	(32)	(49)	(29·0)	(45·0)	(67·0)	(26·0)	(43·0)	(14·0)	(32·0)	(72·0)	(N/A)
Balance of trade ($m)	−110	−3150	+3690	−586	+11 291	+2980	−846	+3706	−8014	+45 370	+4605
Invisibles											
Debt service ($m)	N/A	−380	−1298	N/A	−7950	−1461	−2991	−	−	−	N/A
(as percentage of exports) (gross)	(N/A)	(30·0)	(32·1)	(N/A)	(34·8)	(27·5)	(21·5)				
Other invisibles ($)	+56	+784	−1150	N/A	3614	−796	+2950	−16 673	+13 169	+3 800	N/A
Balance of payment on current account ($m)	−166	−1092	+1242	−19	−273	−723	−887	−12 967	+5 155	+49 170	N/A
Flow of external capital											
Private (net) ($m)	+119	+986	+1560	+400	+2 503	+3393	+5615	−	−	−	−
Public (net) ($m)	"	+13	+90	"	"	+735	+2501	−3 400	−7421	−4 720	N/A
Other information											
GNP per capita ($)	380	380	800	940	1 640	2 000	2 150	8 850	8 460	11 300	N/A

* Primary products includes:
Fuels, minerals and metals
Food
And other primary products.
Source: Compiled from IBRD statistics.

various nations' balance of payments. This is done in Table 38.8. The World Bank groups nations under six headings. We will also consider nations from these categories. The classification is based partly on the GNP per capita and partly upon the type and location of the economy. The first group, which is the low-income economies, is all the nations in which the GNP per capita was less than $400 per annum in 1985.

A feature you should notice for many of the poorer nations is the enormous burden of debt interest which they carry.

Low-income economies

In Table 38.8 the nations with low-income economies are represented by Ghana and Pakistan. With less developed economies one would expect to see a large proportion of their exports devoted to primary products. This is certainly true in the case of Ghana but less so in the case of Pakistan, reflecting Pakistan's growing importance as a producer of manufactured goods such as textiles. The traditional picture of poor countries as exporters of raw materials and importers of manufactured goods is becoming more and more suspect as the West's traditional areas of dominance are taken over, especially by countries around the Pacific Basin.

Nearly all low-income countries run deficits on their balance of payment current accounts and have to rely on imports of capital to keep their payments in balance. This is well illustrated in the figures for Ghana and Pakistan.

Lower middle-income economies

Nigeria and Jamaica both illustrate the case of lower middle-income economies which are heavily dependent upon the export of primary products and the import of manufactured goods. Nigeria's trade surplus is a result of its oil exports but Jamaica is not so lucky. Nigeria borrowed heavily when oil prices were high in the 1970s and was then badly hit as oil prices fell and interest rates rose in the 1980s. Jamaica has ploughed a more independent furrow and the lack of information in the table is partly due to

Jamaica's refusal to co-operate with World Bank and IMF schemes.

Upper middle-income economies

This is a diverse group of economies which includes highly successful economies such as Korea, Malaysia and Singapore. These Pacific basin economies have made spectacular strides in the export of manufactured goods. This group also includes many of the chief debtor nations of the world such as Brazil and Mexico. As you can see from the figures, 34.8 per cent of Brazil's exports were needed to pay just the interest on its debts.

High-income oil exporters

Saudi Arabia heads an exclusive group of nations whose prosperity is based on oil. Others in the group are Libya and the United Arab Emirates. They all have balance of trade surpluses. In the 1970s these trade surpluses were huge due to the high price of oil. In order to balance these surpluses the export of capital was necessary. Much of this capital found its way onto the eurocurrency market. In the 1980s the surpluses were much reduced by the fall in the price of oil but nevertheless visible trade remained comfortably in surplus.

Industrial market economies

Japan and the UK, provide examples of mature industrial economics. Japan provides perhaps the most perfect example of an industrial trading nation drawing in raw materials and exporting manufactured goods. The UK has for many years, relied upon a surplus on invisible earnings from overseas investments to balance deficits on the balance of trade. The growth in the percentage importance of primary products in the UK's exports in recent years is explained by the development of North Sea oil. Within this group is the world's wealthiest nation, the USA, which, as a result of massive balance of payments deficits, was by the end of the 1980s the world's largest debtor nation. The UK and Japan, on the other hand, were, by 1988, the two largest creditor nations in the world.

Non-market industrial economies

It would be interesting to compare the above nations' balance of payments with those of COMECON countries but unfortunately the lack of published material prevents this. They are referred to in IBRD statistics as non-reporting non-member economies.

Summary

1   The traditional pattern of the UK's overseas trade is to import raw materials and to export manufactures. This is changing; on the export side the UK is now an exporter of oil and also relies upon tertiary exports such as banking, while on the import side there is an increasing tendency to import manufactured goods.
2   The terms of trade measure the relative prices of exports and imports.
3   The balance of payments is a summary of all the nation's dealings with the rest of the world.
4   Both deficits and surpluses on the balance of payments create problems.
5   Cures for a deficit can be categorised as *expenditure reducing* and *expenditure switching*.
6   The effect of a depreciation in the external value of a currency upon a country's balance of payments depends upon the combined elasticities of demand for exports and imports.
7   The Keynesian view of the balance of payments is termed the *absorption approach*.
8   Monetarists believe that the origins of balance of payments problems are monetary and stress the need for floating exchange rates and control of the money supply.
9   The structure of a nation's balance of payments is determined by its stage of economic development.

Questions

1   List the possible cures for a balance of payments deficit.
2   Update the figures in Tables 38.3 and 38.5.
3   Consider the effects which different exchange rate regimes will have upon policies to cure balance of payments disequilibriums.
4   Define the expressions *terms of trade* and *balance of trade*. Discuss the possible relationships between the two.
5   Discuss the significance of the foreign trade multiplier.
6   Outline the changes in the UK's balance of payments since 1970.
7   Compare and contrast Keynesian and monetarist ideas of the balance of payments.
8   Consider the information in Table 38.8. What effect do you consider a considerable increase in the price of oil would have upon the balance of payments of the various countries?

9   Assume that a country is in balance of payments equilibrium on current account such that total current debits are $40 000 million and total current credits are $40 000 million. Demonstrate that, as a result of the Marshall–Lerner condition, a depreciation of 10 per cent in the country's exchange rate, *ceteris paribus*, will improve the balance of payments condition to a surplus of $4800 million if the combined elasticities of demand for exports and imports is 1·2 ($E_X + E_M = 1·2$).

Data response   **Atlantica's balance of payments** ━━━━━━━━━━━━━━━━━━━

The figures below are taken from the annual balance of payments statement of Atlantica. Prepare Atlantica's balance of payments to show:

a) the balance of visible trade;
b) the invisible balance;
c) the balance on current account;
d) transactions in external assets and liabilities;
e) the balancing item.

Items	$m
Capital transactions	+ 750
Banking earnings	+1 200
Insurance earnings	+ 500
Interest paid abroad	− 300
Interest received from abroad	+ 900
Exports of manufactures (FOB)	+18 000
Exports of raw materials and fuel (FOB)	+8 000
Imports of manufactures (FOB)	−15 000
Imports of raw materials and fuel (FOB)	−14 000
Shipping earnings (net)	+ 250
Tourist earnings	+ 500
Change in reserves	−1 200

Do these figures point to the fact that Atlantica is an undeveloped country or do they tend to suggest that it is an advanced industrial country? Give reasons for your answer.

39

Exchange rates

The pound is sinking
The peso's falling
The lira's reeling
Feeling quite appalling

Paul McCartney

The subject of international trade is complicated by the existence of different currencies. Money is a complicating factor in studying national economies but in the international sphere we have to contend with different types of exchange rate, exchange control and different units of currency. In this chapter we will examine the different regimes which exist and the problems associated with them.

Exchange rates and nationalism

The problem of exchange rates is often complicated by national pride. Many countries have wasted vast sums of money supporting unrealistic rates. Consider the vocabulary which is used if the exchange rate is high; we are said to have '*a strong pound*'; conversely a low rate is described as '*weak*' and the papers often speak of '*defending the pound*'. These are very emotive words. However, what is important is not that the exchange rate be high or low but that it should be *correct* for the circumstances.

The theory of exchange rates

Although exchange rates are often complicated by government interference, we will first examine how exchange rates are set in a free market situation. This is normally termed a *floating*, or *freely fluctuating*, exchange rate.

An exchange rate is simply the price at which one currency can be traded for another. For example, if the exchange rate is £1 = DM4 then one pound will exchange for 4 Deutschemarks or 1 Deutschemark costs 25 pence.

If people from the UK wish to buy foreign goods then they must obtain the foreign currency with which to effect the purchase. It is no good, for example, offering French vintners pounds sterling for wine; they will demand francs. Similarly if foreigners wish to buy UK goods then UK manufacturers will demand pounds in return for them. The exchange rate will be determined by the demand and supply for exports and imports.

The exchange rate for any particular country is the result the interaction of export demand and import supply.

In Fig. 39.1 we have measured all foreign currencies in dollars. Thus, foreigners wishing to buy UK goods offer dollars for them; this, therefore, constitutes the *demand for sterling*. Conversely, UK people offer pounds in order to purchase foreign goods. Thus the *demand for imports* constitutes the *supply of pounds* to the foreign exchange market.

The exchange rate is now determined like any other price. In Fig. 254 we can see that the exchange rate is £1 = $1.60 or that $1 costs 62.5 pence. It is, therefore, possible for us to analyse changes in exchange rates in the same manner as other prices.

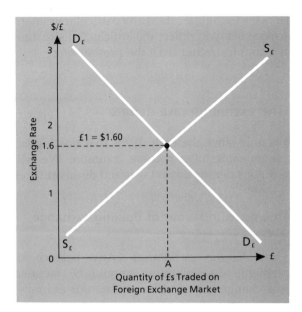

Fig. 39.1 *An exchange rate of £1 = £1.60*
Behind the demand curve lies the USA's desire to buy UK exports, while behind the supply curve is the UK's desire to buy the USA's exports.

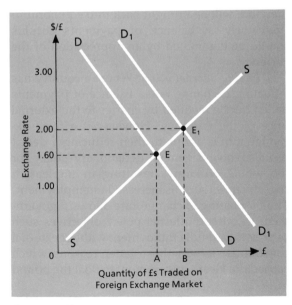

Fig 39.2 *Effect of an increase in demand on the exchange rate*
The effect of the shift of the demand curve from DD to D_1D_1 increases the exchange rate from £1 = \$1.60 to £1 = \$2. \$1 now only costs 50p.

Simple changes

If we consider any one factor then we can illustrate it as a shift rightwards or leftwards of either the demand curve or the supply curve. Figure 39.2 shows the effect of an increase demand for UK exports; foreigners are therefore offering more money so that demand for sterling increases. Thus the price of foreign currency has declined and the pound is said to have *appreciated*. If foreign currency becomes more expensive the pound is said to have *depreciated*.

An appreciation in the rate of exchange could therefore be caused by either:

a) an increased demand for UK exports; or
b) a decreased UK demand for imports.

Alternatively a depreciation in the rate of exchange could be caused by:

a) an increased UK demand for imports;
b) a reduced foreign demand for UK exports.

Complex changes

Many factors may change simultaneously and, therefore, the effect upon the exchange rate may be complex. For example, the advent of North Sea oil had at least two major effects upon the UK exchange rate. Firstly oil reduced the need for imports, thus moving the supply curve to the left, while, secondly, it became an export, thus moving the demand curve to the right. This is illustrated in Fig. 39.3.

The effect of inflation

Let us assume the UK has inflation but West Germany does not. This will mean that the sterling price of UK goods will rise. Thus, other things being equal, the demand for UK goods will decrease, whilst West German goods will now appear cheaper to Britons who will, therefore, buy more. Thus the demand for sterling will decrease while the demand for Deutschemarks will increase, and both the factors will cause a depreciation in the external value of sterling. If, on the other hand, the domestic rate of inflation

519

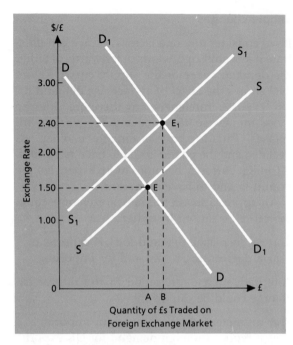

Fig. 39.3 *Effect of North Sea oil*
The exploitation of North Sea oil both increased the demand for £s as oil was exported and decreased the supply of £s as the UK imported less oil. Thus the exchange rate increased from £1 = $1.50 to £1 = $2.40.

is lower than that abroad, these factors may be expected to work in reverse. (See also page 511.)

Non-trade influences

We have, so far, discussed exchange rates as being determined by the demand for imports and exports. However, exchange rates are influenced by many other influences such as invisible trade, interest rates, capital movements, speculation and government activities.

Confidence

A vital factor in determining exchange rates is confidence. This is especially so because most large companies 'buy forward', i.e. they purchase foreign currency ahead of their needs. They are therefore very sensitive to factors which may influence future rates. Key indicators are such things as inflation and government policy.

Thus the exchange rate at any particular moment is more likely to reflect the anticipated situation in a country rather than the present one.

The exchange rate debate

It is only since the early 1970s that floating exchange rates have become common. We will here consider the advantages and disadvantages of them.

Arguments in favour of floating exchange rates

a) *Automatic stabilisation.* Any balance of payments disequilibrium should be rectified by a change in the exchange rate; for example, if a country has a balance of payment deficit then, other things being equal, the country's currency should depreciate. This would make the country's exports cheaper, thus increasing demand, whilst making imports dearer and decreasing demand. The balance of payments therefore will be brought back into equilibrium. Conversely, a balance of payments surplus should be eliminated by an appreciation of the currency.

b) *Freeing internal policy.* Where a country has a floating exchange rate a balance of payments deficit can be rectified by change in the external price of the currency. However if a fixed exchange rate is adopted, then reducing a deficit could involve a general deflationary policy for the whole economy, resulting in unpleasant consequences such as increased unemployment. Thus a floating exchange rate allows a government to pursue internal policy objectives such as growth and full employment without external constraints. It was these latter reasons which caused the Heath government to float the pound in 1972.

c) *Absence of crisis.* The periods of fixed exchange rates were frequently characterised by crisis as pressure was put on a currency to devalue or revalue. The fact that with floating exchange rates such changes occur automatically has removed the element of crisis from international relations.

d) Management. Floating exchange rates have still left governments considerable freedom to manipulate the external value of their currency to their own advantage.

e) Flexibility. Changes in world trade since the first oil crisis of 1973 have been immense and have caused great changes in the value of currencies. It is difficult to imagine how these could have been dealt with under a system of fixed exchange rates.

f) Avoiding inflation. A floating exchange rate helps to insulate a country from inflation elsewhere. In the first place if a country were on a fixed exchange rate then it would 'import' inflation by way of higher import prices. Secondly a country with a payments surplus and a fixed exchange rate would tend to 'import' inflation from deficit countries (see page 510).

g) Lower reserves. Floating exchange rates should mean that there is a smaller need to maintain large reserves to defend the currency. These reserves can, therefore, be used more productively elsewhere.

Arguments against floating exchange rates

a) Uncertainty. The fact that currencies change in value from day to day introduces a large element of uncertainty into trade. Sellers may be unsure of how much money they will receive when they sell goods abroad. Some of this uncertainty may be reduced by companies buying currency ahead in *forward exchange contracts.*

b) Lack of investment. The uncertainty induced by floating exchange rates may discourage foreign investment.

c) Speculation. The day-to-day changes in exchange rates may encourage speculative movements of 'hot money' from country to country, thereby making changes in exchange rates greater.

d) Lack of discipline. The need to maintain an exchange rate imposes a discipline upon an economy. It is possible that with a floating exchange rate such problems as inflation may be ignored until they have reached crisis proportions.

Research by the Group of 30 in 1980 concluded that as far as large business were concerned, the system of floating exchange rates has not proved a major obstacle to development of trade.

Fixed exchange rates

The Gold Standard

A gold standard occurs when a unit of a country's currency is valued in terms of a specific amount of gold. The Gold Standard Act of 1870 fixed the value of the pound sterling such that 1 ounce of gold cost £3.17s.10½d. This remained constant until 1914.

There are several types of gold standard. A *full gold standard* is where gold coins circulate freely in the economy and paper money is *fully convertible* into gold. Such was the case in the UK until 1914. A *gold bullion standard* is when gold is available in bullion form (bars) for foreign trade only. The UK adopted such a standard in 1925 which lasted until 1931. A *gold exchange standard* occurs when a country fixes the value of its currency, not in gold, but in terms of another currency which is on the gold standard. For example, from 1925–31 most Commonwealth and Empire countries fixed their exchange rates by quoting their currency against sterling.

After the 1939–45 war the USA maintained the price of gold at $35 = 1 ounce of gold. However in 1971 the USA was forced to abandon this and it is unlikely that a gold standard of any type will be readopted in the near future.

The gold standard and the balance of payments

One of the most notable features of the gold standard is that a country operating it will experience automatic rectification of any balance of payment disequilibrium.

Consider what would happen if a country had a payments deficit. In order to pay for the deficit, gold would be exported, for gold was, and is, almost universally accepted. However this would reduce the money supply in the country because the money supply is tied to gold. The result of this would be deflation. Deflation would contract the economy and, therefore, mean rising unemployment which would reduce consumers' ability to buy goods, including imports. Deflation would depress the *domestic* price of goods. Thus consumers would tend to buy more home produced goods. Imports would stay the same absolute price but would appear relatively dearer. For these reasons consumers would buy less imports whereas foreigners would buy more of the country's exports because they are cheaper. Other things being equal, this should bring the country's payments back into equilibrium. The effect of a surplus would be eliminated by this process working in reverse through inflation.

The reader will recall that floating exchange rates also automatically regulate the balance of payments. However there is an important difference from the gold standard. With the gold standard an imbalance is rectified by changes in the *internal* level of economic activity and prices. With floating exchange rates the balance is brought about by a change in the *external* value of the currency.

Pegged exchange rates

When a country is not on a gold standard but wishes to have a fixed exchange rate this can be done by the government 'pegging' the exchange rate, i.e. a rate is fixed and then guaranteed by the government. For example, after the UK left the gold standard in 1931 the government fixed the price of sterling against the dollar, in 1932, and made the rate of £1 = $4.03 effective by agreeing to buy or sell any amount of currency at this price.

Exchange control

One of the methods by which a government can attempt to make the stated exchange rate effective is through exchange control. Exchange con-

trol refers to restrictions placed upon the ability of citizens to exchange foreign currency freely; for example in 1966 the UK government would only allow Britons to convert £50 into foreign currency for holidays abroad. The Mitterand government in France imposed similar restrictions in 1983. A more serious restriction in the UK was the *dollar premium*. Under this arrangement any Briton wishing to change money into foreign currency for investment overseas had to pay a premium of 25 per cent. The Conservative government abolished all forms of exchange control in 1979. It was agreed in 1988 that, as a part of the unification of EEC markets, in 1992 there would be free movement of capital between EEC nations. However, people may still find themselves subject to restrictions by other countries, for example, anyone travelling in Eastern Europe becomes acutely aware of strict exchange controls. Very strict controls can make an unrealistic rate effective by imposing a rationing system. The situation was discussed in Chapter 11 on prices (see page 144 and Fig. 11.7).

The adjustable peg

This was the system of fixed exchange rates operated by the members of the International Monetary Fund from 1947 to 1971. Members agreed not to let the value of their currencies vary by more than 1 per cent either side of a parity. Thus, for example, the UK's exchange rate in 1949 was £1 = $2.80 and sterling was allowed to appreciate to £1 = $2.82 or depreciate to £1 = $2.78. The system was termed 'adjustable' because it was possible for a country to devalue or revalue in the event of serious disequilibrium.

Some countries operated a so-called 'crawling peg'. Under this system a currency was allowed to depreciate (or appreciate) by a small percentage each year. Thus if, for example, a limit of 2 per cent was set and the currency devalued by this amount in year 1, it would be allowed to devalue by another 2 per cent in year 2, and so on.

Since the break up of the adjustable peg system various other attempts have been made to fix exchange rates. These are discussed later in the chapter.

Fixed rates evaluated

The chief advantage of fixed exchange rates is that they give certainty to international trade and investors. It is also said that they reduce speculation. Fixed exchange rates also impose discipline on domestic economic policies because, in the event of an adverse balance of payments, deflationary measures will have to be taken to restore the situation.

On the other hand if an exchange rate is fixed incorrectly then this will cause intense speculation against the currency. It can often be an expensive job defending a fixed exchange rate, requiring large reserves of foreign exchange. Defending a currency may also involve raising interest rates, and this can be both costly and damaging to the domestic economy. It is possible, therefore, that a fixed exchange rate may result in domestic policy being subordinated to the external situation.

The equilibrium exchange rate

We have considered some of the factors which can influence exchange rates. However there is no completely satisfactory theory which explains how the equilibrium rate of exchange is established. In Fig. 39.1 we might make the assumption that the equilibrium rate will occur at the intersection of the curves when the balance of payments is in equilibrium, and that imbalances will cause shifts to new equilibriums. However we still would like to explain why the exchange rate occurs at the level it does, i.e. why is it £1 = $2 and not £1 = $3 and so on. The Swedish economist Gustav Cassell, building on the idea of the classical economists and mercantalists, attempted to explain this in terms of purchasing power parity.

The purchasing power parity theory

This theory suggests, for example, that the exchange rate would be in equilibrium if a situation existed where the same 'basket' of goods which costs £100 in the UK cost DM310 in West Germany and the exchange rate were £1 = DM3.10. In order to do this we would have to discount transport costs and tariffs. Thus a measure we might use could appear as:

$$\text{Purchasing power parity} = \frac{\text{West German consumer price index}}{\text{UK consumer price index}}$$

From this we might deduce that a doubling of the general price level in the UK whilst prices in West Germany remained constant would lead to the exchange rate being cut by one half. However no such strict proportionality exists. There are a number of reasons for this.

a) The 'basket' of goods which determines domestic price levels is different from those which are traded internationally. Items which are important domestically, such as housing, bread, rail fares, etc., do not influence foreign trade significantly.

b) Exchange rates are influenced by many other factors such as capital movements, speculation and interest rates.

c) Confidence is also a very significant factor in determining exchange rates.

Thus, we may conclude that although domestic price levels do influence exchange rates, there is no strict proportionality.

Exchange rate stability

The possibility exists that an exchange rate can be inherently unstable. To explain this we must consider the effect of the elasticity of demand for imports upon the supply of sterling to the foreign exchange market. Consider the situation of a West German wine producer who sells wine in West Germany at DM8 per bottle. The same wine is sold in the UK at £2 per bottle when the exchange rate is £1 = DM4. However if the exchange rate were to change to £1 = DM2 then, in order to recover the same DM2 per bottle, the UK price must now increase to £4 per bottle.

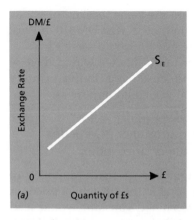 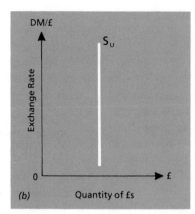 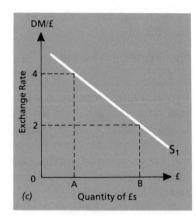

Fig. 39.4 *Elasticity of demand for imports and the supply of £s*
(*a*) When demand for imports is elastic this gives a normal supply curve. (*b*) When demand is unitary the supply of £s remains constant. (*c*) When demand is inelastic this results in a downward-sloping supply curve. This means that as the £ depreciates from £1 = DM4 to £1 = DM2 the supply of £s on the foreign change market increases.

The effect of this price change upon the supply of sterling to the foreign exchange market is determined by the elasticity of demand for wine in the UK. If demand is elastic then people reduce wine consumption substantially and the supply of sterling falls. This is shown in Fig. 39.4 (*a*). If demand is unitary then the amount of sterling offered remains constant and thus the supply curve is vertical. This is shown in Fig. 39.4 (*b*). However, if demand is inelastic then, despite the price rise, people go on drinking and, therefore, in response to a price rise the supply of pounds increases and we thus have a perverse supply curve. If Fig. 39.4 (*c*) you can see that, as the exchange rate has fallen from £1 = DM4 to £1 = DM2, i.e. the price of wine in the UK has *increased*, the supply of sterling has expanded from OA to OB.

In Fig. 39.5 we examine the possible effect of such a perverse supply curve upon the equilibrium rate of exchange. Here, as the result of a trade surplus, there has been an increase in the *demand* for sterling from foreigners. You can see that the result of this *increased* demand is a *fall* in the exchange rate. Such a perverse result is likely to bring instability to the foreign exchange market. In order for stability to be achieved it is necessary for the Marshall–Lerner condition

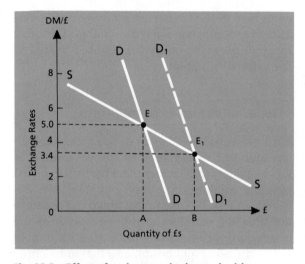

Fig. 39.5 *Effect of an increase in demand with a perverse supply curve*
Despite the fact that the demand for £s has increased from DD to D₁D₁ the exchange rate has fallen from £1 = DM5 to £1 = DM3.4.

to be fulfilled, i.e. the combined elasticities of demand of foreigners' demand for UK exports and UK demand for imports is greater than unity (see page 511). Under such circumstances a floating exchange rate should correct a balance of payments disequilibrium.

Other exchange rate theories

We have discussed exchange rate stability in terms of the demand and supply of imports and exports. However, as we mentioned earlier, there are many other factors which influence the supply and demand for sterling. Other theories have, therefore, been put forward to explain the determination of exchange rates.

a) *The portfolio balance theory*. This theory stresses the importance of international investment flows, including speculative movements, in determining exchange rates. It assumes that large investors are aware of investment opportunities worldwide. They therefore, diversify their portfolios to gain higher yield in different countries. For example, if the yield on, say, Treasury bills in London were to increase then we might expect funds to flow in from other countries. *Ceteris paribus*, this would cause sterling to appreciate until such a time that there was no advantage to be gained from switching funds into pounds. (See also discussion of portfolio balance in Chapter 36.)

The huge amount of highly liquid funds in international markets makes interest rates a key factor in determining exchange rates. However, *expectations* of future interest rates and/or exchange rates may be *more* important than existing rates. This leads us to the interest rate parity theory.

b) *The interest rate parity theory*. In the era of floating exchange rates much currency is bought 'forward'. For example, a company which may need large quantities of deutschemarks in six months' time may place an order for them now and both buyer and seller agree to exchange the currency in six months' time at the rate agreed today. This rate may be higher or lower than today's 'spot' rate depending upon *expectations* of the future. Needless to say there, there is a very large speculative market in currency *futures*.

The interest rate parity theory gets its name from the idea that differences in interest rates between countries will be reflected in the 'discount' or 'premium' at which currency futures are traded. The picture is complicated by the differences between *real* and *nominal* rates of interest, i.e. rates of inflation and expectations of rates of inflation.

Once we have progressed beyond the idea that exchange rates are determined by trade flows we can see the vital importance of other factors such as – *expectations, confidence, interest rates* and *speculation*.

Thus we can see that the determination and explanation of the equilibrium exchange rate is a complex topic. It is very difficult to give a simple answer to the straight forward question, 'What is the correct exchange rate?'

Recent developments

The operation of the International Monetary Fund is discussed in detail in the next chapter. We will here consider how developments since the early 1970s have influenced the UK economy.

Dirty floating

Following the USA's abandonment of the gold standard in 1971 and the failure of the Smithsonian agreement, the UK floated the pound in 1972. The objective of the government was that the development of the economy should be free to continue without the constraint of having to maintain a fixed exchange rate. Although ostensibly the government allowed the exchange rate to find its own level, it in fact interfered to manipulate the exchange rate. This is termed *managed flexibility*, or, more memorably, a *'dirty float'*.

Figure 39.6 illustrates government intervention in the foreign exchange market. Left to itself the exchange rate would be £1 = $1 but the government forces the rate up to £1 = $1.90 by buying sterling on the foreign exchange market, thus shifting the demand curve to the right.

The government agency responsible for intervention in the foreign exchange market is the Exchange Equalisation Account. This was set up in 1932 following the UK's abandonment of the gold standard. It is controlled by the Treasury

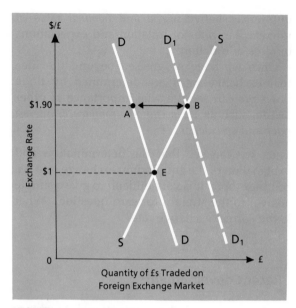

Fig. 39.6 *Dirty floating*
The government forces up the exchange rate from
£1 = $1 to £1 = $1.90 by purchasing AB £s on the
foreign exchange market.

and managed by the Bank of England. Its object is to buy and sell sterling for gold or foreign exchange in order to stabilise the exchange rate. In times of fixed exchange rates the Account has sometimes lost large sums of money defending an unrealistic rate. Since the float of 1972 the operation of the Account has been more muted, but it is its actions which give rise to the term 'dirty float'. Nearly all governments operate a similar system. The Account's operations should not be confused with the official financing of the balance of payments.

Trade weighted indices

When countries are on a gold standard there is a simple way to show the value of their currencies. However with floating exchange rates it becomes difficult. The most widely known measure of the UK exchange rate is that against the dollar, but the dollar itself is floating. It is possible, therefore, for the pound to be rising against the value of the dollar while falling against other currencies such as the yen. *Trade weighted indices*

are an attempt to overcome this problem by providing a measure of a currency in terms of a number of currencies which are weighted in accordance with their importance in trade to the country whose currency is being measured. Table 39.1 shows the Bank of England trade weighted index, known as the *sterling effective exchange rate*, based on 1975. Also in Table 39.1 is the dollar exchange rate. You can see that the two do not always move together. Additionally, Table 39.1 shows the considerable change in the fortunes of sterling in recent years.

Table 39.1 Sterling/US dollar exchange rate and sterling's effective exchange rate

Annual average	US$ to £	Sterling's effective exchange rate index
1975	2.220	100
1976	1.805	85.7
1977	1.9185	81.2
1978	2.0410	81.5
1979	2.2250	87.3
1980	2.3920	96.1
1981	2.0254	95.3
1982	1.7489	90.7
1983	1.5158	83.3
1984	1.3364	78.8
1985	1.2976	78.7
1986	1.4672	72.9
1987	1.6393	72.7
1988 (May)	1.8655	77.9

Source: Bank of England Quarterly Bulletin

Attempts at stabilisation

After the turbulence in currency markets during the 1970s various attempts were made in the 1980s to bring stability to exchange rates. These were mainly confined to the western industrialised nations. The EEC established the European Monetary System (EMS) which effectively fixes the rates of exchange between Common Market countries. The Plaza agreement (1985) and the Louvre accord (1987) attempted to limit the fluctuation in exchange rates between the G5 and G7 nations, respectively. (These systems are discussed more fully in the next chapter.) However, by the end of the 1980s most of the world still operated under a regime of floating exchange rates.

The UK: floating or sinking?

How well has the floating rate worked for the UK? When the UK floated sterling in 1972 the exchange rate was £1 = $2.60; it reached a low of £1 = $1.55 in October 1976, an effective devaluation of 40.4 per cent. This massive drop was not altogether unwelcome to the UK government, who believed it would make exports more competitive. It should be remembered, however, that increasing the price of imports will also increase inflation. It is reckoned that a 4 per cent rise in import prices causes 1 per cent domestic inflation. The UK government, however, seemed happy to settle for a rate of about £1 = $1.70, but no sooner had the rate stabilised around this level than the prospects of North Sea oil brought money flooding into London and the exchange rate soared, much to the displeasure of the government. It appeared that a pound that floated upward was almost as difficult to live with as a sinking one.

The end of the 1970s saw the UK with a large balance of payments surplus and an exchange rate almost back to the 1971 level. The 'over-valued' pound had UK industry screaming for relief. The pound then collapsed, despite a sound balance of payments and in 1983 dropped below £1 = $1.50 for the first time.

This fall continued until in February 1985 the pound dipped briefly below £1 = $1.10. It was during this crisis that the Bank of England reintroduced MLR for one day in an attempt to stop the fall. This crisis for the pound was caused both by the weakness of the UK economy and by the strength of the dollar.

The recovery of the pound over the period 1985–88 was due both to increased confidence in the UK economy and also to the weakness of the dollar. However, at the same time that the pound was rising in value against the dollar the balance of payments was moving into record deficits. The prospect for the pound was, therefore, uncertain.

We may conclude our discussion of floating exchange rates by saying that there have undoubtedly been unprecedented fluctuations in value, but there have also been unprecedented circumstances and it is doubtful if fixed exchange rates could have coped with the situation. For the UK, however, the Single European Market of 1992 meant the prospect of greater currency co-operation with its European partners.

Summary

1 The problem of exchange rates is complicated by national pride.

2 A floating exchange rate is the result of the interaction of export demand and import supply.

3 Exchange rates are also influenced by many non-trade factors such as interest rates.

4 The chief advantage of floating rates is that they free internal policy from external constraints; however this also increases uncertainty.

5 There are many types of fixed exchange rate. Fixed rates increase certainty in trade but can be expensive to defend.

6 The equilibrium exchange rate may be unstable.

7 The purchasing power parity theory attempts to explain the exchange rate in terms of the relative values of currencies.

8 The UK now operates a system of managed flexibility or a 'dirty float'.

9 The problems of floating have brought new measures such as trade weighted indices and the EMS.

10 Since floating there have been great changes in the value of sterling but there have also been big changes in international circumstances.

Questions

1 Discuss the arguments for and against floating exchange rates.
2 Explain the role of the Exchange Equalisation Account.
3 Outline the factors which are responsible for the determination of a nation's exchange rate.
4 Explain the changing fortunes of sterling in the 1970s and 1980s.
5 Assess the weaknesses of the purchasing power parity theory.
6 Explain the circumstances under which a deficit on the balance of payments current account could be accompanied by an *appreciation* of the country's currency.
7 What would be the likely effect of the following upon a country's exchange rate?
   a) An increase in the rate of inflation.
   b) An improvement in the terms of trade.
   c) Increased government spending overseas.
   d) A rise in domestic interest rates.
   e) A surplus on the balance of payments current account.

Data response The sterling exchange rate ▬▬▬▬▬▬▬▬▬▬▬▬

Read the following passage carefully. It is extracted from articles appearing in the press on 5 May 1988

The uncertainty and unpredictability of foreign exchange markets continued yesterday. *Sterling's trade weighted index* stood at 77.9 its highest value for over four years and an effective *revaluation* of 7 p.c. since last year.

The pound-dollar rate remained high at £1 = $1.86 despite *Bank of England intervention* to keep the rate down. The rise in reserves over the year of £20 billion demonstrates the magnitude the Bank's selling activities.

Money market rates point to a further rise in base rates which would certainly bring dearer mortgages.

The crucial *three month inter-bank rate* is already at a level which, if sustained would prompt another half percentage point rise in base rates to 8.5 p.c.

Concern centres on the rise in the inflation rate–now at 5.25 p.c. according to the Government's 'index of home costs', or *GDP deflator*, a more comprehensive index than the Retail Prices Index – and the weakening of the balance of payments running at an annual deficit of £11 billion on current account.

A key date was the day before the Budget in March when the pound was allowed to crash through the 3 Deutschemark barrier. The Chancellor was concerned to keep the pound at a competitive level and to honour agreements with other *G7 nations* while Mrs Thatcher stuck to her view that 'you can't buck the market' and her concern that dropping interest rates would fuel inflation.

Since the pre-Budget fracas between Nos. 10 and 11 Downing Street, the Treasury and the Bank have in theory been engaged in twin policy operation – trying to both to tighten monetary policy and to alter the 'mix' between interest rates and exchange rate levels.

They have raised interest rates significantly, but without dropping the pound to its pre-Budget level against the mark. That the Chancellor has put interest rates up at all is disgraceful. He is, in effect punishing borrowers to try to regain control over the credit boom that his tax cuts for high-income earners only exacerbated.

The present uncertainty in currency markets has increased pressure for the UK fully to join the *EMS* and to reaffirm the spirit of official currency market co-ordination which was contained in the *Plaza Agreement* of 1985

Answer the following questions:

1   Explain the terms in italics.

2   What is the significance of the level of interest rates to the determination of the exchange rate?

3   Paragraph five of the passage refers to the effects of inflation. With reference to the purchasing power parity theory, explain how relative price levels may determine exchange rates.

4   With the aid of a diagram, explain the effect that a deficit on the balance of payments current account is likely to have on the external value of a nation's currency.

5   What are the likely effects upon the economy of the rise in the value of the pound which is referred to in the passage.

6   The final paragraph of the passage refers to arrangements to stabilise exchange rates. Evaluate the benefits of such policies.

7   Under what circumstances may the equilibrium exchange rate be inherently unstable?

40

International institutions

For a'that, an' a' that,
It's coming yet for a' that,
That man to man, the world o'er,
Shall brithers be for a' that.

Robert Burns

Introduction

In July 1944 a conference took place at Bretton Woods in New Hampshire to try to establish the pattern of post-war international monetary transactions. The aim was to try to achieve freer convertibility, improve international liquidity and avoid the economic nationalism which had characterised the inter-war years. The conference was chaired by the secretary of the US Treasury, Henry Morgenthau. The conference was dominated, however, by Keynes and the American Harry Dexter-White.

Keynes had a plan for an international unit of currency. This he called the *bancor*. It was to be a hypothetical unit of account against which all other currencies would be measured. This would be administered by a world bank with which all countries would have an account. In effect this bank would perform the tasks of an ordinary bank, except its customers would be nations: cheques would be written out to settle international indebtedness; money would be *created* to finance trade; and overdrafts could be given to those countries which required them. It was essential to the concept of the bank, however, that it be allowed to determine each country's exchange rate and adjust it to ensure that nations did not fall hopelessly into debt or run gigantic surpluses. The plan foundered because nations, none more so that the UK, were unwilling to allow an international institution to determine the value of their currency.

The result was that two compromise institutions were established: in 1947 the International Monetary fund (IMF); and in 1946 the International Bank for Reconstruction and Development (IBRD). The latter is usually called the World Bank, which is misleading, for it is the IMF which contains the remains of Keynes's idea for the *bancor*, not the IBRD.

The International Monetary Fund

It was the IMF system which dominated the pattern of international monetary payments from 1945–72. The objectives of the Fund were to achieve free convertibility of all currencies and to promote stability in international money markets. Although there is now greater convertibility, there is still much to do. However up until 1972 the IMF system was reasonably stable. The IMF also attempts to give assistance to less developed countries.

In 1988 the IMF had 146 members. These included almost all the countries in the world apart from Switzerland and the Comecon countries (except Rumania and Hungary).

Quotas

Each of the members of the IMF is required to contribute a quota to the fund. The size of the quota will depend upon the national income of the country concerned and upon its share in

Table 40.1 Quotas

Country	Amount (SDR million)	%
USA	12 607·5	21.0
UK	4 387·5	7.3
West Germany	3 234·0	5·4
France	2 878·5	4·8
Japan	2 488·5	4·1
Canada	2 035·5	3·4
Italy	1 860·0	3·1
India	1 717·5	2·9
Netherlands	1 422·0	2·4
Belgium	1 335·0	2·2
Australia	1 185·0	2·0
Others	24 840·0	41·4
	60 000·0	100·0

Figures may not total due to rounding.

world trade. The quota used to be made up of 75 per cent in the country's own currency and 25 per cent in gold. Since the demonetisation of gold the 25 per cent is now subscribed in reserve assets. In this way it was hoped that there would be enough of any currency in the pool for any member to draw on should they get into balance of payments difficulties. Members' quotas are now supplemented by an allocation of SDRs (see below). Table 40.1 shows the size of members' quotas as they were in 1981.

Voting power in the IMF is related to the size of the quota. Each member is allocated 250 votes plus one vote for every 1 000 000 SDRs of its quota. In this way the USA and the other industrialised nations have managed to dominate the Fund for most of its life. It has been necessary to revise the quotas seven times, firstly to increase the overall size of quotas to take account of the growth of world trade and of inflation, and secondly to revise the relative size of members' quotas; for example, the UK's quota was originally 14.9 per cent but now stands at 7.3 per cent of the total.

Borrowing

Originally each member of the Fund could borrow in *tranches* (slices) equivalent to 25 per cent of their quota, taking up to five consecutive *tranches*, i.e. it was possible to borrow the equivalent of 125 per cent of one's quota. Today it is possible to borrow up to the equivalent of 450 per cent of one's quota over a three year period. This is not, however, an unconditional right to borrow, for the Fund may, and usually does, impose conditions of increasing severity upon a member as it increases its borrowing.

The methods of borrowing from the Fund have received several modifications.

a) Standby arrangements. Devised in 1952, this method of borrowing has become the most usual form of assistance rendered by the Fund. Resources are made available to a member which they may draw on if they wish. Attaining a standby facility is often enough to stabilise a member's balance of payments without them actually drawing it, in the same way that the guarantee of a bank overdraft will often stabilise a company's finances. It is still necessary for a member to agree to conditions for each *tranche*.

b) General agreement to borrow (GAB). In 1962 the leading 10 industrialised nations – the Group of 10 – agreed to make a pool of $6 billion available to each other. Although channelled through the IMF, the Group of 10 would decide itself upon whether or not to give assistance, and it also restricted its help to the Group. Since 1984 the size of the pool has been increased to SDR 17 billion and the GAB has agreed to help less developed countries. Switzerland joined the GAB in 1984. Also in 1984 the Saudia Arabian Monetary Agency agreed with the IMF that it would be prepared to consider supplementary lending under the GAB of up to SDR 1.5 billion.

c) Compensatory finance scheme. Started in 1963, this was a system to give loans with fewer conditions to members experiencing temporary difficulties because of delays in the receipt of their export credits. By the early 1980s this accounted for almost one-third of all the Fund's lending.

d) Buffer stock facility. This was a scheme, introduced in 1969, to give loans to members to allow them to pay their subscriptions to buffer

531

stock schemes (see pages 145 and 159). It was principally used by members of the international tin agreement and the international sugar agreement.

e) The extended fund facility. This was a scheme introduced in 1974 to give longer-term assistance to members experiencing more protracted balance of payments difficulties.

f) The supplementary financing facility. This scheme was started in 1979. Its aim was to give longer-term loans to less developed countries. It has a special fund of SDR 7.8 billion made available by 14 of the wealthier countries, including the USA, Saudia Arabia and West Germany.

Special drawing rights (SDRs)

In 1967 it was decided to *create* international liquidity for the first time. This was done by giving members an allocation of special drawing rights. These do not exist as notes but merely as booking entries. When they were introduced in 1970 they were linked to the dollar and thus to gold (SDR1 = $1) and became known as 'paper gold'. However since 1974 the value of a unit of SDR has been calculated by combining the value of leading currencies. Originally based on 16 currencies, this was reduced to 5 in 1981. Table 40.2 shows the weights within the basket in 1981.

Table 40.2 Percentage weight in SDR currency 'basket', 1981

Currency	%
US dollar	42
Deutschemark	19
Japanese yen	13
French franc	13
Pound sterling	13

SDRs are the nearest equivalent so far to Keynes's idea of the *bancor*. (Other hypothetical units of account exist, such as the European currency unit – see page 541).

The functions of SDRs can be summarised as follows.

a) A means of exchange. SDRs can be used to settle indebtedness between nations, but only with the consent of the Fund. However they cannot be used commercially.

b) A unit of account. All IMF transactions are now denominated in SDRs. Several other institutions use the SDR as the unit of account, including the Asian Clearing Union, the Economic Community of West Africa and the Suez Canal Company.

c) A store of value. In 1976 at the Jamaica conference it was decided to reduce the role of gold and make the SDR the principal asset of the IMF.

It can therefore be seen that the SDR fulfils the most important functions of money but only to a limited extent. We could therefore best describe it as quasi-money (see page 420). If world trade is not to be limited by lack of international liquidity, further development of SDRs is required.

The adjustable peg

At the heart of the IMF system was the regime of fixed exchange rates known as the adjustable peg. This was described in Chapter 39 (see page 522). When the UK joined the Fund in 1947 her exchange rate was £1 = $4.03. In 1949 the UK, along with most other countries, devalued against the dollar so that the rate became £1 = $2.80. This rate lasted until 1967 when Britain devalued to £1 = $2.40. The Smithsonian agreement of 1971 was an attempt to patch-up the adjustable peg system and saw the pound revalued to £1 = $2.60. The 1970s, however, saw a collapse of the adjustable peg. We will now have a look at the break-up of this system.

The break-up of the IMF adjustable peg system

The 1967 crisis

Although it was not realised at the time, the UK's 1967 devaluation marked the beginning of the end for the adjustable peg system. The basis of economic power in the world had changed greatly since 1947 when the Fund was set up. At that time the economies of West Germany and Japan lay in ruins, but no changes came about in the IMF system to take account of their subsequent recovery. The UK and the USA solidly refused to *devalue* their currencies while West Germany and Japan refused to *revalue* theirs. In 1967 the UK could resist the pressure no longer and devalued.

This precipitated worldwide uncertainty. Speculators realised that gold was undervalued at $35 = 1 ounce and there was, therefore, great pressure on the USA to devalue. The final attempt to save the gold standard occurred in 1968 when a two-tier rate was established. This meant that the price of gold for monetary purposes was maintained at $35 while the price of gold for commercial purposes was allowed to float upwards.

The USA leaves the gold standard (1971)

The announcement by President Nixon in August 1971 that the USA would no longer exchange dollars for gold at the official price ended the gold standard. This was forced upon the USA by a massive balance of payments deficit. The fundamental reason for this was realignment of the economic power in the world which had led to massive and continuing surpluses and the accumulation of vast reserves by West Germany and Japan. However the situation was made worse for the USA by more immediate circumstances.

a) Inflation. This made the price of gold ever more unrealistic.

b) Speculative pressure. The vast USA deficit meant that there was a large amount of dollars on the foreign exchange market which could be used to speculate upon a rise in the price of gold.

c) The Vietnam war. One of the consequences of the unpopularity of this war was that the US government was not able to increase taxation to pay for it. The war was, therefore, partly financed by running up a deficit on the balance of payments.

d) The 'Watergate' election. President Nixon desperately needed to reflate the economy to win the election of Autumn 1971. This was fatal for the external position of the dollar.

The Smithsonian agreement 1971

The abandonment of the gold standard swept away the adjustable peg system since the world reference point for currencies had disappeared. The Smithsonian agreement of December 1971 was an attempt to re-establish the adjustable peg. This agreement put the value of gold at $38 per ounce, an effective devaluation of the dollar of 8.9 per cent. The new rate for the pound was therefore £1 = $2.60.

The Smithsonian peg allowed a $2\frac{1}{4}$ per cent variation in the value of a currency (as opposed to the 1 per cent of the 1947 system). This meant that the maximum possible variation between three currencies (cross parities) was 9 per cent. The variation was unacceptable to the EEC countries and therefore, on 24 April 1972, they established a variation between their own currencies of half that of the Smithsonian variation. The Smithsonian variation was said to provide the *tunnel* within which the smaller European *snake* moved. The UK joined the snake on 1 June 1972 but left 54 days later when Anthony Barber, the then Chancellor of the Exchequer, announced that the pound was to float.

The Smithsonian agreement was short-lived, as most countries were obliged to float their currencies in 1972 and 1973. However two legacies remain. As it was the last time when most currencies were fixed against each other it is a reference point, and one still finds many references to the *Smithsonian parities*. The other legacy is the European currency snake. Although abandoned in the mid-1970s it became the EMS in 1979 (see page 541).

The oil crises

The instability which was started in 1971 was made much worse by the oil crisis. As a result of **533** the Yom Kippur war of 1973, oil supplies were cut off. When they were resumed the OPEC countries contrived a fourfold rise in price. It is possible to argue that the resulting transfer of money from the developed countries to OPEC nations brought about one of the most fundamental shifts in economic power of all time. It is estimated that this cost the oil importing countries an extra $100 billion per year.

Then in 1978 oil prices were again raised dramatically, this time doubling, and causing a liquidity problem even greater than that of 1973. This price rise was a major factor in the subsequent world depression. This hit the industrialised countries hard but was disastrous for *non-oil exporting developing countries* (NOEDCs). The subsequent slump in oil prices left some less developed oil exporters such as Mexico saddled with large debts which they found it impossible to service.

The Plaza agreement 1985 and Louvre accord 1987

In the mid 1980s there was a concensus of opinion among the leading industrial nations that they would prefer to see a more stable system of exchange rates. The Plaza agreement (so called after the Plaza Hotel, New York) was an agreement by the monetary authorities of the G5 nations (see below) to bring about an orderly decline in the value of the dollar which was then considered overvalued.

The Louvre accord (so called because it was arrived at in Paris) was an agreement among the G7 nations to stabilise variations in their exchange rates within certain limits. These limits were not published. However, they could, at least partly, be deduced from the actions of central banks. For example, in March 1988 it became obvious that the Bank of England was committed to holding the pound below the level of £1 = DM3. In the event this was not possible.

These agreements illustrate the urge to return to a more orderly pattern of exchange rates. The fact that they were not arrived at through the IMF also illustrates its decline in importance.

The terms G5 and G7 may be in need of some explanation. The GAB (1962) was said to have been founded by 'the Group of Ten'. This was abbreviated by journalists to G10. Subsequently the Group of Five leading industrialised nations – the USA, Japan, West Germany, France and the UK – became G5. When, by the addition of Canada and Italy, the Group of Five became the Group of Seven, this was abbreviated to G7.

The problem of international liquidity

When we speak of the problem of international liquidity we are referring to the lack of universally acceptable means of payment. Since the 1939–45 war the dollar and, to a lesser extend, the pound have attempted to fulfill this role. The regime of floating exchange rates has worsened the problem. Today we can summarise the stock of *official* international liquidity as being the gold and foreign currency reserves held by nations, plus their quotas at the IMF and their allocation of SDRs. It could be argued that there has been an excess of *unofficial* liquidity. The expansion of eurocurrency business in the 1970s left many developing nations hopelessly in debt. By the end of the 1980s many of the debtor nations found it impossible to borrow money on the commercial market. However, the scale of the debt problem was so great that the reserves of the IMF and other international agencies were totally inadequate to deal with it. Put more bluntly, the IMF did not have enough funds to help the debtor nations even if it wanted to.

The role of the IMF

In this section we have examined how the orderly arrangements of the IMF broke down in the turbulent times of the 1970s. In 1976 the annual conference of the IMF came to the *Jamaica agreement*. This agreement officially recognised the end of the system of fixed exchange rates. It also 'demonetised' gold, i.e. the official price of gold was abolished. Member countries were no longer allowed to use gold as part of their quota subscriptions to the IMF. In addition to this the IMF agreed to get rid of one third of its stocks of gold. This it did by sales and by transfers to members.

The role of the IMF declined significantly during the 1980s. Many developing nations were considered uncreditworthy by the IMF. In addition to which some nations were unwilling to borrow from the IMF because of the strict austerity programme which the IMF laid down when giving loans. Debtor nations turned to private sources. The *Financial Times* commented in 1987. 'More and more debtors have been winning concessions from their private creditors (i.e. international lending banks) while the IMF has been relegated to a subordinate role. In January (1987) Brazil became the first country without an IMF programme to negotiate a scheduling of its government-to-government debt.'

The role of the IMF with more advanced nations was also reduced. The regime of floating exchange rates lessened the need to borrow foreign currency for official purposes. In addition to this the drop in oil prices got rid of the current deficits of many nations.

Thus by the end of the 1980s we had the anomaly of a major debt crisis in the developing nations but the major international lending agency taking a back seat. (The debt crisis is discussed in Chapter 46).

Eurocurrencies

There is no one institution which is concerned with eurocurrencies. However, it is convenient to consider them in this chapter since they have such an enormous impact on world trade. For example, the amount of transactions in eurocurrencies is far greater than all IMF business.

Defining a eurocurrency

Eurocurrencies were referred to in Chapter 34. We may formalise our definition thus:

A eurocurrency is any deposit in a financial institution which is not denominated in the national currency

For example, deposits of sterling in a French bank which continue to be denominated as sterling and not as francs are eurocurrency – in this case eurosterling. A glance at the balance sheet of any commercial bank (see page 436) will show just how much such business they do. Most eurocurrency deposits are in dollars.

The origins and growth of the markets

The original market was the eurodollar market. This emerged in London in the 1950s to handle the supply of US dollars in Europe. The dollar, you will remember, was then (as now) the most important international unit of account. Therefore companies, not necessarily dealing with the USA, demanded dollars for the purposes of international trade.

Up to 1957 sterling also fulfilled a similar role but in that year the government restricted its use in third-party deals outside the *sterling area*. Merchant banks and others who had specialised in this trade switched to dollars. (Sterling deals in London would not be eurocurrency but dollar deals in London are – see definition.)

a) Growth in the 1950s and 1960s. In addition to the demand from traders for dollars the growth of the eurodollar market was further accelerated by the following factors:

(i) US balance of payments deficits which created a supply of dollars outside the USA.

(ii) Comecon countries preferring to hold their dollar reserves in London rather than the USA.

(iii) Relaxation of exchange controls elsewhere in Europe allowing the holding of foreign currency reserves in London by individuals and institutions.

(iv) Regulation Q which restricted the interest rates which US banks could pay and, therefore encouraged Americans to place deposits in London to gain higher rates. (See also page 144.)

The 1960s also saw the introduction of new **535**

financial instruments such as certificates of deposit which encouraged dealing. In this period we also saw the beginning of trade in other eurocurrencies, notably the eurodeutschemark.

These forces combined to make London the world centre of eurocurrency dealing.

b) *The 1970s.* There was a spectacular growth of the eurocurrency markets in the 1970s. Towards the end of the decade business was expanding at the rate of 30 per cent per year! There were two main reasons for the growth. Firstly the huge rise in oil prices in 1973 and again in 1978 left the oil-exporting countries with huge dollar surpluses (all oil transactions are in dollars). A very large proportion of these surpluses were placed on short-term deposit in Europe. Secondly the regime of floating exchange rates encouraged speculation and freed many currencies from exchange restrictions.

c) *The 1980s.* This period saw a drastic slowing down in the expansion of the markets. This was partly a result of the worldwide recession but more especially of the world debt crisis. Many developing countries who had been borrowers in the 1970s found it impossible to service their debts in the 1980s when real interest rates were much higher.

Despite this slow-down, by the end of the decade the total gross lending in eurocurrencies was over £2000 billion. An amount almost equal to the GDP of the USA and eight times that of the UK.

What and where are the eurocurrency markets?

The leading eurocurrency is the dollar, accounting for something like 74 per cent of the market. The second most important is the deutschemark, other eurocurrencies are the Swiss franc, the yen and sterling. One reason why the pound is a relatively unimportant eurocurrency, while London is the leading market may be obvious to you, i.e. deals in sterling in London would not (by definition) be eurocurrency deals. In addition to this there is only a limited demand for sterling because of the UK's relatively small share of world trade.

We have just mentioned that the yen is a eurocurrency; we have also seen that the leading eurocurrency is the dollar and some of the largest depositors are Arabic. Thus, there is nothing exclusively European about eurocurrencies. This is also reflected in the geographical location of the leading dealing centres. London is the pre-eminent centre. Other centres include Zurich, Hong Kong, Luxembourg, Paris, Tokyo, Singapore, Bahrain and Nassau. (Why isn't New York in the list?)

The importance of the eurocurrency markets

The sheer size of the markets makes them important but activities in the markets have important effects nationally and internationally. The markets are a source of finance for both companies and countries. In particular developing nations such as Brazil and Mexico have borrowed heavily on the eurocurrency markets. The level of interest rates in the markets influence interest rates world-wide. Many loans are at variable interest and are often tied to a key rate such as LIBOR (London Inter-Bank Offered Rate).

The eurocurrency markets are largely beyond the effective control of government but they impinge upon the operation of domestic monetary policy. The fact that banks can switch easily into and out of eurocurrencies makes it very difficult for direct controls (e.g. special deposits) on banks to be effective. This was well illustrated in 1979 when the government abolished the 'corset' (see page 459). The immediate effect of this was a surge in £M3 as banks switched liquidity they had been 'hiding' in eurocurrencies back into sterling. Because of these problems the monetary authorities have to rely to a much greater extent on the control of interest rates as a method of monetary policy.

The mobility of eurocurrency deposits is a source of instability bringing unwelcome changes in the exchange rate. For example, if interest rates were raised in the UK this could lead to a switch from eurodollars to sterling and hence to an appreciation of the pound and/or a growth in the money supply in the UK. Both of these consequences may be unwelcome.

The existence of the eurocurrency markets may, therefore, be another argument for the return to a more stable regime of exchange rates.

Other international institutions

The World Bank (IBRD)

The International Bank for Reconstruction and Development, or World Bank, was set up in 1947 as the sister organisation to the IMF. Its original aim was to make loans to develop the war-shattered economies of Europe. The IMF's purpose is not to give loans to finance development projects; this is the job of the IBRD. One of the chief problems facing the IBRD is its lack of funds. Funds come from three sources.

a) Quotas. The membership of the IBRD is the same as that of the IMF. Members make contributions in relation to their IMF quota. Of the quota, 10 per cent is subscribed while the other 90 per cent is promised as a guarantee for the Bank's loans.

b) Bonds. The World Bank sells bonds on the capital markets of the world.

c) Income. A very small proportion of the Bank's funds come from the Bank's earnings.

As it developed the World Bank turned its attention from Europe to the poorer countries of the world. Today it is almost wholly concerned with helping LDCs. It is a valuable source of advice and information, besides making loans.

The World Bank has also increased its operations by forming new organisations.

a) The International Finance Corporation (IFC). This was set up in 1956 to enable to Bank to give loans to private companies as well as governments

b) The International Development Association (IDA). The object of this organisation, set up in 1960, was to make loans for longer periods and on preferential terms to the LDCs. The IDA has become known as the 'soft loan window'.

c) The Multilateral Investment Guarantee Agency (MIGA). This agency was set up by the G7 nations in 1988 and is operated by the World Bank. The object of the agency is to guarantee long-term private investment in developing countries. The political instability in many nations makes it difficult and expensive for them to borrow. The agency guarantees investors' funds against such things as expropriation by dictators but it does not, however, guarantee them against normal commercial risks. The effect of the agency's guarantee is to level the degree of risk in investments with that in other, more advanced or stable, nations.

As with the IMF, we may conclude that although there is a great need for the services of the IBRD its role is limited. The limitation comes both from lack of funds and from political disagreements. Increasingly the work of the World Bank is overshadowed by that of commercial lending to developing nations.

GATT (the General Agreement on Tariffs and Trade)

At the same time as the negotiations on international payments were taking place at Bretton Woods, other negotiations were underway to set up a sort of worldwide common market to be named the International Trading Organisation (ITO). However, the talks foundered and all that was achieved was the General Agreement on Tariffs and Trade (GATT). Nonetheless GATT has been the most important organisation for the promotion of free trade. GATT came into existence as a result of the Havana Charter in 1948. The main points of GATT are these.

a) 'Most favoured nation.' Every signatory was to be treated as 'a most favoured nation', i.e. trading privileges could not be extended to one member without extending them to all. Existing systems of preference were allowed to continue but could not be increased.

b) Tariffs and quotas. Members agreed to work towards the reduction of tariffs and the abolition of quotas. In the first 30 years of its existence GATT was fairly successful in these objectives, but in recent years protectionism has once again become widespread.

c) Trading blocs. The establishment of common-market-type agreements such as EEC and EFTA were allowed but they were encouraged to be outward looking rather than insular.

Progress in GATT was through a series of rounds of talks, the most famous of which was the *Kennedy round* of the 1960s. In recent years the emphasis has shifted to the gap between the rich northern countries and the poor southern nations. This has become known as the north-south dialogue. The forum for these discussions is now the United Nations Conference on Trade and Development (UNCTAD). The object of the poorer nations can be summed up in the phrase 'trade not aid'. The poor countries are mainly producers of primary products, but they are unable to trade freely with the rich northern countries because they are discriminated against by protectionist policies such as those of the EEC. The depression of the 1970s and early 1980s and increased protectionism amongst the rich has made the plight of the poorer countries worse. The plight of the poor nations of the world is desperate but the high ideals of international cooperation of the immediate post-war years seem to be receding.

OECD (the Organisation for Economic Cooperation and Development)

In 1947 the Organisation for European Economic Cooperation (OEEC) came into existence to administer the European recovery programme ('Marshall aid'). This was an important institution and, amongst other things, helped to establish the European Payments Union (EPU). By 1961 it was thought that the OEEC had succeeded in the task of redeveloping Europe and it became the OECD, a more widely-based organisation. Its objectives are:

a) to encourage growth, high employment and financial stability amongst members;

b) to aid the economic development of less developed non-member countries.

The OECD now has 21 members, including most of the European countries, the USA, Canada, Australia, and Japan who joined in 1965.

One of the most important functions of the OECD is to provide information and statistics. In fact all the international organisations we have discussed in this chapter are important sources of information; the reader may like to consult the OECD *Economic Outlook*, the IMF's *Annual Report* and the IBRD's *World Development Report*.

The Bank for International Settlements (BIS)

This institution is based in Basel, Switzerland. It was set up after a proposal by the Young Committee in 1930. Its original purpose was to enable central banks to coordinate their international payments and receipts. Originally it arose out of the need to regulate German reparations. It is one of the oldest surviving and most successful of international institutions.

Since the 1939–45 war, the BIS has acted like a central bank for central banks. The board of the BIS is made up of representatives of the central banks of the UK, France, Germany, Belgium, Italy, Switzerland, the Netherlands and Sweden. Other countries such as the USA and Japan regularly attend meetings.

The chief functions of the BIS are as follows:

a) the promotion of cooperation between central banks;

b) organising finance for nations in payments difficulties;

c) monitoring eurocurrency markets;

d) provision of expert advice for the OECD and the EMS;

e) administration of the EEC's credit scheme.

Not only is the BIS one of the oldest and most successful of international institutions, it is also a self-supporting and profit-making institution!

The European Economic Community

The origins of the Community

The beginnings of the EEC can be traced back to the foundation of the European Coal and Steel Community (ECSC) which was set up in 1952 by France, Italy, Belgium, Holland and Luxembourg. The UK participated in the negotiations but declined to join. West Germany later joined the ECSC, the object of which was to abolish trade restrictions on coal and steel between member countries and to coordinate production and pricing policies. The outcome of further negotiations was the Treaty of Rome in 1957 and on 1 January 1958 the EEC (usually referred to as the Common Market) came into existence. Once again the UK participated in early negotiations but then withdrew.

After two later abortive attempts to join the EEC the UK finally became a member in 1972, together with Ireland and Denmark. Norway decided, by a referendum, not to become a member. Greece became a member in 1981 and Spain and Portugal in 1986. The introduction of the Single European Act in 1987 should complete the process by which these twelve economies function as one.

The main features of the EEC

There are two main features of the EEC.

a) *Customs union.* The establishment of a full customs union involves both the *abolition of tariffs* between members and the erection of a *common external tariff* to the rest of the world; if each country did not have the same external tariff then imports would simply flood into the community through the member state with the lowest tariffs. To arrive at the common external tariff the general policy has been to take the arithmetic mean of the previous six tariffs. In some cases, e.g. the imports of produce from France's tropical ex-colonies, the lowest duty was adopted since there was no conflict with domestic production. Several of the old colonial states have *associated status* with the EEC. The original arrangements for these states was superseded by the Lomé Convention in 1975. Under this, 46 developing nations in Africa, the Caribbean and the Pacific (ACP states) are allowed to send all their industrial exports and most of their agricultural exports to the EEC duty free.

When the UK joined the EEC it was particularly difficult for her to agree to the common external tariff because she formally enjoyed duty free imports from Australia, Canada and New Zealand. The agricultural products of the highly efficient farmers in these temperate countries were in direct competition with European farmers. The UK was not allowed to join until she agreed to erect considerable tariff barriers against her Commonwealth partners.

b) *Common market.* The EEC is colloquially known as the Common Market, but this is only one aspect of its organisation, although potentially the most important. The term refers to the running of the economies of the members as if they were one, i.e. the common prices and production policy of the ECSC was to be extended to all industries. A common market agreement implies the free movement of labour, capital and enterprise within the EEC. So far it is only in the common agricultural policy (CAP) that there is a truly common policy (see pages 155–56). Despite the fact that the EEC has been in existence since 1957 it is only in 1992 that a true common market should be created. It is possible, however, that subtler forms of non-tariff barriers may continue.

The structure of the EEC

The Treaty of Rome envisaged that the EEC would eventually lead to economic and political unity. Although at present this has become more unlikely than it seemed some years ago, it is possible to discern the four essential components of state organisation.

a) *The Council of Ministers.* This could be described as the executive or cabinet of the EEC. It consists of one minister from each state; **539** which minister it is depends on what is being discussed. If, for instance, the issue were agriculture then it would be the ministers of agriculture who would attend. Voting in the council is weighted; the UK, for example, has ten votes while Luxembourg has only two. The Council is assisted by a committee of permanent representatives (Coreper).

b) *The European Commission.* This consists of 17 permanent commissioners (two from each of the five largest countries and one from each of the other seven). The Commission is the secretariat of the EEC. Behind the Commission there is a staff of about 2,500 people working in the Commission's headquarters in Brussels. The Commission is responsible for the day-to-day running of the Community. It is also responsible for the development of EEC policy. It is proposals by the Commission on such things as food hygiene which provoke outbursts in the UK press about 'the European sausage' or 'the European chicken'. More seriously, things such as the introduction of tachographs into lorry cabs have provoked great opposition from many people in the UK.

c) *The European Parliament.* The institution which meets in Strasbourg is the embryonic legislature of the EEC. Originally it consisted of MPs nominated by national parliaments. However, since 1979, members have been elected directly to the European Parliament. At present there are 518 members of the European Parliament (MEPs), of which the UK elects 81. As yet the Parliament has little authority or power. Its main function is to monitor the activities of other Community institutions.

d) *The European Court of Justice.* Not to be confused with the European Court of Human Rights, the function of the European Court of Justice is to 'ensure that the law is observed in the interpretation of the Treaty of Rome'. It is the final arbiter on all questions involving *interpretation* of the EEC treaties and it deals with disputes between member states and the Commission and between the Commission and business organisations, individuals or EEC officials. It is, thus the judiciary of the EEC.

The UK and the EEC

In 1972 the UK Parliament passed the European Communities Act and in 1973 the UK, together with Ireland and Denmark, joined the EEC. In joining the EEC the UK became part of a community of 260 million people (320 million since the accession of Greece, Spain and Portugal). The economic advantages which the UK gained were enormous and fundamental – those of increased *specialisation* and *comparative advantage* (see Chapter 37), i.e. the potential market for UK goods increased six fold. In many ways it was impossible for the UK to stay out of the EEC since, amongst other things, UK industry had already joined by exporting capital to Europe. The gains from the EEC are not, however, readily appreciated by the average citizen. Real advantages such as an increased rate of growth in GDP may seem abstract whereas minor changes such as those in driving licences and passports cause disproportionate annoyance.

More seriously the common tariff of the EEC prevents us from benefiting from comparative advantage worldwide. The most obvious example is foodstuffs, whereby the UK is condemned to eat expensive European food when it could be imported more cheaply from the elsewhere. This diminution of comparative advantage is termed *trade diversion*.

Despite the 1992 changes complete economic unity is a long way off. Meanwhile the EEC aims at the *harmonisation* of the economies of members. Some of the implications of this for the UK are listed below. The measures considered are an attempt to move towards a true common market in Europe, allowing the free movement of labour, capital and enterprise.

a) *Taxes.* It is EEC policy that there should be no big differences between rates and methods of taxation. One of the reasons why VAT was introduced in the UK was to bring it into accord with the EEC. Differences in taxes can be discriminatory. France, for example, claims that high excise duty on wine in the UK discriminates against French exports.

b) Social security. It is EEC policy that social security benefits and payments be similar and transferable. This will enable people to work more easily in different countries.

c) Competition. EEC law is aimed at regulating competition throughout the EEC. One example of this was the case of the Distiller's Company Ltd, who in 1977 were ordered to stop their practice of selling the same brand of whisky at different prices in different countries of the EEC (see page 220).

d) Metrication. Most of the EEC members have always used similar weights and measures, but for the UK this meant abandoning the old imperial and avoirdupois standards in favour of metric units, e.g. in 1981 petrol began to be sold in litres rather than gallons.

e) Free movement of labour. It is part of EEC policy that its citizens should be free to work anywhere in the EEC. Generally, however, it is necessary to have obtained a job in the country to which one wishes to move before a work permit is granted.

f) Monetary union. It is an objective of the EEC that there should be totally free convertibility between members' currencies, and the estab-lishment of a European monetary union (EMU). (See below.)

g) Free movement of capital and enterprise. There is supposed to be freedom for capital and enter-prise to move anywhere in the EEC. After 30 years of the EEC many barriers to be movement of capital remained. Again it is anticipated that the 1992 changes will lead to a much freer movement of capital.

A comparison of the economies of the members of the EEC can be made by studying the figures in Table 40.3. You can see from the figures in Table 38.3 (see page 503) the increasing depen-dence of the UK upon European trade.

In joining the EEC the UK was only following the trend of her own trade, the European market having occupied a larger and larger share of UK trade since the 1939–45 war. While the EEC may be beneficial to the UK, many third world countries have described it as 'a rich man's club'. This is because the common external tariff seems designed to keep out many primary pro-ducts (see page 631). The USA has also attacked the EEC's protective duties, but since the USA is one of the world's most protectionist nations

Table 40.3 The economies of the EEC members compared.

	Greece	Belgium	Denmark	Germany	France	Ireland	Italy	Luxem-bourg	Nether-lands	United Kingdom	Spain	Portugal
Population (millions 1984)	9.9	9.9	5.1	61.4	54.3	3.5	56.7	0.4	14.3	56.4	38.4	10.1
Employment (per cent, 1983)												
Agriculture	29.4	3.0	8.2	5.6	7.9	16.6	11.9	4.6	5.0	2.6	18.0	23.8
Industry	27.8	30.7	26.7	41.6	33.0	29.2	34.5	35.9	27.1	32.9	32.7	34.0
Services	42.7	66.3	65.1	52.8	59.1	54.2	53.6	59.5	67.9	64.4	49.3	42.2
Gross Domestic Product Average annual growth 1978–83 (per cent)	1.1	1.2	1.4	1.2	1.5	2.2	1.4	0.0	0.3	0.8	1.0	2.9
Per inhabitant in 1983 (PPS)*	5759	11 176	12 053	11 977	11 776	7040	9102	11 833	10 702	10 238	7616	5001
Standard of living Private consumption per head in 1983(ECU)†	2729	6135	6771	7351	6894	3360	4483	5889	6127	5373	3406	1533
Telephones per 1000 inhabitants 1983	338	417	718	570	544	236	406	587	382	521	352	169
Doctors per 100 inhabitants in 1983	2.5	2.6	2.4	2.4	2.1	1.3	3.2	1.7	2.0	1.7	2.5	1.8
Cars per 1000 inhabitants in 1983	110	331	272	399	363	208	364	385	333	318	230	:

* PPS = Purchasing power standard
† ECU = European currency unit

Source: Eurostat

this is not to be taken seriously. The USSR, however, remains opposed to the EEC on political grounds because it does not wish to see a strong united Europe.

The European Monetary System (EMS)

The EEC countries operate a system of exchange rates designed to limit the fluctuations in the value of their own currencies. However, the EEC currency 'snake' (see page 532) is allowed to depreciate and appreciate in terms of other world currencies. The EMS was established on 13 March 1979. All the members of the EEC joined it except the UK. The UK government decided that, at a time when exchange rates were highly volatile, it was not in its interests to join. The EMS is based on a newly devised unit of account called the European currency unit (ECU). The value of one unit is determined by taking a weighted basket of all member currencies. The value of each weight is determined by the size of the member's GDP. Table 40.4 gives the weights in 1987. As you can see, sterling was included in the calculation even though

Table 40.4 The European Monetary System Currency Basket. January 1987

Currency	Amount of national currency equal to 1 ECU	Weight of currency in ECU basket %
Belgium/Luxembourg franc	42·87	9·07
Deutschemark	2·06	34·93
Dutch guilder	2·32	11·04
Danish Kroner	7·82	2·79
French franc	6·88	18·97
Italian lira	1462·93	9·44
Irish punt	0·77	1·13
Sterling	0·73	11·87
Greek drachma	14·00	0·76
Spanish peseta	143·98	–
Portugese escudos	154·47	–
		100·0

Source: Eurostat

it did not belong to the EMS. This is because the UK is a member of the EEC and all EEC transactions are now denominated in ECUs. At the time of writing the Portugese and Spanish currencies had not been incorporated in the value of the ECU.

The value of members' currencies is allowed to fluctuate by plus or minus 2.25 per cent of the central rate established by the value of the ECU (the lira was allowed to fluctuate by 6 per cent).

By 1988 the EMS may be judged to have been relatively successful. The ECU had remained relatively stable against other world currencies in contrast to sterling. The onset of 1992 means that there is a need for a move towards greater monetary union. It was suggested in 1988 that it was time to start considering the possibility of a European central bank.

The Single European Act

The Single European Act 1987

In 1985 the EEC published a white paper which had the objective of abolishing all barriers between members of the Community. This was finally approved by the UK parliament in 1987. It was intended that by 1992 all major obstacles to trade between EEC nations should be removed.

This meant that goods should be free to pass between EEC countries. In addition to this, obstacles to the movement of capital, such as exchange control, would be abolished. These changes also implied the harmonisation of tax policies throughout the community. In essence, this would mean the completion of the process begun in 1957.

The gains

As explained above the gains of a unified internal market should be those resulting from the benefits of comparative advantage across the whole of the Community. The 1992 measures should bring bigger gains than the mere abolition of tariffs. Tariffs are only one of the factors which make producers' cost higher and their prices lower in other EEC countries than in their own country. Profit margins tend to be higher at home than in other EEC countries. This is because, in addition to tariffs, there are a whole range of non-tariff barriers which increase exporters' costs. For example, state subsidies to industry and agriculture and the protection of public purchasing markets for national producers.

The Cecchini Report (1988) estimated that the potential gains of the the 1992 changes were about £150 billion pounds. However, the practical difficulties of abolishing tariffs and harmonising taxes and so on may well reduce this.

Conclusions

For the EEC fully to benefit from the 1992 changes it is necessary that prices of similar products should fall accompanied by reductions in costs and increases in output. There will be a need for national competition and merger laws to be intergrated in order to deal with take-overs within the internal market. It is also likely that investment flows between EEC nations will increase. Take-overs may concentrate investment in the home base or in a host country offering the most attractive location – labour law would be an important consideration in this.

There will also be inward investment from non-EEC counties seeking to gain the benefits of the single market. Examples of this are Japanese motor manufacturers establishing themselves in the UK and the take-over of UK firms such as that of Rowntree by Nestlé.

The single market could be good for one of the UK's leading industries – financial services. However, the UK has gone against its own principle of more deregulation in the EEC in the way in which it has implemented the Financial Services Act, i.e. there seems to be more regulation than there was before. (See page 284).

For the financial services industry and others it is desirable that the UK achieves a much greater degree of stability in its exchange rate. The changes point toward freer money transmission within the EEC, more widespread use of the ECU and UK membership of the EMS. Further into the future we may see monetary union, a common currency and, consequently, common fiscal and monetary policies.

The average person probably thinks most about harmonisation of indirect taxes (cheaper alcohol and tobacco?) but the harmonisation of other taxes such as corporation tax is likely to have more effect upon the economy.

Overall it is calculated that the effect of the changes could add about one per cent to the EEC's growth rate over the seven years after 1992. This may seem unspectacular but, if you refer to Table 40.3 you can see that this could mean the doubling or tripling of the rate of economic growth for many of the EEC countries.

Summary

1 The IMF and the IBRD were set up as a result of the Bretton Woods conference and were aimed at regulating international payments and helping economic development.

2 The IMF system is based on a system of quotas; members may borrow in relation to the size of their quotas.

3 The adjustable peg was central to the IMF system.

4 The 1970s saw a breakdown of the system of fixed exchange rates.

543

5 The SDR is a hypothetical unit of account, similar to Keynes's idea of a *bancor*, and is now the basis of all IMF transactions.

6 Both the IMF and the IBRD are hampered by lack of funds.

7 There has been a decline in the importance of the IMF and the IBRD.

8 The eurocurrency markets are both an important source of finance and of instability in the international system.

9 The EEC is both a customs union and a common market.

10 The present EEC policy is to achieve 'harmonisation' of members' economies.

11 EEC membership, while benefiting the UK, has caused problems because the UK's previous trading relationships differed significantly from those of other members.

12 The 1992 changes present enormous potential for change in European markets.

Questions

1 Explain the reason for the abandonment of the adjustable peg system.

2 What is the problem of international liquidity and how does the IMF help to overcome it?

3 Describe the main functions of the IMF.

4 Trace the reasons for the variations in the level of economic cooperation in the 1970s and 1980s.

5 Examine the implications for the UK of joining the EMS.

6 Compile a table or chart of the UK's (or another country with which you are familiar) 15 most important trading partners at the beginning and end of the last 10 years. Account for the observed changes. (Hint: you will find the figures in the *Balance of Payments* (Pink Book) or the *Annual Abstract of Statistics*.)

7 Outline the activities of the Bank for International Settlement (BIS).

8 Trace the origins and growth of the eurocurrency markets.

9 What are the likely consequences of the Single European Act?

Data response   The united markets of Europe

The following is condensed from a report from the Henley Centre for Forecasting published in June 1988.

The united markets of Europe

It is likely that the creation of a single European market in 1992 will bring disproportionate overseas investment to Britain, but the changes will aggravate the inequality between the North and the South and the rich and the poor.

There is a real danger that Japanese companies will have most to gain from the single market, because their comparative advantage lies in high-tech sectors where the barriers to trade are considered to be greatest.

Furthermore, the gains for what is considered to be one of Britain's leading industries – financial services - will be limited without both a substantial and long-lasting degree of currency stability.

The current spate of mergers in Europe will be ineffective in boosting competitiveness if they are merely being conducted on the basis of 'big is beautiful'.

This is because efficiency results more from plant size and technological factors than from business size.

The South-east region of the UK dominates in all of the industries which are most affected by the 1992 proposals. Consequently, if the UK is to substantially gain from the proposals, it will be the South East rather than any other region that benefits. If the UK does gain, the North – South divide will be exacerbated.

The EEC Commission's proposals for bringing VAT and other indirect taxes into line, which would allow frontiers to come down without creating too many opportunities for cross-border 'tax shopping', will lead to falls in retail prices of about 1.4 per cent and therefore a consequent boost to consumer spending.

However the removal of zero-rating would most affect poorer people in Britain, since a higher proportion of their spending is on zero-rated items such as food and children's clothing.

The most likely outcome of the tax debate is either the scrapping of frontier controls without tax harmonisation – and living with cross–border shopping – or the agreement on tax harmonisation of a core of countries such as Germany, France, Italy and the Benelux, excluding the others.

Answer the following questions:

1   The article speaks of the North – South divide in the UK; what is meant by this? Why might the single European market make this worse?

2   Give two examples of mergers or take-overs of firms which have taken place across state boundaries and explain what you consider to be the reason for the mergers.

3   What does the article mean when it says that 'efficiency results more from plant size and technological factors than from business size'? (Para. 5). Do you agree with this statement?

4   In what way will the creation of the single European market allow nations to benefit from the law of comparative advantage?

5   In what ways does the EEC limit the advantages to be gained from comparative advantage and bring about 'trade diversion'?

6   Explain as fully as possible why the Japanese may have most to gain from the single European market (Para. 2).

7   The article starts by saying (Para. 1) that there will be an inward flow of investment to the UK. Give reasons why this may be so.

8   Which industries in the UK do you consider are most likely to gain from the 1992 changes and which are most likely to be adversely affected? Explain your answers.

9   Why is it likely that the UK will have to join the EMS?

10   The article speaks of the North-South divide in the UK. There is, however, a much greater world North-South divide between the rich nations of the world and the poor. Critically assess what the impact of EEC policies is upon this divide.

3

Macroeconomics
VIII Problems and Policies

41

Direction of the economy and public finance

Using official statistics to govern the country is like looking up today's trains in last year's timetable.

Harold Macmillan

Public finances are one of the best starting points for an investigation of society.

Joseph Schumpeter

Having completed our survey of economics we can now proceed to bring the various strands together. In this chapter we will survey the general nature of problems facing the government and the policy options available. In subsequent chapters we will examine some of the problems, such as inflation, in more detail.

Problems and policies

The major objectives of government policy

Even within political parties, opinions differ as to the correct objectives of policy, but in general terms all governments pursue similar objectives. These we can summarise as follows.

a) The control of unemployment. Until the 1970s, UK governments were successful in achieving near full employment. However in the late 1970s and early 1980s unemployment rose to very high levels (3.4 million or 12.3 per cent in 1986). This has made employment policy important once again, but unemployment remains one of the most intractable problems.

b) The control of inflation. Since the 1939–45 war inflation has proved a continuous problem, reaching a record rate of 26 per cent in 1975.

c) A favourable balance of payments. There is some discussion as to what constitutes a favourable balance of payments. To most people it would mean a surplus on the current account, but, as we saw in Chapter 38, there can be problems associated with this. There can be little doubt, however, that current account deficits were one of the UK's toughest problems in the first 30 years after the 1939–45 war. North Sea oil transformed the balance of payments situation. In the early 1980s this resulted in large current account surpluses and even favourable balance of trade figures. The revenues from North Sea oil disguised the massive import penetration of many of the UK's industries. By the end of the 1980s record deficits were being recorded.

d) Economic growth. We can regard the first three objectives of policy simply as 'good housekeeping', whereas economic growth, i.e. an increase in real national income, is the true objective of economic policy; this allows everyone to enjoy a better standard of living. The boom years of the 1950s and early 1960s gave way to stagnation and even to decline in the 1980s.

However, by the end of the decade the UK was experiencing record rates of growth; ahead of its competitors such as Japan and Germany. The environmentalist lobby would argue that

549

the pursuit of economic growth is mistaken, but for most people it remains the prime objective of policy.

e) Aid to less developed countries. All Western governments pay lip-service to aiding the poorer countries of the world. The Brandt Report of 1981 suggested that each country should aim to contribute the equivalent of 0.7 per cent of their GDP to overseas aid. Few countries attain this. By 1988 the UK was devoting less than 0.3 per cent of GDP to aid. The most generous country was the Netherlands which gave just over one per cent.

Other economic objectives of policy
While working our way through the book we have seen that there are other various ways in which the government intervenes in the economy. We may summarise these as *correcting market failure*. That is to say the government steps in when it considers that the forces of demand and supply do not bring about the most desirable social and economic solution. You can refer back to the fuller discussion of the various points in earlier chapters. To recap briefly, the government is concerned with:

a) The provision of *public goods* such as defence. (*See* pages 316–17.)

b) The provision of *merit goods* and services such as, health care, and the regulation of de-merit goods such as hard drugs. (Merit goods may be tricky to define – *see* page 318.)

c) The adjustment of *externalities.* You will recall that externalities are said to exist when the actions of producers and consumers affect not only themselves but also third parties. The government may try to regulate *negative externalities* such as pollution or promote situations which produce *positive externalities*, e.g. better community health care. (*See* discussion in Chapters 26 and 27.)

d) The application of *cost-benefit analysis* (CBA) to major economic decisions. In such questions as the siting of an airport it is necessary for the government to evaluate the total costs and benefits of a scheme to the economy. (*See* discussion

of CBA in Chapter 27 and also data response question on page 338.)

There is no disagreement about these objectives of policy. The disagreements arise out of how to achieve them and also about the priorities to give to these objectives. Given just one problem, such as inflation, any government can usually solve it, but it must also attempt to achieve the other objectives at the same time. It is not just a problem of priorities but also of *conflict between objectives* because curing one problem often seems to aggravate others; for example, eliminating unemployment might well increase inflation.

Policy options

In Chapter 6 we reviewed the various types of policy which are available to a government, and we have since established various attributes of these policies. We will review the broad policy options before proceeding further.

a) Fiscal policy. This is the direction of the economy through taxation and government expenditure. As we have seen, the most important aspect of this policy is the overall relationship between the governments' expenditure and income. A budget deficit should have the effect of expanding the level of national income and, therefore, might be deemed to be an appropriate policy in times of unemployment. Conversely, a budget surplus should have a contractionary effect upon national income and therefore could be considered to be the correct policy in times of inflation. We saw in Chapter 36 that this is a contentious topic. For example, does expanding the level of aggregate demand have 'real' effects upon the economy or only monetary effects?

b) Monetary policy. This is the direction of the economy through the supply and price of money. Expanding the supply of money and lowering the rate of interest should have the effect of stimulating the economy, whilst contracting the money supply and raising the rate of interest should have a restraining effect upon the economy.

c) Direct intervention. Both monetary and fiscal

policy aim at inducing the economy to conform to the government's wishes. The government could, however, intervene directly in the economy to see that its wishes are carried out. Perhaps the most obvious example of this is a *prices and incomes policy* to restrain inflation. The failure of incomes policies demonstrates that direct intervention is as fraught with difficulties as are other methods of policy; we cannot, for example, legislate against inflation. (Incomes policy is discussed in Chapter 42.)

Fiscal policy – taxation

Before turning to study the problem associated with the operation of fiscal policy we will consider the actual structure of the government accounts. Table 41.1 shows the revenues of central and local government in the UK in 1988–9.

Direct taxes

Direct taxes are those which are levied on the income or earning of an individual or an organisation. These are the most important revenue raisers for the government and can be considered under four headings.

a) Taxes on income. Before taxing an individual's personal income, personal and other allowances can first be deducted. The remaining taxable income is referred to as the *legal tax base*. For example, if a person had an income of £8000 p.a and allowances of £3200, then the legal tax base would be £4800. The *marginal rate of tax* is the amount of tax a person would pay on each successive unit of legal tax base. In 1988–89 a person paid 25 per cent on the tax base up to £19 300. At this figure tax rose to 40 per cent for the rest of the person's income. Such a tax is said to be *progressive* because it takes proportionately more off people with higher incomes. If one takes gross income and expresses the actual tax paid as a proportion of it we arrive at the *effective rate of tax*. We can represent the value of these terms in the following manner:

Table 41.1 Consolidated Fund revenue estimates 1988–89

Item	£m	%
Inland Revenue:		
Income tax	42 100	32.8
Corporation tax	19 800	15.5
Petroleum revenue tax	1 180	0.9
Capital gains tax	1 950	1.5
Development land tax	10	–
Inheritance tax	1 000	0.8
Stamp duties	1 950	1.5
Total Inland Revenue	68 000	53.0
Customs and Excise:		
Value added tax	26 200	20.4
Petrol, derv, etc	8 400	6.5
Cigarettes and other tobacco	5 000	3.9
Spirits, beer, wine, cider and perry	4 500	3.5
Betting and gaming	890	0.7
Car tax	1 260	1.0
Other excise duties	20	–
EEC own resources		
Customs duties etc	1 550	1.2
Agricultural levies	120	0.1
Total Customs and Excise	47 900	37.3
Vehicle excise duties	2 770	2.2
Gas levy	420	0.3
Broadcast receiving licences	1 140	0.9
Interest and dividends	680	0.5
Other*	7 300	5.7
Total Consolidated Fund Revenue	128 200	100.0

Source: Financial Statement and Budget Report HM Treasury

* Includes: Proceeds from privatisation, EEC refund, oil royalties.

$$\text{marginal rate of tax} = \frac{\text{increase in tax paid}}{\text{increase in income}}$$

or

$$\text{marginal rate of tax} = \frac{\triangle \, T}{\triangle \, Y}$$

The effective rate of tax or, we may also say, the average rate of tax is:

$$\text{average rate of tax} = \frac{\text{total tax paid}}{\text{total income}}$$

or

$$\text{average rate of tax} = \frac{T}{Y}$$

With progressive taxes it is the case that the marginal rate is higher than the average rate i.e.:

$$\frac{\triangle\,T}{\triangle\,Y} > \frac{T}{Y}$$

b) *Corporation tax.* This is the tax which is levied on the profits of companies. In 1988 the rate of tax started at 25 per cent and was, thus, in line with income tax. Companies may also be liable for advance corporation tax (ACT). It can be argued that corporation tax is a disincentive to enterprise. However, lowering the rates of tax and more efficient collection considerably increased the revenue from these taxes in the 1980s.

c) *Taxes on capital.* Capital as such is not taxed, although the Labour Party has suggested a wealth tax. Tax is paid when capital is sold or transferred. The most important taxes are *capital gains tax* and *inheritance tax*.

d) *National insurance.* Although not officially classed as a tax, national insurance contributions are in effect a *proportional tax*, i.e. it takes a constant percentage of income at all levels, upon employer and employees alike. Originally contributions used to be a fixed-rate 'stamp', but now they are a percentage of employees' income This may be counted as one of the fiscal successes of the Conservative government. In the financial year 1988–9 the revenue from contributions was estimated at £31.6 billion. During the late 1980s the government was looking at different ways of funding the health service.

Fiscal drag

Where progressive taxes are concerned, inflation will mean that the Chancellor of the Exchequer takes a bigger and bigger portion of a person's income as increased money wages raise them from a lower to a higher tax bracket. This tendency is known as *fiscal drag* and it is to offset this that the Chancellor frequently raises the tax threshold. In 1977 two back-bench Labour MPs,

Jeff Rooker and Audrey Wise, successfully amended the *Finance Act* to bring in indexation of tax thresholds in income tax. This became known as the *Rooker-Wise amendment* by which allowances automatically went up the rate of inflation. Nigel Lawson was able to make much of the fact that he had increased allowances beyond that necessary to compensate for fiscal drag.

There is also a principle known as *fiscal boost*. This refers to the fact that inflation will reduce the real burden of specific taxes such as excise duty.

Indirect taxes

Indirect taxes are usually taxes on expenditure. They are so called because the tax is paid *indirectly*, the consumer paying the tax to the shopkeeper who in turn pays it to the government. For example, in the case of the duty on whisky it is the distiller who must pay the tax, this being referred to as the *impact* (or *formal incidence*) of the tax. The tax is then 'shifted' down the chain of distribution until the *burden* (or *effective incidence*) of the tax falls also upon the consumer. The determination of the incidence of tax is explained on page 146.

These are the main forms of indirect tax in the UK.

a) *Customs and excise duty.* Customs duty may be levied on goods coming into the country but this only accounts for 1 per cent of government revenues. Excise duty is levied on a commodity no matter where it is produced; it is a *specific tax*, i.e. it is levied per unit of the commodity irrespective of its price. The main duties are shown in Table 41.1.

b) *VAT.* The most important of indirect taxes, VAT was first introduced in 1973 when it replaced purchase tax. VAT is an *ad valorem* tax, i.e. it is levied on the selling price of the commodity. There are currently two rates of VAT, zero and 15 per cent. These rates were introduced in the first budget of the Conservative government of 1979 and replaced the system of four rates which had existed previously.

The differences in the rates of indirect taxation present one of the major obstacles before single European market can be achieved. Some nations such as the UK and Denmark have very high levels of tax on some commodities such as alcohol. On the other hand the UK traditionally exempted (zero rated) certain commodities such as food and children's clothing which other nations do not. Under these circumstances harmonisation is difficult. (*See* Data Response Questions on page 544.)

Taxes on expenditure are generally said to be *regressive* i.e. they take a larger percentage of the incomes of the lower paid. With regressive taxes it is the case that the average rate of tax is greater than the marginal rate:

$$\frac{T}{Y} > \frac{\triangle T}{\triangle Y}$$

To the government, however, they are cheap to collect and lack *announcement effect*, i.e. people are often unaware that they are paying tax or how much they are paying. For example, over £5 of the price of a bottle of whisky is excise duty.

Other indirect taxes include car tax, road fund and television licences, betting tax, and stamp duty.

Borrowing

If there is any shortfall between the government's expenditure and income this is made up by borrowing, i.e. the government increases the size of the national debt. If we consider the borrowing both by central and local government, this gives us the *public sector borrowing requirement* (PSBR). The PSBR forms the subject of a separate section in this chapter.

diture up between *central* and *local* government expenditure, or between *capital* and *current* expenditure. Economically speaking the most important distinction is between *real government final expenditure* and *transfer payments*. The "real" expenditure includes the salaries of government employees, the purchase of goods and services and so on. Transfer payments are things such as old age pensions (this is discussed in more detail on page 81). The distinction is that transfer payments do not contribute directly to the GDP whilst 'real' expenditure does. When looking at the proportion of GDP which is disposed of by the government it is usual to exclude transfer payments. Debt interest, which you see included in Table 41.2, is also considered as a transfer payment.

Table 41.2 Public expenditure

	1988–9 Forecast	
	£bill	%
Department		
DHSS – social security	48.5	26.5
DHSS – health and personal social services	20.7	11.3
Defence	19.2	10.5
Education and science	18.0	9.8
Scotland, Wales and Northern Ireland	17.1	9.3
Other departments	34.9	19.1
Privatisation proceeds	−5.0	−2.7
Reserve	3.5	1.9
Public expenditure planning total	156.8	85.7
General government debt interest	17.5	9.6
Other adjustments	8.6	4.7
General government expenditure	182.9	100.0
as a percentage of GDP		41.25

Source: Financial Statement and Budget Report HM Treasury

Fiscal policy – expenditure

Public expenditure may be divided up in various ways. Table 41.2 shows how much money was planned to be spent on what in 1988–9. However, we could equally well have divided expen-

Local authority finance

The rating system

Table 41.3 shows the estimate of local government revenues and expenditure in 1988–9. As

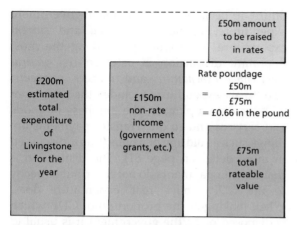

Fig. 41.1 *The rate poundage of Livingstone*

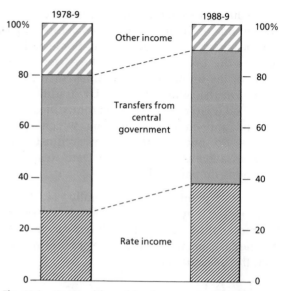

Fig. 41.2 *Composition of local government incomes 1978-89*

you can see a major form of income was transfers from central government. It was a popular misconception that rates were the only source of income for local government. The rating system was a curiosity; it was in fact a tax on the value of property. Each local authority had all the property in it valued by the *Inland Revenue*. The rateable value placed on a property was supposed to reflect the rentable value of the property. When added together this gave a total valuation for the local authority.

In order to determine the level of its rates the local authority compared its expenditure plans with its revenue from non-rate sources, and the shortfall was made up by the rates. In Fig. 41.1 this is explained for the fictional authority of Livingstone. Its revenue expenditure was £200 million whilst its non-rate income was £150 million. This must mean that £50 million must be collected in rates. If the total rateable value of Livingstone was £75 million this means that each ratepayer had to pay £0.66 for each pound of rateable value; for example, if someone had a house with a rateable value of £300 they received a rate demand for £200.

The pattern of finance

Central government financial support for local authorities for local authorities comes mainly in the form of the *rate support grant*. Pressure has been put upon local government to curtail its spending since 1976. This pressure become acute under the Conservative government after 1979. This led to local authorities raising a greater proportion of their revenue as rates. The reluctance, or inability, of local government to make cuts led to more and more draconian measures being taken by the central government. The so called *rate capping Act* of 1984 was seen by many people not just as an attempt to control expenditure but also as an attack upon local autonomy.

Figure 41.2 shows how the proportions of local government revenues changed over the years 1978–89. You will note the increased proportion of revenue from rates. The proportion of money coming from central government remained relatively constant. You may find it a little surprising that the proportion of income from other sources (mainly local authority trading activities) fell at a time when they were being pressed to think more commercially. This fall was due to council house sales which deprived local authorities of income and to other activities being privatised.

The Community Charge (Poll tax)

Rates were often criticised as being unfair be-

Table 41.3 Local authority transactions

	1988–9 Forecast £billion	%
Receipts:		
Rates (net of rate rebates)	19.0	38.1
Rate support grant	13.3	26.7
Other grants from central government	12.4	24.9
Other	5.1	10.3
Total receipts	49.9	100.0
Expenditure:		
Current expenditure on goods and services	35.6	70.6
Current grants and subsidies	6.0	11.9
Interest	4.7	9.3
Net lending and capital expenditure	4.1	8.2
Total expenditure	50.4	100.0

Any errors are due to rounding.
Source: Financial Statement and Budget Report
HM Treasury

cause they were not related to the services the ratepayer receives from the local authority. This is a difficult argument to maintain since few taxes are related to services received. It was also argued that rates were unfair since they only fell on the head of the household. Thus if, for example, there were two identical houses in a borough but in one six people lived whilst in the other only one, the household of six would only pay the same rates as the household of one.

Another criticism of the rating system came from the business community. Rates on business premises in fact raised more money than rates on housing. However, unless the businesspersons happened to live in the same area as their company they got no say in how the money was spent since businesses do not have a vote.

The pattern of local authority expenditure is determined by the services for which it is responsible. The chief form of expenditure for most local authorities is on education, as this is administered at a local level.

The Conservative government of 1987 was committed to the reform, or abolition, of the rating system. Various proposals were put forward such as local income taxes or complete funding from central government. In the end the government opted for the Community Charge. Under this system all people over the age of eighteen living in a local authority area pay the same amount of tax. It was for this reason that it became known as the poll tax because you would pay tax simply as a result of being on the electoral register. The tax is in no way related to income. Relief is given to various categories of people such as full-time students.

The Community Charge was introduced in Scotland in 1988 and it was planned to introduce it in England and Wales in 1990. The domestic Community Charge is determined by the local authority. In addition to this there is an industrial rate which is set nationally. Local authority incomes continue to be supplemented by transfers from central government. Income from other sources continued with central government enforcing council house sales, making local authorities privatise leisure centres and so on.

The Community Charge has been subject to much criticism. It certainly is a highly regressive tax which 'taxes a duke the same as a dustman'. It is hard to see how it accords with the accepted canons of taxation (*see* below). The last time the country had a poll tax was 1381 and this caused the Peasants' Revolt. Of this tax the historian J. R. Green wrote:

To such a tax the poorest man contributed as large a sum as the wealthiest, and the gross injustice of such an exaction set England on fire from sea to sea.

The only concession to modernity in the Community Charge is that it falls, not only on the poorest man but also, on the poorest woman!

The taxation debate

Taxation is a controversial topic. There is disagreement about the purposes of taxes and what **555** constitutes a good tax. More fundamentally there is argument about the effects of taxation upon the economy. In this section of the chapter we will look at these arguments and also examine suggestions for tax reform.

The canons of taxation

Adam Smith laid down four *canons* (criteria) *of taxation*. Although taxes have changed a great deal the principles still remain good today. A good tax, said Smith, should have the following characteristics.

a) Equitable. A good tax should be based upon the ability to pay. Today, progressive income tax means that those with the high incomes not only pay a larger amount but also a greater proportion of their income in tax.

b) Economical. A good tax should not be expensive to administer and the greatest possible proportion of it should accrue to the government as revenue. In general, indirect taxes are cheaper to collect than direct taxes, but they are not, however, so equitable.

c) Convenient. This means that the method and frequency of the payment should be convenient to the taxpayer. The introduction of PAYE made income tax much easier to pay for most people.

d) Certain. The tax should be formulated so that taxpayers are certain of how much they have to pay and when. This information is widely available today, but is often poorly understood.

A good taxation system should be one which is *flexible*, i.e. it should be readily adaptable to changing circumstances. A fiscal system might also be judged on the *welfare principle*, i.e. the extent to which the taxes are received back by the taxpayer as services, and on the principle of *least aggregate sacrifice*, i.e. that inconvenience to taxpayers is minimised. If sacrifice is minimised and welfare maximised, the fiscal system is running on the principle of *maximum social advantage*.

The redistribution of income

All political parties subscribe to the view that

the fiscal system should be used to redistribute income. A right-wing view might be that this should be just sufficient to redress the worst inequalities in the economy while left-wingers might wish to see something more drastic done to effect a fundamental shift from the rich to the poor.

In Table 41.3 you can see that there is great inequality in the distribution of income. You can also see that the combined effect of taxes and benefits is to mitigate the worst effects of poverty. It is also apparent from the Table that pre-tax income became more unevenly distributed over the years 1976–86. The table also makes clear that the progressivity of the fiscal system declined over the period.

The decline in progressivity was partly a result of dropping the high marginal rates of tax. In 1976 the highest rate was 98 per cent. In 1986 the highest rate was 60 per cent and this was reduced to 40 per cent in the 1988 Budget. Such progressivity as does exist in the system comes about mainly as the result of direct welfare payments such as old age pensions and benefits in kind such as health care. Progressivity in direct taxation in the UK is offset by the regressivity of indirect taxes and by tax avoidance.

Table 41.3 Distribution of income in the UK

| | Quintile groups of households | | | | | |
	Poorest fifth	Next fifth	Middle fifth	Next fifth	Richest fifth	Total
Income before taxes and benefits						
1976	0.8	9.4	18.8	26.6	44.4	100
1986	0.3	6.0	17.1	28.0	48.6	100
Income after taxes and benefits						
1976	7.0	12.6	18.2	24.1	38.1	100
1986	6.0	11.1	17.4	24.0	41.6	100

Sources: *Social Trends*, Inland Revenue and National Accounts.

The poverty trap

One of the worst features of the fiscal system is the *poverty trap*. As Margaret Thatcher said in a House of Commons reply in 1984: 'Many people

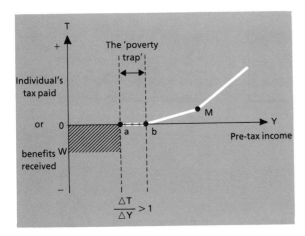

Fig. 41.3 *The poverty trap.* **The shaded area represents flat-rate benefits received. Income tax is paid from income level of *ob*. Between *oa* and *ob* it is possible, due to lost benefits, for an individual to be worse off as their income rises. At *M* individual crosses the threshold to a higher tax bracket.**

are paying income tax and then applying for means-tested benefits from the state.' Such circumstances mean that if a person's income increases, taking them through the tax threshold, they may lose benefit and end up worse off. Then they are effectively paying a marginal rate of tax of more than 100 per cent.

Figure 41.3 presents a simplified diagrammatic explanation of the poverty trap. The vertical axis shows the amount of tax paid or benefits received. On the horizontal axis we have individuals pre-tax income. Below an income level of *oa* individuals receive flat-rate welfare benefits of *ow*. The income tax threshold is set at *ob* and the kink at point M shows a change from a lower to a higher tax bracket, e.g. from paying income tax at 25 per cent to paying tax at 40 per cent.

For simplicity we have constructed the diagram so that the distance *ow* is equal to the distance

ab. As the flat rate benefits are means-tested this means that as an individual's pre-tax income goes beyond *oa* they will lose these benefits. It is thus likely that as a result of a rise in pre-tax income they will be worse off once the loss of benefit is taken into account!

The distance *ab*, therefore represents the poverty trap where the marginal rate of tax is in effect more than one ($\triangle$ T/$\triangle$ Y > 1). The precise distance of this gap will depend upon individual circumstances relating to benefit eligibilty, etc. What should be clear, however, is that the poverty trap is exacerbated by lowering the tax threshold to within the gap *ab*. This is because individuals entering the gap will now be both losing benefit and paying tax. The effective tax rate is thus further increased beyond one for increases in pre-tax income within *ab* and it is now necessary to increase pre-tax income beyond *ab* before any increase occurs in post-tax income.

Direct taxes: a disincentive to work?

Supply side economists argue that taxes are a disincentive to effort. The process is illustrated in Fig. 41.4. It is argued that if taxes are cut this will increase incentives because people will be receiving more for their efforts. Thus people will work harder. This will increase productivity and, as the economy expands, create more employment. There will, therefore, be a rise in the level of real national income. If this is the case then it is possible that a greater total amount of tax may be paid. This was the argument put forward by Laffer. (*See* below and also page 332.)

This argument was accepted by President Reagan and by Chancellor Lawson and was the basis of their tax-cutting budgets. (In the USA at the same time as tax cuts there were massive

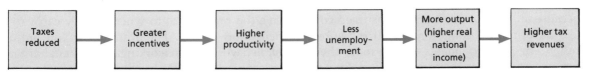

Fig. 41.4 *The supply side argument on taxes.* **Lowering taxes eventually leads to greater tax revenue.**

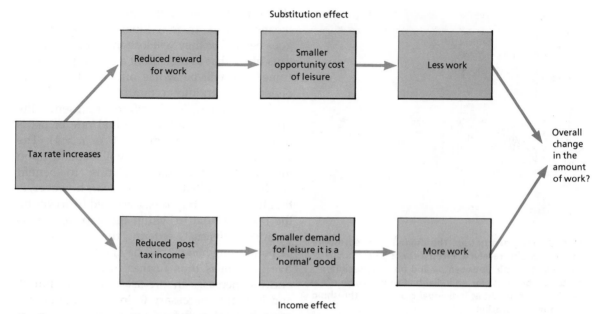

Substitution effect

Income effect

Fig. 41.5 *Income versus substitution effects – non determinancy.*
Raising taxes could cause some people to work harder and others to work less hard. The overall effect depends upon which predominates the income effect or the substitution effect.

budget deficits. Logically, therefore, it would be difficult to separate the supply side effects from those of a conventional Keynesian fiscal boost.)

However, it is important not to accept uncritically anecdotal arguments of the kind, 'We all know that high taxes put people off working'. It is also possible to argue that raising taxes increases effort as people struggle to maintain their level of disposable income. They might not like higher taxes but, at the end of the month, they have to find the money to pay their mortgage, the electricity bill and so on and are thus forced to work harder.

In order to illustrate the two possibilities we will return to the idea of income effects and substitution effects explained in Chapter 9. Suppose that we look at the problem in terms of the 'cost' of leisure. If we raise the rate of tax then we reduce the opportunity cost of leisure because an extra hour's leisure consumed costs less in terms of income forgone. If the substitution effect predominates people may, therefore, work less hard. They are, as it were, 'buying' more leisure because it is cheaper.

Alternatively, we could argue that increasing taxes reduces people's income and we could, therefore, look at demand for leisure from the point-of-view of an income effect. As we know, *ceteris paribus*, if income decreases then the demand for a normal good will decrease. If, therefore, leisure is a normal good then reducing incomes (i.e. raising taxes) will decrease the demand for leisure, i.e. people will work harder. They are, in effect, 'buying' less leisure because they are poorer.

Thus we are in a situation of non-determinancy. If taxes are raised, what will happen to the total amount of effort supplied by the labour force will depend upon whether the income effect or the substitution effect predominates. These alternatives are illustrated in Fig. 41.5.

Apart from the problem of whether people actually regard the situation in this light we have the problem as to whether they can vary their effort at will. For example, if you are a salaried worker then working ten per cent harder (or less hard) probably has little or no effect upon your wage packet. In addition the length of the working day is often beyond the individual employee's control.

The Laffer curve again

The Laffer curve, you will recall, (*see* page 332) attempts to draw a relationship between the rate of taxation paid and the revenue resulting from tax gathering. Obviously if there were a zero rate of tax then there would be zero tax revenue. At the other end of the scale, if the average rate of tax were 100 per cent then there would also be zero revenue because nobody would find it worth working. Laffer, therefore, put forward the idea that there must be a relationship between the two (tax rate and tax revenue). It would follow that there must be an average rate of tax which was most efficient from the tax gathering point of view. This raised the fascinating possibility that it might be possible to lower taxes and increase tax revenue. This could be the result both of increased effort by the workforce and also as a result of decreased tax avoidance. The Laffer curve was one of the chief points of the supply side case. Reduce taxes – encourage work – and gather more taxes at the same time.

If, for the moment we accept the Laffer curve, we can look at it in terms of the income and substitution effects discussed above. In Fig. 41.6 we can argue that when the curve is descending (S–T) the substitution effect is dominating the income effect to such an extent that tax revenue is falling. Thus, an average tax rate of *oa* is the most efficient in terms of tax gathering.

It is possible to speculate on different shapes and slopes for the Laffer curve. In our example the curve is linear up to point R. Thus the tax rate and tax revenue increase hand-in-hand. Beyond this point further increases in the tax rate begin to slow down the increase in tax revenues. However, the government may feel obliged to have higher rates of tax on the grounds of social justice. Thus between points R and S we could say there is an efficiency/equality trade-off. Beyond point S any further increases in taxes are counter-productive.

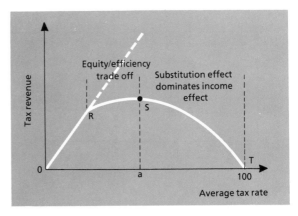

Fig. 41.6 *The Laffer Curve*. **The tax rate which produces the highest revenue is *oa*. The dotted line shows a different view of the relationship with tax revenue increasing in line with increases in tax rate.**

It should be said that there is little empirical evidence on the shape of the Laffer curve. It is possible that it is linear for much of its length. In our example this is shown as the dotted line beyond point R. If this were the case then increasing the rate of tax would also increase tax revenues. In 1985 an OECD report regarded the empirical evidence to be insufficient to support a general proposition that the tax system is undermining the work effort. It is also the conclusion of Professor Charles Brown, one of Britain's leading tax specialists, that recent tax cuts would not increase work effort.

Tax reform

There is much criticism of the fiscal system. The main problems are seen to be that the system is *over complex*, contains many *anomalies* and is *inequitable*. We have already looked at the poverty trap and the problems it creates. (*See* above page 556.) One suggestion for improving both the system of both taxes and benefits is the introduction of a negative income tax.

Negative income tax

The idea of a negative income tax is often supported by monetarists as it avoids the sharp **559**

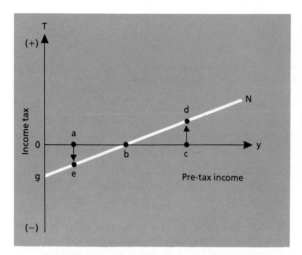

Fig. 41.7 *Negative income tax.* Line N represents a constant rate income tax and negative income tax. At the threshold *b* no tax is paid. Above the threshold at *oc* the amount of tax paid is *cd*. Below the threshold at *oa* negative income tax is received of *ae*.

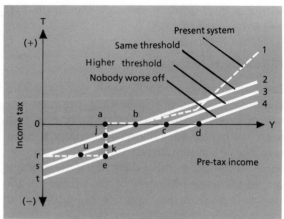

Fig. 41.8 *Negative income tax.* In order for no previous recipients of welfare benefits to be worse off negative income tax must be based on line 4. This involves the government in much greater expenditure.

increase in marginal tax rates caused by flat-rate benefits. As well as abolishing the poverty trap it would be simpler and cheaper to administer. Under this system those above the threshold would pay positive income tax whilst those below it would receive payments (instead of receiving benefits from the Department of Health and Social Security, etc.). Such payments would thus be a *negative income tax*.

We can look at the idea of a negative income tax in terms of the diagram we used to illustrate the poverty trap (*see* Fig. 41.7). In effect, under a negative income tax, everyone in the economy receives a lump sum of *og*. Hence someone who had no earned income at all would have a *negative* tax (i.e. payment from the tax authorities) of *og*. Any earned income is then taxed at a constant rate as shown by the constant slope of the line in the diagram. Thus, if *oa* is received in earned income the payment of income tax on this earned income will have reduced the net payment from the tax authorities to *ae*. At a pre-tax income of *ob* the income tax paid equals the lump sum so that the net payment of tax is zero. Point *b* is thus the break-even point or the threshold past which the net payment of tax to

the authorities becomes positive.

What is important to note is that under such a scheme the marginal tax rate on earned income is constant and thus less than one at all levels of pre-tax income. Thus it always 'pays to work' and the poverty trap has been abolished. Moreover, it is claimed, the system would be cheaper to administer than means tested flat rate benefits and thus be more economical in accordance with Adam Smith's canons of taxation.

A practical difficulty emerges if we superimpose the negative income tax on the present system. This is done in Fig. 41.8. Line 2 shows a constant rate of tax (and negative tax) drawn through the existing threshold *ob*. This, however, has the effect of making a large number of people worse-off as represented by the area *ejr*. This would have adverse political consequences for the government. Line 3 shows what would happen if the government reduced the number of people made worse-off. Even if some people are left worse-off the increased cost to the government is likely to be huge as can be seen by the combined areas of *rus* and *ack* relative to *uke*. The actual net cost will of course depend on the existing distribution of income and the effects on incentives. It can be seen by the shaded areas that a negative income tax scheme which made nobody worse-off than before (line 4) would be extremely expensive.

Apart from these practical problems it can also be argued that a system of negative income tax would be reminiscent of the Speenhamland system of the early nineteenth century which positively encouraged employers to pay low wages, knowing that they would be made up by payments from the public purse. Finally it could be argued that Inland Revenue officials are hardly the best suited people to administer a welfare programme.

A wealth tax

There have been suggestions for an annual tax on wealth, say $\frac{1}{2}$ per cent. This might help to equalise the distribution of wealth and ease the tax burden on earned incomes. It might also close some of the loopholes in capital gains tax. Furthermore, it would not discourage the quest for new wealth because it would be levied on established wealth, much of which, of course, is inherited.

Table 41.4 shows the distribution of wealth in 1976 and 1986. Despite nearly a century of progressive taxation wealth is still very unevenly divided. The slightly more even distribution of wealth in 1986 reflects such things as greater home ownership. However, at the lower end you can see that the poor became relatively poorer. You may like to compare these figures with those for the distribution of income on page 556.

Table 41.4 The distribution of wealth in the UK

Marketable wealth	1976	1986
Percentage owned by:		
Most wealthy 1% of population	24	20
Most wealthy 2% of population	32	27
Most wealthy 5% of population	45	40
Most wealthy 10% of population	60	54
Most wealthy 25% of population	84	78
Most wealthy 50% of population	95	96
Total marketable wealth (£'s billion)	263	1062

Sources: Social Trends and National Accounts.

The reform of national insurance

It is a long time since the system of health and social security was run on actuarial principles. It could be argued that administration could be simplified by incorporating contributions into a unified system of income tax. An alternative to this is to 'privatise' the system as much as possible. Employees could be encouraged, or obliged, to join occupational pension and health schemes thus reducing the burden on the Exchequer. This was the approach taken by the Conservative government in the late 1980s.

The abolition of local rates

The introduction of the Community Charge was discussed on page 554. The collection of the Community Charge is likely to be a costly affair and its administration also has implications for civil liberties.

1992

In order for the single European market to be a reality considerable reform of the fiscal system will be necessary. This affects not only the obvious areas such as VAT and excise duty but also direct taxes. If, for example, taxes on capital and incomes are considerably more liberal in one country than another then, given free movement, businesses will locate to minimise their tax liabilities.

The difficulties of fiscal policy

Having examined the components of government expenditure and income we will turn to look at the difficulties involved in implementing fiscal policy. It should be borne in mind that *a government must have a fiscal policy*. It is easy in the fiscal policy/monetary policy debate to assume that if the government adopts monetary policy as the chief weapon of policy it can abandon fiscal policy. This can never be so because in an economy where the government collects and spends over 40 per cent of the national in- **561** come, *how* this is done must have profound effects upon the economy.

Theoretical problems

We saw in Chapter 36 that there are disagreements between monetarists and neo-Keynesians about the efficacy of fiscal policy. The monetarists claim that budget deficits (or surpluses) will have little or no effect upon real national income whilst having adverse effects upon the rate of interest and upon prices.

The net effects of the budget

The simple Keynesian view is that a budget deficit stimulates the economy, a surplus contracts the economy and a balanced budget has a neutral effect. However, as we saw in Chapter 31, a balanced budget is unlikely to have a neutral effect upon the economy. The theory suggests that equal increases in taxation and spending will raise national income by the amount of the increases in government spending (*see* page 386).

The effect of a budget deficit or surplus is also affected by the type of taxes and the type of expenditure undertaken. If, for example, we imagine a very simple budget in which all the taxes are raised by taxing high incomes whilst all the expenditure is on unemployment benefits, the amount paid could be less than the amount collected so that the budget would be ostensibly in surplus. However, the money that is collected in taxes is the money that would not have been spent, i.e. people with high incomes would probably have saved a good deal of it. On the other hand we can be reasonably certain that all the unemployment benefit will be spent. Thus the government has moved the money from non-spenders to spenders and, therefore, the effect on the economy will be that of deficit, although the budget will be in an accounting surplus.

This would also work the other way round. If, for example, a government's budget is in deficit but its revenue has been raised mainly from taxes on expenditure, such as VAT, and the money thus raised spent mainly on paying interest on the national debt, then the effect of the budget will be that of surplus. This is because the government has, effectively, transferred money from spenders to non-spenders. Thus, when the government announces a deficit or a surplus a much more careful examination of its plans will be necessary before we can decide what the net effect on the economy will be. Put in more general terms we can conclude that:

The net effects of taxes and government expenditure are influenced by the marginal propensities to consume of those being taxed and of those receiving the government's expenditure.

The different propensities to consume of different sectors of the economy will therefore influence the size of the multiplier effect of any budget deficit or surplus.

The inflexibility of government finance.

Adjusting the government's level of economic activity to suit changing circumstances is not as straightforward as it may seem. Much of the government's finance is inflexible. One of the reasons for this is that the major portion of almost any department's budget is wages and salaries, and it is not possible to play around with these to suit the short-run needs of the economy. In addition to this, it would be impracticable, for example, to build a power station one year because more demand was needed, or conversely to stop the construction of a half-built motorway because less expenditure was needed. Much of the government's expenditure involves long-run planning.

Another problem contribution to the inflexibility of government finance is the political problems associated with cuts in expenditure. It would not be easy, for example, to cut old age pensions.

Discretionary and automatic changes

Discretionary changes are those which come about as a result of some conscious decision taken by the government, e.g. changes in tax rates or a change in the pattern of expenditure. Automatic changes come about as a result of some change in the economy, e.g. an increase in unemployment automatically increases government expenditure on unemployment benefits. In fact it is the case that deficits tend to increase automatically in times of recession and decrease in times of recovery. (These fiscal weapons which automatically boost the economy during recession and dampen it in times of recovery are referred to as *build-in stabilisers*.) It is possible for a government to compound the effects of a recession by raising taxes in order to recover lost revenues. This, according to Keynesians, would cause a multiplier effect downwards on the level of economic activity.

Policy conflicts

When devising its fiscal policy, the government must attempt to reconcile conflicting objectives of policy. For example, there is commonly supposed to be a conflict between full employment and inflation, i.e. that the attainment of full employment may cause inflation. This conflict is illustrated by the *Phillips curve* which is discussed in detail in Chapter 42.

Information

It is very difficult to assemble accurate information about the economy sufficiently quickly for it to be of use in the short-run management of the economy. There have been numerous occasions when, for example, the balance of payments has been declared to be in deficit in one quarter but a few months later, when more information is available, it has been discovered that the quarter was in fact in surplus. It is difficult, therefore, for a government to be sure about the accuracy of the information. Even if the figures are accurate, the government still has to decide what they mean. For example, if the balance of payments is still in deficit, is this the beginning of a long-run trend or just a freak result of that month or quarter?

Time lag

One of the chief objectives of fiscal policy is stability, i.e. the government tries to avoid violent fluctuations in the level of economic activity. One way to do this is for the government to have a *counter-cyclical* policy, so that if, for example, the level of economic activity were low, government activity would be high, i.e. they would have a budget deficit. Conversely, if there were a high level of activity then the government would budget for a surplus.

Unfortunately it takes time for a government to appreciate the economic situation, to formulate a policy and then to implement it. This may mean that the government's policy works at the wrong time. For example, if the government decides to reflate the economy during a recession, it could be that by the time the policy works the economy would have recovered anyway. The government's actions therefore have the effect of boosting the economy beyond that which is desirable. When this happens the government decides to clamp down on the economy but, by the time the policy acts, the economy has naturally returned to recession. The government's action therefore makes the slump worse, and so on. This pattern will be familiar to anyone who lived through the *stop-go* policies of the 1950s and 1960s (*see* Fig. 41.9).

A feature of modern fiscal policies has been the imposition of *cash limits*. These were first introduced in the UK in 1976. They consisted simply of laying down aggregate levels of expenditure which could not be exceeded. This reversed the traditional pattern of fiscal policy in that previously it had been usual to draw up expenditure plans first and then raise revenue to meet them. Cash limits were a way of stating how much money is going to be raised before expenditure plans are formulated. It should be stressed that cash limits cannot apply to such things as social security payments.

A neoclassical postscript

It has been explained elsewhere in the book (*see* Chapter 36) that the neoclassical view is that **563**

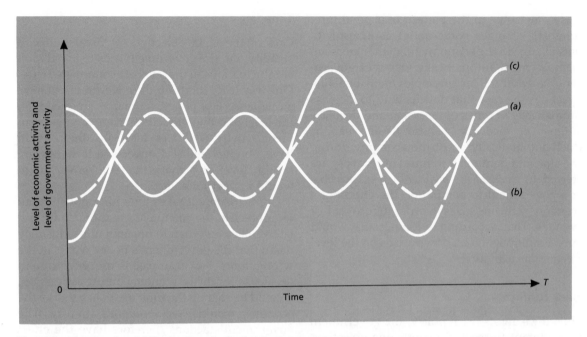

Fig. 41.9 *The time lag.* (*a*) Fluctuations in the level of economic activity without government intervention. (*b*) Proposed pattern of government counter-cyclical activity. (*c*) Worsened fluctuations in the level of economic activity due to government policy acting at the wrong time.

market forces are the best directors of the economy. Positive attempts by the government, it is argued, inevitably make things worse. The correct posture for fiscal policy, therefore, is simply to minimise the role of government thus leaving the largest proportion of the economy possible to be run by market forces.

The public sector borrowing requirement (PSBR)

The PSBR defined

The PSBR is the difference between the income and expenditure of the whole of the public sector. It is made up of the borrowing of the three main arms of the public sector: the central government borrowing requirement (CGBR); the local government borrowing requirement (LGBR); and the public corporation borrowing requirement (PCBR). In Table 41.5 the CGBR and LGBR

Table 41.5 Public expenditure, receipts and borrowing: The PSBR

	1988–9 Forecast £billion
General government expenditure	182.9
General government receipts	184.9
General government borrowing requirement	−2.0
Public corporation's market and overseas borrowing	−1.2
Public sector borrowing requirement	−3.2
PSBR as per cent of GDP	$-\frac{3}{4}$
PSBR excluding privatisation proceeds as per cent of GDP	1.8 $\frac{1}{2}$

Source: Financial Statement and Budget Report HM Treasury

are shown together as the general government borrowing requirement. In the financial year 1987–88 for the first time in many years there was actually a surplus in the public sector. Thus the borrowing was negative, i.e. repayment of the national debt was taking place. The Chancellor therefore suggested that we refer to *Public Sector Debt Repayment* rather than PSBR

Views on the PSBR

The Keynesian view of the economy closely equates the PSBR with the budget deficit and, as such, forms part of the overall strategy of fiscal management of the economy. At one time, for example, it was considered that households tended to save 'too much' whilst firms invested 'too little'; under these circumstances the central government might borrow the savings of households and reinject them into the economy to increase the level of aggregate demand. This *deficit financing* had a central place is fiscal policy for many years.

Monetarists on the other hand have stressed the adverse effects of the PSBR upon inflation. It has also been claimed that public borrowing 'crowds out' private sector investment. Great stress has therefore been laid upon reducing the PSBR. There is thus a fundamental disagreement about the PSBR; neo-Keynesians regard it as a fiscal instrument whilst monetarists concentrate on its monetary effects.

Finance of the PSBR

We may also consider how the PSBR is financed. We can look at this in terms of either the type of security which is sold to raise money – whether, for example, the borrowing is through Treasury bills or 'granny bonds' – or in terms of who has lent the money. In this latter case the most important distinction is between lending by the banking sector and the non-banking sector. These distinctions have consequences when we consider their effect upon the economy.

a) Keynesian and neo-Keynesian views. The traditional Keynesian view paid very little attention to the monetary aspects of the PSBR. The most important effect was always thought to be the effect of the overall deficit or surplus;

the monetary effects were felt only indirectly through changes in the interest rate. The 'new Cambridge' school of economists, associated with the Cambridge Economic Policy Group led by Wynne Godley, have concentrated upon the *net acquisition of financial assets* (NAFA) by each sector of the economy. Overall the deficits and surpluses of each sector must balance out. This was demonstrated earlier in the book (*see* page 358). It can be argued that the distribution of these deficits and surpluses can have adverse effects. The Cambridge Group, for example, argued that an overall debt to the overseas sector would bring about a balance of payments deficit. Thus, it could be argued that, *ceteris paribus*, increasing the PSBR would increase the balance of payments deficit.

b) Monetarist views. Monetarists take a different view of the PSBR, placing the emphasis not upon the direct effect of changing the volume of injections but upon the 'indirect' monetary effects.

An extreme view would argue that each £1 of PSBR adds £1 to the money supply. However, even if this argument is valid it is mitigated by *who buys the financial assets* sold. If financial assets are bought by the non-bank sector then the effects upon the money supply are neutral or even negative. On the other hand if a bank acquires financial assets such as Treasury bills as a result of the expansion of the PSBR, then this will have an expansionary effect upon the money supply since the banks can use these as liquid assets (*see* page 449).

The size of the PSBR

The size of the PSBR in measured in £ billions. However, it is probably more useful to think of it as a percentage of GDP. Both these methods of measurement are shown in Fig. 41.10. The diagram clearly shows the PSBR becoming negative in 1987–8. It should be remembered that at this time government revenues were being boosted by North Sea oil and also by the proceeds from privatisations. The Chancellor found himself repaying the national debt while at the

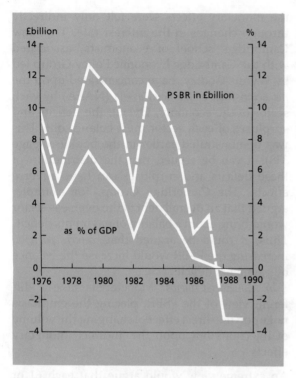

Fig. 41.10 *The PSBR*. The public sector borrowing requirement is shown in aggregate (left-hand scale) and as a percentage of GDP (right-hand scale).

same time demanding spending cuts from other government departments.

Is the national debt too large?

If the government borrows money then this increases the size of the national debt. Most of the national debt is owed to people within the country only a small proportion of it is owed overseas. Figure 41.11 shows how the size of the national debt as a percentage of GDP has declined in recent years.

There is much debate as to whether the national debt is a burden to the country. The national debt can be said to be a burden in three ways:

a) Interest payments. Government must raise revenue to pay interest on the debt. Despite the relative decline in the size of the debt interest payments have remained relatively constant

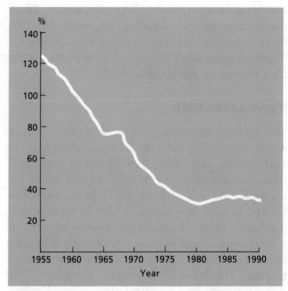

Fig. 41.11 *The National Debt as Percentage of GDP.*

as a proportion of GDP because of the rise in interest rates in the 1980s.

b) Overseas payments. The extent to which the debt is owned overseas presents a real burden to the economy. Surpluses must be generated on the balance of payments to repay the debt and to pay interest on it.

c) Crowding-out. It is argued that government borrowing may starve industry of funds and force up interest rates. This argument is put forward by monetarists and neo-classicists. Although appealing in theory there is little empirical evidence to demonstrate that it has actually taken place.

Monetary policy

We have already examined the operation of monetary policy and the problems associated with it (Chapter 35). In this section we will look at some of the major policy disagreements over monetary policy.

For most of the period since the 1939–45 war, Keynesian orthodoxy ruled and this placed monetary policy as secondary in importance to fiscal policy. Nevertheless governments did use monetary policy to back up fiscal policy, it being seen as part of the overall policy of managing aggregate demand. This view of monetary policy is enshrined in the Radcliffe Report (*The Report of the Committee on the Working of the Monetary System*, 1959). This continued to be the viewpoint into the 1960s. However, increasingly, monetary policy became part of the 'stop-go' cycle, when high interest rates and tight credit control were used in attempts to restrain demand and to protect the exchange rate. It is essential to the Keynesian view that the real impact of monetary policy is thought to be through interest rates because, as we have seen, the neo-Keynesians believe the money supply to be exogenously determined.

The 1970s saw a transformation in government policies, Keynesian ideas being gradually replaced by monetarist ones. Two features are relevant to our discussion here. Firstly, monetary policy came to be regarded as more important and effective than fiscal policy and, secondly, the control of inflation came to be the central concern of economic policy.

The accession of monetarist ideas meant that *control of the money supply* rather than interest rates came to be regarded as the premier object of policy. This is because, as was explained above (*see* Chapter 36), monetarists believed that this and this alone could control inflation.

However it should not be thought that monetarism simply replaced Keynesian demand management. Monetarists do not see monetary policy as a method of stabilising and directing aggregate demand; rather, they see sound money management as a pre-condition for creating the correct climate for improving the economic environment. Thus, emphasis has been switched from short- to medium-term management of the economy. A most important part of government policy became the *medium-term financial strategy* (MTFS). This consisted of making

firm announcements for the growth of the money supply. It was believed that this in itself would reduce inflation by reducing *expectations*. However such monetary targets as were announced were usually not achieved, which led the government to seek for better indications of the money supply. Thus the emphasis was switched from M3 to M1 to M0, and so on, as the goverment sought to find an indicator which would accord with monetarist theories of the money supply. It is likely that their failure was at least in part due to *Goodhart's law* (*see* page 581).

Monetarist policies came to be associated with cutting public expenditure because monetarists believed that there was an *interdependence* between fiscal and monetary policy. This was because it was thought that increasing government expenditure leads to an increase in the PSBR and therefore to an expansion of the money supply. However in a *time of recession* it proved very difficult to cut public expenditure in real terms. It was only in the late 1980s, with the economy relatively prosperous again that the PSBR was brought under control.

Monetarist theory has tended to ignore the rate of interest. It is an elementary principle of economics that we cannot both determine the supply and the price of a commodity simultaneously. Thus emphasis on the control of money supply tends to leave its price (the rate of interest) to look after itself. The Keynesian economist Joan Robinson wrote: 'Changes in the quantity of money are of the utmost importance but the importance lies in their influence upon the rate of interest and a theory [monetarism] which does not mention the rate of interest is not a theory of money at all.' This quote is re-iterating the Keynesian belief that it is the rate of interest which is important. Even if this is now not accepted it must be admitted that control of the money supply has led to high and volatile real interest rates which have had adverse effects upon the economy.

Summary

1 All governments have to deal with similar problems. We may summarise these as the control of unemployment, the control of inflation, the attainment of a satisfactory balance of payments and promoting economic growth.

2 Three main methods of policy are available to governments, i.e. fiscal policy, monetary policy and direct intervention.

3 Taxes may be progressive, proportional or regressive. Progressive taxes take a larger share of higher incomes, proportional taxes take a constant percentage of incomes and regressive taxes take a smaller share of higher incomes.

4 The difference between public expenditure and income is the PSBR.

5 A good system of taxes should be equitable, economical, convenient, certain and flexible.

6 There are many problems associated with the operation of the fiscal system such as the poverty trap.

7 The effect of taxation upon the economy is a controversial topic. For example does increasing direct taxes encourage or discourage effort?

8 The problems associated with fiscal policy may be summarised as calculating the net effects of taxes and spending, the inflexibility of government finance, conflicts of policy, information difficulties and time lags.

9 Neo-Keynesians see public borrowing as part of demand management, i.e. borrowing to finance a deficit is an injection to the circular flow. Monetarists, however, see the chief effect of borrowing as being upon the money supply.

10 Monetary policy now concentrates upon medium-term financial strategy which is based upon setting targets of the growth of the money supply.

Questions

1 What are the main determinants of the pattern of government expenditure? Illustrate your answer with examples from an economy with which you are familiar.

2 Discuss the problems involved in formulating a policy to achieve full employment, low inflation and a favourable balance of payments simultaneously.

3 Consider the merits and demerits of the model of the economy developed in the appendix to Chapter 31 and the analysis developed in Chapter 36 as guides to policy formation.

4 Choose five different taxes and list them in order of progressiveness. Assess the relative importance of these to the government's budget.

5 Assess the merits of the Community Charge as method of local taxation compared with rates and other alternatives.

6 Consider the information given in question 9 at the end of Chapter 33 (*see* page 430). Then examine how the system of taxation influenced these figures.

7 What reform do you think would improve the present system of personal taxation and benefits?

8 This question is based on Table 41.6.

    a) Explain the basis and methods of collection of the various taxes in the table.

Table 41.6 Shares of total UK government revenue raised by Customs and Excise

Type of tax	Name of tax	1963–4 (%)	1983–4 (%)	1988–9 (%)
Specific taxes	Tobacco	13.0	2.8	3.9
	Alcohol	7.0	2.9	3.5
	Hydrocarbon oils	8.5	4.2	6.5
	Total of these	28.5	9.9	13.9
Ad-valorem	Purchase tax	7.5	–	–
	Value-added tax	–	11.5	20.4
	Other	6.5	2.0	3.0
	Total of these	14.0	13.5	23.4
Total Customs and Excise		42.5	23.4	37.3

Source: Financial Statement and Budget Report, *HM Treasury*

b) Comment upon the changing distribution of these two types of tax revenue as fully as possible and upon their relationship to other taxes.

Data response   The budget report ▬▬▬▬▬▬▬▬▬▬▬▬▬▬▬▬▬▬▬▬

Study the information contained in Fig 41.12 which is taken from the Financial Statement and Budget Report of 1988–9. Then answer the following questions.

1 In what ways has the pattern of expenditure changed over the period shown?
2 Which of the taxes shown in Fig. 41.12 are direct and which indirect?
3 What reasons can be put forward to explain the change in the pattern of government income over the period shown?
4 Why has debt interest remained a fairly constant proportion of government expenditure when the relative size of the national debt has declined?
5 What is meant by the poverty trap and how might it be eliminated?
6 Examine the argument that cutting direct taxes stimulates the economy.
7 What objectives does a government have in mind in formulating its expenditure and revenue plans?

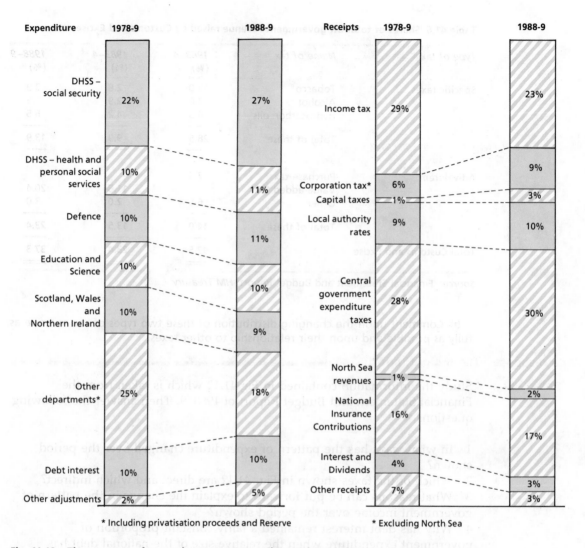

Fig. 41.12 *The structure of general government receipts and expenditure.*

42

The control of inflation

The first panacea for a mismanaged nation is inflation of the currency; the second is war. Both bring a temporary prosperity; both bring a permanent ruin. They both are the refuge of political and economic opportunists.

Ernest Hemingway

In Chapter 33 we defined inflation as a rise in the general level of prices and a fall in the value of money. We examined various measures of inflation such as the RPI. In this chapter we look at the control of inflation as an object of government policy. Since the mid-1970s control of inflation has become the chief objective of government policy. We will first examine the effects of inflation upon the economy.

The consequences of inflation

Inflation and growth

It is argued by monetarists that inflation has a bad effect upon economic growth; this is because it *increases uncertainty* and *discourages savings*. Inflation also means *high nominal rates of interest* which *discourages investment*. Whilst it is undoubtedly true that high rates of inflation are damaging to the economy, the evidence at lower rates of inflation is by no means convincing. Indeed it may be argued that some inflation is conducive to growth. This is because inflation stimulates profits by reducing the costs of business but increasing their revenues. The business costs are usually incurred at a rate which is fixed for a period of time. For example, a business may lease premises at say £10 000 p.a. for ten years. Inflation has the effect of reducing this

rent in real terms whilst the price of the business's product (and therefore its revenues) goes up with inflation.

As we saw in Chapter 29, the high rates of inflation of the 1970s were also accompanied by unprecedented increases in the savings ratio. Increased savings, however, was not accompanied by increased investment, thus increasing the *disequilibrium* in the economy.

Inflation and the balance of payments

Inflation is generally supposed to have an adverse effect upon the balance of payments because it makes imports cheaper and exports dearer. Theoretically this situation may be modified by a reversal of the *Marshall – Lerner condition* (*see* page 511). However it was certainly the experience of the UK in the years after the 1939–45 war that inflation helped to cause recurrent balance of payments crises.

It should be remembered that, as far as the balance of payments is concerned, it is not the absolute but the relative rate of inflation which is important, i.e. the rate of inflation in the UK compared with that of her trading partners. If, for example, the domestic rate of inflation is 5 per cent but that of a trading partner is 10 per cent, then as far as foreign trade is concerned the price of exports will be falling and that of imports rising. Until very recently, however, the UK experienced constantly higher rates of inflation than those of her major trading partners.

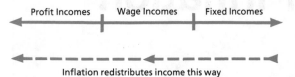

Fig. 42.1 *Inflation and distribution of income in the UK.*

Inflation and the distribution of incomes

A fall in the value of money will remove purchasing power from those living on fixed incomes, such as pensioners, and redistribute it towards those who draw their living from prices. This is illustrated in Fig. 42.1. Wages are seen as being in the middle of the spectrum, and the ability of wage earners to keep up with or ahead of inflation will depend upon the wage earners' bargaining power. This will tend to mean that those whose skills are in demand or who have strong well-organised trade unions, such as doctors and computer operatives, succeed in keeping ahead of inflation while those lacking the correct skills and/or who are poorly unionised, such as shopworkers, agricultural workers and bankers, lag behind.

Inflation and employment

A topic of great controversy is the relationship between the level of inflation and the level of unemployment. For many years it was claimed that there was a trade-off between the two, i.e. reducing inflation would cause more unemployment and vice-versa. Monetarists and neoclassicists stood this relationship on its head by suggesting that reducing inflation would simultaneously reduce unemployment. The controversy surrounds one of the best known hypotheses of recent years – the *Philips curve*. Since this is such an important topic we will now consider this controversy in more detail.

The Phillips curve

The original curve

Professor A. W. H. Phillips (1914–75) published research in 1962 which purported to show the relationship between unemployment, inflation and wage rises in the UK economy, 1862–1958.

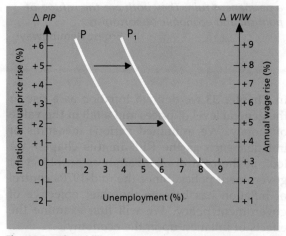

Fig. 42.2 *The Phillips curve.* **This shows the relationship between inflation and unemployment. A rate of wage increase of 3 per cent p.a. is consistent with zero inflation if 3 per cent represents the annual rate of increase of productivity.**

The research appeared to show that the nearer the economy was to full employment the greater would be the rate of inflation. A diagram based upon the original *Phillips curve* is shown in Fig. 42.2. It appeared that if unemployment were at 5·5 per cent then inflation would be zero.

The empirical evidence

Phillip's evidence seemed good for the period he investigated. However since the mid-1960s the relationship seems to have broken down. Figure 42.6 shows the actual relationship between inflation and unemployment. You can see that on a *scatter diagram* it offers very poor evidence for a Phillips curve. Three possible explanations therefore present themselves.

a) No discernible relationship exists between prices and unemployment.

b) A relationship exists, as described in the Phillips curve, but events have caused it to shift rightwards. This is illustrated in Fig. 42.2. As you can see this could also be made to fit reasonably well with the evidence in Fig. 42.6

c) Sherman, a radical US economist, has suggested that the relationship is the other way round, i.e. increasing inflation is associated with increasing unemployment. The shaded area in Fig. 42.6 suggests the possible trend line of the *Sherman curve*.

The adaptive expectations school

Milton Friedman put forward the view that there is a short-run trade-off between unemployment and inflation. That is to say, it is possible for the government, in the short-run, to reduce unemployment by, for example, increasing the money supply. However, in the long-run the jobs market will return to the previous level of employment but with a higher rate of inflation. This phenomenon is caused by the time it takes for people's *expectations* to adjust to the changes in prices and money wages.

The money illusion

This is the tendency of people to be fooled by changes in prices or wages when no *real* change has taken place. For example, if wages double but prices do as well, some people may still believe that they are better-off because they are earning £10 000 a year instead of £5000.

The effect of the money illusion

Suppose that the government, in an attempt to reduce unemployment, increases the money supply. This has the effect of increasing prices but has no immediate effect upon wages. This, therefore, means that prices have gone up but *real wages* have gone down.

We can illustrate the situation using the analysis which we developed in Chapter 36 (*see* pages 475–81). In Fig. 42.3 real wages are on the vertical axis and the quantity of labour demanded

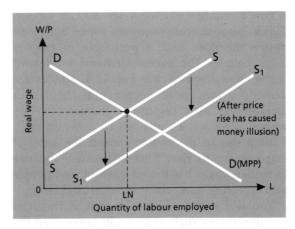

Fig. 42.3 *The effect of inflation with the money illusion.* The real wage is w/p. If prices increase but wages do not then the real wage declines. We can show this as a fall in the supply curve from *SS* to *S,S,* because people are offering their labour at a lower real price not realising that inflation has devalued their wages.

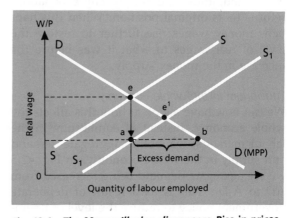

Fig. 42.4 *The Money Illusion disappears.* Rise in prices shifts supply curve to S_1S_1. This creates an excess demand for labour because people are prepared to work for a lower real wage. Short-run equilibrium is e^1. As people demand a higher real wage equilibrium returns to e with the original level of employment of *LN*.

and supplied is on the horizontal axis. The fall in real wages is shown as the shift of the supply curve from SS to S_1S_1. This is to say that people are offering their labour at a lower real wage because they do not appreciate that rising prices have devalued their wages.

In Fig. 42.4 we examine the effect which this has upon the employment situation. There is now a situation of excess demand for labour. This is because real wages are lower and businesses therefore find it profitable to employ more people. The excess demand for labour is shown as distance *ab* in Fig. 42.4. This excess demand draws more people into the labour market and also begins to increase money wages. We reach a short-run equilibrium at e^1. Thus a rise in prices has caused the level of employment to rise. This is because the rise in money wages has fooled unemployed people into accepting jobs which they refused before.

You will note in Fig. 42.4 that at the new equilibrium the real wage is still lower than the original one. The adaptive expectations school argues that this situation can only persist so long as the money illusion continues. In time expectations adapt and people realise that prices have risen; they therefore demand more wages and, thus, the supply curve of labour returns to its original position. When this happens money wages rise further to restore the level of real wages to what it was before the increase in the money supply.

Equilibrium in the whole economy

We can now have a look at how this affects the whole economy. Instead of equilibrium in the labour market(s) we look at aggregate demand and supply in the whole economy. In Fig. 42.5 we see aggregate demand being increased from AD to A_1D_1. This is as a result of deliberate government policy to reduce the level of unemployment. In the short-run the equilibrium changes to e^1 as people accept lower real wages however, as they adapt to the inflationary situation and demand higher real wages we move to equilibrium at e^2. Thus, in the long-run, we have higher prices but only the same amount of employment. It is argued that this is because there is a *natural level of unemployment* for the economy and any attempts to reduce unemployment below this level end in inflation rather than more employment.

The expectations augmented Phillips curve

Friedman has suggested that there is a vertical

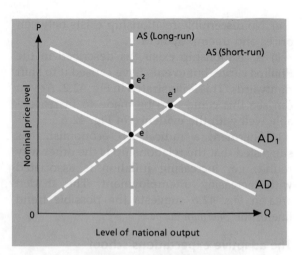

Fig. 42.5 *Equilibrium in the whole economy.* Government policy increases aggregate demand from *AD* to *AD₁*. This creates a short-run equilibrium of e¹ at a high level of output and employment. As people adapt to the new level of prices and demand higher wages, the long-run equilibrium becomes e² – i.e. the same level of output and employment but a higher level of prices. Thus the short-run aggregate supply curve appears to slope but in the long-run is vertical.

long-run Phillips curve (you can see in Fig. 42.6 that the years 1967–75 give reasonable support to this view). The different results are caused by short-run Phillips curves crossing the long-run curve. This possibility is illustrated in Fig. 42.7. The solid vertical curve is situated at the 'natural level of unemployment'.

It is argued that at the natural rate inflation is zero. This being the case, workers *expect* the future inflation rate also to be zero. However if the government considers that OU unemployment is too much it may try to trade-off unemployment against inflation along the Phillips curve P_0, to reach point V, where there is 4 per cent inflation. Employers and unions are willing to settle for this situation because they are under the mistaken belief that their real incomes have risen. But when 4 per cent inflation comes to be anticipated we shift to a new Phillips curve P_4. To maintain unemployment at a reduced level of OZ and to meet expectation of higher real incomes it is necessary to increase aggregate

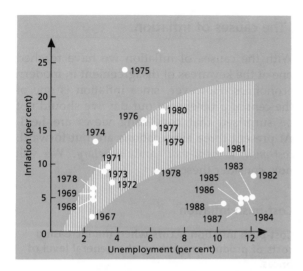

Fig. 42.6 *Inflation and unemployment in the UK.* This shows the relationship between inflation and employment for the years 1967–88. This presents very poor evidence for the Phillips curve. The shaded area, which takes in most of the points of the scattergraph, is possible evidence that unemployment and inflation are positively correlated.

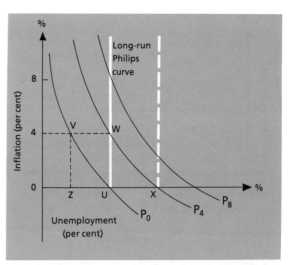

Fig. 42.7 *The effect of expectations upon the Phillips curve.* The natural rate of unemployment is OU. P_0, P_4 and P_8 represent short-run Phillips curves based upon various expectations of inflation. If government decreases unemployment to OZ this causes 4 per cent inflation (point V). If inflation stabilises at 4 per cent employers reduce employment back to point W. However, getting rid of inflation altogether now involves increasing unemployment to OX because the economy has shifted to the expectations-augmented Phillips curve P_4. The heavy dotted vertical line at OX represents an increase in the natural level of unemployment.

demand by increasing the money supply. Thus the Phillips curve is shifted outwards again to P_8 which is consistent with the level of inflation of 8 per cent at the natural level of unemployment.

This rightward shift of the Phillips curve due to increased expectations produces the expectations-augmented Phillips curve.

In order to get rid of this type of inflation Friedman argued that a period of unemployment *above* the natural rate is necessary.

The explanation is as follows. Suppose we are at point V and the government now refuses to expand the money supply. Inflation has now been stabilised at 4 per cent. However employers now realise that they have ZU more workers than they need; thus they move to point W, at the natural rate of unemployment but at 4 per cent inflation. In order to return to zero inflation it is necessary to move to point X, which is a level of unemployment well above the natural rate. This will rid people of their expectations of inflation and the economy can gradually move back to point U.

The rational expectations (new-classical) school

According to this school of thought people are not fooled by changes in the price level. If there is an expansion of the money supply people correctly anticipate the effect on inflation and money wages adjust to keep the real wage the same i.e. there is no money illusion.

In Fig. 42.8 (*a*) the labour market remains in equilibrium because wages adjust in line with inflation. Thus although prices and wages have risen the level of employment has remained at LN. In Fig. 42.8 (*b*) we see the effect upon the whole economy. Here attempts to increase the level of employment lead the government to increase aggregate demand from AD to A_1D_1 but because there is no change in aggregate supply (because people are working the same **575**

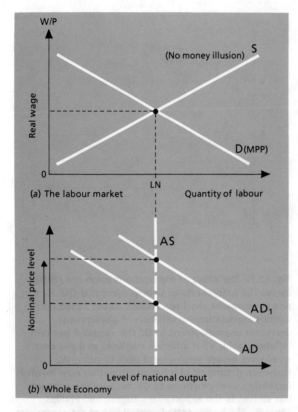

W/P

(No money illusion) S

Real wage

D(MPP)

0

LN

(a) The labour market   Quantity of labour

Nominal price level

AS

AD₁

AD

0

Level of national output

(b) Whole Economy

Fig. 42.8 *The Rational Expectations School.* The labour market remains in equilibrium because wages adjust in line with inflation. In (*b*) we see that attempts to increase employment by increasing aggregate demand from AD to AD₁ only result in inflation. (*See* also page 479).

amount that they did before) the aggregate supply curve AS is vertical and, therefore, the only result is inflation.

Thus, both the adaptive expectations and the rational expectations schools agree that there is no long-run trade-off between inflation and unemployment.

For those who like logical puzzles the rational expectations school presents a nice example of circular logic. For the theory to work people must be able correctly to predict the effect of increases in the money stock upon inflation. This is only possible if the rational expectations model is correct. Thus the model can only be correct if it is correct and is believed to be correct!

The causes of inflation

With the causes of inflation we have reached one of the key areas of disagreement in modern economics. However, since inflation is one of the central problems of our day we should not be surprised that conflicting views are held. At present three explanations are put forward: *cost-push; demand-pull;* and *monetary.* We will now consider these.

Cost-push inflation

Cost-push inflation occurs when the increasing costs of production push up the general level of prices.

This, therefore, is inflation from the supply side of the economy. Evidence for this point of view includes the following.

a) Wage costs. It is widely held that powerful trade unions have pushed up wage costs without corresponding increases in productivity. Since wages are usually one of the most important costs of production, this has an important effect upon prices. Figure 42.9 demonstrates that there is indeed a correlation between earnings and the level of inflation. We should remember, however, that correlation does not imply causation. The precise nature of the connection between wages and prices remains unclear.

b) Import prices. Whatever one's view of inflation, it must be admitted that import costs play some part in it. The huge rise in commodity prices, especially oil, in the 1970s undoubtedly contributed to inflation. It should also be remembered that inflation is a worldwide phenomenon and it is not possible for a nation to cut itself off completely from rising prices in the rest of the world.

c) Exchange rates. As far as the UK is concerned the depreciation in the external value of the pound since the floating of sterling in 1972 has certainly been an inflationary factor. By 1984 the pound had devalued to less than 55 per cent of its 1972 Smithsonian parity against the dollar. An estimate by the Institute of Bankers

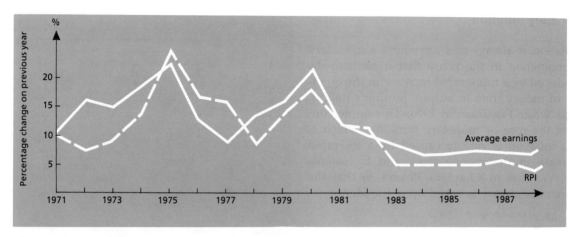

Fig. 42.9 *Earnings and inflation in the UK.* The graph shows a reasonable correlation between the increase in weekly earnings (and therefore employer's costs) and prices.

suggested that each 4 per cent devaluation gave rise to 1 per cent domestic inflation.

d) Mark-up pricing. Many large firms fix their prices on a unit cost plus profit basis (*see* page 219). This makes prices more sensitive to supply than to demand influences and can mean that they tend to go up automatically with rising costs, whatever the state of the economy.

Demand-pull inflation

Demand-pull inflation is when aggregate demand exceeds the value of output (measured in constant prices) at full employment.

The excess demand for goods and services cannot be met in real terms and therefore it is met by rises in the price of goods. Figure 42.10 recapitulates the idea of the inflationary gap introduced in Chapter 30. The aggregate demand line $(C + I + G + (X - M)$ crosses the 45° line at point E which is to the right of the full employment line. Thus at full employment there is excess demand of AB. It is this excess demand which *pulls up* prices.

Those who support the demand-pull theory of inflation argue that it is the result of the pursuit of full employment policies since the 1939–45 war. These policies meant that workers felt free to press for increases in wages in excess of productivity without fear of unemployment. In

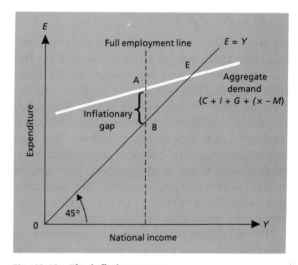

Fig. 42.10 *The inflationary gap.*

addition to this there was the political demand for high levels of public expenditure which were financed by budget deficits. Both these factors, therefore, put excess demand into the economy. From this latter point there may appear to be agreement between Keynesians and monetarists. However in the demand-pull school it is the demand which *brings about* the expansion in the money supply, whereas monetarists see the causality reversed, with the increase in the money stock occuring first.

577

Monetary inflation

Inflation is always and anywhere a monetary phenomenon in the sense that it can *only* be produced by a more rapid increase in the quantity of money than in output' [author's italics]. Thus wrote Friedman in 1970. This quote contains the core of monetary thinking, which is that inflation is *entirely* caused by a too-rapid increase in the money stock and by *nothing else*. We saw in Chapters 33 and 36 that the monetarist theory is based upon the identity:

$$M \times V = P \times T$$

and that this was turned into a theory by assuming that V and T are constant. Thus, we would obtain the formula:

$$M \times \bar{V} = P \times \bar{T}$$

We will briefly examine these two assumptions. Figure 42.11 shows the actual value of V for the UK M0, M3, M4 and M5 money stocks from 1970 to 1988. The velocity is worked out by dividing GDP by the money stock. Naturally, as M0 is considerably smaller than M3, the resultant value of V is much higher. This also emphasises another problem associated with monetarism: What is the correct measure of money stock? As you can see, the measures give quite different rates of change for V, sometimes even moving in opposite directions.

The velocities of the various measures of broad money show a similar pattern of variation to each other. A slowdown in velocity since 1980 is a feature to all broad monetary aggregates and contrasts sharply with the behaviour of velocity through much of the 1970s and earlier. Apart from the sharp fall in 1971–73, which was soon reversed, the velocity of broad money had risen through most of the post-war period up to 1979.

When, after this date, the velocity of M3 slowed down, it was important for the then authorities to establish why this was so. Did it mean that there was not a reliable connection between the growth of the money supply and inflation which the monetarists said there was? The Governor

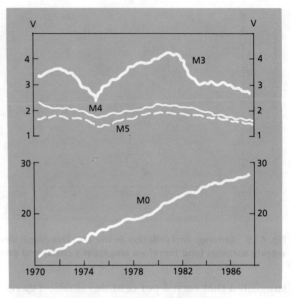

Fig. 42.11 *Velocity of monetary aggregate.*
Source: BEQB

of the Bank of England quoted in the Bank of England Quarterly Bulletin of December 1986 said:

The targeting of broad money aggregates is itself an intermediate objective, (*see* page 454) the fundamental aim of policy being to squeeze out inflation progressively and create a strong and growing economy: and this objective has been chosen in the belief that there was a reasonably stable relationship between the rate of growth of broad money and the rate of growth of nominal incomes. Since 1980, however, this relationship in the UK has become increasingly unpredictable, with the velocity of money falling and that of M3 falling at an increasing rate.

The reasons for the fall of the velocity were varied, but in general terms they were due to a changes in savings behaviour. This in turn may be attributed to greater competition between financial intermediaries for depositors, resulting in more attractive ways for investors to keep money with a bank or building society. It may also be attributed to high real interest rates throughout the 1980s.

As you can see from Fig. 42.11 there was a

steady and continuous rise in the velocity of M0. In 1970 it was only just over 10 but by the end of the 1980s it was approaching 30.

Bear in mind that a relatively small change in V could cause large changes in money national income; for example, if GDP were £280 billion and M were £80 billion this would give us the value $V = 3.5$. Under these circumstances a rise in V to 3.6 would cause an increase in money GDP of £8 billion whilst an increase to 4.0 would increase GDP by £50 billion. *Ceteris paribus*, this is equal to a rate of inflation of over 18 per cent.

Thus, as you can see the idea that V is constant, or even stable, is dubious. Important criticisms of Friedman's views were raised in an article for the *Bank of England Quarterly Bulletin* in December 1983 by Hendry and Ericsson. In the event the Bank did not publish this article because it was too much at variance with the authorities' views at that time. Subsequently their arguments seem, at least in part, to have been accepted as you can see from the quote from the Governor of the Bank of England above. The most devastating claim Hendry and Ericsson make is that Friedman adjusted the figures for the money supply and for price levels to produce a constant V. Without a constant V there will be no predictable relationship between money, national income and prices.

Professor Hendry likens the velocity of circulation to a drunken man walking home. He heads roughly in the right direction but one can never predict whether his next step will be backwards, forwards or sideways. It is a 'random walk'.

The second assumption of monetarism is that T is constant. Put another way, it is the belief that the economy will tend towards a full-employment equilibrium. This being the case, any increase in M can only result in price changes and not real changes in national income. Unemployment is caused by a temporary lack of adjustment in the economy when there is confusion between real national income and money national income – the *money illusion*. The unemployment of the 1980s is perhaps stretching the word 'temporary' to its limits.

Figure 42.12 shows the relationship between sterling M3, M0 and inflation. It is Friedman's contention that an increase in the money stock will cause a rise in inflation 18 months to 2 years later. As you can see the graph shows conflicting evidence. There does seem to be a close correlation between M0 and the RPI during the 1980s. The period considered in the graph is too brief for a fair appraisal of Friedman's proposition. He obtained very good results for a whole century in the USA. However, even if there

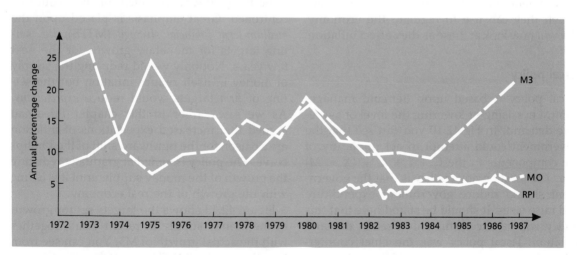

Fig. 42.12 *The money stock and inflation in the UK.*
The graphs trace the annual percentage change in M3, M0 and the index of retail prices.

is a good fit it does not prove that one thing *causes* the other. Also we have just seen above that the empirical basis of Friedman's research has been subject to criticism.

Multi-causal inflation

Having worked through the chapter the student might now legitimately ask, 'What does cause inflation then?' The answer is probably that inflation has a number of causes – increases in the money supply, excessive wage demands, excess demand and so on. It is also probably true that what may be the chief cause of inflation in one year may not be in the next. At this stage we need more research to separate out the different strands of inflation.

If inflation does have many causes, an important conclusion stems from this and that is that a variety of policy measures will be needed to deal with it. Thus a policy which places its trust entirely upon monetary control or entirely upon wage restraint is unlikely to be successful.

The control of inflation

As we said in the beginning of Chapter 41 governments have three main areas of policy which they can use to regulate the economy. We will now look at these as they affect inflation.

Fiscal policy

Fiscal policy is based upon demand management, i.e. raising or lowering the level of aggregate demand. In Fig 42.10 you can see that the government could attempt to act upon any of the components in the $C + I + G + (X - M)$ line. The most obvious policy is that the government should reduce government expenditure and raise taxes. It should be stated here that this policy will be successful only against demand inflation. Fiscal policy was the chief counter-inflationary measure in the 1950s and 1960s. One of the reasons for its failure then was the

clash of objectives. Governments were usually prone to put full employment higher on their list of priorities than control of inflation. Thus, after a short period of fiscal stringency, unemployment was likely to mount and this repeatedly caused governments to abandon tight fiscal policy and go over to expansion of the economy before inflation had been controlled.

The rise of monetarist ideas has meant that fiscal policy is seen as important only in so far as it affects the money supply. Thus in recent years emphasis has been placed upon reducing the size of the PSBR. This was discussed in the previous chapter.

Monetary policy

For many years monetary policy was seen as only supplementary to fiscal policy. The Radcliffe Report's conclusion, that 'money is not important', was widened into 'money does not matter'. Clearly this was an overstatement and we can see, for example, that the rapid expansion of the money supply in the 1970s was undoubtedly one of the causes of inflation.

If monetary policy had a role, Keynesians saw it as being through the rate of interest. The monetarist prescription is to control the supply of money. This, as we have seen, was believed to be the *only* way in which inflation could be controlled. Great emphasis is placed upon the *medium-term financial strategy* (MTFS), i.e. setting targets for monetary growth for the next few years. Not only would reducing the supply of money in itself reduce inflation but the setting of *firm* targets would reduce *expectations*. As we saw earlier in this chapter Friedman argued that increased expectations of inflation are a reason for the rightward shift of the Phillips curve. The policy is aimed at gradually reducing the growth of the money supply until it is in line with the growth of the real economy.

Figure 42.13 shows the targets set for growth in the money supply in recent years, together with the actual growth of M3. You can see from the diagram that MTFS targets were generally greatly exceeded and it was this which, in the

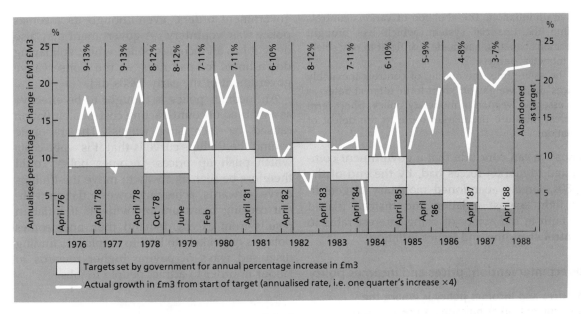

Fig. 42.13 *Monetary targets and monetary growth in the UK.*

end, lead to the abandonment of M3 as a monetary target. As we mentioned earlier, one of the problems in controlling the money supply is choosing the correct measure of it. Should it be M1, M2, M3, etc. The danger is that once policy is aimed at controlling one of these variables it may tend to distort it. A Bank of England official, Goodhart, formulated a principle based upon this difficulty.

Goodhart's law states that any statistical regularity will tend to collapse once pressure is placed upon it for control purposes.

In other words a measure such as M3 is a good guide so long as we do not make its control the object of policy.

At the end of the 1980s the government had fixed on M0 as the measure to control in its MTFS. M0 proved to be a stable and predictable measure of the money supply but, as you can see from Fig. 42.13 the value of V for M0 was increasing rapidly. Thus, using the MV = PT formula, it was still possible to have large increases in the nominal level of national income whilst keeping a strict control on M0.

By the late 1980s inflation had fallen below 5 per cent. Is it possible that we can attribute this to control of the money supply, whichever measure we take? The work of Hendry and Ericsson suggests that this is not so. They argue that the excessive growth of money supply such as that of the 1980s can even be restrictive! If this conclusion is correct it would make it virtually impossible for governments to formulate money supply targets. Their findings also tend to repudiate the idea of the *exogeneity of the money supply* which is vital to Friedman's arguments (*see* page 465). Professor Hendry concluded: 'We have not been able to find any evidence that money supply creates either income growth or inflation.' If this were the case then the decrease in the rate of inflation must be due to some other factor, perhaps unemployment moderating wage demands.

The government itself was disinclined to accept such a neo-Keynesian conclusion. Despite disillusionment with monetary targets it remained convinced of the primacy of monetary policy. Speaking in 1988 Nigel Lawson said:

Experience in the '80s has demonstrated that . . . monetary policy is the only weapon for bearing **581** down on inflation. The abolition of various controls within the financial system, which has brought enormous benefits, has made it difficult to rely solely on monetary targets.

At the same time, the ending of controls inevitably places more weight on short-term interest rates as the essential weapon of monetary policy. Short-term interest rates are the market route to the defeat of inflation.

Thus we can conclude that a government committed to market forces had, by the end of the 1980s, largely abandoned monetary targets in its fight against inflation and instead placed its faith in the ability of rising interest rates to control spending and hence inflation.

Direct intervention: prices and incomes policy

A prices and incomes policy is where the government takes measures to restrict the increase in wages (incomes) and prices.

Like other counter-inflationary measures, a prices and incomes policy tries to ensure that wages and other incomes do not rise faster than the improvement in productivity in the economy. If incomes can be kept below that level there is the added bonus of extra resources which are freed for investment.

There are two main types of prices and incomes policy.

a) Statutory. This occurs when the government passes legislation to limit or to freeze wages and prices. Such policies are unusual in the UK, although a statutory freeze was imposed in 1967.

b) Voluntary. This is where the government tries through argument and persuasion to impose a wages and prices policy. Features of such a policy may include the setting up of a prices and incomes board to examine wage and price increases, exhortations to firms and unions to restrict increases and securing the cooperation of bodies such as the TUC and CBI.

The distinctions between voluntary and statutory policies are not always clear. On several occasions, e.g. 1975–6, the government took actions against firms, such as blacklisting for government orders, even though its incomes policy was 'voluntary'. A government may also deny it has an incomes policy whilst still laying down limits for pay rises, as the Conservative government of the early 1980s did.

An incomes policy is thought to be effective as a method of counteracting cost-push inflation caused by increasing wages. The rationale behind the Phillips curve is that it is wage costs which push up prices. Incomes policy could therefore be seen as a way to move the Phillips curve leftwards, achieving lower inflation without causing more unemployment. If inflation results from excess demand then an incomes policy is only likely to lead to employers finding disguised ways of paying higher rewards to labour in order to attract people to jobs.

Appraisal of prices and incomes policy

Problems of prices and incomes policy

a) Confrontation. The imposition of a prices and incomes policy, voluntary or statutory, risks the possibility of confrontation with trade unions. The most notable example of this in recent years was the confrontation between the Health government and the miners in 1973–4.

b) Discrimination. Incomes policies often tend to be more effective in the public sector, thus restricting incomes there more than in the private sector.

c) Distortion of market forces. If all workers receive similar increases then this will tend to distort market forces in the labour market. Expanding sectors will find it hard to attract labour while contracting sectors will hang on to labour for too long.

d) Differentials. Many incomes policies have been based on flat – rate increases, e.g. £4 per week maximum increases. This increases the wage rate of lower paid workers relatively more than those of the higher paid. This narrowing of differentials tends to stimulate wage claims from the formerly higher paid workers to restore the differentials.

e) *Wages drift*. This refers to the tendency for *earnings* to rise faster than *wage rates*. This is because earnings are a compound of wages, overtime, bonuses, etc. Incomes policy tends to worsen wages drift in those industries which are trying to attract labour, i.e. industry will be tempted to comply with the incomes policy by only raising wage rates by the stipulated amount but increasing bonuses, fringe benefits and so on.

Incomes policies in the UK

Sir Stafford Cripps, a Chancellor of the Exchequer in the 1945–51 Labour government, introduced the first incomes policy with his White Paper *Statement on Personal Incomes, Costs and Prices* in 1947. This was successful for a while but collapsed in the inflation of 1950–1. The Conservatives, when they came to power (1951), abandoned incomes policy in favour of fiscal and monetary measures. Incomes policy was not reintroduced until Selwyn Lloyd, the Conservative Chancellor, brought in the 'pay pause' in 1961. In the years 1961 to 1978 there was some kind of incomes policy for 12 out of the 17 years. A pattern may be discerned in this which the economist Michael Stewart has named the 'Jekyll and Hyde' syndrome. Incomes policies, voluntary or statutory, are always unpopular, but Stewart says that governments found it increasingly impossible to govern without them. The result of this is that, whatever platform the government is elected on, it adopts an incomes policy within a short time. The opposition then promises that if it is returned there will be no incomes policy. When the opposition comes to power, e.g. the Conservatives under Heath in 1970, it abolishes restraints and this results in inflation. The government is then forced to reintroduce an incomes policy. The party in opposition now declares its opposition to this and when it in turn is returned to power, e.g. the Labour Party under Wilson in 1974, it abolishes restraints but a short while later has to

reintroduce them, and so on. This pattern was repeated again when the Conservative government was elected in 1979 on a policy of free collective bargaining. Although it continued to state that there was no incomes policy, the government soon began to suggest norms for pay rises and to impose cash limits on public sector pay settlements.

Stewart's solution to this is somewhat utopian in that he suggests that we agree that some issues are too important to be decided by party politics and that the two main parties agree on a long-term strategy for the economy.

Effectiveness of prices and incomes policies

The UK experience of prices and incomes policies seem to have been that, although they may be successful for a short period, they tend to store up trouble for the future, i.e. incomes policies may restrain inflation and wage claims for a short time but the moment the policy is relaxed a flood of price rises and wage increases is unleashed. It has been suggested that this is at least partly caused because producers and unions see prices and incomes policies as temporary and that if they are permanent, as in such countries as Austria and Sweden, this problem would not occur. It could also be argued that prices and incomes policy may fail, as may fiscal policy and monetary policy, if it is relied upon as the only method of controlling inflation, and that what is needed is a combination of policies.

Conclusion

We have demonstrated in this chapter that inflation can have a number of causes. The failure adequately to contain inflation except at the cost of other objectives of policy such as full employment may be at least partly attributable to treating inflation as if it were monocausal, i.e. inflation is entirely caused by excess demand or entirely caused by expansion of the **583** money supply. If inflation has a number of causes it seems likely that we need a '*package*' of measures, both fiscal, monetary and direct, to deal with it.

We must also consider the problem of inflation in the broader sphere. Firstly, for the last two decades inflation has been a worldwide problem (*see* page 427). Whatever measures have been taken domestically, it has been impossible to isolate the domestic economy. This points to the obvious conclusion, that inflation must also be cured on a worldwide basis. Secondly, we may see the problem of inflation alongside our desire to achieve other objectives of policy such as full employment or economic growth. At the end of the 1980s the problem of inflation seemed to have been contained not only in the UK but in most other industrialised nations. However, there were at the same time levels of unemployment which a decade previously would have been considered unthinkable. There still remained fundamental differences of opinion about the causes of inflation.

Summary

1 Inflation may have adverse consequences for economic growth, the balance of payments, the distribution of incomes and employment.

2 The Phillips curve shows the relationship between inflation and unemployment. Monetarist theory suggests that expectations of inflation shift the Phillips curve rightwards.

3 The adaptive expectations school maintains that, because of the money illusion, there may be a short term trade-off between inflation and unemployment. But in the long run attempts to reduce unemployment below the natural level result in inflation rather than jobs.

4 The rational expectations school argue that there is no money illusion and hence no trade-off between inflation and unemployment.

5 There are three concurrent theories of inflation: demand-pull, cost-push and monetary inflation.

6 Fiscal policy has been used to control inflation by regulating aggregate demand. Policy in the 1980s came to regard fiscal policy as important only as a part of monetary policy.

7 The monetarist approach to monetary policy was based upon strict control of monetary aggregates. At the end of the 1980s monetary policy became almost entirely reliant upon control through interest rates.

8 Incomes policies can be either voluntary or statutory.

9 If inflation has a number of causes it is likely that a 'package deal' of various policy measures is necessary to deal with it.

Questions

1 Distinguish between cost-push and demand-pull inflation.
2 Discuss the usefulness of the Phillips curve as a guide to economic policy.
3 To what extent are the consequences of inflation undesirable?
4 What part do expectations play in the determination of the rate of inflation?
5 Explain the monetarist theory of inflation and state its prescription for the cure.
6 Assess the effectiveness of prices and incomes policies.

7 Distinguish between the adaptive expectations and the rational expectations views of inflation.
8 'Inflation is always and everywhere a monetary phenomenon.' Critically assess Milton Friedman's statement.
9 Examine the relationship between public borrowing and inflation.
10 In what ways may the control of interest rates be used to control inflation?

Data response   What's the attraction of Little Mo?

Read the following article which was condensed from articles appearing at the time of the 1988 Budget.

What's the attraction of little Mo?
'None of the M's is a perfect guide to the underlying guide to the concept they seek to represent'. When Nigel Lawson said this in his first Mansion House speech as Chancellor of the Exchequer, he was referring to the fallibility, not of his Prime Minister, but of her monetary aggregates – M1, M3, and other definitions of the money supply.

It sounded like an echo of the Prime Minister herself. One recalls that she amazed Brian Walden and the Sunday morning viewers of Weekend World by chatting animatedly about various M's as if they were a rather wayward troupe of performing circus animals. Echoing in turn her guru, Professor Alan Walters, she was then taken with the rather obliging behaviour of the smallest money supply of them all, MO, which had obligingly stood on its pedestal and hardly moved for a year.

It was M0, pronounced 'M-nought', but christened 'little Mo' by the TV commentators, remains the one monetary target to which the government is committed. M0 is almost entirely notes and coins, 90 per cent of them in circulation and the rest in bank tills. It is also known as 'wider monetary base'.

Now M0 is the 'key indicator of the growth of narrow money,' according to the Chancellor. The other M's he indicated, have all been misbehaving. The Treasury bravely adjust their targets – up rather than down – and interpret the overruns which often occur.

M3, once the main target, is very sensitive to switches of funds between banks and building societies as it includes bank time deposits but not those of building societies. A difference in interest rates could therefore lead to large transfers of funds.

M1, which is notes and coins plus sight deposits in banks, used to perform rather well. But it is now out of favour, because 25 per cent of it is interest-bearing over-night money, which has been rising rapidly. But the adoption of M0 in this Chancellor's first Budget was surprising since the Bank of England had said that 'movements in cash are unlikely to be helpful as a guide to general economic or financial conditions.'

The superficial attraction of M0 is that it grows much more slowly than any of the other M's. M0 increases in line with personal disposable income in money terms (Treasury model) or personal consumption (Bank of England model), but not as fast. But it is unpredictable. The black economy may require more banknotes, but credit cards and payment of wages by credit transfer – both spreading fast – are a move the other way, to the cashless society.

What will the Chancellor do if M0 rises too fast? He can hardly order incomes or consumption to stop rising. Nor can he tell the Bank of England to stop printing banknotes – unless he wants to start a run on the banks. He has indicated that he will raise interest rates. According to the Treasury model, it takes a 2 per cent rise in deposit rate to cut the growth of notes and coins by about 1 per cent. But the Bank of England view is that: 'It has not proved possible to find a stable econometric relationship between interest rates and cash balances in this country.'

Using interest rates to control M0 could be using a sledgehammer to crack a nut. It would mean a heavy price in terms of deflation of the real economy. The M0 target of 0–4 per cent for next year is lower than all other targets.

Monetary targets have become a three-ring circus. As the Chancellor said, fiscal policy, funding policy and the exchange rate are now all part of monetary policy too – and a more important part. The most important of the M's for the credibility of economic policy, is and always has been, the Big M – Margaret Thatcher.

Money supply and National Income

Year	M0 £ million	GDP at market prices £ million
1981	11,926	254 103
1982	12,341	276 409
1983	13,081	300 973
1984	13,834	320 120
1985	14,412	351 869
1986	15,188	374 895
1987 (Dec)	15,847	

Source: National Accounts *and* CLSB

Answer the following questions.

1 What reasons does the article give for the adoption of M0 as a monetary target?

2 The article says that M0 is composed mainly of notes and coins in circulation. What else is included in the measure?

3 Explain what is meant by the 'Treasury model' and the 'Bank of England model.' Does it matter that they differ?

4 There is reference in the article to 'narrow money'. What is meant by this?

5 Why does the inclusion of interest-bearing deposits in the definition of M1 reduce its usefulness?

6 Determine V for the M0 money stock in 1981 and 1986. Explain how you arrived at your answer.

7 For what reasons has the value of V of the M0 money stock increased over the period shown in the table? What has happened to the value(s) of V for the broad money stock over the same period.

8 How useful do you consider the control of monetary aggregates to be as a method of combatting inflation?

9 What in, your opinion, have been the causes of inflation in the last two decades?

10 Assess the success of government policies since 1979 in combatting inflation.

43

The attainment of full employment

*The enormous anomaly of unemployment in a
world of wants.*

J. M. Keynes, *Essays on Persuasion*

The meaning of full employment

Background

In many ways the control of unemployment is at the core of modern macroeconomics; it was the concern with unemployment which gave rise to the new economics of Keynes and his contemporaries during the 1930s. It is not hard to understand why this was so. In the years 1921 to 1939 the average level of unemployment in the UK was 14 per cent; it was never less than 10 per cent and in the worst years was over 20 per cent. In 1943 *The Times* said: 'Next to war unemployment has been the most widespread, most insidious and most corroding malady of our generation: it is the specific social disease of western civilisation in our time.' The pursuit of full employment as the prime objective of policy was specifically adopted by Western governments at the end of the 1939–45 war and they adopted Keynesian demand management policies as the means of achieving it. Compared with all previous eras this policy was successful, unemployment remaining at very low levels throughout the 1950s and 1960s, so much so that other objectives of policy such as the control of inflation came to be regarded as more important. Many people thought that mass unemployment was a pro-blem which had been banished for ever. However by the early 1980s the UK had a greater number of people unemployed than in the 1930s and the attainment of full employment was once more at the centre of the stage.

The employed and the unemployed

Obviously not everyone in the economy works; the young, the old, some housewives, etc., may not be in employment. Thus when we speak of employment we are speaking of those who are in some form of paid work and when we say the unemployed we are speaking of those who are actively seeking jobs. As we saw in Chapter 4, the working population comprises all those who are working or who are seeking work. In 1988 the working population was 27·8 million and of those 2·7 million were unemployed and seeking work. The post-war high was hit in December 1986 with a total of 3·4 million registered employed.

These figures may be slightly deceptive in that the figure for unemployment includes only those who have to register as available for work at employment offices. Many people such as married women lose their jobs but do not register as unemployed. In addition to this the government excluded certain categories of unemployed from the figures; for example, those over 60

587

Table 43.1 Changes in the unemployment statistics

Date	Change	Effect
10/79	Fortnightly payment of benefits	+20 000
11/81	Men over 60 offered higher supplementary benefit to leave working population	−37 000
10/82	Registration at job centres made voluntary. Computer count of benefit claimants substituted for clerical count of registrants	−190 000
3/83	Men 60 and over given national insurance credits or higher supplementary benefit without claiming unemployment benefit	−162 000
7/85	Correction of Northern Ireland discrepancies	−5000
3/86	Two-week delay in compilation of figures to reduce over-recording	−50 000
		424 000
Total effect of changes to seasonably adjusted figure without school leavers in 4/87		458 000
7/86	Inclusion of self-employed and HM forces in denominator of unemployed percentage	−1·4%

were not required to register as available for work, even though they were still able to draw unemployment benefit.

The number of people who are unemployed in the sense of wanting a job as opposed to the number on the official register is a controversial topic. Supply-siders argue that many of the registered unemployed are not actively seeking work at all. An extreme view, such as that of Professor Patrick Minford, would argue that there is no involuntary unemployment (*see* page 482). The government in the late 1980s tended to favour the annual Labour Force Survey (LFS) or that drawn up by the International Labour Organisation (ILO) which give figures well below those on the official register. The LFS excludes many who are work seekers but do not claim benefit because they are not entitled to (e.g. married women) or because they choose not to.

The history of unemployment since 1981 has become hard to follow because of the frequent changes in the way the statistics are compiled (*see* Table 43.1). Each change has been defensible on the grounds of greater accuracy or practicality. Yet all the changes, except on minor one, have had the effect of reducing published unemployment totals by a cumulative 424 000. Also the inclusion of HM Forces and the self employed in the size of the working population

knocked 1·4 per cent off subsequent figures for unemployment. In addition to these revisions we must also remember the 400 000 or so who are on special job creation schemes.

It is therefore possible to have several different measures of unemployment. Table 43.2 based on the 1986 LFS gives several different estimates. As you can see this could put the unemployed percentage anywhere between 10·6 per cent and 14·3 per cent. If we added to this those who simply wanted a job we would get an even higher figure. In a Commons' written reply in May 1987 a deputy minister said that the total of those which were unemployed in the sense of those who wanted a job could be as high as 5·3 million!

Defining full employment

It may seem the simplest thing in the world to say that full employment must be where there is zero unemployment. However in practice this can never be so. There will always be some unemployment. In his book *Full Employment in a Free Society* (1944) Beveridge defined full employment as being when no more than 3 per cent of the working population were unemployed. However for many years after 1945 there was less than 3 per cent unemployment; thus, there could be said to have been *over-full employment*.

Table 43.2 Criteria for being unemployed

	Claiming benefit	Sought work week	last 4 weeks	Wants a job	Available for work	Worked in week	last 4 weeks	Number 000's
1	Yes	Yes	–	–	Yes	No		2002
2	No	Yes	–	–	–	No		826
3	Yes	–	Yes	–	Yes	–	No	101
4	No	–	Yes	–	Yes	–	No	47
5	Yes	–	No	–	Yes	–	No	859
6	Yes	–	No	–	Yes	–	Yes	206

Note: A dash indicates that the criterion at the head of the column does not form part of the definition summarised by the row.

Alternative definitions of unemployment

			000's	%*
Labour Force Survey (LFS) estimate	1 + 2	=	2828	10·6
Alternative (ILO/OECD) estimate	1 + 2 + 3 + 4	=	2976	11·2
UK national definition: claimants	1 + 3 + 5 + 6	=	3168	11·7
Widest definition	1 + 2 + 3 + 4 + 5 + 6	=	4041	14·3

* Per cent of employed labour force plus unemployed
Source: 1986 Labour Force Survey

As we saw in the previous chapter this is one of the factors which is thought to have accounted for *wages drift* and *demand-pull inflation*.

Before producing his book on full employment, Beveridge had chaired the committee which produced the report *Social Insurance and Allied Services* (1942), usually known as the Beveridge Report. This report had stressed that the only way any viable system of unemployment benefit and health insurance could be financed was if there was full or near-full employment. When Parliament adopted this report it committed itself to the maintenance of 'a high and stable level of employment'. Governments in the 1980s have discovered just how difficult it is to finance the social services when there is such heavy unemployment.

Although Beveridge's definition became the bench-mark for subsequent policies, a single numerical definition can have its drawbacks. Table 43.3 shows the regional unemployment figures for 1964. Even though national unemployment figures for 1964. Even though national unemployment was only 1·8 per cent, some regions were above the stipulated 3 per cent.

Another method of defining full employment

Table 43.3 Regional rates of unemployment in the UK, 1964

Percentage unemployed				
N Ireland	Scotland	Wales	N England	UK
6·6	3·7	2·6	3·4	1·8

would be to relate it to the number of job vacancies. Thus if the numbers of jobs available were greater than the number of unemployed we could say that there was full employment. There are, however, two shortcomings to this definition.

a) The regional disparities described in Table 43.3 could apply with vacancies in one area of the country and surplus labour in another. This could work out as follows:

Area	Vacancies	Unemployed
A	90 000	10 000
B	10 000	90 000
Total	100 000	100 000

Under these circumstances not only would people in area B find it very difficult to get a job **589** but also there is a shortage of labour in Area A which may exert inflationary pressure upon the economy.

b) Even when the vacancies and unemployed match up numerically in an area, the unemployed are likely to lack the necessary skills for the jobs which are on offer.

Figure 43.1 shows the relationship between unemployed and vacancies from 1955 to 1988. You can see that the graph plots the regular cycle of recession and recovery which was the pattern until the mid-1960s. After this date the plunge of the curve shows the descent of the economy into slump and the beginnings of recovery.

Thus we could conclude that any statistical definition of full employment is likely to prove unsatisfactory. We might therefore adopt a more rule-of-thumb definition such as:

Full employment exists when everyone who wants a job and is capable of doing a job is able to find one.

Types of unemployment

Unemployment is not a uniform phenomenon, it exists for a number of reasons. When we list those reasons we are therefore considering the *causes of unemployment.*

Frictional

This refers to people displaced by the normal working of the economy. It is inevitable in a developing economy that people will, from time to time, change jobs and may perhaps be unemployed for some weeks as they wait to take up the next job.

Seasonal

Some jobs are dependent upon the weather and the season. Facetiously, we might say that this refers to deck-chair attendants being unemployed in the winter or hot-chestnut salespeople being

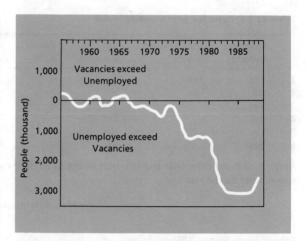

Fig. 43.1 *Vacancies and unemployment in the UK.* The graph shows the relationship between registered unemployed and the vacancies notified to employment offices. Such vacancies are only about a third of total vacancies.

unemployed in the summer. However, on a more serious level the construction industry is the most badly hit by seasonal unemployment, with tens or even hundreds of thousands of workers laid-off in the winter when the bad weather makes work difficult.

Residual

There is thus always a *residue* of unemployment, due to frictional and seasonal causes, which we cannot reduce. In addition to these causes there are, of course, a number of people who are simply unwilling to work but register as unemployed in order to receive benefit. The existence of residual unemployment further complicates our definition of full employment.

There is also the problem of attempting to quantify residual unemployment. In the full employment times of the 1950s and 1960s it was estimated that it amounted to between 100 000 to 200 000 people, depending on the time of year. In the late 1960s, however, the base line for unemployment rose to around 600 000.

In Chapter 42 we saw that the concept of the *natural level of unemployment* is used in monetarist thinking. However, although this is a useful theoretical tool and might be thought to equate with the residual unemployment we have just discussed, we can see that it is a very difficult idea to quantify. What factors, for example, account for the discrepancy between the residual (or natural) level of unemployment of one hundred thousand in the 1950s and of one million and more in the 1980s.

In the 1980s prophecies were made of unemployment in the millions to the end of the century with, perhaps, never a return to the levels of the immediate post-war years. It is *not* suggested, however, that this huge reservoir of unemployment is due to frictional or seasonal causes; it is due to the more profound causes which we will now consider.

Structural

This is unemployment resulting from a change in the structure of the economy; for example, it could be the result of the imbalance caused by the decline of one industry and (hopefully) the rise of another. Unemployment results when new industries do not create enough jobs to employ those made redundant, or because the new industry is in a different area or requires different skills.

Structural unemployment has plagued the UK economy for most of this century. For most of the period it has been caused by the decline of the *old staple industries* such as coal-mining, iron and steel and textiles. These industries tended to be concentrated in the coalfields and thus, because of this heavy regional specialisation, structural unemployment manifested itself as *regional unemployment*.

In the 1970s and 1980s new forms of structural unemployment came about as previously prosperous industries such as motor vehicles were hit by foreign competition. This has made the incidence of unemployment more widespread. For example, the West Midlands, which until recently was one of the most prosperous areas of the country, became one of the most profoundly depressed.

General or cyclical

All of the types of unemployment we have considered so far are the result of changes in the economy which we would not necessarily wish to oppose, although we may seek to lessen the impact and the hardship caused. However, the most severe unemployment, that of the 1930s and of the 1980s, is a result of the general depression of the whole economy. This is unemployment which we have traditionally associated with the *trade cycle*, hence its name. The causes of these periodic depressions are a subject of much controversy. Students should at this stage, if they have not already done so, acquaint themselves with the content of Chapter 32, all of which is relevant to our discussion here.

A disturbing trend in recent years has been suggestions that we may see the revival of the economy but with no fall in the level of unemployment. Previously a fall in the number of unemployed has been seen as the indicator of economic recovery.

Technological

This occurs when improvements in technology reduce the demand for labour. There is nothing new about technological unemployment; the spinning jenny, for instance, allowed one person to do the work previously done by 100. What is new at the moment is the speed and breadth of technological change. The new technology associated with the microchip affects almost all industries and jobs. The new technology affects unemployment in two ways, firstly by doing away with jobs and skills and secondly by creating new jobs which many of the unemployed are incapable of doing.

Let us consider the new technology as it affects one industry – banking. We have already seen computerised accounting, electronic transfer of funds, cash dispensers and so on. Now we have EFTPOS (electronic funds transfer, point of sale), whereby people's bank accounts are automatically debited from a terminal in the shop. Also to come soon are speaking computers **591** which customers will be able to telephone for statements of their accounts, etc. All these developments save on labour so that, although banking is one of the UK's fastest growing industries, its total workforce is not increasing. The new technology also produces a division in the workforce, creating a new managerial class of those able to comprehend and to control the technology on the one hand and, on the other, a class of semi-skilled people whose job is to feed the machines. Whole areas of intermediate skills such as book-keeping are being swept away. This pattern is being repeated throughout whole sectors of the UK industry and the potential for development seems to be showing no signs of slowing down.

Job prospects have also been adversely affected in the UK by the new technology, in that the UK has failed to keep pace with the manufacturing side of the industry. The manufacture of microchips, for example, is effectively dominated by just two countries, the USA and Japan. Thus the UK and many other traditional manufacturing countries such as West Germany and France are placed at a disadvantage. One encouraging sign is the dominance which the UK seems to be achieving in software. This may be at least partly attributable to the wholeheartedness with which many Britons have taken to microcomputers.

Table 43.3 Percentage rates of unemployment in the UK

Region	1974	1982	1988
North	4·6	16·5	13·4
Yorkshire and Humberside	2·5	13·4	10·7
East Midlands	2·2	11·0	8·3
East Anglia	1·9	9·9	5·8
South East	1·5	8·7	5·9
South West	2·6	10·8	7·2
West Midlands	2·1	14·9	9·9
North West	3·4	14·7	11·9
Wales	3·7	15·6	11·9
Scotland	3·8	14·2	12·6
N. Ireland	5·4	19·4	17·7
UK	2·6	12·2	9·1

Source: CSO, Annual Abstract of Statistics, HMSO and Employment Gazette

Regional unemployment

There are considerable differences in the rates of unemployment in the various different regions of the UK. These figures also disguise much worse conditions in particular places. In Corby, for example, adult unemployment was greater than 50 per cent in 1984. This was not an untypical figure for the worst hit towns. In a time of general unemployment, then, we must first consider whether there is a case for a special regional policy.

Arguments for regional policy

a) The failure of market forces. Advocates of free market economics argue that the price mechanism will eventually abolish these disparities. Unemployment will reduce wage and other costs in the regions and this will eventually attract industry. However it appears that, over any reasonable period of time, market forces are as likely to accentuate regional disparities as to remove them.

Neo-classical economists would also argue that the movement of workers should lessen regional differences, i.e. people will move out of the depressed regions thereby reducing the supply in that area and increasing it in other areas. Unfortunately, to the extent to which this is true, it tends to be the young and vigorous workers which move out of the depressed regions. This therefore leaves an older and less adaptable workforce. This may further add to the reluctance of firms to move to the region.

b) Cumulative decline. The depressed areas often have a legacy of labour troubles which are a result of the decline of the old staple industries. Thus this history of trade union disputes may discourage firms from moving there. In addition to this the social capital of these areas, e.g. housing, transport and communications, often tends to be run down. These factors further discourage firms from moving to these areas. There is therefore a need for positive government policy to encourage firms to move to these regions.

c) Inflationary pressures. If national measures are taken to stimulate the economy in order to reduce unemployment it is quite likely that they will have an inflationary effect. Consider the following situation:

	Percentage employment of capacity in industry	
Area	*X*	*Y*
A	100	–
B	–	70

Industrial capacity in industry X is fully employed in area A but area B is dependent upon another industry (Y) and in this there is considerable unemployment. If the government tries to cure this by stimulating the general level of demand, this is likely to cause inflationary pressure in industry X before it cures the unemployment in industry Y.

d) Social costs. A firm in choosing its location is likely to consider only its *private costs*. Socially, however, it must be considered that there is already enormous pressure upon resources in congested areas. Roads, schools, hospitals and housing are all much more expensive to provide in the prosperous areas, whilst in the depressed areas of the country there is often spare capacity. It may be worthwhile, therefore, encouraging firms to go to these regions in order that society may benefit from these lower social costs.

Government policy

The main choice which confronts the government is that of taking *'workers to the work'* or *'work to the workers'*. Methods of taking workers to the work include removal and relocation grants, retraining schemes and Job centres. Since the Special Areas Act 1935 the majority of government regional policy has been aimed at encouraging firms to locate in the less prosperous regions. Over the course of the 1980s the government reduced the scale of regional aid until it could be said that it was virtually relying on the market forces approach. The details of government regional policy are to be found on pages 168–70.

The efficacy of regional policy

There is little evidence to show that government policy had much success up until 1963. After that date there was a more aggressive regional policy.

Table 43.4 Unemployment in the Regions

Region	Unemployment			
	1979		1986	
	% unemployed	*% above (+) or below (−) national average*	*% unemployed*	*% above (+) or below (−) national average*
North	7·9	+61·2	17·1	+43·7
Yorkshire and Humberside	5·1	+4·1	13·8	+16·0
East Midlands	4·0	−18·4	11·3	−5·0
East Anglia	3·7	−24·5	9·1	−23·5
South East	3·0	−38·7	8·7	−26·9
South West	4·8	−2·0	10·2	−14·3
West Midlands	4·8	−2·0	14·0	+17·6
North West	6·1	+24·5	14·5	+21·8
Wales	6·5	+32·7	14·5	+21·8
Scotland	6·9	+40·8	14·3	+20·2
Northern Ireland	9·1	+85·7	18·8	+58·0
United Kingdom	4·9	–	11·9	–

Source: Regional Trends *HMSO*

This policy succeeded for some time in reducing regional disparities but it was overtaken by the general depression in the economy in the early 1980s and then by the government's abandonment of regional policy.

Table 43.4 shows figures for unemployment in the regions in 1979 and 1986. It is possible to argue from these figures that the disparities between the regions have diminished, i.e. that for most regions the percentage deviation from the nation average has declined. However, this has to be seen against the background of much higher rates of unemployment nationally. It would be little comfort for the unemployed in the North region to be told that, although the rate of unemployment had increased to 17.1 per cent this was only 43 per cent above the national average whereas the 1979 rate of 7.9 per cent was 61 per cent above the national average.

(A map of the regions appears on page 169. See also comments on the North-South divide below.)

The costs and benefits of regional policy

The most important criticism of regional policy is that it creates inefficient units of production. For example, Chrysler (now Talbot) were persuaded by the government to build a new factory at Linwood outside Glasgow rather than in Coventry where they would have preferred to build it. Car engines were made in Coventry, transported to Scotland to be put into bodies and then transported south again to be sold. The eventual closure of the Talbot Linwood plant in 1981 requires little further comment. Whilst the creation of inefficient plants may be tolerated in the economy as a way of coping with unemployment, it has very bad consequences for our external trade because it destroys our comparative advantage.

However, if we look at regional policy in the context of the whole economy there are several points to be borne in mind. Firstly, although firms might choose to locate in the South East, they often ignore the very high *social costs* in these areas. Housing, for example, is in very short supply in the South East and is consequently extremely expensive, whilst elsewhere in the country houses stand empty. Furthermore, as aid is put into the regions it should regenerate the areas to such an extent that their *recovery becomes self-sustaining*. The lessons of the 1930s also teach us that there is a great *danger in concentration*. Diversification is a good safeguard against changes in demand, even if it is slightly less efficient.

The North-South Divide

It is often asserted that, over recent years, the discrepancies between different regions have become more pronounced. The prosperous areas tend to be in the south of the country and the depressed ones in the north – hence the name. The existence of the north-south divide is vigorously denied by many politicians. However we observed in Table 43.4 that there were considerable differences in rates of unemployment between the regions. You can also see from Table 43.5 that there are considerable differences in earnings and also that these have been becoming more pronounced.

We have already mentioned that the decline of the northern regions began with the decline of the old staple industries and was compounded by the decline of newer industries such as motor vehicles. In the 1980s there have been rapid improvements in productivity which also caused industries to shed labour.

It is certainly true that the depressed areas are attracting new industry but they are not doing it fast enough to offset the other trends. These trends tend to exacerbate other factors such as house prices which have rocketed in the south-east. This in turn makes it more difficult for the people in the north to move south in search of work.

This is not just a UK trend. It seems that Europe is experiencing relative decline at its edges. Prosperity in the EEC is mainly concentrated in the 'golden triangle' which takes in northern Germany and France, the Benelux countries and the south-east of England.

Table 43.5 Index of average weekly household incomes

Region	1979–80	1984–85
North	89·0	82·4
Yorkshire and Humberside	87·0	86·6
East Midlands	101·0	98·3
East Anglia	97·6	99·0
South East	114·2	119·9
South West	92·6	101·0
West Midlands	99·5	93·0
North West	95·5	88·6
Wales	92·4	90·5
Scotland	94·3	95·9
Northern Ireland	84·3	83·6
United Kingdom	100·0	100·0
	= £134·1	= £206·8

Source: Regional Trends HMSO

The unemployment of the 1980s

The growth of unemployment

Examination of Tables 43.6 and 43.7 (page 601) will show you that unemployment in the 1980s reached unprecedented levels. A young person at the threshold of a career will hardly need reminding of this, while at the other end of the career spectrum people made redundant in the second half of their working life could only look forward to a life on the dole.

Table 43.6 shows the surge of unemployment during the 1970s and 1980s. The table also shows the figures for all those working. By comparing the unemployed and the employed figures between 1976 and 1988 you can see that although unemployment rose by 1 270 000, the employed total rose by 367 000. This was caused by the growth of the relative size of the working population and was due to such factors as the changing age distribution of the population and the increased proportion of women working. We may even be faced with the curious paradox of employment and unemployment growing simultaneously.

The origins of unemployment

We must now turn to consider the reasons for this rise in general unemployment. No single explanation is satisfactory but the following factors are significant.

a) *Deficiency of aggregate demand*. The Keynesian explanation of unemployment attributes it to lack of aggregate demand. Whilst it must be true that unemployment is due to lack of demand, this begs the questions of what causes the depression of demand and also whether deficit financing to raise the level of aggregate demand would alleviate it.

b) *Increase in structural and frictional unemployment*. Commentators have pointed to several factors in labour markets which have increased unemployment. The rise in social security benefits relative to wages has made unemployment more tolerable for some. The increase in unemployment has also made firms less willing to retrain employees or take on older ones, while employment protection legislation and redundancy payments have made them more cautious about taking on labour.

We have already mentioned the decline in some UK industries which has increased unemployment. This has been particularly noticeable

Table 43.6 Unemployment and employment in the UK

Year	Total unemployed (thousand)	Percentage unemployed (%)*	Employed labour force (thousand)
1976	1266	5·5	24 844
1977	1359	5·8	24 865
1978	1343	5·7	25 014
1979	1234	5·3	25 393
1980	1513	6·8	25 327
1981	2395	10·5	24 344
1982	2770	11·6	23 908
1983	2984	11·7	23 610
1984	3030	11·7	24 060
1985	3179	11·9	24 445
1986	3229	11·9	24 542
1987	2953	10·6	25 142
1988	2536	9·1	25 211

* Method of calculation subject to revision.
Source: Employment Gazette DoE

in the manufacturing sector (*see* page 47). The unemployment caused by these structural changes has been made worse by the difficulty that many people have when attempting to move to the south-east in search of jobs because of high housing prices.

c) International aspects. Unemployment in the UK cannot be considered in isolation. Rates of unemployment have also been significantly higher in most of the UK's trading partners. This therefore contributed to the general depression of demand. Another international aspect is the import penetration of the UK's manufacturing industries such as iron and steel, motor vehicles and electronics. Exports on the other hand have often been hindered by a too-high exchange rate for the pound. This caused producers to cut prices, even though real wages were rising at the same time, so that profits were often squeezed to the point where firms closed down.

d) Oil prices. The OPEC price rise in 1973 played a significant part in the rise in inflation and unemployment in the mid-1970s. The 1978 oil price rises had even more dramatic effects, increasing costs dramatically and thus squeezing profits still further. The 1978 oil price rise was a major factor in precipitating the world-wide depression of the early 1980s. The subsequent collapse in oil prices helped some of the UK's main trading rivals such as Japan and Germany who are major oil-importers but further damaged the UK which is an oil exporter.

e) Technology. We have already seen that improvements in technology have reduced the demand for labour (*see* also the discussion on page 591). However, we may hope that in the long run improvements in technology and the resultant increases in productivity will create jobs by leading to an expansion of the economy. (*See* page 244.)

f) Government policy. Up until the mid-1970s government policy was aimed at reducing unemployment by expansionary fiscal and monetary policies. However at this time government began to adopt contractionary policies, with the aim of squeezing inflation out of the economy. These policies therefore contributed to unemployment. Further we saw in Chapter 42 that monetary thinking points to the necessity of raising unemployment as a method of eliminating inflation. Government policies must therefore be seen as a major factor in the rise of unemployment.

Changes in measurement and population

We discussed earlier in the chapter the many changes in measurement during the 1980s which make it difficult to say precisely what is happening to unemployment. Estimates by Christopher Johnson of Lloyds Bank suggest that unemployment was reduced by 400 000 by statistical redefinitions and that special employment measures such as YTS accounted for a further 400 000.

It is also the case that many of the new jobs created were part-time jobs. Also some of these part time jobs were in fact second jobs for those already employed. There were a growing tendency for newly-created jobs to go to women. This could be, at least in part, because the jobs were part-time and/or low paid. However, while there were 1 139 000 less men employed in 1986 than in 1979 there were, in fact, 289 000 more women employed.

Because of demographic changes the population of working age was rising by about half a per cent a year, that is a figure of about 1.5 million for the period 1979–87.

The unemployment figures have also been distorted by changes in the activity rate, that is the percentage of those of working age who are working or seeking work. In the early 1980s the activity rate dropped to 77.5 per cent but rose again to reach 80.2 per cent in 1987. This made the unemployment figures worse. On the other hand the official policy of discouraging benefit claims kept the activity rate below that which it would otherwise have been.

The control of unemployment: the supply side view

Introduction

For most of the period since the 1939–45 war attempts to alleviate unemployment have centred on neo-Keynesian demand-side management policies. For example, running a budget deficit was supposed to boost demand and reduce unemployment. During the late 1970s and 1980s various supply-side schools of economics gained acceptance in government, not only in the UK but in the USA and most major western economies. They argued that, not only were demand-side policies ineffective but, they made matters worse. Budget deficits created inflation and, in the end, created more unemployment not less.

There are various supply side schools – monetarist, neo-classical, new classical and so on. While there are significant differences between them (*see* discussion on the *adaptive expectations* and the *rational expectations* schools on pages 573–77) there are common features and policy prescriptions and it is on these that we will concentrate in this section.

Supply-side economics emphasises the 'natural' competitive forces in the economy. It is believed that the economy is essentially self-regulating. (*See* page 463.) Problems arise because these 'natural' competitive forces are thwarted by government interference and by restrictive practices by firms and by unions. In short, we need to concentrate on the costs of production (hence supply-side). This will reduce costs, control inflation and, in the long-run, promote employment.

One central idea of the supply side schools is that there is a natural level of unemployment and that it is the vain attempts to reduce this level that have been a key element in creating inflation. Only when the natural level has been achieved can we expect the economy to be operating efficiently and achieving the economic growth which will create more jobs. (*See* discussion of this in Chapters 36 and 42.)

Common supply side policy prescriptions are:

a) reduced welfare payments, such as unemployment benefits;

b) lower levels of direct taxation;

c) reduction of employee and trade union rights;

d) abolition of wage floors.

e) the promotion of training and retraining schemes

We have already discussed the argument on lowering tax rates (*see* pages 557–9) we will now consider the other points listed above.

Reducing welfare payments to the unemployed

It is argued that welfare benefits may be pitched at a level which is above the equilibrium wage rate in the lower paid labour markets. This being the case some people will not work since they would be worse-off if they did so. Thus, welfare payments have artificially increased the level of unemployment.

In Fig. 43.2 the 'benefits floor' is set at a level of oc which is above the equilibrium wage in that labour market of ob. This being the case only OL_1 will be employed instead of OL_2. Thus welfare benefits have created $OL_3 - OL_1$ registered unemployed.

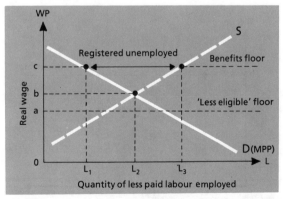

Fig. 43.2 *Effects of welfare benefits on unemployment.* A benefits floor set at oc which is above the equilibrium wage rate results in only OL_1 being employed instead of OL_2. However, $OL_3 - OL_1$ claim benefits thus there is less employment and a number of registered unemployed are created. Lowering the benefits floor to the 'less elligible' level eliminates the unemployment.

597

In order to eliminate the unemployment it is necessary to reduce the welfare benefits below the level of the lowest wage available in the labour market. In our example this could be *oa*. This argument contrasts with the Beveridge unemployment insurance argument that welfare insurance should sustain a person at or near their working standard of living whilst they are (temporarily) out of work.

The idea of making the level of welfare benefits less than the lowest standard of living achievable by those in work is not new, it is the principle of 'less eligibility' on which the Poor Law of 1834 was founded.

Reducing trade union rights

Many supply-siders believe that over-strong trade unions through such things as closed shop agreements hold the wage rate above the equilibrium. In Fig. 43.3 union power has lifted the wage rate to *ob* this is above the equilibrium rate *oa*. As a result of this employers now only wish to employ OL_1 workers rather than OL_2 at the equilibrium. (*See* discussion of this point page 257.)

Supply-side policies also aim at increasing productivity by reducing union power. For

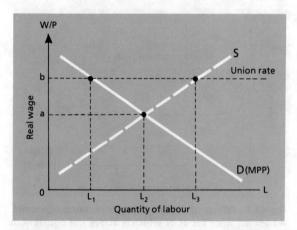

Fig. 43.3 *Wages and union power.* Over-strong unions impose a wage rate at *ob* which is above the equilibrium *oa*. Legislation to weaken unions allows the wage rate to return to the equilibrium and more employment to be created. (*See* also Fig. 43.4.)

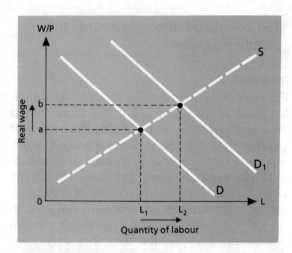

Fig. 43.4 *The effect of increased productivity.* Productivity increases resulting from the reduction of restrictive practices such as demarcation, and/or improvement of the quality of the labour force through improved training shifts the demand curve for labour to the right. This results in both higher wages and increased employment.

example, the ending of demarcation agreements and overmanning is said to have a positive effect on both wages and employment. This is illustrated in Fig. 43.4 here you can see that improvements in productivity have shifted the demand curve for labour to the right. Thus, before the ending of restrictive practices the equilibrium wage was *oa* and the quantity of labour employed was OL_1 after the resultant rises in productivity the wage rate has risen to *ob* and the quantity of labour employed to OL_2.

There were substantial improvements in productivity during the 1980s – (*see* page 603).

Training schemes

It is an obvious supply-side point that improving the quality of factor inputs should improve productivity and output. Thus schemes to train and retrain labour must have beneficial effects upon the economy. We can illustrate this point by reference to Fig. 43.4. The result of better trained labour should be to shift the demand curve for labour to the right as it becomes more productive.

Governments during the 1980s introduced many training schemes such as TOPS, YOPS and YTS. These were politically controversial with many left wingers claiming that real training was not being given and that the schemes were a method of keeping people off the unemployment register.

It need hardly be said that the policy prescriptions described above are hotly disputed by neo-Keynesians. They would see measures such as cutting wages as more likely to increase unemployment by creating a deficiency in demand. However, we may accept all the measures described above as effective and still be left with a problem. You will recall from our definition of labour as a factor of production that it has the unique characteristic of being 'the human factor.' Thus we may find that we have policy measures which are economically sound but which are politically or morally indefensible. This insight was one of the key starting points for Keynes. We will now go on to look at the more traditional neo-Keynesian prescriptions for the control of unemployment.

The control of unemployment: neo-Keynesian views

Fiscal policy

Keynesian and neo-Keynesian policies emphasise the primacy of fiscal policy in the direction of the economy. The fiscal prescription for the cure of unemployment is to raise the level of aggregate demand and so to close the deflationary gap. This is illustrated in Fig. 43.5. Most usually this would be done by running a budget deficit. However, two sets of problems are associated with this. First there are the problems of forecasting and implementation which were discussed on pages 561–64. These problems raise the possibility that fiscal policy may actually make the problem worse rather than better. Second, there is the problem that deficits in times of full or near-full em-

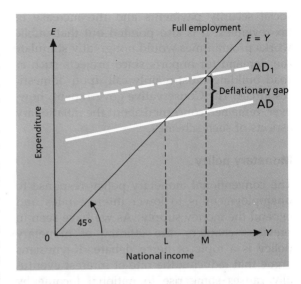

Fig. 43.5 *A deflationary gap*. Unemployment occurs when the equilibrium level of national income (OL) is below the full employment level (OM). Unemployment could be eliminated by increasing the level of aggregate demand from AD to AD_1 ($AD = C = I + G + (X - M)$).

ployment tend to cause inflation. It is for these reasons that fiscal policy fell out of favour and monetary policy gained the ascendancy. We are here drawing together many threads of the argument. Assiduous readers should make sure that they are familiar with the contents of Chapter 36 and also with the discussion of the Phillips curve in Chapter 42. You will also find an aggregate supply and demand treatment of this argument in Chapter 44.

It should be remembered, however, that both problems considered above are most likely to occur at or near full employment. The problems associated with a finely-balanced counter-cyclical fiscal policy can hardly be said to exist at a time of mass unemployment. It is also to be doubted whether expansionary policies would have the same inflationary effects when unemployment is at levels in the 3 millions area.

Many people have argued for an expansionary programme of public works. This would increase the level of aggregate demand and thus reduce unemployment. The cost of such schemes would be at least partly offset by the decrease in **599** social security payments and the increase in tax revenues. It is also pointed out that public works programmes would not greatly stimulate the demand for imports since projects such as road building must mainly call upon domestic resources. The Conservative government, however, remained concerned about the inflationary aspects of such schemes.

Monetary policy

The conventional monetary policy response to unemployment is to lower interest rates and expand the money supply. As we have seen in previous chapters, the efficacy of monetary policy is a topic of fierce debate. Keynesians argue that reducing the rate of interest eventually causes some rise in national income by stimulating investment. You will recall from Chapters 36 and 42 that monetarists and neo-classicists reject the idea that employment can be created either by expanding the money supply or through budget deficits.

Incomes policy

The term neo-Keynesian embraces a wide spectrum of views and certainly not all would favour incomes policy. Incomes policy is usually regarded as an anti-inflationary device. We can see, however, from the arguments above concerning fiscal and monetary policies that the main reason for not stimulating the economy by such measures is fear of the inflationary consequences. If, therefore, inflation could be restrained by incomes policy whilst fiscal and monetary policies stimulated demand this could be a major contribution to the cure of unemployment.

Protection

The Cambridge Economic Policy Group has argued for protectionist measures to reduce unemployment in the UK, i.e. aggregate demand could be boosted without causing a severe current account deficit on the balance of payments. Conventionally, economists oppose calls for protection since these limit the benefits to be gained from comparative advantage. However there may be justification in the protectionist argument when we consider that many other countries, such as Japan, are taking measures to prevent the UK's exports entering their country.

The political dimension

For 30 years after the 1939–45 war *positive economics* was concerned with making statements which were scientifically verifiable. Increasingly it came to be recognised that major economic questions have a political dimension to them. If, for example, there is a trade-off between unemployment and inflation, as suggested by the Phillips curve, then whether it is more desirable to have zero inflation and 14 per cent unemployment or 5 per cent unemployment and 10 per cent inflation is a question which cannot be definitively answered by economics.

International aspects

Table 43.7 shows the rates of unemployment for the seven major OECD countries in 1967, 1982 and 1987. These figures well illustrate the depression of the early 1980s. You can see that it was the UK which was hardest hit by this depression. It can also be seen that the subsequent recovery has affected different countries in different ways. Despite a strong economy unemployment in Germany increased. The worst record is that of France where, in 1987, unemployment hit an all-time high. *Le chômage* remains the number one political issue in France while in the UK it has been politically defused.

The success of the USA and to a lesser extent of the UK in reducing unemployment is a matter of controversy. Supporters of supply-side Reagonomics claim that it is a result of tax-cutting and other supply-side measures. As we have already mentioned (page 557) these were accompanied in the USA by massive budget deficits which could be seen as having Keynesian type effects on the level of aggregate demand.

Table 43.7 Percentage rates of unemployment in the leading OECD countries

Country	1967	1982	1987 (3rd Qtr)
USA	3·7	9·5	5·9
Japan	1·3	2·4	2·8
West Germany	1·3	6·1	7·0
France	9·1	8·0	10·8
UK	3·3	12·8*	9·8
Italy	5·3	8·9	10·5
Canada	3·8	10·9	8·8

* OECD basis of calculation.
Source: Economic Outlook, *OECD*

The figures in Table 43.7 show the international nature of the problem. It is unlikely that one nation can step out of the pattern by following policies which are radically different from those of its chief trading partners. The attempts of the Mitterand government in France in the early 1980s to expand their economy unilaterally demonstrated the difficulties in trying to go it alone.

If we turn to consider unemployment in less developed countries it becomes a much more difficult problem to quantify. This is because many of these countries suffer from *under employment*. This occurs when a person may have a job, such as farming, but this is insufficient to keep them fully occupied. The problem of under-employment is of significant dimensions in all nations where there is a considerable proportion of peasant agriculture. What we can be reasonably sure of, however, is that the depression of the 1980s had very dire consequences for many of the poorest countries (*see* discussion in Chapter 46).

Conclusion

Having considered the problem of unemployment we may note that it has a national and international aspect. Whatever its causes, unemployment can only be cured if there is a significant increase in the growth of real national income. This forms the subject of Chapter 45 of the book.

Summary

1 The best-known definition of full employment is that of Beveridge, i.e. 3 per cent unemployment. However this is beset with difficulties because of regional differences and mismatches in skills. Similarly the definition based on the unemployed and vacancies is also difficult to justify.
2 There are many different types, or causes, of unemployment, e.g. frictional, seasonal, structural, cyclical and technological. Structural and cyclical unemployment are the legitimate targets of government policy.
3 There are a number of valid reasons why governments should have a policy specifically designed to deal with regional unemployment. The efficacy of these policies, however, is open to debate.
4 There are many causes of the present high level of unemployment. The cure for it, however, is a matter of great controversy. The main concern is that attempts to expand the economy might fuel inflation.
5 The supply-side school places great emphasis on the promotion of competitive forces in the economy as the way to reduce unemployment.
6 Neo-Keynesians favour demand management and other interventionist measures to reduce unemployment.
7 Inflation is an international as well as a national problem. It is unlikely, therefore, that a purely national solution can be found to the problem.

Questions

1 What problems are encountered in defining full employment?

2 Discuss the view the regional unemployment would be best solved by the price mechanism.

3 In the 1930s Keynes advocated that the government should 'spend its way' out of depression. Do you think that this view is still valid today and, if not, why not?

4 Study the figures in Table 43.5 (page 595) and then suggest reasons for the observed differences.

5 There was a considerable economic recovery in the UK in the late 1980s but the number of unemployed remained high in historical terms. What are the implications of this for government policy?

6 In 1988 there were 2.7 million people unemployed in the UK. Attempt to assess the magnitude of the various types of unemployment involved, i.e. frictional, structural, etc.

7 What is meant by the term mobility of labour? Would increasing the mobility of labour reduce unemployment, and if so how?

8 Describe what measures supply-side economists might favour to reduce unemployment.

9 Throughout much of the last two decades employment was rising and so was unemployment. Explain how this was possible.

10 Outline the changing pattern of employment during the 1980s.

Data response Changes in employment, unemployment and productivity

Study carefully the information contained in Table 43.8 and in Fig. 43.6. Then attempt the following questions:

Table 43.8 Changes in employment and unemployment 1979–87 in Great Britain

		March 1979 A 000's	March 1987 B 000's	Change (B–A) 000's
1	Manufacturing employees	7 129	5 075	−2054
2	Other employees	15 413	16 182	+769
3	All employees	22 542	21 257	−1285
4	Self employed	1 843	2 644	+801
5	HM Forces	314	320	+6
6	*Employed Labour force*	24 699	24 221	−478
7	Unemployed	1 199	3 116	+1917
8	Working population	25 898	27 337	+1439
9	Inactive population	6 672	6 730	+58
10	*Working age population*	32 570	34 067	+1497
	Activity ratio 8/10	79·5%	80·2%	

$$1 + 2 = 3, \quad 3 + 4 + 5 = 6, \quad 6 + 7 = 8, \quad 8 + 9 = 10$$

1 Distinguish between an increase in productivity and an increase in production. Illustrate you answer by reference to the information in Fig. 43.6 and Table 43.8.

2 Why do you consider that productivity in manufacturing rose so much more rapidly than in the economy as a whole during the 1980s? In your

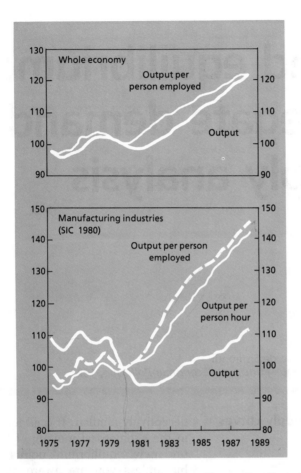

Fig. 43.6 *Indices of output, employment and productivity. (Seasonally adjusted (1980 = 100))*
Source: Employment Gazette

answer make it clear how an increase in productivity can be associated with a fall in output.

3 With the aid of a diagram explain how improvements in productivity could improve *real wages* and the level of employment.

4 With reference to the figures in Table 43.8 explain what is meant by the 'activity rate'.

5 Explain as fully as possible the reasons for the growth of the working population over the period.

6 In what ways has the study of unemployment been made more difficult by changes in statistical definitions?

7 Explain the reasons for the rise in unemployment during the early 1980s.

8 What supply-side measures might a government take to reduce unemployment?

9 Assess the success of government policy on employment during the 1980s.

44

Policy and equilibrium: An aggregate demand and supply analysis

Let us beware of this dangerous theory of equilibrium which is supposed to be automatically established. A certain kind of equilibrium, it is true, is re-established in the long run, but it is only after a frightful amount of suffering.

Simonde de Sismondi
Nouveaux Principes d'Economie Politique, 1827

Aggregate demand and supply curves

Introduction

It has become fashionable to represent macro-economic interactions in terms of aggregate supply and demand diagrams. Not so long ago textbooks dealt only with demand determined Keynesian macro models, thus the supply side of the economy was virtually ignored. It is important that supply conditions be considered. Indeed understanding of the various neo-classical variants and recent economic policy requires an appreciation of models in which aggregate demand adjusts more or less passively to supply determined levels of output and employment. Nevertheless there are also dangers in the approach of representing macro-economic adjustment in terms of supply and demand diagrams.

To the student who has read through the micro sections of a textbook the aggregate demand and supply curve diagrams will look deceptively familiar. It is all too easy to engage in the geometrical moving of lines in order to find new 'equilibrium' points of intersection. But unless you are aware of the theoretical underpinning of such curves you are doing little more than moving a ruler across a page. Of course the same consideration is true in the case of micro demand and supply diagrams and it was for this reason that so much time was devoted to the theories of consumers and firms equilibrium. What is important is that you always thinks about what lies behind these curves and to realise that different schools of thought may offer alternative interpretations.

You will no doubt be relieved to learn that the theoretical underpinnings of aggregate demand and supply have already been largely established in this book (in particular, *see* Chapters 36, 41, 42 and 43). Indeed we have already used this approach more or less explicitly in several places. Thus, if you do not understand the conclusions in this section the cross references should be used to locate and re-read the relevant pages. We have been at pains to explain what lies behind such aggregate curves so as to avoid introducing them in the manner of rabbits from a magician's hat as occurs in many other books. In this section we gather together what we have learned and investigate the varying interpretations of these aggregate supply and demand curves.

It should be pointed out that demand and supply analysis tends to impart a neo-classical bias. For example, strictly speaking, supply and demand curves imply that firms and consumers are *price takers* as in perfect competition. Nevertheless so useful (convenient) is this approach that economists of virtually all persuasions will resort to it from time to time. Moreover the concept of a supply curve can be stretched in order to represent different theories, but it must be said that such an approach can sometimes distort rather than elucidate the perspective of some schools of thought.

The derivation of the aggregate demand curve

The derivation of the aggregate demand curve in neo-classical and neo-Keynesian models is fairly straightforward. As the level of prices fall the real money supply is expanded (this assumes a 'given' or exogenously set nominal money supply). The precise monetary transmission mechanism may vary (*see* pages 471–74) but the end result of this expansion is an extension of demand for the output of the economy. Depending on the exchange rate regime the demand for exports may also increase as the domestic price level falls relative to foreign markets. In addition there might be a decrease in the demand for imports as domestically produced goods become cheaper. In short *we can expect the aggregate demand curve to be downward sloping*.

The derivation of the aggregate supply curve

The shape of the aggregate supply curve depends crucially on the assumptions we make. In neo-classical schools, such as monetarist and new classical, *perfect competition is assumed*. Thus the labour market clears at the level of employment which corresponds to profit maximisation i.e.:

$$W = MPP \times P$$

or in real terms:

$$\frac{W}{P} = MPP$$

In the short-run the stock of capital (and land) is fixed, hence this level of employment also corresponds to a definite level of output. Under new-classical rationale expectations assumptions (*see* page 575) *the aggregate supply curve is thus vertical* and an increase in the nominal money supply which increases aggregate demand will simply cause nominal prices to increase. This continues until the *real* money supply is what it was before and aggregate demand has contracted back to meet the unchanged level of aggregate supply again. This 'classical dichotomy' in which the monetary or nominal sector of the economy is independent of real forces was illustrated by Fig. 36.8 and Fig. 42.8.

Under 'gradualist' monetarist or adaptive expectations assumptions money illusion can occur. This allows a *temporary trade-off between inflation and unemployment*, i.e. while the money illusion persists there is a temporary increase in output and employment. This was illustrated in Fig. 42.3, 42.4 and 42.5. Nevertheless, in the long run the classical dichotomy is re-established.

Unemployment

A neo-Keynesian view of the aggregate supply curve

Neo-Keynesians often modify the aggregate supply curve by assuming that money wages are downwardly sticky perhaps because of institutional rigidities or union resistance. In the **605**

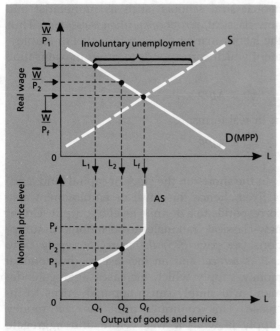

Fig. 44.1 *The aggregate supply curve.* At price level p_1, employers will only employ L_1 labour. Increases in prices lower the real wage and more labour is employed (L_2). At price level P_f full employment is reached and the supply curve becomes vertical.

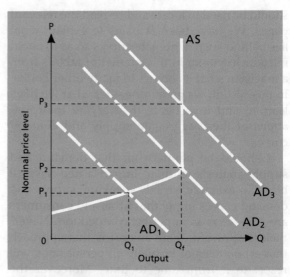

Fig. 44.2 *Neo-Keynesian aggregate demand on supply analysis.* Increase in aggregate demand (AD_1 to AD_2) causes some inflation but a large increase in employment. At full employment (Q_f) any further increase in aggregate demand (e.g. to AD_3) is turned entirely into inflation with no rise in output or employment.

absence of inflation in the prices of goods and services the real wage might thus be 'stuck' at too high a level for the labour market to clear. This is illustrated in Fig. 44.1. The assumption that money wages will not decrease is indicated by the bar on the symbol for money wage, i.e. $\overline{W}$. It can be seen that at a price level of P_1 the real wage is above the equilibrium. Thus employers are prepared to employ only L_1 of labour and there is an excess supply of labour, i.e. involuntary unemployment. In neo-classical models this excess supply would simply force down money wages until the equilibrium real wage is reached. In this neo-Keynesian case this cannot happen because of the downward stickiness of money wages and hence the involuntary employment can persist.

Figure 44.1 also shows the solution to the unemployment. Although money wages will not fall the real wage can be lowered by an increase in the price level of goods and services.

Hence, if the government increases the aggregate demand for goods and services through fiscal or monetary means this will tend to increase their prices and thereby lower the real wage. As the real wage is thus lowered it becomes profitable for firms to employ more workers. As the level of employment increases so will the output of goods and services. Thus, for any given value of the money wage, we can derive an *upward sloping aggregate supply curve.* Notice, however, that once full employment is reached by raising the price level to P_f the model reverts to the neo-classical case. This is because there is nothing to prevent an *increase* in the money wage. Hence any further increase in the price level tending to produce excess demand in the labour market would simply cause money wages to increase so as to hold the real wage and the level of employment and output constant.

In Fig. 44.2 we show aggregate demand and supply based on neo-Keynesian sticky money wage assumptions. As can be seen, increasing aggregate demand from AD_1 to AD_2 results in a mild inflation of the price level and a substantial increase in output (and employment). But once full employment has been reached a further increase in aggregate demand to AD_3 will be absorbed wholly by an increase in the price level as there is no increase in output.

A neo-Keynesian recession

A common fear among neo-Keynesians is that money wages will begin to rise before full employment is reached. This will cause the AS curve to shift upwards with increases in AD. Thus government attempts to lower the real wage by reflating the economy might be thwarted. For this reason neo-Keynesians are usually also keen advocates of incomes policies.

Some writers have challenged the neo-Keynesian interpretation of Keynes' work which identifies downwardly rigid money wages as the critical assumption in Keynes' theory. If this were the sole reason that Keynes had given for the persistence of unemployment then we can hardly speak of a 'Keynesian Revolution' in economics. As the Swedish economist Axel Leijonhufvud writes in his IEA Occasional Paper 'Keynes and the Classics':

Any pre-Keynesian economist, asked to explain the phenomenon of persistent unemployment, would automatically have started with the assertion that its proximate cause must lie in too high wages that refuse to come down.

Some Keynesian economists have thus focused on Keynes' distinction between nominal and effective demand as holding the key to his analysis. Thus it may be the case that even if the real wage is at the level at which the labour market could nominally clear, the effective demand for labour is constrained by lack of demand in the markets for goods and services. This was illustrated in Fig. 36.9. This interpretation clearly breaks with the assertion that unemployment is caused by too high a level of the real wage. In this interpretation the 'prices are right' and it would nominally be profitable for firms to employ all the labour wishing to work. This does

not happen, however, as it is only profitable to employ the labour if the products so produced can be sold. If the produce of labour cannot be sold because of lack of aggregate demand then it is not profitable to employ labour whatever the level of the real wage.

If a lack of aggregate demand for goods and services is the problem then a fall in wages could actually worsen unemployment i.e. a reduction in the spending power of workers might further reduce aggregate demand thereby further constraining effective demand in the labour market. This in turn would cause more unemployment and thus aggregate demand would be subject to a downward multiplier cycle as more workers are deprived of spending power.

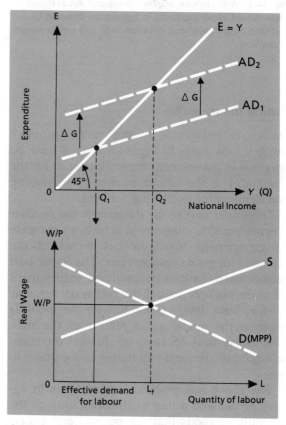

Fig. 44.3 *Curing a Keynesian recession.* **Lack of effective demand keeps employment below the full employment equilibrium. This is cured by an increase in government expenditure ($\triangle$G) increasing the level of aggregate demand.**

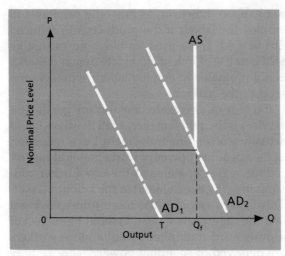

Fig. 44.4 *A Keynesian aggregate supply.* An extreme view would allow increases in aggregate demand to increase output, without inflation until full employment is reached.

Curing the recession

As is so often the case the analysis of a problem suggests the cure. In Fig. 44.3 we see how an increase in government expenditure can lift the constraint in the labour market by increasing the demand for goods and services.

The upper part of the diagram is the familiar Keynesian 45% diagram in which an increase in government injections has increased the demand for goods and services. The lower part shows that this allows the profitable employment of more workers even if the real wage remains at the same level. Once full employment is reached the model again reverts to the neoclassical vertical AS case, i.e. further increases in aggregate demand will simply cause prices to rise.

The above interpretation of increases in aggregate demand acting to lift constraints on the quantity of goods that can be sold and consequently the amount of labour employed implies an AS curve as shown in Fig. 44.4.

As can be seen, in this interpretation increases in AD can increase output until full employ-

ment is reached without the need for any price changes or reduction in the real wage.

A neoclassical view

The transmission mechanism

If we stick of the assumption of perfectly competitive markets for goods and services and flexible wages there is a monetarist rebuttal to the Keynesian assertion that a lack of AD can forever prevent full employment being reached. If markets are perfectly competitive the lack of effective demand would cause a persistent downward pressure on prices as firms try to sell more than consumers can afford to buy. Thus, given a constant *nominal money supply* the *real supply of money* will be constantly increasing. As we saw from our discussion of monetary *transmission mechanisms* (pages 471–74) in the Keynesian model this will only increase interest rate sensitive expenditure. Thus even when interest rates become zero due to the expanded money supply AD might only reach point T in Fig. 44.4, i.e. demand may still be less than that needed for full employment even when prices have fallen as low as possible. But you will recall that in the monetarist version of the transmission mechanism excess money balances can spill over *directly* into spending on consumption (*see* Fig. 36.5). This will increase AD until eventually full employment is reached.

The Pigou effect

The increase in consumption due to increased real money balances described above is known as the real money balances or 'Pigou effect' after the economist who used it to challenge the assertion of Keynes' 'General Theory' that the economy could remain permanently at less than full employment. Many Keynesian economists have responded by accepting its validity as a theoretical solution but insisted that the process would take far too long for policy purposes and that hence the increase in aggregate demand would have to be 'artificially' hastened by government induced reflation.

The effect of pricing policies

If we drop the assumption of perfectly competitive markets the Pigou effect loses much of its persuasiveness that a free market capitalist economy is ultimately self correcting. For example, it has been known for a long time that most firms are not engaged in marginal cost pricing but in fact set their price according to a predetermined mark-up on average cost. Now much empirical evidence suggests that average cost is fairly constant for most firms over a wide range of output. Thus reality may not consist of firms moving up their marginal cost curves in response to increased prices, but instead firms may use some 'rule of thumb' mark-up pricing formula and then sell as much as they can at this price. Hence, as Fig. 44.5 shows increases in demand may be met by firms increasing their output in response to increased sales without any upward pressure on prices.

Similarly firms may respond to decreases in aggregate demand by cutting back output without any change in price. Thus, unlike in perfect competition, there is not necessarily a tendency

for prices to fall as aggregate demand falls. If, following depressed sales, firms competed with one another for increased sales, then the real money supply may again be increased leading ultimately to a real balance effect. But, particularly in highly concentrated markets, firms may resist the temptation to cut prices for fear of precipitating a self defeating price war. (*See* discussion of oligopoly behaviour in Chapter 17.)

Mark-up pricing can also be used to explain why the aggregate supply curve might begin to slope, and increase in slope, as full employment is approached. For example, as firms near their maximum potential output production might become less efficient causing unit costs to rise. Alternatively, as resources become more fully utilised input costs might rise again causing unit costs to increase. In either case the increase in unit cost will be passed on as a price rise if a constant mark-up is maintained.

Conclusion

Some post-Keynesian economists have gone further and suggested that the very concept of equilibriums brought about by the interaction of supply and demand is a misleading one. Joan Robinson in the foreword to 'A Guide to Post-Keynesian Economics' (edited by A. Eichner) writes:

When Keynes was writing *The General Theory*, his main difference from the school from which he was struggling to escape lay in the recognition of the problem of effective demand, which they ignored . . . After the book was published, he drew the line differently. He saw that the main distinction was that he recognised, and they ignored, the obvious fact that expectations of the future are necessarily uncertain.

It is from this point that post-Keynesian theory takes off. The recognition of uncertainty undermines the traditional concept of equilibrium

Enough has now been said for the reader to appreciate that there is more than one interpretation of aggregate demand and supply diagrams

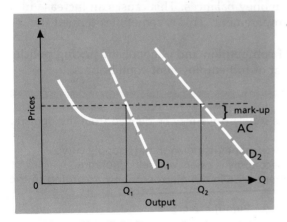

Fig. 44.5 *The effect of mark-up pricing.* **The existence of a flat-bottomed AC curve and mark-up pricing policies means large changes in demand have no effect upon price. This means that excess capacity can exist without affecting prices. Thus the market might not be self-correcting.**

and hence they should not be not be used unthinkingly. Nevertheless they can provide a convenient way of demonstrating likely macroeconomic interactions. For example, a reduction in the cost of an important raw material can be expected to increase aggregate supply thereby causing an increase in output and a reduction in the price level.

Summary

1 For many years macroeconomic analysis focused on aggregate demand, following the work of Keynes. The neoclassical school has moved the emphasis to aggregate supply.

2 Deceptively simple, aggregate demand and supply curves should be treated with caution. Many assumptions may be used when constructing them, such as that of perfect competition.

3 A fall in the level of prices causes the real money supply to increase, which results in an extension of demand for the output of the economy. Thus the aggregate demand curve is downward sloping.

4 The neoclassical view is that the aggregate supply curve is vertical. The neo-Keynesian view is that the aggregate supply curve slopes upwards until full employment is reached when it becomes vertical.

5 Neoclassical schools of thought emphasise the self-regulating nature of the economy. Changes in the level of real wages ensure full employment. Keynesians argue that a lack of effective demand in the economy may cause unemployment.

6 Neo-Keynesians argue for the need for governments to increase the level of aggregate demand to cure unemployment. The neoclassical view is that this causes inflation not employment.

7 Neoclassicists argue that any lack of effective demand causes prices to fall and thus an increase in real money balances. This causes an increase in demand and eliminates the unemployment. This is sometimes termed the Pigou effect.

8 Uncertainty, imperfections of competition and oligopolistic pricing policies may interfere with the attainment of full employment equilibriums.

Questions

1 Demonstrate how the aggregate supply curve may be derived from the demand curve for labour.

2 Contrast the different views of the shape of the aggregate supply curve.

3 Discuss the view that the macroeconomy is essentially self-regulating.

4 How may persistent unemployment arise in the macroeconomy according to the neo-Keynesian school of thought.

5 What is the real money balances (or Pigou) effect?

6 Contrast neoclassical and neo-Keynesian views on policies to reduce unemployment.

7 Use aggregate demand and supply curves to demonstrate how inflation occurs.

8 'If the Treasury were to fill old bottles with banknotes, bury them at suitable depths in disused coalmines which are then filled up to the surface with town rubbish, and leave it to private enterprise on well-tried principles of *laissez-faire* to

dig the notes up again . . . there need be no more unemployment and with the help of the repercussions, the real income of the community, and its capital also, would probably become a good deal greater than it actually is.'

Do you agree with this statement taken from Keynes's *General Theory*? Give reasons for your answer.

Data response   The Chancellor speaks ▬▬▬▬▬▬▬▬▬▬▬▬▬▬▬▬▬▬▬

The following article is taken from the *Financial Times* of 22 July 1988. Read it carefully and then attempt the questions which follow.

Public finances must balance for stability

Mr Nigel Lawson, the Chancellor, yesterday gave a lengthy exposition of the Government's economic policy at a gathering of the Institute of Economic Affairs in London.

In the first part of his speech he dealt with the economy the Government inherited in 1979 and the measures it has taken to reinstate a 'market economy'. In short: 'A much smaller State sector, less interference in industry, fewer regulations and controls, and fewer tax-induced distortions'. What follows is an extract of the final section of his speech headed 'Markets and macro-economic policy'.

The Government has to take responsibility for maintaining the value of the currency – avoiding inflation – not least because it is the monopoly supplier of currency . . . We have accepted that the state has a clear responsibility to maintain the internal value of the currency – that is, to avoid domestic inflation – and, within that context, to maintain the external value of the currency – the exchange rate.

There is nothing new about these dual responsibilities. The heyday of the market economy in the second half of the last century and the early part of this was accompanied by a firm financial framework secured by two disciplines. The first was that the state ran a balanced budget. The second was that currencies were linked to gold, which maintained both their internal and their external value. The first of those disciplines has now, I am glad to say, been restored . . .

As for monetary policy, the ultimate objective – stable prices – is not in doubt. But means of getting there – how monetary policy should be operated – has proved more complex.

Experience in the '80s has demonstrated that, while the essential thesis – that monetary policy is the only weapon for bearing down on inflation – remains as valid as ever, the practical process of monetary control has become more complicated. The abolition of the various controls within the financial system which I described earlier, and which has brought enormous benefits, has made it difficult to rely solely on monetary targets.

At the same time, the ending of controls inevitably places more weight on short-term interest rates as the essential instrument of monetary policy. To attempt to reinstate the direct controls of earlier years would not only be needlessly damaging to the financial sector. It would also be ineffective . . .

Short-term interest rates are of course the market route to the defeat of inflation . . .

I mentioned a moment ago that we have to assess monetary conditions as a whole. With separate national currencies in an international financial marketplace, it is inevitable that the exchange rate plays an important part in determining monetary conditions. So governments have to come to terms with the behaviour of the foreign-exchange market. Left entirely to its own devices, we have seen in recent years how destabilising and disruptive that behaviour can be.

Governments are a part of this particular market, whether they like it or not, not least because they are the monopoly manufacturers of the currencies being traded. And they can afford to take a long view. The experience of the '60s and the '70s showed conclusively the folly, and indeed futility, of governments' trying to maintain exchange rates regardless of changes in the economic fundamentals.

But what the authorities of the major nations have sought to do with the dollar, with some success, through the Plaza and Louvre accords, has been to help to keep them in line with fundamentals . . .

The Government's job, then, is to deal with the financial framework which it can influence . . . I would maintain that, provided the overall fiscal, monetary and exchange-rate framework work is sound, and markets are working effectively, the results of the private sector's economic activity should not normally be something in which it is sensible for the Government to interfere.

If that is so, it has considerable relevance to the topical issue of the current account of the balance of payments. It is clear . . . that there are very considerable differences between the present period of current-account deficit and previous episodes in the UK – or indeed the present experience in the United States. For in the UK now, the Government's own finances are very sound indeed.

The public-sector finances are more or less in balance, even before taking account of the proceeds of privatisation. So the current-account deficit is clearly not associated with excessive spending and borrowing by the Government. No doubt a part of the deficit reflects the fact that the UK economy is currently growing a little too fast, above its sustainable rate, and will have to slow down . . . As it does, the deficit will diminish. But that is only part of the story. For there is no iron law that the private sector's finances must be in balance, in any given year or period of years. Sometimes savings will exceed investment; sometimes the reverse will happen . . .

Net capital flows are inevitable and indeed desirable, given differing propensities to save and differing investment opportunities . . .

The main reason for the present deficit appears to be that the UK economy has entered a phase which combines a set of circumstances we have not seen together for some considerable time.

Investment is rising rapidly . . . Individuals have seen their wealth rise sharply in the 1980s.

It is thus not surprising that individuals now feel they can safely spend more – in many cases by adding to their borrowing rather than by spending their capital.

1   Explain the assumptions about the nature of the macroeconomy upon which Nigel Lawson was basing his comments and policy.
2   When the Chancellor spoke of the 'current-account deficit' which account was he referring to and what did he suggest were the reasons for it?
3   What is the relationship between the exchange rate and the domestic economy?
4   If, as the neo-classical theorists argue, the aggregate supply curve is vertical what policies should a government pursue to promote economic growth?
5   Discuss the role of interest rates in regulating the level of economic activity.
6   How does the existence of monopolies affect the neo-classical view of the economy? What are the implications for public policy.
7   At the time the Chancellor was speaking there was a budget surplus. How had this been achieved?

45

Economic growth

The rate of growth at a given time is a phenomenon rooted in past economic, social and technological developments rather than determined fully by the coefficients of our equations.

M. Kalecki

What is economic growth?

Defining growth

When we speak of economic growth we mean an increase in the GDP of a nation. However we must first distinguish between *real* and *nominal* increases. For example between 1961 and 1986 the GDP of the UK increased from £24·4 billion to £319·1 billion, an increase of 1307 per cent. However when the effect of inflation is taken into account this amounts to an increase of only 52 per cent.

We must also consider the effect of population growth. Consider the case of a nation whose GDP is growing at 5 per cent per year but whose population is growing at 10 per cent. In this case in real terms the average GDP per capita is declining. Thus the usual definition of economic growth is:

An increase in the real GDP per capita of a nation.

The distribution of income

Our simple GDP per capita definition of economic growth is modified by the distribution of income within a country. If the increase in GDP is concentrated mainly amongst the rich then this will obviously have very little effect upon the average *living standard*. As we saw in Chapter 7,

income tends to the more unevenly distributed in poor countries and this therefore further exacerbates the problems of underdevelopment.

Environmental considerations

We too often assume in economics that *more is better*. As we saw in Chapter 7, economists are becoming increasingly concerned with the fact that the production of *economic goods* also involves the production of *economic bads* such as pollution. Chapter 7 also considered measures such as MEW and NEW which are designed to take account of this. This topic was further explored in Section IV on welfare economics, where we examined the dichotomy between private costs and social costs. It is the case, therefore, in many advanced economies that environmental considerations are now being given much more weight when assessing economic progress.

If we turn to the very poor nations of the world it is understandable that they tend to downgrade environmental considerations in their fight against the extreme poverty which exists in their countries. It is unfortunately the case, however, that it is in many of the less developed nations that the finite resources of the world such as tin, copper and zinc are being most ruthlessly exploited, thus possibly leading to future further impoverishment of these nations.

The importance of economic growth

Why worry about economic growth? The answer is that it is this very economic growth that enables us to enjoy a better *standard of living*. As we saw in the early chapters of the book, we assume that *people are acquisitive*, wishing to acquire more goods, more leisure, more entertainment, etc. All of these acquisitions are made possible by economic growth, as are better education, health care and so on. Thus, whilst there are many who condemn the materialistic society, there are few who would deny that they would like a better standard of life.

Economic growth has important *political* and *military* dimensions. It is the wealthy nations of the world which dictate policies. Thus the USA and the USSR contend with each other in the sphere of economic growth because it is this growth which enables them to finance their incredibly expensive military machines with which they confront each other. It is no accident that the UK's relative political and military influence in the world has declined along with its decline in the economic league table. In this connection we might also mention the immense adverse effects which military spending has upon the poorest nations of the world. No political value judgments are involved in saying that if only one-tenth of the expenditure which goes on the arms race was directed to the development of the poorer nations, then many of the problems of underdevelopment could be solved.

Stages of economic growth

Many attempts have been made to classify the pattern of economic growth as a passage through a number of definable stages. The most famous of these is Marx's classification. He saw societies as passing through the following stages: *primitive communism; slavery; feudalism; capitalism;* and, finally, *socialism* and *communism*. Another famous classification is that which appears in W. W. Rostow's *Stages of Economic Growth* which envisages a development of an economy up to the time when there is a 'take-off into self-sustaining growth'.

While these ideas may be illuminating, it is now regarded as fallacious by all but hard-line Marxists to see economies as passing through definite stages. Indeed, it could be argued that the idea that economies *must* pass through certain stages has been harmful when these ideas have been rigorously applied to the economic policies of governments.

International comparisons

Between 1965 and 1980 the UK economy grew by only 38 per cent in real terms. Historically this compares well with growth in the nineteenth century. However, when we compare it with growth of our main trading partners it is very poor indeed. This is illustrated in Table 45.1. As you can see the UK was comfortably bottom of this league table.

It is important to realise that relatively small differences in rates of growth can have very significant differences upon GDP when considered over the medium-term or long-term. Over the period 1965–80 the average annual growth in real GDP per capita of the UK was 2·2 per cent whilst that of Japan was 6·3 per cent. These might appear only minor differences, but now consider the information in Table 45.2. Let us assume that the UK is represented by the 2 per cent column, and Japan by the 7 per cent column. If 1980 is the base year we can see how quickly the GDPs begin to diverge. In ten years'

Table 45.1 Percentage growth rate in real GDP over the period 1965–80 of selected countries

Country	%
Japan	165
Canada	101
Spain	101
France	88
Australia	85
Netherlands	78
Italy	68
West Germany	65
USA	53
UK	38

Source: *IBRD*

Table 45.2 How growth rates affect incomes

Year	Index of national income based upon growth rate (%) per year of (1980 = 100)			
	2%	3%	5%	7%
1980	100	100	100	100
1990	122	135	165	201
2010	182	246	448	817
2030	272	448	1218	3312
2050	406	817	3312	13 429
2080	739	2009	14 841	109 660

time the UK's GDP increases by 22 per cent but Japan's doubles. After 30 years the UK's GDP is 82 per cent higher but Japan has increased by a *factor of eight*. After a century the differences are staggering, with all the implications this has for standards of living and political and military power.

Table 45.2 is also useful in explaining the vast differences which exist between the rich and the poor nations. While the UK, the USA and West Germany have experienced more than two centuries of continuous economic growth, many of the poor nations have experienced very little growth. It is small wonder therefore that if, for example, we compare the GDP per capita of the USA in 1985 we find that it is 61 times greater than that of India (*see* pages 87–93 for discussion of the difficulties of international comparisons).

Factors influencing growth

Theories of growth

There are a number of theories of economic growth which attempt to explain the causes and rates of economic growth. Prominent amongst these are the following: the Harrod-Domar model; that of Smith and Malthus; the Ricardo-Marx-Solow model; and that of Leontieff. None of these theories is a satisfactory explanation of the growth problems of advanced or less developed economies. An examination of the mathematics

of them is also beyond the scope of this book, although the interested student may care to pursue them in more advanced texts. What we can say is that there are a number of factors which are definitely known to have an influence upon the growth rate, and we will now proceed to examine these.

Investment

It is undoubtedly true that investment determines the rate of growth. We can see in Fig. 23.1 (*see* page 273) that increasing the rate of investment (capitalisation) should increase the rate of growth. However there appears to be no simple relationship between the rate of investment and the rate of growth. This is well illustrated by the figures in Table 45.3. It is obvious that the high rate of investment in Japan in the period 1965–80 must have been significant in accounting for its place at the top of the table. It is also apparent that the average rate of investment of the first five nations in the table is significantly higher than that of the second five. The figures for the 1980–5 period in Table 45.3 illustrate the world-wide depression. The high rates of investment which the USA and the UK achieved over the 1980–5 period were to be rewarded by higher growth rates later in the decade.

Nonetheless, it is clear from the figures in

Table 45.3 Growth and investment in selected countries

Country	Average annual growth (%) in real GDP		Average annual growth (%) in investment	
	1965–80	1980–85	1965–80	1980–85
Japan	6·3	3·8	6·7	2·4
Spain	4·8	1·6	4·0	–2·6
Canada	4·8	2·4	4·9	0·4
Ireland	4·7	1·5	6·8	–1·0
Norway	4·4	3·3	2·7	2·9
USA	2·9	2·5	1·8	5·2
Denmark	2·8	2·4	1·3	4·9
Sweden	2·7	2·0	1·1	0·5
UK	2·2	2·0	1·1	5·3
Switzerland	2·0	1·2	0·8	0·9

Source: IBRD

615

Table 45.3 that, as far as the UK is concerned, the low rate of investment over most of the period is matched by very poor performance in the growth league. Whether the higher rate of investment in the 1980s will lead to a significantly improved growth performance in the long term remains to be seen. There are many imponderables on the horizon. For example, what will be the effect on investment of the single European market?

Difficulties of comparison

The relationship between investment and growth will also be affected by our old friend *the law of diminishing returns*. Other things being equal, the principle of *marginal productivity* tells us that as we apply more and more investment to an already-large stock of capital, the extra output achieved should diminish. This might partly explain why a wealthy country such as Switzerland sees a relatively poor return on its investment whilst a relatively poorer country such as Spain sees a much better return for less investment.

We can also point out that a low rate of growth may appear less burdensome to a rich country than a poor country. Let us consider an analogy with individual incomes. Suppose we consider two individuals, one with an income of £5000 per year and the other with £50 000 per year. If both their incomes increase by 10 per cent then the first individual has an extra £500 to spend whilst the second's will increase by £5000. Thus rich countries with low growth rates may be able to sustain much higher increases in their real living standards than those of poor nations with high growth rates. In 1985, for example, the GDP per capita in Spain was $4290 but that of Switzerland was four times this amount.

It is also possible to consider that geographical conditions may have an effect upon investment. Countries with inhospitable climates or terrains may find that the physical problems of development are disproportionately high. Amongst the advanced countries, this may affect nations such as Austria, Switzerland and Finland.

Gross and net investment

A major factor influencing the relationship between investment and growth is that of the difference between *gross* and *net investment*. Much investment may simply be to replace obsolete equipment and, thus, will therefore have no effect upon the rate of growth; it is only *net investment* which increases the wealth of a nation (*see* page 81). This is a problem which particularly affects a mature industrial nation such as the UK, since much investment must be to replace out-of-date equipment. This, therefore, compounds the problem associated with the UK's low rate of investment.

The quality of investment

Units of investment are not homogeneous and it does not follow that there is a constant capital/output ratio even within one industry. For example, it has frequently been the case that investment per worker in a particular industry in the UK has been the same as that in West Germany, and yet productivity has been higher in West Germany. We must therefore consider *the quality of investment*. An often repeated argument is that at the end of the 1939–45 war the UK was left with much obsolete and worn-out equipment and investment consisted of patching and infilling. On the other hand, West Germany and Japan, where the destruction of capital had been almost total, investment was in all-new integrated plant. More significantly in the last part of the twentieth century is the speed at which the UK is investing (or not investing) in the new technology.

Defence expenditure

All economics is a question of allocating scarce resources in the optimal manner. A significant factor when we come to compare growth rates is defence expenditure. If a nation is devoting a proportion of its precious GDP to defence this must consist of resources which could be used for investment to increase the living standard directly. Table 45.4 shows the proportion of

Table 45.4 Defence expenditure of selected countries 1985

Country	Defence expenditure as percentage of GDP
Austria	1·2
Spain	1·4
New Zealand	2·0
West Germany	2·8
Australia	2·9
Netherlands	2·9
USA	6·1
UK	10·5
Israel	27·0

Source: *IBRD*

GDP devoted to defence expenditure in various countries.

Again it is impossible to draw any simple relationships between defence expenditure and growth. However, in the case of the UK we can say that it is yet one more factor restricting economic growth. Of course it is impossible to estimate the value of defence expenditure to the community in terms of the security it offers. There are also spin-offs in terms of arms sales, etc. However the burden of defence expenditure can be disproportionately high because it ties up highly-trained personnel as well as some of the most young and vigorous of the workforce. Israel has been included in the table simply because it is the nation which devotes the largest proportion of its GDP to defence. It should also be said that defence expenditure is a factor inhibiting the growth of many of the less developed countries.

People and growth

Population growth

As far as advanced economics are concerned it may be debated whether population growth is a spur to economic development or whether increased standards of living have increased population. Figure 4.7 on page 50 shows that, theoretically, there is an optimal size for a population, although the discussion also showed how difficult it is to define this in practical terms. We could argue, for example, that at the moment the stagnation in population growth in Western Europe has some connection with the lack of economic growth.

If on the other hand we turn to less developed countries, there can be little doubt that population growth is one of the main inhibiting factors in increasing GDP per capita. It would appear that any major advance in living standards will, for many countries, depend upon limiting the size of families. In recent years the country to take this most seriously has been China, the most populous nation on earth, where draconian measures have been taken to limit population growth.

Population structure

As we learned in Chapter 4, it is not just the size of the population which is important but also its age, sex and geographic distribution. These factors all have important considerations for economic growth. If, as is the case in most advanced countries, there is an increasing proportion of dependent population (the old, the young, etc.), then resources will have to be devoted to caring for them. Thus, valuable investment resources will be channelled into projects of very low productivity such as old people's homes. It could be argued that extra investment put into education will pay dividends in the long-run, but such projects will not be conducive to high rates of growth in the short- and medium-term. When we examine the nations with low growth rates in Table 45.3 such as Switzerland and the UK, it is noticeable that these are countries which have, since the 1939–45 war, placed a high priority on welfare projects.

In considering the effect of population upon growth, we must also consider *participation rates*, i.e. the proportion of the population which is economically active. In this respect the UK has one of the highest participation rates of any advanced country. Participation rates are governed by such things as school-leaving age, the attitude towards working women, the facilities which exist for child care, the age of retirement, and so on.

The average age of the population may also affect economic growth. By and large, an ageing population tends to inhibit economic growth since older people tend to be more conservative and less inclined to take risks. Again it is possible to argue that the ageing of the UK's population over this century has inhibited growth.

Migration

Migration also has an effect upon economic growth. The effects of overall immigration and emigration upon the UK were discussed in Chapter 4, where we noted that immigrants tend to be of working age and therefore beneficial to the economy, whereas the UK has tended to lose highly trained personnel such as doctors by emigration.

If we make comparisons between the UK and her immediate neighbours such as France, West Germany and Italy, a fact which is apparent is that each of these countries has a large reservoir of labour to draw on, i.e. a drift of the agricultural population to the towns, and in the case of West Germany there was for a time the defection of people from East Germany. Thus, in each case these countries has a pool of relatively cheap easily-assimilable people which can be drawn upon. The immigration which the UK has experienced from overseas has been small by comparison but has posed problems of cultural and social differences. These problems have also been experienced by France and, to a lesser extent, by West Germany. Since the recent depression, reduced job opportunities have exacerbated these problems.

Education and training

It is often said that the wealth of a country lies in the skill of its population. This being the case, the education, training and attitude

Table 45.5 Number enrolled on higher education as percentage of age group. Selected OECD nations

Country	1965	1984
	%	%
USA	40	57
Canada	26	44
Sweden	13	38
Japan	13	30
West Germany	9	29
France	18	27
Spain	6	26
Ireland	12	22
UK	12	20

Source: IBRD

of a country's population must be a significant factor in determining its rate of growth. Whilst it may appear unpleasant to speak of investment in people as if they were machines, nonetheless it is important that a nation makes sure that it has the adequate skills it needs to advance its economy.

Table 45.5 shows the participation rates in higher education for a number of OECD countries. That is the percentage of people in the age group receiving higher (university or polytechnic) education. The UK has the lowest rate for any advanced industrial economy. This must eventually have an adverse effect upon growth. We might also regard education, as opposed to training, as a component in the quality of life. Thus those receiving higher education are consuming an economic product which will improve their standard of living by improving their quality of life.

If you are just embarking upon higher education it will doubtless come as a great comfort to know that there is also a marked correlation between higher education and higher earnings later in life!

The British disease

There can be little doubt that in the years since the 1939–45 war the UK has possessed many of the advantages which were desirable for economic growth and yet, although it has done well compared with many Third World countries, it has not done well compared with its peers such as France and West Germany. The reasons for this are not to be found in complex mathematical models of growth, but rather in a combination of socioeconomic factors which have inhibited the growth of the economy.

Government policy

'Stop-go' policies and the variation in the objectives of government policies have had adverse effects upon growth. Government preoccupation with control of the money supply is just the latest in a long line of different policy objectives.

Trade unions

It has often been the case that all the problems of the UK's industry have been blamed on trade unions. Whilst this is an exaggeration, restrictive practices and excessive wage demands have certainly had adverse effects upon growth.

Management

On the whole, UK management has been uninventive and unadventurous. In particular, there has been an unwillingness to invest in the future. For example, research and development has decreased in real terms. This is, of course, not true of all firms, but for industry in general it has been a significant factor.

Complacency

The UK, being the first country to industrialise, has often tended to rest on its laurels and be unwilling to make changes.

Low status of engineers and scientists

Technical skills have often tended to be demoted while those with qualifications in the arts have often tended to be promoted.

Overall there still persists a belief that somehow economic progress can be 'muddled through' and improvised, while, on the contrary, there is a need for scientific management and co-ordinated research and development.

The outflow of capital

You may recall from the chapter on the balance of payments that the UK is a net exporter of capital. It can be argued that this flow of funds abroad starves the domestic economy of investment. There is little evidence to demonstrate that this is so. Rather it may be the case that the other factors discussed combine to limit investment opportunities.

Short-termism

There is evidence to show that the performance of the economy is damaged by the fact that investment managers go for quick returns on their funds and that this deprives long-term research and development of the investment it needs. The Bank of England has expressed concern about this.

Recent experience

In the late 1980s the prospect on growth in the UK economy looked a lot better. Table 45.6 shows the UK at the top of the growth league. This is, at least in part due to government supply-side measures although we should not forget our enormous good fortune in North Sea oil. The government would doubtless claim credit for

45.6 Average annual growth in real GDP

	1980–85	1986
Country	%	%
United States	2·5	2·9
Japan	3·8	2·4
Germany	1·3	2·5
France	1·1	2·0
United Kingdom	2·0	3·3
Italy	0·8	2·7
Canada	2·4	3·3

Source: IBRD and OECD.

reducing the power of trade unions and for re-introducing a spirit of competition into the economy.

If you look at the information in Data Response in Chapter 43 you will see that there were also great improvements in productivity. However, these were, in part due to the elimination of large amounts of capacity in manufacturing, leaving the economy with the most efficient rump of the sector. Productivity gains elsewhere in the economy were less spectacular and there was huge import penetration of manufacturing industries. We should also remember that the economy was recovering from the worst depression for fifty years when we ought to expect rapid growth.

It remained to be seen whether the government's 'hand's off' policies would sustain growth in the 1990s. Other problems in the list above – lack of education, lack of research and development, poor management etc. – remained to be tackled. And for the millions still unemployed there remained the all important question of when economic growth would reach them.

Summary

1 Economic growth is an increase in the real GDP per capita of a nation.

2 An increase in economic growth may not be the same thing as an increase in economic welfare. We must also consider such factors as the distribution of income and the exploitation of the environment.

3 Whatever its relative merits, economic growth is vital to the improvement of the real standard of living of a nation, either in terms of material wealth or other considerations such as leisure and the general state of well-being.

4 Since the 1939–45 war the UK's economic growth has been rapid but it has nevertheless been much slower than that of her main trading partners.

5 Investment is crucial to economic growth but there is no simple relationship between the rate of investment and the rate of economic growth.

6 The efficacy of investment is affected not only by its quantity but also by its quality and type.

7 Economic growth is affected by the size and structure of a population.

8 Although the roots of economic growth are difficult to define, when we examine the UK experience we find that despite improvements in the late 1980s the economy is still lacking in many areas. Thus, whatever factors we consider, it is clear that there is much to do if the UK's economic growth is to be improved. On the other hand there are many prominent economists such as Galbraith and Mishan who would argue that we need to come to terms with a no-growth situation. Such points of view, however, sell at a discount in the poor nations of the world.

Questions

1 What factors are significant in influencing the growth rate of a nation?

2 Study the information in Table 45.7. Construct Lorenz curves to show the distribution of income in these nations. What other information would be useful in assessing the living standards of these nations?

Table 45.7 Distribution of income in selected countries.

Country	Lowest 20 per cent	Second quintile	Third quintile	Fourth quintile	Highest quintile	Highest 10 per cent
Kenya	2·6	6·3	11·5	19·2	60·4	45·8
India	7·0	9·2	13·9	20·5	49·4	33·6
Mexico	2·9	7·0	12·0	20·4	57·7	40·6
UK	7·0	11·5	17·0	24·8	39·7	23·4
USA	5·3	11·9	17·9	25·0	39·9	23·3
Sweden	7·4	13·1	16·8	21·0	41·7	28·1

Source: IBRD

3 What is the relationship between investment in a country and the rate of growth?

4 Study the information in Table 45.8 and then complete this table. Having done this, comment upon the effects of overseas borrowing upon these economies.

Table 45.8 Debt service ratios of selected countries

Country	Interest payments on external debt ($m)		Exports of good and services ($m)		Interest payments as a percentage of exports of goods and services (%)	
	1970	1985	1970	1985	1970	1985
Mexico	283	9436	1 024	21 866		
Brazil	224	7950	1 064	25 637		
Yugoslavia	104	1625	481	10 700		
Nigeria	28	1298	502	12 567		

Source: IBRD

5 What is meant by the North–South dialogue? How has it been affected by the rise in oil prices in the 1970s?

6 How would you account for the UK's relatively poor growth performance since the 1939–45 war?

7

The sources of social welfare are not to be found in economic growth *per se*, but in a far more selective form of development which must include a radical reshaping of our physical environment with the needs of pleasant living and not the needs of traffic or industry foremost in mind.

E. J. Mishan, The Costs of Economic Growth

The anti-growth movement and its accompanying excessive concern with the environment not merely leads to a regressive change in the distribution of resources in the community, it also distracts attention from the real issues of choice which society has to face.

Wilfred Beckerman, In Defence of Economic Growth

Compare and contrast these views of economic growth, stating what role the economist should play in attempting to answer the opposing views of the problems they pose.

Data response   Mrs Thatcher's gains – and her losses ▬▬▬▬▬▬▬▬▬▬▬▬

The following article is taken from the *Guardian* of 4 March 1988. Read it carefully and then attempt the questions which follow.

There is accumulating evidence that some of the supply-side policies introduced since Mrs Thatcher came to power in 1979 have helped the British economy halt and even reverse its century-long relative economic decline, but some areas which still need action will require the government to abandon its reluctance to intervene in the market.

This is the key conclusion of a series of academic studies investigating the long-run economic performance in Britain, published today in the Oxford Review of Economic Policy.*

The findings are likely to be particularly influential because the review represents main-stream economic thinking, and is edited by Dr Christopher Allsopp of New College, Oxford, a leading policy economist who also advises the Labour front bench on economic matters.

The overall assessment, by Professor Nicholas Crafts, is broadly sympathetic to the government's changes but it says that some of the long-term problems of the economy arise in areas in which markets fail to deliver socially desirable results, notably in training and research and development.

'The solution of these difficulties can be expected to require a greater degree of successful government action and initiative than has hitherto been the case,' Professor Crafts concludes.

The main evidence cited for the view that Britain's relative economic decline has ended is that the growth of real output per worker in Britain between 1979 and 1986 was 1.8 per cent per year, and exceeded the equivalent growth rates of the other main industrial countries, except Japan with 2.8 per cent per year. This is in sharp contrast to the relatively poor performance between 1964 and 1973, and again between 1973 and 1979.

However, Professor Crafts notes that economic history suggests that short periods of five to eight years can experience unduly sluggish or rapid growth in response to shocks to demand and are not necessarily good guides to underlying long-run supply-side performance or growth potential. He cites the slow growth in 1899–1907 and the fast growth between 1932 and 1937.

'The period 1973–81 was affected by adverse shocks, and comparisons between the 1980s and 1970s need to be made cautiously at present.'

The historical record also provides ample reasons for discarding the notion of any simple panacea for reversing relative economic decline, since different factors were operating at different times.

The professor points out that the Victorian and Edwardian economies were very lightly taxed but were outperformed by competitor countries which adopted new technology, the scale of advantages of the modern corporation and management techniques. However, the assessment finds that there appear to have been 'serious and persistent weakness on the supply-side' which were not tackled by post-war governments.

Chief among these were the obstacles which demarcation-obsessed craft trade unions posed to the proper use of new technology, the shortfall in vocational and technical education and training, and the shortfall in research and development by industry.

Professor Craft cites evidence that some improvement has been made on the trade union front: about a third of managers are still constrained in their prerogative to organise work, but this compares with 47 per cent of managers at the time of the Donovan Commission at the end of the Sixties.

'To its credit the present government has in some key respects improved supply-side policy and relative decline appears to have ceased.

At the same time there remain significant problems in these areas, despite nine years of Thatcher administrations'.

Opportunities to promote efficiency through competition when state enterprises were privatised had been passed up, regional mobility had been reduced because of the housing market, and skill shortages had probably been exacerbated.

In education and technical training, remedies had been inadequate.

The weaknesses of post-war government policy in failing to foster long-term growth lay primarily in the failure to rectify supply-side problems, rather than in the destabilising impact of policies on the demand side – such as hire purchase controls – which became characterised as stop-go.

Professor Crafts argues that Keynesian policies may be criticised for offering a commitment to full employment based on cooperation with trade unions and management, which effectively meant that managers could not tackle union intransigence in demarcation disputes. Thus it was conducive to over-manning and restrictive practices.

This does not imply, he says, that given an appropriate supply-side policy, demand management should be discarded as inimical to good long-run performance.

Oxford Review of Economic Policy, vol 4, no 1, Spring 1988; Oxford University Press.

1   The article says that government policy has been based on non-interventionism. In what areas important to growth are market forces likely to fail to provide optimal results?

2   What evidence does the article put forward to suggest that there has been a halt in Britain's relative decline? Do you agree with this? Give reasons for your answer.

3   What does the article suggest were the chief weaknesses of the post-war British economy? How far have these been tackled by the Thatcher governments? Illustrate your answer with examples of the measures which have been taken.

4   What factors do you consider important to the promotion of economic growth? How would you suggest improving these?

5   Is it possible that supply-side measures alone will not ensure long term economic growth? Explain your answer as fully as possible.

46

Development and underdevelopment

*For unto everyone that hath
shall be given, and he shall
have abundance; but from him
that hath not shall be taken
away even that which he hath.*

St. Matthew 25:29

In this penultimate chapter we shall look at the problems of economic development as they affect the poorer countries of the world. We will take a brief look at the controversial area of development economics, at the factors influencing development and at the international debt crisis. To begin with we will look at what we mean by a developing nation.

What is a developing country

Terminology

There are a number of different ways in which the nations of the world are categorised. These categories sometimes cut across one another and categorisations are often rejected by nations. For example, many years ago we sometimes spoke of *backward countries* or of *underdeveloped nations*. These terms were considered perjorative and are not now used.

One of the broadest classifications is that of the *three worlds*. The *First World* is the advanced industrial economies including most of those of Europe, Canada, the USA, Australia, New Zealand and Japan. The *Second World* being the communist countries of eastern Europe, the

USSR and China. This leaves the *Third World* as all the remaining countries of Africa, Asia and Latin America.

Another expression which is used is that of the '*North-South Divide*'. This refers to the fact that the rich countries tend to be in the Northern Hemisphere while the poor are in the Southern. To be accurate the Southern Hemisphere would have to start well north of the Equator in Africa and Asia to include some of the world's poorest nations. Australia and New Zealand, obviously, do not fit into this classification.

An expression which is still in wide use is that of *Less Developed Country* (LDC). This term is now also slipping from use and nowadays we tend to use the expression *developing countries* to describe the poorer nations.

A developing country is one where real per capita income is low when compared with that of industrialised nations such as the USA and Japan.

Within this term there are distinctions. The very poorest such as Ethiopia and Bangladesh are, in fact, not developing at all and for them the term must be a bitter irony. To those which have experienced rapid economic development in recent years, such as Korea and Singapore, we give the name *newly industrialising countries* (NICs).

GDP per capita

One of the easiest ways to classify economies is by their GDP per capita. This is the method used by the World Bank. This classification is described at the end of the chapter on the balance of payments (*see* pages 513–16). All values are shown in dollars and the poorest nations are those whose GDP per capita was (in 1985) less than $400. In 1985 thirty seven nations fell into this category from Ethiopia with $110 to Zambia with an income of $390 dollars per head. If you have not already done so, make sure that you are familiar with the problems of measuring national income and of making international comparisons. These were described at the end of Chapter 7.

The standard of living

There is not an exact correlation between the standard of living and the GDP per capita, although the fact that in 1985 it was only $110 in Ethiopia whilst in Switzerland it was $16 370 tells use something pretty fundamental about the two nations. Table 46.1 is extracted from a wealth of statistical information put out by the World Bank. It draws together a number of indicators which are significant in assessing the present standard of living and the potential for development.

The first ten nations all fall within the World Bank's category of 'low-income economies'. Nations 11–13 are in the 'lower middle-income category' and 14–18 are in 'upper middle-income category' and could also be classed as NICs. Data for the UK and Switzerland is added for comparison. You may note, however, the huge difference between GDP per head in the UK and Switzerland which is adequate testimony to the UK's lacklustre growth performance over the last forty years.

Comparison of some of the other indicators such as education and medical services confirms the huge discrepancy between the rich and the poor. In Ethiopia, for example, a newborn baby had a 1 in 6 chance of not making it to the age of

one and a further 4 per cent chance of being dead before reaching the age of 5. This gives an overall infant mortality figure (age 0–4) for Ethiopia of 206 per thousand compared with a figure of 9 for the UK.

The economic and social organisation of the nation can significantly modify the picture presented by the GDP per capita figures. If you track the lower columns in Table 46.1 from left to right you will find that they behave much as you might expect, e.g. infant mortality decreases, calorie intake increases and so on. However, two countries create serious hiccups in the pattern. These are the two communist nations, China and Yugoslavia. Note how in life expectancy, infant mortality, calorie intake and number of doctors they are both well out of the pattern having figures only achieved by nations with significantly higher GDPs per capita. This evidence conflicts with the World Bank's own conclusions (World Development Report 1987) that development is linked to the degree of free enterprise in the organisation of the economy.

We may, thus, conclude this section of the chapter by saying that economic development and improvements in the standard of living are influenced by social organisation, choices made and goals set as well as by growth in the real GDP per head.

Development economics

What's special about development economics?

We have looked at many branches of economics in this book such as monetary economics, foreign trade and so on. It should come as no surprise, therefore, that there is a specialised branch of economics concerned with development. There is also here, as elsewhere, controversy. The argument is concerned with whether or not the principles and policies which apply to advanced economies also apply to very poor ones.

Table 46.1 Indicators of development

Indicator	Year	1 Ethiopia	2 Bangladesh	3 Mali	4 Zaire	5 India	6 Kenya	7 Sudan	8 China	9 Ghana	10 Pakistan	11 Indonesia	12 Nigeria	13 Jamaica	14 Brazil	15 Yugoslavia	16 Mexico	17 Korea	18 Singapore	19 United Kingdom	20 Switzerland
Population (millions)	1985	42.3	100.6	7.5	30.6	765.1	20.4	21.9	1040.3	12.7	96.2	162.2	99.7	2.2	135.6	23.1	78.8	41.1	2.6	56.5	6.5
GNP per capita (dollars)	1985	110	150	150	170	270	290	300	310	380	380	530	800	940	1640	2070	2080	2150	7420	8460	16 370
Growth of GNP per capita (per cent)	1965–85	0.2	0.4	1.4	-2.1	1.7	1.9	—	4.8	-2.2	2.6	4.8	2.2	-0.7	4.3	4.1	2.7	6.6	7.6	1.6	1.4
Percentage of labour force in agriculture	1965	86	84	90	82	73	86	82	81	61	60	71	72	37	49	57	50	55	6	3	9
	1980	80	75	86	72	70	81	71	74	56	55	57	68	31	31	32	37	36	2	3	6
Total external debt (millions of dollars)	1985	1 869	6526	1 469	:	35 460	4219	:	:	:	12 695	35 761	18 348	3775	106 730	19 382	97 429	47 996	:	:	:
Debt service as a percentage of export of goods and services	1970	11.4	:	1.4	:	25.1	:	:	:	16.1	23.3	16.5	7.1	:	21.8	19.7	44.3	20.4	:	:	:
	1985	10.9	16.7	16.6	:	12.7	:	:	:	4.1	30.0	25.1	32.1	:	34.8	21.2	48.2	21.5	:	:	:
Official development assistance (dollars) & receipts as percentage of GNP	1985	16.8	11.4	50.6	10.6	1.9	21.5	51.5	0.9	16.1	7.8	3.7	0.3	76.0	0.9	0.5	1.8	-0.2	9.3	:	:
	1985	15.1	7.1	34.9	7.5	0.7	7.9	15.6	0.4	4.1	2.2	0.7	.	10.0	0.1	.	0.1	0.1	0.1	:	:
Government expenditure as percentage of GNP	1972	13.7	9.4	:	19.8	:	21.0	19.2	:	19.5	16.5	15.1	10.2	:	17.6	21.1	12.0	18.3	16.8	32.7	13.3
	1985	15.1	:	:	23.3	16.7	26.6	:	:	12.5	19.0	20.2	:	:	21.1	6.7	24.9	18.4	26.3	41.1	19.9
Crude birth rate per thousand population	1965	43	47	56	47	45	51	47	39	49	48	43	51	38	39	21	44	35	31	18	19
	1985	46	40	48	45	33	54	45	18	46	44	32	50	25	29	16	33	21	17	13	11
Crude death rate per thousand population	1965	20	21	26	21	20	21	24	13	20	21	20	23	8	11	9	11	11	6	13	10
	1985	15	15	20	15	12	13	17	7	14	15	12	16	6	8	9	7	6	5	12	9
Life expectancy at birth (years) (females)	1965	43	44	40	45	44	46	41	55	49	44	45	43	67	59	68	61	58	68	74	75
	1985	47	51	48	53	56	56	50	70	55	50	57	52	76	67	75	69	77	75	77	80
Infant mortality rate (aged under 1)	1965	165	153	200	135	151	112	160	90	120	149	138	177	49	104	72	82	63	26	20	18
	1985	168	123	174	102	89	91	112	35	94	115	96	109	20	67	27	50	27	9	9	8
Daily calorie supply per capita	1965	1 832	1964	1 860	2 188	2 100	2 287	1 874	2034	1 949	1 747	1 792	2 185	2232	2 405	3 287	2 643	2 255	2214	3346	3 413
	1985	1 681	1899	1 788	2 154	2 189	2 151	1 737	2602	1 747	2 159	2 533	2 038	2585	2 633	3 602	3 177	2 841	2771	3131	3 432
Population per physician	1965	70 190	8400	49 200	35 000	4 880	12 820	23 500	3780	13 670	:	31 740	44 230	1980	2 500	1 200	2 020	2 700	1900	870	710
	1981	88 120	9700	26 450	:	3 700	10 140	9 800	1730	7 250	2 910	12 300	12 000	2700	1 300	700	1 200	1 390	1100	680	390
Numbers enrolled in secondary education as percentage of age group	1965	2	13	4	5	27	4	4	24	13	12	12	5	51	16	65	17	35	45	93	95
	1984	12	19	7	57	34	19	19	37	36	15	39	29	58	55	82	55	91	71	71	98
		E	B	M	Z	I	K	S	C	G	P	N	J	B	Y	M	K	S	UK	S	

It is argued that the problems of developing economies are different from those of developed economies. First because poor economies are starting out in a world in which there are already rich countries. Thus, for example, models based on the experience of the UK in the industrial revolution, when Britain was already the richest country in the world are unlikely to be of use. Second many people argue that there is a special case for state intervention and coordination in the economies of poor nations the arguments for which are considered below.

On the other hand, there has, in recent years, been a tendency to absorb development economics back into mainstream economics and argue that the principles are no different. This, for example, has been the point of view of the World Bank. This accords with the neo-classical movement back towards market orientation elsewhere in the subject of economics.

A full treatment of development economics is beyond the scope of this book and the syllabus. We will, however mention some of the main points. We will consider why it is argued that development economics is a special discipline demanding different theory.

Pioneers and latecomers

It can be argued that developing countries have the advantage of 'free' access to the ideas and inventions which the advanced nations pioneered. There is, as it were, a 'book of blueprints' which they can draw on. However, it may be doubted whether this access is free and whether the 'book of blueprints' is appropriate to developing nations. For example, the adoption of industrial techniques often throws thousands of skilled artisans out of work.

Some nations, however, have made a spectacular success of borrowing the blueprints, for example, Japan and later Korea and other Pacific basin countries.

Balanced and unbalanced growth

Those arguing for *balanced growth* say that there is a need for central coordination and state con-

trol. The experience of the USSR is often quoted. With all its disasters central coordination lifted the Russians from feudalism to superpower within a lifetime. Central control can direct scarce capital resources to where they are most needed, ensure that education is appropriate, restrict wasteful consumption and so on.

On the other hand those arguing for *unbalanced growth* urge the use of market forces in directing the economy. It is said the market forces will maximise the rate of growth. Some infrastructure projects may be neglected but in the long run the benefits created by a high, if unbalanced, rate of growth will 'trickle down' to the rest of the economy.

The dual economy

Attention has been focused on the fact that development can create a dual economy. In one section is the *subsistence economy* where wages are very low or zero and the other section is the *newly industrialising* one utilising capital. The existence of the first is important to the second in that it provides a pool of labour. In effect the industrialising sector can operate with a perfectly elastic supply of labour.

As the industrialising sector expands so it draws in a greater and greater percentage of the population. This process will be hindered if the expansion of the industrialising significantly increases wages. The successful expansion of the industrial sector increases the dualism.

Dualism existed in economies such as the UK during the industrial revolution. However, the relatively slow introduction of labour saving technology kept the process in check.. With a developing economy the ability to adopt the latest technology at once may dramatically increase dualism.

Growth and trade

Early thinking on development economics argued that the terms of trade tended to move against latecomers especially where they are producers of primary products. This stems from

627

a combination of low price and income elasticities of demand for primary products and a tendency towards the saving of raw materials as technology improves in industrialised countries. To this we may add the 'learning by doing argument' which says that, whatever the level of technology a latecomer adopts it only becomes good at producing the goods through the experience of doing so. By the time the latecomer has learnt the developed countries are likely to have moved on. For both these reasons, therefore, the latecomer (developing country) is likely to be at a disadvantage when trading.

The debate is thus whether, on the one hand, a developing country is at an advantage in the terms of trade by being able to adopt the latest technology and benefit from low wage costs or, on the other hand, the terms of trade are likely to move against it for the reasons stated above. If evidence did support the view that the terms of trade do move against the latecomer this could be an argument for (temporary) protection of infant industries in the 'learning by doing case'. On a non-theoretical basis it could be an argument for better organisation of primary producers.

Protection and cost-benefit analysis

In those Third World economies which have grown significantly since the 1939–45 war we find that both the pace and the pattern of industrial growth has been influenced by a plethora of protective tariffs, subsidies, rebates quotas and licences as well as direct investments by activist states. These interventions attracted the attention of development economists from the 1960s onwards. Many focused on the effects of intervention on incentives and resource allocation. The pattern revealed was higgledy-piggledy. The only discernible regularity was the taxation of agriculture and the subsidisation of industries, especially those producing consumer goods.

However, while a country is free to subsidise or protect an industry, it is still important for it to be able to assess its true opportunity cost. This is especially true for an economy attempting a balanced growth scenario. Thus, it becomes necessary to undertake cost-benefit analyses based on world market prices. The difficulties of such analysis (see pages 333–35) may be another reason for the reversion to the market forces viewpoint.

Conclusion

The study of developing economies is not just a one way process, some of what has been learned studying developing economies has improved our understanding of mature economies.

In all of the points made above you can see that the central question governments face is, 'to intervene or not to intervene?' If the answer is believed to be intervention then does this mean wholesale direction of the economy or more discreet manipulation of markets? The evidence on which is better as a method of forwarding development, market forces or direct intervention is not conclusive. Often when a market is seen as efficient it is operating in the wider context of a macroeconomy which is not subject to market forces and, thus, any outcome cannot, in general, be assessed as efficient or otherwise. We may perhaps conclude that whether governments should interfere, and in what form, will depend on circumstances. However, this sort of pragmatic thinking will not appeal to doctrinal purists of right or left.

Perspectives on development

Population

The developing nations account for 80 per cent of the population of the world but only 16 per cent of total world output. Again, although accounting for 80 per cent of the population developing nations account for only 54 per cent of the land area. This situation is bound to get worse as the century draws to its close. If, as predicted, world population reaches six billion by the year 2001 the developing nations are likely to account for 84 per cent of the population and an even smaller share of output.

Population growth is centred in the developing nations. Advances in science have reduced infant mortality and increased lifespan but, as yet, birth rates remain high. (*See* discussion of this and population momentum on pages 39–41.)

The predictions of Malthus seem to be upon us once again (*see* page 37). It seems unlikely that there will be a drastic slow down in population growth until twenty years or so into the next century. If, therefore, we are to avoid being overtaken by the law of diminishing returns it is vital that productivity be drastically improved in developing nations.

Pollution and non-renewable resources

The gloomy picture which population growth presents us with is compounded when we consider two other factors. Firstly greater output implies greater pollution – more acid rain, more Chernobyls and so on. Secondly many of the earth's non-renewable resources are being used up – oil, tin, copper etc. Also the renewable resources – the rain forests, fish stocks, etc. – are also shrinking rapidly. The combination of depletion and pollution could create a crisis not only for the poor nations of the world but for the whole Earth.

If these latter points are taken seriously then what is implied is not more economic growth but less. In which case the only way to preserve the planet and alleviate world poverty would be a drastic redistribution of the wealth of the world.

The idea of a halving of living standards has not yet caught on in the industrialised nations!

Export dependence

Many developing countries are 'one-horse' economies that is to say they are very dependent for their export earnings on one or two products. For example, for the countries in Table 46.2 75

Table 46.2 Export dependence of developing nations 1985

Country	Chief Export	Chief export as percentage of total exports
Uganda	Coffee	99
Zambia	Copper	96
Ethiopia	Coffee	64
Bangladesh	Jute	59
Surinam	Bauxite	55

Source: IBRD

per cent of Bangladesh's export earnings came from one crop, jute while Zambia was dependent for over 90 per cent of its export earnings on copper. This can be fortunate for the country if the price of the product goes up and very unfortunate if it comes down. Either way it makes life unstable and unpredictable.

The terms of trade

As we saw in the section on the theory of development economics the terms of trade can

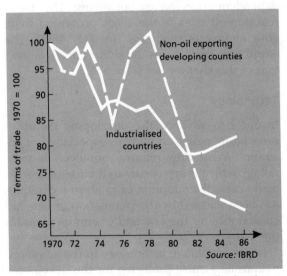

Fig. 46.1 *The terms of trade.* The rise in oil prices in 1973 caused the terms of trade to deteriorate for all oil importing nations. After recovering in the late 1970s, the terms of trade for developing nations plunged following the oil price rise of 1978 and the depression of the early 1980s. *Source*: IBRD

629

present special problems for developing economies. This is illustrated in Fig. 46.1. Here you can see that after a dip in the early 1970s, the terms of trade of developing countries took a dramatic plunge following the OPEC oil price rise in 1973. A swift recovery followed after 1975 and then the second oil price rise in 1978 sent the terms of trade for non-oil exporters plunging. This drop was compounded by the world depression of the early 1980s which depressed the demand for primary products. The collapse of oil prices was good news for the developed nations and brought some relief to developing nations but the continued depression in commodity prices kept the terms of trade against them.

A poor nation such as Bangladesh had to export 15 per cent more in 1985 than it did in 1980 just to pay for the same volume of imports. When the rise in interest rates is considered the situation was even more desperate.

Interest rates

Many of the less developed countries are heavily dependent upon foreign borrowing. The rise in real interest rates in the 1980s presented them with enormous problems (*see* Fig. 46.2). The world debt crisis forms the subject of a later section of this chapter (*see* page 634).

Technology

In order to advance the developing countries must adopt new technologies especially in agriculture. What they require, however, is technology which is *appropriate* to their situation. In many cases the adoption of modern techniques has been rejected by the population or else has created jobs for the few and unemployment for the many.

Improvements in technology in the advanced nations also cause problems for the developing nations. New processes replace old products as, for example, when synthetic fibre replaced jute in carpets. Additionally better technology facilitates economies in the use of materials as, for example, with the introduction of much thinner

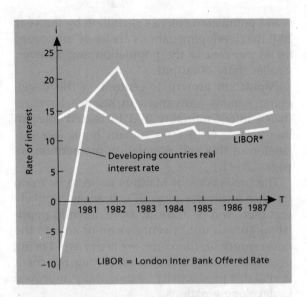

Fig. 46.2 *Interest rates 1980–87.* The graphs show that real interest rates were negative at the beginning of the 1980s – it was this which spelt disaster for many developing nations. *Source*: IBRD

tin cans. Such developments have the effect of depressing the demand and therefore the price of primary products.

Cartelisation

The success of the OPEC oil price rise in 1973 dramatically demonstrated the effects of a successful cartel upon the price of a product. Never has there been a swifter redistribution of wealth from one group of countries to another. This lesson was well learned by the producers of other primary products but they have so far been unsuccessful in organising similar cartels.

A factor which works against the developing nations is that the buyers of primary products are frequently more organised than the sellers. The price of jute, for example, can effectively be set by a small group of people on the London Commodity Exchange. The position of the peasant producing the crop is often undermined by being heavily in debt and having sold the crop a year in advance.

When it comes to imports the developing nation is likely to find the situation reversed with the oligopolistic producers of manufactured goods much better organised. Consider the case of motor vehicles. It is the marketing requirements of the industrialised nations which determine the design and price of cars and these often bear little relation to the needs (or income) of developing nations.

The problem of agriculture

We might expect in a simple economic model that the Third World would produce food to sell to the industrialised First World, this, however, is not the case. Rather it is the industrialised world which sells food to the developing world.

In the days of peasant agriculture people produced much of what they required themselves. In the push for development they have been encouraged to produce cash crops. Their livelihood then becomes subject to the variations in market price of the crop. However, this market price is not freely determined. Massive intervention by governments in the developed world effectively precludes many Third World producers from the rich markets. Consider, for example, the variable import levy of the CAP which ensures that imported agricultural products are at least the same price as those domestically produced. Worse than this the CAP produces food surpluses which further depress world price if they are released.

Defence expenditure

The performance of many developing countries is obstructed by high defence expenditure. Much of their precious foreign exchange goes on importing military hardware. The most celebrated case in recent years must be that of Ethiopia, the poorest country on Earth, which while Bob Geldorf was raising money for it, was involved in a bloody and expensive civil war.

Governments are naturally a little coy about disclosing their expenditure on defence. However, for Pakistan in 1985 we find that defence accounted for 33 per cent of the budget. If, as you can see from Table 46.2, it also had to spend 30 per cent of its exports just to pay the service

of its loans you will realise that it does not leave a lot of latitude for other programmes. In fact only 1.1 per cent of government expenditure went on health care in that year.

Sacred cows

It is a familiar theme in developed economies that development in the Third World is hindered by the people clinging to the practices of their forebears. A case is cited of where resettled peasants in Ethiopia left their purpose built houses and hundreds of new tractors to return to their traditional ways and practices.

However, bear in mind that economic development is about increasing the quality of life. This is made up not only of the consumption of material goods but also of social wellbeing. Would you, if you could be one hundred per cent assured of a better material life – a new car, a holiday home and so on – be prepared to go and live in Russia? Almost assuredly the answer is no. People will not even move from the south of England to the north to obtain these same things.

What is necessary for development

The four elements of development

Despite the disagreements on both theory and practice most people are agreed that there are four wheels to the development vehicle.

a) Human resources. We must be concerned with the health, nutrition and education of the work force. There is a growing recognition that investment in people is a key to development.

b) Natural resources. The discovery of gold is doubtless a great boon but natural resources are not the key to development. The richest nation in Table 46.1 is Switzerland which is almost devoid of mineral resources, has a terrible climate (unless you are skier) and an impossible terrain. On the other hand there are oil-rich nations with money gushing out of the ground but which are

631

still, to all intents and purposes, undeveloped – poor schools, health, roads and so on.

Perhaps for the underdeveloped country the key resource is agricultural land. Moreover, land ownership patterns are a key to providing farmers strong incentives to invest in capital and technologies that will increase their land's yield.

c) *Capital formation.* It is perhaps an obvious tautology that the rich are rich because they have wealth. Again we may turn to Switzerland as an example, it lacks almost everything except that it has enormous stocks of capital. The problem for a developing nation is how to accumulate capital. If possible the best way is the savings of its own people, Singapore and Korea provide excellent examples of this. But, for the poorest nations of the world this is impossible. If a nation is already reduced to the bare minimums of existence depressing current consumption to accumulate capital is inviting mass starvation.

We can say that the poorest nations of the world are caught in a *vicious circle of poverty*. Low incomes lead to low saving; low saving retards the growth of capital; inadequate capital prevents rapid growth in productivity; low productivity leads to low incomes and so on. Other elements in poverty are self-reinforcing. Poverty is accompanied by low levels of skill, literacy and health; these in turn prevent the adoption

of new processes and technologies. (*See* Fig. 46.3.)

The alternative therefore is the importation of capital from abroad. This is turn is beset with problems as we shall see in the section on debt.

d) *Technology.* The adoption of the appropriate technology is a difficult and controversial topic. (*See* discussion on pioneers and latecomers in the section on the theory of development economics page 627.)

World Bank policy

As we said in the section on the World Bank (*see* page 537) it is not itself big enough to make a significant contribution to the problems of developing nations. However, we may take its attitude as being generally symptomatic of the approach of the developed nations towards the developing world.

In the early years of its development the World Bank concentrated on projects to improve the infrastructure of developing countries – irrigation projects, transport, power and like projects. The emphasis has now changed. In the 1980s the World Bank became more concerned with the significance of improved health, nutrition and education in bringing about economic growth. It regards them, not only as important for economic development but desirable in themselves.

As to whether the World Bank has achieved anything in this direction is another question. Despite its stated objectives the Bank has been obsessed with the debt of developing countries and imposing sound financial packages on them in accordance with the policies of monetarist and neo-classical policies in the advanced world. Other international organisations such as the IMF have followed a similar line. The commercial banks who have lent billions to the Third World have also pressed financial stringency on developing nations. Thus, desperately poor nations have been constrained to deflate their economies, devalue their currencies, rein in government spending – in short to apply classic supply-side economics to their problems.

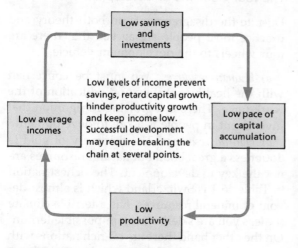

Fig. 46.3 *The vicious circle of poverty.*

Reporting on a speech made by Mr Seaga the prime minister of Jamaica in 1985 the *New York Times* said as follows:

Mr Seaga added that his country had done everything that supply-siders or free-enterprisers could desire. It had devalued its currency to make exports more competitive; it had diverted government programs to the private sector; even including garbage collection and hospitals; it had got rid of burdensome regulations; rebuilt tourism, increased agricultural output and exports, and reached record levels of investment. Yet all this had not solved the nation's debt problem.

Does aid help?

There are two question to be addressed when aid is considered: 'How much is given?' and 'Does it do any good?'

The targets are not ambitious. UNCTAD suggested that the developed nations should give 0.7 per cent of their GDP in aid. In fact, of the OECD nations in 1986 only five – the Netherlands, France, Denmark, Sweden and Norway – managed to reach this target. The UK managed only 0.33 per cent. The USA was second from the bottom of the list with 0.23 per cent.

On the second point several doubts have been cast on the efficacy of aid. Firstly aid is usually given to governments or government agencies and thus may be perverted into the political aims of that regime. For example, if the government is buying millions of dollars worth of arms from overseas, is not aid just aiding the finance of these purchases in a roundabout way. Secondly there is a tendency for aid to be spent on prestigious projects rather than the more mundane developments in the economy which may yield better results. Finally there is concern as to whether aid really furthers development or whether it undermines the self-reliance of a nation.

Bolivia: A measure of the problem

It would seem reasonable to ask how well policies are working. There are undoubtedly some success stories, the progress of Korea, for example, has been spectacular. For the many of the poorest countries, however, the last few decades have been very bleak indeed. Where there has been growth in the economy it has often been swallowed by debt repayments. The policy prescriptions, however remain the same devaluation, deflation and financial stringency. In other words to apply First World solutions to Third World problems. Let us consider an analogy. Obesity is a problem in many of the advanced nations. A policy to persuade people to eat less would improve their health, free resources for other uses and so on. The recommendation of the same policy to a family already existing on half the required calorie intake is unlikely to yield similar benefits.

Whatever may be the causes of poverty and whatever the correct theory of development, policy, for the poorest nations, has clearly failed!

To illustrate this point let us consider one of the poorest Latin American countries Bolivia. World Bank statistics show that it had a negative growth rate of −0.2 per cent over the decades 1965–85. This, however, is a bland cloak over economic chaos. There is a massively unequal distribution of income, huge debt repayment problems and a chaotic political system. Add to this a rate of inflation which reached 25,000 per cent (!), the collapse of tin prices and a 'black' economy out of control. It is estimated that exports of hard drugs (cocaine) account for $4

Table 46.3 Some changes in Bolivian food prices 1975–85

	Hours worked to purchase 1000 calories	
	1975	1985
Barley	0·07	0·59
Quinua (buckwheat)	0.11	0·40
Sugar	0·16	0·51
Wheatflour	0·21	0·52
Dried beans	0·22	3·47
Bread	0·28	0·51
Oil	0·28	0·59
Potatoes	0·76	2·35
Onions	1·02	3·22
Powdered milk	1·05	3·95

Source: Susan George. *A Fate Worse Than Debt*. Pelican

billion dollars a year which is seven times the value of legal exports. It is also estimated that at least a third of the country's economy is illegal and/or underground when one counts smuggling, drug trafficking, speculation, tax evasion and capital flight.

Between 1980 and 1984 real salaries shrank for all Bolivians, sometimes by as much as 75 per cent. They were obliged to work much longer hours to earn enough to buy basic staple foods. Table 46.3 shows some changes in food prices between 1975 and 1985. The figures indicate how many hours one needed to work, at a minimum salary to purchase 1000 calories of various foodstuffs. Obesity is not a problem in Bolivia!

Table 46.3 shows, for example, that it was necessary to work for 2.35 hours to buy 1000 calories worth of potatoes. To gain some measure of what this means we may compare it with the UK. If we take a low wage in the UK as, say, £100 per week (i.e approximately half average earnings in 1988) then a kilo of potatoes would have to cost £5.88 to be as expensive as in Bolivia. In fact a typical family in the UK buys about 3 kilos of potatoes a week but the total cost of these is only about £1.

The world debt crisis

Origins

International debt is no bad thing. To borrow to develop your economy can be a sensible policy, the economy of the USA, for example, was greatly aided by borrowing from the UK in the nineteenth century. The problem of international debt is that it has now got out of hand. There is little hope of all the interest being paid on the debt and no hope at all of it ever being repaid.

The debt is a legacy of unwise borrowing and lending during the 1970s. The oil crisis made conditions extremely difficult for many Third World countries. For the same reason the eurocurrency markets were awash with money (*see* page 535) and real interest rates were low. There-

fore, poor countries needed to borrow and banks were anxious to lend where they could get a better return than on the domestic market. You will note from this that the bulk of lending was by banks and *not* by international institutions such as the IMF and World Bank. This has the consequence that, while an international institution could write-off the debt, it is very difficult for commercial ones to do so.

Much of the money which was borrowed was not used for development purposes but simply to balance the books for the nations' overseas payments. Little found its way into the sort of projects which development economics would suggest.

The problem turned into a crisis in the early 1980s. As the world fell into recession this hit the debtor nations particularly hard. As we have pointed out many developing economies are highly dependent on the export of primary products and the price of these dropped dramatically (*see* Fig. 46.1). At the same time real interest rates rose sharply and most of the debt was at variable interest. The debtor nations were thus caught in a vice between falling income and rising costs. When this happened the banks which had been so anxious to lend in the 1970s were no longer willing to do so. It was as if you had borrowed money to pay your grocery bills or for your holiday, promising to pay it back next year. But when next year came your income had been halved but the bank had doubled the rate of interest.

This meant that the debtor nations had to turn to international agencies for help. As we remarked on page 632 the international agencies do not have sufficient funds substantially to affect the situation. For such help as they were able to give they demanded very stringent conditions. As we have seen above these deflationary conditions have often further impoverished the debtor nations.

The size of the problem

The total size of the Third World debt is incalculable, however, the World Bank estimated that the total amount of government debt of low and middle income economies in 1985 was $627 billion dollars. The interest payment on this amounted to $43 billion per year. In addition to this debtors had to find money to repay loans.

A key measure to observe in assessing a nation's debt problem is the *debt service ratio*. This expresses the amount of money a nation has to repay each year as a percentage of the value of its exports of goods and services.

One of the largest debtor nations is Mexico and it illustrates well the problems involved. Mexico is an oil-producing nation and in the 1970s it found bankers falling over themselves to lend money. With the collapse of the oil price in the early 1980s it found it had huge debts and not the money to pay for them. You can see from Table 46.1 that in 1985 Mexico's debt service ratio was 48.2 per cent. In other words virtually a half of all that it exports was needed in order to service its debts.

Reverse transfers

We might conventionally think of the richer countries helping out the poorer through lending and investment and also by the giving of aid. However, this is not so. So great is the interest burden on debts that there is a massive net trans-fer of money from the poor countries of the world to the rich. This phenomenon is known as a *reverse transfer*.

The overall transfer of resources from the Third World in fact disguises much larger trans-fers from a number of key debtors, offset by positive flows to many others. Figure 46.4 illus-trates the situation as far as the seven largest debtor nations are concerned. As you can see it is estimated that in 1990 a net transfer of almost $40 billion dollars takes place.

On the IMF's figures the reverse transfers from countries with debt servicing problems such as Mexico, Brazil and Zaire, totalled $189·5 billion between 1983 and 1987. Meanwhile their external debt rose from $494 billion to $586 billion as they at least managed to extract some new lending to meet a part of the interest and prin-cipal payments.

The consequences for these economies con-tinue to be dire. For the 17 most highly indebted countries, imports have contracted at an average annual rate of 6.2 per cent since 1980. GDP has grown by only 1 per cent per year, about half the growth in population. Consumption per person has fallen by 1.6 per cent each year. Much of the burden of under and unemployment has fallen precisely on those groups who benefited least from debt-led growth, and which are least able to bear it.

The results of this debt-imposed poverty are none too good for the creditor nations either. The Federal Reserve Bank of New York esti-mated that the 40 per cent drop in US exports to Latin America in the wake of the 1982 Mexico crisis cost 250 000 American jobs. UNCTAD es-timates are much higher. The unemployment is caused because the flood of imports from debtor nations, which are necessary to service their debts, are not matched by a counterflow of exports. Thus the people in the industries which would have produced those exports lose their jobs.

After the 1914–18 war Keynes had explained in his *Economic Consequences of the Peace* how rep-arations would impoverish the victors. In the same way reverse flows from debtor nations

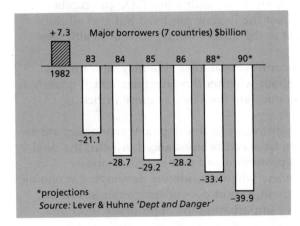

Fig. 46.4 *Reverse transfers*: **Net flow to borrowers of new lending minus interest and capital payment.**
Source: **Lever + Huhne '*Debt and Danger*'**

cause the markets of the developed nations to diminish.

The whole business is only sustained because the banks of the developed nations fear that the debtors will default on their debts. There have already been defaults and moritoria but each time the banks have stepped in to lend just enough to keep the ship afloat. Mass defaults would spell ruin for the economies of the creditor nations.

Conclusion

For readers who have worked their way through this chapter the views of the author on the problem of economic development have probably become clear. We see here the moral and political aspects of economics which have become so much more clearly articulated in recent years. Left-wing economists have frequently claimed the moral high ground. However, in recent years the right wing has put forward the moral

benefits of acquisitiveness. Such views are associated with economists such as the Austrian school and with new right-wing radical politicians such as Margaret Thatcher. But, perhaps the best-known defence is the fictional one put forward by Michael Douglas in the film *Wall Street*.

Which works best? Harnessing the natural acquisitiveness of the human race to maximise growth as described by Adam Smith two centuries ago (*see* page 55) is one way. Alternatively, do we need central direction of developing economies with a massive planned transfer of wealth from the rich to the poor? Can you make the poor rich by making the rich poorer?

Whatever *your* point of view the question must ultimately be a moral one, for as we debate millions starve. If *you* wish to take the moral high ground you can do no worse than to return to the quotation which starts this chapter. However, I recommend that you then read the remaining 17 verses of the chapter from which it is taken.

Summary

1 Many different terms are used to describe the poorer nations of the world. Whatever terms are used the poor are those with a low GDP per capita.

2 The standard of living is not just the income per head but also all the other things which are important to the quality of life, such as health care and literacy.

3 Development economics is a controversial topic. We may sum up this controversy by saying that it is about whether the principles which govern the development of poorer economies are the same as those in rich economies.

4 Some of the major areas of controversy in development economics are as follows: Pioneers and latecomers; balanced or unbalanced growth; the dual economy; growth and trade and protection and cost benefit analysis.

5 Topics which need special review when considering developing economies are those such as: population growth; export dependence; interest rates; cartelisation; agriculture and (very importantly) the appropriate level of technology.

6 The four elements of development are: human resources; natural resources; capital formation and technology.

7   There are serious doubts about the policy of international agencies such as the World Bank towards developing countries.
8   The world debt crisis threatens to overwhelm debtors and creditors.
9   Reverse transfers mean that it is the Third World that is sending money to the First and not *vice versa*.
10   Nowhere else in economics are the moral and political dimensions of the subject seen so starkly.

Questions

1   What is meant by the term 'a developing nation'?
2   Evaluate the arguments for developing economics being a special branch of the subject.
3   What factors do you consider most important in aiding the development of poor nations?
4   'Trade not aid.' Evaluate this slogan as a prescription for development.
5   Take an example of a successful newly industrialising nation and analyse the reasons for its success.
6   Discuss the importance of environmental factors in development economics.
7   What is meant by the international debt crisis and what should be done about it?
8   How might reform of agricultural policy in the advanced nations aid the development of poorer nations?
9   If as Fig. 46.1 shows, the terms of trade have moved against both industrialised countries and developing ones, in whose favour have they moved?
10   What does the principle of comparative advantage have to tell us about development economics?
11   What should be the role of international agencies such as the World Bank in alleviating world poverty?
12   The problem of the debt is fundamentally political, more than financial, and should be confronted as such. What is at stake is not the accounts of the international creditors, but the lives of millions of people who cannot endure the permanent threat of repressive measures and unemployment that bring poverty and death.

Cardinal Paulo Evaristo Arns,
Archbishop of Sao Paulo, Brazil 1985

The poor populations cannot pay intolerable social costs, sacrificing the right of development, which for them remains elusive, while other nations enjoy opulence.

Pope John Paul II
Bogata, 1986

Assess the implications of these statements for the formulation of policy on dealing with the world problem of poverty.

Data response   A fate worse than debt

The following extract is taken from Dr Susan George's book *A Fate Worse than Debt* published by Pelican. The book is about world poverty and the debt crisis. The extract is from the beginning of the concluding chapter.

637

A philosophical afterword

A new scientific truth does not triumph by convincing its opponents and making them see the light, but rather because its opponents eventually die, and a new generation grows up that is familiar with it.

Max Planck.

In the foregoing pages I've tried to show that Third World countries have fallen deep into debt because they have accepted, internalised and followed the model promoted by the World Bank, the IMF and similar institutions. The debt crisis is a particularly ugly, acute manifestation of a chronic condition, the predictable outcome of economic strategies concerned far more with the world market than with local needs. Like an outbreak of carbuncles, it is spectacular on the surface but also a sure sign of underlying infection.

By any normal standards we ought to be able to affirm confidently that this model has failed, since it has plunged countries adopting it into a quagmire from which few show signs of escaping and has caused immeasurable suffering for their people. Yet these same countries are now told, by those in a position to enforce their advice, that they must apply the same policies, only more so, in order to qualify for further loans and continuing membership of the international community. It is like prescribing of cyanide as an antidote to arsenic.

As I've worked on this book, I've grown increasingly intrigued and troubled by the sheer illogic of much of what passes for sober thought, by the nearly seamless consensus position of those who matter on the 'development' scene. One has to put that word in quotes now – it has become too embarrassing to use otherwise. One must also wonder that such a high visibility débâcle, of which the debt crisis is a part, has not yet provoked general dismay and a search for theories which could lead a way out. I am not sure how one can induce changes in dogma and mindsets. I am, however, certain that millions of poor people will continue to pay for the absence of a theoretical revolution.

In the physical and natural sciences world views change because science has criteria, on which everyone can usually agree, for validating and substantiating its claims. Frameworks exist within which scientists look at nature – often called paradigms – are not immutable, but they last as long as they can accommodate a greater number of observed phenomena than any rival paradigm. Scientific truth may not be eternal, but, for a time, at least, it works or it doesn't; observations fit or they don't. Every science must develop ways of recognising error and correcting it, otherwise it will not remain a science and will become more of an amusement, like astrology, or will be discarded entirely, like alchemy.

Max Planck, quoted at the beginning of this Afterword, is pessimistic about the timescale, but he still affirms that new scientific paradigms will triumph, if only after the demise of the stone-wallers. Young scientists with brilliant, unorthodox and often unwelcome insights find it trying to wait – if, indeed, they must – for the last diehards to die, but if their hypotheses stand up to experimental scrutiny and explain more phenomena than previous ones, they will eventually prevail.

Since the pursuit of 'development' is, presumably, a rational activity, can we hope for – or even count on – a similar revolution in our understanding of, and solutions for, hunger and poverty? I would like to believe so. I fear, however, that mainstream development theorists and practitioners, unlike *scientists, have so far been unable or unwilling to establish criteria for recognising, correcting and avoiding error*. For this reason, development theory hews closer to astrology than to astronomy.

Scientists are trained to distrust their models and to rely on them only when they are borne out by rigorous observation. Normally development theorists should be trained to test their models by observing *what they do to people*, since human welfare is theoretically the goal of development. 'People' in this context means not well-off, well-fed elites but poor and hungry majorities whose fundamental needs are presently not being met.

When the reigning development model, or paradigm, has been applied for decades and has failed to alleviate human suffering and oppression – or, worse still, has intensified them – it should be ripe for revolution.

1 What, according to Dr George, are the causes of the debt crisis?
2 Is there an argument for treating the economics of developing countries differently from that of developed nations.
3 Trace the development of the world debt crisis.

Having read the passage from Susan George read also the passage from Keynes which concludes the first chapter of this book. Then attempt the following questions.
4 What is the different between scientific method and economic method?
5 What do these extracts tell us about the use of paradigms in economics?
6 In the extract from Keynes he speaks of the power of vested interests. Are these the cause of the problem of the deteriorating condition of the poorest nations or is it that, as he and Susan George say, that we do not correctly understand the problem?
7 What alternative models of development exist to those currently pursued by agencies such as the World Bank and the IMF?

47

Radical political economy

*The communists disdain to conceal their views
and aims. They openly declare that their ends
can be obtained only by forcible overthrow of
all existing social conditions. Let the ruling
classes tremble at a communist revolution. The
proletarians have nothing to lose but their
chains. They have a world to win. Working men
of all countries unite!*

Karl Marx and Friedrich Engels

What is political economy

Introduction

Despite the number of points of view we have
examined, such as Keynesian and neo-classical,
the bulk of this book has been concerned with
what we may term *mainstream economics*. In this
chapter we consider more controversial viewpoints where we may say that views give way
to *vision*.

In Chapter 1 we defined economics as:

**The human science which studies the relationship
between scarce resources and the various uses
which compete for these resources.**

This emphasis on scarcity and choice is vital
when defining the area of interest of the majority
of modern day economists. Nevertheless there
is a substantial body of 'radical' economists who
are seeking to revitalise the classical concept of
'political economy'. For these writers economics
cannot be separated from the wider analysis of
society as a whole. The allocation of resources
between competing uses is seen as interesting,
but only a very small part of the wider economic
and social dynamics that shape the evolution of
societies. Of more importance to the political

economist is the analysis of power and its interaction with political, social and economic life.

'Radical' can be used to describe writers of
very different political complexions (*see* also the
'Austrian School' page 335), but the term 'radical
political economist' has usually been used to
refer to writers who express opposition to capitalism. Of course, radical economists have their
own divisions; there are many assorted socialist
amalgams which have been influenced by
religions, great thinkers, revolutionaries and
the experiences of many political movements
both before and after the work of Karl Marx
(*see* below). Here we can present little more than
a caricature but the interested reader can be
assured that there is no end of further relevant
reading!

Radical methodology

As we saw in Chapter 1, economics is characterised by controversy. In the eyes of mainstream
economists (i.e. neo-Keynesians and the various
modern versions of neo-classical economists)
debates are seen as technical arguments amongst
expert practitioners. In contrast, radical economists emphasise differences in philosophical
and ideological positions. Radical economists
tend to regard mainstream economics as at best

shallow, but at worst a sophisticated form of propaganda which attempts to deny its own ideological origins and obscures the true nature of social relations within capitalist societies.

Mainstream economists emphasise empirical research as a means of settling debates. Radical political economists also gather empirical data but they believe that it is naïve to think that such evidence can provide a neutral and unbiased means of distinguishing between 'correct' and 'incorrect' theories. This does not mean that radical political economists believe that all theories are equally valid or that validity is purely a matter of opinion. Rather they argue that most 'facts' can be interpreted differently according to the theory which is applied to them. Not only do they tend to question the philosophical basis of the positive/normative distinction they argue that even if it were accepted in principle positive and normative aspects are inextricably entwined in practice.

The methodological position of radical political economists is thus in stark contrast to the positive/normative distinction that has traditionally been emphasised in economics textbooks, e.g. Lipsey's famous text *Positive Economics*. Despite some shifts in position on their part, mainstream economists would regard the radical position as leaving no means of discriminating between 'wheat and chaff'. Nevertheless, many mainstream economists would concede much of the following:

a) Whether someone is deemed unemployed or not is ultimately a moral question.

b) Whether or not (in national income accounting) something represents a 'final good' is often an arbitrary judgement. (*See* page 81.)

c) People *might* respond differently to a certain tax rate according to their perception of its justification.

d) An incomes policy *could* 'work' if there were sufficient consensus.

Such considerations blur the distinction between the so called positive and normative aspects of phenomena.

Mainstream and radical visions

In accordance with their methodological position, radical political economists see schools of economic thought as being built upon deeply held, and often implicit, beliefs regarding the nature of human beings and the societies within which they live. There is nothing new in this. For many hundreds of years people judged economic society only in so far as it related to their religious beliefs. Economic rationality was not paramount, Adam Smith was, after all, a professor of moral philosophy.

Today, however, the economic theories and prescriptions of mainstream economics are seen as stemming from the view that human beings can only be consistently motivated by individual material reward; a belief which is then combined with liberal principles of individual freedoms and liberties (in particular the right to private property) to produce an economics which seems to 'prove' the virtues of free market competition.

Thus, in a nutshell, mainstream economics provides a vision of capitalism in which individuals, knowing their own best interest better than anyone else, are allowed freely to engage in mutually beneficial transactions. The end result of all these millions of transactions is an outcome (equilibrium) which reflects the choices of the individuals themselves. The pursuit of self interest and the play of market forces has enabled everyone to be as well off as is possible without infringing the property rights of others.

This 'neo-classical' vision can be summarised as:

Scarcity ⇒ Choice ⇒ Harmony

(*See* also Section IV.)

The vision of the radical political economists is somewhat different; they reject the vision of capitalism as markets working smoothly to satisfy 'God given' and individualistic wants. They claim that it is misleading to characterise modern capitalism as a sea of perfect competition distorted here and there by a few isolated whirlpools of monopoly. Some radical economists also follow Keynes's emphasis on uncertainty **641** and identify the assumption of perfect knowledge (or known probabilities) as an additional major flaw of mainstream economics. To this is often added the assertion that smooth substitutions between goods and production techniques in response to changing relative prices is another fallacy of mainstream economics. Cambridge University has a tradition of great economists who dissent from the traditional text book portrayal of the price mechanism as 'a marvellous computer' which efficiently balances the unlimited wants of consumers against the use of scarce resources. One such economist is Joan Robinson who wrote in her book *A Guide to Post-Keynesian Economics*:

The slogan that the free play of market forces allocates scarce resources between alternative uses is incomprehensible. At any moment the stocks of means of production in existence are more or less specific. The level of output may be higher or lower with the state of demand but there is very little play in the composition of output. Changes in the adaption of resources to demand can come about only through the process of investment; but plans for investment are made in the light of expectations about the future which are rarely perfectly fulfilled, and therefore have to be drawn up with a wide margin of error.

Instead of emphasising the role of mutually beneficial, and therefore harmonious, market exchanges, radical political economists see modern capitalism as consisting of concentrations of financial and industrial monopoly power which maintain an unequal access to the means of production. This exploitative situation is seen to be manifest in unequal distributions of income, wealth, power and control. In place of the harmonious equilibriums of mainstream economists, radical political economy focusses on conflicts of interest and recurring crises.

The evolution of society

Radical political economists do not emphasise static, 'timeless' equilibriums in which everybody is 'doing what they want to do' (given the constraints they face). Instead, social evolution is stressed in which 'human nature' and socio-economic institutions and relationships undergo change. For them (particularly the more Marxist), the dynamics of such social evolution can best be explained and understood as a consequence of class struggle. According to this view, human history has revolved around the struggle of subordinated classes to escape the exploitation of more powerful dominant classes. (*See* Data Response 1.) These dominant classes, however, attempt to use their power to maintain a social order in which their own interests prevail. Minor concessions might be made in order to dampen down dissent, but a dominant class never voluntarily relinquishes the power relationships within the existing social order by which an economic surplus is expropriated from the subordinated class.

Most radical political economists see themselves as working toward a radically new social order which will be far more egalitarian and yet truly liberating; differences in material wealth and political power would be limited and people set free from the domination of others and the confines of socially determined roles so that they can achieve their true potential as members of the human species. It is facile to dismiss this as mere utopian fantasy for it is an essential part of this radical vision that our perceptions, and hence attitudes, are conditioned by the existing socio-economic environment (which is itself seen as determined by the prevailing 'mode of production'). Hence human behaviour is not seen as determined by an inalterable 'human nature'; it is accepted that in a system founded on the pursuit of capitalist profit people will appear 'naturally' greedy and selfish but within the new socialist order people will likewise appear to be 'naturally' concerned with the collective good. Thus the greedy 'rational economic man' of mainstream economics (*see* page 55) is often seen as a product of capitalism and not as a non-controversial non-normative starting point for economic analysis.

It should be clear that radical political economists are unlikely to be satisfied with an economics which merely reduces the 'evils' of capitalism. They argue that the roots of the 'problem' must be attacked. Thus they tend to support political movements of the 'subordinated' class that attack the very foundations of unequal social orders by seeking to counter and ultimately eliminate the sources of power of the dominant class. This does not mean, however, that all such radicals are supporters of violent revolution or supporters of those regimes which use oppressive powers in order to maintain totalitarian power in the name of socialism. One of Britain's best known socialists, Tony Benn, wrote in his *Arguments for Socialism*:

British socialism . . . [is] . . . a blend of theory and practice built up out of many centuries of effort and thought; drawing its inspiration from many sources and absorbing them all into a belief in basic human equality and freedom, to be expressed in the democratic forms of chapel, union and Parliament, to which all power should be accountable.

Any consideration of socialism would be sadly incomplete without a study of Karl Marx. We will conclude this chapter with a brief look at the work of Marx. It should be remembered, however, that there are as many views of Marxism as there are of Christianity.

Marx's economics

The influence of Marx

Karl Marx (1818–1883) was far more than an economist. His lifelong collaborator, friend and financial benefactor Friedrich Engels, described Marx's work as a synthesis of German philosophy, French socialism and English political economy. Marx was indeed a learned man. Karl Marx is still by far the most influential of radical political writers (indeed he is one of the most influential writers of all time). Not all radical political economists would regard themselves as 'Marxist', but few if any would disown Marx as an influence on their own thought.

Marx created, refined and developed the 'vision' of radical political economy that we have outlined above. We do not have space to examine the full extent or depth of this vision as seen by a man who was as much an historian, philosopher, sociologist and revolutionary political activist as an economist. Nevertheless, it is a central theme of his vision that it is impossible to totally separate economics from the rest of his ideas.

Stages in the evolution of society

Marx identified four stages through which the relations of production and society had passed namely, *primitive communism, slavery, feudalism* and *capitalism*. He argued that under feudalism the produce of labour was expropriated (by the lords from the serfs), through a complex social system based on hierarchies of land ownership. In Western Europe by the mid-19th century this system of expropriation had been overthrown by the emerging capital owning-class and replaced by a social system which served their interests instead i.e. capitalism. Just as feudalism had generated its own ideology 'obligation' and 'divine right', so the ideology of the great liberal thinkers such as Adam Smith and John Stuart Mill was used to justify this new mode of production and social structure. Just as serfs had largely accepted their lot as inevitable and ordained by God so workers typically are not aware of capitalist exploitation.

Marx then saw that workers within capitalist systems would typically question their wages rather than the wage system which is at the root of their exploitation. For change to come about it was thus necessary to lay bare the 'laws of motion of capitalist society' so that the workers could recognise and rally around their class interests. The raising of class consciousness would then allow the workers to organise the revolutionary overthrow of the capitalist mode of production. Marx himself recommended armed revolution on the part of the proletariat and took an active part in organisations dedicated to this end, but it has to be said that Marx was responding to the political reality of the nineteenth century when there was no prospect of advance through democratic means.

643

Communism would result when all the classes in society had been absorbed into the proletariat. In this ideal society the state would have withered away and each person would contribute according to ability and receive according to needs. This Utopia envisaged by Marx is the stage of economic development which follows from capitalism and socialism.

Exploitation

The ideology of the liberal thinkers emphasised the right to equality under the law. Marx agreed that workers are equal to capitalists in the sense that they can exchange their labour power in the market place in exchange for its market value. They can thus withhold their services from an employer who does not pay this rate. Indeed, for Marx the distinguishing feature of capitalism *is* that labour power is sold in the market in *exactly* the same way as any other commodity, in contrast, say, to the ownership of a slave or the feudal obligation of a serf.

This equality in exchange, however, hides the inequality in production. If workers exercise their freedom to refuse to sell their labour power they have no other means of providing for their subsistence. This is because workers have no other access to the prevailing means of production i.e. capital. In the limit workers can exercise their freedom to refuse to work until starvation, in this sense slaves are equal to their masters! Thus the capitalist's monopoly of the means of production enforces *wage-slavery* on the working class.

Obviously, given the profits of capitalists, workers would prefer to sell the products they produce rather than their labour power. For Marx then, the exchange of labour power in the same way that other commodities are exchanged via market transactions pre-supposes the monopoly of the means of production on the one hand and a class of wage-slaves on the other. It is this social relationship that identifies capitalism as a particular mode of production and exploitation as distinct from slavery or feudalism. Hence the very categories of analysis, e.g. profit

and wages, used by mainstream economists (who Marx called 'bourgeois economists'), are derived from the existence of social relations and social classes as they exist under capitalism and yet the method of analysis employed, i.e. individualistic maximisation based on personal choice, ignores these social realities. In the first volume of *Das Kapital* Marx argued that:

The categories of bourgeois economics consist precisely of forms of this kind. They are forms of thought which are socially valid, and therefore objective, for the relations of production belonging to this historically determined mode of social production. The whole mystery of commodities, all the magic and necromancy that surrounds the products of labour on the basis of commodity production, vanishes therefore as soon as we come to other forms of production.

For Marx then, workers are not exploited because they are paid less than the market value of their labour power, although this might be true in specific instances. Workers are equal in exchange but unequal in terms of their access to the means of production, i.e. 'capital'. It is through the ownership of capital that an economic surplus is extracted from the labour power of workers by capitalists. Thus workers are exploited in that they must sell their labour power to the capitalist. Hence, even if they receive the full market value of their labour or perhaps a little more, they do not receive all the fruits of their labour power. To understand this point we must understand Marx's version of the labour theory of value. (*See* page 244.)

The labour theory of value

Use value and exchange value

Marx developed the labour theory of value from the value theory of Smith and Ricardo. Following Smith, Marx distinguished between 'use-value' and 'exchange-value'; for something to have use-value it simply has to be wanted, but even the most useful things, such as air and water, may have little or no exchange-value i.e. they cannot be exchanged for other things which have exchange value. Obviously, for a commodity to have exchange value it must have use-value, unless it is a form of money i.e. a medium of exchange.

A consistent set of exchange-values must satisfy certain everyday numerical rules of equivalence e.g. if A exchanges for B then 2A must exchange for 2B, if A exchanges for B and B exchanges for C then A exchanges for C etc. Physical properties such as weight could perhaps satisfy such relationships, but the property that Marx saw all commodities as having in common is that ultimately they are the product of human labour.

What determines values?

Following Ricardo, Marx analysed exchange-values in terms of the labour-time necessary to produce commodities. By this he did not mean that a commodity would be increased in value by working more slowly to produce it; rather its exchange-value reflects the 'socially necessary' labour required to produce it. Socially necessary labour-time is the labour-time required to produce something under the conditions of production normal for a given society and with the average degree of skill and intensity of effort prevalent in that society. Thus advances in the technology of producing a particular commodity will tend to reduce its exchange value relative to other commodities where the necessary labour time in production is unchanged. In principle then, but subject to many qualifications, a commodity which, with the prevailing technology, necessitates twice as much labour time as another will have an exchange value twice that of the latter.

As labour-power under capitalism is exchanged in the same way as any other commodity it must have use-value to the capitalist. Marx saw that the use-value of labour-power is that it is the *creator* of exchange values. A capitalist would not use his money to employ factors of production unless it produced a value of output greater than the value of the money he so invested. Indeed, Marx's definition of capital centred on this expansion of value, hence money, commodities and factor inputs are all regarded as capital when used in this self expanding value circuit of production. It follows that one or more of the inputs purchased by the capitalist must create in production more value than it costs. If we start from a labour theory of value there can only be one input which contributes more labour-time, and hence value, to output than it itself cost in terms of labour-time to produce and that is labour-power itself.

Inputs other than labour-power will be reflected in the value of output as these inputs required labour-time for their production. But if only labour-power can create value, then these other inputs add no more to the value of output than the past value of the labour-time necessary to produce them. In contrast the cost of producing labour-power, i.e. the labour-time necessary to produce the commodities which sustain life and health, is less than the labour-time which the labour-power so produced can contribute to the value of output. To reduce this to a simple example, a farm labourer might be able to work for a month producing food whilst sustained by a quantity of food which took only a week to produce. Hence, according to the labour theory of value the value of the labourer's work would be only one week of labour-time but the value of his or her output would be one month of labour-time. Thus the worker receives, in wages, value equivalent to one week of labour-time, but the capitalist farmer can exchange the output for value equivalent to one month of labour-time. The rate of exploitation of the labourer is thus given by the ratio 'surplus labour' to necessary labour i.e. 3 to 1.

Capitalist crises

Underconsumption

Marx described capitalist production as anarchic. By this he meant that the links between the various components of the system are precarious. Hence, because of the interdependencies **645** within the system, general crises of the capitalist system would recur. For example, Marx accepted the notion of 'underconsumption' in which a break in production halts the flow of money around the system. If for what ever reason (e.g. large changes in demand, foreign competition or failures of the financial credit system) workers and capitalists do not receive their regular flow of money income, then they will cut their money expenditures. This in turn means that others do not now receive a regular money income and they in turn cut their expenditure and so on. If this becomes generalised a slump in economic activity is caused by underconsumption, i.e. a general lack of expenditure and hence demand for commodities (see also Chapter 30 on the economics of Keynes).

Concentration of capital

An important theme in Marx's work is his stress on 'competitive capital accumulation'. Capitalists compete with each other through time by accumulating capital and applying labour saving technology. Each capitalist seeks to defend themself against competitors or steal an advantage by reducing their costs of production. This capital accumulation reduces the costs of the capitalist by reducing the labour-time necessary for the production of his commodities. But as each capitalist adopts the more capital intensive production technique the socially necessary labour-time for the production of commodities is reduced. Thus the value of the commodity falls and the profits of all capitalists producing that commodity falls with it. Those smaller capitalists left behind in the accumulation race are competed out of business by those capitalists who have accumulated more capital or adopted a more advanced labour saving technology. The rule is accumulate or die as the control of capital is concentrated more and more into the hands of fewer and larger centralisations of capital.

Unemployment

Marx argued that the constant tendency of competition to expel labour from the production process would cause a continuous flow of workers into unemployment. As output expands the total level of employment might expand, but even while this is happening capitalist competition and accumulation will condemn workers in many regions and industries to unemployment. Workers in depressed regions or with redundant skills will become surplus to the requirements of capitalists, Marx called these people an 'industrial reserve army of the unemployed.' Within this army will develop a core of the permanently unemployed who will be condemned to relative poverty and misery.

Revolution

Marx hoped that as the extent of this misery grew, and as capitalism appears increasingly unable to provide for workers, the class consciousness of the working class (or 'proletariat') would develop, even among workers whose material conditions were being improved by the capitalists' development of the means of material production. When the proletariat recognised its class interest it would use the economic and political strength that capitalism had unwittingly bestowed upon it through the concentration of workers into places of mass production. The ensuing revolution would overthrow the capitalist order and replace it with a 'dictatorship of the proletariat' whereby the productive power developed through capitalist accumulation would be 'socialised' and co-ordinated to provide for the good of all.

Marx's 'law' or tendency for the rate of profit to fall

Although, for Marx, the 'anarchy' of capitalist production made crises likely, the inevitability of crises is predicted by his law of the tendency of the rate of profit to fall. This tendency rests upon Marx's assertion that only labour-power creates value and that production will be by increasingly capital intensive means.

The capital that a capitalist must advance for the purposes of production can be divided into two parts. Part must be used to buy buildings, machines and raw materials. This part Marx called 'constant capital' because, although its value (i.e. the past labour-time that was necessary to produce it) can be passed on as part of the value of the capitalist's output, its value does not vary during production. In contrast, the other part of the capital advanced must be spent on the necessary labour-time for the planned production of commodities. It is this part alone which produces surplus value. This part Marx called 'variable capital' as its value varies because it contributes more value to output than it costs as an input.

As the technical ratio of constant capital to labour-time is increased by capital accumulation, so the value of the constant capital that must be advanced by the capitalist tends to grow in relation to the value of the variable capital that must be advanced. This ratio of constant capital value to variable capital value was termed the 'organic composition' of capital by Marx. Of course, if the labour-time necessary for the production of constant capital were to fall greatly then the value of each unit of constant capital would itself fall. This might prevent the organic composition of capital rising even if the technical ratio of constant to variable capital increased. On the other hand, the labour-time necessary for the production of the commodities to produce labour-power would also fall. Thus although it is not a logical certainty, we can expect that there will be many periods in which the organic composition of capital will substantially increase.

Because only variable capital produces surplus value, a rise in the organic composition of capital will tend to decrease the profit of the capitalist in relation to his total capital advanced i.e. the rate of profit will fall. Of course there may be offsetting factors such as cheaper raw materials obtained from exploiting colonies or third world producers. Raising the rate of exploitation might also counteract the tendency of the rate of profit to fall. But there will be limits to how far the real or relative wage can fall without inducing widespread resistance and political dissent among workers. In contrast the organic composition of capital can rise without limit even

reaching infinity in fully automated processes! In short, although most production problems will be overcome if profits are high, recurring crises caused by declining profits are, for practical purposes inevitable. It will be during one of these periodic crises that, according to Marx, the proletariat will revolt.

Criticisms of Marx's analysis

Problems with the labour theory of value

Many admirers of Marx on the left of the political spectrum disagree with aspects of his analysis. Joan Robinson used the famous battle cry of revolutionary Marxists 'Workers of the world unite, you have nothing to lose but your chains!', to comment wryly on Marx's apparently false prophesy of increasing proletarian misery:

'You have nothing to lose but the prospect of a suburban home and a motor car' would not have been much of a slogan for a revolutionary movement.

However, she also says in the same work:

. . . no point of substance in Marx's arguments depends upon the labour theory of value.

Post-Keynesians such as Joan Robinson argue that if the point of Marx's analysis was that profits arise from the exploitation of workers by capitalists who own the means of production, then this can be done without reference to labour values or the concept of surplus value. The irrelevance of the labour theory of value to an analysis of capitalist exploitation is hotly disputed by Marxists. Critics of Marx who are not from the left have gone further as, for example Paul A Samuelson in his *Economics* says:

The internal logic of Marx's economics was flawed at the core.

The transformation problem

The most common criticism of Marx's analysis concerns the 'Transformation Problem' whereby **647** labour-time values are transformed into market prices. Here there appears to be a logical inconsistency between Marx's assertion that competition in the labour market will tend to equalise the rate of exploitation across labour markets and his acceptance that competition will also tend to equalise the rate of profit across the economy. As only the variable capital advanced by the capitalist can produce value, it follows that if the rate of exploitation (i.e. the ratio of surplus to necessary labour) is constant across industries then the rate of profit cannot be, i.e. the rate of profit will be lower in industries in which constant capital is a higher proportion of the capital advanced and higher in industries in which constant capital is a smaller proportion.

The significance of the transformation problem remains a controversial area. It is only fair to remind the reader, however, that logical problems arise with mainstream economics (e.g. *see* the 'reswitching debate' page 277). Those who wish to remain close to Marx's original analysis emphasise that the power of Marx's insights are far more important than any 'algebraic' puzzles that remain to be solved. It can be argued that concentrating on the mathematics of market exchanges, in the manner of mainstream economists, obscures the nature of the social relations revealed by Marx. For example, Ben Fine in *Marx's Capital* says:

Market prices will be modified by differing capital-labour ratios, scarcities, skills, monopolies, and tastes. These influences have been the prime object of study of orthodox economists since the neo-classical revolution of the 1870s, with little advance being made on Adam Smith's ideas of the 1770s. They were not ignored by Marx, but they are irrelevant . . . for uncovering the social relations of production specific to capitalism. If this cannot be done on the assumption that commodities exchange at their values, it certainly cannot be done in the more complicated case when they do not.

In conclusion

Whether or not the reader finds this defence of Marx convincing or not, the debate rages on and emotions often run high. Sometimes marxist ideas appear to be gaining support at other times they seem to lose ground. Many more controversies should be examined here, such as Lenin's assertion that Marx's analysis should be modified to allow for the rising real wages of workers in established industrialised countries at the expense of less developed countries, but space (and examination syllabuses!) forbids. What is clear is that the ideas of Karl Marx, for better or worse, continue to exert influence and have not, as some writers claim, been consigned to the graveyard.

Select bibliography

General works

Bannock, G., Baxter, R. E. and Rees, R., *The Penguin Dictionary of Economics*, Penguin

Donaldson and Farquhar, *Understanding the British Economy*, Pelican

Dunnett, A., *Understanding the Economy*, Longman

Economist (The), *Economist Briefs: Money and Finance; Britain's Economy under Strain; The EEC; The World Economy; European Economies*

Hardwick, P., Khan, B. and Longmead, J., *An Introduction to Modern Economics*, Longman

Heathfield, D., *Modern Economics*, Philip Allan

Heilbroner, L. and Thurow, L., *The Economic Problem*, Prentice-Hall

Heilbroner, L. and Thurow, L., *Economics Explained*, Prentice-Hall

Hunt and Sherman, Economics: An Introduction to Traditional and Radical Views, Harper and Row

Lipsey, R. G., *An Introduction to Positive Economics*, Weidenfeld & Nicolson

Lipsey and Harbury, *First Principles of Economics*, Weidenfeld and Nicolson.

Manchester Economics Project, *Understanding Economics*, Ginn

Maunder, P. *et al.*, *Economics Explained*, Collins

McCormick, B. J. *et al.*, *Introducing Economics*, Penguin

Pennant, R., and Emmott, B., *The Pocket Economist*, Martin Robertson and *The Economist*

Powell, R., *'A' Level Economis: Course Companion*, Letts

Samuelson, P. A., and Nordhaus, W. D., *Economics (Ed. 12)*, McGraw-Hill

Stanlake, G. F., *Introductory Economics*, Longman

Wonnacott, P. and Wonnacott, R., *Economics*, McGraw-Hill KogaKusha

Official statistics and publications

UK economy

Annual Abstract of Statistics, HMSO

Bank of England Quarterly Bulletin, Bank of England

CSO, *Economic Trends*, HMSO

CSO, *Financial Statistics*, HMSO

CSO, *Monthly Digest of Statistics*, HMSO

Department of Trade and Industry, *Employment Gazette*, HMSO

HM Treasury, *Financial Statement and Budget Report*, HMSO

National Income and Expenditure, HMSO

United Kingdom Balance of Payment, HMSO

International

OECD Economic Outlook, OECD

World Development Report, Oxford

More specialised and/or advanced texts

Ackley, G., *Macroeconomics: Theory and Policy*, Collier Macmillan

Atkinson, A. B., *The Economics of Inequality*, Oxford University Press

Baumol, W. J., *Economic Theory and Operations Analysis*, Prentice-Hall

Beckerman, W., *National Income Analysis*, Weidenfeld & Nicolson

Blaug, M., *The Cambridge Revolution: Success or Failure?* Hobart Paperback No. 6, I.E.A.

Black, J., *The Economics of Modern Britain*, Martin Robertson

Brandt Commission, *North–South: A Programme for Survival*, Pan

649

Brooman, F. S., *Macroeconomics*, Allen & Unwin

Brown, C. V. and Jackson, P. M., *Public Sector Economics*, Martin Robertson

Carter, H. and Partington, I., *Applied Economics in Banking and Finance*, Oxford University Press

Cole, C. L., *Microeconomics*, Harcourt Brace Jovanovich

Copeman, H., *The National Accounts: A Short Guide*, HMSO

Crockett, A., *Money: Theory, Policy and Institutions*, Nelson

Donaldson, P., *Economics: A Simple Guide to the Economics of the Early Eighties*, Pelican

Dunnett, A., *Understanding the Market*, Longman

Fine, Ben, *Marx's Capital*, Macmillan

Friedman, M. and Schwartz, A., *A Monetary History of the United States 1867–1960*, Princeton University Press

Galbraith, J. K., *The Affluent Society*, Pelican

Galbraith, J. K., *Economics and the Public Purpose*, Pelican

Galbraith, J. K., *The New Industrial State*, Pelican

Grant, R. M. and Shaw, G. K. (eds), *Current Issues in Economic Policy*, Philip Allan

Green W., and Clough, D., *Regional Problems and Policies*, Holt, Rinehart & Wilson

Hartley, K., *Problems of Economic Policy*, Allen & Unwin

Haverman, R. H., *The Economics of the Public Sector*, Wiley

Jones, H., *An Introduction to Modern Theories of Economic Growth*, Nelson

Kindleberger, C. P. and Lindert, P. H., *International Economics*, Homewood

Koplin, H. T., *Microeconomic Analysis*, Harper & Row

Laidler, D., *Microeconomics*, Philip Allan

Levačić, Rosalind, *Economic Policy Making*, Wheatsheaf Books

Levačić and Rebmann, *Development in Economics: An Introduction to Keynesian and Neoclassical Economics*. Macmillan

Lewis, D. E. S., *Britain and the European Economic Community*, Heinemann.

Lancaster, K., *An Introduction to Modern Microeconomics*, Rand McNally

Leijonhufvud, A., *On Keynesian Economics and the Economics of Keynes*, Oxford University Press

Mishan, E. J., *The Economic Growth Debate: An Assessment*, Allen & Unwin

Milner, C. and Greenaway, D., *An Introduction to International Economics*, Longman

Morgan, B., *Monetarists and Keynesians—Their Contributions to Monetary Theory*, Macmillan

Mulvey, C., *The Economic Analysis of Trade Unions*, Martin Robertson.

Pearce, D. W., *Cost-Benefit Analysis*, Macmillan

Pearce, D. W., *Environmental Economics*, Longman

Peston, M. H., *The British Economy*, Philip Allan

Prest, A. R. and Coppock, D. J. (eds.) *The UK Economy: A Manual of Applied Economics*, Weidenfeld & Nicolson

Prest, A. R. and Barr, N. A., *Public Finance in Theory and Practice*, Weidenfeld & Nicolson

Price, C. M., *Welfare Economics in Theory and Practice*, Macmillan

Robbins, L. C., *Nature and Significance of Economic Science*, Macmillan

Ryan, W. J L. and Pearce, D. W., *Price Theory*, Macmillan

Stanlake, G. F., *Macroeconomics: An Introduction*, Longman

Stewart, J., *Understanding Economics*, Hutchinson

Thurow, L., *The Zero-Sum Society: Distribution and the Possibilities for Economic Change*, Penguin

Trevithick, J. A., *Inflation: A Guide to the Crisis in Economics*, Penguin

Vane, H. R. and Thompson, J. L., *Monetarism*, Martin Robertson

Westaway, A. J. and Weyman–Jones, T. G., *Macroeconomics: Theory, Evidence and Policy*, Longman

Index